SECONDARY SCHOOLS AND BEYOND

*Transition of Individuals
with Mild Disabilities*

☙ ☙ ☙

SECONDARY SCHOOLS AND BEYOND
Transition of Individuals with Mild Disabilities

Anna Gajar

Libby Goodman

James McAfee

PENNSYLVANIA STATE UNIVERSITY

Merrill, an imprint of
Macmillan Publishing Company
New York

Maxwell Macmillan Canada
Toronto

Maxwell Macmillan International
New York Oxford Singapore Sydney

Cover art/photo: Nate Krupko
Editor: Ann Castel
Production Editor: Linda Hillis Bayma
Art Coordinators: Peter A. Robison, Vincent A. Smith
Artist: Jane Lopez
Text Designer: Anne Flanagan
Cover Designer: Robert Vega
Production Buyer: Patricia A. Tonneman
Electronic Text Management: Ben Ko, Marilyn Wilson Phelps

This book was set in New Baskerville by Macmillan Publishing Company and was printed and bound by Arcata Graphics/Martinsburg. The cover was printed by Phoenix Color Corp.

Macmillan Publishing Company
866 Third Avenue
New York, NY 10022

Macmillan Publishing Company is part of the
Maxwell Communication Group of Companies.

Maxwell Macmillan Canada, Inc.
1200 Eglinton Avenue East, Suite 200
Don Mills, Ontario M3C 3N1

Library of Congress Cataloging-in-Publication Data
    Secondary schools and beyond : transition of individuals with mild
disabilities / Anna Gajar, Libby Goodman, James McAfee.
      p. cm.
    Includes bibliographical references and index.
    ISBN 0-675-21373-8
    1. Handicapped youth—Education (Secondary)—United States.
2. Post compulsory education—United States. 3. Vocational
education—United States. 4. Vocational guidance for the
handicapped—United States. I. Goodman,Libby, 1947- .
II. McAfee, James. III. Title.
LC4031.G35 1993
371.91'0973—dc20   92-27482
                                                  CIP

Printing: 1 2 3 4 5 6 7 8 9   Year: 3 4 5 6 7

Photo credits: Larry Hamill/Macmillan, p. 407; The Pennsylvania State University Archives, pp. 1, 95, 255, 339.

Dedicated to:

Jano Bician ("Seventh after Jano"), the last of a great Slovak heritage;

❦

My husband and son, Bob and Robbie;

❦

Donna, whose optimism is abounding;

❦

and Gerard, who persevered and engineered his own successful transition into adulthood.

✿　✿　✿

Preface

Transition, which involves the movement of students from school to post-secondary environments and pursuits, has become a major focus in special education. In many people's minds, transition is an issue related to those with moderate and severe impairments. This perspective is too restrictive and does disservice to students with mild disabilities. Historically, services have been provided for persons with severe disabilities from infancy to adulthood. This has not been true for people with mild disabilities.

Ample research describes the many difficulties that individuals with mild disabilities face when they attempt to assume the responsibilities of adulthood. Schools play a vital part in preparing all students with disabilities for transition. Federal initiatives already encompass individuals who are mildly impaired, as well as those who are severely disabled, in definitions of eligible populations for experimental and exploratory programs in transitional services—an important and timely acknowledgment that transition is a major concern for all learners with disabilities. Growing interest in the transitional needs of individuals with mild disabilities is symptomatic of a pressing demand for current and useful information on this critical topic. This need has arisen among parents, teachers, other professionals, and individuals with mild disabilities themselves.

Our purpose for this text is to provide a comprehensive and cohesive book that synthesizes up-to-date information on theory and practice in transition for persons with mild disabilities, teachers in training, and professionals on the job. The text is organized into five major parts. In order to focus the reader's attention to key concepts and facilitate understanding and retention, each part begins with a preview, and each chapter ends with a summary. To underscore the real-life implications of transitional training, each part preview includes a vignette or a series of vignettes about individuals with mild disabilities whose histories illustrate the key issues of the chapters included in the section.

In Part I we address the rationale, definitions, components, and subcomponents of transition, legislative history, models, related models, as well as supports for and barriers to transition.

We accentuate the relationship of secondary and postsecondary special education to transition in Part II. Secondary transition models of special education and the pertinent subcomponents of the area—including foundations, academic guidance, assessment and programming at the secondary and postsecondary levels of education, and follow-up—are presented. In addition, the role of special education as a component of transition is discussed.

In Part III we address the relationship of vocational education and vocational rehabilitation to the transition of persons with mild disabilities. Pertinent subcomponents including foundations, programming at the secondary and postsecondary levels of education, job placement, and follow-up are presented. This section of the text also includes the role of vocational education and vocational rehabilitation as components of transition.

The emphasis in Part IV lies on the career education (extravocational) components of transition, including the subcomponents of work support skills, independent living skills, and citizenship skills.

In Part V we stress the major issues involved with transition within different environments and levels of interaction, including society, institutions, family, agencies, interagency relations, and recreation. The importance of long-term effects is highlighted. The future of transition is discussed for mildly disabled persons at the secondary, postsecondary, and adult levels.

Because of the current rapid growth of interest in the area of transition for persons with mild disabilities, many questions concerning the relationship between theory and practice and between practice and efficacy have not been resolved. Consequently, approaches to educating students with mild disabilities in secondary and postsecondary environments vary greatly. To understand this phenomenon, a comprehensive overview of the process of transition and the issues that exist are presented. How educational and rehabilitational theories affect practice at each stage of the transitional process is shown, with emphasis on successful application of theory.

We have attempted to provide an overview of transition. Simultaneously, we have offered in-depth analysis of some specific, important, and often neglected aspects of transition such as individual responsibility. We have not attempted to consider in depth all topics related to transition, for, truly, *all* instruction is related to transition. Further, we believe that there are many excellent sources of information on some topics (e.g., traditional academic instruction). What we have tried is to identify, discuss, and offer methodology for those aspects of transition that are new, nontraditional, and critical to the adult success of persons with mild disabilities.

ACKNOWLEDGMENTS

Many people helped to create this text. We would especially like to recognize Pam Smith for her assistance with library research and positive messages when they were needed; Debbie Carnuccio and Delores Wiant for tracking down "fugitive" references; Glenda Carelas for assistance with formatting; and Tony Zilz for his indexing and editing.

We would like to extend our appreciation to the following reviewers for their suggestions and comments: Lesley P. Graham, Bradley University; John Langone, University of Georgia; Anjali Misra, State University of New York at Potsdam; Kathy Peca, Eastern New Mexico University; and Eleanor B. Wright, University of North Carolina at Wilmington.

Contents

PART III
Vocational Support for Transition   255

PART V
Issues in Transition   407

Chapter 17
Current and Future Research Priorities   411

Chapter 18
The Future of Transition: Theoretical and Practical Issues   427

PART I

Background and Foundations

The beginnings of transition. College students practice ambulance skills during World War I. Disabled veterans of World War I were instrumental in initiating legislation for adults with disabilities. The 1990 Americans with Disabilities Act is the culmination of legislative efforts in this area.

*B*ackground and foundations of the transition of individuals with mild disabilities are presented in five chapters (chap. 1: "Rationale and Definitions"; chap. 2: "History and Legislation"; chap. 3: "Models of Transition and Related Areas"; chap. 4: "The Process of Transition"; chap. 5: "Transition Barriers and Supports"). In the following narrative we present a rationale for each chapter and a conceptual overview.

❦ ❦ ❦

CHAPTER 1

Educators are notorious for creating synonymous and redundant terms and concepts. Special educators are no exception. In order to communicate effectively, however, they need definitions. In addition to facilitating effective communication, definitions also are tied to federal, state, and local regulations, to funding sources, to the existence of services for persons with mild disabilities, and to client and provider characteristics and job descriptions. Based on this rationale and following a discussion of the justification for the need for transition for individuals with mild disabilities, a number of definitions related to transition and the mildly disabled are presented. The reader is referred to a transitional schemata (Figure 1–1) for the mildly disabled that encompasses the transitional components and subcomponents of career, special and vocational education, and vocational rehabilitation.

❦ ❦ ❦

CHAPTER 2

Although the term *transition* was not used before the 1980s, a number of individuals concerned with young adults with disabilities designed and initiated secondary programs and curricula for "life after high school." A historical overview of these programs is beyond the scope of this text. Students with mild disabilities, however, have rights and needs. These are supported within the cultural context encompassing history and legislation. Efforts of parents and a number of national and local organizations (e.g., the Association for Retarded Citizens, the Learning Disabilities Association) have influenced the development of transitional services for students with mild disabilities. Legislative enactments have provided a major impetus for establishing transitional services for students with disabilities. As a background to the current interest and mandated support for transition, an overview of these pertinent historical and legislative events is given. The chapter concludes with a presentation of federal involvement in the area of transition for students with mild disabilities.

❦ ❦ ❦

CHAPTER 3

In this chapter we present the major transition models that have evolved from federal legislation. Transition includes not only that from secondary special education into employment but also the transition from secondary education into adulthood (encompassing postsecondary education, employment, community, leisure, and retirement). A number of models from related disciplines that have evolved from the foundations of transitional components are also described here (e.g., career and vocational models).

✻ ✻ ✻

CHAPTER 4

Working from the concepts of individuals, methods, settings, and setting agents associated with the models of transition described in chapter 3, we have conceptualized a process of transition in chapter 4. This process is enacted by the student with mild disabilities and a person or persons who we have identified as facilitators of the transitional process. These individuals interact with agents within specific settings, such as the community or the workplace, and utilize a variety of methods, such as consultation, cooperation, and advocacy. Chapter 4 addresses this process. The reader is referred to the schemata for the process of transition (Figure 4–1), which illustrates the interactions among the various components.

✻ ✻ ✻

CHAPTER 5

Supports for and barriers to transition are presented in this chapter within the systems framework described by Bronfenbrenner (1977). The four systems are actually social environments or contexts within which the student with mild disabilities develops and interacts with pertinent individuals, institutions, and society.

Bronfenbrenner (1977) defines the ***microsystem*** as a "complex of relations between the developing person and environment in an immediate setting containing that person. . . . The factors of place, time, physical features, activity, participant and role constitute the elements of a setting" (p. 514). Supports and barriers to transition, such as attitudes and expectations created by individuals (parents, coworkers, or special education teachers) interacting with the student with mild disabilities, are presented in this context.

The ***mesosystem*** is defined as "interrelations among major settings containing the developing person at a particular point in his or her life" (Bronfenbrenner, 1977, p. 515). Supports and barriers to transition, such as academic and agency requirements, created by the various vocational and special education components related to transition within the mesosystem are presented.

Bronfenbrenner (1977) defines the ***exosystem*** as

an extension of the mesosystem embracing other special social structures both formal and informal, that do not themselves contain the developing person but impinge upon or encompass the immediate settings in which that person is found, and thereby influence, delimit or even determine what goes on there. These structures include the major institutions of society both deliberately structured and spontaneously evolving, as they operate at a concrete local level. They encompass, among other structures, the world of work, the neighborhood, the mass media, agencies of government. (p. 515)

Presented within this social context are supports and barriers to transition, such as interagency agreements, interagency consultation, and cooperation, created by communication across agencies and institutions involved with the individual with mild disabilities.

The *macrosystem* is defined by Bronfenbrenner (1977) as

the overarching institutional patterns of the culture or subculture, such as the economic, social, educational, legal and political systems, of which micro-, meso-, and
exo-systems are the concrete manifestations. Macro-systems are conceived and
examined not only in structural terms but as carriers of information and ideology
that both explicitly and implicitly endow meaning and motivation to particular
agencies, social networks, roles, activities and their interrelations. (p. 515)

A discussion of cultural supports and barriers to or for transition (legal mandates, economic and financial trends, political and social issues) concludes this chapter.

※ Vignettes ※

(a) "My daughter is severely learning disabled with multiperceptual motor deficits and social skills difficulties.

"To date, she is unemployed in Maine since there seems to be no jobs in this area that she can successfully participate in. There is also no public transportation. There are some very excellent facilities in this area for those with severe mental disabilities but she would not meet that criteria for eligibility.

"In 1988, she was referred to Vocational Rehabilitation by the Social Security Administration. However, it seems that Vocational Rehabilitation Services in this northern area of Maine leave much to be desired.

"To date, two options have been suggested to us. The first is placement in Goodwill Industries in Portland, which is 250 miles away. The second option offered on February 7, 1989, was for some new facility in Bangor. We are waiting further information on this program.

"Since a residential program seems to be the best long-range placement for our daughter, we find that there are no programs in Maine exclusively for the learning disabled; however, various out-of-state facilities are listed in a recent publication" (Smith, 1989, p. 121).

(b) "My son was/is most interested in attending a vocational school. His school counselor advised young Phil to seek vocational counseling after graduating (1987). It has been one disappointment after another. Young Phil's words (age 22): 'I was told a professional counselor would team up with me, explore employment options, decide on vocational goals, write a program plan. Here's the results: 2 years out of school, 3 fast food jobs, making more big money—$3,000 for 1 year. Where's the help?'" (Smith, 1989, p. 111).

(c) "My son has a reading problem. He was in a regular classroom. He did not get into a Resource Room until eighth grade. He was okay in everything except the subjects which required a lot of reading. In high school, he was on the football team and the baseball team and made all-star teams. If it wasn't for sports, I think he would have wanted to drop out of school.

"I am writing because I realize LD is a hidden handicap and too many kids are bypassed because teachers and counselors do not know enough about learning disabilities. I had to keep after the schools to give him help with his reading. According to the school, as long as he read at the sixth grade level when he graduates that was good enough. I wanted him to read better. My son feels ashamed that he does not read well.

"He was graduated in June and got a tutor in January. It is over a year and he is still being tutored. The principals, counselors, and regular classroom teachers all need to be enlightened about LD. I did not like the attitudes of the school counselors I had contact with. We wouldn't have so many LD adults unprepared for work if the schools would change their ways and do more to prepare the LD student for working and everyday living" (Smith, 1989, p. 122).

These vignettes are parts of unsolicited letters from parents of individuals with disabilities who are in transition from school to postsecondary pursuits. The reports are not encouraging. The three young adults who are mildly disabled are living at home, unemployed, and apparently dependent on family support and assistance. Reports of this type are not surprising. Many individuals with disabilities leave school and stay unemployed for long periods. Those who acquire employment usually do so in jobs that require limited skills, offer low salaries, and produce low job satisfaction. In addition, many individuals with disabilities lead unfulfilled lives in several areas of adult functioning. Currently, interest in the transition of individuals with disabilities from school to adult life and employment is receiving national attention.

REFERENCES

Bronfenbrenner, U. (1977). Toward an experimental ecology of human development. *American Psychologist, 32,* 513–531.

Smith, J. O. (1989). *Access to rehabilitation services by adults with learning disabilities.* Unpublished doctoral dissertation, Pennsylvania State University, University Park.

Chapter 1

❦ ❦ ❦

Rationale and Definitions

I n this chapter, we will provide a rationale for the new interest in transition, a description of the major components and subcomponents associated with transitional programming, and definitions of some basic concepts related to mild disabilities. We will conclude the chapter with some of our own definitions, which will be used throughout this text.

❦ ❦ ❦

RATIONALE

Transition from school to adult life for individuals with disabilities has become a national priority. School dropout rates, underachievement, lack of appropriate career/vocational/counseling assessments and programs, limited parental involvement and work experiences, and the lack of cooperative programming and support systems have resulted in serious unemployment and other problems that hinder an efficient and satisfying adult existence. Economically, the burden affects not only the individual who is disabled but each taxpayer as well.

According to the U.S. Commission on Civil Rights (1983), unemployment among persons with disabilities was estimated to be between 50% and 75% compared to 7% among nondisabled individuals. Bowe (1978) reported that 63% of individuals with disabilities were at or near the poverty level. Brolin and Elliott (1984) disclosed that over 7 million adults with disabilities did not have a personal income, and over 4 million earned less than $3,000 a year. Of the adults with disabilities who were employed, average earnings were approximately $2,000 less than their nondisabled peers. In addition, many of the 500,000 students with disabilities who exit the educational system yearly do so "woefully unprepared to acquire satisfactory societal roles in occupational, avocational, and daily living activities" (p. 12).

Rusch and Phelps (1987) cite the results of a Harris telephone survey of 1,000 individuals with disabilities conducted in 1985:

- Of the respondents, ages 16 to 64, 67% were not working.
- If an individual with a disability was working, that person was 75% more likely to be employed part-time than a nondisabled person.
- Of those persons with disabilities not working, 67% said that they wanted to work.

The result of unemployment and inadequate transition of persons with disabilities is an increased burden on society. Razeghi (1979) indicates that the annual cost for dependent individuals with disabilities exceeds $115 billion. Support programs such as sheltered workshops, day-care services, and unemployment benefits at times exceeded $12,000 annually per individual (Phelps, Blanchard, Larkin, & Cobb, 1982; Walls, Zawlocki, & Dowler, 1986). Undoubtedly, inflation has now doubled that figure. Will (1983) reports that "approximately 8% of the gross national product is spent each year in disability programs, with most of this amount going to programs that support dependence" (p. 1).

Although one would assume that this type of dependency would be prevalent only among persons with severe disabilities, the prognosis for those with mild disabilities leaves much to be desired. In a review of career outcomes for students with mild disabilities, McAfee and Mann (1982) draw the following conclusions:

- Employment rates of individuals who are mildly disabled leaving secondary schools range from 30% to 92%.
- A majority of people with disabilities are likely to change jobs over three times in a 2-year period following graduation.
- Interpersonal problems are the most common cause for dismissal.
- The longer young adults with disabilities are in the work force, the more likely it is that they will obtain stable employment.
- A small percentage of youths with disabilities enter skilled occupations upon leaving school.
- Once in the work force for a period of time, an adult with disabilities has a greater probability of obtaining a skilled position.
- Employed workers with disabilities are likely to be generally satisfied with their jobs, with the major source of dissatisfaction being the lack of opportunity for advancement.
- The modal earning level of workers with disabilities is estimated to be only slightly higher than the minimum wage.

Owings and Stockling (1985), in a comparison of students with and without mild disabilities leaving secondary education, report the following:

- Of the 1980 sophomores, 18.6% as compared to 12.6% of the students without disabilities had dropped out of school between their sophomore and senior years.
- Of these sophomores, 45% were in the lowest quartile on combined vocabulary, reading, math, and science tests, compared to only 19% of the nondisabled.
- Only 29.4% were enrolled in vocational education programs.

Clearly, the pressing need and rationale for transition intervention and planning has been demonstrated.

Although a number of transition programs and services are funded and provided for all levels of disabling conditions, our position is that transition efforts that will result in a positive prognosis for the individuals who fall in the mild to moderate range of disabling conditions can and should be emphasized. Individuals in these categories include those with moderate/mild mental retardation (MR), learning disabilities (LD), and emotional disturbance (ED). Backing for this position can be found in reports of federally funded projects supporting transition. Those projects served 9,816 LD students and 755 ED students between 1984 and 1988. Out of 18,877 students served during that period, 14,912 were identified as either LD, MR, or ED (Dowling & Hartwell, 1988).

❦ ❦ ❦

TRANSITIONAL COMPONENTS AND DEFINITIONS

To establish a common point of reference, we will now present basic definitions of transition, a brief discussion of the four components related to transition (career education, vocational education, special education, and vocational rehabilitation), and transitional subcomponents (see Figure 1–1). Then we will describe categories of mild disabilities: mental retardation, learning disabilities, and emotional disturbance. The relationship between definitions and the components of transition is presented, followed by the definitions of transition and related terms that we will use throughout this text.

Transition

The *American Heritage Dictionary* (1982) defines *transition* as "the process or an instance of changing from one form, state, activity, or place to another" (p. 1287). The process of transition from school to adult life for individuals with disabling conditions is almost always more difficult than for their nondisabled peers. In addition, difficulty of transition is compounded by the different meanings of transition. This is further complicated by the severity of the disabling condition and the perception of the individual and professionals of the importance of resources or services needed to accomplish the process.

A widely accepted definition of transition is presented by Will (1984):

> The transition from school to working life is an outcome-oriented process encompassing a broad array of services and experiences that lead to employment. Transition is a period that includes high school, the point of graduation, additional postsecondary education or adult services, and the initial years in employment. Transition is a bridge between the security and structure offered by the school and the opportunities and risks of adult life.
>
> Any bridge requires both a solid span and a secure foundation at either end. The transition from school to work and adult life requires sound preparation in the secondary school, adequate support at the point of school leaving, and secure opportunities and services, if needed, in adult situations. (p. 3)

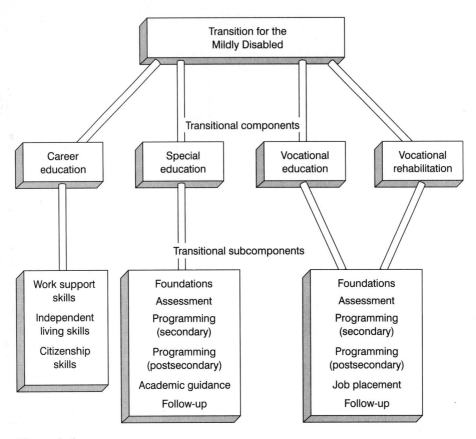

Figure 1–1
Transition schemata

Will's definition has been criticized as too narrow by others such as Halpern (1985):

> What the authors of this policy seem to be suggesting is that the nonvocational dimensions of adult adjustment are significant and important only in so far as they contribute to the ultimate goal of employment. Such a position can be challenged both philosophically and empirically. (p. 480)

Halpern adds two additional components to the definition that emphasize the importance of the quality of the "residential environment" and the "social and interpersonal network."

Career Education

In 1971, Sidney Marland, Jr., former U.S. commissioner of education, introduced but did not explicitly define the term *career education* at a speech presented before the annual convention of the National Association of Secondary School Principals. The concept sparked the imagination of many educators, and since that time a number of diverse definitions have been proposed. As with the definition of transition, career education has been viewed from narrow and broad perspectives. The narrow perspective limits the definition to a vocational focus, whereas the broad perspective reflects a life approach.

Definitions encompassing a narrow perspective of career education include the following:

1. The U.S. Office of Education in 1975 defined career education as "the totality of experience through which one learns about and prepares to engage in work as part of his or her way of living" (Hoyt, 1975, p. 4).
2. Hoyt (1977) has stated that career education is "an effort aimed at refocusing American education and the actions of the broader community in ways that will help individuals acquire and utilize the knowledge, skills, and attitudes necessary for each to make work a meaningful, productive, and satisfying part of his or her way of living" (p. 5).

A broader perspective can be seen in the following definition written for the U.S. Office of Career Education. This definition extends the concept of a career beyond just an occupation and includes the work of volunteers, students, and housewives:

> The sequence of major positions occupied by a person throughout his preoccupational, occupational, and postoccupational life; includes work-related roles such as those of student, employee, and pensioner, together with complementary avocational familial, and civic roles. Careers exist only as people pursue them; they are person-centered. (Super, 1976, p. 20)

A more widely accepted definition of career education appears in a position paper by the Council for Exceptional Children (1978):

> Career education is the totality of experiences through which one learns to live a meaningful, satisfying work life . . . . career education provides the opportunity for children to learn, in the least restrictive environment possible, the academic, daily living, personal-social, and occupational knowledge and specific vocational work skills necessary for attaining their highest levels of economic, personal and social fulfillment. The individual can obtain this fulfillment through work (both paid and unpaid) and in a variety of other societal roles and personal life styles . . . as a student, citizen, volunteer, family member and participant in meaningful leisure-time activities. (p. 1)

Thus, in the broad sense, career education is concerned with the total person and with his or her adjustment for community working and living. Related to this broad conceptualization of career education, Brolin, Elliott, and Corcoran (1984) offer the following key components:

1. It begins in early childhood and continues through the retirement years.
2. It encompasses the total curriculum of the school and provides a unified approach to education for life.
3. It focuses on the various life roles, settings, and events that are important in the productive work life of the individual.

4. It encourages all members of the community to have a shared responsibility and a mutual cooperative relationship among various disciplines.
5. It includes learning in the home, in private and public agencies, in the employment community, as well as in the school.
6. It encourages all teachers to relate their subject matter to its career implications.
7. It recognizes the need for basic education, citizenship, family responsibility, and other important educational objectives.
8. It provides for career awareness, career exploration, and skills development at all levels and ages.
9. It provides a balance of content and experiential learning with substantial hands-on activities.
10. It provides a personal framework to help individuals plan their lives through carefully conceived career decision making.
11. It promotes the opportunity for students to acquire a saleable entry-level occupational skill before leaving school.
12. It actively involves the parents in all phases of education.
13. It actively involves the community in all phases of education.
14. It requires a lifelong education based on principles related to total individual development.

The components of career education relate to the four phases or stages of life cited by Cegelka (1985), which include (a) career awareness, (b) career exploration, (c) career preparation, and (d) career placement/follow-up/continuing education. Cegelka summarizes the relationship of career education to special education: "Special educators have embraced career education as the missing link between academic and vocational preparation, and as the means for developing an integrated approach to the total preparation of the handicapped student" (p. 575).

Special Education

The major parts of a definition of special education would include all of the elements involved in educating exceptional children. A concise definition of the field, however, can be found in the *Encyclopedia of Special Education* (Reynolds & Mann, 1987):

> Exceptional children, i.e., handicapped or gifted individuals between the ages of birth and 23, constitute (depending on various types of estimation) nearly 10% of children and adolescents who receive educational services throughout the world. The field of endeavor concerned with this education is generally designated as special education. (p. xvii)

The field of special education has expanded tremendously since the passage in 1975 of PL 94-142, the Education for All Handicapped Children Act (known since 1990 as the Individuals with Disabilities Education Act). The first part of this act is paraphrased by Kirk and Gallagher (1979) as follows:

We hold these truths to be self-evident, that all children handicapped and non-handicapped, are created equal; that they are endowed by their creator with certain inalienable rights, among these are the right to equal education to the maximum of each child's capability. To secure these rights, Public Law 94-142 was established. We, the people of the United States, solemnly declare that all exceptional children shall be educated at public expense, and that their education will be in the least restrictive environment. (p. xi)

Historically, special educators have been involved with preparing individuals with disabilities to lead productive and satisfying lives. Special education's interest in career education and transition reaffirms this commitment. Within the broad definition of transition, options can range from sheltered workshops to college entrance for those with mild disabilities. Training within these options involves a close relationship with vocational education and vocational rehabilitation.

Vocational Education

Definitions of vocational education are also numerous and varied. In addition, many practitioners mistakenly equate vocational education with career education. In an overview of career education, Kokaska (1983) points out that vocational education includes training in a wide variety of specific technical skills essential in performing work roles. "This training is supervised by specialists who qualify for such occupational areas as accountant, secretary, or electrician. Training begins at the secondary level and is defined in terms of courses within an instructional program" (p. 194).

Cegelka (1985) defines vocational education as providing specific vocational skill training and vocational adjustment. The following definition is included in PL 94-142:

Vocational education means organized educational programs which are directly related to the preparations of individuals for paid or unpaid employment or for additional preparation for a career requiring other than a baccalaureate or advanced degree. (Section 121a.14[b][3])

In addition, vocational education is "included as special education" if it consists of specially designed instruction, at no cost to the parents, to meet the unique needs of a handicapped child. (Section 121.14[a][3])

Hoyt, Evans, Mackin, and Mangum (1974) outline five stages of vocational education. These stages are appropriate today when defining vocational education from a broad perspective that includes the following points:

1. Awareness of primary work roles played by persons in society
2. Exploration of work roles that an individual might consider as important, possible, and probably for him- or herself
3. Vocational decision making (which can go from a highly tentative to a very specific form)
4. Establishment (including preparing for and actually assuming a primary work role)

5. Maintenance (all of the ways in which a person gains—or fails to gain—personal meaningfulness and satisfaction from the primary work role he or she has assumed)

Vocational Rehabilitation

Historically, the field of vocational rehabilitation has involved adults with disabilities. Currently, however, vocational rehabilitation counselors are becoming involved with secondary students who have disabilities and are in the transitional process. The field of vocational rehabilitation includes three elements: rehabilitation, vocational education, and vocational guidance. In order to understand the relationship of vocational rehabilitation to transition, each of these elements needs to be addressed. Brutting (1987) defines rehabilitation as

> any process, procedure or program that enables a disabled individual to function at a more independent and personally satisfying level. This functioning should include all aspects—physical, mental, emotional, social, educational, and vocational—of the individual's life. . . . The range of disabilities is wide and varied, including such conditions as autism, mental retardation, muscular dystrophy and a variety of neurological and orthopedic disorders. (p. 1329)

Historically, vocational guidance has been an important part of vocational rehabilitation. Vocational guidance encompasses not only directing clients to vocational training but also identifying job opportunities and placement services. As early as the 1930s, in a manual for case workers, guidance was emphasized:

> One of the most important services given by a rehabilitation agent is that of counsel and advisement. It is a continuous service designed to assist the disabled person in choosing, preparing for, entering upon and making progress in an occupation. (U.S. Department of the Interior, 1934, p. 49)

The problems encountered by vocational rehabilitation counselors in their role involving vocational guidance is aptly portrayed by the following paraphrased segments of an account given by a vocational guidance counselor cited by Payne, Mercer, and Epstein (1974, p. 54). The counselor's hopes are related not only to vocational rehabilitation but also to the field of transition:

> "Several years ago I was hired as a vocational rehabilitation counselor and I can readily recall my first day on the job. I was assigned a caseload of handicapped clients. . . . I was instructed to read the policy manual and find the clients. 'What do you mean, "find the clients"'? I responded. The response was 'The last counselor left unexpectedly and the first thing you need to do is find out who and where your clients are.'"
>
> The counselor was told, by the client's former employer, that the individual had walked off the job. Following the encounter with the employer, the counselor concluded, "I hope counselors [will learn] to understand business routine, schedule, and business thinking." It took the counselor 4 days to find the client. "He was at home, unshaven, watching television, and feeling sorry for himself. He

was living in a place which smelled like urine and looked like a pigsty." The counselor concluded, "I hope [that counselors will learn] about people." Within 1 year, the client walked off of five jobs. The counselor concluded, "I hope [that counselors learn] something about evaluation and training."

After talking to an employer who was upset about a client breaking a window, the counselor concluded, "I hope [that counselors will learn] about how to approach an employer."

After talking to other counselors who had placed six clients on a job in 1 day and found that they had left a month later, the counselor concluded, "I hope [that counselors will learn] about follow-up."

After a client working at the local humane society released all the animals because he did not like to see them caged, the counselor concluded, "I hope that the counselors will understand people's feelings."

After a client who had been incarcerated for stealing bicycles found successful employment in a bicycle shop, the counselor concluded, "You know, I hope [that counselors] really [do learn] about people, all types of people."

In short, a number of problems were encountered by the counselor. The solutions to these problems involved a predictable mixture of success and failure.

Summary and Discussion

A number of common themes can be extracted from the aforementioned definitions and descriptions of components associated with transition. Transition can be viewed as a lifelong process encompassing critical transition periods in an individual's life, including the sequence of transition from home to elementary education, to middle school, to secondary education, to postsecondary education or employment, and to retirement. Transition can be viewed from the narrow perspective (transition from school to employment) or from the broader perspective (including all the environmental, social, family, community, employment, and leisure components that in combination define an individual's life).

These two themes can be seen in the definitions associated with career education and vocational education and to a lesser degree in vocational rehabilitation. The topics of this text are confined to the transitional period from school to adult life, a time considered to be one of the most critical periods in the life of an individual with a disability. In addition, we view transition and related areas from a broad perspective. In short, our position is that the objectives of transition must take into account not only employment but all the environmental, community, and social variables that influence an adult's life, including the ones so aptly described by the vocational rehabilitation counselor. In addition, secondary transition for a person with mild disabilities does not end at the time that a person achieves employment or parenthood but continues throughout the person's life span.

In the following section we present definitions and characteristics of this population.

❦ ❦ ❦

DEFINITIONS OF MILD DISABILITIES

Most disabling conditions can be viewed on a continuum from severe to mild. The focus of this text is on the majority of individuals with disabilities who fall in the moderate to mild range in the categories of learning disability, emotional disturbance, and mental retardation.

Learning Disability

The term *learning disability* is considered a recent addition to the list of disabling conditions. It was first coined by Samuel Kirk in the 1960s, although the characteristics of an individual who might today be identified by this label were addressed in the literature as early as 1850 (Hallahan & Kauffman, 1977). At that time, the young man in question addressed his problem as a mental weakness. Subsequent terms for individuals who could not learn at expected rates and who exhibited behaviors that might be considered as stemming from a neurological base included *brain injured, minimal brain dysfunction, hyperactive, attention deficit disorder, neurologically impaired,* and *dyslexic.* These conditions are subsumed under the current federal definition:

> Specific learning disability means a disorder in one or more of the basic psychological processes involved in understanding or in using language, spoken or written, which may manifest itself in an imperfect ability to listen, think, speak, read, write, spell or do mathematical calculations. The term includes such conditions as perceptual handicap, brain injury, minimal brain dysfunction, dyslexia and developmental aphasia. The term does not include children who have learning problems which are primarily the result of visual, hearing, or motor handicaps, of mental retardation, or of environmental, cultural or economic disadvantage. (*Federal Register,* 1977, p. 42478)

In 1981, the National Joint Committee on Learning Disabilities (NJCLD) formulated the following definition (Hammill, Leigh, McNutt, & Larsen, 1981). This new NJCLD definition was not designed to set up operational criteria for identifying individual cases of learning disabilities but to serve as a theoretical basis for the discipline. The definition is as follows:

> Learning disabilities is a generic term that refers to a heterogeneous group of disorders manifested by significant difficulties in the acquisition and use of listening, speaking, reading, writing, reasoning, or mathematical abilities. These disorders are intrinsic to the individual and presumed to be due to central nervous system dysfunction. Even though a learning disability may occur concomitantly with other handicapping conditions (e.g., sensory impairment, mental retardation, social and emotional disturbance) or environmental influences (e.g., cultural differences, insufficient/inappropriate instruction, psychogenic factors), it is not the direct result of these conditions or influences. (p. 336)

A great deal of controversy has arisen over the definition of learning disabilities, partly because many students who do not have a learning disability are identified and served within this category. This overidentification occurred because of the availability of funding and the lack of services for under-achieving students. Although overidentification is not justifiable, the premise that theoretical definitions result in or necessarily include criteria for identification also is not defensible. The preceding NJCLD definition is a theoretical one, and identification and diagnostic criteria call for further research and study.

Emotional Disturbance

As with the category of learning disabilities, the definition of emotional disturbance leaves much to be desired in terms of identification and diagnostic relevance. The Group for the Advancement of Psychiatry (1966) proposes no fewer than 24 different methods of classifying emotional disturbance. Basically, a child is considered to have an emotional disturbance when he or she does not behave in an acceptable fashion or when someone judges his or her behavior to be inappropriate. This definition could conceivably include a myriad of behaviors and, consequently (as in the area of learning disability), a myriad of children.

By definition, personality and social adjustment disorders are associated with children classified as emotionally disturbed. Historically, a major problem in this area has been the lack of an acceptable method of classifying emotional disturbance. Schemes of classification have been based on descriptive adult psychiatry. Terms such as *childhood schizophrenia, neurosis,* and *depression* have been associated with emotionally disturbed children and young adults. In the 1960s and 1970s, classification systems began to take childhood disorders into account. Phillips, Draguns, and Bartlett (1975) outline three challenges facing those trying to classify emotional disorders of children: (a) an emancipation from models of psychopathology; (b) a need to classify behaviors and disorders, not individuals, since maladaptive behaviors of children have the potential for rapid modification; and (c) a need to incorporate data on childhood disorders and normal progressions of development. Recently, Cummings and Maddux (1987), in their discussion of mild emotional disturbance, address six different approaches to the condition: (a) the psychodynamic or psychoeducational, (b) the sociological, (c) the ecological, (d) the biological, (e) the behavioral, and (f) the countertheory.

An overview of these approaches suggests that there exists a continuum of disabilities ranging from severe to mild. The young adults (16–25) addressed in this text fall in the subcategory that is often referred to as mild behavioral disorders and/or socially maladjusted. The definition of emotional disturbance incorporated into PL 94-142 (*Federal Register,* 1977) concentrates on the severe end of the continuum. As with the definition of learning disabilities, however, the definition is presented as the basis for a theoretical framework for this category:

> (i) The term means a condition exhibiting one or more of the following characteristics over a long period of time and to a marked degree, which adversely affects

educational performance; (a) an inability to learn which cannot be explained by intellectual, sensory, or health factors; (b) an inability to build or maintain satisfactory interpersonal relationships with peers and teachers; (c) inappropriate types of behavior or feelings under normal circumstances; (d) a general pervasive mood of unhappiness or depression; or (e) a tendency to develop physical symptoms or fears associated with personal or school problems.

(ii) The term includes children who are schizophrenic or autistic. The term does not include children who are socially maladjusted, unless it is determined that they are seriously emotionally disturbed. (Section 121a.5, p. 42478)

Mental Retardation

In 1973, the definition of mental retardation formulated by the American Association on Mental Deficiency was revised to exclude previously identified individuals. The definition (Grossman, 1983) included in PL 94-142 reads as follows:

Mental retardation refers to significantly subaverage general intellectual functioning existing concurrently with deficits in adaptive behavior, and manifested during the developmental period . . . . significantly subaverage refers to performance which is two or more standard deviations from the mean or average of the test. (p. 11)

This definition excludes previously included children with IQ scores of 71 to 85. It is not unrealistic to hypothesize that youngsters within this IQ range, who would have been identified as mentally retarded prior to 1973, are currently being considered learning disabled. In addition, maladaptation as an identifying criterion also is difficult to assess. It has been proposed that if a child's behavior violates the teacher's norms, he or she is referred for psychological evaluation and then is judged to be maladapted (Mercer, 1973). Students falling into the IQ range of 71 to 85 and exhibiting maladaptive behavior could and often are identified as being learning disabled.

Summary and Discussion

Controversy over definitions (especially those of mild disabilities) exists. We believe that definitions can only serve as a theoretical framework rather than as a basis for identification or intervention for transition. Identification and transition intervention for these students must be individualized and take into consideration those characteristics and discrepancies that might hinder successful adult functioning. The identification of such characteristics must be based on what is needed for acceptable adult functioning. Individualized identification and intervention within a normal framework might result in the identification of transition subtypes within or across traditional categories. For the present, however, the fact remains that the majority of secondary students with disabilities are mildly retarded, learning disabled, or mildly emotionally disturbed.

❦ ❦ ❦

DEFINITIONS AND TRANSITIONAL SUBCOMPONENTS

Figure 1–1 shows a number of transitional subcomponents that are related to the four transitional components. Subcomponents such as work support skills, independent living skills, and citizenship skills, although listed under career education, are related to each transitional component. The skills are listed under career education in order to facilitate discussion and present the reader with an organizational diagram. Definitions and discussions of the subcomponents are addressed in subsequent sections of this text.

In the following section of this chapter, we present our definitions of the terms related to transition that we will use throughout this text.

Transition

Transition for the mildly disabled is the process or movement through secondary education into adulthood and encompasses a number of critical periods in an individual's life, including the sequence from secondary education, to postsecondary education or employment, and on to retirement. Transition includes all of the environments (social, family, community, employment, leisure, etc.) that in combination influence and define a person who is mildly disabled as an individual. Transition is the movement from the protection and dependence of childhood to the risk and independence of a fully realized adulthood.

Special Education

Special education is the educational services provided in the "least restrictive environment" to individuals in a secondary setting. These include, but are not limited to, special placements such as a resource room setting; individualized curricula and instruction; Individualized Education and Transition Plans; individualized assessment; individualized academic, personal, and employment training; as well as counseling and guidance.

Career Education

Career education includes experiences and opportunities provided to persons with mild disabilities that assist and facilitate in determining the various roles and positions that each individual will occupy throughout his or her life span.

Vocational Education

Vocational education entails educational services and training provided to secondary and postsecondary students within a vocational program. This includes training necessary for employment and on the job adjustment.

Vocational Rehabilitation

Vocational rehabilitation services are provided to adolescents and adults with disabilities during critical transitional periods, such as that from secondary to postsecondary education or employment. Services include such areas as financial assistance, guidance, advisement, and they encompass all areas related to independent living. These services are provided through state vocational rehabilitation agencies.

Mild Disabilities

Mild disabilities are those in the moderate to mild range on the continuum of severity of a disabling condition, in the categories of learning disability, emotional disturbance, or mental retardation. The definitions of the three categories as stated in PL 94-142 are used in this text (see the Emotional Disturbance section earlier).

REFERENCES

American Heritage Dictionary (2nd college ed.). (1982). Boston: Houghton Mifflin.

Bowe, F. (1978). *Handicapping America: Barriers to disabled people.* New York: Harper & Row.

Brolin, D. E., & Elliott, T. R. (1984). Meeting the lifelong career development needs of students with handicaps. *Career Development for Exceptional Individuals, 7*(1), 12–21.

Brolin, D. E., Elliott, T. R., & Corcoran, J. R. (1984). Career education for persons with learning disabilities. *Learning Disabilities, 3*(1), 1–14.

Brutting, L. K. (1987). Rehabilitation. In C. R. Reynolds & L. Mann (Eds.), *Encyclopedia of special education* (Vol. 3, p. 1329). New York: Wiley.

Cegelka, P. T. (1985). Career and vocational education. In W. H. Berdine & A. E. Blackhurst (Eds.), *An introduction to special education* (pp. 572–612). Boston: Little, Brown.

Cummings, R. W., & Maddux, C. D. (1987). *Career and vocational education for the mildly handicapped.* Springfield, IL: Thomas.

Council for Exceptional Children. (1978). *Position paper on career education.* Reston, VA: Author.

Dowling, J., & Hartwell, C. (1988). Overview of secondary transitional services in the United States. *Interchange, 4*(8), 1–5.

Federal Register. (1977, August 23). Washington, DC: U.S. Government Printing Office.

Grossman, H. (Ed.). (1983). *Manual on terminology and classification in mental retardation.* Washington, DC: American Association on Mental Deficiency.

Group for the Advancement of Psychiatry. (1966). *Psychopathological disorders in childhood: Theoretical considerations and a proposed classification.* New York: Author.

Hallahan, D. P., & Kauffman, J. M. (1977). Categories, labels, behavioral characteristics: ED, LD, and EMR reconsidered. *Journal of Special Education, 11*(2), 139–149.

Halpern, A. S. (1985). Transition: A look at the foundations. *Exceptional Children, 51*(6), 479–486.

Hammill, D. D., Leigh, J. E., McNutt, G., & Larsen, S. C. (1981). A new definition of learning disabilities. *Learning Disability Quarterly, 4*(4), 336–342.

Hoyt, K. B. (1975). *An introduction to career education: A policy paper of the Office of Education.* Washington, DC: U.S. Office of Education.

Hoyt, K. B. (1977). *A primer for career education.* Washington, DC: U.S. Government Printing Office.

Hoyt, K. B., Evans, R. N., Mackin, E., & Mangum, G. L. (1974). *Career education: What is it and how to do it.* Salt Lake City: Olympus.

Kirk, S. A., & Gallagher, J. J. (1979). *Educating exceptional children* (3rd ed.). Boston: Houghton Mifflin.

Kokaska, C. J. (1983). Career education: A brief overview. *Teaching Exceptional Children, 15*, 194–195.

Marland, S. (1971). *Career education now.* Paper presented at the annual convention of the National Association of Secondary School Principals, Houston, TX.

McAfee, J. K., & Mann, L. (1982). The prognosis for mildly handicapped adults. In T. Miller & E. E. David (Eds.), *The mildly handicapped student* (pp. 461–496). New York: Grune & Stratton.

Mercer, J. R. (1973). *Labeling the mentally retarded.* Berkeley: University of California.

Owings, J., & Stockling, C. (1985). *Characteristics of high school students who identify themselves as handicapped. High school and beyond: A national longitudinal study for the 1980s.* Washington, DC: National Center for Education Statistics.

Payne, J. S., Mercer, C. D., & Epstein, M. H. (1974). *Education and rehabilitation techniques.* New York: Behavioral.

Phelps, L. A., Blanchard, L. C., Larkin, D., & Cobb, R. B. (1982). *Vocational programming and services for handicapped individuals in Illinois: Program costs and benefits.* Springfield: Illinois State Board of Education.

Phillips, L., Draguns, J. G., & Bartlett, D. P. (1975). Classification of behavior disorders. In N. Hobbs (Ed.), *Issues in the classification of children: Vol. 1.* San Francisco: Jossey-Bass.

Razeghi, J. A. (1979). *Final report of supplement to consumer involvement in career and vocational education.* Washington, DC: American Coalition of Citizens with Disabilities.

Reynolds, C. R., & Mann, L. (Eds.). (1987). *Encyclopedia of special education: Vol 1.* New York: Wiley.

Rusch, F. R., & Phelps, L. A. (1987). Secondary special education and transition from school to work: A national priority. *Exceptional Children, 53*(6), 487–492.

Super, D. E. (1976). *Career education and the meanings of work* (Monographs on Career Education). Washington, DC: U.S. Department of Health, Education, and Welfare, Office of Education.

U.S. Commission on Civil Rights. (1983). *Accommodating the spectrum of disabilities.* Washington, DC: U.S. Commission on Civil Rights.

U.S. Department of the Interior. (1934). *Manual for case-workers* (Bulletin No. 175, Vocational Rehabilitation Series No. 23). Washington, DC: U.S. Government Printing Office.

Walls, R. T., Zawlocki, R. J., & Dowler, D. L. (1986). Economic benefits as disincentives to competitive employment. In F. Rusch (Ed.), *Competitive employment issues and strategies* (pp. 317–329). Baltimore: Brookes.

Will, M. (1983). *OSERS programming for the transition of youth with disabilities: Bridges from school to working life*. Washington, DC: Office of Special Education and Rehabilitative Services.

Will, M. (1984, June). Bridges from school to working life. *Interchange*, 2–6.

Chapter 2

❀ ❀ ❀

History and Legislation

*I*n this chapter we present an overview of historical and legislative events affecting people with disabilities. These events serve as a backdrop for the current interest in transition. The chapter concludes with a look at the federal interest in transition. The reader should note that in this chapter we use the language of the original legislation (e.g., "handicapped individuals") rather than the currently more acceptable term ("individuals with disabilities"). We do this to reflect more accurately the content of the legislation and to avoid confusion.

❀ ❀ ❀

HISTORICAL BACKGROUND: 1917–1970

Phase 1

During the 1800s and early 1900s and prior to pertinent federal legislation, services and schools for individuals with disabilities were dependent on the interest of private firms, individuals, or benefactors. In 1917, based on the concern that disabled World War I veterans would become a burden on society, the U.S. Congress passed the Smith-Hughes Act (PL 64-347), which provided for vocational rehabilitation and employment for disabled veterans. This act was the first in a series of federal laws that strongly influenced the provision of services for the disabled. In addition, the act provided for the first federally supported vocational education curriculum in the secondary schools in the areas of agriculture, home economics, trade, and industrial education. A year later, Congress passed the Smith-Sears Act (PL 65-178), which provided additional rehabilitation support for disabled veterans. Finally, in 1920, Congress passed the Smith-Fess Act (PL 66-236), which offered vocational training for civilians disabled while engaged in civil employment. Although funding for the programs provided under the three acts was minimal (resulting in limited participation and benefit to adults with disabilities), the acts did provide a framework and incentives for future legislation.

During the late 1920s and 1930s, following the advent of unemployment and the Great Depression, interest and funding for disability programs subsided. Two pieces of legislation in the late 1930s, however, added somewhat to the slowly growing federal commitment to individuals with disabilities. The Wagner O'Day Act of 1938 provided for the purchase of certain commodities made by persons who are blind, and the Social Security Act Amendments of 1939 provided financial grants to states for vocational rehabilitation.

Phase 2

In 1943, President Franklin D. Roosevelt signed into law the Bardon-LaFollete Act (PL 77-113). The stimulus for this legislation was the need for manpower in war-related industries. It provided vocational training for individuals with disabilities who did not qualify for military service and, for the first time, included medically related services, such as examinations, corrective surgery, and prosthetic devices. As landmark legislation, the act expanded the concept of rehabilitation to include services for persons with mental retardation. These services, however, were sparse. For example, 10 years later a National Association for Retarded Children subcommittee on sheltered workshops identified only 10 in existence (Miller, Ewing, & Phelps, 1980).

The Vocational Rehabilitation Amendments (PL 83-565) were signed in 1954. They included provisions for the expansion and improvement of vocational and rehabilitation programs. In addition, they provided funds for research and professional training. The existence of work-study programs during the 1950s has been cited as the major vehicle for preparing adolescents with disabilities for the world of work (Brolin, Clark, Hull, as cited in Miller et al., 1980). One of the initial programs was located at Southern Illinois University and included a controlled work experience in school, job placement and experience, and eventual employment (Kolstoe, as cited in Miller et al., 1980). The 1950s also witnessed the first research efforts in employment of persons with mental retardation. In 1955, the first sheltered workshop study was approved by the Office of Vocational Rehabilitation.

Phase 3

During the Kennedy era, a report of the President's Panel on Mental Retardation (1962) advocated vocational training and related services for every youth with mental retardation. The report stated:

> Vocational services should include funding for instruction in appropriate vocational areas, cooperative work study experience programs, on-the-job training programs, and vocational guidance. Obstacles to training the handicapped included (1) failure of cooperation among the various institutions and agencies serving the handicapped and (2) the lack of available job opportunities. (pp. 119–120)

In his 1962 State of the Union address, President John F. Kennedy (U.S. Government Printing Office, 1963) emphasized the findings of the panel by stating, "To help those less fortunate of all, I am recommending a new program of public welfare, stressing service instead of support, rehabilitation instead of relief, and training . . . instead of prolonged dependence" (p. 8).

Following President Kennedy's address, the Vocational Education Act of 1963 included provisions for expanded development of vocational programs and areas of training for the handicapped. In 1964, the commitment to unemployed handicapped and disadvantaged individuals was expanded by the passage of the Economic Opportunity Act. President Lyndon B. Johnson, in his 1964 State of the Union message, stated that the nation was directed toward ensuring all individuals of the opportunity to become healthy and productive members of society. As in earlier periods, however, funding for the necessary programs to meet the stated need was sparse and sporadic, resulting in limited benefits to the handicapped individual (U.S. Government Printing Office, 1965).

The 1960s witnessed the passage of two additional pieces of legislation: the Vocational Rehabilitation Amendments (PL 90-99) of 1967, which provided funds for research and model programs for the rehabilitation of disabled migrant workers and established a national center for the deaf and blind; and the enactment of the Vocational Rehabilitation Amendments of 1968 (PL 90-391), which extended funding and rehabilitation programs and services. Major provisions of the 1968 amendments included:

- funding for rehabilitation, research, demonstration, and training projects;
- creation of programs for the recruitment and training of rehabilitation service providers; and
- authorization of up to 10% of the funds for vocational and rehabilitation programs for the handicapped.

Summary

The 53-year span from 1917 to 1970 included national recognition of the needs of Americans with disabilities in the form of pertinent legislation (see Figure 2–1). Funding for the necessary programs and services, however, was minimal, resulting in limited impact on the plight of individuals with disabilities. In addition, although the Vocational Education Act of 1963 and the Vocational Rehabilitation Amendments of 1968 indicated that vocational training for the handicapped was a priority, programs provided limited access and did not include training in personal, social, and daily living skills necessary for successful adult adjustment (Evans & Clark; Mann, Goodman, & Weiderholt; & Phelps, as cited in Miller et al., 1980; Olympus Research Corporation, 1974; Weisenstein, 1976).

❦ ❦ ❦

HISTORY AND LEGISLATION: THE 1970s

In a historical overview of career and vocational services, Miller et al. (1980) emphasize the limited impact on the transition of handicapped youth of the legislation passed in the 1960s. Their review of Martin's study conducted in

---

Phase I

1800s to early 1900s. No legislation for people with disabilities; schools and services dependent on private firms, individuals, and benefactors

1917	Smith-Hughes Act, PL 64–347
1918	Vocational Rehabilitation Act (Smith-Sears Act), PL 65–178
1920	Vocational Rehabilitation of Persons Disabled in Industry (Smith-Fess Act), PL 66–236
1938	Committee on Purchases of Blind-made Products (Wagner-O'Day Act), PL 75–739
1939	Social Security Act Amendments, PL 76–379

Phase 2

1943	Vocational Rehabilitation Act Amendments (Bardon-LaFollete Act), PL 77–113
1954	Vocational Rehabilitation Amendments, PL 83–565

Phase 3

1962	President's Panel on Mental Retardation Report President Kennedy's State of the Union Address Manpower Development and Training Act, PL 87–415
1963	Vocational Education Act, Colo. L. 146–1–1 et seq.
1964	Economic Opportunity Act, PL 88–452 President Johnson's State of the Union Address
1967	Vocational Rehabilitation Amendments, PL 90–99
1968	Vocational Rehabilitation Amendments, PL 90–391

Figure 2–1
Legislative and historical background

the early 1970s showed that only 21% of youth with disabilities would be fully employed or going on to college, 26% would be unemployed, 40% would be underemployed, and 13% would be dependent on family or community services.

The Vocational Education Act of 1963 and the 1968 Vocational Rehabilitation Amendments indicated that vocational education for persons with disabilities was a priority. In reality, few targeted youngsters benefited or were given access to specified training or services. Tindall (1977) reports that states did not use the 10% of the vocational education funds available, as specified, for persons with disabilities. Weisenstein (1976) observes that handicapped students were not being served appropriately in vocational programs, separate programs were most common, and there was a shortage of trained personnel in the area. A report by the Olympus Research Corporation (1974) shows that even though federal funding was available, the goals and needs of handicapped individuals were not being defined or identified. In addition, vocational programs for these students were not being developed and consequently were not being implemented.

Next we provide an overview of major federal legislation enacted during the 1970s, a most important legislative period.

PL 93-112

The Rehabilitation Act of 1973, although emphasizing services for individuals with severe disabilities, yielded landmark regulations for all handicapped adults. Section 504 of the act provided for significant changes in the training and hiring of handicapped individuals. Specifically, it stated:

> No otherwise qualified handicapped individual in the United States . . . shall, solely by reason of his handicap, be excluded from the participation in, be denied the benefits of, or be subjected to discrimination under any program or activity receiving Federal financial assistance.

Based on this statement, the law guaranteed entrance of "otherwise qualified" handicapped students into colleges and universities when those colleges and universities received federal money from any source.

Section 503 of the act stipulated that businesses with federal contracts were to initiate an affirmative action plan for the purpose of hiring, recruiting, training, and promoting handicapped individuals. Bies (1987) provides the following objective summary of other provisions of the law:

- to promote expanded employment opportunities for the handicapped in all areas of business and industry;
- to establish state plans for the purpose of providing vocational rehabilitation services to meet the needs of the handicapped;
- to conduct evaluations of the potential rehabilitation of handicapped clients;
- to expand services to handicapped clients as well as to those who have not received any rehabilitation services or received inadequate services;
- to increase the number and competence of rehabilitation personnel through retraining and upgrading experiences. (p. 33)

This act also emphasized the need for rehabilitation services for those with the most severe handicaps.

PL 93-203

The Comprehensive Employment and Training Act of 1973 (CETA) subsumed many of the programs and functions established under the Manpower Development and Training Act of 1962 (PL 87-415) and the Economic Opportunity Act of 1964 (PL 88-452). The latter act established and funded seven major programs, including: (a) the Job Corps, (b) Work Training programs, (c) College Work-Study programs, (d) Urban and Rural Community Action programs, (e) Adult Basic Education, (f) Education of Migrant Children, and (g) Adult Work Experience programs.

In essence, the primary purpose of CETA was to provide comprehensive manpower services intended to alleviate the high unemployment rates of the early 1970s. According to Bies (1987), "The act was aimed at hard-core unemployed youths and adults who had no occupational skills and thus were not contributing to the development of the nation's economy" (p. 37). Subsequent legislation included the CETA Reauthorization Act of 1978 (PL 95-524), the Youth Employment and Demonstration Projects Act (PL 95-93), the Youth Employment Demonstration Amendments of 1981 (PL 97-14), and the Job Training Partnership Act of 1982 (PL 97-300). Although not specifically aimed at handicapped youth, this legislation provided services, programs, and training opportunities in which handicapped individuals could participate.

PL 94-142

On November 29, 1975, President Gerald Ford signed the Education for All Handicapped Children Act (PL 94-142). This legislation was a culmination of events and efforts of the previous two decades to reduce the disparities in educational opportunities between exceptional children and nonexceptional children. In order to receive federal funding, states were required to offer free public education to all handicapped children. Additional stipulations included developing extensive child identification procedures, providing special education in the least restrictive environment, ensuring nondiscriminatory testing and evaluation, and writing an individualized program for each and every handicapped child. The implication of this legislation for adolescents and young adults reaching the period of transition included providing career and vocational education for this population, if such an education was deemed to be appropriate and prescribed for the student in his or her Individualized Education Plan (IEP). Prior to the passage of this act, little effort at both the local and state levels was directed toward providing funding and programs for the secondary-aged handicapped individual. As a result, many handicapped students dropped out of school prior to graduation (Malouf & Halpern, 1976).

In addition to directing school systems to provide an education for all handicapped children, the law provides extensive guidelines for ensuring the rights of handicapped children and their parents and guardians. States must outline procedures for parents to examine all records with respect to identification, evaluation, and educational placement of their children; provide the public with outlines of how handicapped children are identified, evaluated, and placed; and allow parents to express concerns or complaints with respect to any matter related to identification evaluation or educational placement. This provision has been extremely instrumental in parental efforts to convince local school boards of the necessity of providing secondary career, vocational and occupational training for handicapped youngsters.

PL 94-482

The Education Amendments of 1976 were signed into law by President Ford and increased the funding for vocational education programs, with 10% designated for the handicapped. Additional stipulations of the amendments included the curtailment of sexual discrimination in vocational education programs and the establishment of cooperative relationships between vocational education and labor programs such as those administered under CETA.

The Impact of 1970s Legislation

As in previous decades, the 1970s witnessed the passage of mandates designed to promote the education and employment of the handicapped (see Figure 2–2). Despite these efforts, the education and employment problems of handicapped youth were not alleviated. Miller et al. (1980) have observed:

> Despite passage of legislation designed to promote education of the handicapped during the 1970s there continued to be considerable disenchantment with the quality, quantity, and direction of vocational programs serving handicapped learners. Appropriate vocational programs for the handicapped had not developed rapidly or consistently. Numerous barriers to the delivery of vocational services to the handicapped had been identified. Several problems have slowed the development of vocational programming for the handicapped: lack of trained personnel, inadequate and incomplete needs assessment, limited interagency communication, few direct teacher certification initiatives, and little differentiated vocational curricula for the handicapped. (pp. 352–353)

Taking into account the growing recognition of the need to provide occupational and transitional services and programs for the handicapped, the 1980s became the decade of the special federal initiative in the area of transition. In the following two sections, we describe legislation, programs, and funding that have emerged as a result of this initiative.

❦ ❦ ❦

FEDERAL INITIATIVE: THE 1980s

Two major pieces of legislation enacted during the early 1980s directly addressed a number of transition issues affecting the employment and

---

1973	Rehabilitation Act, PL 93–112; Section 503; Section 504
	Comprehensive Employment and Training Act (CETA), PL 93–203
1975	Education for All Handicapped Children Act, PL 94–142
1976	Education Amendments (Vocational Education Act), PL 94–482
1977	Youth Employment and Demonstration Projects Act, PL 95–93
1978	Comprehensive Employment and Training Act Amendments (CETA Reauthorization Act), PL 95–524

Figure 2–2
Legislation of the 1970s

training of handicapped youth: the Education of the Handicapped Act Amendments of 1983 (PL 98-199), and the Carl D. Perkins Vocational Education Act of 1984 (PL 98-524). In addition, a significant number of projects and programs have been funded by these and previous mandates.

PL 98-199

Section 626 of the 1983 amendments entitled "Secondary Education and Transitional Services for Handicapped Youth" authorized $6.6 million annually in grants and contracts for the purpose of supporting and coordinating educational and service programs designed to assist handicapped youth in the transition from secondary to postsecondary education, employment, and services. Rusch and Phelps (1987) have summarized the major objectives of this section, which include provisions to (a) stimulate the improvement and development of programs for secondary special education and (b) strengthen and coordinate education, training, and related services to assist in the transition process to postsecondary education, vocational training, competitive employment, continuing education, or adult services. One of the results of this legislation has been the creation of the Secondary Transition Intervention Effectiveness Institute at the University of Illinois at Urbana that was contracted to study the problems related to secondary education and transitional services through 1990. (The current activities of the Institute will be discussed in subsequent chapters.)

PL 98-524

The Carl D. Perkins Vocational and Technical Education Act was signed into law on October 19, 1984. The act was designed to

> assure that individuals who are inadequately served under vocational education programs are assured access to quality vocational education programs, especially individuals who are disadvantaged, who are handicapped, men and women who are entering non-traditional occupations, adults who are in need of training and retraining, individuals who are single parents or homemakers, individuals with limited English proficiency, and individuals who are incarcerated in correctional institutions. (PL 98-524, 98 Stat. 2435)

In short, the act extended the provisions of the Vocational Education Act of 1963 by mandating vocational assessment, counseling, support, and transitional services for students identified as handicapped and disadvantaged. In addition, the act mandated planning and coordination with other federally funded programs. Vocational goals and objectives are to be included in the student's IEP, training is to be provided in the least restrictive environment, and records must be kept on the number of handicapped students served. It is interesting to note that the definition of *disadvantaged* was restricted to economic and academic. Cultural disadvantage was excluded on the premise that a person's culture, even though different from the major culture, is not a hindrance but a positive contribution to the development of the individual. We *strongly* support this restriction.

🌿 🌿 🌿

LEGISLATION OF THE 1990s

Two major pieces of legislation (see Figure 2–3) enacted during the early 1990s include a number of provisions that provide additional impetus to transition services for the mildly disabled: the 1990 amendments to the Education of the Handicapped Act (PL 101-476) and the Americans with Disabilities Act of 1990 (PL 101-336).

PL 101-476

On October 30, 1990, President George Bush signed the Education of the Handicapped Act (EHA) Amendments of 1990 (PL 101-476). The act was later renamed the Individuals with Disabilities Education Act (IDEA). Section 626 of the 1990 amendments addresses the provision for secondary education and transitional services for youths with disabilities.

The 1990 amendments revised previous mandates by including community and independent living as transition foci. Authorization also is provided for activities that address issues related to assistive technology devices and services. Future funded projects may now include the development and dissemination of "exemplary programs and practices that meet the unique needs of students who utilize assistive technology devices and services as such students make the transition to postsecondary education, vocational training, competitive employment and continuing education of adult services." In addition, the amendments direct the funding of demonstrations models "designed to establish appropriate methods of providing or continuing to provide, assistive technology devices and services to secondary school students as they make the transition to vocational rehabilitation, employment, postsec-

1981	Youth Employment Demonstration Amendments, PL 97–14
1982	Job Training Partnership Act, PL 97–300
1983	Education of the Handicapped Act Amendments, PL 98–199, Section 626
1984	Carl D. Perkins Vocational Education Act, PL 98–524
1990	Amendments to the Education of the Handicapped Act, PL 101–476
1990	Americans with Disabilities Act of 1990, PL 101–336

Figure 2–3
Legislation of the 1980s and 1990s

ondary education or adult services" and establish a new state grant program to improve transitional services (National Association of State Directors of Special Education [NASDSE], 1990, p. 12).

The state grant program authorized by the 1990 amendments enables state education agencies and vocational rehabilitation agencies or other state agencies to apply jointly to "develop, implement and improve systems to provide transition services for youth with disabilities from age 14 through the age they exit school" (NASDSE, 1990, p. 12). Funds can be used for (a) increasing the availability to transitional services for young adults who are disabled; (b) improving the ability of pertinent others such as parents, professionals, and advocates to work with youngsters involved in the transition process; and (c) ameliorating the working relationships among agencies and individuals involved in the delivery of transitional services.

PL 101-336

On July 26, 1990, President Bush signed the Americans with Disabilities Act (ADA). This act broadly expands the nation's civil rights laws. The legislation extends federal civil rights laws that apply to women and minorities (including race, national origin, and religion) to over 43 million Americans who have some form of disability. The legislation prohibits discrimination in employment, public services, and public accommodations and transportation, and it provides for telecommunications relay services.

In the area of employment, the ADA prohibits employers with 15 or more employees from discriminating against persons with disabilities because of their disability. This prohibition pertains to applications for employment, hiring, advancement, discharge, compensation, and training. In addition, employers must guarantee reasonable accommodations for qualified employees with disabling conditions. In the area of public services, the ADA bans state and local governments from excluding or denying access to services, programs, or activities to individuals with disabilities. This prohibition includes access to public bus and rail systems and privately owned bus and van companies. Public accommodations such as places of lodging, restaurants, theaters, grocery stores, clothing stores, shopping centers, laundromats, banks, barber shops, offices of accountants, lawyers, health care providers, museums, libraries, zoos, and so forth must be accessible. Operators of these facilities are also prohibited from discrimination on the basis of disability.

The ADA directly influences the transition concerns of young adults who are mildly disabled. Employers, public service providers, agencies, and businesses cannot discriminate or deny access to services for this population.

The 1983 amendments to the Education of the Handicapped Act and the 1984 Carl D. Perkins Vocational Education Act served as cornerstones to the federal initiative for transition in the 1980s (see Figure 2–3). The 1990 amendments to the Education of the Handicapped Act and the 1990 Americans with Disabilities Act serve as further steps in building a foundation for the transition process.

❦ ❦ ❦

FUNDED PROGRAMS AND PROJECTS

As illustrated by the historical overview of mandates passed prior to 1980, legislative direction for transition has been provided over a period of time. The results of these mandates were limited because of a lack of adequate financial, federal, and social commitment to the area. Appropriations for recent mandates, however, have increased substantially (over $835 million designated for PL 98-524, $6.6 million for Section 626 of PL 98-199; Rusch & Phelps, 1987). Based on these appropriations, a number of transition projects and programs have been initiated. Rusch and Phelps (1987) summarize the projects that have resulted from the federal initiative of the 1980s. These are presented in Figure 2–4.

Authorizing Legislation/Grant Program

Section 626 of PL 98–199, Education of the Handicapped Act, 1983 Amendments

Secondary Education and Transitional Services for Handicapped Youth: Service Demonstration Projects (84.158A)
Fiscal Year 1984—16 grants awarded

Secondary Education and Transitional Services for Handicapped Youth: Cooperative Models for Planning and Developing Transitional Services (84.158B and 84.148C)
Fiscal Year 1984–86—37 grants awarded

Postsecondary Educational Programs for Handicapped Persons: Demonstrations (84.078B and 84.078C)
Fiscal Year 1984–86—43 grants awarded

Section 641–642 of PL 98–199, Part E of the Education of the Handicapped Act (20USC 1441–1442)

Handicapped Children's Model Program: Youth Employment Projects (84.023D)
Fiscal Year 1984—12 grants awarded

Handicapped Children's Model Program: Postsecondary Projects (84.023G)
Fiscal Year 1984—15 grants awarded

Section 311(A)(1) of PL 93–112, Rehabilitation Act of 1973, as amended

Rehabilitation Services: Special Project (84.128A)
Fiscal Year 1984—5 grants awarded

Figure 2–4
Grant programs awarded since the 1984 enactment of PL 98-199

Source: From "Secondary Special Education and Transition from School to Work: A National Priority" by F. R. Rusch and L. A. Phelps, 1987, *Exceptional Children, 56*(6), p. 22. Copyright 1978 by the Council for Exceptional Children. Adapted by permission.

Summary

A substantial amount of funding has been designated for the area of transition as a result of mandates enacted in the 1980s and early 1990s. As in previous decades, problems related to definition, assessment, curriculum, service coordination, personnel training, and types of programs persist. There exists a need for a theoretical framework for transition and increased cohesion of services. The theoretical framework presented in this text is that students with mild disabilities must be evaluated and provided with intervention in employment related skills *and* in prevocational, vocational, career, leisure, community, family citizenship, and social skills. Within this framework, the need for evaluation and intervention throughout a person's life span is indicated.

In the remaining section of this chapter, we discuss other aspects of federal interest in transition. The chapter concludes with a summary of legislation and programs related to transition in education, employment, health, housing, income, nutrition, social service, transportation, and vocational rehabilitation.

❦ ❦ ❦

FEDERAL PRIORITY

A key figure in establishing a national priority in the area of transition for the handicapped has been Madeline Will, former assistant secretary of the Office of Special Education and Rehabilitative Services (OSERS). In a number of articles (Will, 1984a, 1984b, 1984c, 1984d), she has stated that an enormous effort would have to be made "to create or totally reorganize a system of services for disabled people in our nation" (Will, 1984a, p. 11). According to Will, the major challenge facing this effort "is to *will* the means to accomplish our ends. One of these involves looking beyond traditional service boundaries to collaboration among human service delivery systems" (Will, 1984a, p. 12). In order to integrate service delivery systems, an effort to establish working relationships must, according to Will, be exerted by every involved sector dealing with individuals who are disabled. "We need partnership, not only between the Office of Special Education and the Rehabilitation Services Administration, but with government at every level, with the private sector, and as well with the community of disabled citizens" (Will, 1984a, p. 12).

Will (1984a) continued her discussion of transition by stating that recent legislation had established a new priority, which is "to strengthen and coordinate education, training, and support services for handicapped youth in order to foster their effective transition from school to the adult world of work and independent living" (p. 12). She enumerates four barriers that she sees to the achievement of this priority:

> These barriers, which disabled Americans know well, are not primarily physical, but are intellectual, moral, organizational, statutory, and regulatory. They involve problems of inadequate and inaccurate communications. I challenge special education (and commit OSERS) to breaking down these four artificial barriers in the next decade.

1. The barrier between special and regular education.
2. The barrier to full integration of handicapped individuals in a heterogeneous society.
3. The barrier between the nursery and the school.
4. The barrier between the school and the work place. (pp. 12–13)

The fourth barrier emphasizes Will's employment goal as the eventual outcome of transition for the disabled. This interpretation of transition has been criticized as being too narrow (Halpern, 1985). Will (1984b) defends her position by stating:

> This concern with employment does not indicate a lack of interest in other aspects of adult living. Success in social, personal, leisure, and other adult roles enhances opportunities both to obtain employment and enjoy its benefits. (p. 1)

> The focus on employment as a central outcome of effective transition provides an objective measure of transition success. (p. 2)

Will (1984a) suggests several specific recommendations related to transition. These include creating a secondary curriculum that is relevant to the transition to the workplace, improving postsecondary services, and providing employer incentives. In regard to improving postsecondary services, she states:

> The array of post-secondary services available in any community should be broad enough to enable each student with a disability to enter employment, either immediately after leaving school, or after a period of further education or adult services. Like other citizens, people with disabilities should have access to appropriate educational opportunities that are relevant to individual interests and to the job market. Community colleges, vocational-technical schools, and other institutions of higher education can respond by reducing barriers to participation, developing relevant programs, and providing needed accommodation. (1984a, pp. 15–16)

Finally, Will introduces the OSERS Transition Model. She addresses its underlying assumptions and presents a conceptual framework for transition. Besides the OSERS program, four other models have been cited in the literature: the Halpern Transition Model, the Vocational Transition Model, the Brown and Kayser Model, and the Project Interface Model. These models differ in focus and basic assumptions, and they along with related models from other disciplines are discussed in chapter 3.

❦ ❦ ❦

SUMMARY

This chapter presents a chronological account of the historical and legislative events leading to transition, with each period being summarized. In order to understand the importance of history and legislation, however, a chronological account of legislation may not highlight the importance of these mandates within pertinent transition categories. Table 2–1 summarizes the pertinent legislation presented in this chapter and related legislation and programs within the categories of education, employment, health, housing, income maintenance, nutrition, social service, transportation, and vocational rehabilitation.

Table 2–1
Summary of Legislation and Programs Related to Transition

Legislation	Program
Education	
1. Education for All Handicapped Children Act (PL 94–142), 1975	(a) Basic state grants for handicapped education (b) Regional resource centers
2. Higher Education Act (PL 89–329)	(a) Community service and continuing education
3. Vocational Education Act (PL 88–210), 1963	(a) Basic grants to states for vocational education
4. Vocational Education Act Amendments of 1976	(a) Increased funding for the disabled in vocational education
5. Education of the Handicapped Act Amendments, 1983/1990	(a) Grants to support transition from school to work programs (b) Grants to improve secondary programs (c) Grants for community and independent living programs (d) Funding for assistive technology devices and services in the transition process
6. Carl D. Perkins Vocational Education Act, 1984	(a) Expanded provisions of 1963 act to include handicapped and disadvantaged individuals
7. National Library Service for the Blind and Physically Handicapped	(a) Free braille and recorded materials. Services presently available for students identified as dyslexic and/or reading disabled
Employment	
1. Comprehensive Employment and Training Act Title II CETA of 1973 (PL 93–203)/Youth Employment and Demonstration Projects Act, 1977/CETA Reauthorization Act, 1978/Youth Employment Demonstration Amendments, 1981/Job Training Partnership Act, 1982	(a) Comprehensive employment and training services (b) Special populations (c) Employment demonstration programs (d) Job Corps
2. Fair Labor Standards Act of 1938 (PL 89–601 and 95–151)	(a) Minimum wage regulation
3. Small Business Act of 1953 (PL 92–595 and 95–89)	(a) Workshop loans (b) Handicapped-owned business

Source: From *Services for Developmentally Disabled Adults* (pp. 113–120) by R. L. Schalock, 1983, Baltimore: University Park Press. Adapted by permission.

Table 2–1, continued

Legislation	Program
4. Americans with Disabilities Act of 1990	(a) Expands Civil Rights bill of 1964 to include disabled citizens (b) Disabled individuals cannot be discriminated against in employment, etc.

Health

Legislation	Program
1. Social Security Act amendments, Title V	(a) Maternal and child health services
2. Social Security Act Amendments of 1965, Part A, Title 18	(a) Hospital insurance (b) Supplementary insurance
3. Grants to states for medical assistance/Social Security Act Amendments of 1965	(a) States mandated to provide some services to categorically needy Medicaid recipients

Housing

Legislation	Program
1. U.S. Housing Act of 1937	(a) Rent subsidies
2. Housing Act of 1949	(a) Rural housing for elderly and disabled (b) Rural rent assistance
3. Housing Act of 1959	(a) Loans to nonprofit agencies to provide housing and services for handicapped
4. Housing and Community Development Act of 1974	(a) Grants to remove architectural barriers and construct special public facilities

Income Maintenance

Legislation	Program
1. Social Security Disability Insurance Social Security Act of 1935	(a) Disability insurance benefits (b) Adult disabled child program (c) Rehabilitation services
2. Supplemental Security Income Social Security Act of 1935 as amended	(a) Basic supplemental security income program (b) Rehabilitation, treatment, referral, counseling

Nutrition

Legislation	Program
1. National School Lunch Act of 1946	(a) School lunch program
2. Food Stamp Act of 1977	(a) Food coupons for social security disability insurance and supplemental security income recipients

Table 2–1, *continued*

Legislation	Program

Social Service

1. Social Services Program (Title XX)
    (a) Grants to assist social service agencies
    (b) Social services training (staff)

2. Developmental Disabilities Assistance and Bill of Rights Act
    (a) Basic grants to states for services
    (b) Grants to protection and advisory services
    (c) Special projects grants

3. Domestic Volunteer Service Act, 1973
    (a) Grants to harness resources of volunteers to help disabled individuals

Transportation

1. Urban Mass Transportation Act, 1964
    (a) Transportation facilities must be useable by disabled

Vocational Rehabilitation

1. Smith-Hughes Act, 1917
Smith-Sears Act, 1918
Smith-Fess Act, 1920
    (a) Vocational rehabilitation and employment for disabled veterans
    (b) Vocational training for citizens engaged in civil employment

2. Social Security Amendments, 1939
    (a) Aid to states for vocational rehabilitation

3. Bardon-LaFollete Act, 1943
Vocational Rehabilitation Act Amendments
    (a) Vocational training for individuals who did not qualify for military service
    (b) Concept of rehabilitation expanded to mentally retarded

4. Vocational Rehabilitation Act Amendments of 1954, 1967, 1968
    (a) Expanded aid for vocational and rehabilitation training
    (b) Funds for research and professional training
    (c) Funds for demonstration programs

5. The Rehabilitation Act of 1973 (PL 93–112)
    (a) Basic federal-state voc/rehab grants
    (b) Special programs and supplementary services
    (c) Employment opportunities
    (d) Comprehensive services for independent living
    (e) Protection and advocacy
    (f) Centers for independent living

6. Wagner O'Day Act (PL 75–739), 1938
    (a) Procurement of services and commodities from workshops serving handicapped persons

REFERENCES

Americans with Disabilities Act, PL 101-336 (1990).

Bies, J. D. (1987). The impact of federal legislation on vocational special needs programming. In G. D. Meers (Ed.), *Handbook of vocational special needs education* (2nd ed., pp. 29–46). Rockville, MD: Aspen.

Carl D. Perkins Vocational Education Act, PL 98-524, 98 Stat. 2435 (1984).

Committee on Purchases of Blind-made Products (Wagner O'Day Act), PL 75-739, 52 Stat. 1196 (1938).

Comprehensive Employment and Training Act of 1973 (CETA), PL 93-203, 87 Stat. 839 (1973).

Comprehensive Employment and Training Act Amendments of 1978 (CETA Reauthorization Act of 1978), PL 95-524, 92 Stat. 1909 (1978).

Economic Opportunity Act of 1964, PL 88-452, 78 Stat. 508 (1964).

Education Amendments of 1976 (Vocational Education Act), PL 94-482, 90 Stat. 2081 (1976).

Education for All Handicapped Children Act of 1975, PL 94-142, 89 Stat. 773 (1975).

Education of the Handicapped Act Amendments of 1983, PL 98-199, 97 Stat. 1357 (1983).

Education of the Handicapped Act Amendments of 1983, PL 98-199, Section 626, 97 Stat. 1357, 1367–1368 (1983).

Halpern, A. S. (1985). Transition: A look at the foundations. *Exceptional Children* 51(6), 479–486.

Job Training Partnership Act, PL 97-300, 96 Stat. 1322 (1982).

Malouf, D., & Halpern, A. S. (1976). Review of secondary level special education. *Thresholds in Secondary Education*, 2.

Manpower Development and Training Act of 1962, PL 87–415, 76 Stat. 23 (1962).

Miller, S. R., Ewing, N. J., & Phelps, L. A. (1980). Career and vocational education for the handicapped: A historical perspective. In L. Mann & D. A. Sabatino (Eds.), *The fourth review of special education* (pp. 341–366). New York: Grune & Stratton.

National Association of State Directors of Special Education. (1990). *Education of the handicapped act amendments of 1990 (P.L. 101-476): Summary of major changes in parts A through H of the act.* n.p.: Author.

Olympus Research Corporation. (1974). *An assessment of vocational programs for the handicapped under Part B of the 1968 Amendments to the Vocational Education Act.* Salt Lake City: Author.

President's Panel on Mental Retardation. (1962). *Report to the President—A proposed program for national action to combat mental retardation.* Washington, DC: U.S. Department of Health, Education, and Welfare Public Health Service.

Rehabilitation Act of 1973, PL 93–112, 87 Stat. 355 (1973).

Rehabilitation Act of 1973, PL 93–112, Sections 503, 504; 87 Stat. 355, 393, 394 (1973).

Rusch, F. R., & Phelps, L. A. (1987). Secondary special education and transition from school to work: A national priority. *Exceptional Children, 53*(6), 487–492.

Schalock, R. L. (1983). *Services for developmentally disabled adults.* Baltimore: University Park.

Smith-Hughes Act, PL 64–347, 39 Stat. 929 (1915–1917).

Social Security Act Amendments of 1939, PL 36–379, 53 Stat. 1360 (1939).

Tindall, L. W. (1977). *Vocational/career education programs for persons with special needs in Wisconsin's vocational, technical, and adult districts. (A part of project: Modifying regular programs and developing curriculum materials for the vocational education of the handicapped, No. 19001151147(A).* Madison: Wisconsin State Board of Vocational, Technical, and Adult Education.

U.S. Government Printing Office. (1963). *Public papers of the Presidents of the United States—John F. Kennedy—Containing the public messages, speeches, and statements of the President, January 1 to December 31, 1962.* Washington, DC: Office of the Federal Register National Archives and Records Service General Services Administration.

U.S. Government Printing Office. (1965). *Public papers of the Presidents of the United States—Lyndon B. Johnson—Containing the public messages, speeches, and statements of the President.* (Book 1: November 22, 1963–June 30, 1964). Washington, DC.: Office of the Federal Register National Archives and Records Service General Services Administration.

U.S. Office of Education. (1977). Education of handicapped children: Implementation of Part B of the Education of the Handicapped Act, *Federal Register, 42*(163), 42474–42518.

Vocational Education Act, Colo. Rev. Stat. 1963, 146–1–1 et seq.

Vocational Rehabilitation Act (Smith-Sears Act), PL 65–178, 40 Stat. 617 (1917–1919).

Vocational Rehabilitation Act Amendments of 1943 (Bardon-LaFollete Act), PL 77–113, 57 Stat. 374 (1943).

Vocational Rehabilitation Amendments of 1954, PL 83–565, 68 Stat. 652 (1954).

Vocational Rehabilitation Amendments of 1967, PL 90–99, 81 Stat. 250 (1967).

Vocational Rehabilitation Amendments of 1968, PL 90–391, 82 Stat. 297 (1968).

Vocational Rehabilitation of Persons Disabled in Industry (Smith-Fess Act), PL 66–236, 41 Stat. 735 (1919–1921).

Weisenstein, G. R. (1976). Vocational education for exceptional persons: Have educators let it drop through a crack in their services continuum? *Thresholds in Secondary Education, 2,* 16–17.

Will, M. (1984a). Let us pause and reflect—but not too long. *Exceptional Children, 51*(1), 11–16.

Will, M. (1984b). *OSERS programming for the transition of youth with disabilities: Bridges from school to working life.* Washington, DC: Office of Special Education and Rehabilitative Services.

Will, M. (1984c). *Supported employment for adults with severe disabilities: An OSERS program initiative.* Washington, DC: Office of Special Education and Rehabilitative Services.

Will, M. (1984d, June). Bridges from school to working life. *Interchange,* 2–6.

Youth Employment and Demonstration Projects Act of 1977, PL 95-93, 91 Stat. 627 (1977).

Youth Employment Demonstration Amendments of 1981, PL 97–14, 95 Stat. 98 (1981).

Chapter 3

❦ ❦ ❦

Models of Transition and Related Areas

*F*ive models of transition based on the federal initiatives considered in chapter 2 are presented in this chapter. The description of these models is followed by a discussion of related models developed within career, vocational, and rehabilitation education areas. These related models encompass activities with the potential for contributing to the creation and delivery of services to persons with mild disabilities during the transitional period. The chapter concludes with a description of the mission of the Secondary Transition Intervention Effectiveness Institute.

❦ ❦ ❦

MODELS OF TRANSITION

The OSERS Transition Model

Assumptions.   Will (1983) presents three assumptions that underlie the Office of Special Education and Rehabilitative Services (OSERS) program: "complexity of post school services . . . focus on all students with disabilities, . . . goal of employment" (pp. 2–3). In addressing the complexity of postschool services, Will states:

> The OSERS program assumes that students in transition from school are leaving a somewhat organized provider system and entering a more complex and confusing world, not fully understood by most service professionals, much less parents or consumers. This complexity is necessary, if adult services are to offer opportunities for normal adult living and working to all individuals with disabilities. Effective transition requires that relevant community opportunities and service combinations be developed to fit individual circumstances and needs. (p. 3)

In addressing the second assumption, Will (1983) explains that the focus of the model is on identifying the services needed "that will assist the transition of all persons with disabilities from school to working life" (p. 3). She

41

estimates that this will affect an estimated 250,000 to 3,001,000 students leaving special education each year.

In regard to the third assumption, Will (1983) believes that sustained employment is the "important outcome of education and transition for all Americans. The goal of OSERS programming for transition is that individuals leaving the school system obtain jobs, either immediately after school or after a period of post-secondary education or vocational services" (p. 3). This last assumption is based on the premise that employment provides the means for successful integration into the mainstream of society. The workplace provides the opportunity for socialization; salaries supply the purchasing power needed for successful integration.

Description. The OSERS Transition Model uses a bridge concept from high school to employment (see Figure 3–1). The bridges contain three clusters of transitional services that include (a) transition without special services, (b) transition with time-limited services, and (c) transition with ongoing services. The left side of the figure shows high school as the foundation of a successful transition program. This foundation includes secondary special education, vocational, and other school-based services that are utilized to develop the "skills, attitudes, personal relationships, and employer contacts that determine much of the success of later transition" (Will, 1983, p. 5). Will adds that "curriculum content in special education and vocational education affects whether or not students leave school with entry level job skills that are saleable in the local community" (p. 5).

The first bridge (no special services) addresses the services, along with special accommodations for the disabled incorporated within these generic services, that are available to anyone in the community. Postsecondary services such as community colleges, 4-year colleges, and vocational training schools

Figure 3–1
The OSERS Transition Model

Source: From A. S. Halpern (1985), "Transition: A Look at the Foundations," *Exceptional Children*, *51*(6), p. 480. Copyright 1985 by the Council for Exceptional Children. Used by permission.

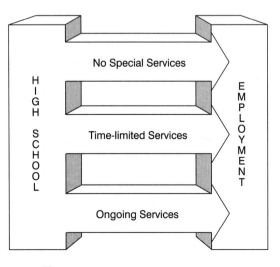

would fit into this "no special services" cluster. It is assumed that the majority of students with disabilities leaving high school would be served via this route.

The second bridge (time-limited services) includes "temporary services that lead to employment . . . services such as vocational rehabilitation, post-secondary vocational education, and other job training programs to gain entry into the labor market" (Will, 1983, p. 6). The services available in this cluster are usually terminated after the person has obtained employment. Individuals qualifying for these services must have exhibited the potential for employment. Vocational rehabilitation is cited as perhaps the best-known service in this time-limited cluster.

The third bridge (ongoing special services) includes what has recently been labeled *supported employment.* Prior to the development of this concept, services for the severely disabled included nonvocational or custodial care or services aimed at possible future employment. Will (1983) states:

> Consistent with the assumptions defined earlier, the alternative proposed here is employment, with whatever ongoing support is necessary to maintain that employment. For example, an individual using this bridge from school to working life might leave school and obtain employment as part of a small team of disabled individuals in an electronics manufacturing plant, where the state agency responsible for ongoing services paid for a work supervisor in the company. (p. 7)

The right side of Figure 3–1 shows employment as the designated goal, or final foundation, in the transition process. The availability of employment opportunities is essential to achieving this goal. Will (1983) believes:

> consequently, programming for transition from school to working life cannot be addressed adequately without simultaneous attention to such labor issues as minimum wage levels, business incentives to offer employment, equal employment opportunity, and efforts to address structural unemployment problems. (p. 8)

Implications. In order to operationalize the OSERS Transition Model, Will (1983) presents specific activities to be conducted in each of the five areas: (a) high school, (b) no services, (c) time-limited services, (d) ongoing services, and (e) employment.

In the high school foundation area, efforts would be concentrated on research, development, demonstration, and replication of projects aimed at all high school service areas. According to Will (1983):

> Particular interests include: renewed efforts to develop cooperative programs with vocational education and vocational rehabilitation to serve all students with disabilities; improvement of community-based job training and placement with the school's vocational preparation program; and development of service models for all students that allow regular and frequent contact with non-disabled peers. (p. 8)

In the no special services area, efforts would be directed to postsecondary education: "While emerging post-secondary programs will no doubt address the needs of all disability groups, OSERS is particularly concerned with stimu-

lating research and program development for persons with learning disabilities and other mild educational handicaps" (Will, 1983, pp. 8–9).

In the time-limited services area, Will (1983) emphasizes the efforts of
OSERS to initiate "cooperative relationships between special education, vocational rehabilitation, and vocation education" to facilitate changes in service
delivery (p. 9). Innovations in on-site job training and placement would be
supported.

In the ongoing services area, the emphasis of OSERS is shifting from day
activity programs, via prevocational activities, to employment alternatives.
Support for staff training, program development, and demonstration would
be provided.

Finally in the area of employment, the emphasis of OSERS would involve
"cooperative initiatives with other agencies" (Will, 1983, p. 9). A major thrust
would be to provide incentives to employers who are willing to hire individuals
with disabilities and who may need "special equipment, building modifications, longer training periods, or other investments" (p. 9).

In addition to these activities, OSERS would attempt to determine the
number of students successfully crossing each of the three bridges toward
employment and evaluate each of the three routes, including changes in the
number of students who use each of the service paths.

The Halpern Transition Model

Halpern's (1985) model builds on the assumptions of the OSERS program.
The model, however, challenges the assumption that the ultimate goal of transition is employment. According to Halpern, the ultimate goal of transition
should be *community adjustment*. Based on this goal, two additional dimensions
must be added to the employment dimension of transition: (a) the residential
environment and (b) the social and interpersonal networks of persons with disabilities (see Figure 3–2). The three dimensions are viewed as supporting the
goal of community adjustment.

In his discussion of the three dimensions, Halpern (1985) indicates that
employment, the first pillar supporting community adjustment, has been
described by the OSERS Transition Model. The issues of this component
include "job finding networks, job search skills, minimum wage levels,
employer incentives, job discrimination and structural unemployment" (p.
481). However:

> The second pillar of residential environment is equally complex. In addition to the
> satisfactoriness of a person's actual home, one must also consider the quality and
> safety of the neighborhood in which the home is located as well as the availability
> of both community services and recreational opportunities within reasonable prox-
> imity to the home. (p. 481)

Halpern (1985) considers the third pillar, social and interpersonal networks, as *most* important. "It includes major dimensions of human relation-

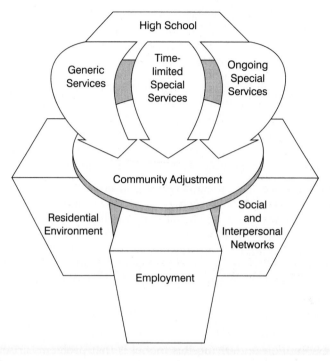

Figure 3–2
A revised transition model

Source: From A. S. Halpern (1985), "Transition: A Look at the Foundations," *Exceptional Children*, *51*(6), p. 481. Copyright 1985 by the Council for Exceptional Children. Used by permission.

ships such as daily communications, self-esteem, family support, emotional maturity, friendship, and intimate relationships" (p. 481).

The importance of the three dimensions outlined by Halpern (1985) is recognized by individuals involved with young adults with disabilities. OSERS' position that success in employment will lead to success in the other dimensions can be challenged. Halpern presents evidence to support this position:

> In other words, success in one area was often unrelated to success in either of the others. This means that successful programmatic efforts aimed at a single dimension of community adjustment are not necessarily going to produce improvements along the other dimensions. If our three-dimensional model is correct, this also means that success along only one or even two dimensions is not likely to be sufficient to support the desired goal of community adjustment. Programs will need to be directed specifically toward specific services. (p. 482)

The Vocational Transition Model

Assumptions underlying the Vocational Transition Model proposed by Wehman, Kregel, and Barcus (1985) include the following:

(a) members of multiple disciplines and service delivery systems must participate, (b) parental involvement is essential, (c) vocational transition planning must occur well before 21 years of age, (d) the process must be planned and systematic, and (e) the vocational service provided must be of a quality nature. (p. 26)

The three-stage model proposed by Wehman et al. (1985) includes school instruction, planning for transition, and job placement. It emphasizes the importance of career and vocational training throughout the school career of the individual with a disability. The model is most often viewed as targeted toward persons with severe disabilities, although many of the subjects of Wehman et al.'s research more properly meet the criteria of moderately/mildly disabled:

> With the increased federal emphasis on transition, it is essential that service providers and agencies do not focus exclusively on the transition process while ignoring the quality of the foundation services offered by public schools and the range of vocational alternatives offered by community agencies. Previous efforts at interagency agreements which purported to ameliorate transition problems actually resulted, in all too many cases, in movement of a student from one inadequate school program to another inadequate adult program. (pp. 26–27)

The Brown and Kayser Model

A fourth model of transition has been proposed by Brown and Kayser (1982). The basic assumption underlying this model is that problems arise during the secondary transition phase of an individual's life mainly because the characteristics of the individual do not match the demands of the environment. In order to overcome this mismatch, it is up to the educator to use a number of strategies: (a) correction (correcting the constraints imposed by the environment), (b) compensation (increasing individual strengths and assets so that the match between student and environment is compatible), and (c) circumvention (altering the student-environment interaction so that it occurs at beneficial levels). The model involves four activities: (a) assessment, of both the individual and the institution; (b) planning, which involves aiding the individual in meeting the demands of the institution and the institution in meeting the needs of the individual; (c) implementation, using the three strategies of correction, circumvention, and compensation; and, finally, (d) evaluation.

The Project Interface Model

The basic assumption of this model created by D'Alonzo, Owen, and Hartwell (1985) is that individuals with disabilities leaving school need a comprehensive model for gaining productive employment. For the objectives of this model to be accomplished, linkages must be established between the individual leaving the secondary school environment and community-based training programs and services. These linkages occur through the creation of job banks and information clearinghouses. The model involves four major activities: (a) identification of secondary students with disabilities; (b) intervention, including intake, vocational evaluation, employment training, and job placement; (c) employment, including following client progress and crisis intervention; and (d) follow-up, including continuous monitoring of employment and adjustment.

Model Comparison

The five models just described address the major issues faced in the transition of students from schooling to adult life. The OSERS Transition Model concentrates on the goal of employment for persons with disabilities. The Halpern Transition Model concentrates on the goal of community adjustment. As such, both the OSERS and the Halpern models are conceptualizations of transition, whereas the latter three models are more technical descriptions of how transitional activities should occur. The Vocational Training Model (Wehman et al., 1985) emphasizes transitional services throughout the student's school environment. The Brown and Kayser Model stresses the match between the student with a disability and the environment and how the environment can be modified to meet individual needs. The Project Interface Model concentrates on providing students who are not ready for competitive employment with links or access to community training programs. We believe that although the emphasis of the five models differs, the ultimate goal of each is the achievement of what has been labeled *normalization*—an adult life as close to normal as possible.

❦ ❦ ❦

RELATED MODELS

The Lifelong Career Development Model

This model, developed at the University of Missouri at Columbia, includes transition centers located in community college settings. The underlying rationale for the centers, according to Brolin (1984), is that many individuals with mild disabilities either do not qualify for vocational rehabilitation services or do not want to continue being identified as disabled. The community college setting provides a "normal" setting in which individuals who are disabled can interact with nondisabled peers. In addition, the center provides comprehensive services not only for the young adult but throughout the life span. Services are offered in eight areas: (a) career assessment, (b) instruction in vocational skills, (c) assistance with independent living and personal adjustment, (d) professional training to improve services, (e) information and referral to other community resources, (f) career development planning, (g) collection of resources for the service needs of persons with disabilities, and (h) advocacy.

The Lifelong Career Development Centers are an outgrowth of many years of work by Donn E. Brolin and his associates in developing what has become known as the Life-centered Career Education (LCCE) Competency-based Curriculum Model (Brolin, 1982, 1983; Kokaska & Brolin, 1985). The curriculum and its relationship to secondary and postsecondary education is addressed in detail in Parts II and III of this text. Its relationship to Lifelong Career Development Centers as an approach to transition involves providing training and services in three major areas: (a) skills and competencies needed for successful community living; (b) identification and location of school, community, and home resources; and (c) assistance in various levels of career development.

Competencies. Outlined in detail are 22 major competencies and 102 subcompetencies, within three curriculum areas: (a) daily living skills, (b) personal-social skills, and (c) occupational guidance and preparation skills (see Figure 3–3).

A. Daily Living Skills Curriculum Area

    1. Managing Family Finances

    2. Selecting, Managing, and Maintaining a Home

    3. Caring for Personal Needs

    4   Raising Children, Enriching Family Living

    5. Buying and Preparing Food

    6. Buying and Caring for Clothing

    7. Engaging in Civic Activities

    8. Utilizing Recreation and Leisure

    9. Getting around the Community (Mobility)

B. Personal-Social Skills Curriculum Area

    10. Achieving Self-Awareness

    11. Acquiring Self-Confidence

    12. Achieving Socially Responsible Behavior

    13. Maintaining Good Interpersonal Relationships

    14. Achieving Independence

    15. Achieving Problem-solving Skills

    16. Communicating Adequately with Others

C. Occupational Guidance and Preparation Curriculum Area

    17. Knowing and Exploring Occupational Possibilities

    18. Selecting and Planning Occupational Choices

    19. Exhibiting Appropriate Work Habits and Behaviors

    20. Exhibiting Sufficient Physical and Manual Skills

    21. Acquiring a Specific Salable Job Skill

    22. Seeking, Securing, and Maintaining Employment

Figure 3–3

Twenty-two career education competencies

Source: From *Life Centered Career Education: A Competency Based Approach* (p. 12) by D. E. Brolin, 1978, Reston, VA: Council for Exceptional Children. Copyright 1978 by the Council for Exceptional Children. Used by permission.

Resources. Counselors or consultants at the centers emphasize the integral involvement of the community college staff, family members, other service agency members, and business and industry personnel in the design and implementation of an individual's program.

Career Stages. Four levels of career development are (a) awareness; (b) exploration; (c) preparation; and (d) placement, follow-up, and continuing education. These stages progress through basic education to late adulthood. The third and fourth stages are especially pertinent during the secondary transitional period of an individual's career. Work-study, competitive work, and noncompetitive work roles are emphasized. Figure 3–4 illustrates the four stages of career development and how they relate to the competencies and various subject and community resource areas. The model places importance on the involvement of school, home, and community in this endeavor.

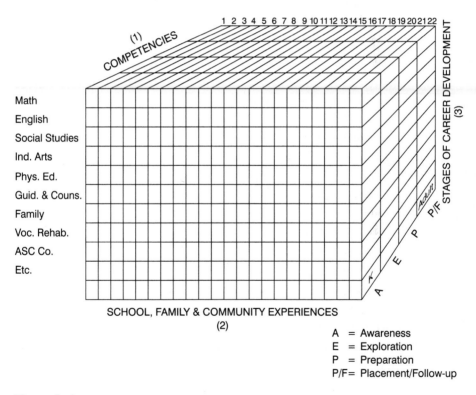

A = Awareness
E = Exploration
P = Preparation
P/F = Placement/Follow-up

Figure 3–4
Career competency-based model for infusing education into the curriculum

Source: From *Career Education for Handicapped Children and Youth* (p. 45) by D. E. Brolin and C. J. Kokaska, 1979, New York: Merrill/Macmillan. Adapted with the permission of Merrill, an imprint of Macmillan Publishing Company. Copyright 1985 by Macmillan Publishing Company. Copyright 1979 by Merrill Publishing Company.

In their evaluation of the LCCE curriculum, Cummings and Maddux (1987) state, "We believe that the LCCE approach represents the most substantial contribution to date to the career and vocational education of handicapped individuals" (p. 142). Extending this statement to secondary transition, we believe that the use of the LCCE approach within the transition model of the Lifelong Career Development Centers, located in community college settings, is one of the most promising for the mildly disabled. (The Lifelong Career Development Model has been initiated, and results of the effort based on a research base should be available in the near future.)

The Transition Service Activity Center

Browder (1987) has proposed an alternative to the Lifelong Career Development Centers—Transition Service Activity Centers—based on research indicating that personal relationships and the support of informal networks contribute to successful life adjustment. She states that the proposed alternative would be cost effective and efficient in that the approach would use professionals as facilitators and liaisons in the formation of informal, personal support relationships rather than as primary service providers. The resulting relationships then would serve as focal points for issues associated with transition.

The Activity Center approach is similar to that of the Lifelong Career Development Center in that the centers would be located in the community and would be accessible to individuals with and without disabilities. The centers differ in that the primary activities of the Activity Center would be conducted within a social-recreational context rather than from a curriculum base.

Figure 3–5 shows the proposed social-recreational context around which a number of transitional areas might be addressed. These include adult edu-

Figure 3–5
Proposed model for Transition Service Activity Centers

Source: From "Transition Services for Early Adult Age Individuals with Mild Mental Retardation" by P. M. Browder, 1987, in R. N. Ianacone and R. A. Stodden (Eds.), *Transition Issues and Directions* (p. 86), Reston, VA: Council for Exceptional Children. Copyright 1987 by the Council for Exceptional Children. Used by permission.

cation, individual and group counseling, advocacy and referral to other community resources, and outreach to other adults who may be hospitalized, home bound, and so forth.

The proposed approach to establishing a Service Activity Center model for transition is based on the following premises (Browder, 1987):

1. Those benefiting from the services should determine what services are offered, when, by whom, and how.
2. Services should accommodate the full range of life adjustment needs of adults with disabilities.
3. Transitional services should be adaptable to changing issues faced by young adults.
4. Transitional services should be open-ended.
5. Transitional services should be flexible.
6. Transitional services should be provided in integrated settings.
7. Transitional services should be provided as an integral part of the ongoing activities of an individual's life.

Browder (1987) presents a strategy for implementing the proposed model that includes (a) establishing a neighborhood base of operations, (b) identifying neighborhood leaders, (c) identifying the core of service recipients, (d) gaining support and participation for the center, and (e) establishing the center.

A weakness is that the characteristics of the person or persons who would initiate this strategy and/or who would be responsible for the center's operation are not identified. An organizational chart, including a board of directors and a career director followed by coordinators and a series of specialists, is presented. How a career director is identified and how or who initiates the process of developing the initial Activity Center is not specified.

The Experience-based Career Education Model

The Experience-based Career Education (EBCE) model has been used for students with and without disabilities at the secondary level. Basically, it is an individualized alternative to traditional education. The program involves placing a student in a series of community work settings for 1 to 3 hours a day for 2 to 3 weeks. A work coordinator works with the students to identify placements and experiences. Larson (1982) identifies five aspects of the model: (a) the program is community based, (b) scheduling is individualized, (c) employer participation is voluntary, (d) experiences are exploratory, and (e) academics are developed in conjunction with the site. The program or approach relies heavily on the cooperation of the school, family, and community.

Clark's School-based Model

Clark's (1981) model for career education is school based. Although the model emphasizes early education, a number of its components are pertinent to the secondary transitional period of students with mild disabilities: (a) values, attitudes, and habits; (b) human relationships; (c) occupational information; and (d) acquisition of jobs and daily living skills (see Figure 3–6).

At the secondary level of education, options during the transition process include (a) college preparation, or general education, (b) vocational and/or technical training, (c) fine arts, (d) cooperative or work-study programs, and

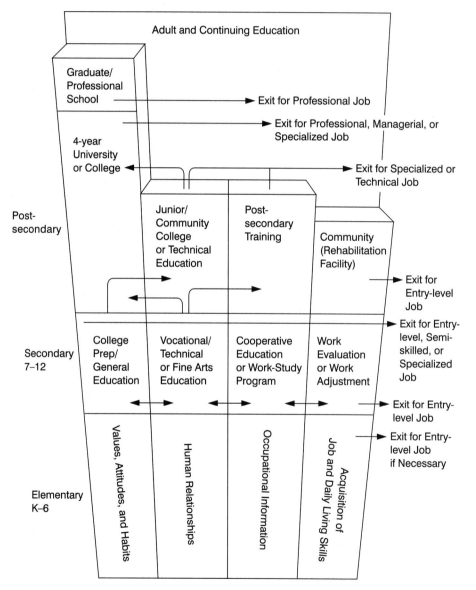

Figure 3–6
A school-based career education model for the disabled

Source: From *Career Education for the Handicapped Child in the Elementary Classroom* by G. M. Clark, 1979, Denver: Love.

(e) work evaluation or work adjustment. These options lead to postsecondary levels of education including university, junior college or technical training, or referral to vocational rehabilitation and/or other services.

A major contribution of this model is its emphasis on personal values, attitudes, habits, and human relationships. Clark (1981) indicates that the processes involved in establishing values and relationships are essential prerequisites to a successful life adjustment.

The Secondary Transition Intervention Effectiveness Institute

Since 1984, a large number of models dealing with secondary transition for persons with mild disabilities have been developed and implemented by various federally funded programs. Most of the models, however, are variations of the major and related models described here. Information about additional transition models can be obtained from the Transition Library located at the University of Illinois at Urbana-Champaign.

The Secondary Transition Intervention Effectiveness Institute at the University of Illinois at Urbana-Champaign has conducted a number of evaluations of federally funded programs and models dealing with transition. As stated in chapter 1, the Institute was formed in August 1985 to evaluate and extend the impact of the federal transition initiative. This initiative was stimulated under the 1983 Education of the Handicapped Act Amendments, Section 626 of PL 98-199 entitled "Secondary Education and Transitional Services for Handicapped Youth."

The activities of the Institute are a natural extension of a number of projects, which have been conducted by the College of Education at the University of Illinois at Urbana-Champaign, dealing with vocational education of people with disabilities and other transition issues. One of the college's projects funded by the Office of Special Education and Rehabilitation, the National Network for Professional Development in Vocational Special Education, resulted in the publication of a number of issues of *Interchange,* a professional journal dealing with career education. Currently *Interchange* is published by the Institute and includes articles dealing with evaluation and research findings of all federally funded transition projects.

In addition to publishing *Interchange,* the Institute annually publishes a *Compendium of Project Profiles,* which provides information about the model programs funded under the Secondary Education and Transition Services Initiative. Over 200 projects have been cited in the *Compendium,* including a report of project development and implementation on a range of service delivery models that focus on facilitating the transition of youths and adults with disabilities. Finally, a number of publications are available dealing with the Institute's study of issues and problems related to secondary education and transitional services. Additional information about projects and publications available from the Institute can be obtained from Dr. Frank R. Rusch, Director, Transition Institute at Illinois, University of Illinois at Urbana-Champaign, 110 Education Building, 1310 S. Sixth St., Champaign, IL 61820.

❦ ❦ ❦

SUMMARY

Based on the rationale for transition presented in chapter 2, five models of transition have been presented in this chapter. The OSERS Transition Model based on the federal initiative formulated by Will during the 1980s concentrates on the goal of employment as a final objective during the transition process from secondary education for individuals who are disabled. The Halpern Transition Model challenges the assumption that the goal of transition should be limited to gaining employment. In addition to employment, the residential environment and the social and interpersonal networks of individuals should be addressed for the ultimate goal of community adjustment. The Vocational Transition Model proposed by Wehman et al. (1985) concentrates on the secondary school environment as an important aspect of the transition from secondary education into employment. The Brown and Kayser Model places additional emphasis on the match between the characteristics of the individual who is disabled and the transitional environment of that individual. The developers of the Project Interface Model propose community training programs and/or linkages for students who leave the secondary school system and find themselves in need of additional training and support.

Related models of transition include the Lifelong Career Development Model in which the establishment of transition centers within community college settings is proposed. Services offered by the centers would span the individual's lifetime and would be concerned with needs experienced at various developmental levels throughout adulthood. On the same principle as the Lifelong Career Development Model, Browder has proposed the establishment of Transition Service Activity Centers. Activity Centers would facilitate the establishment of informal networks and support programs rather than providing formal service. The Experience-based Career Education Model concentrates on providing students with employment exploratory experiences during secondary education as a major stepping stone for choosing an occupation upon graduation from high school. Clark's School-based Model is somewhat similar to the Experience-based Career Education Model in that it emphasizes the school environment during the transition process. Additional models of transition have been identified, monitored, and evaluated by the Secondary Transition Intervention Effectiveness Institute.

The models presented in this chapter include activities and services that reflect different definitions of transition. Models in which employment is the major objective of transition show services at the secondary level concentrated on gaining an occupation. Models that encompass the entire range of experiences and adult adjustments throughout the lifetime as ongoing objectives include services that are ongoing and available on a longitudinal basis.

REFERENCES

Brolin, D. E. (1978). *Life centered career education: A competency based approach.* Reston, VA: Coucil for Exceptional Children.

Brolin, D. E. (1982). *Vocational preparation of persons with handicaps* (2nd ed.). New York: Merrill/Macmillan.

Brolin, D. E. (1983). *Life centered career education: A competency based approach* (rev. ed.). Reston, VA: Council for Exceptional Children.

Brolin, D. E. (1984). *Preparing handicapped students to be productive adults.* Paper presented at the Western Regional Resource Center Topical Conference, Serving Secondary Mildly Handicapped Students, Seattle.

Brolin, D. E., & Kokaska, C. J. (1979). *Career education for handicapped children and youth.* New York: Merrill/Macmillan.

Browder, P. M. (1987). Transition services for early adult age individuals with mild mental retardation. In R. N. Ianacone & R. A. Stodden (Eds.), *Transition issues and directions* (pp. 77–90). Reston, VA: Council for Exceptional Children.

Brown, J. M., & Kayser, T. F. (1982). *The transition of special needs learners into post-secondary vocational education.* Minneapolis: University of Minnesota, Department of Vocational and Technical Education, Minnesota Research and Developmental Center for Vocational Education.

Clark, G. M. (1979). *Career education for the handicapped child in the elementary classroom.* Denver: Love.

Clark, G. M. (1981). Career and vocational education. In G. Brown, R. L. McDowell, & J. Smith (Eds.), *Educating adolescents with behavior disorders* (pp. 25–39). New York: Merrill/Macmillan.

Cummings, R. W., & Maddux, C. D. (1987). *Career and vocational education for the mildly handicapped.* Springfield, IL: Thomas.

D'Alonzo, B. J., Owen, S. D., & Hartwell, L. K. (1985). *School to work: Transition models for persons with disabilities.* Unpublished manuscript. (Available from the Secondary Transition Intervention Effectiveness Institute, University of Illinois, 110 Education Building, 1310 S. Sixth St., Champaign, IL 61820)

Education of the Handicapped Act Amendments of 1983, PL 98-199, Section 626, 97 Stat. 1357, 1367–1368 (1983).

Halpern, A. S. (1985). Transition: A look at the foundations. *Exceptional Children, 51*(6), 479–486.

Kokaska, C. J., & Brolin, D. E. (1985). *Career education for handicapped individuals* (2nd ed.). New York: Merrill/Macmillan.

Larson, C. (1982). Personal communication regarding the EDCE-MD/LD models, 1981. (Cited in D. E. Brolin, 1982, *Vocational preparation of persons with handicaps* [2nd ed.]. New York: Merrill/Macmillan.)

Wehman, P., Kregel, J., & Barcus, J. M. (1985). From school to work: A vocational transition model for handicapped students. *Exceptional Children, 52*(1), 25–37.

Will, M. (1983). *OSERS programming for the transition of youth with disabilities: Bridges from school to working life.* Washington, DC: Office of Special Education and Rehabilitative Services. (ERIC Document Reproduction Service No. ED 256 132)

Chapter 4

❦ ❦ ❦

The Process of Transition

A number of individuals, methods, settings, and setting agents are associated with each of the various models (presented in chap. 3) and cited in the transition literature. These can be viewed as components of the process of transition. Figure 4–1 presents a schematic overview of the relationships among the individuals, methods, settings, and setting agents for a point of reference for the discussion that follows.

In this chapter we present information related to the individuals and methods of the transition process and how these two components are related to the various special education, career education, vocational education, and vocational rehabilitation models.

❦ ❦ ❦

INDIVIDUALS

Mildly Disabled

The definition and characteristics of individuals with mild disabilities have been presented in chapter 2. We have defined this population as secondary students and adults who have been identified with a moderately to mildly disabling condition such as learning disability, emotional disturbance, or mental retardation.

Individuals with mild disabilities should not be considered as the passive focal point of transition but rather as active participants in all aspects of the process. They have an intimate knowledge of their disabilities and how these affect their ability to function in various settings. The information they possess concerning their own strengths, weaknesses, and unique problems can be invaluable in designing, developing and implementing their Individualized Transition Plans (ITPs). Likewise, their input can be vital in evaluating the success or failure of the various components of their ITPs. The interactions

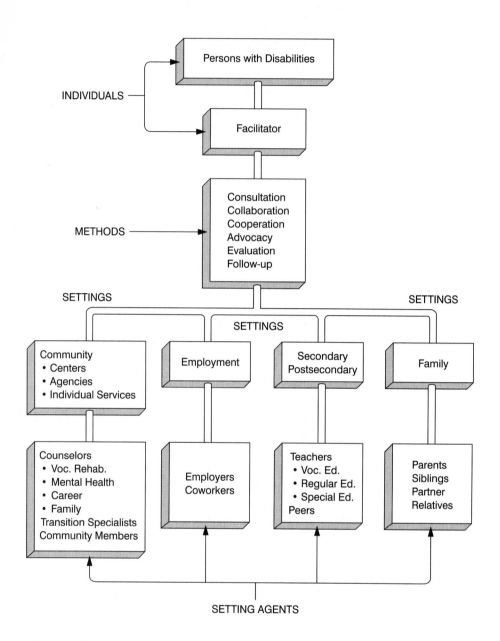

Figure 4–1
The process of transition

among individuals, the facilitator, methods, settings, and setting-related agents will continue to be addressed throughout this text.

Facilitator

The facilitator is a person or group that facilitates the transition process. The concept of a facilitator of transition and that person's or group's responsibilities have been alluded to in each transition model and in several state standards. However, there is not usually a person whose title is "facilitator" but rather a role that may be filled by persons with many job titles.

Transition models emphasize the need for linkages among the home, community, employers, and schools. The developers of the models, however, are unclear as to who will be responsible for developing and initiating these connections. State departments of education, because they must reflect federal requirements, also conceptualize transition as a bridge between school programs and the opportunities of adult life. Thus, a number of states have standards such as Pennsylvania's that indicate that "the school district shall designate persons responsible to coordinate transition activities" (Department of Education of Pennsylvania, 1990, p. 19). How these individuals will be selected and what discipline they should represent is not clear. In addition, specific transitional activities to be coordinated by these individuals are not defined.

Related models of transition allude to counselors, consultants, center directors, and/or work coordinators as responsible for facilitating the process of transition. In addition, transition specialists, consulting teachers, work-study coordinators, personnel directors, boards of directors, career education special needs committees, transition teams, and parent organizations are mentioned in the literature. These various individuals and groups are responsible for delivering and/or coordinating transitional services for young persons with disabilities. Specific criteria for personnel selection, job descriptions, and employment of these individuals, however, remain undefined and variable.

It is often mistakenly assumed that the secondary special education teacher will assume the responsibilities of the transition facilitator. Adding the responsibilities and skills of a facilitator to the job description of the secondary special education teacher is an unrealistic expectation. Currently, secondary special educators are expected to be consultants, tutors, cooperating teachers, and curriculum developers. They cannot take on the responsibility of facilitators of transition. *The necessity for creating a position, a job description, and training in this area is obvious.*

Palmer, Velleman, and Shafer (1984), in a review of transition, outline what they called "Transition Specialist's Functions." These include (a) planning and coordination of interdisciplinary efforts surrounding the transition to work and community living; (b) training of school personnel, adult service workers, and family members; (c) job placement training and follow-up; (d) case management; and (e) advocacy (pp. 49–50). In order to function effectively, the transition specialist should utilize methods of service delivery including consultation, collaboration, cooperation (between individuals and agencies), advocacy, evaluation, and follow-up. These then become the facilitator's roles. They should be fulfilled by an independent entity supported by state or local funds. The facilitator provides the linkages among settings (community, employment, school, and family) and setting agents including teachers, parents, and employers.

❦ ❦ ❦

METHODS

Consultation and Collaboration

Consultation refers to the relationship between two individuals or a group of individuals in which either (a) one party provides a service or expertise aimed at improving the functioning of the other or (b) views and expertise of each individual are exchanged or the individuals collaborate. The use of consultation in providing educational services for students who are mildly disabled has grown significantly in the past decade. In fact, entire issues of professional journals have been dedicated to this topic (see, e.g., Blankenship & Jordan, 1985; Brown & Kurpius, 1985; Hresko, 1988; Nelson, Neel, & Lilly, 1981).

A number of theoretical perspectives of consultation in school settings are presented in the literature (Conoley & Conoley, 1988). The **mental health perspective** includes consultants working toward the goal of improving student learning and behavior. Consultants work with teachers and adult care givers for the purpose of changing attitudes and characteristics that influence the difficulties experienced by youths with mild disabilities (Conoley & Gutkin, 1986).

In the **behavioral perspective,** consultants teach teachers how to work with individuals or groups of children. Social learning, behavioral, and cognitive-behavioral approaches are utilized (Bergan, 1977).

In the **process perspective,** consultants work with teachers and adults to help them understand how events and individuals in the environment affect learning. Emphasis is placed on developing group management skills (with parents, children, other educators) and on alerting individuals to the process involved when groups of individuals participate in solving problems and making decisions (Schein, 1969). In short, the mental health, behavioral, and process perspectives all include a relationship in which one individual or a group of professionals confers with others in seeking information, training, or guidance when working with individuals with mild disabilities. Each of these perspectives can be utilized during the transition process and are referred to in subsequent sections of this text.

Collaborative Consultation

Collaborative consultation, curriculum consultation, and problem-solving methods involving mutual give-and-take between individuals or groups are viewed as outgrowths of the three perspectives of consultation (Conoley &

Conoley, 1988). The collaborative consultation method is the most appropriate for incorporation into the transition process.

Collaborative consultation is defined by Idol, Paolucci-Whitcomb, and Nevin (1986) as

> an interactive process which enables people with diverse expertise to generate creative solutions to mutually defined problems. The outcome is enhanced, altered, and produces solutions that are different from those that the individual team members would produce independently. The major outcome of collaborative consultation is to provide comprehensive and effective programs for students with special needs within the most appropriate context, thereby enabling them to achieve maximum constructive interaction with their nonhandicapped peers. (p. 1)

Three purposes of collaborative consultation are described by West, Idol, and Cannon (1988): (a) the prevention of learning and behavioral problems, (b) the remediation of learning and behavioral problems, and (c) the coordination of instructional programs. The third purpose is most appropriate for transition and involves integrating programs of instruction and services across settings and setting agents.

The school collaborative consultation process (West & Idol, 1990) can be applied to the various stages of transition. The process can be used by the transition facilitator when working with individuals or setting agents in community, school, family, and employment settings. In essence, the facilitator acts as the consultant in establishing the collaborative consultation process. The process, as West and Idol describe it, entails

> an equal relationship characterized by (a) mutual trust and open communication, (b) joint approaches to problem identification, (c) the pooling of personal resources to identify and select strategies that will have some probability of solving the problem that had been identified, and (d) shared responsibility in the implementation and evaluation of the program or strategy that has been initiated. (p. 23)

All parties involved in the collaborative consultative process have a shared responsibility for the success of their endeavors. West and Idol (1990) state that when individuals work with each other individually or in groups, they create a powerful force called "mutual empowerment." This means that each individual in the relationship has a vested interest in the success of the program.

Collaborative consultation in transitional programs in school settings is concentrated on the relationships among professionals and "important others" in the lives of students with mild disabilities. In Figure 4–1, the transition process is conceptualized as a collaborative consultative relationship not only with the facilitator across settings and setting agents but also with the student who is mildly disabled. Student input, either through the facilitator or directly to settings and setting agents, is an important aspect of transition. The notion that students who are mildly disabled can function as consultants to important others in their environment and as participants in the collaborative process may be criticized as an inappropriate extension of what is meant by collaborative consultation. Our rationale for including the secondary student in the method is based on the premise that these students must experience the independence of self-direction in order to attain satisfactory adjustment. It is probable that the lack of opportunity to make decisions is one of the factors responsible for the large number of adjustment problems of this group. If this is the case, the expertise that the student brings to the collaborative consultation process is essential, and the collaborative consultation process is doomed to failure if the student is not extensively included. Students who are mildly disabled can assist in defining problems, in participating in the design of programs, and in evaluating the impact of these programs on their lives. Furthermore, eventually all decisions are theirs to make.

Collaborative Consultation Stages

Six problem-solving stages used in the collaborative consultation method in school settings are described by Idol et al. (1986) and West et al. (1988). Based on West and Idol's (1990) summary, the following stages are presented for use in the transition process:

Stage 1: Goal/Entry. In this stage, the responsibilities, roles, objectives, and expectations of each member involved are described. This stage can occur among individuals or among groups involved in the settings outlined in Figure 4–1. The facilitator's role during this stage would be to contact pertinent individuals in a specific setting and assist with establishing the collaborative model. For example, in the secondary school setting, the individuals involved might include the vocational rehabilitation counselor, a guidance or career counselor, the vocational education teacher, the special education teacher, and the student. Contracts, both formal or informal, would be developed at this stage.

Stage 2: Problem Identification. During this stage, each member acquires a clear understanding of the problem and/or related problems. In the secondary school setting, the problem might be identifying a vocation or determining a career direction for the student.

Stage 3: Intervention Recommendations. During this stage, each member of the process contributes to generating recommendations or intervention strategies. Potential successes or failures are considered and a plan of operation is developed. West and Idol (1990) state:

> Written, measurable objectives are developed to (a) specify intervention details for each aspect of the problem, (b) identify criteria for determining if the problem has been solved, and (c) delineate activities and procedures for consultant, consultee, and client and identify resources needed to implement intervention strategies. (p. 25)

In the secondary school setting example, it might be concluded that the student has the potential for employment that would require a postsecondary education. The members involved in the collaborative model then would develop an ITP that would include objectives directed toward achieving this goal (e.g., preparing for, selecting, and gaining admission to a 4-year college). The ITP includes long- and short-term objectives, materials, resources, and individual responsibilities for the successful accomplishment of each objective. In addition, the reader is reminded that ITPs can include objectives, materials, resources, and individuals from community, employment, and family settings as well.

Stage 4: Implementation Recommendations. During this stage, the plan of operation (or the ITP) is carried out and/or modified dependent on success or failure of each specified long- or short-term objective. Individual responsibilities during this stage vary. The facilitator's role, dependent on circumstances, might include modeling and training and is phased out as the collaboration process becomes firmly entrenched and as the individuals involved in the transition process have gained the confidence and expertise to consult and collaborate with each other.

Stage 5: Evaluation. During this stage, the interventions recommended and carried out are evaluated. Each part of the process is assessed, including each objective and each participant. The facilitator is responsible for evaluating transition across settings and individuals.

Stage 6: Redesign. The plan of operation and/or the major objectives of the ITP are reconsidered, changed, or maintained. As mentioned in the evaluation stage, it is up to the transition facilitator to decide if different strategies are necessary for successful transition.

Cooperation

Cooperation among individuals or agencies often is mistaken as an indication of a collaborative relationship. As stated by West and Idol (1990), it is important to make a distinction between *collaboration* and *cooperation*. Collaboration involves a process that combines the expertise and interests of each individual in defining and solving a common problem. This is accomplished by designing appropriate programs for an individual student. In the area of transition, it involves combining the interests and expertise of each individual in an effort to create a successful transition for a student who is mildly disabled. In short, each party involved is responsible and has authority for the basic decisions that are made. Cooperation, on the other hand, involves individuals or groups of individuals with separate programs agreeing to work together toward the goal of making each individual program more successful (Hord, 1986).

Secondary special education and regular teachers often engage in a cooperative relationship. The special educator tutors the student in a subject or provides accommodating services. The regular teacher presents the content for the course. The two teachers agree to engage in a cooperative teaching relationship in which one teacher presents the content of the course and the other supplies the study skill training necessary for student mastery. Each teacher is interested in making her or his program work for the student. This is accomplished by *cooperation.*

In the employment setting, the job trainer will cooperate with the employer to ensure success for each individual's program. The employer is interested in hiring a productive individual; the trainer is interested in teaching employment skills. Agencies serving the young adult also participate in cooperative arrangements (agency cooperative arrangements will be addressed in subsequent chapters). Although collaboration often evolves from cooperation, the mutual responsibility for problem identification, intervention, evaluation, and follow-up of a student is not an intrinsic part of cooperation.

Advocacy

The historical legislative background for transition has been presented in chapter 2. Mandates and models of transition evolved because of individual and group concerns for the rights of persons with disabilities. Throughout the past three to four decades, advocacy has played an important role in assuring that the rights of individuals with disabilities are guaranteed. Advocacy, especially as part of the role of the facilitator, is an important method associated with transition.

Advocacy groups, such as the Council for the Retarded Child founded in 1933, were initially formed by groups of concerned parents. Lippman and Goldberg (1973) have identified three major effects of these early parental advocacy efforts, including (a) providing emotional support and information about resources to families with retarded members; (b) encouraging legislation and funding for public school programs; and (c) developing model preschool, school, and adult programs.

During the 1960s and 1970s, additional advocacy groups of parents, volunteers, legal advocates, and professionals were organized. Presently, various groups and professional associations advocate for the interests of individuals with disabilities including those who are mentally retarded, learning disabled, deaf, blind, emotionally disturbed, autistic, and physically or medically disabled. Advocates concentrate on disseminating information, supporting and initiating legislation, raising funds, and to a lesser extent providing direct services (Roos, 1983).

Herr (1983) describes different kinds of advocacy as they may be related to transition as follows:

1. *Self-advocacy:* The individual is encouraged and supported in becoming involved in the transition process. It is essential for the individual who is mildly disabled to become involved in the collaborative process of transition. This involvement includes self-advocacy. If necessary, training for this role is provided by the facilitator.
2. *Family advocacy:* Historically, parents and family members have created the foundation for advocacy. Family efforts toward ensuring a productive and

successful adult life for individuals with disabilities have become the cornerstone for the present interest in transition.

3. *Friend advocacy:* This is also referred to as *citizen advocacy.* In the community setting, citizen advocates for transition would include neighbors, friends, and other individuals concerned about the interests of people with disabilities.

4. *Disability rights advocacy:* This type of advocacy involves individuals who have been trained and are specialists in advocating for individual needs and service systems. The transition facilitator should be trained in this capacity.

5. *Human rights advocacy:* This type of advocacy involves individuals who serve on review committees for various governing and service agencies (e.g., an advisory board for employees with disabilities). The committees are usually composed of volunteers and professionals.

6. *Internal advocacy:* This term refers to advocacy within a service agency. These individuals are sometimes called *ombudsmen* and serve in the capacity of monitoring or guaranteeing the rights of the client with mild disabilities.

7. *Legal advocacy:* This type of advocacy involves public interest law projects (usually nonprofit) and may include private and government lawyers.

It is important to point out that professionals, such as special education teachers or vocational rehabilitation counselors advocating for the transition rights of people with mild disabilities, may find themselves in conflict with their professional role (Bateman, 1982). For example, a professional may find that the agency for which he or she works discriminates against persons with disabilities in employment. To be an effective advocate, the professional must emphasize the advocacy role. Current knowledge of legal, ethical, and educational developments in transition should result in successful advocacy not only for those with mild disabilities but also for the professional who often is asked to assume responsibilities above and beyond what one individual can accomplish (e.g., expecting a secondary special educator or rehabilitation counselor to function as the facilitator across transitional settings and agents).

Evaluation

Each of the models of transition presented in chapter 3 includes a reference to evaluation. The methods of transition evaluation for people with mild disabilities are varied and multidimensional. Evaluation of ITPs or Individualized Work Plans and assessment of specific academic, vocational, and extravocational skills are discussed in subsequent chapters. The responsibility for evaluating whether or not specific variables related to transition across settings and setting agents are successful rests primarily with the facilitator and the individual who is mildly disabled. Secondary participants in the evaluation method include the setting agents involved in specific settings (community, employment, family, school) and collaborative relationships.

It is beyond the scope of this narrative to describe the variety of evaluation models that can be utilized within the process of transition. The evaluation of transition, however, must include what various authors describe as *responsive evaluation* (Guba & Lincoln, 1981; Idol et al., 1986). Responsive evaluation involves the concerns and issues pertinent to the individual and the prescribed program. In responsive transition evaluation, evaluative information is collected by various techniques, synthesized, and interpreted to determine whether the transition concerns and issues related to the individual have been addressed and/or accomplished.

Evaluation of the transition process for a student includes evaluating (a) the student within a setting (community, family, school, employment), (b) the setting agents (counselors, transition specialists, community members, employers, coworkers, teachers, peers, family members), and (c) the program components within each setting and across setting agents. Dimensions of evaluation presented by Baer, Wolf, and Risley (1968) are relevant to this process:

1. The *applied* dimension. The behavior to be changed should be important to the secondary student involved in the transition process.
2. The *behavioral* dimension. Behaviors should be observable and measurable in reliable terms. In other words, if two people observe the same behavior and agree that the behavior has or has not been exhibited, then the observation is reliable.
3. The *technological* dimension. The training procedures are clearly described so that any qualified individual can implement or take over intervention.
4. The *conceptual* dimension. The intervention is based on what is expressed in the literature and current knowledge in the field.
5. The *generality* dimension. The target behaviors are such that they can be demonstrated in different settings, across people and time, and across related behaviors.
6. The *effective* dimension. The change in behavior should be significant and valuable to the individual.
7. The *analytic* dimension. Evaluation of behaviors should be based on methods that determine whether the intervention procedures have been effective.

Idol et al. (1986) describe seven strategies that are vital for effective evaluation. These seven strategies are pertinent in evaluating the transition process and include the following:

1. *The evaluation system should provide information on the overall program.* This means that the ITP for a student should encompass each pertinent setting and input from relevant setting agents. The facilitator in conjunction with the student should determine the goals and objectives for achieving an integration of settings and setting agents. Input from agents involved in various settings will result in a comprehensive plan and methods of evaluation.

2. *Student evaluation should match goals and objectives of the ITP.* It is important to remember that the ITP will contain not only student-specific objectives but also objectives that have been identified by the collaborative process across settings. The evaluation of the student's progress in each setting needs to be included.

3. *Criterion levels of performance should be identified.* Criterion levels for defining success of intervention techniques need to be established for each setting and for each setting agent's interaction with a student with disabilities. Appropriate criterion levels should be determined prior to transition implementation.

4. *The mediator should be involved in the evaluation process.* Throughout the transition process, the facilitator (mediator) functions as a key individual. This person, along with individuals involved in the collaborative consultative relationship in each setting, must be actively involved in evaluating transition objectives.

5. *Data collection systems should be simple and easy to administer.* The facilitator is responsible for monitoring the overall transition data collection system input, processing, and output across settings. Although data pertinent to a specific setting will be collected and evaluated, the summative data obtained from each setting should be easy to interpret and conducive to generalization across settings.

6. *Evaluation data should be closely monitored.* The facilitator is responsible for overall transition program evaluation. In specific settings, however, individual persons must be designated as being responsible for monitoring student progress. For example, in the secondary vocational education environment, the vocational education teacher would be responsible for evaluating the acquisition of specific vocational skills.

7. *Results of transition plans across settings must be shared.* It is up to the facilitator to collate and report the student's progress across settings and setting agents. This information sharing should result in strengthening consulting collaborative relationships. It is extremely important that each person involved in the transition process be willing and capable of evaluating his or her own progress as well as the student's and the facilitator's and setting agent's accomplishments.

Follow-up

Various follow-up methods have been alluded to in each of the models of transition. Literature documenting the progress of students who are mildly disabled throughout the secondary transitional period is not generally available.

The method of follow-up is closely associated with the evaluation method. The pertinent question is, What is the outcome of transition for an individual student? The transition literature abounds with citations of successful employment outcomes for individuals who are disabled. These reports, however, are based on short- rather than long-term goals. Students who are mildly disabled have been placed in employment settings and have been shown to be capable of acquiring a limited set of specific vocational skills. Reports of success, however, usually end at this point. Successful transition to adult life has not been reported. Six months after being taught a vocational skill or being employed, the student who is mildly disabled may be out of a job, divorced, and/or unable to solicit additional assistance from the transition process.

❧ ❧ ❧

SETTINGS AND SETTING AGENTS

We have identified four specific settings—community, employment, secondary/postsecondary education, and family—that we feel are relevant for any individual who is making the transition through secondary education into adulthood. If we analyze all of the basic and related models of transition in combination (see chap. 3), we find that these four settings have been variously identified as critical milieus for the transition process. While all of us function in these settings and eventually make a more or less successful transition, the situation for the individual who is mildly disabled differs in the manner and degree to which setting agents (counselors, employers, teachers, parents, etc.), in conjunction with the facilitator, must intervene to structure and manipulate these settings in order for that person to accomplish the transition process successfully.

Setting agents may be divided into *professional* and *nonprofessional* categories. Professional setting agents (regular, special, and vocational education teachers; vocational rehabilitation, mental health, career, and family counselors; and transition specialists) are considered to be experts in the theories and methodologies associated with their respective professions. It is their responsibility to

- know the characteristics, demands, requirements, and expected outcomes of the setting(s) in which they operate;
- assess the various strengths and weaknesses of the individual as they apply to attaining normalcy within the setting(s);
- utilize the body of theory and methodology associated with his or her profession to design, develop, and implement an appropriate ITP that allows the person with a mild disability to function successfully in the setting(s);
- provide pertinent information to nonprofessional setting agents (employers, coworkers, peers, parents, siblings, partners, etc.) so that they may positively affect, support, and reinforce the individual's efforts to function successfully within the transitional setting(s); and

- utilize the methods of transition (consultation, collaboration, cooperation, advocacy, evaluation, and follow-up) to establish effective working relationships with reciprocal participants (the facilitator, the individual with a mild disability, and other professional setting agents) in the transition process.

Nonprofessional setting agents differ from professional setting agents in that they have not been formally trained and certified to assume the roles they play in the transition process. Some (e.g., employers, spouses, friends) make a conscious decision to become involved in the life of an individual who is mildly disabled. For others (community members, coworkers, peers, parents, siblings, etc.), circumstances establish a relationship between them and the person with a mild disability, and they are therefore automatically made active participants in the transition process. In large part, it is the beliefs and attitudes of these people that affect the nature of their interactions with the individual who is mildly disabled. If negativism is manifested, then it is imperative that the professional setting agents and facilitator utilize their expertise in conjunction with the methods of transition to change these beliefs and attitudes and, more importantly, their behaviors. In addition, the setting agents must make the person with a disability realize that he or she can directly influence the nature and quality of relationships and interactions with others. If the individual lacks appropriate social skills and behaviors, those must be taught.

❦ ❦ ❦

SUMMARY

The person who is mildly disabled and the facilitator are key individuals in the transition process. While the facilitator coordinates the activities of all those who participate in the process, the individual with a mild disability must be regarded as the major information resource whose input concerning problem definition and program design, development, implementation, and evaluation is vital to the success of the transition process. Although the theoretical concept of a facilitator is included in many models of transition, steps need to be taken to operationalize the concept. The role of the facilitator must receive detailed conceptual analysis so that

1. appropriate training programs can be developed to impart the theoretical perspectives, methodologies, and skills needed to effectively coordinate transition programs for people who are mildly disabled; and
2. specific criteria for job description, personnel selection, and employment of these individuals can be established.

The methods utilized in the transition process (consultation, collaboration, cooperation, advocacy, evaluation, and follow-up) stimulate the interchange of information among the various participants (facilitator[s], the individual with a mild disability, and setting agents) and foster the development of an atmosphere that encourages the use of a team approach in identifying and ameliorating the transition problems of persons who are mildly disabled.

The transition process occurs across a number of different settings: community, employment, secondary/postsecondary education, and family. Each setting has its own group of setting agents. In conjunction with the facilitator, these are the team members who directly influence the nature and quality of the individual's passage through the transition process.

REFERENCES

Baer, D. M., Wolf, M. M., & Risley, T. R. (1968). Some current dimensions of applied behavior analysis. *Journal of Applied Behavior Analysis, 1*, 91–97.

Bateman, B. (1982). Legal and ethical dilemmas of special educators. *Exceptional Education Quarterly, 2*(4), 57–67.

Bergan, J. R. (1977). *Behavioral consultation.* New York: Merrill/Macmillan.

Blankenship, C., & Jordan, L. (Eds.). (1985). *Teacher Education and Special Education, 8*(3).

Brown, D., & Kurpius, D. J. (Eds.). (1985.) Consultation [Special issue]. *The Counseling Psychologist, 13*(3).

Conoley, J. C., & Conoley, C. W. (1988). Useful theories in school-based consultation. *Remedial and Special Education, 9*, 14–28.

Conoley, J. C., & Gutkin, T. B. (1986). Educating school psychologists for the real world. *School Psychology Review, 15*, 457–465.

Department of Education of Pennsylvania. (1990). Title 22, Education Part XVI, Standards, Chap. 342. In *Special education services and programs* (pp. 20–21). Harrisburg, PA: Author.

Guba, E. G., & Lincoln, Y. S. (1981). *Effective evaluation improving the usefulness of evaluation results through responsiveness and naturalistic approaches.* San Francisco: Jossey-Bass.

Herr, S. S. (1983). *Rights and advocacy for retarded people.* Lexington, MA: Lexington Books.

Hord, S. M. (1986). A synthesis of research on organizational collaboration. *Educational Leadership, 44*, 22–26.

Hresko, W. P. (Ed.). (1988). *Remedial and Special Education, 9*(6).

Idol, L., Paolucci-Whitcomb, P., & Nevin, A. (1986). *Collaborative consultation.* Rockville, MD: Aspen.

Lippman, L., & Goldberg, I. I. (1973). *Right to education: Anatomy of the Pennsylvania case and its implications for exceptional children.* New York: Teachers College Press.

Nelson, C. M., Neel, R. S., & Lilly, M. S. (Eds.). (1981). Consultation as a support system for behaviorally disordered pupils and their teachers. *Behavioral Disorders, 6*(2).

Palmer, J. T., Velleman, R., & Shafer, D. (1984). *The transition process of disabled youth: A literature review.* Albertson, NY: Human Resources Center. (Illinois Transition Institute Document No. 723)

Roos, P. R. (1983). Advocate groups. In J. L. Matson & J. A. Mulick (Eds.), *Handbook of mental retardation* (pp. 25–35). New York: Pergamon.

Schein, E. H. (1969). *Process consultation: Its role in organization development.* Reading, MA: Addison-Wesley.

West, J. F., & Idol, L. (1990). Collaborative consultation in the education of mildly handicapped and at-risk students. *Remedial and Special Education, 11*(1), 22–31.

West, J. F., Idol, L., & Cannon, G. (1988). *Collaboration in the schools: Communicating, interacting and problem solving.* Austin, TX: PRO-ED.

Chapter 5

❦ ❦ ❦

Transition Barriers and Supports

*T*he process of transition as described in chapter 4 includes four essential components: individuals, methods, settings, and setting agents. Within each of these four components various barriers and supports for transition exist across different environments and social systems. For example, an individual who is mildly disabled may experience attitudinal barriers in a number of social contexts (leisure, family, agency, political, legal, etc.).

Bronfenbrenner (1977) describes four social contexts or systems that affect individuals as they progress through the life cycle: the microsystem, the mesosystem, the exosystem, and the macrosystem. In this chapter, barriers to and supports for transition are presented within a systems framework. The four systems have been described in some detail in the preview to Part I.

Bronfenbrenner's four systems have been applied to various individuals and environments. For example, Rusch and Mithaug (1985) apply this systems analytic approach to transitional programming for students with severe disabling conditions. Gajar (1992) employs it in a discussion of model programs for postsecondary students with learning disabilities. In the ensuing discussion, the four systems are addressed separately. The reader is reminded that these four social systems and the four components of the process of transition overlap and influence each other.

❦ ❦ ❦

MICROSYSTEM

The microsystem for an adult who is mildly disabled is the individual's immediate interactions with pertinent others including peers, family members, transition facilitators, employers, fellow employees, teachers, guidance counselors, and community members. Among the major objectives at this level are identifying career and personal goals. Major barriers or supports for transition within this context involve the facilitator's and setting agents' attitudes, awareness of needs, and willingness to provide services and become involved with the adult who is mildly disabled. Self-awareness and self-advocacy can also be barriers or supports within this system depending on the individual's skills in those areas.

Supports and barriers to transition within the microsystem (e.g., stereotypes and adequate social skills) are presented in the following narrative.

Stereotypes

Research has shown that successful interactions with others (peers, family, community members, etc.) play an important role in the transition process for people who are mildly disabled. Parker and Asher (1987) state that "studies suggesting a link between problematic childhood, peer relationships, and adult maladjustment have accumulated slowly but more or less continuously since the early 1930s" (p. 357).

Stereotyping of individuals who are disabled presents a barrier to successful interactions at the microsystem level of society. For example, studies show that children who are disabled are more likely to be rejected by their classmates than their nondisabled peers because of characteristics associated with labels and special placements. Lundstrom (1988), in a series of interviews related to transition, found that a number of parents reported that their children with mild disabilities were often picked on and teased by mainstreamed students because they were in special education classes. Parents of regular education peers also displayed negative attitudes toward these students. Lundstrom relates a disabled boy's parents' conversation with a parent of a nondisabled schoolmate:

> "She called me and she said, 'Mrs. ———, your son asked my daughter out. . . . Maybe I should explain something to you. My daughter is not in his type of classroom, if you understand what I mean.' And I said, 'Oh, are you trying to tell me she's not a special ed kid?' And she said, 'Well, now I don't want to hurt your feelings.' I said, 'Oh, thank God you told me, we don't let our child date "normal" girls.' . . . I was the one who had to go to him and say, 'I'm really, really sorry but . . .' and I explained the situation." (p. 11)

Browder (1987) points out that labels (especially during the secondary period of education) separate individuals from age peers and raise immediate doubts about competency and worth. In a study of adults who were mildly retarded and their families, Zetlin and Turner (1985) found that respondents felt "different" and questioned their own competence. These feelings influenced self-esteem. Browder observes that because of this feeling of "different," a number of individuals with mildly disabling conditions regard the exit from secondary education as an escape from the label. Longitudinal studies of this population reveal that a number of students with mild disabilities "disappear from official view after high school and apparently require no special services" (p. 82). Perhaps they do not look for the services because they know that a negative label often comes with them. In support of this position, May and Hughes (1985) state:

> Failure to make a good escape at this time is to invite a double penalty, since to be reassigned to the category of mentally handicapped is also to be confined to a childlike status, judged incompetent and irresponsible, held in a subordinate and dependent position and excluded from the mainstream of social life. (p. 157)

The barrier that comes from being labeled in high school overlaps with the barrier presented by stereotypical views held by regular and vocational educators and employers concerning the occupational and learning capabilities of individuals who are mildly disabled. Plue (1984) analyzed jobs held by 3,177 individuals who were mildly disabled. The results indicated that jobs held by these individuals required unskilled or semiskilled capabilities such as sorting, separating, assembly line contributions, and so forth. Commenting on this analysis, Cummings and Maddux (1987) ask:

> Do mildly handicapped individuals end up in jobs of this type because their personalities and interests lead them to seek out such work environments, or because vocational programs, counselors, educators in general, and other helping professionals hold a *stereotypic* view of suitable jobs for the handicapped, and thus make decisions about career/vocational education and job placements that result in the continuation of the stereotype? (p. 152, our emphasis)

Studies of vocational interests of individuals who are mildly disabled show that their interests and vocational skills are as varied as those of nondisabled individuals. Training programs, therefore, should be based on a comprehensive analysis of vocational interests, personalities, strengths, and weaknesses exhibited by the individual rather than on a stereotypical label (Cummings & Maddux, 1987).

The stereotypical characteristics associated with an individual who is disabled can influence interactions and attitudes of pertinent others within the microsystem. In the following section parental attitudes as an example of attitudinal barriers and/or supports within this context are examined.

Parental Attitudes.   Parental roles and attitudes toward the young adult who is disabled play an important part in the transition process (Hill, Seyfarth, Orelove, Wehman, & Banks, 1985; Nitzberg, 1974; R. C. Smith, 1983). Despite the popular belief that upon diagnosis of a disability in a child, "adjustment to life without undue stress" follows a period of "disequilibrium," Wikler (1981) has observed that many families do experience disequilibrium throughout the individual's development. Discrepancies between ability and expectations periodically create disruptions and stress in family environments. The disruption and stress created during the transitional period and the stereotypical characteristics associated with the individual can create a barrier to successful adult life for the young person who is disabled, especially during transitional periods.

Johnson, Bruininks, and Thurlow (1987) state that parent participation during the transitional period is less than what is needed. Lynch and Stein (1982) have observed that parents of older students participate less in Individual Education Plan (IEP) conferences than parents of younger children. Goldstein and Turnbull (1982), McKinney and Hocutt (1982), and Browder (1987) have found that employment failure by adolescents who are disabled is often viewed by parents as a result of the disability rather than as a necessary step toward employment. An understanding that the maturation needed for employment takes time and experience and that failure is a usual part of this experience is accepted for nondisabled peers. However, failure on the part of the young worker with a disability often leads toward discouraging the child to attempt vocational success, lowering expectations, and building a transition barrier.

The failure of schools to produce explicit IEP expectations for "normalization" and an inadequate "sink or swim" attitude in the mainstream leads many parents, students, and secondary school personnel to become discouraged, which results in increased stereotyping. The failure of remedial expectations in elementary settings is also discouraging for parents and teachers.

On the other hand, Cummings and Maddux (1987) propose that because of a lack of information and often poor counseling from educators, parents may hold "unrealistically high expectations," especially parents of young adults who have been identified as learning disabled. According to Cummings and Maddux, these parents may overemphasize academics at the expense of important socializing and transition experiences.

Unrealistically low expectations by employers, peers, and parents of individuals who are mildly disabled present barriers to transition. Simultaneously, barriers created by unrealistically high expectations and a belief that a child will "outgrow" a disability occur in cases where the disability is denied.

The influence of positive family attitudes and support for transition is reported in the literature. Schalock et al. (1986), in a follow-up evaluation of employment and living status of 108 individuals who were disabled, found that family involvement was a strong predictor of employment success. Schalock and Lilly (1986) recommend family involvement in job-exploration training and placement. On the other hand, Turnbull and Turnbull (1982) point out that parents can at times be overwhelmed by what is expected: "The implication is clear; to be a good parent, one must have skills comparable to a master's level special educator, and still have time for IEP participation, self-fulfillment, individual and system advocacy, employment, and other family responsibilities" (p. 119).

Discussion. Stereotypes of individuals who are disabled undoubtedly lead to barriers within the microsystem context. Peers, employers, teachers, and administrators all exhibit negative attitudes toward individuals who are disabled. White (1985) concludes that despite media campaigns, employers continuously demonstrate prejudices against people with disabilities.

Fast and simple solutions to attitudinal barriers have been presented. For example, military service for individuals who are mildly disabled has been suggested. Harnden, Meyen, Alley, and Deshler (1980), however, found that only 19% of a group of high school students with learning disabilities scored high enough on armed services aptitude tests to qualify for the Army, and only 4% qualified for the Air Force.

In American culture we often look for quick and easy solutions to difficult problems. When early identification and IEP objectives do not solve the problems faced by individuals who are disabled, parents, employers, and others within the microsystem revert to accepting the stereotypical characteristics. Importantly, however, Browder (1987) concludes:

(a) Participation in normative activities and interaction with nondisabled persons are related to successful adult adjustment.
(b) The life domains of work, home and family, leisure, and community are interrelated such that the inability to transition successfully in one domain has spill over effects to other domains.
(c) Transition success is strongly related to the assistance of a benefactor or positive support system.
(d) Positive social relationships are important contributors to successful adjustment. (p. 84)

Social Skills

Kernan and Koegel (1984) have found that vocational success depends on an individual's access to a strong support system, either family members or support from a service agency. Mithaug, Horiuchi, and Fanning (1985) report that independent living and participation in social and community activities are skills necessary for a "better life." Kaufman (1984) has observed that a high degree of satisfaction with life of persons with mild disabilities is positively related to having nondisabled friendships, chronological age, employment, the willingness to consider other persons with disabling conditions as friends, and self-esteem. White (1985) supports the position that the lack of social skills can be a deterrent to successful functioning for people with mild disabilities. It has been noted in many studies that individuals who are mildly disabled have problems making friends and communicating with others such as family members, coworkers, and peers.

Zigmond and Brownlee (1980) define social skills as those interactions that enhance interpersonal relationships. Appropriate or adequate social skills play an important part in successful transition into employment and adult living for an individual who is mildly disabled. Schumaker, Pederson, Hazel, and Meyen (1983) indicate that problems with social skills may be more detrimental to successful employment and adult functioning than academic or job performance deficits. In a survey of employers and personnel officers of corporations, Wilms (1984) found that adequate social skills, good work habits, and positive attitudes toward employment were more important than specific job skills. Many employers contend that job skills can be taught more easily on the job if positive work habits and attitudes have been instilled by the public school system.

Cummings and Maddux (1987) have observed that information about social skills has often been derived from anecdotal accounts rather than experimental inquiry. In addition, they state that "social skills have been replaced with the current concern for transitional programs" (p. 160). There is no doubt that certain issues in education are at times popular and that often promising research is abandoned because of revised funding priorities. However, the tremendous interest in transition, which encompasses many skills, does not negate the importance of social skill training or research in spite of the observation that such training is neglected in career-vocational education (Cummings & Maddux, 1987).

In summary, within the microsystem stereotypical expectations, labels, and the absence of social skills have consistently created transitional difficulties for individuals with disabilities.

❦ ❦ ❦

MESOSYSTEM

Barriers and supports within the mesosystem include academic and agency requirements, characteristics across agencies, an absence of longitudinal involvement, and the large number of sometimes competing service agencies available to the individual who is mildly disabled.

Agency Requirements

Each secondary, community, and/or employment agency imposes various requirements for an individual to participate. Requirements within certain disciplines can present either supports or barriers to transition. For example, Okolo and Sitlington (1986) indicate that an increasing emphasis on academic and interpersonal skills by vocational programs presents a barrier to the inclusion of youth with disabilities into vocational education. Admission criteria often include successful performance in prerequisite academic courses and adequate performance on basic skill examinations. Many vocational programs use texts and lectures that require proficiency in academic related skills and often preclude success within the vocational curriculum (Sherrell, 1981; Sitlington, 1981). Special education resource room programs, on the other hand, often provide secondary students who are mildly disabled with tutoring in order to "get them through" the curriculum (Anderson & Strathe, 1987). Follow-up studies reveal that this approach has not been very successful. Institutional policies and criteria also lead to underrepresentation in secondary and postsecondary vocational education and technical programs, and community college and university programs.

Attitudes of teachers about the capability of students who are disabled to handle the curriculum influence the requirements for admission into secondary programs. For example, in vocational education teachers' perceptions of the effects of students with disabilities on other students, personal liability, the need for equipment modification, accountability, lack of training, and the possibility of lower academic and vocational standards have been cited as reasons for limiting the number of students who are disabled in vocational education classes (Camaren, 1975; Dahl & Lipe, 1978; Hughes, 1978; Meers, 1977; Minner, 1982; Rumble, 1978; Whiteford & Anderson, 1977).

On the other hand, Okolo and Sitlington (1986) point out that vocational educators do not always exhibit or express negative attitudes toward individuals who are disabled and that consultation and in-service activities facilitate the acceptance into vocational education of these individuals.

Agency Characteristics

Secondary school, community, and employment agency characteristics can either support or present barriers to the transition process. The differences between secondary school settings and human service agency settings can create impediments to transition such as the following:

1. Schools operate under the mandate of inclusion (all children are eligible for services). Human service agencies operate on the basis of exclusion, usually using socioeconomic status and/or disability type to determine eligibility.
2. Schools are organized under a single administrative unit. Each human service agency operates independently of any other agency.
3. Services provided by schools are well defined. Services offered by human service agencies are often variable.
4. Schools are financed by taxes. Agencies are supported by a number of sources, fees, taxes, donations, and so on, and are therefore more dependent on current economic trends.
5. School personnel assume that their responsibility ends when a student leaves school and that service agencies will automatically pick up on needed services. Service agencies assume that adults with disabilities know about services and if the need arises, they will apply for them (Anderson & Strathe, 1987).

Differences in agency characteristics can be formidable and confusing. Competitive employment settings present another situation in which the characteristics of the agency providing the training or assistance can either hinder or facilitate the transition process. Problems encountered in these settings include the following:

1. In secondary training situations, such as the resource room, or in vocational training programs that include special needs students, feedback and reinforcement can be provided on a one-to-one basis and a high degree of performance can be guaranteed. In competitive employment situations, these types of support are difficult to maintain.

2. Social skill deficits jeopardize successful functioning within a competitive employment environment. Ford, Dineen, and Hall (1984) found that 42% of the individuals identified as mentally retarded who lost their jobs did so because of poor relationships with employers and colleagues, emotional outbursts, and poor language. Inadequate grooming skills, inability to deal with transportation, child care, health care, and housing situations are all problems that can affect work performance.

3. Finally, continuing services for the disabled often do not exist. However, employment-related problems continue long after employment begins.

Ford et al. (1984) recommend guidelines to be followed by agencies (such as secondary school, community, and employment-based service programs) involved with providing services for competitive employment in order to enhance effectiveness:

1. The training program must provide on-the-job training for clients involving close monitoring of performance levels.
2. There should be long-term follow-up to ensure maintenance.
3. Support services such as recreational programs should be provided at hours when clients are not working.
4. Financial support needs to be made available for long-term follow-up. Services and agencies need to provide and be funded for maintenance as well as for initial placement.

Absence of Follow-up Activities

The lack of follow-up or longitudinal studies by responsible agencies presents another barrier to transition within the mesosystem. For example, when a student who is mildly disabled graduates, the school system's responsibility is finished. The same holds true for vocational rehabilitation services, vocational education, and the like.

This gap is mainly based on the principle of "normalization." Emphasis on normalization encompasses identifiers such as "mainstreaming," "least restrictive environment," and "regular education initiative." Within this milieu of normalization the identifier of "competitive employment for the disabled" has become the goal for service providers. Once employment has been accomplished, however, the individual is in essence "normalized" and therefore abandoned. Maintenance or follow-up of successful employment is sorely lacking. According to Ford et al. (1984), "Mentally retarded clients who have been trained to competitive levels in vocational skills remain handicapped by the lack of adequate systems for maintaining them on the job and assuring that the quality of their lives is in fact enhanced by competitive employment" (p. 291).

Number of Available Agencies and Services

Finally, the variety of agencies and organizations offering services, the array of services offered (e.g., counseling, recreation, vocational, medical), and the varying eligibility and operating requirements across agencies deter the young adult who is mildly disabled from effective learning of availability, meeting requirements for eligibility, and even knowing how to apply for the necessary service. For example, a survey of adults with learning disabilities concerning postschool status and vocational rehabilitation needs revealed that a large group of the respondents were found to be ineligible for rehabilitation services or were dissatisfied with the services they received (e.g., they were trained for menial jobs). Rehabilitation counselors lacked training in the area of learning disabilities. Generally, respondents' knowledge of their rights in the vocational rehabilitation application/eligibility process was limited (J. O. Smith, 1989, p. iv).

Edgar, Horton, and Maddox (1984) have identified a number of other possible factors within the mesosystem that create barriers to effective transition. These include (a) different organizational patterns across agencies, (b) different geographical areas covered by various programs, (c) different application procedures across agencies for service eligibility, and (d) varying planning cycles and fiscal years. In short, the extended number of service-oriented agencies and the absence of agency procedures that would ensure involvement with an individual over an extended period of time contribute to the array of transition barriers.

❧ ❧ ❧

EXOSYSTEM

The transition exosystem involves interactions among agencies. Although the individual is not directly involved in the interactions, he or she is directly influenced by the quality and outcome of those interagency relationships. Supports and barriers, such as adequate or inadequate consultation and collaboration and high- or low-quality interagency agreements, are possible in this context.

Interagency Consultation and Collaboration

Federal and state laws require interagency agreements among federal, state, and local agencies. Interagency consultation and collaboration have been mandated by a number of laws such as the Job Training Partnership Act (PL 97-300), the Carl D. Perkins Vocational Education Act (PL 98-524), and the Education of the Handicapped Act Amendments of 1986 (PL 99-457). In spite of this legislation, however, the lack of collaboration between agencies continues to be a barrier to many service recipients. The lack of coordination has been identified by parents and service providers as a major barrier to effective transition (Calkins et al., 1985; Johnson et al., 1987; McDonnell & Hardman, 1985). In addition, McDonnell, Wilcox, and Boles (1983) report that parents of secondary students who are disabled seldom receive information about adult services or agencies.

Tindall and Gugerty (1989) state that one reason for the problems encountered is the "shear enormity of the array of federal services for persons with disabilities" (p. 129). Figure 5–1 presents a list of agencies and associated programs providing services to individuals with disabilities; its length helps provide a perspective on the scope of the problem.

Advocacy groups add to the number of agencies dealing with transition issues. According to Tindall and Gugerty (1989), "The list of advocacy agencies is as long and varied as the types of persons with disabilities that they serve" (p. 129). Advocacy agencies for adults who are mildly disabled include the Association for Retarded Citizens (ARC), the Learning Disabilities Association (LDA), and the Council for Exceptional Children (CEC). These and other groups have been instrumental in working with federal and state personnel to develop needed legislation. Coordination among advocacy groups and governmental agencies, although at times successful, often presents a barrier because of the large number of such groups and the rules governing their operations.

Schalock (1986) observes that service delivery to persons with disabilities is often duplicated, fragmented, and inefficient. He cites the following reasons for these phenomena:

1. Overlapping legislation and lack of a clear national policy
2. Multiple funding sources without financial coordination
3. Multiple planning bodies accompanied by inadequate control and responsibility
4. Lack of reliable data on program benefits and effectiveness (p. 115)

State Level. Federal initiatives in the form of mandates to establish interagency agreements for the purpose of improving the coordination of services affects not only federal agencies but state agencies as well. Johnson et al. (1987) state that more than 35 states have interagency agreements among special education, vocational education, vocational rehabilitation, and other service agencies. In spite of these agreements, there is little evidence to show whether these agreements are effective or whether they provide cooperative services at the local level. An analysis of a number of state interagency agreements (Johnson et al., 1987) reveals that they are more descriptive than prescriptive. In short, state agency agreements are often ambiguous in delineating responsibilities and/or plans of action for achieving precise service outcomes. Wehman, Kregel, Barcus, and Schalock (1986) identify terminology and eligibility differences among agencies, duplication of services, political, and attitudinal barriers, protection of "turf," and the fear of possible program termination or cuts as reasons for the ambiguous nature of state interagency agreements.

Greenan and Phelps (1982), in a survey of state directors of vocational and special education concerning what problems currently confront the provision of vocational education to special populations, found that the problems most often listed included

• interagency cooperation and agreements;

U.S. Department of Education

1. Education of Handicapped Children
2. Vocational Rehabilitation
3. Vocational Education
4. National Institute of Handicapped Research
5. Rehabilitation Services—Service Projects
6. Centers for Independent Living
7. Handicapped Media Captioned Films
8. Handicapped-Innovative Development
9. Deaf Blind Centers
10. Secondary Education and Transitional Services
11. Client Assistance Program
12. Handicapped Regional Resource Centers
13. Postsecondary Education Programs

Social Security Administration

1. Social Security Disability Insurance
2. Supplemental Security Income

Department of Health and Human Services

1. Developmental Disabilities—Basic Support and Advocacy
2. Developmental Disabilities—University Affiliated Facilities
3. President's Committee on Mental Retardation
4. Developmental Disabilities—Special Projects
5. Architectural and Transportation Barriers Compliance Board

Small Business Administration

1. Handicapped Assistance Loans 164
2. National Council on the Handicapped
3. President's Committee on Employment of the Handicapped

Figure 5–1
Federal agencies involved directly or indirectly with transition

Source: From "Collaboration among Clients, Families, and Service Providers" by L. W. Tindall and J. J. Gugerty, 1989, in D. E. Berkell and J. M. Brown (Eds.), *Transition from School to Work for Persons with Disabilities* (p. 130), White Plains, NY: Longman. Copyright © 1989 by Longman Publishing Group. Adapted by permission from Longman Publishing Group.

- funding and fiscal policy;
- service delivery and program alternatives;
- personnel preparation;
- state legislation, plans, and policies;
- attitudes; and
- program evaluation and improvements.

Most problems were in the areas of interagency cooperation and agreements and funding and fiscal policy. Emphasis on these two problems results from recent mandates that highlight "expanded efforts to work cooperatively in providing a continuum of vocational education opportunities and services for the handicapped population" (p. 410).

Local Level. The same difficulties involved in getting pertinent agencies to cooperate and communicate at federal and state levels surface in academic units and agencies at the local level. For example, one of the factors presenting a barrier to transition within the secondary school environment is the lack, or infrequent, communication between special education and vocational education (Okolo & Sitlington, 1986). In support of this position, Halpern and Benz (1984) found that many special education teachers in Oregon were not involved with vocational education. In addition, 60% of the administrators surveyed believed that special educators should coordinate vocational and special education, whereas only 30% of the special educators felt that this responsibility was included in their job description. Anderson and Strathe (1987) indicate that it is unclear how two different systems such as education and human service agencies can interface and collaborate. Their missions, organizational structures, sources of funding, methods of service delivery, and so forth are so different that collaboration is therefore nearly impossible. Edgar et al. (1984) found that inadequate coordination among school, social service, and health agencies is the norm rather than the exception.

A major problem in developing a collaborative and cooperative atmosphere among agencies is that the answers to the following crucial questions, concerning interagency collaboration, have not always been agreed upon by program developers:

    (a) When should postsecondary services agencies become involved in the transition process?
    (b) What criteria should be used to determine transition success?
    (c) Which agency will be responsible at each step of the transition process?
    (d) What roles will each agency play during phases of the transition process? (Stodden & Boone, 1987, p. 540)

In addition, cooperative planning between agencies is hindered by the following factors:

    (a) Conflicting agency classification, labeling and counting procedures
    (b) Differing agency language systems that typically lead to misunderstandings, gaps in service provision, and overlap in service delivery

(c) Differing agency philosophies that resulted in differing criteria for determining student/client success (p. 540)

Wehman, Kregel, and Seyfarth (1985) also observe that interagency agreements are ineffective. Creating interagency agreements is difficult because of "turf" issues and the fear of losing funding and community support. In short, territorial issues inhibit effective planning across service agencies (Johnson et al., 1987).

❦ ❦ ❦

MACROSYSTEM

The macrosystem for the adult who is mildly disabled includes the individual's rights and needs within American culture. Special educators, community members, parental advocates, and the efforts of a number of national and local organizations (LDA, CEC) have influenced the development of transitional services. Legislative enactments, presented in chapter 2, have provided a major impetus for establishing the mandate for transition. As a result of legislation, a number of model programs dealing with transition have been funded by the U.S. Department of Education, and great strides have been made in providing transitional services in the past two decades. A number of barriers within the macrosystem, however, continue to exist. Political-economic and social-philosophical issues still abound and affect transition.

Political-Economic Issues

Financial Considerations. Economic support for transition can be either a barrier or support. Historically, political and economic support for special education and transition was based on the moral argument that such services were necessary from the humanistic standpoint, which resulted in a number of legislative mandates. The 1980s, however, saw a shift from the moral argument to an economic one: whether the cost for these services is warranted. The change was partially due to the fact that the increase in political and economic support has resulted in a rise in the number of individuals identified for services and in the demand for transitional services. Moreover, there has not been widespread improvement in the lot of persons with mild disabilities.

A review of the literature (Crowner, 1985) in the area of special education finance shows that critics of the present system question whether the current system is "the most efficient and effective way to support services for exceptional students." Questions such as "(a) Who are the disabled? (b) Is the rapid growth of services for the mildly disabled cause for concern? (c) Should fiscal support occur at the expense of other needy students? (d) What is the best way to pay for these services?" have not been resolved (p. 503).

On the other hand, proponents of the present system oppose reducing current political and economic supports for transition. Breakthroughs in awareness, attitudes, and political and economic support for transition involved years of struggle against resistance from local, state, and federal administrators and agencies. A return to limited spending in this area and to the position that transition of people with mild disabilities can be handled effectively within the mainstream and without special services and financial support is unacceptable. Certainly, mainstream vocational programs have been terribly ineffective for youths with disabilities, and a return to a "benign neglect" model is threatening.

The Labor Market.   Knowledge of the labor market is pertinent to the study of transition because this information is necessary to make decisions about resources and to minimize barriers presented by diminishing resources. In a chapter entitled "Economics of Transition," Passmore (1989) examines a number of aspects of the labor market that affect employment of people with disabilities. These include (a) the structure of the market, (b) the economic factors that affect the supply of labor, and (c) the economic factors that influence the demand of labor.

The structure of the labor market.   The market's structure is difficult to analyze by any individual seeking employment. Knowledge of the longevity of employment, working conditions, promotion, wages, and alternative employment is not readily available. Adults with disabilities are at a greater disadvantage. Labor market information available to potential employees may not include pertinent data concerning the requirements of employment that may preclude hiring, promotion, or retention of an individual with a disability. According to Passmore (1989), the elusive structure of the labor market warrants consideration of supply and demand that may "aid vocational planning for people with disabilities" (p. 51).

Supply of labor.   Supply of labor is defined by Passmore (1989, p. 51) as the number of people willing to work at current wages. He analyzes the supply of labor from the macro- and microeconomic perspectives. On the macro level, educators and trainers involved with the transitional period of individuals with disabilities need to consider the prevailing supply of employees within an occupation, the potential for entering the occupation, and the flow of employees leaving the occupation. Passmore (1989) suggests that the U.S. Bureau of Labor Statistics (BLS) model shown in Figure 5–2 can be utilized in "planning and policy deliberations about employment of people with disabilities" (p. 53).

Based on the BLS model, entries into an occupation, the current supply of employees, and separation from the occupation can be analyzed from a number of views. For example, a study of a particular occupation may indicate that a large number of individuals from other occupations or returning adults are entering the occupation with relative ease. The current supply of employees may be relatively stable, with few individuals leaving or being promoted to different positions. Even though training costs for this occupation

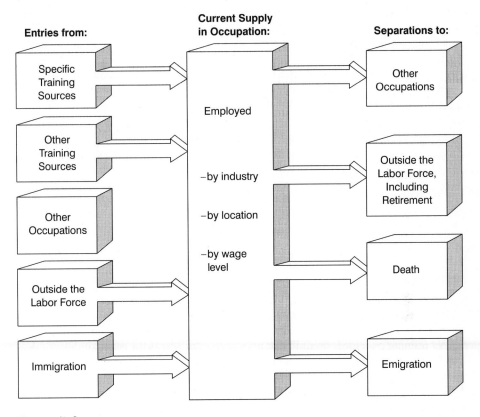

Figure 5–2
U.S. Bureau of Labor Statistics (BLS) model of occupational supply structure

Source: From D. L. Passmore (1989), "Economics of Transition" by D. L. Passmore, 1989, in D. E. Berkell and J. M. Brown (Eds.), *Transition from School to Work for Persons with Disabilities* (p. 52), White Plains, NY: Longman. Copyright © 1989 by Longman Publishing Group. Used by permission from Longman Publishing Group.

may be low, the probability of employment and the recuperation of funds expended for training may be nonexistent. Developing a training program for such an occupation would be, to say the least, counterproductive.

From the microeconomic perspective of the labor force, individuals who are disabled are often eligible for public assistance. Support programs of this kind are designed for individuals who cannot achieve gainful employment or who are below the poverty levels of employment. A number of studies indicate that public assistance programs may function as a disincentive to gainful employment for adults with disabilities and therefore present a barrier to transition (Berkowitz, Johnson, & Murphy, 1975; Passmore, 1987).

On the other hand, the benefits of using financial resources for training individuals with limited employment potential as opposed to providing public assistance has been questioned. As Passmore (1989) states:

With no limitations on resources, both income support and rehabilitation could be provided for all people with disabilities . . . in this era of budget deficits, trade deficits, high rates of consumer debt, and social program cuts. . . . Choices must be made.

Choices that influence the labor supply of people with disabilities raise some fundamental questions about how to use public resources for the well-being of people with disabilities. . . . What are the most cost-beneficial means for reaching these ends? (p. 56)

Since choices must be made, it is our position that redirecting resources to train and facilitate the transition of individuals who are mildly disabled is a viable alternative. According to Levitan and Taggart (1977):

In the face of the limited employment potential of the most severely handicapped and the considerable resources investment needed to prepare them for gainful employment, consideration might be given to whether they might be better served with income support, so that scarce rehabilitation resources can be focused on others who might be helped more in the labor market. (p. 118)

Cummings and Maddux (1987) support this position:

The mildly handicapped generally have a more positive prognosis with regard to potential for success in semiskilled and skilled jobs, . . . their potential for normalization is greater than that for the moderately/severely handicapped. . . . the thrust of training programs should be to help prepare students for eventual independent functioning with limited or with no further support. (p. 151)

Demand for labor.   Passmore (1987) defines the demand for labor as the number of workers needed to produce goods and services for society. On the macro level educators and trainers involved with the transitional period of individuals with disabilities need to consider the "transactions among industries." According to Passmore (1987), Leontief's (1936) model should be used when planning transition for individuals with disabilities. This model divides the input of a particular industry, such as land, capital, and labor, for the purpose of producing an output that in turn other industries use to meet their input requirements. Passmore (1987) believes that if Leontief's input-output model of labor demand by industry is used in conjunction with the BLS model of supply, employment training and identification of the important components of transition programs for people with disabilities would be facilitated.

The demand for labor in a certain occupation can also be supplemented by information from the *Dictionary of Occupational Title* (*DOT*). The *DOT* contains information about physical and mental requirements for successful performance within a particular occupation. In short, the needs of an industry can be cross-referenced with the information contained in the *DOT* to determine the feasibility of occupational training for individuals who are mildly disabled. The study of occupational demands and employment requirements, by transition facilitators, may result in determining whether certain occupations could be redesigned to accommodate individuals who are mildly disabled. Selection of training for occupations that are "relatively insensitive to fluctuations in the economy" would be facilitated (Passmore, 1989, p. 60).

From the microeconomic perspective of labor demand, Passmore (1989) addresses employment discrimination and employer incentives. Studies regarding attitudes and discrimination by employers, consumers, and others against individuals who are disabled have been considered within the microsystem narrative. Stereotypes of individuals with disabling conditions are prevalent and affect not only the individual who is disabled but often the employer as well. According to Passmore (1989), "employment discrimination against people with disabilities hurts the employer, and retaliation against the employer reduces the welfare of people with disabilities" (p. 60).

A second consideration within the microeconomic level of labor demand includes the availability of incentives for employers who hire disabled individuals. Such incentives include hiring individuals at lower than minimum wage and receiving tax credits. The rationale for incentives includes transferring some of the presumably high cost of hiring an individual who is disabled to the public. According to Passmore (1987), many employers do not use or apply for available incentives because of prohibitive costs associated with the paperwork and application procedures.

Social and Philosophical Issues

Within the macrosystem context, Cummings and Maddux (1987) point out the lack of a theoretical base for career development approaches with populations who are disabled. The concern over an absence of a philosophical base in career education for people with disabilities is also expressed by Conte (1983) and Phillips, Strohmer, Berthaume, and O'Leary (1983). The authors center their concerns on the fact that many programs are based on stereotypes rather than on a theoretical viewpoint.

Career development for the nondisabled has been based on a number of theoretical foundations. Cummings and Maddux (1987) discuss theory in terms of four theoretical approaches: (a) personality, (b) developmental, (c) social systems, and (d) trait factor. They apply the relevance of each approach to populations with disabilities. The discussion of theoretical approaches for nondisabled individuals and the application of these approaches to those with mild disabilities is relevant to the discussion of barriers within the macrosystem and to future directions for transition. The four theoretical approaches, therefore, presented by Cummings and Maddux, are addressed in detail in Part V of this text.

Finally, the successful integration of young people with disabilities into nondisabled segments of the population often depends on reducing the misconceptions associated with labels and stereotypes. Stereotyping seems to override many of the other problems, and stereotypical misconceptions often present insurmountable barriers. It is our position that part of the responsibility for creating stereotypical misconceptions rests with the media. Too often individuals with disabilities have been portrayed as objects of pity (telethons) or as super-heroes who achieve in spite of adversity (consider, e.g., the quiz show question "What do Einstein and Leonardo da Vinci have in common?") rather than as individuals who are not essentially different from other ordinary citizens. A realistic approach to individuals with disabilities in the media would greatly reduce the misconceptions and stereotypes associated with this population.

❦ ❦ ❦

SUMMARY

Two major barriers to transition—stereotyping and the difficulties involved in collaboration and cooperation among individuals, methods, settings, and setting agents—have been discussed across four social contexts (micro-, meso-, exo-, and macrosystems) identified by Bronfenbrenner (1977). The characteristics (stereotypes) associated with individuals who are mildly disabled influence every aspect of transition. On the microsystem level, stereotypes associated with persons with disabilities influence the attitudes held by peers, family, employers, and service providers. The individual who is mildly disabled and the transition facilitator face parental, family, employer, peer, teacher, supervisor, service provider, and counselor perceptions that affect the transition process. In addition, the presence or absence of positive social skills bears an influence on successful interactions within this context.

Within the meso- and exosystem, attitudes and stereotypical impressions held by agency employees and program developers influence the success of interagency collaboration and cooperation. On the macrosystem level, stereotypical beliefs are often influenced by the mass media and create barriers to economic, social, and political progress for individuals who are mildly disabled.

The difficulties of collaboration and cooperation among agencies and agency personnel (referred to as settings and setting agents in chap. 4) are identified as the second major barrier to transition. Although mandates include collaborative and cooperative statements among agencies at the federal, state, and local levels, these agreements are often nonfunctional. Differences in agency philosophy, methods, requirements, "turf," funding, purpose, and the interactions among characteristics of and the vast number of involved agencies and advocacy groups preclude collaborative success.

Political-economic concerns such as the structure of the market and supply and demand of labor also come into play. In addition, the absence of a theoretical base and the ensuing social-philosophical issues have been considered here.

REFERENCES

Anderson, R. J., & Strathe, M. I. (1987). Transition from school to work and community. In G. D. Meers (Ed.), *Handbook of vocational special needs education* (2nd ed., pp. 315–329). Rockville, MD: Aspen.

Berkowitz, M., Johnson, W. G., & Murphy, E. H. (1975). *Policy and the determinants of disability*. Princeton, NJ: Rutgers University Press.

Bronfenbrenner, U. (1977). Toward an experimental ecology of human development. *American Psychologist, 32*, 513–531.

Browder, P. M. (1987). Transition services for early adult age individuals with mild mental retardation. In R. N. Ianacone & R. A. Stodden (Eds.), *Transition issues and directions* (pp. 77–90). Reston, VA: Council for Exceptional Children.

Calkins, C. F., Walker, H. M., Bacon-Prue, A., Gibson, B., Martinson, M. C., & Offner, R. (1985). *The learning adjustment process: Implications of a national profile of adult development*. Logan: Utah State University, Developmental Center for Handicapped Persons.

Camaren, R. J. (1975). *Guidelines for improvement of vocational programs and resources to serve needs of handicapped students* (Final Report). Englewood, CO: Performance Management Specialists.

Carl D. Perkins Vocational Education Act, PL 98-524, 98 Stat. 2435 (1984).

Conte, L. D. (1983). Vocational development theories and the disabled person: Oversight or deliberate omission? *Rehabilitation Counseling Bulletin, 26*(5), 316–328.

Crowner, T. T. (1985). A taxonomy of special education finance. *Exceptional Children, 51*(6), 503–508.

Cummings, R. W., & Maddux, C. D. (1987). *Career and vocational education for the mildly handicapped*. Springfield, IL: Thomas.

Dahl, R. R., & Lipe, D. (1978). *Overcoming barriers to mainstreaming: A problem-solving approach* (Final Report). Palo Alto, CA: American Institutes for Research in the Behavioral Sciences.

Edgar, E., Horton, B., & Maddox, M. (1984). Postschool placements: Planning for public school students with developmental disabilities. *Journal of Vocational Special Need Education, 6*(2), 15–18, 26.

Ford, L., Dineen, J., & Hall, J. (1984). Is there life after placement? *Education and Training of the Mentally Retarded, 19*(4), 291–296.

Gajar, A. H. (1992). University based models for students with learning disabilities: The Pennsylvania State University Model. In F. R. Rusch, L. Destefano, L. Chadsey-Rusch, L. A. Phelps, & E. Szymanski (Eds.), *Transition from school to adult life: Models, linkages, and policy* (pp. 51–70). Sycamore, IL: Sycamore.

Goldstein, S., & Turnbull, A. P. (1982). Strategies to increase parent participation in IEP conferences. *Exceptional Children, 45*, 360–361.

Greenan, J. P., & Phelps, L. A. (1982). Delivering vocational education to handicapped learners. *Exceptional Children, 48*, 408–411.

Halpern, A., & Benz, M. (1984). *Toward excellence in secondary special education: A statewide study of Oregon's high school programs for students with mild disabilities*. Unpublished manuscript, University of Oregon, Eugene.

Harnden, G., Meyen, E. L., Alley, G. R., & Deshler, D. D. (1980). *Performance of learning disabled high school students on the Armed Services Vocational Aptitude Battery* (Research Report No. 24). Lawrence: Institute for Research in Learning Disabilities, University of Kansas.

Hill, J. W., Seyfarth, J. P., Orelove, F., Wehman, P., & Banks, P. D. (1985).

Parent/guardian attitudes toward the working conditions of their mentally retarded children. Richmond: Virginia Commonwealth University, School of Education, Rehabilitation Research and Training Center.

Hughes, J. (1978). *Mainstreaming the handicapped in preparatory occupational education programs in North Carolina* (Final Report). Chapel Hill, NC: System Sciences.

Job Training Partnership Act, PL 97-300, 96 Stat. 1322 (1982).

Johnson, D. R., Bruininks, R. H., & Thurlow, M. L. (1987). Meeting the challenge of transition service planning through improved interagency cooperation. *Exceptional Children, 53*(6), 522–530.

Kaufman, S. (1984). Friendship, coping systems and community adjustment of mildly retarded adults. In R. Edgerton (Ed.), *Lives in process: Mildly retarded adults in a large city* (pp. 73–92). Washington, DC: American Association on Mental Deficiency.

Kernan, K., & Koegel, P. (1984). Employment experiences of community-based mildly retarded adults. In R. Edgerton (Ed.), *Lives in process: Mildly retarded adults in a large city* (pp. 9–26). Washington, DC: American Association on Mental Deficiency.

Leontief, W. (1936). Quantitative input-output relations in the economic system of the United States. *The Review of Economics and Statistics, 43*, 105–125.

Levitan, S. A., & Taggart, R. (1977). *Jobs for the disabled* (Policy Studies in Employment and Welfare No. 28). Baltimore: Johns Hopkins University Press.

Lundstrom, F. (1988, December). *Parents of young persons with special needs in transition—Results of Phase I*. Paper presented at the Fourth Annual Meeting of the Transition Institute Project Directors, Washington, DC.

Lynch, E. W., & Stein, R. (1982). Perspectives on parent participation in special education. *Exceptional Education Quarterly, 3*(2), 56–63.

May, D., & Hughes, D. (1985). The prospects on leaving school for the mildly mentally handicapped. *British Journal of Special Education, 12*, 151–158.

McDonnell, J. J., & Hardman, M. (1985). Planning the transition of severely handicapped youth from school to adult services: A framework for high school programs. *Education and Training of the Mentally Retarded, 20*(4), 275–284.

McDonnell, J. J., Wilcox, B., & Boles, S. M. (1983). *Issues in the transition from school to adult services: A study of parents of secondary students with severe handicaps*. Eugene: University of Oregon, Center on Human Development, Specialized Training Program Model School and Community Services for People with Severe Handicaps. (ERIC Document Reproduction Service No. ED 240 381)

McKinney, J. D., & Hocutt, A. M. (1982). Public school involvement of parents of learning disabled children and average achievers. *Exceptional Education Quarterly, 3*(2), 64–73.

Meers, G. D. (1977). *Development and implementation of program models for assisting vocational teachers in dealing with the educationally disadvantaged, handicapped, and minorities*. Lincoln: University of Nebraska.

Minner, S. (1982). The influence of educational labels and behavioral descriptors on secondary vocational educators. *Journal of Vocational Special Needs Education, 4*, 7.

Mithaug, D., Horiuchi, C., & Fanning, P. (1985). A report on the Colorado statewide follow-up survey of special education students. *Exceptional Children, 53*, 397–404.

Nitzberg, J. (1974). The resistive parent behind the resistive trainee at a workshop training center. *Special Children, 6,* 5–29.

Okolo, C. M., & Sitlington, P. (1986). The role of special education in LD adolescents' transition from school to work. *Learning Disability Quarterly, 9*(2), 141–155.

Parker, J. G., & Asher, S. R. (1987). Peer relations and later personal adjustment: Are low-accepted children at risk? *Psychological Bulletin, 102,* 357–389.

Passmore, D. L. (1987). Theory: Adapting human resources to organizational change. In R. A. Swanson & D. Gradous (Eds.), *Human resources and organizational change.* Alexandria, VA: American Society for Training and Development.

Passmore, D. L. (1989). Economics of transition. In D. E. Berkell & J. M. Brown (Eds.), *Transition from school to work for persons with disabilities* (pp. 42–63). White Plains, NY: Longman.

Phillips, S. D., Strohmer, D. C., Berthaume, D. L. J., & O'Leary, J. (1983). Career development of special populations: A framework for research. *Journal for Vocational Behavior, 22,* 12–29.

Plue, W. (1984). Employment patterns of the mildly retarded. *The Journal for Vocational Special Needs Education, 7*(1), 23–28.

Rumble, R. R. (1978). *A survey of the attitudes of secondary vocational teachers toward the mainstreaming of handicapped learners.* Portland, OR: Portland Public Schools.

Rusch, F. R., & Mithaug, D. E. (1985). Competitive employment education: A systems-analytic approach to transitional programming for the student with severe handicaps. In K. C. Lakin & R. M. Bruininks (Eds.), *Strategies for achieving community integration of developmentally disabled citizens* (pp. 177–192). Baltimore: Brookes.

Schalock, R. L. (1986). Service delivery coordination. In. F. R. Rusch (Ed.), *Competitive employment issues and strategies* (pp. 115–127). Baltimore: Brookes.

Schalock, R. L., & Lilly, M. A. (1986). Placement from community-based mental retardation programs: How well do clients do after 8-10? *American Journal of Mental Deficiency, 90*(6), 669–676.

Schalock, R. L., Wolzen, B., Ross, I., Elliott, B., Werbel, G., & Peterson, K. (1986). Postsecondary community placement of handicapped students: A five-year follow-up. *Learning Disability Quarterly, 9*(4), 295–303.

Schumaker, J., Pederson, C. S., Hazel, J., & Meyen, E. L. (1983). Social skills curricula for mildly handicapped adolescents: A review. *Focus on Exceptional Children, 16*(4), 1–16.

Sherrell, E. (1981). Long neglected factor: Reading ability of vocational students. *Phi Delta Kappan, 42,* 115–188.

Sitlington, P. L. (1981). Vocational and special education in career programming for the mildly handicapped adolescent. *Exceptional Children, 47,* 592–598.

Smith, J. O. (1989). *Access to rehabilitation services by adults with learning disabilities.* Unpublished doctoral dissertation, Pennsylvania State University, University Park.

Smith, R. C. (1983). *Seven special kids: Employment problems of handicapped youth* (Contract No. DOL 300-81-2608). Chapel Hill, NC: MDC, Inc. (ERIC Document Reproduction Service ED 237 688)

Stodden, R. A., & Boone, R. (1987). Assessing transition services for handicapped youth: A cooperative interagency approach. *Exceptional Children, 53*(6), 537–545.

Tindall, L. W., & Gugerty, J. J. (1989). Collaboration among clients, families, and service providers. In D. E. Berkell & J. M. Brown (Eds.), *Transition from school to work for persons with disabilities* (pp. 127–160). White Plains, NY: Longman.

Turnbull, A. P., & Turnbull III, R. (1982). Parent involvement in the education of handicapped children: A critique. *Mental Retardation, 20*(3), 115–122.

Wehman, P. H., Kregel, J., Barcus, M. J., & Schalock, R. L. (1986). Vocational transition for students with developmental disabilities. In W. E. Kiernan & J. A. Stark (Eds.), *Pathways to employment, for adults with developmental disabilities* (pp. 113–127). Baltimore: Brookes.

Wehman, P. H., Kregel, J., & Seyfarth, J. (1985). Transition from school to work for individuals with severe handicaps: A follow-up study. *Journal of the Association for Persons with Severe Handicaps, 10,* 132–136.

White, W. J. (1985). Perspectives on the education and training of learning disabled adults. *Learning Disability Quarterly, 8,* 231–236.

Whiteford, E. B., & Anderson, D. H. (1977). The mainstreaming of special needs students: Home economics teachers are coping. Report of a Minnesota survey. *American Vocational Journal, 52*(50), 42–44.

Wikler, L. (1981). Chronic stresses of families of mentally retarded children. *Family Relations, 30,* 281–288.

Wilms, W. W. (1984). Vocational education and job success: The employer's view. *Phi Delta Kappan, 65*(5), 347–350.

Zetlin, A., & Turner, J. (1985). Transition from adolescence to adulthood: Perspectives of mentally retarded individuals and their families. *American Journal of Mental Deficiency, 89,* 570–579.

Zigmond, N., & Brownlee, J. (1980, August). Social skills training for adolescents with learning disabilities. *Interchange,* 6-12.

PART II

❧   ❧   ❧

Academic Support for Transition

This freshman class of 1892 had been suspended for playing baseball during class.
They mocked the suspension by setting up a camp, cooking their meals, making ice
cream, and sleeping in tents. Ultimately the students were reinstated. As in the days of
Camp Suspension, students must perceive their education as relevant and functional if
learning is to take place.

❧   ❧   ❧

I n Part II we explore academic programming at the secondary and postsecondary levels. The nature and content of the secondary school program are vital to the successful transition of youth with mild disabilities. It is important, therefore, to assess the current status of secondary school academic and transitional programs and to ascertain the degree to which such programs adequately address the transition needs of people with mild disabilities. Where shortcomings exist, appropriate directions for future development of programs and services must be found.

❦ ❦ ❦

CHAPTER 6

In chapter 6 we address three important issues related to academic programming for persons with mild disabilities in our secondary schools: minimum competency testing (MCT), the dropout phenomenon, and the role of the special education teacher. Minimum competency testing has broad implications for students who are mildly disabled. Practices vary greatly across the country, but some consensus has emerged as to appropriate provisions and procedures to ensure fair and equitable treatment of disabled learners. A review of MCT practices and the performance of learners with disabilities on MCT to date is included in chapter 6.

Students with disabilities drop out of school at an alarming rate. In our discussion, we describe the dropout phenomenon, dropout rates, dropout reasons, the consequences of dropping out, and prevention of dropping out.

The role and responsibilities of the special education teacher in transitional programming are discussed at length. Different perspectives on the teacher's role are presented. The question of role assignment is essential to the successful implementation of transition programs and services; however, designation of the special education teacher as the "transition facilitator" may not be the appropriate solution to this pressing problem.

❦ ❦ ❦

CHAPTER 7

The mounting concern for appropriate transitional services has brought secondary school educational programs under scrutiny. Chapter 7 deals with the academic foundations for transitional programming in our secondary schools. Current models of academic instruction are discussed, and the strengths and weaknesses of each model relative to the transition process are explored. The essential components for secondary-level transition programs are also discussed, with attention directed toward the discrepancy between what exists and what needs to be provided in order to achieve optimal instructional programming to meet the academic and transitional needs of disabled students. Three model transition programs that illustrate implementation of transition planning programs at the school and district level are reviewed.

❦ ❦ ❦

CHAPTER 8

Assessment is a critical component of both instructional and transitional programming. Emerging assessment trends for transition planning, notably the curriculum-based vocational assessment model, are described, discussed, and contrasted with curriculum-based assessment in special education. Assessment practices of federally funded transition projects provide an invaluable perspective on the variety and nature of assessment procedures actually being used across the country. A summary of the data gathered from the federally funded projects is included in this chapter. Current and relevant information on the individual education and transition planning (IEP/ITP) process is discussed, and selected ITP formats are presented.

❦ ❦ ❦

CHAPTER 9

Our knowledge about effective instructional practices at the secondary school level has increased greatly in recent years. In particular, directive and active teaching methods appear to be instructionally effective for students with mild disabilities. In chapter 9 we explore this methodology. The interrelationship between current instructional methods and the functional curricular model is carefully considered.

❦ ❦ ❦

CHAPTER 10

Discussion of academic programming for those with mild disabilities would be incomplete without consideration of the opportunities for continued academic training. Therefore, chapter 10 is devoted to an examination of formal academic programs at community colleges and 4-year institutions of higher learning that are open to students with disabilities. Program availability, admission requirements, and institutional accommodations to encourage the attendance of students with disabilities are discussed. Intervention techniques that foster students' academic success (e.g., study skills, self-management, effective time management) are also included. Data on student performance in college and university programs are used to clarify the nature of the support structures that students with mild disabilities require to achieve success in programs of advanced academic study.

As the reader proceeds into the chapters on academic programming, we urge him or her to reflect on Kalvin, the student who is the subject of the introductory vignette to Part II. This student's experience underscores the need for an honest and insightful appraisal of academic programming in our secondary schools. Clearly, the secondary educational system had failed to tap the abilities of this young man and to channel them into a productive direction. Special education services had been provided but were inappropriate and/or inadequate, and as a result Kalvin became one of many casualties of the educational system. Our intentions may be well founded, but the services we provide must be evaluated ultimately against human and real-life outcomes.

❧ *Vignette* ❧

It was October when Mrs. Jacobs discovered that she had left the keys to her classroom at home. Her thoughts that morning had been preoccupied with the problems of starting the first self-contained high school class for adolescents with disabilities. Previously her students had been enrolled in an upper-level class for the retarded at a local elementary school. The school board had created the high school class at the insistence of teachers and a few parents who did not want their elementary-age children going to school with 14- and 16-year-old retarded youngsters. The high school principal had informed Mrs. Jacobs that her teaching evaluation would be based on how well she could *"keep those retards contained in their classroom"* and from *"disrupting the orderly functioning"* of the school. Considering the fact that the high school was located in the midst of a midwestern metropolitan area with high crime and dropout rates, Mrs. Jacobs had been somewhat taken aback by the principal's comments. The problem at hand, however, involved opening the door to her classroom so that she could get the list of students eligible for the morning breakfast program at the school. At that particular moment, Kalvin appeared in the hallway.

Kalvin was one of the students in Mrs. Jacobs's classroom who would soon be 16. She had visited his home prior to the school year and had helped his mother gain medical assistance for his little sister. Kalvin, one of 16 teens in her class, used his influence to keep the other students from disrupting the orderly functioning of the classroom. When Mrs. Jacobs explained her problem to Kalvin, he quickly produced a package of tools from his pocket and with great dexterity opened the classroom door.

After school that day, Kalvin approached Mrs. Jacobs and asked her not to let anyone know about what had happened. He told her about his "business." Living close to the railroad freight yards, Kalvin made money by stealing cartons of cigarettes from the biweekly freight shipment. He knew the details of the security system and how to pick locks. A number of students at the school were in his employ. The students would sell a package of cigarettes for 15 cents. They would keep 5 cents, and he would make 10 cents on each package. He showed Mrs. Jacobs the notebook in which he kept track of each transaction (a basic form showing debits and credits). Kalvin was the same student who had scored a 59 IQ on the Stanford-Binet and had failed miserably when given a third-grade addition/subtraction worksheet.

Mrs. Jacobs spent the next week trying to decide what to do. One of her students was running an illegal business. Yet she had given her word not to tell. If she did tell, would anyone believe the story? And, if they did, what would happen to Kalvin? After a great deal of thought, Mrs. Jacobs had an idea. She spent the next month visiting local department stores, hardware stores, and small locksmith shops in the area. Trying to convince an employer to hire a student with mental retardation on a trial basis was not easy! One small locksmith business, however, agreed to hire Kalvin as a stock boy after school and on weekends. Kalvin agreed to curtail his cigarette business and took the job.

Epilogue

Kalvin dropped out of school when he reached his 16th birthday. He continued to work for the local locksmith who, after finding out about Kalvin's *ability* to pick locks, promoted him to the position of all-around troubleshooter. Kalvin informed Mrs. Jacobs that he was saving his money so that *maybe* someday he could open his own locksmith business.

Kalvin's story is nonfictional. We do not know if Kalvin ever opened his locksmith shop. If he did and was successful, his story would be quite unique and contrary to the outcomes facing most high school dropouts, especially those with mild disabilities who leave school unprepared for the demands of adult life.

Chapter 6

❦ ❦ ❦

Issues in Academic Programming and Transition

*T*he vast majority of secondary students with mild disabilities will receive their education in a public secondary school. There are a number of relevant issues bearing on the academic and transitional programming for the secondary student who is mildly disabled that demand our attention. The implications of performance standards, in the form of minimum competency testing (MCT), at the secondary school level must be addressed. Additionally, students with disabilities are not at all immune to problems that are widespread among secondary school–age youth (e.g., drug abuse, delinquency, and, in the achievement realm, dropping out of school). Minimum competency testing of those with disabilities and the dropout phenomenon are two important and timely issues of which the reader should have some knowledge and understanding. These important topics are explored in this chapter. The role of the special education teacher in the transition process is central to the entire discussion of transition and is also discussed here.

❦ ❦ ❦

ACADEMIC PERFORMANCE STANDARDS

The most recent and comprehensive figures indicate that 40 states have enacted MCT programs (Education Commission of the States, 1985). Recognizing that the decision regarding MCT comes under each state's purview, it should come as no surprise that the nature of MCT programs and requirements varies greatly across the country. Some state programs are well established; others are still in the early stages of development. Some states enforce uniform requirements, while others share the decision making regarding MCT with local districts, which thus creates considerable variability not only across but also within state boundaries.

The MCT movement, initially a response to the public outcry for higher performance standards and teaching accountability (Haney & Madaus, 1978) is now well beyond the "should we or shouldn't we" stage of debate, as the number of states committed to MCT attests. From the outset there was great concern about the inclusion or exclusion of children with disabilities in MCT programs (Amos, 1980; Linn, Madaus, & Pedulla, 1982; McCarthy, 1983; McDill, Natriello, & Pallas, 1985, 1986; Safer, 1980; Smith & Jenkins, 1980) and the impact that MCT would have on those students. Satisfactory answers to all of the concerns have not been achieved by any means. Some preliminary data on the performance of students with disabilities in selected states reveal how the states are dealing with the inclusion/exclusion questions. Other related and important issues deal with testing modifications and adaptations, provision of remediation, and the legal perspective on MCT for the disabled learner.

State MCT Options

Vitello (1988) has organized current state policies regarding students with disabilities and MCT testing into five categorical options:

1. Students with disabilities are required to pass MCT in order to receive a high school diploma (8 states).
2. Students with disabilities may obtain a high school diploma upon completion of their individual IEP requirements (21 states).
3. Differential tests are applied to students with disabilities (1 state).
4. The decision regarding competency testing of students with disabilities is made at the local school level (5 states).
5. Policies and procedures are being formulated (5 states).

Three of the five options warrant closer scrutiny as they raise a number of legal and educational issues.

Option 1, which requires students with disabilities to pass MCT in order to receive a regular high school diploma, has spawned litigation in which state departments of education and local school districts have been cast in adversarial roles. For example, New York state is one in which MCT requirements apply to students who are disabled and those who are not. In *Board of Education of Northport-East Northport Union Free School District v. Ambach* (1981) (cited in Vitello, 1988) the district awarded high school diplomas to two students with disabilities upon their successful completion of the requirements stated in their IEPs. Litigation between the state and school district followed. The state commissioner of education sought to have the diplomas revoked because the students had not passed the state's MCT. The school district sued on behalf of the two disabled students. The case was finally resolved at the state supreme court, which upheld the state's right to set regulations regarding graduation from high school, to establish basic competency standards, and to withhold a high school diploma from students, including those who are disabled, who do not pass minimum competency tests (*Education for the Handicapped Law Report*, 1983). Option 1 and the litigation that followed highlight the issue of credibility—the credibility of a high school diploma.

The MCT movement was fueled, in part, by a desire to reestablish the credibility of the high school diploma as a guarantee of students' attainment of certain minimal levels of performance and competencies in essential skill areas. "At commencement ceremonies this year, thousands of high school students will receive diplomas that are virtually counterfeit. After 12 years of schooling, they have not learned minimum skills in reading, writing and mathematics" (Cannell, 1983, p. 549). Cannell's appraisal may well hold true for many students, both disabled and nondisabled. The use of MCT as a criterion for determining who shall and who shall not receive a high school diploma has been challenged on the basis of the Education for All Handicapped Children Act of 1975 (PL 94-142), Section 504 of the Vocational Rehabilitation Act of 1973, and the due process and equal protection provisions of the 14th Amendment. Challenges to state-imposed MCT requirements have, for the most part, failed. The courts have upheld the right, indeed the responsibility, of the states to establish educational standards.

Citing cases in Georgia, Illinois, and New York, Pullin (1985) sees a consistent trend in the legal findings. The high court in each state upheld the use of MCT as the basis for awarding high school diplomas. Further, the justices found that the application of MCT requirements to students with disabilities is not per se unconstitutional or discriminatory. In certain instances the courts have ordered relief for particular students when it was determined that school districts had acted in an arbitrary or discriminatory manner. But these isolated decisions in no way impinge on the state's right to go forward with MCT programs. The courts have held that an individual with disabilities has no inherent right to a high school diploma in the absence of the ability to meet academic standards (*Education for the Handicapped Law Report*, 1983; McCarthy, 1983).

Although the courts have clearly upheld the right of the states to impose MCT requirements as a precondition for graduation with a regular high school diploma, they have spoken out and taken action against state-imposed practices that are arbitrary and/or discriminatory. It is clear that modifications to MCT to circumvent the impact of the individual's disability and to allow him or her to demonstrate a true level of skill must be allowed (e.g., adequate time to prepare for MCT, exposure to MCT content in course work, modified testing procedures, etc.), as long as the basic integrity of the test is not compromised.

Morissey (1978), an early and outspoken advocate of MCT modifications for students with disabilities, has articulated three approaches to modification of MCT tests and four categories of "procedural modifications." The basic alterations include (a) exemption, (b) application of different criteria, and (c) procedural modifications. She has expressed her preference for "procedural modifications" as the most equitable and challenging of the three alternative approaches to MCT modifications. Procedural modifications were categorized under the headings of (a) environmental modifications, (b) performance adjustments, (c) flexible pacing, and (d) format modifications. More recently, Grise, Beattie, and Algozzine (1982) demonstrate that simple test modifications (e.g., added examples, hierarchical ordering of items) led to improved MCT performance for students who were learning disabled. Scott (1983), in a study involving 50 students who were learning disabled, also reports positive results from test format modifications. Scott added modifications to those applied in the Florida study and found that on the average these students performed 16 points higher on the modified version of the test.

A study by Mick (1989) on the effect of test modifications offers conflicting results. She studied the effect of format modifications only on the MCT performance of secondary-age students with learning disabilities or educable mental retardation. The data showed that these students performed better on the unmodified version; the students with learning disabilities performed significantly better on only one subtest of the modified MCT test. The author speculates that the difference in results between her and other studies of MCT modifications may reflect the age of the students involved. The youngsters in the Grise et al. (1982) and Scott (1983) studies were elementary age, while the subjects of the Mick study were secondary age. Older students may have a greater degree of "testwiseness" that lessens the impact of test modifications. Limitations of the study's design, such as small sample size and questionable test equivalency, may have been a contributing factor also. The research on MCT modifications is very limited at this time, but it is clearly an area that needs to be explored further. We do not know from any of the studies to date exactly which modifications, singly or in combination, brought about any positive effects, and Mick's study raises the issue of the interaction of student characteristics with test modifications.

Option 2, adopted by 21 states, exempts the student with disabilities from MCT. These states grant a regular high school diploma to students who are disabled based on successful completion of the individual's IEP. Some states award a special diploma for completion of the IEP in lieu of the regular high school diploma. Some professionals believe that the special diploma carries an undeniable stigma (McCarthy, 1983; McClung & Pullin, 1978). Safer (1980) reports that, according to the U.S. Department of Labor, a high school diploma is required for entry into virtually all jobs. Further, some preliminary data on employer's attitudes reveal that basic generalizable skills are highly desired in job applicants (Algozzine, O'Shea, Stoddard, & Crews, 1988).

Lack of a high school diploma may become a formidable obstacle to employment for many people with disabilities, but employer bias may be mitigated if some means is found to match individual skills and abilities with specific job requirements. In contrast to the negative sentiments expressed in some circles, Westling (cited in Grise, 1980) reports positive findings regarding the receipt of a special diploma, instead of a regular high school diploma, for students with disabilities in Florida's class of 1977. The special diploma, which is very similar in wording and appearance to the regular diploma, apparently incurred no stigma or negative reaction from prospective employers, community college programs, and military service recruiters for the group of students studied. Some employers are already cognizant of the untapped potential of disabled workers (e.g., the McDonald Corporation's McJobs program), but many more need to become aware. In this regard, the U.S. Department of Labor estimates of slow growth in the available work force, particularly among the 16- to 24-year-olds who traditionally represent the new entrants into the labor market, should improve job prospects for those who are disabled (L. Ellis, 1990). In a tight labor market, as is projected for the next decade, increasing numbers of employers may turn toward employees with disabilities, and the importance of the "diploma" may diminish if the individual is capable of doing the job.

Option 3 involves the use of differential competency standards and tests for students with disabilities. To date, only Florida has followed this path. (The results of Florida's MCT program will be discussed later in this chapter.) The apparent unpopularity of this approach suggests that it does not adequately address the problem of differential standards at the same time that it highlights the philosophical and pedagogical differences that distinguish special and regular education. Benz and Halpern (1987) have suggested that the use of differential diplomas for documenting school completion creates the need for proficiency standards in vocational, independent living, and personal social content areas "to serve as a curricular framework for the development of differential graduation requirements" (p. 512). They add that such standards would be the product of joint efforts between state and local school personnel and that regular, special, and vocational educators would be prime contributors.

The use of differential diplomas raises the issue of the inherent value of any standard. To be useful and fair to all parties involved, do standards have to be uniform? This is the central issue on which opinions regarding differential standards and diplomas diverge. In the final analysis, Archer and Dresden's (1987) observation that MCT pits uniformity and accountability against recognition of individual student differences may have hit the mark. It is obvious that further research is needed on the impact, short- and long-term, of MCT on students with disabilities as a prelude to the development of appropriate educational policy and practices.

MCT Performance of Students with Disabilities

Early data on the performance of students on MCT reveal, as expected, that those who are disabled lag far behind their nondisabled peers. However, on closer inspection, the data reveal some interesting trends and lead to some probing questions about the continued use of MCT with populations with mild disabilities.

Serow and O'Brien (1983) compared the MCT performance of students who were disabled with those of nondisabled students in North Carolina. The students with disabilities included the learning disabled (LD), persons with other disabilities (mostly orthopedically impaired), and those who were educable mentally retarded (EMR). The percentage of nondisabled students passing MCT was 80.5% compared to 27.7% for the students with disabilities.

The percentage difference was large (but not unexpected), and perhaps not as surprising as the degree of variability found among the three populations of students with disabilities. Among those classified as LD, 51.3% passed the MCT tests. Those who were categorized as "other handicapped" performed even better, with a passing rate of 60%. For those labeled EMR the passing rate was a mere 3.5%. Thus the aggregated rate of 27.7% masks the extreme variability among the three student groups. On subsequent testing (states that require MCT generally allow students additional opportunities to pass the tests), most of the students classified as LD or otherwise impaired achieved eligibility for graduation with a regular high school diploma. Most of those students labeled EMR failed the MCT on all three attempts; many subsequently dropped out of school.

In a study of MCT outcomes in Florida, Crews, Algozzine, and Schwartz (1989) conducted an ex post facto analysis of the MCT performance of randomly selected 10th graders. The students were divided into four groups: nonhandicapped, LD, emotionally handicapped, and EMR. Performance on MCT was studied for both communications and mathematics proficiency. Of the students who were not disabled, 87% achieved mastery on both the communications and mathematics standards. Among those with learning disabilities, 44% and 38% achieved mastery on the communications and mathematics standards, respectively. Approximately 40% mastery in both performance areas was achieved by those labeled emotionally handicapped. Among the EMR students, less than 5% achieved mastery in either communications or mathematics skills. The categorical differences in this study mirror those found in the Serow and O'Brien (1983) investigation. In both studies the EMR students performed at an extremely low level as a group and exerted an overall depressing impact on the aggregated scores for all the participants with disabilities. In the Serow and O'Brien study remediation apparently benefited all students. Remediation produced a 20% increase in MCT scores for both the group with disabilities and the nondisabled, but the relative standing did not change. Remediation had the least beneficial effect for EMR students; from the first to the third testing the percentage of these students passing the MCT increased from 3.5% to 10.7%.

The data from Serow and O'Brien (1983) and Crews et al. (1989) demonstrate that satisfying MCT requirements is particularly difficult for the student who is mildly retarded and that the weight of failure falls particularly heavily on this subgroup. The mandatory inclusion of students with mild retardation in MCT needs to be reconsidered, a suggestion put forth by many concerned special educators (Archer & Dresden, 1987; Serow & O'Brien, 1983). Archer and Dresden believe that MCT may be contributing to the high disabled dropout rate by producing a new kind of dropout. That is,

> students with poor academic backgrounds who have the willingness to stay in school and graduate, but who will be denied a diploma because they do not meet the minimum standards. These students may become frustrated and quit school or they may remain in school only to receive a certificate of attendance. (p. 278)

The dropout rate among students with disabilities is so severe that any means of mitigating the loss of students prior to graduation needs to be considered. Levin, Zigmond, and Birch (1985), in a study of adolescents with learning disabilities from a large urban high school, found a dropout rate of 47%. In a follow-up study of ninth graders who should have been in the graduating class of 1982, Zigmond and Thornton (1985) reported a dropout rate of 54.2% for students with learning disabilities. In the prior two studies the comparative dropout rate for nondisabled students was 36% and 32.8%, respectively. The role of MCT in the dropout phenomenon needs further investigation.

Algozzine et al. (1988) also compared the MCT performance of students with and without disabilities in Florida but delved deeper into the types of questions passed and not passed by these students and the relationship of their performance to employers' attitudes about the importance of certain skill categories. They analyzed the performance of 10th graders on basic communication skills. Using a statewide sample of disabled ($N = 1,098$, LD only) and nondisabled ($N = 934$), they found that the mastery rate in communication skills was 91% for students who were not disabled and 49% for the LD students. The authors ascertained employers' valuation of the communication skills tested and found that more than 50% of the LD students had mastered 80% of the communication skills designated by employers as important and job related. The data also revealed that the students with learning disabilities performed better on some types of reading tasks than others, notably reading tasks at the literal level. The study raises some interesting questions about the congruence between MCT content and curricular content and the relationship of MCT content to job-related skills. The results of the Algozzine et al. study have utility for curricular planning and program evaluation; "teachers can use this information to organize and plan functional reading and writing objectives for their communications programs, and, without 'teaching to the test,' modify instruction appropriately" (p. 159).

❦ ❦ ❦

THE DROPOUT PHENOMENON

The dropout phenomenon is a major problem confronting all of public education. For those with mild disabilities it may well be a tragedy of even greater proportions. School personnel cannot effectively develop or implement transition plans for students who are intermittently truant or permanently removed from the school setting. Premature termination of schooling disrupts transition in a number of ways:

1. Termination of schooling undermines the entire transition planning process that seeks to bridge the gap between school and postschool experiences.
2. The negative consequences of poor preparation for postschool pursuits are exacerbated by early withdrawal from school.

3. Completion of the secondary school educational and/or vocational training programs is the stepping-stone for postsecondary training and/or employment.

An understanding of the dropout phenomenon and its implications for students with mild disabilities requires consideration of dropout rates, characteristics of dropout students, the consequences associated with school termination, and dropout prevention programs and strategies.

How Many Students Drop Out?

Discussion of the dropout phenomenon among both regular and special education students is complicated by a lack of common definitions, terms, and consistent counting procedures (Clements, 1990; Morrow, 1986). Dropouts or school leavers are defined and counted differently at the state and school district levels. The Educational Data Improvement Project (EDIP), a joint effort of the Council of Chief State School Officers and the National Center for Educational Statistics, is attempting to standardize data collection procedures nationwide to improve the data base used in decision-making processes at all educational levels. Among its initiatives is a recommended definition for use in the identification and counting of dropouts. The EDIP defines a dropout as "a student who for any reason other than death leaves school before graduation without transferring to another school district" (Clements, p. 20).

Neither this definition nor any other is uniformly employed. Furthermore, states, even individual school districts, differ on such issues as the point at which a truant becomes a dropout, the inclusion or exclusion of student subgroups (e.g., incarcerated youth, students pursuing the GED, and juveniles in mental institutions), the age at which students can be classified as dropouts, and the inclusion of returning students (e.g., former dropouts who return to school) (Clements, 1990; Hammack, 1986; Rumberger, 1987). Nor are students with disabilities uniformly included or excluded when dropout rates are determined. The exclusion of students with disabilities is likely to lower the dropout rate for the state or district in question.

Methods of calculating the number of dropouts also vary. The most common approaches are the 1-year cross-sectional and longitudinal or cohort counting methods (Wolman, Bruininks, & Thurlow, 1989). The 1-year cross-sectional method reveals the number of students who dropped out of school in any given year. The calculation involves dividing the number of dropouts by the total enrollment for all the grade levels of a single year (Hammack, 1986; Morrow, 1986) and answers the question "What percentage of the students dropped out this year?" (Doss & Sailor, 1987, p. 9).

In the longitudinal cohort method a designated group of secondary students is monitored over a number of school years to determine the percentage of students who meet graduation expectations as compared to the percentage of students who drop out (Doss & Sailor, 1987). The calculation in the longitudinal cohort procedure involves dividing the cumulative number of dropouts by the number of students in the initially designated class and answers the question "What percentage of students entering the ninth grade in a certain school district drop out after X years?" (Doss & Sailor, p. 9). The longitudinal method will generally produce a higher dropout rate. In addition, the longer the follow-up term, the higher the resulting dropout rate is likely to be (Stephenson, 1985).

Notwithstanding the differences in calculation methods, the national dropout rate is consistently reported to be in the 25% to 30% range (*National Center for Educational Statistics Bulletin*, 1983; Seidel & Vaughn, 1991; Weber, 1988). The dropout rates reported for large urban areas are generally higher, often exceeding 40% (Seidel & Vaughn). Dropout rates for special education students equal or exceed those reported for regular education. The national dropout rates for students with disabilities as reported in the *Tenth, Eleventh,* and *Twelfth Annual Reports to Congress on the Implementation of the Education for the Handicapped Act* were 26%, 25%, and 27%, respectively. Comparative data from the National Longitudinal Transition Study reveal a dropout rate of 36.4% among students with disabilities (Butler-Nalin & Padilla, 1989).

Closer inspection of the data reveals that the dropout rate among the categories of exceptionality vary greatly and that the dropout rate for certain categories of exceptionality are much higher than the national average. Of particular concern are the dropout rates for the "mildly handicapped" categories of LD, emotionally disturbed (ED), and EMR. Data contained in the 12th annual report reveal that 92% of the total population of students with disabilities who dropped out of school during the 1987–88 school year were LD, ED, or EMR (60,429 students out of a total disabled student dropout population of 65,395). For each of the 2 preceding years the number of LD, ED, and EMR student dropouts combined represented 91% of the total population of students with disabilities who left school. School termination rates reported by individual researchers for smaller and more selective populations of students with disabilities yield even higher dropout rates and further attest to the magnitude of the dropout problem among these students. For example, for students with learning disabilities, noncompletion rates of 54% (Zigmond & Thornton, 1985), 51% (Levin et al., 1985), 37% (Hoffman et al., 1987), and 42% (Edgar, 1985) have been documented. Comparison data for nondisabled students are provided by Zigmond and Thornton (32.8%) and Levin et al. (36%). For students labeled ED, Edgar (1985) reports a school-leaving rate of 42%, and Bruininks, Thurlow, Lewis, and Larson (1988) cite a noncompletion rate of 73%. Studies of nondifferentiated groups of students with mild disabilities have disclosed dropout rates of 31% (Fardig et al., 1985) and 28% (Hasazi, Gordon, & Roe, 1985). Wolman et al. (1989), based on a review of 21 research studies and national surveys, have identified two trends in the dropout research for special education students: (a) Students with disabilities, whether attending special or regular school, are more likely to drop out of school than students without disabilities; and (b) among the various categories, students with learning disabilities and emotional disturbances are at greatest risk of dropping out.

In a reaction to the data on the magnitude of the dropping-out population among students with disabilities reported in the *Tenth Annual Report to Congress*, Wyche (1989) offers four reasons for the renewed interest:

1. The dropout rate has been relatively constant over time, but two ethnic minority groups (African-Americans and Latinos) are experiencing significant increases.
2. Nationally, increasing minority populations will further fuel the minority dropout rate.
3. The increased academic requirements associated with the educational reform movement will add to school failure and thus school dropout rates.
4. Increasing educational requirements of the workplace will subject dropouts to an even greater degree of economic disadvantage.

The impact of early school departure on the prospects for successful transition is further reason to be concerned about dropouts with disabilities. It has been suggested that dropout rates for regular education have lost their "shock value" (Weber, 1988) and that educators are resigned to the fact that fully a quarter or more of their students will not successfully complete high school. Weber states also that the magnitude of nationally reported dropout rates has been relatively constant since the 1970s. The tone of the current special education rhetoric conveys a distinct attitude of concern and alarm at the magnitude of the dropout phenomenon among those with disabilities. The growing emphasis on the transition from school to adult life and recognition of the critical role of education in the successful completion of the transition process should cause greater concern and action within special education on behalf of students at risk for dropping out.

Factors Associated with Student Dropouts

A variety of social, academic, and economic factors have been implicated in the dropout phenomenon. The relevant research evolves along two lines of inquiry. Traditionally, researchers held to a student-centered perspective and attempted to identify personal characteristics that predisposed certain students to dropping out. More recently, investigators have broadened the research agenda to include the organizational and social dimensions of schools that impact on students staying and leaving behavior (Rumberger, 1987; Wehledge & Rutter, 1986). It is becoming increasingly apparent that an interactive relationship exists between school and student factors and that both components contribute to the dropout phenomenon.

Student Characteristics. The student-centered factors often cited in relation to at-risk students are poor academic record and lack of basic skills (Bearden, Spencer, & Moracco, 1989; deBettencourt & Zigmond, 1990; Ekstrom, Goertz, Pollack, & Rock, 1986; Weber, 1988; Wehledge & Rutter, 1986); low socioeconomic status (Bearden et al., 1989; Ekstrom et al., 1986; Weber, 1988; Wehledge & Rutter, 1986); disciplinary problems including expulsion, suspension, and excessive absenteeism (Bearden et al., 1989; deBettencourt & Zigmond, 1990; Ekstrom et al., 1986; Wehledge & Rutter, 1986); and race/ethnicity (Blackorby, Edgar, & Kortering, 1991; Ekstrom et al., 1986; Rumberger 1983, 1987). The dropout rate among minorities (i.e., Latinos and African-Americans), far exceeds that of whites; the rate among males generally exceeds that of females (Rumberger, 1983).

A number of familial factors that contribute to early school leaving have been identified. These include educational attainment of parents, income level, and family structure (i.e., a higher dropout rate is associated with single-parent households), family size (i.e., larger families tend to have a greater incidence of children dropping out of school) (Rumberger, 1983, 1987). The interaction of familial and economic factors is a potent force. For example, family background accounts for virtually all racial differences in dropout rates (Rumberger, 1983); when familial factors are controlled, race is no longer predictive of school termination (Wehledge & Rutter, 1986). Socioeconomic and familial factors predispose large numbers of minority youth to dropping out. Among males the need to contribute to the economic support of the family is a major factor in the decision to drop out of school. A family-related factor that figures prominently in the dropout rate among females is pregnancy and, to lesser extent, marriage. Pregnancy is the single most important precipitating factor for dropping out among female students (Scholl & Johnson, 1988; Wehledge & Rutter, 1986). In general, familial factors have the strongest influence on youths from lower socioeconomic backgrounds (Rumberger, 1983).

Additional characteristics believed to place students at risk of early school leaving are poor academic record (Bearden et al., 1989; Weber, 1988; Wehledge & Rutter 1986), grade retention (Afolayan, 1991; Zigmond & Thornton, 1985), low self-esteem (Ekstrom et al., 1986), and general alienation from school as evidenced in poor relationships with teachers and peers and/or negative attitudes toward school (Bearden et al., 1989; Miller, Leinhardt, & Zigmond, 1988).

The characteristics of students with disabilities at risk for dropping out have not received as much attention as the problem among at-risk students in regular education. The research available portrays a striking similarity in the characteristics associated with student dropouts in both regular and special education (Butler-Nalin & Padilla, 1989). From the existing data base, Wolman et al. (1989) have gleaned a list of indicators that may predispose students to dropping out. The factors that place students with disabilities at risk include

- negative attitudes toward school,
- low participation in school-related activities,
- low achievement and aptitude measures,
- grade repetition,
- poor attendance and disruptive behavior, and
- socioeconomic factors.

All of the factors cited for students with disabilities have previously been associated with the general population of at-risk students. Wolman et al. (1989) suggest that large numbers of students who are disabled may, in fact, hold membership in both at-risk populations. There is reason to question the utility of the distinction imposed between dropouts with disabilities and those without for preventive and intervention efforts. However, Edgar (1985) suggests that the categorical distinctions have some basis. He justifies the separation of students who are mildly mentally retarded from a combined grouping of those with learning disabilities and behavioral disorders on the basis of gender differences, employment rate, engagement rate, and dropout rate differences. He maintains that those who are mildly mentally retarded are a distinct category of exceptionality that may require different interventions at the secondary level.

School Characteristics. When surveyed, students express numerous reasons for dropping out of school. For example, a 1982 survey of high school dropouts reported by Ekstrom et al. (1986) revealed that students' major reasons for dropping out of school included the following:

> did not like school
> poor grades
> offered job and chose to work
> getting married
> could not get along with teachers
> had to help support family
> pregnancy
> expelled or suspended (p. 363)

A more recent survey of dropouts yielded results quite similar to those reported by Ekstrom et al. Additional reasons not previously cited by students included these:

> absent for too many days
> could not get along with family
> school was boring
> unable to keep up with school work
> teachers did not care
> no one helped me (Bearden et al., 1989, p. 115)

The students' reasons for dropping out of school echo many of the student-focused characteristics already noted. However, the student responses not only reveal personal, financial, and familial problems but also allude to shortcomings within the school that contributed to their decision to drop out (e.g., "school was boring," "no one helped me," and "unable to keep up with school work"). To date much of the research on dropouts has been dominated by a student-centered research perspective that views dropping out as the student's problem, even "a form of social deviance" (Wehledge & Rutter, 1986, p. 375). The schools and school personnel are not implicated, that is, not seen as contributing to the problem. Wehledge and Rutter challenge that point of view and urge research efforts directed at understanding how school characteristics contribute to the rate of dropping out. Their scrutiny of data from the High School and Beyond Study reveals problems associated with school discipline, curricular offerings, and the schools' credibility and legitimacy in the eyes of students. They offer three recommendations for increasing the holding power of school:

1. Increase accountability among educators for all students
2. Establish disciplinary practices and policies that will be viewed as both fair and effective by the students and thus will help reestablish the legitimate authority of the institution
3. Redefine schoolwork so that a greater number of students can achieve success and satisfaction

Other researchers have also studied the influence of school factors on the rate of student dropouts. Bryk and Thum (1989) investigated the relationship of structural and normative features on student absenteeism, which is repeatedly cited as one of the strongest predictors of dropping out. They found absenteeism to be less prevalent in secondary schools of smaller size where there was a strong emphasis on academics, an orderly environment, and a considerable amount of positive interaction between teachers and students. Schools with lower absentee rates also engaged in less differentiation and stratification among students on the basis of inherent student characteristics. The research findings of Bryk and Thum build on the work of Wehledge and Rutter (1986) and others (Natriello, Pallas, & McDill, 1986) and substantiate a relationship between organizational, structural, and procedural characteristics of a school and the school's climate.

School climate, in turn, is related to student feelings of belonging or alienation. Student alienation has been identified as a risk factor for dropping out (Seidel & Vaughn, 1991; Wehledge, 1983). School practices and policies that greatly define a school's climate or ethos have been associated with the degree of student alienation (Natriello et al., 1986). Conversely, integration—that is, the student's sense of belonging and comfort level within the school—is seen as an important antidote for the dropout problem. A sense of belonging among students can be fostered by the school's ability to accommodate student needs. Miller et al. (1988) found that a school's level of accommodation was associated with the students' engagement and the dropout rate. Schools in which there was greater accommodation to student needs experienced lower dropout rates. In these schools "teachers and administrators consciously tried to limit the demands made on students or to provide alternative means by which students could meet those demands" (p. 482). Less accommodative schools registered a higher rate of dropping out. Miller et al. acknowledge the potentially negative effects of accommodation (e.g., lower academic standards, student dependency, tutorial instructional model, boredom, and lack of challenge). Further research is needed to identify accommodations with the greatest holding power and least negative consequences for secondary students with mild disabilities.

The emerging, more balanced perspective of the dropout problem, one that takes into account both student and school factors, has increased educators' understanding of the factors contributing to student dropout decisions and establishes a basis for the development of effective interventions.

Consequences of Dropping Out

The consequences of dropping out are far-reaching and affect both the individual and society at large. Of the diverse social, personal, and economic consequences that are related to dropping out, employment outcomes have received the greatest amount of attention. Wehledge and Rutter (1986) state that "increasingly the lack of a high school diploma is tantamount to a denial of employment" (p. 375). Employment figures for dropouts alone or contrasted to those for graduates bear witness to the importance of school completion for future employment opportunities. It is important to remember that the research amply demonstrates that the employment opportunities, employment rates, remuneration for employment, and the like, for graduates with disabilities already lag well behind those for nondisabled graduates. Contrasting employment figures for dropouts and graduates with disabilities need to be viewed within this context.

Zigmond and Thornton (1985), in a study of individuals with learning disabilities, found an employment rate of 74% for graduates as compared to an employment rate of 46% for nongraduates. The corresponding employment figures for graduates and nongraduates without learning disabilities were 82% and 50%, respectively. In another study involving students with learning disabilities, Hewitt (1981) found that 44% of the dropouts were employed as compared to 58% of the graduates. Edgar (1985) reports an employment rate of 61% for graduates and 30% for a combined category of learning disabled and behaviorally disordered (LD/BD) dropouts. Regarding the general category of students who are mildly handicapped, Hasazi et al. (1985) found that 60% of the graduating students were employed, while the employment rate for the nongraduating varied from 30% to 51% depending on the age at which the student left school. Interestingly, the younger dropouts seemed to fare better in the workplace. In other studies involving rural students with disabilities (Fardig et al., 1985) and black students (Felice, 1981), the highest grade of school completion, rather than age, was identified as a strong predictor of later employment status. Graduate or nongraduate status impacts not only on employment per se but also important aspects of employment (e.g., part-time and seasonal work vs. full-time work, salary level) (Hewitt, 1981) and type of job held (Lichtenstein, 1987). The research suggests that students who are mildly disabled and do not complete their schooling experience even greater employment disparity than is associated with disabling conditions in general.

Limited employment opportunities impact on lifetime earnings. Catterall (1987) estimates that the lifetime dollar loss to the individual that results from early school leaving is approximately $200,000. And McDill et al. (1986) report the average lifetime lost earnings for males and females as $260,000 and $211,000, respectively. Earnings loss impacts on society as well as the individual. It has been estimated that each year's class of high school dropouts costs society $296 billion in lost productivity and forgone taxes in the students' lifetimes. The lifetime lost taxes from the class of 1981 was estimated at $68.4 billion (Catterall, 1987). Dropping out has direct economic impact and is related to social and personal consequences such as poverty, crime rate, drug abuse (Bearden et al., 1989; Ehrlich, 1975; Levin, 1972), and diminished cognitive development (Alexander, Natriello, & Pallas, 1985).

Dropout Prevention Programs and Strategies

There is a dearth of information on dropout prevention or intervention programs specifically designed for students with disabilities (Butler-Nalin & Padilla, 1989; Wolman et al., 1989). Thus it is necessary to draw on the available literature for the general population of at-risk students. Two strategies prevail in prevention programs: predictive and alternative strategies (Fortune, Bruce, Williams, & Jones, 1991). Predictive programs, based on the identified characteristics of dropout students, address student needs in an effort to keep the at-risk students in school, by providing academic assistance, counseling, child care, and so forth. Alternative programs generally offer the student a choice between the traditional school setting and an alternate program. Alternative programs may be totally removed from the traditional academic setting or follow a school-within-a-school concept. Reentry or recovery programs for students who wish to reverse the dropout decision is another intervention alternative. Diversity of program options is necessitated by the diversity within the at-risk and dropout student population.

The most common elements of dropout programs have been discussed by numerous authors. Key elements identified include alternative classes or programs, counseling and advising, work-related activities, parental involvement, referral, and outreach systems (Bearden et al., 1989; Beck & Muia, 1980). Hamilton (1986) states that effective dropout prevention programs have four common elements:

1. They separate potential dropouts from other students.
2. They have a strong vocational component.
3. They utilize out-of-class learning.
4. They are intensive; that is, they are small, offer individualized instruction, have low student-teacher ratios, and offer more counseling than regular schools.

Wolman et al. (1989) see many facets of dropout prevention programs that coincide with identified "good practices" in special education, for example, early identification, individualized instruction, small classes with lower student-teacher ratios, counseling, and a strong vocational component including vocational training, employment preparation, and job training. Dropout prevention and intervention programs may already provide the basic structure and instructional methodology needed by the at-risk student with mild disabilities as well as the student not labeled as at risk. Parallel and separate programs may not be necessary, which would thus permit limited resources to be focused on the combined at-risk population.

On a less optimistic note, Jay and Padilla (1987) asked why the dropout rate in special education programs is so high if exemplary instructional practices are already in use. They suggest that the high dropout rate may indicate problems with the adequacy of implementation of special education programs for secondary-age students.

There is general agreement that dropping out is the final step in a cumulative process of alienation and withdrawal from school (Ruben, 1989; Wehledge & Rutter, 1986) and that dropout prevention efforts must begin early (Rumberger, 1983; Sansone & Baker, 1990; Schmidt, 1988). Certain stages in a student's academic career have been identified as critical in predisposing particular students to the risk of dropping out. The ninth-grade experience has been identified as a critical factor in school completion (Zigmond & Thornton, 1985). Sansone and Baker (1990) investigated the ninth-grade experience for students in a large urban high school. They describe the ninth-grade year as difficult, impersonal, and confusing, with the students having much difficulty making the transition into the high school and integrating into the school community. The authors pinpointed current school practices related to student orientation, school rules and discipline, attendance policies, and academic scheduling that impeded ninth-grade students' progress. Their recommendations included the following:

- development of specific informational and orientation activities for ninth graders to be delivered prior to and during the course of the school year,
- clear and meaningful communication of school rules and procedures,
- flexible academic scheduling with adjustments permitted after the academic year has begun,
- provision of special supports and incentives for ninth-grade teachers,
- proactive as well as reactive staffing procedures to address the needs of at-risk students, and
- sufficient individual attention for ninth-grade students at key points during the school year.

Vocational training and preparation are emphasized as critical elements of successful dropout prevention programs (Weber, 1988). Paid work experiences while in school are closely tied to students' postschool employment success (Hasazi et al., 1985; McAfee & Mann, 1982). In addition, parents and teachers place a high value on vocational education and view it as a major deterrent to dropping out (Brannon, 1988). The importance attributed to vocational training programs is undoubtedly tied to parental and student concern for future economic and employment prospects.

The instructional appeal of vocational education may be tied to a delivery mode that is more suited to the needs and characteristics of mildly disabled and at-risk students than traditional classroom instruction. Data from a national survey of vocational and nonvocational classrooms support Weber's (1988) contention that "vocational classrooms are more student-centered, more activity-based, and more individualized than other classrooms, three characteristics deemed important when dealing with at-risk youth" (p. 38). The potential for student-centered rather than teacher-centered classrooms within vocational education has other proponents (Eschenmann, 1988). Weber has described collaborative efforts between academic and vocational teachers in Ohio that resulted in academic teachers teaching applied academic classes in vocational schools. Students received relevant basic skills instruction and earned credits toward graduation. In contrast to secondary school classrooms, the composition and climate of vocational classrooms may indeed offer a hospitable learning environment for innovative teaching as well as essential vocational knowledge and training needed by at-risk students with mild disabilities. The holding power of transitional services and programs is unknown at this time. The potential exists for dropout prevention programs to be a deterrent if they too, like vocational programs, are highly valued by students and parents.

The disabled dropout population represents a diverse student population with regard to student characteristics and reasons for dropping out of school. Dropout prevention programs and strategies will have to respond to this diversity with an array of programs and strategies. The response to the dropout problem will necessitate preventive efforts based on identified characteristics of at-risk students as well as programs for the returning student as substantial numbers of dropouts with disabilities return to school. Blackorby et al. (1991) report that 12% of graduating students with disabilities had interrupted their schooling at least once. The prevalence of interruptions in the school histories of the students led them to conceptualize a "drop out cycle" (p. 109) wherein school leavers return to the academic setting. Dropout prevention programs for the returning student very likely will differ from pre-dropout preventive programs. Diversity and flexibility in approaches and strategies will be needed.

❦   ❦   ❦

ROLE AND RESPONSIBILITY OF THE SPECIAL EDUCATION TEACHER

The special education teacher is portrayed as the central figure in the transition process. However, there is a lack of clarity as to what the nature and extent of the special education teacher's role and responsibilities are or ought to be.

Benz and Halpern (1986) conducted a statewide survey in Oregon involving administrators, teachers, and parents concerning the vocational opportunities and status of vocational education for students with disabilities. Portions of the data related to the perceptions of these three constituent groups regarding the roles and responsibilities of the special education teacher. Both administrators and teachers pinpointed the special education teacher as the person most frequently assumed to be responsible for coordinating vocational activities for students who are disabled. Work experience coordinators were the second choice cited by both administrators and teachers.

The rankings alone mask the degree of disparity that existed between administrators and teachers' perceptions of the roles and responsibilities of the teaching staff; the percentage of response gave a more accurate picture. First- and second-place ratings among administrators were 60% for special education teachers and 28% for work experience coordinators; first and second ratings among teachers were 29% for special education teachers and 18% for work experience coordinators, respectively. In addition, 19% of the teacher respondents indicated their belief that no one was responsible for the coordination of vocational activities for those who are disabled; the administrators' response to that option was 0%.

These data are not encouraging; they are suggestive of the depth of the problem that exists regarding the delegation of responsibility for coordination of vocational and transitional process activities. The data also reveal that the literature focuses heavily on vocational preparation and transition to employment. The prominence of vocational training and employment concerns in the following discussion is a reflection of the literature as it currently exists and not a reflection of the authors' own view of the scope of the transition process. We have and will argue for a much broader perspective of the transition process.

Numerous authors have discussed and/or defined the role of the special education teacher, most frequently in the context of vocational programming and employment. For example, Gill and Edgar (1990) stress the importance of quality in vocational programming to postschool success of the disabled. They view special education as an "instructional support" with special education teachers supplementing the ongoing instructional program of vocational education by stressing vocabulary building, essential math operations, and coordinated movements. Cummings and Maddux (1987) state that "the thrust of the training for regular and special educators should be an emphasis on integrating career and vocational concepts into the regular curriculum's academic activities" (p. 167). The statements of Gill and Edgar and Cummings and Maddux relegate special education to a support system for vocational education. Given the prominence of vocational preparation in the literature on transition, this posturing of vocational and special education is not surprising.

Other authors describe the role of the special education teacher in more expansive terms, but the preeminence of vocational preparation is still obvious. Kerr, Nelson, and Lambert (1987) describe the role of the secondary special education teacher in terms consistent with the ancillary role depicted earlier. However, they ascribe an even greater range of responsibilities to the special educator:

> Thus, in the classroom, your role involves providing a meaningful curriculum based on each student's IEP, updating and devising IEPs consistent with preparing each

pupil for adult living, and generalizing relevant academic, social, and vocational skills beyond your classroom. In addition, you [the special education teacher] should assume a major role in writing students' individual transition plans. (p. 296)

The authors assign additional responsibilities to the special education teacher, specifically monitoring and following up former special education students and interagency contact and transfer of school records. The authors intimate that these latter responsibilities are being relegated to the special education teacher because no one will do them otherwise. Okolo and Sitlington (1986) also envision a large scope of responsibilities for the special education teacher with regard to vocational preparation and transition planning. They indicate that the responsibilities of the special educator entail

1. providing instruction in job-related academic and interpersonal skills;
2. "offering . . . a comprehensive set of vocationally relevant services to equip LD adolescents with needed experiences and skills and to increase coordination and cooperation between special and vocational education in the delivery of services" (p. 148), which includes
   a. occupational awareness, exploration, and basic work experience,
   b. in-depth career/vocational assessment,
   c. instruction in job-related academic skills,
   d. instruction in job-related interpersonal skills,
   e. support services to other disciplines involved in vocational programming, and
   f. postschool placement and follow-up.

Okolo and Sitlington (1986) assign the leadership role for the coordination between the two disciplines to special education because they view vocational education as lacking the necessary training and resources (the level of training of special educators and the extent of special education resources is also open to question) that the job demands. Consequently, "the responsibility for forging such a partnership rests with secondary special education teachers, who are the case managers and advocates for the LD adolescent" (p. 150).

It would appear that the special education teacher has been singled out for the lion's share of responsibility for transition by default. This approach is one we discourage. Although we recognize the need for someone to assume a leadership role in the transition planning process, we believe that targeting the special education teacher as the "obvious" (or most convenient) candidate for this role and the attendant responsibilities belies the complexity and difficulty of the transition process and, in the long run, will be counterproductive for the students involved.

Our position on the issue of the teacher's role and responsibilities was initially stated in chapter 4. We reiterate that it is often "mistakenly" assumed that the secondary special education teacher will or should assume the responsibilities of the transition "facilitator." The "job descriptions" offered by Kerr et al. (1987) and Okolo and Sitlington (1986) represent an "overload" of responsibility for the special education teacher and for special education.

We support the concept of a transition team, that is a body of relevant professionals representing multiple constituencies that have a stake in the student's success who work cooperatively toward a successful transitional experience. This "collaborative ethic" (Gill & Edgar, 1990) fosters collaboration and cooperation not only between special and vocational education but also many other critical service providers. It is not an exaggeration to state that there is virtually universal support for the collaborative or team approach. In fact, the transition team is viewed as one of the essential components of successful transition planning and programming.

Collaboration takes place at different levels, and the constellation of professional participants involved will vary accordingly. Collaborative efforts between special and vocational educators at the district and school building level are especially important. Each of the two disciplines has its strengths and weaknesses vis-à-vis the transition process. For example, Cummings and Maddux (1987) indicate that special education can be restrictive and prepare pupils for menial jobs. Regular vocational education starts at too late an age for most students with disabilities, and many vocational programs require prerequisite skills that students lack. Vocational educators typically have had a limited number of teacher education courses and need more training and assistance in instructional methodology to instruct the special needs student effectively (Greene, Albright, & Kokaska, 1989). Greene et al. have suggested four generic instructional strategies that can be used by vocational instructors to improve the quality and effectiveness of vocational education for special needs learners:

1. Collaborative approaches such as IEP/ITP planning, team teaching, and job coaching
2. Cooperative learning
3. Tutoring by peers or adults
4. Task analysis

These instructional strategies will be quite familiar to most special educators but are not commonplace among vocational educators. To explore the example further, the authors describe task analysis as a four-stage process: (a) organizing the curriculum, (b) designating specific skill areas, (c) identifying specific tasks and skills to be taught, and (d) specifying behaviors that can be linked together and sequentially taught to achieve mastery. The entire process of task analysis, from curricular analysis through instructional interventions, should be in every special education teacher's methodological repertoire. Greene et al. believe that vocational educators can cope with the first two stages of the task analysis process but lack competency in stages 3 and 4. Special educators will readily recognize that stages 3 and 4 of the process represent the actual instructional components where accommodations, adjustments, and so forth, to meet the needs of individual students will be called for. Finally, the "basic skills" of special education may not match the "basic skill" needs of vocational education (Greenan, 1983). These few examples are sufficient to illustrate the range and variety of barriers that can impede cooperation and collaboration among professionals representing different disciplines.

The examples also highlight the need for adequate personnel preparation, an area that may present particularly thorny problems. Sitlington (1981) has proposed a model of joint cooperation between vocational and special education personnel that begins with career awareness in the elementary school, career exploration at the junior high level, and career preparation at the secondary school level. In keeping with Deno's Cascade Model (Reynolds & Birch, 1977), Sitlington envisions a continuum of services in which student needs would be matched to specific services with sufficient flexibility to allow for the movement of students among more and less restrictive environments. The continuum extends from full integration of the student with a disability into the regular vocational training program to participation in separate programs especially designed for the special needs learner.

Personnel preparation for transition will inevitably focus heavily on the preparation of adequately trained teachers, both special and vocational educators. But to focus on teachers alone is, we believe, the wrong path to follow. A much larger array of personnel, school-based and others, must be involved in the training effort. For example, West (1988) indicates the possible constituencies from which participants for the transition team (or task force, to use her terminology) could be drawn; they include "special education, vocational education, vocational rehabilitation, guidance, administration, support services, community, human services, parents, and other related agencies" (p. 5). Regarding the actual program planning and teaching for individual students, Greene et al. (1989) identify the following individuals who could be involved in the collaborative and planning effort: vocational rehabilitation counselor, vocational placement coordinator, teacher of the special education student, regular vocational instructor, parents of the student, instructional assistant, job coach, community representative, and rehabilitation counselor (p. 4). The authors even entertain the inclusion of the student and other persons who would be essential for meaningful student participation to occur (e.g., interpreter for students who are deaf or hard of hearing) in the collaborative process. It is obvious that the special education teacher is but one among many who ought to be part of the transitional team.

The complexity of the transition process will demand well-trained leadership personnel. Chadsey-Rusch (1988) recommends that the preparation of leadership personnel for transition should flow from the factors associated with successful competitive employment. Drawing from work done by Heal, Haney, DeStefano, and Rusch (1988) at the University of Illinois Transition Institute, Chadsey-Rusch posits five variables that differentiate successful from unsuccessful employment of disabled students:

- student attitude,
- job match,
- follow-up support,

- creative placement specialist, and
- team effort.

The author believes that leadership personnel in transition should master and share the core competencies related to the five key variables. Each individual would not be equally expert in all areas, but as a group a transition team should have the knowledge and skills to address each of the key variables. For example, in discussing creative employment specialists, Chadsey-Rusch describes them as "proficient in making good job matches between workers and their jobs. In addition, they must be flexible, have autonomy in decision making, and exhibit competent management skills" (p. 31). Winking, DeStefano, and Rusch (cited in Chadsey-Rusch, 1988) expand the job-related qualifications of the creative placement specialist (or job coach). The key points of their lengthy description are that this individual

> must be able to meet both the demands of the business world and the ideals of the social service world, be competent in applied behavior analysis to effectively train and evaluate vocational and social skills, be able to advocate for the handicapped to promote integration, have good communication skills to interact effectively with the business community, be proficient in paperwork. (p. 31)

In sum, the creative placement specialist must be competent in instruction, management, and consulting.

The role of the creative placement specialist as described above clearly suggests not only a degree of knowledge and skills that few special education or vocational education teachers are likely to possess, but also a degree of flexibility with regard to working conditions (e.g., hours, locations) that are inconsistent with teacher positions, which presently are bound by school location, school schedules, and class loads. We think it unlikely that significant numbers of classroom teachers will achieve the degree of flexibility required to do the job of the creative placement specialist discussed here. We along with others advocate for the creation of new and somewhat specialized positions within our schools to address the needs of the transition process. Cobb and Hasazi (1987) recommend that there be specially trained resource room teachers who would have the freedom of time and movement to serve as consultants to both special and regular education classroom teachers. Another approach is embodied in the designated vocational instructor (Gill, Cupp, & Lindquist, 1986), which is "a building level position that is responsible for coordinating the actions of vocational and special education. A special education teacher position is essentially redirected to provide direct instructional support to handicapped students currently enrolled in vocational education programs and classes" (p. 27).

From just these two examples, it is apparent that school districts are approaching the problem of "staffing" for transition in various ways; some by redirecting a teaching position, others by creating new positions and filling them with persons who possess the skills and knowledge required. The designated vocational instructor or creative placement specialist cannot simply be "add on" roles to the existing job descriptions of classroom teachers. They are specialty areas in their own right requiring a full-time commitment from professionals with the training and experience for the job to be done.

❦ ❦ ❦

SUMMARY

Academic programs for students with mild disabilities must address the issue of performance standards as embodied in minimum competency testing (MCT). Individual states and local school districts clearly have the responsibility and the latitude to establish testing programs that ensure that students meet minimal levels of performance as a prerequisite for promotion, graduation, and receipt of a high school diploma. The decision to include or exclude students with disabilities from competency testing is made at the state level. To date a significant number, but not yet a majority, of states have opted to exempt students with disabilities from MCT and to grant diplomas to these students on the basis of the completion of individual IEPs.

In some states and school districts, a special diploma is granted in lieu of the regular high school diploma. There are arguments for and against the special diploma. Some see such documents as discriminatory and stigmatizing, whereas others hold fast to successful performance on MCT as a prerequisite for receiving a regular high school diploma. The issue is far from resolved. There is, however, widespread support for modifications in testing to allow the students who are disabled a fair opportunity to demonstrate their level of competency without compromising the test content or standards. Initial data on the MCT performance of students with disabilities from a handful of states have indicated that they generally perform well below the level of performance achieved by others—an outcome to be expected. More surprising was the finding of intercategorical differences. It appears that students with mild retardation as a group perform very poorly on MCT—far below the level of others with mild disabilities. Minimum competency testing requirements present an insurmountable obstacle for many such students and may be contributing to the alarmingly high rate of dropouts among them as well as other secondary students with mild disabilities.

The school dropout with a mild disability is likely to be male, a member of an ethnic minority, and of lower socioeconomic background who is labeled learning disabled or emotionally disturbed. For a female student, pregnancy and to a lesser extent marriage may have been the precipitating factors in the decision to quit school. The dropout is likely to be a member of a family headed by only one parent whose own level of educational attainment is limited. Financial pressures will have a major influence on the family and its decisions relative to education. The student may already be contributing to the family's financial support. In school, the student may have been a truant or have a history of excessive absenteeism. The academic record will be poor with low and/or failing grades and a distinct possibility of grade retention. The student is likely to evidence a negative attitude toward school and poor relationships with teacher and peers. There is a high probability of prior disciplinary problems.

The magnitude of the dropout phenomenon among students with disabilities, the highest for any subgroup of secondary-age youth, cannot be ignored. The social, economic, and personal consequences for the individual and society are staggering. Diverse programs will be needed to meet the variety of needs within the student group. It would appear, however, that preventive programs may not be needed to serve students with and without disabilities separately. Components of effective dropout prevention programs appear to be effective for both populations.

REFERENCES

Afolayan, J. A. (1991). Retention policy and school dropout rate: Implications for professional educators. *The High School Journal, 74*(4), 220–224.

Alexander, K. L., Natriello, G., & Pallas, A. M. (1985). For whom the school bell tolls: The impact of dropping out on cognitive performance. *American Sociological Review, 50,* 409–420.

Algozzine, B., O'Shea, D. J., Stoddard, K., & Crews, W. B. (1988). Reading and writing competencies of adolescents with learning disabilities. *Journal of Learning Disabilities, 21*(3), 154–160.

Amos, K. M. (1980). Competency testing: Will LD students be included? *Exceptional Children, 47*(3), 194–197.

Archer, E. L., & Dresden, J. H. (1987). A new kind of dropout: The effect of minimum competency testing on high school graduation in Texas. *Education and Urban Society, 19*(3), 269–279.

Bearden, L. J., Spencer, W. A., & Moracco, J. C. (1989). A study of high school dropouts. *The School Counselor, 37,* 113–120.

Beck, L., & Muia, J. A. (1980). A portrait of a tragedy: Research findings on the dropout. *The High School Journal, 64*(2), 65–72.

Benz, M. R., & Halpern, A. S. (1986). Vocational preparation for high school students with mild disabilities: A statewide study of administrator, teacher, and parent perceptions. *Career Development for Exceptional Individuals, 9*(1), 3–15.

Benz, M. R., & Halpern, A. S. (1987). Transition services for secondary students with mild disabilities: A statewide perspective. *Exceptional Children, 53*(6), 507–514.

Blackorby, J., Edgar, E., & Kortering, L. (1991). A third of our youth? A look at the problem of high school dropout among students with mild handicaps. *Journal of Special Education, 25*(1), 102–113.

Brannon, D. R. (1988). Our piece of the dropout puzzle. *Vocational Education Journal, 63*(6), 12, 14.

Bruininks, R. H., Thurlow, M. L., Lewis, D. R., & Larson, N. W. (1988). Post-school outcomes for students in special education and other students one to eight years after high school. In R. H. Bruininks, D. R. Lewis, & M. L. Thurlow (Eds.), *Assessing outcomes, costs and benefits of special education programs* (pp. 9–111). Minneapolis: University of Minnesota, University Affiliated Programs.

Bryk, A. S., & Thum, Y. M. (1989). The effects of high school organization on dropping out: An exploratory investigation. *American Educational Research Journal, 26*(3), 353–383.

Butler-Nalin, P., & Padilla, C. (1989, March). *Dropouts: The relationship of student characteristics, behaviors, and performance for special education students.* Paper presented at the meeting of the American Educational Research Association, San Francisco.

Cannell, J. (1983). *Brookhart et al. v. Illinois State Board of Education et al.*: Denial of standard diploma for handicapped students. *Education Law Reporter, 8*, 549–553.

Catterall, J. S. (1986). *On the social costs of dropping out of school.* (ERIC Document Reproduction Service No. ED 271 837)

Catterall, J. S. (1987). An intensive group counseling dropout prevention intervention: Some cautions on isolating at-risk adolescents within high schools. *American Educational Research Journal, 24*(4), 521–540.

Chadsey-Rusch, J. (1988). Personnel preparation for leadership in transition. *The Journal for Vocational Special Needs Education, 11(1)*, 29–32.

Clements, B. S. (1990). What is a dropout? *The School Administrator, 47*(3), 8–22.

Cobb, B., & Hasazi, S. B. (1987). School-aged transition services: Options for adolescents with mild handicaps. *Career Development for Exceptional Individuals, 10*(1), 15–23.

Crews, W. B., Algozzine, B., & Schwartz, S. E. (1989). How do adolescents perform on a statewide minimum competency test? *Diagnostique, 14*(3), 163–173.

Cummings, R. W., & Maddux, C. D. (1987). *Career and vocational education for the mildly handicapped.* Springfield, IL: Thomas.

deBettencourt, L. U., & Zigmond, N. (1990). The learning disabled secondary school dropout: What teachers should know. What teachers can do. *Teacher Education and Special Education, 13*(1), 17–20.

Doss, D. A., & Sailor, P. J. (1987). *Counting dropouts, it's enough to make you want to quit too!* (Publication No. 86.39). Austin, TX: Austin Independent School District.

Edgar, E. (1985). How do special education students fare after they leave school? A response to Hasazi, Gordon and Roe. *Exceptional Children, 51*(6), 470–473.

Education Commission of the States. (1985). *Clearinghouse notes. State activity: Minimum competency testing as of November 1985.* n.p.: Author.

Education for the Handicapped Law Report. (1983, December). [Entire issue]. *554*, 220

Ehrlich, I. (1975). On the relation between education and crime. In F. T. Juster (Ed.), *Education, income, and human behavior* (pp. 313–337). New York: McGraw-Hill.

Ekstrom, R. B., Goertz, M. E., Pollack, J. M., & Rock, D. A. (1986). Who drops out of high school and why? Findings from a national study. *Teachers College Record, 87*(3), 356–373.

Ellis, L. (1990, July 3). Depending upon the disabled. *The Philadelphia Inquirer*, pp. A1, A15.

Eschenmann, K. K. (1988). Structuring classrooms for success. *Vocational Education Journal, 63*(6), 46–47.

Fardig, D. B., Algozzine, R. F., Schwartz, S. E., Hensel, J. W., & Westling, W. L. (1985). Postsecondary vocational adjustment of rural, mildly handicapped students. *Exceptional Children, 52*(2), 115–121.

Felice, L. G. (1981). Black student dropout behavior: Disengagement from school rejection and social discrimination. *Journal of Negro Education, 50*, 415–424.

Fortune, J. C., Bruce, A., Williams, J., & Jones, M. (1991). What does the evaluation of your dropout prevention program show about its success? Maybe not enough. *The High School Journal*, *74*(4), 225–231.

Gill, D., & Edgar, E. (1990). Outcomes of a vocational program designed for students with mild disabilities: The Pierce County Vocational/Special Education Cooperative. *The Journal for Vocational Special Needs Education*, *12*(3), 17–22.

Gill, H., Cupp, D. E., & Lindquist, D. A. (1986). A consortium of vocational educational and special education. *The Journal for Vocational Special Needs Education*, *9*(3), 25–28.

Greenan, J. P. (1983). *Identification of generalizable skills in secondary vocational programs* (Executive Summary). Urbana: Illinois State Board of Education.

Greene, G., Albright, L., & Kokaska, C. (1989). Instructional strategies for special education students in vocational education. *The Journal for Vocational Special Needs Education*, *12*(2), 3–8.

Grise, P. (1980). Florida's minimum competency testing program for handicapped students. *Exceptional Children*, *47*, 186–191.

Grise, P., Beattie, S., & Algozzine, B. (1982). Assessment of minimum competency in fifth grade learning disabled students: Test modifications make a difference. *Journal of Educational Research*, *76*(1), 35–40.

Hamilton, S. F. (1986). Raising standards and reducing dropout rates. *Teachers College Record*, *87*(3), 410–429.

Hammack, F. M. (1986). Large school systems' dropout reports: An analysis of definitions, procedures, findings. *Teachers College Record*, *87*(3), 324–341.

Haney, W., & Madaus, G. (1978). Making sense of the competency testing movement. *Harvard Educational Review*, *48*, 462–484.

Hasazi, S. B., Gordon, L. R., & Roe, C. A. (1985). Factors associated with the employment status of handicapped youth exiting high school from 1979 to 1983. *Exceptional Children*, *57*(6), 455–469.

Heal, L., Haney, J., DeStefano, L., & Rusch, F. (1988). *A comparison of successful and unsuccessful placements of secondary students with mental handicaps into competitive employment*. Champaign: University of Illinois, Transition Institute.

Hewitt, S. K. N. (1981). *Learning disabilities among secondary in-school students, graduates, and drop-outs*. Unpublished doctoral dissertation, University of Minnesota, Minneapolis.

Hoffman, F. J., Sheldon, K. L., Minskoff, E. H., Sautter, S. W., Steidle, E. F., Baker, D. P., Bailey, M. B., & Echols, L. D. (1987). Needs of learning disabled adults. *Journal of Learning Disabilities*, *20*(1), 43–52.

Jay, E. D., & Padilla, C. L. (1987). *Special education dropouts: The incidence of and reasons for dropping out of special education in California* (SRI Project No. 2544). Menlo Park, CA: SRI International.

Kerr, M. M., Nelson, C. M., & Lambert, D. (1987). *Helping adolescents with learning and behavior problems*. New York: Merrill/Macmillan.

Levin, E., Zigmond, N., & Birch, J. (1985). A follow-up study of 52 learning disabled students. *Journal of Learning Disabilities*, *18*, 2–7.

Levin, H. (1972). *The costs to the nation of inadequate education* (Report to the Select Committee on Equal Education Opportunity, U.S. Senate). Washington, DC: U.S. Government Printing Office.

Lichtenstein, S. J. (1987). *A study of selected post-school employment patterns of handicapped and nonhandicapped graduates and dropouts.* Unpublished doctoral dissertation, University of Illinois, Urbana-Champaign.

Linn, R. L., Madaus, G. F., & Pedulla, J. J. (1982). Minimum competency testing: Cautions on the state of the art. *American Journal of Education, 91,* 1–35.

McAfee, J. K., & Mann, L. (1982). The prognosis for mildly handicapped students. In T. L. Miller & E. E. Davis (Eds.), *The mildly handicapped student* (pp. 461–496). New York: Grune & Stratton.

McCarthy, M. M. (1983). The application of competency testing mandates to handicapped children. *Harvard Educational Review, 53,* 146–164.

McClung, M. S., & Pullin, D. (1978). Competency testing and handicapped students. *Clearinghouse Review, 11,* 922–927.

McDill, E. L., Natriello, G., & Pallas, A. M. (1985). Raising standards and retaining students: The impact of the reform recommendations on potential dropouts. *Review of Educational Research, 55*(4), 415–433.

McDill, E. L., Natriello, G., & Pallas, A. M. (1986). A population at risk: Potential consequences of tougher school standards for student dropouts. *American Journal of Education, 94*(2), 135–181.

Mick, L. B. (1989). Measurement effects of modifications in minimum competency test formats for exceptional students. *Measurement and Evaluation in Counseling and Development, 22,* 31–36.

Miller, S. E., Leinhardt, G., & Zigmond, N. (1988). Influencing engagement through accommodation: An ethnographic study of at-risk students. *American Educational Research Journal, 25*(4), 465–487.

Morissey, P. A. (1978, April). *Adaptive testing: How and when should handicapped students be accommodated in competency testing programs?* Paper presented at the American Educational Research Association Topical Conference, Washington, DC.

Morrow, G. (1986). Standardizing practice in the analysis of school dropouts. *Teachers College Record, 7*(3), 342–355.

National Center for Educational Statistics Bulletin. (1983). High school dropouts: Descriptive information from high school and beyond. Washington, DC: National Center for Educational Statistics.

Natriello, G., Pallas, A. M., & McDill, E. L. (1986). Taking stock: Renewing our research agenda on the causes and consequences of dropping out. *Teachers College Record, 87*(3), 430–439.

Okolo, C. M., & Sitlington, P. (1986). The role of special education in LD adolescents transition from school to work. *Learning Disabilities Quarterly, 9,* 141–155.

Pullin, D. (1985). Minimum competency testing and special education: Evolving judicial standards. *Education Law Reporter, 20,* 811–819.

Reynolds, M. C., & Birch, J. W. (1977). *Teaching exceptional children in all America's schools.* Reston, VA: Council for Exceptional Children.

Ruben, A. M. (1989). Preventing school dropouts through classroom guidance. *Elementary School Guidance & Counseling, 24,* 21–29.

Rumberger, R. W. (1983). Dropping out of high school: The influence of race, sex, and family background. *American Educational Research Journal, 20*(2), 199–220.

Rumberger, R. W. (1987). High school dropouts: A review of issues and evidence. *Review of Educational Research, 57*(2), 101–121.

Safer, N. D. (1980). Implications of minimum competency testing standards and testing for handicapped students. *Exceptional Children, 46*(4), 288–290.

Sansone, J., & Baker, J. (1990). Ninth grade for students at risk for dropping out of high school. *The High School Journal, 73*(4), 218–231.

Schmidt, J. (1988). Guidance for dropout prevention. *Vocational Education Journal, 63*(6), 48–49.

Scholl, M. F., & Johnson, J. R. (1988). Keeping pregnant teens in school. *Vocational Education Journal, 63*(6), 42–43, 52.

Scott, C. S. (1983). The effect of test format modifications on the minimum competency test performance of mildly handicapped students. *Dissertation Abstracts International, 44*(9), 2737-A.

Seidel, J. F., & Vaughn, S. (1991). Social alienation and the learning disabled school dropout. *Learning Disabilities Research & Practice, 6*, 152–157.

Serow, R. C., & O'Brien, K. (1983). Performance of handicapped students in a competency based testing program. *Journal of Special Education, 17*, 149–155.

Sitlington, P. L. (1981). Vocational and special education in career programming for the mildly handicapped adolescent. *Exceptional Children, 47*(8), 592–598.

Smith, J. D., & Jenkins, D. S. (1980). Minimum competency testing and handicapped students. *Exceptional Children, 46*(6), 440–443.

Stephenson, R. S. (1985). *A study of the longitudinal dropout rate: 1980 eighth-grade cohort followed from June, 1980 through February, 1985.* Miami, FL: Dade County Public Schools.

Vitello, S. J. (1988). Handicapped students and competency testing. *Remedial and Special Education, 9*(5), 22–28.

Weber, J. M. (1988). The relevance of vocational education to dropout prevention. *Vocational Education Journal, 63*(6), 36–38.

Wehledge, G. G. (1983). At-risk students and the need for high school reform. *Education, 107*(1), 18–28.

Wehledge, G. G., & Rutter, R. A. (1986). Dropping out: How much do schools contribute to the problem? *Teachers College Record, 87*(3), 374–392.

West, L. L. (1988). Designing, implementing and evaluating transition programs. *The Journal for Vocational Special Needs Education, 11*(1), 3–7.

Wolman, C., Bruininks, R., & Thurlow, M. L. (1989). Dropouts and dropout programs: Implications for special education. *Remedial and Special Education, 10*(5), 6–20, 50.

Wyche, L. G. (1989). The tenth annual report to Congress: Taking a significant step in the right direction. *Exceptional Children, 56*(1), 14–16.

Zigmond, N., & Thornton, H. (1985). Follow-up of postsecondary age learning disabled graduates and drop-outs. *Learning Disabilities Research, 1*(1), 50–55.

Chapter 7

❧ ❧ ❧

Academic Foundations for Transition in the Secondary School

G rowing awareness of the importance of transitional services for the older
student with disabilities has focused sharp, and often critical, attention on
the secondary school and its contribution to the transition process. A rising
chorus of professional voices is urging educators, particularly special educators, to recognize that a successful transition from school to adult life is
founded in the academic years and that special education has a critical role to
play in the preparation of students for the world of work and other adult pursuits (Benz & Halpern, 1987; Halpern, 1985; Okolo & Sitlington, 1986; Rusch
& Phelps, 1987; Wehman, Kregel, & Barcus, 1985). In addition, research is
beginning to shed light on the plight of students who exit school ill prepared
for adult life. The data paint a rather bleak picture of the future for the unprepared student who is mildly impaired (McAfee & Mann, 1982; Rusch &
Phelps, 1987; U.S. Commission on Civil Rights, 1983).

The importance of transitional services and programs has been addressed
in federal legislation. There is a long history of legislation in support of vocational training and employment services for those with disabilities, though the
condition of those who are mildly disabled has received far less attention than
that of those who are moderately and severely impaired. Despite federal legislation and financial incentives, transitional services and programs at the secondary level are still rare (Rusch & Phelps, 1987). Models of service delivery,
theoretical perspectives on secondary education, and instructional methodologies are still in a formative stage (Carlson, 1985; Masters & Mori, 1986;
Zigmond & Sansone, 1986). Additional evidence of the newness of secondary
programs for students who are mildly disabled can be found in the fact that
well-known texts that address elementary-level students with mild disabilities
are in their third, even fourth, printing, while textbooks that address secondary populations with mild disabilities are of a more recent vintage.

Examination of the academic foundations for transition in our secondary
schools involves three major topics. The first concerns the models of service that
currently predominate in secondary school settings. The second topic focuses

on the essential programmatic components for effective transitional services. The third concern involves the contrast between "what is" and "what ought to be" and the degree of discrepancy between current and desired levels of service.

❦ ❦ ❦

MODELS OF SERVICE

The variety of program models currently in vogue for the secondary student with a mild disability is not easily conceptualized or categorized. Zigmond and Sansone (1986) have recently suggested a useful two-dimensional framework for conceptualizing program options for the secondary-school learning-disabled adolescent that is useful for understanding school-based programs for all types of students with mild disabilities (see Figure 7–1).

The two dimensions of Zigmond and Sansone's (1986) framework involve the temporal and curricular aspects of various service models. The temporal dimension represents the extent to which the student spends class time with special education teachers in a designated special education placement. The self-contained classroom in contrast to the totally mainstreamed program would reflect the two extremes of the temporal dimension, that is, total instructional time in a special education setting versus no time at all in a special education placement. The second dimension, the curricular, denotes the degree to which curricular and program content deviate from that of the regular educational curriculum and program. A student with a disability working within the regular curriculum with minimal adaptations would exemplify one end of the curricular dimension, while another such student working in an alternative curriculum with highly specialized material or methods (e.g., survival skills curriculum) would represent the other end of the curricular dimension.

Zigmond and Sansone (1986) have plotted a number of different program options within their two-dimensional framework. It is apparent that the lower right quadrant encompasses special education programs that deviate markedly from regular education programs, while the upper left quadrant encompasses program options that vary little if at all from regular education offerings in terms of setting and content. One could hypothesize further that students whose disabilities are severe and whose functional levels are very low would be concentrated in programmatic options falling within the lower right quadrant and that program choices for students whose disabilities are less severe and whose functional levels are more intact would fall within the other quadrants. The upper left quadrant would encompass programs for students whose disabilities and resultant functional limitations were only moderate (as opposed to severe) or who were good candidates for reintegration into regular education.

The framework helps clarify the range of programmatic options currently available at the secondary school level. The framework as presented does, for the most part, address traditional secondary goals, that is, academic and vocational training. The clearly "special education" programmatic options (highly restrictive as to setting and utilization of alternative curriculum and instruc-

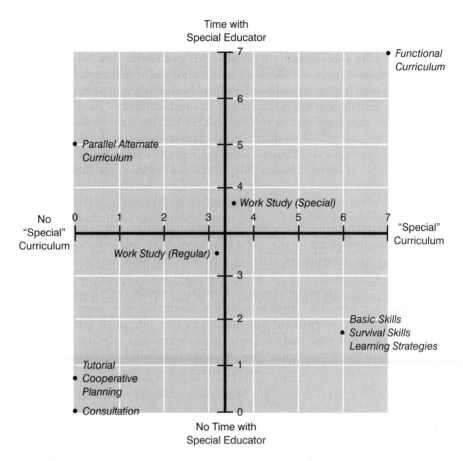

Figure 7–1
Program options at the secondary level

Source: From "Designing a Program for the Learning Disabled Adolescent" by N. N. Zigmond and J. Sansone, 1986, *Remedial and Special Education*, 7(5), p. 13. Copyright 1986 by PRO-ED, Inc. Reprinted by permission.

tional methods) do not abandon these goals. Rather, there is recognition that preparation for adult functioning may involve restricted educational settings and altered curricular content and methodology in keeping with individual learning needs. It remains to be seen how transitional programming (and the range of program options that individual student characteristics will demand) can be integrated into the existing status quo of program options or the extent to which the demands of the transition process impact on and alter traditional service delivery models.

Zigmond and Sansone (1986) have indicated various program options. Their list is illustrative, not necessarily exhaustive. Lists of secondary program options (generally referred to as models or approaches) are readily found in the literature. Six programmatic models have been culled from the disparate lists for further description and discussion. The models selected were those that appeared on at least two independent lists, embodied a recognizable perspective on the etiology of disability, and espoused a well-founded methodology of intervention. The instructional focus, strengths, and weaknesses of each model are summarized in Table 7–1.

Basic Skills Model

The basic skills model provides developmental or remedial instruction for basic academic skill deficits (Alley & Deshler, 1979). It includes a variety of activities, techniques, and practices intended to eliminate or strengthen the basic source(s) of weakness that is interfering with successful learning (Masters & Mori, 1986; Smith, Price, & Marsh, 1986). The scope of the remediation included within the basic skills model may be more or less restrictive depending on the perspectives and orientation of various authors. Goodman and Mann (1976) advocate for a strong academic focus and totally eschew any "formal process training" at the secondary level. Other authors allow greater latitude for remediation of "psychological processes deemed important to learning the fundamental skills" (Masters & Mori, 1986, p. 55).

Controversy over the appropriate focus of remedial intervention for students with mild disabilities, in particular those who are learning disabled, was prevalent during the 1970s and early 1980s (Ewing & Brecht, 1977; Ysseldyke & Salvia, 1974). The differences of opinion are still evident in more recent sources, which indicates that the controversy has never been totally resolved. For the most part, however, the professional community, bolstered by the weight of the research literature, supports intervention with a curricular focus on the remediation of academic, behavioral, and social skill deficits and opposes psychological process or ability training (Arter & Jenkins, 1977).

The ultimate goal of the basic skills model is to prepare the student for reentry into the mainstream of regular education (Sabatino & Mann, 1982; Smith et al., 1986). The basic skills model emphasizes instruction in the tool subjects of the elementary school—mathematics, reading, and other language arts. The instructional methods employed stress remedial activities and techniques aimed at eliminating the basic source of the weakness or deficiency that is hampering the student's academic progress (Marsh, Gearheart, & Gearheart, 1978). Instruction begins at the student's level of functioning and proceeds through the scope and sequence of the various subjects. Functional literacy, computation, and knowledge are the academic goals.

At the elementary level, the basic skills model is, and ought to be, the preeminent choice for most students who are mildly disabled. The choice is more problematic at the secondary level. For many secondary-level students with mild disabilities, academic deficiencies are so severe that there may not be sufficient time left within the academic program to make meaningful progress under this model of instruction. In short, continued remediation of basic skills at the secondary level frequently may lead to disappointment if students cannot

Table 7–1
Instructional Models for Secondary-Level Disabled Students

Model	Instructional Focus	Instructional Features
Basic skills	Remediation/development of basic academic skills Functional literacy	Continuation of traditional academic curriculum Classroom-based approach
Functional	Skill development for independent adult living (e.g., vocational, social, homemaking)	Community-based integration instruction Use of learning theory/principles for effective instruction
Learning strategies	Strategies for effective learning/problem solving across content domains, tracks, settings, and situations	Teaching of both task-specific and generic strategies Learner's sense of responsibility increased for his or her own learning Emphasis on study and survival skills Metacognition
Tutorial	Successful completion of regular education class assignments/requirements	Special education teachers assume responsibility for content subject instruction
Compensatory	Continuation of academic progress	Teaching to preferred learning style and stronger learning capabilities Assessment of performance without bias because of limited sensory, manual, speaking skills Accommodative teaching and compensatory techniques (e.g., response or presentation mode) to facilitate progress
Vocational	Preparation for employment	Specific job functions and job-related skills emphasized Career exposure and working experiences

Table 7–1, continued

Strengths	Weaknesses
Preparation for continued post-secondary education	Lack of preparation for important aspects of adult life
Attainment of high school diploma	Possibility of course failure and grade retention places students at risk of dropping out
Opportunities for integrating into regular education	
	Skill deterioration after leaving school because of inadequate development
Preparation for independent living	Possible underdevelopment of student strengths and capabilities
Enhanced employability	
Enhanced student motivation because of relevance of curricular content	Restricted curricular content of postschool educational options
	Interaction with more capable students
Enhanced student ability to work effectively and independently	Does not address underlying deficiencies (e.g., decoding skills) that can impede learning
Enhanced student ability to deal with secondary content subjects	
	Does not compensate for a general lack of knowledge
	Does not address noncognitive variables
Maintenance of students with disabilities in academic mainstream	Limited subject-matter expertise of special education teachers
Attainment of credits toward graduation	Does not address deficiencies that precipitated student referral
	Diminishes regular education's responsibility for comprehensive curriculum
	Questionable use of special education resources
	Departmentalized special education programs with lowered academic standards
Individualization of instruction	Lowered performance standards/requirements
	Limited accommodative ability of regular education teachers
	Student ability to function in nonaccommodating environments
Enhanced employability	Restrict postschool educational opportunities
Supervised/supported work experience	Limited access to vocational programs for students with disabilities
	Difficulty level of regular educational vocational programs for many students with disabilities

meet subject matter demands (Sabatino & Mann, 1982). Further, Alley and Deshler (1979) point out that continued remediation of a very narrow range of elementary-level skills (probably involving instruction to which the student has already been overly exposed without success) undercuts the instructional time and attention that can be given to critical areas of instruction (e.g., social skills, vocational skills) essential to secondary and postsecondary functioning.

Functional Curricular Model

The primary focus of the functional curriculum is to equip the student to function in society and to cope with the immediate demands of daily living. The instructional emphasis of the functional curriculum is the training of functional skills in real-life situations and environments (Boyer-Stephens & Kearns, 1988; Valletutti & Bender, 1982; Wehman et al., 1985). The scope and content of the functional curriculum will vary depending on the degree of disability. For some students, a functional level of literacy may not be attained, and training in survival skills will be essential. For the student who is mildly disabled, the functional curriculum should address the skills associated with all potential adult roles (consumer, spouse, parent, citizen, etc.). In addition, vocational training and specific job-related skills must be a central component of a comprehensive training program.

Pursuit of a functional curricular model for a student with mild disabilities is generally determined only after academic remediation or direct tutoring of basic skills has failed (Sabatino & Mann, 1982). The decision to abandon a traditional academic course sequence should be based on the student's learning history, current academic status, and future goals. The parents and student should be intimately involved in this decision-making and planning process.

Alley and Deshler (1979) point out both the positive and negative aspects of the functional curriculum. On the positive side they see (a) preparation for independent living, at least for the immediate future, (b) preparation for a specific designated job that can enhance the immediate employment possibilities for the individual, and (c) the suitability and relevance of the functional curriculum for the severely disabled. On the negative side, Alley and Deshler point to (a) the possible underdevelopment of student strengths, (b) the assumption that survival skills can be identified and are stable over time, (c) the degree of restrictiveness of the functional curriculum that can inhibit student interaction with more able and nondisabled peers, and (d) the heavy responsibility placed on the classroom teacher for both the development and implementation of the functional curricular program.

Learning Strategies Model

The goals of the learning strategies model are to empower students as learners (Archer & Isaacson, 1990; Harris & Pressley, 1991), to enable them to achieve a significant degree of independence in the management of their own learning, and to successfully meet the demands of the school and postschool environments (Hermann, 1990). These goals are achieved by teaching students "how to learn" rather than specific subject-matter or curricular content that is likely to be quickly forgotten or become outdated. Strategies, the means to this end, have been defined as "an individual's approach to a task; it includes how a person thinks and acts while planning, executing, and evaluating performance on a task and its outcomes" (Lenz & Deshler, 1990, p. 84).

Training in learning strategies is theoretically rooted in cognitive psychology, developmental cognitive psychology and, at the applied level, metacognition (Wong, 1986). The conceptualization of metacognition, that is, the awareness and control of one's own thinking processes, emphasizes the student as an active participant in the learning process (Harris & Pressley, 1991). The learning strategies model requires the student to assume a significant degree of responsibility for his or her own learning (Alley & Deshler, 1979).

Two overriding facts emerge from the research literature: (a) students with disabilities have strategy deficiencies that may involve either the lack of strategies or the inability to apply strategies effectively (Gerber, 1983; Hall, 1980) and (2) strategies are amenable to training among those who are mildly disabled with corresponding positive impact on learning and performance (Graham & Harris, 1989; Harris & Pressley, 1991; Schumaker, Deshler, Alley, & Warner, 1983; Sheinker, Sheinker, & Stevens, 1984; Wong & Jones, 1982). The latter finding has broad implications for instructional practice.

Strategies are learning tools. The range, nature, and type of strategies vary greatly. Weinstein and Mayer (1986) have categorized learning strategies into eight categories:

- rehearsal strategies (basic and complex),
- elaboration strategies (basic and complex),
- organizational strategies (basic and complex),
- comprehension monitoring, and
- affective/motivational strategies.

Strategies have also been differentiated as task-limited strategies, that is, used in very restricted and highly specific situations or across domain strategies that have far greater generalizability (Pressley, Goodchild, Fleet, & Zajchowski, 1989). An example of a task-limited strategy would be a mnemonic strategy to facilitate memory of a list of facts or words. An example of an across-domain strategy would be a proofreading strategy that could be applied to a wide range of written material. Instructional strategies can be subject-specific (e.g., reading comprehension strategies) or more general (e.g., memory or attentional strategies). There are innumerable sources for the teacher interested in pursuing strategies instruction (Pressley et al., 1989).

There are limitations to the application of learning strategies instruction. Learning strategy deficiencies do not provide an adequate explanation for all learning problems displayed by learners with disabilities. For example, learning strategies do not adequately address the decoding problems that impede the academic functioning of many students (Torgesen, 1979, 1982).

Strategies training does not compensate for inadequacy of a student's general fund of knowledge (Weinstein & Mayer, 1986). Research has demonstrated that the individual's fund of information and level of strategies usage are interrelated, with greater knowledge being associated to the use of more elaborate and higher order strategies (Chi, 1981; Wong, 1985). Learning strategies do not address noncognitive variables such as academic self-concept, achievement expectation, and locus of control, which influence learning and performance (Battle, 1979; Boersma & Chapman, 1981; Hiebert, Wong, & Hunter, 1982; Wong, 1986). Another potential "limitation" of strategies instruction involves the ability of teachers to provide effective instruction in this area. There is general recognition that teachers require extensive preparation for the role of strategy instructor (Archer & Isaacson, 1990; Ellis, 1990; Pressley et al., 1989; Sheinker et al., 1984). It has even been suggested that teacher preparation for their role in strategies instruction may require the reconfiguration of existing preservice and in-service training approaches (Lenz & Deshler, 1990).

Tutorial Model

The primary goal of the tutorial model is to help students succeed in meeting the academic demands of the regular education program (Sabatino & Mann, 1982). Traditionally, the instructional focus of the tutorial program involved the provision of assistance with specific academic course content (e.g., preparing for or administering tests, completing written assignments) (Almeida, 1988; Masters & Mori, 1986; Wujeck, 1981). The special education resource room program is often the setting in which assistance is provided. Another form of the tutorial model involves the creation of departmentalized or parallel special education programs that address secondary academic course requirements for learners with disabilities (Carlson, 1985; Howell, Kaplan, & O'Connell, 1979).

Under the tutorial model, the role of the special education teacher can vary from a supportive function only (e.g., offering academic assistance but not grading) to a more central role involving both instruction and course grading (Brozovich & Kotting, 1984). If the special education teacher has only an ancillary function, his or her role may be limited to helping students complete assignments or prepare for tests and the like.

The tutorial model is widespread in secondary special education. Deshler, Lowrey, and Alley (1979) conducted a nationwide survey of secondary-level special education teachers and found that 24% of the programs surveyed followed a tutorial approach. In another survey, Wells, Schmidt, Algozzine, and Maher (1983) found that 27% of the special education teachers at the junior high level and 42% of those at the senior high level reported spending most of their time involved in subject-matter tutoring. Very few teachers at either the junior or senior high school levels disavowed any involvement in subject matter tutoring—14% and 16%, respectively. More recently, McKenzie (1991a) has reported that the tutorial model was widely employed in 41 states.

Despite the widespread use of the tutorial approach, the appropriateness of this instructional model has been questioned by many special educators. There is concern about special educators' lack of experience in the subject matter of the secondary school curriculum (Carlson, 1985; Cline & Billingsley, 1991; Goodman & Mann, 1976; Sabatino & Mann, 1982). The training and experience of most special education teachers has not equipped them, either in content knowledge or instructional methodology, to teach secondary school curricular subjects adequately. In a multistate survey of special education teachers, 41% of the teacher-respondents indicated that they were not certified to teach courses in which they were providing instruction (Cline & Billingsley, 1991). Departmentalized or parallel special education programs are viewed by some as essentially a tracking system for special education students accompanied by watered-down standards for special education course offerings (Carlson, 1985). One cannot help but wonder if these adjustments are made solely to meet student needs or are also a response to the teachers' limited expertise.

The degree of segregation associated with the two tutorial models—skill focused versus content focused—is a matter of concern. McKenzie (1991b), in a survey of special education teachers involved in skill-focused and content-focused secondary tutorial programs, found no substantive curricular or methodological differences between programs but did find that the content-focused special classes fostered a far greater degree of student segregation. The data also revealed that students in content classes were more rejected by their nondisabled peers and themselves expressed more negative attitudes toward special education than their counterparts in skill-focused classes. McKenzie (1991b) suggests that these manifestations may reflect true "sociometric differences between content and skill models" (p. 469).

Another problem of the tutorial model involves excessive referrals and placements of underachieving and/or misbehaving, but nondisabled, students in special education (Sabatino & Mann, 1982). The tutorial model encourages referrals to special education. And, as special education becomes the placement option for a vast array of students with learning problems, the tolerance of the regular education teacher for individual student differences is diminished—it becomes easier to remove the problem than to deal with it. In addition, the tutorial model does not address the deficiencies and/or difficulties that were the basis of the student's referral and placement in special education to begin with (Carlson, 1985; Sabatino & Mann, 1982).

Finally, the appropriateness and cost effectiveness of expending special education resources on programs and services that legitimately fall under the rubric of regular education is cause for concern. Many special educators view the tutorial model as the least desirable of all the secondary school program models (Sabatino & Mann, 1982).

Compensatory Model

The goal of the compensatory model of instruction is continued student progress in his or her academic program. *Compensatory teaching* refers to a process whereby the learning environment or task demands are altered to facilitate the learning process despite fundamental weaknesses or deficiencies within the student (Marsh, Gearheart, & Gearheart, 1978). In contrast to remedial instruction, which implies a cure or restoration of a person's skill to a normal or near-normal level (Cartwright, Cartwright, & Ward, 1989), compensatory instruction emphasizes substitution of stronger skills for weaker ones and alteration of learning environments to facilitate learning. Compensatory strategies will vary from specific subject-matter alterations for reading, handwriting, spelling, and so forth, to accommodations in school procedures or policies that unfairly hinder students with disabilities (e.g., scheduling flexibility and modified testing procedures). The compensatory model embodies the philosophy of individualization that permeates all of special education.

The emphasis in instruction is likely to shift from remedial to compensatory as students become older or as disabilities remain resistant to intervention efforts. Application of the compensatory model at the secondary level acknowledges the fact that functional difficulties persist and require accommodations or modifications in the instructional methods used if the student is to be able to meet the requirements of his or her secondary academic and vocational classes. The degree of functional disability of the individual student will determine if compensation can be provided in the regular classroom setting (e.g., orally administering tests) or if the student must participate in a specialized program (e.g., offering departmentalized special education or parallel curriculum). A compensatory instructional model undoubtedly raises the issue of modified performance standards and graduation requirements. Modifications and accommodations to enable students with disabilities to perform need not involve a lowering of performance standards, only adjustments in the way information is communicated and the means by which the student demonstrates mastery. If performance standards are altered, then the student may ultimately earn a certificate of attendance or completion rather than a standard diploma.

Vocational Model

The objective of the vocational model for the student with a mild disability is to prepare for immediate or short-term employment (Smith et al., 1986). The vocational model becomes the option of choice for many students with mild disabilities late in their academic careers when the prospect of employment after high school becomes a very pressing concern for both the student and his or her parents. Commitment to the vocational model signals the decision to set aside academic goals such as continued attempts at functional literacy in favor of preparation for independent living and successful employment.

For many years, a major problem associated with vocational training programs was one of access. Regular educators, for a variety of reasons, were reluctant to admit students with disabilities into vocational training programs. Students who are mildly disabled are beginning to participate, in significantly increasing numbers, in prevocational and vocational programs that were largely out of their reach for many years. Recent legislation (e.g., ADA, Section 504 of the Vocational Rehabilitation Act and the Carl D. Perkins Act) has greatly reduced barriers based on prejudice and stereotypical thinking (Cummings & Maddux, 1987).

Access to vocational programs has brought to light another barrier facing persons with disabilities: regular vocational training programs may be too difficult for them (Sitlington, 1981). The success of students who are mildly disabled in such training programs often depends on the availability of support services and the degree of accommodation that will be made to meet individual needs. Vocational special needs programs that Meers (1987) describes as part of the general vocational education delivery system are designed to provide the instruction and support services needed by special students if they are to succeed in vocational or prevocational programs. According to Meers, special needs programs can take many forms:

1. A separate vocational special needs course such as vocational English or vocational mathematics
2. A regular vocational class with support materials or modified materials for use by special needs students
3. A regular vocational class with a resource teacher in the class to assist the vocational instructor
4. A regular vocational class with a special needs resource center for use by special needs students

The effectiveness of various vocational training programs has typically been measured by initial placement after completion of the high school program. The nature of the placement as well as the longevity in the job are not taken into account. In light of research data indicating that job loss is high and job satisfaction is low for many persons who are mildly disabled, the short-sighted criterion of programmatic success needs to be reevaluated (Smith et al., 1986).

Summary

As a group, the current programmatic options for secondary youth with mild disabilities are best described as "traditional" and "restrictive." The traditional label applies to those programs that are clearly an extension of elementary programs and methodologies to the secondary school (basic skills model, compensatory model). Even those options that are clearly divorced from the elementary school curriculum primarily serve the academic needs of the traditional secondary school curriculum (tutorial model) for those students still striving to satisfy secondary school academic demands. Even the learning strategies model, the newest of the program approaches, is curriculum bound and focuses on fundamental skills generally contained within the standard elementary curriculum. The vocational model and functional curriculum model hold much promise for the secondary students who are mildly disabled. If the stereotypical thinking and prejudice that have characterized vocational programs give way to full access for students with disabilities and if innovative approaches to training and service are implemented, the promise of vocational programming may be realized. If the functional curricular approach can be expanded to address the full range of instructional needs of these students, it too holds much promise for this population.

To the extent that all of the secondary models fail to prepare students with mild disabilities for successful adult living, they are "restrictive"; that is, failure to prepare secondary students for full participation in adult living necessarily restricts those students to a lesser quality of life. Thomas (1980), in discussing programming for students who are mentally retarded, observes that the least restrictive environment is the one that is most productive for the student. The same logic applies to programs for all students with mild disabilities; the least restrictive programs are those that help them achieve the greatest degree of independence in their adult lives. Ultimately the issue of importance will be whether current models of secondary school education and future-oriented models of needed transitional services can be merged to create a unified and comprehensive model of service that will effectively guide the student from the dependence of adolescence to independent functioning as an adult.

❦ ❦ ❦

SECONDARY PROGRAMS: ESSENTIAL COMPONENTS

Many of the approaches to secondary programming, as described here, are both limited and limiting. Secondary programs in general have been characterized as inadequate and out of touch with the postschool needs of the students being served (Edgar, 1985; Heller, 1981; Hoffman et al., 1987). Dowdy, Carter, and Smith (1990) portray secondary programs as minimally related to the students' lives after high school. The authors based their conclusion on the self-reports of Alabama high school students with learning disabilities regarding their school experiences, future goals, and transitional needs. Most of the students were anticipating entry into the job market upon leaving school, not continued training or education. Over 65% of the students surveyed had a career goal, but many of the same students lacked marketable skills. The students felt they needed more instruction in career exploration, job seeking, and independent living skills. In general, "LD students view their parents, friends and regular education teachers as most helpful in postsecondary transition activities" (p. 347), a finding that the authors found very disconcerting.

The heavily academic orientation of secondary programs for students with mild disabilities has been criticized (Edgar, 1987). However, the academic focus of secondary programs seems highly resistant to change. A study of teachers who worked with students with learning disabilities conducted by Deshler et al. (1979) revealed that 45% of the respondents were committed to basic skills remediation as the primary programming option.

Additional teacher surveys by Wells et al. (1983), Houck, Geller, and Engelhard (1988), and Cline and Billingsley (1991) corroborate the original findings of Deshler et al. Teachers of students with learning disabilities and emotional disorders surveyed reported spending the major portion of their time on basic skill instruction. Instruction in content subjects also accounts for a significant portion of instructional time and effort (Cline & Billingsley, 1991; Wells et al., 1983). In addition to current teacher and classroom focus, Cline and Billingsley sought data on what teachers and supervisors thought the primary instructional focus of the classroom ought to be. Interestingly, the authors found that teachers' and supervisors' perception of the most important instructional focus for the classroom was changing from a primary concern for content area instruction to a greater concern for career/vocational education.

Such findings bode well for the development of transitional programs and services. However, the academic needs of students with mild disabilities cannot be totally dismissed. Adults with learning disabilities (mean age 23 years, 2 months) reported significant problems with basic academic skills (e.g., reading, math, spelling, and written composition) (Hoffman et al., 1987). In the same survey, employers viewed reading disabilities as deleterious to vocational adjustment. The persistence of academic deficiencies argues for comprehensive school programming for an array of adult needs. Although three of the models discussed—basic skills, compensatory, and tutorial—have a strong academic focus, four models—basic skills, compensatory, tutorial, and learning strategies—do not address many of the transition issues raised in this text. The two exceptions, the vocational and functional curricular models, partially address the transition needs of the student who is mildly disabled. A conceptualization of an appropriate and comprehensive transition model has been presented.

"The achievement of satisfactory transition outcomes depends upon the quality and appropriateness of both the high school curriculum and the transition services provided to help students achieve their goals" (Benz & Halpern, 1987, p. 507). Special education programs that are isolated and insular and deal with immediate curricular issues only, as do most of the secondary models commonly associated with the secondary school, will not adequately prepare students for successful transition into their adult lives. Transitional programs must be future oriented; that is, their success or failure can only be determined sometime after the students leave the school setting. In regular education, the adult accomplishments of graduates is seen as a positive reflection on the schools from which those students came. The noteworthy endeavors and accomplishments of former students are followed for years after graduation. Special education has not followed this tradition. Graduation or the completion of the academic career terminates not only the school's responsibility but also interest in the future status and pursuits of special education students. Follow-up, when it occurs, usually extends only as far as the initial job placement, and it is usually conducted for research purposes by university researchers and not by secondary schools that have any real interest in the status of their special education graduates.

There is a growing realization that the acid test of success or failure lies in the adult accomplishments of our special education graduates no less than in the adult accomplishments of regular education graduates. The bleak statistics on the rate of unemployment, underemployment, socialization difficulties, involvement in the criminal justice system, and so forth, clearly indicate that special education has a long way to go toward achieving meaningful success. In these early stages of development, insight into the essential components of effective transition programs is valuable for those educators who must create programs where none exist or improve programs already under way. Descriptions of the essential components of effective transitional programs follow.

Assessment

The assessment component of the transitional program should help identify the appropriate instructional options for the individual student. Program options should address a diverse range of postschool pursuits, since postsecondary school options for students who are mildly disabled minimally include continued academic training, vocational and/or technical training, military service, and competitive employment (Benz & Halpern, 1987). Assessment must also go beyond academic skills and aptitudes to include student personality and interests. Adequate assessment will provide the basis for the matching of student to job and personality type to job type. Vocational assessment of the disabled has stressed the former and generally overlooked the latter. In addition, vocational assessment has been notoriously restricted and biased by the supposed identification of "job aptitudes" that are more properly reflections of an individual's experience rather than innate ability.

Cummings and Maddux (1985, 1987) and Heller (1981), among others, decry the stereotypical assignment of individuals who are disabled into a very narrow range of job options. The outcomes of a survey of employment patterns in Mississippi among persons who are mildly mentally retarded reported by Plue (1984) is relevant to this issue. Data on 3,177 individuals collected over a 6-year period reveal that the jobs in which those with disabilities were most often placed required "unskilled or semiskilled" work involving physical and concrete tasks that emphasized "sorting, motor speed, manipulation of parts, separating, matching, assembly and tool use" (p. 26). Jobs of this type are all too commonly the lot of persons with disabilities.

Cummings and Maddux (1987) suggest that the use of Holland's theory of personality and career choice offers "a basis for formulating ways of looking at handicapped individuals in a nonstereotypic manner" (p. 5). Holland's theory posits six categories of personality and job environment: realistic, investigative, artistic, social, enterprising, and conventional. The jobs identified by Plue (1984) as prevalent fall, for the most part, into Holland's "realistic" category. Cummings and Maddux (1987) found a similar pattern in job placements of 50 adults who had borne the label of learning disabilities during their school years. Cummings and Maddux (1987) also found that the range of vocational personality and interests were as diverse among a group of 96 students who were learning disabled as they were among a comparison group of nondisabled individuals.

It is obvious that the job placements found in the "realistic" category represent a very restrictive range of employment opportunities. If job success and satisfaction are tied to the match between job type and personality type—and the evidence points to this conclusion—vocational assessment needs to be expanded to include student personality characteristics and interests. The restriction of persons with disabilities to one type or category of vocational placements has no justification; in fact, it is contradicted by the available research evidence. (Better methods of vocational assessment involving job experience are described in Part III.)

Social Skills Training

The importance of social skills, both on and off the job, cannot be overemphasized. Lack of adequate social skills for the job site is a major obstacle to successful employment among adults with disabilities (Alley & Deshler, 1979; Gardner, Beatty, & Gardner, 1984; Irvine, Goodman, & Mann, 1978; Lignugaris/Kraft, Rule, Salzberg, & Stowitschek, 1986; White, 1985). The importance of social skills is obvious not only to prospective employers but also to persons with disabilities themselves who feel the impact of inadequate social skills.

In a study involving 560 18- to 36-year-old students who were learning disabled, social relationships and skills were identified as the area of greatest need for assistance (Chelser, 1982). Work-related social problems exhibited include getting along with coworkers or bosses, inability to accept responsibility for one's own life and career, a tendency to blame others for one's own failures, lack of understanding of self-related work problems, and inappropriate work attitudes (Gardner et al., 1984). The list of social skill deficits specifically associated with people who are mildly disabled includes inability to make friends (Fafard & Haubrich, 1981; Gray, 1981), dissatisfaction with family relationships (White et al., 1980), restricted range of social contacts (Fafard & Haubrich, 1981), and a variety of emotional and psychological problems. One could easily extend the composite list, but we believe the point is well made.

In light of the importance of social development for people with disabilities, Cummings and Maddux (1987) deplore the "cooling" of interest in social skills training and the fickleness of federal funding priorities. They believe that federal funding policies create "hot topics" and short-term funding rather than long-term programs. They are concerned that social skills training may be ignored or underemphasized rather than recognized as an essential component of secondary-level transitional programming. (Social skills training is addressed further in Part IV.)

Parental Involvement

Parents must continue to be the primary advocates for their children through their secondary school years. Unfortunately, the level of parental involvement at the secondary level tends to be low (Benz & Halpern, 1987), yet active parental involvement is even more important as the entitlements guaranteed under PL 94-142 cease to exist after the student leaves school. This change in the rules is an important issue for parents and students to understand.

During the school years, particular rights of parents and children are protected under federal legislation, most notably PL 94-142, and both parents and school personnel have an advocacy role to play. The advocacy role of the parent is apparent; that of the school is less so. But PL 94-142 specifies that school districts shall engage in child find activities and provide appropriate programs and services, and it permits schools to initiate the due process mechanism to compel evaluation and placements when parents are reluctant or opposed to special education for a child clearly in need of such services. The schools can initiate due process actions on behalf of children even if parents cannot or will not do so, and many do take on this advocacy responsibility.

Beyond the age of 21 or at the point of termination of the school program, the guarantees and protection of PL 94-142 and the central organization of the school give way to a broad array of agencies, institutions, service providers, and numerous and varied sets of regulations. In addition, and perhaps most important, the entitlement factor is gone. The adult with a disability must take the initiative to seek out services in his or her own behalf. Many service providers do not actively seek clientele; rather, they respond only to client-initiated requests for service. Many service providers require cooperation from the individual and/or family as a condition for providing services. And many service providers only carry on programs to the extent that funding is available. The agencies, institutions, and various providers do not have the same seek, find, and serve obligations as the public schools. Such a complex and complicated network of agencies can overwhelm the individual with mild disabilities. Benz and Halpern (1987) stress that in the transitional process parents must still serve as the advocates for their child and take on the role of case manager as well.

Increased parental involvement throughout the school career of the student with a disability would help diminish the problem of unrealistic parental expectations. Cummings and Maddux (1987) discuss this problem at length. They feel that parents of students who are mildly disabled often hold unrealistic expectations, expectations that may be too low but more often too high. The parents of a student with a severe learning disability who insist on only continued academic programming (basic skills or tutorial model) are creating a situation that is potentially devastating for the student and disappointing to the family. Critical time during the secondary school years may be lost, as well as the opportunity to prepare the student for more appropriate and productive postschool endeavors. A well-designed transitional program will address the needs of parents as well as those of their children, and parents can provide much needed continuity.

Transition Planning

According to Benz and Halpern (1987) "Effective transition planning formalizes a question asking process directed at determining what the student will be doing, where he or she will be living, and what type of support will be needed to accomplish his or her goals" (p. 508). Clearly, the transition process is guided by the postschool goals of the student and family. The schools have a critical role to play in the transition planning process.

One measure of a school's transition services can be found in individual education plan (IEP) documents. In an exploratory study of the vocational components, vocational goals, and vocational assessment in the IEPs of educable mentally impaired (EMI) and learning disabled (LD) students, Cobb and Phelps (1983) found that fewer than half of the IEPs for these students contained at least one vocationally related annual goal. Vocational goals were more often found in the IEPs of the EMI students than in those of the LD students. As to placement options, the majority of the students (51.1%) were placed in special vocational classes; placements in special work study programs was the second placement choice (30.3%), followed by placements in regular vocational education classes (16.2%).

The data certainly suggest that students are being placed into vocational programs without delineation of appropriate vocational goals. The data also indicate that the full impact of the least restrictive environment has yet to be felt in the realm of vocational education. No doubt the lack of integration for students with disabilities in regular vocational education training programs is a holdover from the extremely restrictive policies used to bar those students from participation. It will take time to overcome this legacy of discrimination and teach vocational educators how to accommodate the needs of students with special needs. A significant shift in the placement of the majority of students with mild disabilities from specialized and segregated programs to integrated regular education programs with support services will be an important and tangible indication of progress in transition services.

Finally, the Cobb and Phelps (1983) study reveals extremely limited involvement of vocational education personnel in the team planning process and limited vocational assessment data. The authors conclude that vocational service delivery models being created by school personnel are "more oriented toward meeting administrative rather than individual student needs" (p. 63).

The schools bear a major responsibility for transition planning, but they do not bear the entire burden. As students phase out of the educational arena, other agencies and service providers assume the primary role in providing ongoing support and service. A statewide survey of secondary-level administrators, teachers, and parents of high school students with mild disabilities provides some useful data (Benz & Halpern, 1987). The authors report that two-thirds of the administrators felt that transitional services were important, but only one-third of these same administrators believed that it was important for the school district to assume responsibility for transitional services. Many authorities who address the organizational and structural issues involved in the provision of transitional services stress the need for the designation and creation of a transition team with responsibility for coordinating and monitoring services if effective transition is to occur (Benz & Halpern, 1987; Cox, Frank, Hocutt, & Kuligowski, 1984; Johnson, McLaughlin, & Christenson, 1982; Wright, Padilla, & Cooperstein, 1981).

Interagency Agreements

Another essential component of transitional planning at the secondary level is the existence of interagency agreements. Clearly, students' need for support does not end with graduation. Linkages to those agencies with the resources to provide the services needed must be forged while the student is still in school. Formal agreements can greatly enhance and facilitate the provision of services for the secondary school graduates. Unfortunately, the data show that formal written agreements are the exception rather than the rule (Ballantyne, McGee, Patton, & Cohen, 1984; Benz & Halpern, 1987; Cox et al., 1984).

Those who favor the development of interagency agreements face a variety of obstacles; these "restraining forces" have been discussed by many authors (Elder & Magrab, 1980; Johnson et al., 1982). They vary from a lack of a centralized data base and variability in client eligibility to competition among existing institutions. (The reader is referred back to chap. 5 in which barriers to transition are discussed within a systems framework.) Despite the obstacles, the task of developing interagency agreements must go forward. Interagency collaboration at the federal level (e.g., the "Memorandum of Understanding" between the Office of Special Education and the Office of Civil Rights to coordinate services to states in the implementation of PL 94-142 and PL 93-112, Section 504) should serve as a model to spur interagency cooperation and coordination of service delivery systems at the state and local levels. The potential benefits of interagency cooperation and coordination of service delivery systems will not only help students with disabilities but include economic benefits for the community at large (Johnson et al., 1982).

Teacher's Role

The special education teacher at the secondary level is a central figure in the transitional planning process. Many administrators and teachers believe that the special education teacher is the individual to whom responsibility for coordinating transitional services should be delegated (Benz & Halpern, 1987; Okolo & Sitlington, 1986). But there is little discussion as to how the teacher is to fulfill the responsibilities of this important task. Teachers work under the provisions of contracts and job descriptions that clearly designate them as instructional personnel. The realities of day-to-day teaching bind them to their classrooms and teaching rosters. The coordination of transitional planning and services would expand the traditional classroom-bound role of the teacher into a managerial, possibly quasi-administrative role. Unless provisions are made to alter teachers' schedules and specialized training is provided, teachers may find themselves caught between old and new responsibilities—and coming up short on both. Alternatives to merely "adding on" transition-related responsibilities to the role of special education teachers include the development of new professional positions within school staffing patterns specifically to provide and coordinate transitional services (e.g., transition facilitators [Palmer, Velleman, & Shafer, cited in Chadsey-Rusch, 1988] or creative employment specialists [Winking, DeStefano, & Rusch, 1988]) and the development of transitional teams that support the entire school-based transitional effort (Gill & Edgar, 1990). (The reader is referred back to chaps. 4 and 6 for fuller discussion of these issues.)

Follow-up

A glaring weakness in school transitional services is the lack of systematic follow-up of students. Follow-up is essential to the monitoring and evaluation of program effectiveness. Observations and insights gleaned from follow-up studies provide direction for the improvement of secondary programs and services. The number of follow-up studies available at this time is still limited, but additional research reports seem to appear in the professional journals with every new issue. The data we have are beginning to give us a picture of the lives of individuals with disabilities after they leave school (Birenbaum & Re, 1979; Brimer & Rouse, 1978; Hasazi, Gordon, & Roe, 1985; Hasazi, Gordon, Roe, Hull, et al., 1985; Hasazi, Johnson, Hasazi, Gordon, & Hull, 1989; Mithaug, Horiuchi, & Fanning, 1985; Rogan & Hartman, 1990; Vetter, 1983; Zigmond & Thornton, 1985).

The follow-up studies that have been done emphasize vocational outcomes for the most part. We believe that this is a very narrow perspective of postschool adjustment. A notable exception is a paper by Horn, O'Donnell, and Vitulano (1983) in which the authors review long-term follow-up studies of adults with learning disabilities from 1960 to the early 1980s. In 10 of the studies the researchers assessed vocational adjustment; 8 of these reported average or above-average attainment levels for the majority of the former students with learning disabilities using the general population as the standard for comparison. Fifteen of the 17 (88%) studies reviewed revealed that basic skill deficits continue among this population. Five researchers considered emotional-behavioral functioning, three reported poor functioning, and two reported good emotional-behavioral adjustment.

More recent follow-up studies generally identify employment-related problems, for instance, high frequency of part-time jobs (Fafard & Haubrich, 1981; Hasazi, Gordon, & Roe, 1985; Mithaug et al., 1985), low job satisfaction, and low job status (Vetter, 1983; White, Schumaker, Warner, Alley, & Deshler, 1980), and unemployment (Hasazi, Gordon, & Roe, 1985; Mithaug et al.,

1985). More follow-up research that embodies a broad perspective of all the important areas of adult functioning is sorely needed.

❦ ❦ ❦

MODEL SECONDARY-BASED TRANSITIONAL PROGRAMS

There are two broad types of transitional programs for students who are mildly disabled. One type is concerned with assisting these students, primarily those who are learning disabled, to gain admittance and succeed in programs of higher education at community colleges and universities. Transitional programs of this kind are numerous and widespread around the country; they will be discussed at length in chapter 10.

The second type of transitional program is concerned with less academically oriented students and their preparation for adult life. Transitional programs of this type are a recent phenomenon, spurred by the growing awareness of the needs of students who are mildly disabled. They are few in number and represent innovative and pioneering efforts to meet the needs of a large population of special needs students. The non-college-oriented programs about which we have adequate information are limited in number and so diverse in their approaches to the transitional process that there is not, at this time, any viable way to categorize them.

At this early stage of program development it is more appropriate merely to provide brief descriptions of selected transitional programs culled from the available literature. Three model programs will be described here, and other programs are detailed in varying degrees of specificity in Parts III and IV. Only programs clearly earmarked for students with mild disabilities and that include initial data on student outcomes are noted. It was not our purpose to rehash information regarding transitional programming for the moderately or severely impaired, as a large body of literature exists and many authors have written extensively on this topic. We sought instead to ferret out information regarding new and innovative approaches to transitional programming for youths with mild disabilities based on our belief that successful programs for this population will differ in significant respects from those designed for the more impaired student.

Skyline Vocational Training Project

The primary goal of this program (White, Smith, Meers, & Callahan, 1985) is to help disabled students make the transition from school to gainful employment. The project embodies a very strong commitment to community-referenced employment opportunities with frequent job openings and projected growth.

The Skyline Vocational Training Project is being carried out in the Great Falls School District, an agriculturally based community in rural north central Montana. The effects of economic recession in 1982 called attention to deficiencies within the existing comprehensive vocational work-study program. Two major problems were evident: (a) many students with learning disabilities were finding employment in occupations that did not match their interests or abilities, and the jobs were limited as to type with little opportunity for further training and advancement; and (b) lower functioning students with employability deficits (e.g., poor attendance record, poor grooming habits) frequently were unable to get or keep jobs and were falling back into sheltered employment with little hope of permanent gainful employment. To respond to these problems, project personnel combined the successful practices from both vocational and special education. "The blending of vocational and special education practices enabled the staff to interface with the community in a new way while retaining the instructional methods which have been applied successfully to the classroom with disabled learners" (White et al., p. 16).

An area labor market survey, a vocational strategy, revealed employment opportunities in the Great Falls area as well as emerging national employment trends. Students thus were trained for jobs in their immediate geographical region as well as for those available nationwide. Ten occupational training areas were selected: auto parts clerk, bus person, electrical assembly, janitor-sanitizer, punchcard and ticket builder, cashier, grocery courtesy clerk, fast foods worker, medical records filing clerk, and motel-hotel housekeeper. Training stations were built to correspond to the 10 vocational areas. An advisory council helped identify the critical work factors for each occupation. These in turn became the foundation for the Vocational Skills Training Model.

Prototype curricula were developed. Students were first trained at the simulated work stations prior to being placed in work sites in the community. Two methodologies from special and regular education were utilized to enhance the "power" of the instructional program, namely precision teaching and direct instruction. These instructional methodologies are widely used in special and regular education, and their effectiveness is well documented (Englert, 1984; Gersten, 1985; Goodman, 1990).

Student training commenced in 1983 in the simulated training stations. Each student received an orientation and comprehensive assessment and was assigned to an appropriate training station. Intensive instruction followed. After demonstrating competency on required skills, the students were placed in work sites in local businesses, and generalization training commenced. Employers certified when students had acquired the skills needed to function successfully in the occupation. The final phase of the training program involved identification of potential employers and assistance in job seeking.

Program evaluation was based on comparison of student employment outcomes for the 5 years preceding the project and the outcomes for students who had had the opportunity to participate in the project. Permanent private sector placements for hard-to-place students increased from an average of 2.2 (range of one to four placements per year over a 5-year period) to 9.0 placements during the project's first year of implementation. The number of students employed in the private sector increased from a 5-year average of 16 to 28 placements during the first year of operation. Terminations remained about the same (18.2 vs. 18) for both student groups, but only two of the terminated students had participated in the training project. Other findings revealed increased wage levels, a greater variety of job placements, and permanent career-ladder positions for a greater proportion of graduated students from the work-study program.

The Skyline Vocational Training Project has a unidimensional focus on vocational preparation. The data suggest that the project has enjoyed a measure of success in its mission to help students with mild disabilities make a successful transition from school to gainful employment. The intensive training of students for community-referenced entry-level occupations, which offers hope of advancement, is a strong feature of the project. The collaboration between vocational and special education sectors is another strong point, as is the selection and utilization of proven instructional methods to more effectively teach vocational content and skills to learners with disabilities.

Job Training and Tryout Model

The Job Training and Tryout Model (JT&T) (Neubert & Tilson, 1987; Neubert, Tilson, & Ianacone, 1989) is a time-limited, collaborative transitional model for individuals who are learning disabled or mildly mentally retarded. The model, initiated in 1984, encompasses four phases of transitional planning and instruction.

Phase 1 involves the utilization of previous assessment data and development of an individualized employment success plan (IESP). From a base of existing data supplemented by additional assessment of job-relevant aptitudes, interests, and dexterity, JT&T staff develop an initial IESP that is revised or expanded as needed.

Phase 2 involves employability skills training (EST). Project participants are engaged in an 8-week-long instructional program focused on job-seeking skills and exploration of postsecondary training and employment opportunities in the local community. The training is conducted in an adult training facility. There is an emphasis on appropriate adult behavior throughout the project's activities. The EST curriculum is focused on four major topics: "(1) occupational and self awareness; (2) job seeking skills; (3) personal, social and work adjustment skills; and (4) effective communication and decision making skills" (Neubert & Tilson, 1987, p. 5).

At the conclusion of the EST, a plan is developed for placing participants in job tryouts within the local business community. The IESP is reviewed and amended. Parental involvement and interagency collaboration are stressed. Students are engaged in two 6-week job tryouts, 10 to 12 hours per week for which they receive a tuition stipend. The job tryouts serve several important purposes:

1. To expose participants to new occupational experiences;
2. To assess the participant's work, social, and personal skills in a real work environment (situational assessment);
3. To expose employers to this population as potential and viable workers;

4. To gather additional data useful in making job placement decisions; and
5. To provide participants with references and work experiences to be documented on their resumes. (Neubert & Tilson, 1987, p. 5)

After two job tryouts, JT&T staff, the student, his or her parents, and the vocational rehabilitation counselor confer. Based on the student's job tryout performance, a plan for job placement is devised. The JT&T staff provide assistance to the student in his or her job search.

Phase 3 involves the actual placement of the student in a job site. A JT&T transition specialist-trainer or employment specialists help the student at the job site and maintain weekly contact with the employer. Employers and participants are encouraged to contact the JT&T staff person if any job-related problems arise. The JT&T staffer will act as mediator when required to do so. A variety of job-related problems and/or work adjustment problems did, in fact, come to light, most of which were related to inappropriate work and social behaviors, not task-related problems. Most of these problems were identified by the JT&T staff through their follow-up activities rather than by the employer, participants, or parents. An added support mechanism was the Job Club, which participants were required to join once they were employed. The Job Club met one evening per month and provided a forum for discussion of a variety of job-related issues (e.g., promotions, independent living).

Phase 4 encompasses job change and job advancement. Despite the intensity of support provided to each participant, it became apparent that the time-limited nature of the JT&T project was a detriment. For persons who are mildly disabled, changes in job status or job situation ought to be expected as part of the normal course of career development. The reasons for job changes may vary from terminations initiated by the employer to the participant's desire for an improved working situation (e.g., better wages, hours, location). Individuals with mild disabilities need assistance to manage job changes. It became apparent to the JT&T staff that their students need access to ongoing but periodic assistance. Such a support system would help many workers with mild disabilities to move beyond entry-level jobs.

Neubert et al. (1989) provide much descriptive data on the employment patterns of 66 students with mild disabilities who participated in the JT&T project. All of the participants were in high school special education placements with an exceptionality label of either severe learning disability or mild mental retardation. Their IQ scores (WAIS or WISC-R) fell between 50 and 95, with a mean of 73. Thirty-nine participants were females, and 27 were males. The mean age of the group was 22 years. Forty-four percent of the participants were learning disabled, whereas 56% of the group was considered mildly mentally retarded. The mean reading grade level was 4 to 9 (range 1–3 to 9–9), and the mean math achievement level was 4 to 4 (range 1–4 to 11–0).

The majority of the initial placements were in the clerical and sales sector (48%) and service sector (25%). A variety of job types accounted for the remaining placements. Wages ranged from a low of $3.35 to a high of $6.09 per hour; the mean wage level was $4.40 per hour. Fifty percent of the initial placements were part-time, and therefore many of the participants did not receive health or medical benefits through their employment. The amount of staff time devoted to on-the-job support over a 4-week period steadily decreased from an average of 4.7 hours to 47 minutes per week. There was considerable variability among the participants in the level of staff support required. The highest weekly amount for any participant was 12.5 hours; the lowest was 5 minutes. From the first to the fourth week, there was an 83% decrease in the amount of JT&T staff time devoted to on-the-job support. Job-related difficulties did occur for 49 of the 66 participants; 92% were task related, 71% involved work-adjustment skills, and 12% were health related. (The percentages exceed 100% because some participants exhibited multiple problems.) Most problems were identified by the JT&T staff.

Job retention is of major concern. For the purposes of this project, job retention was defined as "a participant's ability to secure a full- or part-time remunerative job and to remain employed continuously from the time of initial placement" (Neubert et al., 1989, p. 498). Job changes were permitted provided the time lapse between jobs did not exceed 1 month. The mean length of time that participants remained on their initial job placements was 10 months. Of the 45 participants who had the opportunity for at least 1 year of employment within the time frame of the project, 64% remained employed for 1 year. Sixteen (of the 45 participants) were terminated or quit their jobs and did not regain employment. Of the 29 participants who remained continuously employed for 1 year, 15 sought assistance from the JT&T staff to find alternate employment. Five to 10 hours of staff time per participant were devoted to helping participants locate new jobs and for on-the-job support during the first day or two in the new work situation. Participants' reasons for changing jobs varied: five were fired because of work adjustment problems, four were laid off as a result of budget cuts, four participants quit in favor of better job opportunities, one participant quit because of an inability to maintain the work pace, and there was one lateral move within the same company.

The descriptive data highlight some of the employment issues of particular importance. Underemployment is a reality for many persons who are mildly disabled. Efforts are needed to help such persons who are capable of doing so to improve their job status and as a result maintain a reasonable level of job satisfaction. Time-limited programs can exacerbate the problem of underemployment by failing to provide the pattern of assistance that persons with mild disabilities require. It is evident that job changes are a natural part of the job process and can be a means to better jobs, higher wages, and so forth. Persons with mild disabilities need access to periodic support, not just initial intensive assistance to achieve their first job placement. Neubert et al. (1989) state, "Therefore transition or employment outcomes should be viewed in terms of economic self-sufficiency, not simply as an individual's ability to access an initial job" (p. 499).

The Job Training and Tryout Model is primarily concerned with employment of young adults who are mildly disabled. A pattern seems to be emerging among transition programs for those with mild disabilities that attests to the paramount importance attached to employment outcomes. The descriptive data provide invaluable information about employment patterns and highlight the complexity of adequate transitional services for this group. Assumptions that transition from school to work is easier for those who are mildly disabled than for the more severely impaired and that time-limited programs can adequately serve the needs of this population are not supported by the data presented.

Pierce County Vocational/Special Education Cooperative

The Pierce County Vocational/Special Education Cooperative (PCC) (Gill, Cupp, & Lindquist, 1986; Gill & Edgar, 1990) encompasses 12 independent school districts in western Washington state. The purpose of the PCC is "the development of job entry level skills and/or the foundation for postsecondary vocational involvement" (Gill et al., p. 25). The consortium of school districts fosters reciprocal relationships that facilitate the delivery of quality vocational services. An underlying premise of the PCC is that the quality of vocational education is critical to later employment success. Gill and Edgar state:

> If vocational education is to have any meaningful impact on the postschool status of students, the vocational education involvement needs to consist of a carefully planned and implemented sequence of experiences. This needs to include a definable range of options, a sequential offering of course work leading to a marketable set of skills, well-trained vocational and special education teams, a process which promotes communication and planning between vocational and special education personnel, and an ongoing support team. (p. 18)

The goals of the PCC are achieved through the unique organizational and operational structure of the district consortium. The model contains information and strategies that may be useful to others who could benefit from interdistrict cooperative efforts.

A written constitution and by-laws guide the activities of the Cooperative. Special and vocational education are equally represented within the organization. Twenty-four vocational and special educators from the 12 member districts form the nucleus of an advisory committee. Ex officio members of the advisory committee represent a local parent advocacy organization, the district superintendents, and Educational Service District 121, which has oversight responsibility for the PCC regarding legal, fiscal, and other such matters. There are two cochairpersons, one each from special and vocational education, who preside at monthly executive committee meetings and bimonthly advisory committee meetings. There is a program manager supported by monetary contributions from the 12 member districts. State supplemental monies were applied to start-up and excess cost expenditures. The program manager is ultimately responsible to both the Educational Service District 121 and the advisory committee.

The PCC combines inter- and intradistrict functions. Interdistrict functions address data collection, staff development, and on-site consultative assistance. Intradistrict applications allow flexibility and local discretion needed to tailor programs to meet local needs. The combination of inter- and intradistrict functioning has proven to be cost-effective. Cost estimates for the services provided by the PCC were derived on a per student and per teacher basis as part of the Cooperative's National Diffusion Network validation. To duplicate the services provided by the Cooperative, each member district would have to spend approximately an additional $1,700 to match the per pupil and per teacher services (Adelman & Petry, 1989).

The Cooperative initially targeted students with mild disabilities as it commenced operations during the 1983–1984 school year. The sheer number of such students in need of transitional assistance was the justification for this decision. Expansion to other populations in the future is anticipated. The project was guided by six major goals during its first operational year:

1. To establish and maintain a data base
2. To develop and initiate local district-level implementation plans
3. To establish and maintain a vocational/special education resource information center within Pierce County
4. To determine the nature and extent of interagency cooperation/involvement in the career-vocational development of disabled persons
5. To increase vocational education involvement in local district individualized education program development and implementation
6. To explore the related vocational instructor–liaison teacher concept

The second and third years of the project added two dimensions to its mission: (a) a regularly scheduled series of seminars and (b) sponsorship of internships with industry for teachers in the participating districts. The focus of the seminars was interdisciplinary dialogue at the school building level. The internships involved 5 days in an industrial setting for selected teachers with the expectation for substantive changes in classroom practices as a result.

Evaluation of project effectiveness was based on a comparison among PCC graduates with mild disabilities; a baseline group of similar students who had graduated from Pierce County secondary schools during the 3 years prior to the Cooperative's implementation; and a cohort group from the University of Washington Study comprised of students who were mildly mentally retarded, learning disabled, behavior-disordered, and health-impaired and who had graduated from districts throughout the state during the period from 1984 to 1986. Each of the three groups contained 120 students.

Analysis of the data on student employment outcomes revealed that the PCC graduates were employed at a significantly higher level than the UW cohort group. There was no significant difference between the PCC graduates and the PCC baseline group on this variable. However, PCC graduates were employed in more skilled jobs than the PCC baseline group. When data for students with learning disabilities only were examined, the PCC graduates' level of employment exceeded that of both the PCC baseline group and the UW cohort group. The data also revealed that the PCC graduates enrolled in postsecondary education programs at a higher rate than the UW cohort group and at a rate equivalent to that of the PCC baseline group. On degree of engagement (working or in school, or both working and in school), the PCC graduates were significantly more engaged than students in both of the comparison groups. Based on data such as this, Gill and Edgar (1990) conclude that the PCC graduates experienced better postschool outcomes than either of the other comparison groups.

The authors attribute the success of the PCC graduates to well-planned and -implemented vocational education programs. They emphasize that four crucial components underlie the successful collaborative effort between special and vocational education:

- multiple course work options providing sequential experiences leading to marketable skills,
- staff training to fill in the instructional gaps of vocational educators and the knowledge gaps about vocational content and expectations among special educators,
- ongoing staff support,
- open and ongoing communication and planning between vocational and special education.

The PCC transitional program echoes the vocational thrust and concern for employability that we have seen in the preceding model programs. In this instance interdistrict cooperation and interdisciplinary collaboration were mainstays of the venture. Apparently, cooperative ventures of this kind can be both instructionally effective and cost-effective.

❧ ❧ ❧

SECONDARY TRANSITIONAL PROGRAMS: WHERE ARE WE NOW?

Fairweather (1989) has surveyed school districts nationwide to obtain data on the kind and number of traditional and nontraditional transitional services and programs offered to exceptional secondary school students. Traditional vocational services in the study include vocational education, counseling, occupational and physical therapy, and a vocational rehabilitation (VR) staff member assigned to the local educational agency (LEA). Nontraditional transition services include an LEA staff member assigned to help students find job placements and a specially designed transitional program.

The data reveal, not unexpectedly, the prevalence of traditional, vocationally oriented services. More than 50% of all secondary LEAs provide at least one of the traditional vocational services. Less than 50% of all LEAs offer at least one transition-related service. Approximately 33% of all LEAs claim to have a staff member who helps students find jobs. And 45% of the LEAs report having a transitional program. The figures on service availability speak to both the availability *and* absence of services. If 33% of the LEAs report the employment of a staff member who helps locate jobs for students with disabilities, then approximately 67% of the surveyed LEAs have no such staff person. Fairweather (1989) has found that the availability of traditional and nontraditional services are related to district size and wealth. Services of any kind are more likely to be found in larger districts and districts with a higher per pupil expenditure.

These data reveal that secondary school transitional services for students who are mildly disabled are far below the level needed and, further, that transition programs are not, nor are they likely to be, equitably distributed across school districts. The influence of district size and wealth on availability, and thereby access, to transitional services has implications for future program/service development. Smaller and less wealthy districts, and rural school districts in particular, may lack the resources to implement appropriate and demonstrably effective transitional programs. In the absence of resource allocations or innovative approaches to service delivery to overcome economic disparities, students' access to transitional services and the quality of services provided may be determined simply by virtue of the district of residence (Fairweather, 1989).

The status quo represents both problems and opportunities. A widespread lack of services and inequitable distribution of emerging transitional programs and services are problems already. As discussed earlier, equitable access to appropriate and effective transitional services for all students with disabilities may be a major problem as transitional models and programs evolve. Also, we have little insight into the comparative effectiveness of different transitional services or the most effective services to meet the needs of subsets of students. We cannot assume that one model will serve all students who are mildly disabled. Differentiation in response to student diversity is likely to be essential for maximally effective service delivery.

Another problem involves the many individuals with mild disabilities who will "miss the boat" on transitional services and whose adult quality of life will be the worse for it. The speed with which school districts gear up for transitional programs can diminish the number of students who will be adversely affected.

❧ ❧ ❧

SUMMARY

A variety of instructional models are currently available for secondary students with mild disabilities. Instructional models can be viewed in terms of the amount of time students spend in special versus regular education and the degree of specialization and individualization of methodology and curriculum. The more restrictive and/or specialized the curriculum, the farther removed from regular education the particular instructional program is likely to be. Instructional programs can also be gauged in terms of transitional programming, that is, the extent to which instruction adequately prepares students for their postschool lives. Most secondary curricular approaches are still strongly biased toward traditional academic programming. Some, notably the functional curriculum and vocational curriculum, are more closely aligned with the emergent perspective of transition. But neither the functional nor the vocational curricular model, as currently conceived, provides adequate training for the full range of adult roles for which students with mild disabilities must be prepared.

A full complement of traditional and nontraditional instructional and supportive services will be needed to fully prepare individuals who are mildly disabled for transition. The research data reveal that transitional services and programs are generally in an early stage of development. Survey data indicate that district size and wealth are tied to the level and range of transitional services provided (Fairweather, 1989). Students who reside in larger and wealthier districts have a distinct advantage and enjoy greater access to transitional services. This finding suggests that concerted efforts will be needed to counteract the effects of the endemic educational inequality that characterizes public education in our society. Equal and necessary access to transitional services for all students who require it may thus be ensured.

Opportunities lie in the mobilization of forces in support of transitional programming to develop quality programs and services from the outset. Transitional services for students who are mildly disabled are nonexistent in many school districts. But it is sometimes easier to create a new structure where none exists than to dismantle and replace present structures. The need for transitional services is beyond question, and the urgency is fueled by federal legislation and initiatives as well as stark data on adult outcomes for those who did not have the benefit of transitional programs during their secondary school years.

The literature on transition, by no means complete, provides guidelines for program and service development:

1.   The postsecondary school options for students who are mildly disabled must expand to encompass a broad spectrum of vocational and educational training opportunities. The interests and personalities of these students are as varied as those found among nondisabled students. Options available must not be based on stereotypical ideas about what people who are mildly disabled can and cannot do, as such thinking is too easily translated into policies and procedures that restrict what those who are disabled are permitted to do.

2.   Transitional programs must prepare students with mild disabilities to function in all areas of adult living. The narrow focus on vocational training does nothing to prepare students for their adult roles as citizens, parents, and so forth.

3.   Current instructional models emphasize a traditional curricular orientation (i.e., continued academic skill development, as in the basic skills model, or

support to the regular curricular program, as in the tutorial model). According to Okolo and Sitlington (1986), youth with mild disabilities, particularly those with learning disabilities, are unemployed or underemployed for three primary reasons: "(a) lack of interpersonal skills, (b) lack of job-related academic skills, [and] (c) lack of specific vocational skills to perform more than entry level service jobs" (p. 143). Most of the current secondary service models do not address these skill development needs. Even vocational programs do not adequately address all of the job-related skill development needs, and the skill training provided may only prepare students for a very restricted range of low-level jobs.

The challenge of merging secondary school programs with transitional services looms large before us. Special educators, in cooperation with regular and vocational educators, should take advantage of the current focus on transitional services to develop and implement programs for youths with mild disabilities. Transitional services have had a pronounced effect on the education of students who are moderately and severely impaired. The sheer numbers of students who are mildly disabled suggests that transitional services can have a greater and more visible impact for both them and the community at large. The preparation of all students to lead productive and meaningful lives is the common goal of special, vocational, and regular education (Benz & Halpern, 1987). Every student goes through the transition process; some just need more help than others.

Three model programs have been described. All three emphasize employability and job placement; one also offers a promising model for interdistrict cooperative services. Initial data on student outcomes are encouraging, yielding evidence of improved performance for students with mild disabilities on important outcome variables (e.g., range of job placements, wage levels, job stability, continuation of training beyond high school, attainment of career-ladder positions). Data on student outcomes also yield valuable feedback for program planners. For example, the data reveal the inadequacy of time-limited programs for students with mild disabilities. Many such students require periodic assistance over an extended period of time, as opposed to concentrated but short-term services over a limited period of time, to help with the job changes that inevitably occur as they do among the nondisabled population.

Overall, secondary academic programming and transitional programs have a long way to go in fulfilling the needs of youths who are mildly disabled. Interface between academic and transitional programming is essential to the development of focused and individually appropriate programs of instruction that will give students the skills they require for independent and satisfying adult lives.

REFERENCES

Adelman, N. E., & Petry, C. A. (1989). *Case study of the Pierce County Vocational/Special Education Cooperative*. Paper prepared for National Assessment of Vocational Education, U.S. Department of Education. Washington, DC: Policy Studies Associates.

Alley, G., & Deshler, D. (1979). *Teaching the learning disabled adolescent: Strategies and methods*. Denver: Love.

Almeida, D. A. (1988). Teaching content area courses in the resource room. *ACLD Newsbriefs, 174*, 5–6.

Archer, A. L., & Isaacson, S. L. (1990). Teaching others how to teach strategies. *Teacher Education and Special Education, 13*(2), 63–72.

Arter, J. A., & Jenkins, J. R. (1977). Examining the benefits and prevalence of modality considerations in special education. *Journal of Special Education, 11*(3), 281–298.

Ballantyne, D., McGee, M. Patton, S., & Cohen, D. (1984) *Report on cooperative programs for transition from school to work* (Contract No. 300-83-0158). Waltham, MA: Harold Russell Associates.

Battle, J. (1979). Self-esteem of students in regular and special classes. *Psychological Reports, 44*, 212–214.

Benz, M. R., & Halpern, A. S. (1987). Transition services for secondary students with mild disabilities: A statewide perspective. *Exceptional Children, 53*(6), 507–514.

Birenbaum, A., & Re, M. A. (1979). Resettling mentally retarded adults in the community—Almost 4 years later. *American Journal of Mental Deficiency, 83*(4), 323–329.

Boersma, F. J., & Chapman, J. W. (1981). Academic self-concept, achievement expectations, and locus of control in elementary learning-disabled children. *Canadian Journal of Behavioral Science, 13*, 349–358.

Boyer-Stephens, A., & Kearns, D. (1988). Functional curriculum for transition. *Journal for Vocational Special Needs Education, 11*(1), 13–18.

Brimer, R. W., & Rouse, S. T. (1978). Post-school adjustment: A follow-up of a cooperative program for the educable mentally retarded. *Journal of Special Education and Mental Retardation, 14*, 131–137.

Brozovich, R., & Kotting, C. (1984). Teachers' perceptions of high school special education programs. *Exceptional Children, 50*(6), 548–550.

Carlson, S. A. (1985). The ethical appropriateness of subject-matter tutoring for learning disabled adolescents. *Learning Disabilities Quarterly, 8*(4), 310–314.

Cartwright, G. P., Cartwright, C. A., & Ward, M. E. (1989). *Educating special learners*. Belmont, CA: Wadsworth.

Chadsey-Rusch, J. (1988). Personnel preparation for leadership in transition. *The Journal of Vocational Special Needs Education, 11*(1), 29–32.

Chelser, J. C. (1982). ACLD vocational committee completes survey of LD adults. *ACLD Newsbriefs, 146*(5), 20–23.

Chi, M. T. H. (1981). Interactive roles of knowledge and strategies in development. In S. Chipman, J. Segal, & R. Glaser (Eds.), *Thinking and learning skills: Current research and open questions* (Vol. 2) (pp. 457–483). Hillsdale, NJ: Erlbaum.

Cline, B. V., & Billingsley, B. S. (1991). Teachers' and supervisors' perceptions of secondary learning disabilities programs: A multi-state survey. *Learning Disabilities Research & Practice, 6*(3), 158–165.

Cobb, B., & Hasazi, S. B. (1987). School-aged transition services: Options for adolescents with mild handicaps. *Career Development for Exceptional Individuals, 10*(1), 15–23.

Cobb, R. B. (1983). A curriculum-based approach to vocational assessment. *Teaching*

Exceptional Children, 15(4), 216–219.

Cobb, R. B., & Phelps, L. A. (1983). Analyzing individualized education programs for vocational components: An exploratory study. *Exceptional Children, 50*(1), 62–64.

Cox, J. L., Frank, N. L., Hocutt, A. M., & Kuligowski, B. A. (1984). *An exploration of issues regarding transition services for handicapped students in secondary schools.* Research Triangle Park, NC: Center for Educational Studies, Research Triangle Institute.

Cummings, R. W., & Maddux, C. D. (1985). The Holland theory. *Journal for Vocational Special Needs Education, 8*(1), 3–6, 10.

Cummings, R. W., & Maddux, C. D. (1987). *Career and vocational education for the mildly handicapped.* Springfield, IL: Thomas.

Deshler, D. D., Lowrey, N., & Alley, G. R. (1979). Programming alternatives for LD adolescents: A nationwide survey. *Academic Therapy, 14*(4), 389–397.

Deshler, D. D., & Schumaker, J. B. (1986). Learning strategies: An instructional alternative for low-achieving adolescents. *Exceptional Children, 52*(6), 583–590.

Dowdy, C. A., Carter, J. K., & Smith, T. E. C. (1990). Differences in transitional needs of high school students with and without learning disabilities. *Journal of Learning Disabilities, 23*(6), 343–348.

Edgar, E. (1985). How do special education students fare after they leave school? A response to Hasazi, Gordon and Roe. *Exceptional Children, 51*(6), 470–473.

Edgar, E. (1987). Secondary programming in special education: Are many of them justifiable? *Exceptional Children, 53*(6) 555–561.

Elder, J. O., & Magrab, P. (Eds.). (1980). *Coordinating services for handicapped children: A handbook for interagency collaboration.* Baltimore, MD: Brookes.

Ellis, E. S. (1990). What's so strategic about training teachers to teach strategies? *Teacher Education and Special Education, 13*(2), 59-62.

Englert, C. S. (1984). Effective direct instruction practices in special education settings. *Remedial and Special Education, 5*(2) 38–47.

Ewing, N., & Brecht, R. (1977). Diagnostic/prescriptive instruction: A reconsideration of some issues. *Journal of Special Education, 11*, 323–327.

Fafard, M., & Haubrich, P. (1981). Vocational and social adjustment of learning disabled young adults: A follow-up study. *Learning Disabilities Quarterly, 4*, 122–130.

Fairweather, J. S. (1989). Transition and other services for handicapped students in local education agencies. *Exceptional Children, 55*(4), 315–320.

Gardner, D. C., Beatty, G. J., & Gardner, P. L. (1984). *Career and vocational education for mildly handicapped and disadvantaged youth.* Springfield, IL: Thomas.

Gerber, M. M. (1983). Learning disabilities and cognitive strategies: A case for training or constraining problem solving? *Journal of Learning Disabilities, 16*(5), 255–260.

Gersten, R. (1985). Direct instruction with special education students: A review of evaluation research. *Journal of Special Education, 19*(1) 41–58.

Gill, D., & Edgar, E. (1990). Outcomes of a vocational program designed for students with mild disabilities: The Pierce County Vocational/Special Education Cooperative. *Journal for Vocational Special Needs Education, 12*(3), 17–22.

Gill, H., Cupp, D. E., & Lindquist, D. A. (1986). A consortium of vocational educational and special education. *Journal for Vocational Special Needs Education, 9*(3), 25–28.

Goodman, L. (1990). *Time and learning in the special education classroom.* New York: State University of New York Press.

Goodman, L., & Mann, L. (1976). *Learning disabilities in the secondary school.* New York: Grune & Stratton.

Graham, S., & Harris, K. R. (1989). Improving learning disabled students' skills at composing essays: Self-instructional strategy training. *Exceptional Children, 56,* 201–214.

Gray, R. A. (1981). Services for the LD adult: A working paper. *Learning Disabilities Quarterly, 4*(4), 426–434.

Hall, R. J. (1980). Cognitive behavior modification and information-processing skills of exceptional children. *Exceptional Education Quarterly, 1*(1), 9–15.

Halpern, A. S. (1985). Transition: A look at the foundations. *Exceptional Children, 51,* 479–486.

Harris, K. R., & Pressley, M. (1991). The nature of cognitive strategy instruction: Interactive strategy construction. *Exceptional Children, 57,* 392–404.

Hasazi, S. B., Gordon, L. R., Roe, C. A. (1985). Factors associated with the employment status of handicapped youth exiting high school from 1979 to 1983. *Exceptional Children, 51,* 455–473.

Hasazi, S. B., Gordon, L. R., Roe, C. A., Hull, M., Finck, K., & Salembier, G. A. (1985). A statewide follow-up on post high school employment and residential status of students labeled "mentally retarded." *Education and Training of the Mentally Retarded, 20,* 222–234.

Hasazi, S. B., Johnson, R. E., Hasazi, J. E., Gordon, L. R., & Hull, M. (1989). Employment of youth with and without handicaps following high school: Outcomes and correlates. *Journal of Special Education, 23*(3), 243–255.

Heller, H. W. (1981). Secondary education for handicapped students: In search of a solution. *Exceptional Children, 47*(8), 582–583.

Hermann, B. A. (1990). Teaching preservice teachers how to model thought processes: Issues, problems, and procedures. *Teacher Education and Special Education, 13*(2), 73–81.

Hiebert, B., Wong, B. Y. L., & Hunter, M. (1982). Affective influences on learning disabled adolescents. *Learning Disability Quarterly, 5*(4), 334–343.

Hoffman, F. J., Sheldon, K. L., Minskoff, E. H., Sautter, S. W., Steidle, E. F., Baker, D. P., Bailey, M. B., & Echols, L. D. (1987). Needs of learning disabled adults. *Journal of Learning Disabilities, 20*(1), 43–52.

Horn, W. F., O'Donnell, J. P., & Vitulano, A. (1983). Long-term follow-up studies of learning disabled persons. *Journal of Learning Disabilities, 16,* 542–555.

Houck, C. K., Geller, C. H., & Engelhard, J. (1988). Learning disabilities teachers' perceptions of educational programs for adolescents with learning disabilities. *Journal of Learning Disabilities, 21*(2), 90–97.

Howell, K. W., Kaplan, J. S., & O'Connell, C. Y. (1979). *Evaluating exceptional children: A task-analysis approach.* New York: Merrill/Macmillan.

Irvine, P., Goodman, L., & Mann, L. (1978). Occupational education. In L. Mann, L. Goodman, & J. L. Wiederholt (Eds.), *Teaching the learning-disabled adolescent* (pp. 263–292). Boston: Houghton Mifflin.

Johnson, H. W., McLaughlin, J. N., & Christenson, M. (1982). Interagency collaboration: Driving and restraining forces. *Exceptional Children, 48*(5), 395–399.

Lenz, B. K., & Deshler, D. D. (1990). Principles of strategies instruction as the basis of effective preservice teacher education. *Teacher Education and Special Education, 13*(2), 82–95.

Lignugaris/Kraft, B., Rule, S., Salzberg, C., & Stowitschek, J. (1986). Social interpersonal skills of handicapped and nonhandicapped adults at work. *Journal of Employment Counseling, 23*(1), 20–29.

Marsh, G. E., Gearheart, C. K., & Gearheart, B. R. (1978). *The learning disabled adolescent: Program alternatives in the secondary school.* St. Louis: Mosby.

Masters, L. F., & Mori, A. A. (1986). *Teaching secondary students with mild learning and behavior problems: Method, materials, strategies.* Rockville, MD: Aspen.

McAfee, J. K., & Mann, L. (1982). The prognosis for mildly handicapped students. In T. L. Miller & E. E. Davis (Eds.), *The mildly handicapped student* (pp. 461–496). New York: Grune & Stratton.

McKenzie, R. G. (1991a). Content area instruction delivered by secondary learning disabilities teachers: A national survey. *Learning Disabilities Quarterly, 14,* 115–122.

McKenzie, R. G. (1991b). The form and substance of secondary resource models: Content area versus skill instruction. *Journal of Learning Disabilities, 24*(8), 467–470.

Meers, G. D. (1987). *Handbook of vocational special needs education.* Rockville, MD: Aspen.

Mithaug, D. E., Horiuchi, C. H., & Fanning, P. N. (1985). A report on the Colorado statewide follow-up survey of special education students. *Exceptional Children, 51,* 397–404.

Neubert, D. A., & Tilson, G. P. (1987). The critical stage of transition: A challenge and an opportunity. *Journal for Vocational Special Needs Education, 10*(1), 3–7.

Neubert, D. A., Tilson, G. P., & Ianacone, R. N. (1989). Postsecondary transition needs and employment patterns of individuals with mild disabilities. *Exceptional Children, 55*(6), 494–500.

Okolo, C. M., & Sitlington, P. (1986). The role of special education in LD adolescents transition from school to work. *Learning Disabilities Quarterly, 9,* 141–155.

Palmer, J. T., Velleman, R., & Shafer, D. (1984). *The transition process of disabled youth: A literature review.* Albertson, NY: Human Resources Center.

Plue, W. (1984). Employment patterns of the mildly retarded. *Journal for Vocational Special Needs Education, 7*(1), 23–28.

Pressley, M., Goodchild, F., Fleet, J., & Zajchowski, R. (1989). The challenges of classroom strategies instruction. *Elementary School Journal, 89*(3), 301–342.

Rogan, L. L., & Hartman, L. D. (1990). Adult outcomes of learning disabled students 10 years after initial follow-up. *Learning Disabilities Focus, 5*(2), 91–102.

Rusch, F. R., & Phelps, L. A. (1987). Secondary special education and transition from school to work: A national priority. *Exceptional Children, 53*(6), 487–492.

Sabatino, D. A., & Mann, L. (1982). *A handbook of diagnostic and prescriptive teaching.* Rockville, MD: Aspen.

Schumaker, J. B., Deshler, D. D., Alley, G. R., & Warner, M. M. (1983). Toward the development of an intervention model for learning disabled adolescents: The University of Kansas Institute. *Exceptional Education Quarterly, 4*(1), 45–74.

Sheinker, A., Sheinker, J. M., & Stevens, L. J. (1984). Cognitive strategies for teaching the mildly handicapped. *Focus on Exceptional Children, 17*(1), 1–15.

Sitlington, P. L. (1981). Vocational and special education in career programming for the mildly handicapped adolescent. *Exceptional Children, 47*(8), 592–598.

Smith, T. E. C., Price, B. J., & Marsh, G. E. (1986). *Mildly handicapped children and adults*. St. Paul, MN: West.

Thomas, M. A. (1980). Most productive environment for mentally retarded individuals. *Journal of Research and Development in Education, 13*, 8–14.

Torgesen, J. K. (1979). Factors related to poor performance on memory tasks in reading disabled children. *Learning Disabilities Quarterly, 2*(3), 17–23.

Torgesen, J. K. (1982). The learning disabled child as an inactive learner: Educational implications. *Topics in Learning and Learning Disabilities, 2*(1), 45–52.

U.S. Commission on Civil Rights. (1983). *Accommodating the spectrum of disabilities*. Washington, DC: Author.

Valletutti, P. J., & Bender, M. (1982). *Teaching interpersonal and community living skills: A model for handicapped adolescents and adults*. Baltimore, MD: University Park Press.

Vetter, A. (1983). *A comparison of the characteristics of learning disabled and nonlearning disabled young adults*. Unpublished doctoral dissertation, University of Kansas, Lawrence.

Wehman, P., Kregel, J., & Barcus, J. M. (1985). From school to work: A vocational transition model for handicapped students. *Exceptional Children, 52*(1), 25–37.

Weinstein, C. E., & Mayer, R. E. (1986). The teaching of learning strategies. In M. C. Wittrock (Ed.), *Handbook of research on teaching* (3rd ed., pp. 315–327). New York: Macmillan.

Wells, D., Schmidt, R., Algozzine, B., & Maher, M. (1983). Teaching learning disabled adolescents: A study of selected teacher and teaching characteristics. *Teacher Education and Special Education, 6*, 227–234.

White, W. J. (1985). Perspectives on the education and training of learning disabled adults. *Learning Disabilities Quarterly, 8*, 231–236.

White, W., Schumaker, J., Warner, M., Alley, G., & Deshler, D. (1980). *The current status of young adults identified as learning disabled during their school career* (Research Report No. 21). Lawrence: University of Kansas, Institute for Research in Learning Disabilities.

White, S., Smith, H., Meers, G., & Callahan, J. (1985). The key to transition: Merging vocational and special education. *Journal for Vocational Special Needs Education, 8*(1), 15–18.

Winking, D., DeStefano, L., & Rusch, F. R. (1988). *Supported employment in Illinois: Job coach issues* (Vol. 3). Champaign: University of Illinois, Transition Institute.

Wong, B. Y. L. (1985). Potential means of enhancing content acquisition in learning-disabled adolescents. *Focus on Exceptional Children, 17*(1), 1–8.

Wong, B. Y. L. (1986). Metacognition and special education: A review of a view. *Journal of Special Education, 20*(1), 9–29.

Wong, B. Y. L., & Jones, W. (1982). Increasing metacomprehension in learning disabled and normally achieving students through self-questioning training. *Learning Disabilities Quarterly, 5*, 228–240.

Wright, A. R., Padilla, C., & Cooperstein, R. (1981). *Local Implementation of P.L. 94-142: Third year report of a longitudinal study*. Menlo Park, CA: SRI International.

Wujeck, M. (1981). *Study of secondary special education program effectiveness* (SRI Document No. 24). Menlo Park, CA: SRI International.

Ysseldyke, J. E., & Salvia, J. A. (1974). Diagnostic prescriptive teaching: Two models. *Exceptional Children, 41*, 181–186.

Zigmond, N., & Sansone, J. (1986). Designing a program for the learning disabled adolescent. *Remedial and Special Education, 7*(5),13–17.

Zigmond, N., & Thornton, H. (1985). Follow-up of postsecondary age learning disabled graduates and drop-outs. *Learning Disabilities Research, 1*(1), 50–55.

Chapter 8

❦ ❦ ❦

Academic Assessment and Planning for Transition

A ssessment is an essential part of a comprehensive transition process. Assessment activity provides the critical information and data on which the instructional decision-making process rests (Salvia & Ysseldyke, 1988; Ysseldyke & Algozzine, 1982; Zigmond, Vellacorsa, & Silverman, 1983). Assessment encompasses a broad range of methodologies, instrumentation and practices. Salvia and Ysseldyke state that assessment activity serves five evaluative functions: (a) referral, (b) screening, (c) classification, (d) instructional planning, and (e) evaluation of pupil progress. Many authors have found it useful to dichotomize assessment functions into the two broad categories of assessment for classification and/or placement and assessment for instructional planning (Goodman, 1990; Wallace & Larsen, 1978; Zigmond & Miller, 1986; Zigmond et al., 1983).

Assessment for classification and/or placement is primarily concerned with establishing a student's eligibility for special services, designation of a disability label, and identification of an appropriate placement and/or service delivery option. For example, a student is evaluated, deemed exceptional within the learning disability category, and placed in a part-time resource room program. Assessment activity of this kind relies heavily on formalized testing procedures and standardized test instruments. A number of different professionals are likely to participate in the evaluation of the student, contributing data to the cumulative file and possibly participating in a multidisciplinary teaming.

In contrast, assessment for instructional planning is classroom oriented, with the teacher in the prime diagnostic role. The focus of the ongoing assessment process is the promotion of student performance and the monitoring of student progress toward preset instructional goals in cognitive, social-behavioral, and academic domains. Informal, as opposed to formal, testing procedures will predominate (e.g., criterion referenced, curriculum based, teacher made, direct observation). The choice of specific testing methods will be dictated by the purpose for testing (Cobb, 1983; Salvia &

Ysseldyke, 1988) and the educational utility of the test instruments (i.e., the immediate relevance of the data produced to the ongoing instructional program [Wallace & Larsen, 1978; Wallace & McLaughlin, 1979]). Assessment data fuel a test-teach-test instructional cycle widely accepted as an effective teaching practice among special educators (Zigmond et al., 1983). In Figure 8–1 assessment for the purpose of classification and/or placement is contrasted with assessment for instructional planning, highlighting the differences in test instruments used and outcomes of the two assessment processes.

The special education perspective of assessment, which distinguishes between assessment for classification/placement and assessment for instruction, is gaining acceptance in educational arenas other than special education. Stodden, Meehan, Bisconer, and Hodell (1989), in the realm of vocational assessment, draw a distinction between "diagnosis for placement" and "data collection for instructional programming" (p. 31). Albright and Cobb (1988) interpret the special needs provision of the Carl D. Perkins Act to mean "assessment and planning services that are directly related to the interaction

---

Academic Problem:

Reading difficulties

Assessment for Classification/Placement	Assessment for Instructional Planning
Assessment Tools:	
Individual Intelligence Test	Diagnostic battery of reading skills: phonics, sight-word vocabulary, word attack skills, fluency, etc.
Standardized Reading Achievement	
Individual Reading Inventory	Curriculum-based Reading Inventory
Vision/hearing screening	Interest Inventory
	Direct observation of reading behaviors
Assessment Outcomes:	
Confirmation of severe reading discrepancy	Individual profile of reading strengths and weaknesses
Eligibility for special education	Individual performance data on a variety of reading and related behaviors
Identification of appropriate categorical label and placement option	Identification of instructional level
	Performance data from which to establish long-range goals and instructional objectives

---

Figure 8–1

Assessment for classification/placement versus assessment for planning

between the student and his/her respective vocational curriculum" (p. 13). Cobb and Danehey (1986) espouse an assessment process for vocational transition planning that is "conceptually analogous to special education assessment" (p. 6) and one in which "measurement outcomes must have direct implication for program planning and implementation" (p. 5). Clearly, assessment practices being utilized as part of the transition planning/programming process have much in common with special education assessment methodology.

This chapter will encompass three important assessment and transition planning issues: the current status of assessment in transitional programs, traditional versus emerging transitional assessment practices, and the link between assessment and instructional planning for the individual education program/individual transition plan (IEP/ITP) process. Once again, the strong vocational bias of the transition literature emerges in the subset of literature pertaining to assessment practices. The following discussion draws heavily from the vocational educational literature.

❦ ❦ ❦

TRADITIONAL VERSUS CONTEMPORARY ASSESSMENT

Assessment for transition has been, for the most part, focused on vocational issues. The current literature reveals that vocational assessment for transition is divided between traditional and emergent perspectives of assessment practices. Discussions of vocational assessment have been complicated by controversy over terminology (Cobb, 1983; Cummings & Maddux, 1987; Veir, 1987). A major point of contention involves the terms *evaluation* and *assessment*. Digression into the controversy that surrounds terminology in vocational assessment is beyond the scope of this chapter. Suffice it to say that we concur with others who believe that one evaluates programs and assesses children (Cobb, 1983; Cobb & Larkin, 1985; Cummings & Maddux, 1987). Furthermore, the term *assessment* is compatible with student-oriented assessment under the rubric of assessment for instructional planning. In the discussion that follows, *assessment* will be used in preference to *evaluation*.

Traditional vocational assessment has evolved from an adult services rehabilitation model (Ianacone & Leconte, 1986). The purpose of traditional vocational assessment is to determine the vocational capability of the individual and predict success or failure of the individual or disability group in particular work situations (Stodden & Ianacone, 1981). Terminology differs, but the scope of vocational assessment is generally the same among various authorities (Cummings & Maddux, 1987). Kokaska and Brolin (1985) identify the major components of vocational assessment as clinical assessment, work evaluation, work adjustment, and job site evaluation. The testing domains for vocational evaluation encompass interests, aptitudes, and achievement (Cobb, 1983). Assessment in these three domains addresses the requirement for evaluation of interests, abilities, and special needs as stipulated in the Carl D. Perkins Act (Veir, 1987).

Traditional vocational assessment relies heavily on formal procedures and standardized testing instruments. It is essentially a static process that adheres to a predictive paradigm. Measures of aptitude, interests, and traits at one point in time are used to predict future learning, performance, and adjustment (Veir, 1987). Gugerty and Crowley (1982) point out that the "results of comprehensive but short term evaluations are often of little use in on-going instructional planning" (p. 217).

Veir (1987) terms newer, emerging assessment practices in vocational education as "contemporary" in contrast to the "traditional" practices just described. Contemporary assessment "employs techniques which link assessment to the classroom and the instructional process. Contemporary assessment requires the outcomes to have direct implications for program planning" (p. 220). The Curriculum-based Vocational Assessment (CBVA) Model is at the forefront of evolving transitional planning and assessment practices in vocational education.

Curriculum-based Vocational Assessment

Curriculum-based vocational assessment is "a process for determining students' career development and vocational needs based upon their ongoing performance within existing course content" (Ianacone & Leconte, 1986, p. 116). This approach is viewed as an alternative to commercial assessment programs that capture the status of the student at only one point in time, may or may not have relevance for the student within social and employment contexts, and predict future performance/adjustment with varying degrees of accuracy (Albright & Cobb, 1988; Ianacone & Leconte, 1986; Peterson, 1986). The CBVA Model promotes ongoing data collection, decision making, and program planning within a comprehensive service delivery model (Porter & Stodden, 1986). Ianacone and Leconte delineate a six-step process that provides a structure for the development of a formalized CBVA process within any designated school and community setting. The process is comprehensive and complex in that it addresses student needs and evaluation, identification of key personnel and resources, the community context, as well as development of an operational plan for implementation and evaluation. At each stage of the process, the authors pose key questions to guide other educators wishing to embark on the development of a CBVA approach. (See Figure 8–2 for a presentation of the process in its entirety.)

At the classroom level CBVA focuses on vocationally relevant data on student skills, attitudes, and interests. According to Stodden and Ianacone (1981), vocational assessment should encompass the three components of readiness, assessment, and application. Readiness involves career awareness and exploration in a wide range of career clusters. Next, assessment shifts to in-depth work role assessment and provides important information about the individual's skill level within specific work roles. The individual is given the opportunity to explore various occupational avenues and refine his or her perceptions of specific jobs and related job skills. The final assessment component

1. Identify key development personnel.
   - Who are the key personnel needed to conceptualize, develop, and validate a curriculum-based vocational assessment model?
   - Who are the key personnel needed to operate and develop the vocational assessment model?
   - What disciplines and administrative personnel are critical to implementation and need to be represented?
2. Conduct a comprehensive search of program models, research literature, vocational evaluation/assessment instrumentation, and pertinent legislation.
   - What research is available concerning the efficacy of vocational assessment services in school-based settings?
   - What program models currently exist, and what factors have influenced their effectiveness within the local education community and employment settings?
   - What factors influence validity and reliability in the collection of assessment data?
3. Establish basic considerations for the model based on previous research; analyze and synthesize the programmative needs. These considerations include tenants (i.e., vocational assessment):
   - Should be an integrated part of the total delivery of career/vocational services
   - Should reflect preassessment readiness needs of the student and provide developmental growth information
   - Should be a student-centered process with a career development orientation consisting of experiences to increase one's awareness, exploration, and understanding rather than a strict predictive procedure providing isolated ability data
   - Should be based on the assessed employment needs of the local community and the applicable skills of the student to ensure key validity and efficacy factors contributing to the structure of the model
   - Should measure key situational factors specific to work roles that can be critical determinants for interest and performance
   - Should produce a wide variety of demonstratively useful information that can be assessed and used by several disciplines, the student, and the parents
   - Who should coordinate and use the assessment information to make placement and programming decisions?
   - How will this information be applied to the development of individualized educational and vocational planning and program development?
4. Establish an operational plan to implement the process.
   - Where will vocational assessment activities occur?
   - Who will be assessed?

Figure 8–2

Key steps to curriculum-based vocational assessment

Source: From "Career Development for Exceptional Individuals" by R. N. Ianacone and P. J. Leconte, 1986, *Career Development for Exceptional Individuals, 9*, pp. 117–118. Adapted by permission.

- What information will be collected?
- How will vocational assessment information be collected (instruments, activities, techniques)?
- Who will conduct vocational assessment activities?
- How will the vocational assessment information be gathered and organized?
- Who will be responsible for coordinating information gathering, which includes facilitating, providing support, and monitoring?
- Who will analyze, synthesize, and interpret vocational assessment findings to appropriate decision-making groups?
- What time frame will be used for vocational assessment activities?
- How will data collection be integrated and formalized as part of the instructional process?
- How will the vocational assessment instrumentation be developed?
- What specific competencies and specific related behaviors will be assessed?
- How should the collected data be formatted and displayed for optimal application and use?
- What evaluation criteria will be used to measure competency attainment and behaviors?

5. Pilot and evaluate the CBVA implementation activities.
   - What school(s) and personnel should be involved in field testing?
   - What steps need to be taken (additional inservice training, technical assistance, and ongoing support) to ensure the appropriate climate and expertise for full integration and application of the vocational assessment process in the pilot sites?
   - What criteria will be used to evaluate the process, instrumentation, and overall impact at the pilot site?
   - What modifications need to be made to the process, instrumentation, or support mechanisms as a result of the pilot test?
   - Who will make the modifications?

6. Implement, evaluate, and expand options.
   - What additional steps need to be taken on a systemwide basis for full integration and application of the curriculum-based vocational assessment model and process?
   - What specific evaluation data will be collected?
   - What implementation and evaluation checkpoints need to be established?
   - What additional course and activity settings would yield relevant career and vocational assessment information?
   - What additional steps are needed to assist teachers to view their instructional processes and outcomes in a career or vocational context?

Figure 8–2, *continued*

is that of application, which involves interpretation and evaluation of specific occupational assessment information to enhance the individual's chances for successful employment. Involvement of service providers who will assist the student after conclusion of his or her school program is important at this final phase of the school-based assessment process. The content and emphasis of assessment will vary according to individual needs, abilities, and the mediating influence of community factors (e.g., job possibilities, level of interagency cooperation). The CBVA process "increases the handicapped student's awareness and understanding of self in relation to work" (Porter & Stodden, 1986, p. 123). The ultimate goal is successful integration of the special needs individual into the working world.

The CBVA Model will impact on the classroom teacher who will be called on to demonstrate expertise in a range of classroom and/or curriculum-based assessment (CBA) methodologies and function in a collaborative and cooperative role with others, most notably vocational educators. The collaborative role is not a new one for special education teachers. But collaboration between special and vocational educators to date has been limited. The degree of collaboration required between special and vocational educators to effectively promote successful transition for students with mild disabilities will be a challenge for all.

Proponents of CBVA envision many benefits for students evolving from new assessment approaches. Ianacone and Leconte (1986) highlight the intrinsic benefits that, they believe, result from the CBVA process:

1. Maximizes the likely impact on instruction and curriculum.
2. Internalizes the process with all staff and helps focus on career and vocational outcomes.
3. Allows for the ongoing collection of data during the career development of the student (Cobb & Larkin, 1987).
4. Generates an ongoing career and vocational assessment base that affects and guides the development of the student's individual education plan (Stodden & Ianacone, 1981).
5. Gathers information at various stages of career orientation, exploration, and preparation.
6. Uses a rich ongoing source of assessment data for career planning and vocational decision making.
7. Allows for continued self-awareness and realistic goal setting for students. (pp. 118–119)

CBVA and CBA

The similarity of the CBVA approach in vocational education and the CBA approach in special education is striking. Albright and Cobb (1988) define CBVA as a "continuous process used to answer questions about the instructional and special services needs of individual students as they enter into and progress through specific vocational education programs" (p. 14). It relies on the use of informal and direct assessment procedures to determine student achievement in the curriculum of his or her vocational program.

Curriculum-based assessment in the realm of special education is, in its simplest terms, testing what is taught (Salvia & Hughes, 1990). The CBA assessment process involves "the practice of obtaining direct and frequent measures of a student's performance on a series of sequentially arranged objectives derived from the curriculum used in the classroom" (Blankenship & Lilly, 1981, p. 81).

The essential component evident in definitions of both CBVA and CBA is assessment of the student's progress in the curriculum of the classroom. Its presence in both definitions confirms Cobb's (1983) perception that vocational assessment and special education assessment are conceptually the same process. In practice the assessment approaches share a number of other features as well. Both CBVA and CBA rely primarily on informal classroom-oriented assessment techniques and espouse a data-based decision-making and instructional planning process.

Data-based instruction in special education is discussed by Rosenberg and Sindelar (1982), who identify its four components as (a) instructional pinpointing, (b) direct and continuous measurement, (c) charting student performance data, and (d) data interpretation and utilization. Data-based instruction requires that specific student behaviors be targeted or pinpointed for intervention. Behaviors must be operationally defined in behavioral (i.e., observable and measurable) terms. Trait labels such as *learning disabled, hyperactive, perceptually impaired,* and the like, that provide general behavioral descriptions of little instructional value are avoided.

Ideally, measurement of student behavior under data-based instruction is direct and continuous (Van Etten & Van Etten, 1976). It involves testing of what has been taught by the person who instructed the students and a schedule of assessment that is ongoing and frequent enough to provide reliable and useful data on student progress. Frequency of evaluation will be a function of the severity of the student's disability and the nature of the skills being taught. For students with mild disabilities, twice weekly assessment of progress in key academic areas is generally sufficient (Fuchs & Fuchs, 1986). Visual display of student performance data facilitates the decision-making process (Tawney & Gast, 1984) and enhances student achievement (Fuchs & Fuchs, 1986). Application of criteria for interpretation of visual data (Alberto & Troutman, 1990), in conjunction with decision rules (White & Haring, 1980), greatly enhances the teacher's use of student performance by encouraging evaluation and modifications to meet individual student needs. Benefits for the instructional program to be expected from the application of data-based instruction include educational accountability, instructional methods verification, and efficacy (Rosenberg & Sindelar, 1982).

Data-based instruction is supported by vocational educators (Woolcock, Stodden, & Bisconer, 1992). In their conceptualization of the transitional process from school to adult life, Woolcock et al. stress the importance of assessment for instruction. They conceptualize the assessment process as an integrative decision-making procedure involving processes and outcomes.

Processes refers to the use of effective and appropriate instructional strategies; *outcomes* refers to goals and objectives of the transitional program for the individual student.

Woolcock et al. (1992) view assessment as a critical link between systematic teaching strategies and attainment of outcomes. Data collection and analysis are viewed as concurrent activities that are, in turn, prerequisites for successful program implementation. In their discussion of the assessment process, Woolcock et al. stress the importance of diagnostic assessment for instructionally useful information, data collection, visual and graphic display of data, and application of decision rules—components of data-based instruction also applied in special education assessment. Ongoing assessment coupled with effective instruction moves the student through three stages of learning: acquisition, proficiency, and generalization/maintenance.

For the most part, special educators would be comfortable with the various descriptions of assessment gleaned from the vocational education literature. The emphasis on diagnosis for instructional purposes, data-based instruction, and so forth, echo basic tenets of special education assessment philosophy and practice. In addition to a shared perspective of "best practices" in classroom-based assessment, special and vocational education points of view converge on other important issues, including ecological perspectives of the learner and learning process and concern for functional curriculum (Schloss & Sedlak, 1986; Woolcock et al., 1992). As special and vocational educators become more aware of their shared perspectives and values regarding the appropriate direction for instruction of special needs students, the prospects for collaboration and cooperation between them on behalf of students with mild disabilities is enhanced.

❧ ❧ ❧

ASSESSMENT PRACTICES IN FEDERALLY FUNDED TRANSITION PROJECTS

Data on current assessment practices used in federally funded transition projects for secondary youth with disabilities has been compiled and reported by Linn and DeStefano (1986) under the auspices of the Transition Institute of the University of Illinois, Urbana-Champaign. The following discussion summarizes their research findings.

The research effort involved 114 federally funded transition projects. Information was extracted from project applications and by means of a survey of project personnel. The review of project applications yielded a composite listing of 142 different assessment devices and procedures employed across the 114 project sites. The composite list was subsequently segregated into 12 student characteristics/competencies categories:

general ability/intelligence
special ability

vocational skills
academic achievement
language
adaptive behavior/survival skills
social skills
career interest
motor skills/dexterity
life-style/consumer satisfaction
daily living skills
other

The survey instrument addressed (a) the student competencies assessed, (b) assessment instruments used, (c) how assessment information was used, and (d) utility of the assessment information. Respondents rated the 12 assessment categories on a 4-point scale ranging from "highly useful" (score of 4) to "not useful" (score of 1). Respondents were also asked to indicate how assessment information was used. Choices included (a) initial assessment for placement, (b) assessment for program planning, (c) ongoing assessment/monitoring of student progress, and (d) evaluation of program outcome measures.

The projects served a wide range of students with disabilities from severe to mild. Projects varied in terms of their primary purpose and focus within the area of transition: transition from high school to work, high school to post–high school training program, high school to college, college to work, and development of cooperative models among agencies (Heal & Phelps, cited in Linn & DeStefano, 1986).

Linn and DeStefano (1986) report that a variety of tests were used within each of the 12 characteristics/competencies categories. Tests of general ability and vocational skills were employed most often. In the general ability category, the WAIS-R and WISC-R were most often the instruments of choice. In the area of vocational assessment, the instruments used most often were the VALPAR Work Sample, McCarron-Dial Work Evaluation System, and the Microcomputer Evaluation Screening Assessment System. The Wide Range Achievement Test was the most widely used achievement measure (27 projects). Other measures cited by at least 10 projects included the Woodcock-Johnson Psychoeducational Battery, Becker Reading-Free Interest Survey, Wide Range Interest and Opinion Test, the Purdue Pegboard, the Peabody Picture Vocabulary Test, the Street Survival Skills Questionnaire, and the Social and Prevocational Information Battery.

Many of the tests used in these transition projects, particularly in the categories of achievement and social skills, are widely used in special education. The technical adequacy of tests used in special education assessment has been questioned, studied, and found wanting (Ysseldyke et al., 1983). Questionable testing procedures and inappropriate testing instruments have contributed to problems of misclassification, misidentification, and inappropriate instructional placement and programming among those who are mildly disabled (Ysseldyke & Algozzine, 1982). Special educators are confronted with the need to upgrade assessment procedures through the selection of technically adequate instruments and the adherence to accepted testing and evaluation methods for both formal and informal testing (Bennett, 1982; Salvia & Ysseldyke, 1991).

The importance of valid and reliable data as the basis for the decision-making process cannot be overemphasized. Schloss and Sedlak (1986) maintain that "errors in any phase of the instructional process generally results from either inadequate data or improper interpretation of data" (p. 83). Linn and DeStefano's (1986) extensive report of transition assessment practices contains individual reviews of each of the 142 test instruments used in the transition projects. The reader is referred to this valuable resource.

The authors report respondents' utility ratings for the 12 assessment categories. As expected, ratings varied across categories and reflected a pattern of association between type of assessment data and degree of student disability. For example, the mean utility rating for general ability tests was 2.80 (3 = moderately useful) but the utility ratings for general ability tests applied to those with severe disabilities was lower (mean = 2.42) than the utility rating for such tests used for students who were mildly disabled (mean = 3.04). Of the 12 assessment categories, social and daily living skills were judged the most useful. Generally speaking, "patterns of test use seems quite consistent with the goals of transition projects" (Linn & DeStefano, 1986, p. 14).

The cumulative data on current assessment practices among federally funded transition projects reveal concern for a broad range of student characteristics and functioning and, at the same time, reliance on traditional formal assessment measures and methods. Thirty-four of the projects did report the use of locally developed test measures, but no additional information on the nature and use of these testing procedures was provided. On the plus side, the use of locally developed tests suggests a willingness among some transition project personnel to incorporate informal testing procedures, possibly curriculum based, along with the more widely used formal assessments. The broad range of assessment categories is encouraging as it suggests the expansion of transition programming beyond vocational evaluation and preparation to a broader conceptualization of adult functioning.

Overall, the pattern of test use is not yet in step with the emerging CBVA Model, which relies heavily on informal, criterion-referenced, or curriculum-referenced assessments. Additionally, the projects yielded little evidence of "contemporary situational assessment" (Linn & DeStefano, 1986, p. 6). Assessment of students in multiple and natural environments is an important component of the CBVA Model. To the extent that federally funded transition projects represent the status quo or the vanguard of transition programming and assessment technology, one must conclude that the assessment approach embodied in the CBVA Model is gaining professional support but has not yet been embraced by the vocational education practitioner.

❦ ❦ ❦

INDIVIDUAL EDUCATION PROGRAM/ INDIVIDUAL TRANSITION PLAN

The legislative mandate for the development of IEPs is, of course, contained in PL 94-142, which sets forth a process for the documentation of each student's IEP. The primary legislative mandate for transition planning and documentation is contained in the Carl D. Perkins Act (PL 98-524). The law requires that students who are disadvantaged or disabled, upon enrolling in vocational education, be assessed in the areas of interests, abilities, and special needs to promote successful completion of their vocational education program. Unlike PL 94-142 regarding the development of IEPs, PL 98-524 does not provide specific guidelines as to how this goal is to be accomplished (Cummings & Maddux, 1987; Ianacone & Leconte, 1986). The Carl D. Perkins Act does not have the clout (legal or monetary) of PL 94-142 and is more accurately viewed as a legislative incentive rather than a legislative mandate.

Ideally, the ITP should evolve as a natural and timely extension of the student's IEP in a continuous IEP/ITP process. Two questions that arise immediately concerning the IEP/ITP planning process are what should be contained in the ITP and at what point in the student's academic program the ITP should be developed. A response to the latter question is more readily available. Transition planning is generally associated with entry into the high school program (i.e., 9th grade) and/or attainment of the age of 14. Severity of disability may dictate that serious transition planning begin at an earlier age (Brown, cited in Veir, 1987).

The required contents of an IEP are well known to special educators but perhaps less well known to vocational educators. The IEP must contain the following (U.S. Department of Health, Education, & Welfare, 1977):

- a statement of the child's present level of educational functioning,
- annual goals and short-term instructional objectives,
- a description of the specific educational services to be provided to the child,
- a statement of the extent to which the child can participate in regular education,
- the projected date for initiation and anticipated duration of the services,
- objective evaluation criteria and procedures, and
- a schedule for annual review of the child's program.

Individual states may impose additional IEP requirements.

Nowhere are the contents of the ITP clearly stipulated. Kerr, Nelson, and Lambert (1987) state that the ITP should contain annual goals, short-term objectives, and the transition services to be provided. Brody-Hasazi, Salembier, and Finck (1983) recommend that the ITP include future residential and employment options, services needed to achieve desired transition outcomes, the names of the service agencies to be involved, and time lines for the completion of activities. Aase and Price (1986) view the ITP as "picking up" where the secondary IEP leaves off to help students achieve appropriate vocational, academic, and social goals for their lives in postsecondary school settings. They recommend that the ITP contain the following components:

- past services,
- current services,
- vocational goals
- postsecondary goals, and
- specific objectives to be completed.

The emphasis on ITP development and the contents of such documents imply that IEPs, as currently developed, fall short in addressing the transitional needs of secondary students. There is some evidence that this may be the case. In a study of Alabama secondary students with learning disabilities, Dowdy, Carter, and Smith (1990) found that the content of IEPs had little relationship to life after high school and did little to make students aware of vocational rehabilitation services. Most of the students surveyed intended to pursue employment after high school but lacked marketable skills. The students themselves expressed a need for more instruction in career exploration, job-seeking skills, and independent living skills.

Gerber and Griffin (1983) examined the content of secondary vocational programs and found that almost three-fourths of the students received no prevocational education and that approximately 60% of the IEPs for these students contained no vocational goals. In a study that investigated the effect of vocational assessment on IEP content, Stodden et al. (1989) found no significant change in the number and quality of vocational goals and objectives on IEPs before and after vocational assessment. Stodden et al. offer recommendations, based on the CBVA approach, to improve vocational assessment practices:

1. development of data collection procedures wherein vocational assessment is conducted by teachers as a part of the student's daily educational program;
2. development of vocational rating instruments that
   a. represent vocational opportunities that are available in a given community,
   b. are valid and reliable, and
   c. are readily translated into educational programming;
3. development of standard procedures for housing and disseminating vocational assessment information to teachers and IEP writers;
4. coordination between the availability of vocational assessment information and the writing of the IEP. (pp. 35–36)

Indeed, ITPs do need to "pick up" for IEPs that are incomplete or inadequate statements of appropriate transition goals and related instructional objectives in vocational and other areas. Even though we have specifications regarding the content of IEPs, quality in IEPs is still elusive. At best, we have informal criteria by which to gauge their quality. Tymitz-Wolf (1982) offers a number of quality guidelines, one of which states that the IEP should address all areas in which the student is deficient. The limited employability of persons with disabilities is directly related to deficiencies in interpersonal, social, job-related, and specific vocational skills (Okolo & Sitlington, 1986). The research reveals that IEPs are deficient in these critical skill areas. The criteria of completeness and relevance are appropriately applied to ITPs as well as IEPs.

Sample formats for transition plans and planning documents are presented in Figures 8–3 through 8–9. The reader will see considerable variety among the forms, testimony to the fact that transitional planning is still in an early stage of development and that the process reflects different perceptions as to goals, desired outcomes, and requisite components of successful transition programs. The common feature of all the formats, however, is a strong emphasis on vocational goals and preparation.

If we judge by the transition planning formats we have seen thus far, we are forced to conclude that the concept of transition as preparation for multiple adult roles has not yet had a significant impact. Stodden (1989) takes a broad view of the transition process. He offers a training process to assist school personnel in the development and implementation of joint IEPs and ITPs. Cobb and Hasazi (1987) also view transition planning as an extension of the IEP planning process. Combined attention to IEPs and ITPs in one training module underscores the need for coordination and continuity between school-based and postschool planning.

The process entailed in development of IEPs/ITPs is described by Greene, Albright, and Kokaska (1989). They view the IEP/ITP planning process as a collaborative technique, the end product of which is "a formal plan drafted for the student specifying the instructional activities, types of community services needed, and steps required to access community services in order to facilitate successful transition from school to independent living" (p. 4).

It bears repeating that collaboration is a cornerstone of successful transition programming. What degree of collaboration exists between special and vocational educators? In a statewide survey of vocational educators in Indiana, Sitlington and Okolo (1987) found that attitudes among vocational staff toward students with disabilities were generally positive but that their involvement in the IEP process was limited. The vocational educators surveyed felt that they had had little input into placement decisions or involvement in the IEP development for those students assigned to their classes. And Gill, Cupp, and Lindquist (1986) report that fully three-fourths of 192 secondary vocational education staff who had students with disabilities in their classes reported "no meaningful involvement in the development of the IEPs that accompanied the students" (p. 27). Greene et al. (1989) wholeheartedly support collaborative IEP/ITP planning and suggest team teaching and job coaching as vehicles for achieving collaboration between vocational and special education teachers. Specialized materials to promote collaboration have been developed by Asselin (1987) and Sarkees and Scott (1985).

Individualized Transition Plan

and

Individualized Educational Plan

VOCATIONAL/EDUCATION SERVICES

Student _____

Social Security # _____

Date of Birth _____

School _____

Date of ITP Meeting _____

ITP Coordinator _____

Year in School _____

Expected Year of Completion _____

ITP Team Members (Discipline)   Relationship to Student   Signature

_____   _____   _____

_____   _____   _____

_____   _____   _____

_____   _____   _____

_____   _____   _____

_____   _____   _____

_____   _____   _____

Figure 8–3

Sample of an ITP/IEP for vocational/educational services

Source: From *Individualized Transition Plan (ITP)/Individualized Education Plan (IEP): A Planning Process Assisting School to Community Transition* by R. A. Stodden, 1989, Honolulu: International Education Corporation (P.O. Box 89338, Honolulu, HI 96830-9338). Reprinted by permission.

181

VOCATIONAL/EDUCATION SERVICES

Individualized Transition Plan

Student _____   Date of ITP Meeting _____

ITP Coordinator _____

ANNUAL ACTION PLAN TO ACCESS SERVICE GOAL

Vocational/ Educational Service Goal	Sequence of Action	Action	Step	Person Responsible (S,F,A)	Time Frame	Date Accomplished
___ Independent Employment	Awareness					
___ Military	1. Values Clarification					
___ Community College	2. Service Options Inquiry					
___ University	3. Assessment(s)					
___ Supported Employment	4. Career Awareness					
___ Sheltered Employment	Exploration					
___ Pre-Voc Training	5. Community Support Service Options					
___ Day Treatment	6. Transportation Options					
___ Other	7. Assessment(s)					
	8. Skill Training					
	Integration					
	9. Assessment of Values and Service Options					
	10. Site Visits					
	11. Program Application					
	12. Transportation					
	13. Assessment(s)					
	14. Skill Training					
	Access/Mastery					
	15. Support Services					
	16. Transportation					
	17. Assessment(s)					
	18. Skill Training					
	19. Employment/Advance Placement					

Figure 8–4

Sample of an ITP for vocational/educational services

Source: From *Individualized Transition Plan (ITP)/Individualized Education Plan (IEP): A Planning Process Assisting School to Community Transition* by R. A. Stodden, 1989, Honolulu: International Education Corporation (P.O. Box 89338, Honolulu, HI 96830-9338). Reprinted by permission.

CITIZENSHIP AND GUARDIANSHIP

Individualized Transition Plan
and
Individualized Educational Plan

Student _____

Social Security # _____

Date of Birth _____

School _____

Date of ITP Meeting _____

ITP Coordinator _____

Year in School _____

Expected Year of Completion _____

ITP Team Members (Discipline)	Relationship to Student	Signature
_____	_____	_____
_____	_____	_____
_____	_____	_____
_____	_____	_____
_____	_____	_____
_____	_____	_____
_____	_____	_____

Figure 8–5
Sample of an ITP/IEP for citizenship and guardianship

Source: From *Individualized Transition Plan (ITP)/Individualized Education Plan (IEP): A Planning Process Assisting School to Community Transition* by R. A. Stodden, 1989, Honolulu: International Education Corporation (P.O. Box 89338, Honolulu, HI 96830-9338). Reprinted by permission.

CITIZENSHIP AND GUARDIANSHIP

Individualized Transition Plan

Student _____

Date of ITP Meeting _____

ITP Coordinator _____

ANNUAL ACTION PLAN TO ACCESS SERVICE GOAL

Citizenship and Guardianship	Sequence of Action	Action	Step	Person Responsible (S,F,A)	Time Frame	Date Accomplished
___ Self as Guardian	Awareness					
___ Public Guardianship Person	1. Values Clarification					
	2. Options Inquiry					
	3. Assessment(s)					
	4. Civic/Consumer Awareness					
___ Private Guardianship Property	Exploration					
	5. Options Exploration					
	6. Support Service Options					
	7. Transportation Options					
___ Self Advocate	8. Assessment(s)					
	9. Skill Training					
___ Public Advocate	Integration					
	10. Assessment of Values and Options					
	11. Service Application					
	12. Transportation					
___ Private Advocate	13. Assessment(s)					
	14. Skill Training					
	Access/Mastery					
	15. Service(s) Secured					
	16. Support Services					
	17. Transportation					
	18. Skill Training					

Figure 8–6
Sample of an ITP for citizenship and guardianship

Source: From Individualized Transition Plan (ITP)/Individualized Education Plan (IEP): A Planning Process Assisting School to Community Transition by R. A. Stodden, 1989, Honolulu: International Education Corporation (P.O. Box 89338, Honolulu, HI 96830-9338). Reprinted by permission.

Transition Plan

Name _____   Date _____

Address _____   Phone Number _____

_____   Social Security # _____

Post Grad Plans _____

SERVICE	NAME OF AGENCY	ADDRESS	PHONE
Educational/Technical			
Training/Evaluation			
Residential/Housing			
Counseling Services			
Employment Services			
Transportation Services			
Leisure/Recreational Services			

THIS PLAN HAS BEEN EXPLAINED TO ME AND I UNDERSTAND ITS CONTENT

_____   _____

Parent Signature   Student Signature

_____   _____

CETVE Staff   Date

cc: CETVE, VE, EM

Figure 8–7
Competitive employment through vocational experience cooperative service delivery model

Source: From "Transitional Services for Mildly Handicapped Youth" by D. W. Test, P. K. Keul, and T. Grossi, 1988, *Journal for Vocational Special Needs Education*, *10*(2), p. 9. Adapted by permission.

Student Information

Name _____ D.O.B. _____ Age _____ Grade _____

Address _____ Home Phone _____

Parent/Other Legal Guardian _____ Work Phone _____

Conference Participants

Name	Position
_____	_____
_____	_____
_____	_____
_____	_____
_____	_____
_____	_____

I agree to work toward the interim/transition objectives by participating in the activities stated on the attached page.

Student _____ Date _____

Parent _____ Date _____

Transition Counselor _____ Date _____

Comments/Recommendations

Figure 8–8
Interim transition plan

Source: From *Using Appropriate Documentation within the Secondary/Postsecondary Transition Process with Learning Disabled Adolescents and Adults* by S. Aase and L. Price, 1986, Minneapolis: University of Minnesota. (ERIC Document Reproduction Service No. ED 280 225) Adapted by permission.

Career/Vocational Goals _____   _____

Is vocational counseling needed? ___ No ___ Maybe ___ Yes

Is vocational assessment needed? ___ No ___ Maybe ___ Yes

Does student have previous job experience?

___ No ___ Yes, but volunteer work only ___ Yes, paid employment

Has student previously received vocational services? ___ No ___ Yes

Postsecondary Goals

Degree: ___ uncertain ___ voc tech certificate ___ AA ___ BA, BS

___ MA, MS ___ Ph.D., M.D. ___ Obtain job/no education

Major Program Area: _____   _____

Postsecondary Schools Considering: _____   _____

_____   _____   _____

Needed Postsecondary Accommodations/Services

___	1. New student orientation	___	2. Early syllabus
___	3. Early registration	___	4. Extra time for course work
___	5. Library assistance	___	6. Note takers
___	7. Alternative assignments	___	8. Extra time for tests
___	9. Adapted tests	___	10. Support group
___	11. Word processing	___	12. Individual tutoring
___	13. Academic counseling, advisor	___	14. Vocational counseling
___	15. Personal counseling	___	16. Diagnostic testing
___	17. Taped texts	___	18. Taped lectures
___	19. Study skills assistance	___	20. Advocacy assistance
___	21. Financial aid assistance	___	22. Time management
___	23. Housing	___	24. Transportation
___	25. Disability-related counseling	___	26. Other: _____
___	27. Physical accessibility	___	28. Basic skill development

Comments/Recommendations

Figure 8–8, continued

Interim Transition Plan for _____ Date _____		
Date Initiated/Completed	Specific Objectives	Responsible Party

Figure 8–8, *continued*

Student _____

Date of Plan _____

Current Classroom Placement _____

Projected Graduation Date _____

Concerns	Objective	Activities	Personnel Responsible	Completion Date
Income: Ability of person to support himself/herself				
Job & Job Training: Ability of person to hold a job on his/her own				
Living Arrangements: Ability to live independently				
Recreation & Leisure: Ability to participate in community recreation and leisure activities				
Transportation: Ability to travel from home to work, postsecondary programs, community activities, etc.				
Medical Needs: Person's medical needs are met				
Friends/Advocates: Ability to develop and maintain friendships with peers and advocates				
Long-Term Planning: Adequate provision made for long-term care/supervision needs				
Family Relationships: Person can maintain contact with his/her family				
Insurance: Adequate provision made for health and other types of insurance				

Figure 8–9

Transition plan

Source: From "School-aged Transition Services: Options for Adolescents with Mild Handicaps" by B. Cobb and S. B. Hasazi, 1987, *Career Development for Exceptional Individuals, 10*(1). Reprinted by permission.

The importance of collaboration and involvement in the IEP or IEP/ITP planning process for both special and vocational educators lies in the relationship between involvement and attitudes. Claxton (1986) surveyed trade and industrial teachers and found that teachers who had participated to a greater degree in IEP development had more positive attitudes toward students with disabilities. She also reported that positive attitudes were significantly related to the use of specialized materials. The IEP process originally and the combined IEP/ITP currently are vehicles for collaboration that can be used to build on an existing foundation of positive attitudes toward students with disabilities (Claxton, 1986; McDaniel, 1982; Moorman, 1980) to increase student participation in and the effectiveness of instruction in transitional courses and programs. Collaboration in the IEP/ITP planning process is an arena in which special and vocational educators can make a crucial contribution to the success of the entire transitional process.

❦ ❦ ❦

SUMMARY

Assessment encompasses a broad array of evaluative activities, tests, and methodologies. Increasingly, assessment practices are being gauged against a standard of educational utility, that is, the extent to which assessment yields information and data that have direct implication and application for the development and delivery of the instructional program. A dichotomy between assessment for classification/placement and assessment for instruction is generally acknowledged in special education. The dichotomy helps to focus the practitioner's attention on the relationship among purpose, methods, and outcomes. According to Cobb (1983), "the purposes of vocational assessment actually determine the setting, the instrumentation, the interpretation, and the timing of assessment activities more than any other single variable" (p. 217). There is additional evidence that vocational educators are "borrowing" from special education assessment philosophy and practices. Regarding vocational education, Peterson and Petersen (1986) identify the instructional benefits of vocational assessment that embodies a diagnostic-prescriptive and developmental perspective. Such assessment will, they state,

   a. develop instructional goals and objectives (these include long-term vocational developmental goals and short-term enabling goals and objectives);
   b. identify appropriate program placements that will assist students to meet their goals and objectives (this may include academic course selection, vocational education, special prevocational curricula, etc.);
   c. identify suggested instructional methods, behavior change techniques, and curriculum adaptations;
   d. provide relevant support services (such recommendations, if soundly based, can assist tremendously in providing effective instruction); and
   e. provide a valuable data base, consisting of effectively aggregated vocational assessment information, to use in school curriculum revision and program development. (p. 14)

Formalized and static evaluation of work aptitudes, abilities, and job skills carried out by other than the classroom teacher in environments removed from the classroom and actual work sites is losing favor in vocational education in much the same way that the standardized psychoeducational battery that categorizes (stigmatizes?) and places children with disabilities has lost favor among special education teachers. Newer classroom- and instructionally oriented models of assessment are emerging. The CBVA Model—characterized by a strong focus on assessment for instruction, evaluation of student progress in the curriculum, informal testing techniques, and more—is gaining acceptance. The similarity of CBVA to CBA is evidence that proven generic assessment methodology transcends disciplinary boundaries. An analogous situation can be found in the applicability of effective teaching methodology to both regular and special education classrooms and more recently to vocational education.

Finally, Woolcock et al. (1992) remind us that "transition is a highly value-driven process" in which the values of educators and of the student and family may, at some points, differ (p. 18). The process of goal setting, program development, and implementation can be enhanced if critical decisions at key decision points are made jointly and based on valid, reliable, and relevant data.

REFERENCES

Aase, S., & Price, L. (1986). *Using appropriate documentation within the secondary/postsecondary transition process with learning disabled adolescents and adults*. Minneapolis: University of Minnesota (ERIC Document Reproduction Service No. ED 280 225).

Alberto, P. A., & Troutman, A. C. (1990). *Applied behavior analysis for teachers* (3rd ed). New York: Merrill/Macmillan.

Albright, L., & Cobb, R. B. (1988). Curriculum-based vocational assessment: A concept whose time has come. *Journal for Vocational Special Needs Education*, *10*(2),13–16.

Asselin, S. B. (1987). *Making the transition: A teacher's guide for helping students with special needs*. Arlington, VA: American Vocational Association.

Bennett, R. E. (1982). Cautions for the use of informal measures in the education of exceptional children. *Exceptional Children*, *15*, 337–339.

Blankenship, C., & Lilly, M. S. (1981). *Mainstreaming students with learning and behavior problems: Techniques for classroom teachers*. New York: Holt, Rinehart, & Winston.

Brody-Hasazi, S., Salembier, G., & Finck, K. (1983). Directions for the 80's: Vocational preparation for secondary mildly handicapped students. *Teaching Exceptional Children*, *15*(4), 206–209.

Claxton, S. B. (1986). Determining attitudes of trade and industrial teachers toward handicapped students. *Journal of Industrial Teacher Education*, *23*(3), 55–63.

Cobb, R. B. (1983). A curriculum-based approach to vocational assessment. *Teaching Exceptional Children*, *15*(4), 216–219.

Cobb, R. B., & Danehey, A. (1986). Transitional vocational assessment. *Journal for Vocational Special Needs Education*, *6*(2), 3–7, 12.

Cobb, R. B., & Hasazi, S. B. (1987). School-aged transition services: Options for adolescents with mild handicaps. *Career Development for Exceptional Individuals, 10*(1), 15–23.

Cobb, R. B., & Larkin, D. (1985). Assessment and placement of handicapped pupils into secondary vocational education programs. *Focus on Exceptional Children, 17*(7), 1–14.

Cummings, R. W., & Maddux, L. D. (1987). *Career and vocational education for the mildly handicapped.* Springfield, IL: Thomas.

Dowdy, C. A., Carter, J. K., & Smith, T. E. C. (1990). Differences in transitional needs of high school students with and without learning disabilities. *Journal of Learning Disabilities, 23*(6), 343–348.

Fuchs, L. S. (1986). Monitoring progress among mildly handicapped pupils: Review of current research and practice. *Remedial and Special Education, 7*(5) 5–12.

Fuchs, L. S., & Fuchs, D. (1986). Effects of systematic formative evaluation: A meta-analysis. *Exceptional Children, 53*(3), 199–208.

Gerber, P. J., & Griffin, H. C. (1983). Vocational education practices with secondary school learning disabled and mildly handicapped students. In W. M. Cruickshank & E. Tash (Eds.), *Academics and beyond* (Vol. 4, pp. 135–145). New York: Syracuse University Press.

Gill, H., Cupp, D. E., & Lindquist, D. A. (1986). A consortium of vocational educational and special education. *Journal for Vocational Special Needs Education, 9*(3), 25–28.

Goodman, L. (1990). *Time and learning in the special education classroom.* New York: State University of New York Press.

Greene, G., Albright, L., & Kokaska, C. (1989). Instructional strategies for special education students in vocational education. *Journal for Vocational Special Needs Education, 12*(2), 3–8.

Gugerty, J. J., & Crowley, C. B. (1982). Informal vocational assessment for special needs students. *Journal for Vocational Special Needs Education, 3*(1),16–18.

Ianacone, R. N., & Leconte, P. J. (1986). Curriculum-based vocational assessment: A viable response to a school based service delivery issue. *Career Development for Exceptional Individuals, 9*, 113–120.

Kerr, M. M., Nelson, C. M., & Lambert, D. (1987). *Helping adolescents with learning and behavior problems.* New York: Merrill/Macmillan.

Kokaska, C. J., & Brolin, D. E. (1985). *Career education for handicapped individuals* (2nd ed.). New York: Merrill/Macmillan.

Linn, R., & DeStefano, L. (1986). *Review of student assessment instruments and practices in use in secondary transition projects.* Champaign: Transition Institute of the University of Illinois. (ERIC Document Reproduction Service No. ED 279 123)

McDaniel, L. (1982). Changing vocational teachers' attitudes toward the handicapped. *Exceptional Children, 48*, 377–378.

Moorman, J. (1980). Vocational education for the handicapped: A study of attitudes. *Journal for Vocational Special Needs Education, 2*, 25–26.

Okolo, C. M., & Sitlington, P. (1986). The role of special education in LD adolescents' transition from school to work. *Learning Disabilities Quarterly, 9*, 141–155.

Peterson, M. (1986). Work and performance samples for vocational assessment of special students: A critical review. *Career Development for Exceptional Individuals, 9*, 69–76.

Peterson, M., & Petersen, D. (1986). Assessment: A resource in vocational instruction of special needs students. *Journal for Vocational Special Needs Education, 6*(2),13–16.

Porter, M. E., & Stodden, R. A. (1986). A curriculum-based vocational assessment procedure: Assessing the school-to-work transition needs of secondary schools. *Career Development for Exceptional Individuals, 9,* 121–128.

Rosenberg, S. R., & Sindelar, P. T. (1982). Educational assessment using direct and continuous data. In J. T. Neisworth (Ed.), *Assessment in special education* (pp. 83–100). Rockville, MD: Aspen.

Salvia, J., & Hughes, C. (1990). *Curriculum based assessment.* New York: Macmillan.

Salvia, J., & Ysseldyke, J. E. (1988). *Assessment* (4th ed.). Boston: Houghton Mifflin.

Salvia, J., & Ysseldyke, J. E. (1991). *Assessment* (5th ed.). Boston: Houghton Mifflin.

Sarkees, M. D., & Scott, J. L. (1985). *Vocational special needs* (2nd ed.). Homewood, IL: American Technical Publications.

Schloss, P. J., & Sedlak, R. A. (1986). *Instructional methods for students with learning and behavior problems.* Boston: Allyn & Bacon.

Sitlington, P. L., & Okolo, C. M. (1987). Statewide survey of vocational educators: Attitudes, training, and involvement with handicapped learners. *Journal of Career Development, 13*(4), 21–29.

Stodden, R. A. (1989). *Training packet for implementing individualized transition plans.* Honolulu: International Education Corporation.

Stodden, R. A., & Ianacone, R. N. (1981). Career/vocational assessment of the special needs individual: A conceptual model. *Exceptional Children, 47,* 600–608.

Stodden, R. A., Meehan, K. A., Bisconer, S. W., & Hodell, S. L. (1989). The impact of vocational assessment information on the individualized education planning process. *Journal for Vocational Special Needs Education, 12,* 32–36.

Tawney, J. W., & Gast, D. L. (1984). *Single subject research in special education.* New York: Merrill/Macmillan.

Test, D. W., Keul, P. K., & Grossi, T. (1988). Transitional services for mildly handicapped youth: A cooperative model. *The Journal for Vocational Special Needs Education, 10*(2), 7–11.

Tymitz-Wolf, B. (1982). Guidelines for assessing IEP goals and objectives. *Teaching Exceptional Children, 14,* 198–201.

U.S. Department of Health, Education, and Welfare. (1977). Education of the handicapped children: Implementation of Part B of the Education of the Handicapped Act. *Federal Register, 42*(163), 42474–42518.

Van Etten, C., & Van Etten, G. (1976). The measurement of pupil progress and selecting instructional materials. *Journal of Learning Disabilities, 6,* 469–480.

Veir, C. A. (1987). Vocational assessment: The evolving role. In D. D. Meers (Ed.), *Handbook of vocational special needs education* (pp. 213–255). Rockville, MD: Aspen.

Wallace, G., & Larsen, S. C. (1978). *Educational assessment of learning problems: Testing for teaching.* Boston: Allyn & Bacon.

Wallace, G., & McLaughlin, J. A. (1979). *Learning disabilities: Concepts and characteristics* (2nd ed.). New York: Merrill/Macmillan.

White, O. R., & Haring, N. G. (1980). *Exceptional teaching* (2nd ed). New York: Merrill/Macmillan.

Woolcock, W. W., Stodden, R. A., & Bisconer, S. W. (1992). Process- and outcome-focused decision making. In F. R. Rusch, L. DeStefano, J. Chadsey-Rusch, L. A. Phelps, & E. Szymanski (Eds.), *Transition from school to adult life* (pp. 219–244). Sycamore, IL: Sycamore.

Ysseldyke, J. E. (1983). Current practices in making psycho-educational decisions about learning disabled students. *Journal of Learning Disabilities, 16,* 226–233.

Ysseldyke, J. E., & Algozzine, B. (1982). *Critical issues in special and remedial education.* Boston: Houghton Mifflin.

Ysseldyke, J. E., Thurlow, M., Graden, J., Wesson, C., Algozzine, B., & Deno, S. (1983). Generalizations from five years of research on assessment and decision making: The University of Minnesota Institute. *Exceptional Education Quarterly, 4*(1), 75–93.

Zigmond, N., & Miller, S. E. (1986). Assessment for instructional planning. *Exceptional Children, 52*(6), 501–509.

Zigmond, N., Vellacorsa, A., & Silverman, R. (1983). *Assessment for instructional planning in special education.* Englewood Cliffs, NJ: Prentice-Hall.

Chapter 9

❦　❦　❦

Academic Programming

S tudents with mild disabilities face important curricular choices during their secondary school years. The primary decision involves a choice between academic and functional curricular programs. The academic program entails a continuation of the traditional course sequence leading to graduation and a regular high school diploma. The majority of high school graduates go on to some type of postsecondary educational program; U.S. census data for 1990, for example, indicate that 59.9% did so (U.S. Department of Education, 1992). Although the comparative rate of enrollment in postsecondary schools exceeds 2 to 1 in favor of those with no disabilities (55.7% nondisabled vs. 22.5% disabled; Marder, 1991), increasing numbers of students with learning disabilities are enrolling in college programs (Dalke & Schmitt, 1987; Mangrum & Strichart, 1984). Aspirations among students with disabilities for continued education beyond high school are strong. In one survey of students who had learning disabilities, 67% expressed a desire to continue in some type of educational activity after high school (White et al., 1982).

In contrast to the academic curriculum, the functional curriculum focuses on specific skill development to prepare the student to function adequately in the adult world. Vocational education and job training will be essential components of the functional curriculum. However, while vocational education is narrowly focused on specific job or job-related skills, the functional curriculum for people who are mildly disabled should provide skills training for multiple adult roles—consumer, homemaker, citizen, as well as employee. Upon completion of the functional curriculum, the student may or may not receive a regular high school diploma. The awarding of certificates of completion or attendance, in lieu of the regular high school diploma, is not uncommon (Vitello, 1988).

Both the academic and functional curricula represent viable choices for secondary students with mild disabilities. Zigmond and Sansone (1986) have emphasized the importance of careful consideration of student characteristics when choosing among curricular options for secondary-age students with disabilities. The most important of these traits to curricular selection include the student's past exposure to special education, growth patterns in academic skills before high school, student goals, and behavioral response to the demands of high school. Increasingly, secondary programmatic choices are being made with sensitivity to transitional needs, that is, the extent to which the curriculum will adequately prepare the student for his or her postschool endeavors. An appropriate curricular choice for the student is one that reflects the student's educational history and learner characteristics and has the potential to prepare the student for postschool pursuits. The remainder of the chapter is devoted to further discussion of important instructional dimensions of each curriculum and their relationship to the transition process.

❧ ❧ ❧

THE ACADEMIC CURRICULUM

The academic curriculum continues the traditional course sequence leading toward the goal of high school graduation. Instruction can be delivered in a variety of settings along two dimensions: restrictiveness from regular education and degree of departure from the regular curricular content and methodology (see the discussion of the two-dimensional curricular schema of Zigmond & Sansone [1986] in chap. 6). At the secondary level, students who are mildly disabled receive the majority of their instruction in regular education classes (Wagner, 1990). However, restrictive, departmentalized special education courses paralleling regular ones are also found at the secondary school level (Carlson, 1985). Instructional setting alone, however, does not guarantee effective or appropriate instruction (Cooley & Leinhardt, 1980). Effective instruction for secondary-level students is the object of increasing interest and research activity and warrants further discussion.

Effective Instruction

Summaries and listings of the essential components of effective instruction are plentiful (Brophy & Good, 1986; Emmer, Evertson, Sanford, Clements, & Worsham, 1984; Evertson, Emmer, Clements, Sanford, & Worsham, 1984; Good & Brophy, 1987; Hawley & Rosenholtz, 1984; Medley, 1979; Rosenshine, 1983). Although the primary focus of the effective schools literature has been elementary-level instruction within regular education, attention to effective instruction for disabled populations is increasing (Bickel & Bickel, 1986; Borich, 1992; Christenson, Ysseldyke, & Thurlow, 1989; Goodman, 1985, 1990; Larrivee, 1986; Zigmond & Sansone, 1986). The effective schools literature does yield instructional themes that cut across the various categories of exceptionality and address the instructional needs of secondary-age students: (a) interactive teaching, (b) lesson delivery and structure, (c) time and classroom management, and (d) curricular integration of basic skills. Each of these topics contributes to the overall effectiveness of the secondary academic curricular program.

Interactive Teaching. Interactive teaching is associated with an active, directive, and involved teaching style. The teacher, not the students, is clearly in control of the ongoing instructional activity. Students spend proportionately more class time in teacher-directed instructional activities rather than working alone or unsupervised; research indicates this improves student performance (Brophy, 1979). Teacher-student interaction is high, which also has been associated with enhanced student achievement (Good & Brophy, 1987; Stallings, 1975; Stallings, Needels, & Stayrook, 1979). Such interaction primarily focuses on the ongoing academic activities rather than classroom or behavioral management. Data indicate that interactions devoted to classroom or student behavioral management are negatively associated with student achievement (Rosenshine & Stevens, 1984; Stallings et al., 1979). Talk in the classroom is teacher directed and academically focused and devoted to lesson delivery (e.g., demonstration, explanation, reviewing student work, questioning, and monitoring student work) (Hawley & Rosenholtz, 1984). Student attentiveness to task typically diminishes during independent or seatwork activities (Rosenshine, 1979). The teacher maintains a brisk pace, giving students many opportunities to respond and practice the academic tasks. Brisk lesson pacing (Brophy, 1979; Carnine, 1981; Englert, 1984; Rosenshine, 1979) and active student participation (Hall, Delquadri, Greenwood, & Thurston, 1982) help produce higher levels of student achievement. Therefore, the teacher strives for maximum engagement and the active academic participation of all students—two hallmarks of effective instruction strongly linked to student achievement.

The effectiveness of an interactive teaching style and practices for secondary-age students has been demonstrated by Stallings et al. (1979) in an investigation of reading instructional practices among secondary school teachers. Stallings et al. found that classes characterized by interactive and supportive instruction were associated with greater reading gains among secondary-age students. Students reading initially at the first- to fourth-grade level gained up to 2 years in reading proficiency during one school year (Stallings, 1981). The teaching style was also related to a lower student absentee rate. Interactive teaching behaviors included a higher amount of time spent in instruction, discussion of homework, questioning students, provision of supportive feedback, drill and practice, and having the lowest functioning students read aloud in small instructional groupings. Noninteractive teaching in those classrooms that produced lower reading gains was characterized by higher rates of written assignments, silent reading, limited teacher-student interaction, and social or managerial interactions.

In a more recent study, Wong, Wong, Darlington, and Jones (1991) effectively taught revision skills to adolescents with learning disabilities. The positive results achieved with an initial group of five adolescents was replicated with a second group of six. The highly structured and directive remedial methodology included interactive dialogues, teacher questioning, and teacher modeling of revision strategies.

The use of interactive teaching practices varies greatly among secondary teachers of students with disabilities. Rieth, Polsgrove, Okolo, Bahr, and Eckert (1987) have gathered observational data from 52 urban secondary special education resource rooms. Their data reveal that the activities to which teachers devoted the most class time are planned demonstrations and lectures (20.6%), responding to student requests for assistance (19.5%), giving directions regarding assignments (13.7%), and supervising seatwork (16.1%). Comparatively little time was devoted to giving academic feedback (2.1%) or academic monitoring (8.0%). Teachers were the source of instruction 43.9% of the time, and students were involved in pencil-and-paper activities or with other media and computers for 40.7%, 5.3%, and 3% of the time, respectively. The data uncover a pattern of instruction in secondary resource rooms that depends heavily on seatwork or other student-directed activities, with little academic feedback from or monitoring by the teachers. The level of responding to student requests for assistance also raises some question about instructional effectiveness, as it suggests that initial presentation and/or directions were ineffective. As a group, these resource rooms do not present a strong picture of interactive teaching. Research and training efforts are needed to define interactive teaching methodology at the secondary level and to encourage adoption of interactive teaching strategies by more secondary-level teachers of students with mild disabilities.

Interactive teaching, as the term is being used in this text, subsumes the array of teaching methodologies that fall under the heading of direct instruction. Direct instruction has been broadly defined by Rosenshine (1979) in reference to "academically focused, teacher-directed classrooms using sequenced and structured materials" (p. 147). Direct instruction also applies to specific curricular programs that embody the essential principles of the methodological approach; DISTAR is perhaps the best known exemplar. Another example of direct instruction is found in *Direct Instruction Reading* (Carnine, Silbert, & Kameenui, 1990) and *Direct Instruction Mathematics* (Silbert, Carnine, & Stein, 1981). These texts are not self-contained curricular programs such as *Corrective Reading Program* (Engelmann et al., 1978); rather, they offer the teacher a master plan for instructional delivery emphasizing three key instructional components: organization of instruction, program design, and presentation techniques. *Direct Instruction Reading* or *Direct Instruction Mathematics* enables the teacher to teach any curriculum of his or her choosing more effectively.

In practice, direct instruction has its roots in elementary and compensatory education; indeed, it is viewed by some as "a form of elementary school teaching" (Corno & Snow, 1986, p. 622). Special educators have been receptive to direct instruction for learners with disabilities (Englert, 1984; Gersten, 1985). The points of compatibility between direct instruction and special education are many (e.g., structured lesson presentation, clear and precise delineation of instructional objectives, corrective feedback, active student responding, careful sequencing of instructional activities). Schloss and

Sedlak (1986) include the topic of direct instruction in their methods text for students with mild disabilities. Direct instruction is defined by them as

> a student-centered as opposed to a student-directed approach that links pupil per-formance data to systematic teaching procedures. Direct instruction involves a comprehensive set of educational principles that address the structure of the learning environment, the differentiation of teaching practices on the basis of learner characteristics, the effective use of motivating consequences, and the sys-tematic articulation of instructional objectives. (p. 82)

Schloss and Sedlak's (1986) definition embodies components of the struc-tured and active approach we have termed interactive teaching and tenets of instruction central to special education methodology (e.g., individualization, specification of instructional objectives). Within the special education realm, it appears that direct instruction is evolving into a set of generic methodological principles applicable to many instructional situations. Applications of direct instruction methodology in secondary-level special education hold much promise but are still quite limited (Englert, 1984; Gersten, 1985). Secondary-level applications are rare and tend toward students who are severely and/or moderately disabled (Horner, Jones, & Williams, 1985; Horner & McDonald, 1982) rather than those with mild disabilities (Gersten & Maggs, 1982).

Lesson Delivery and Structure.   The secondary school day is structured in a series of class periods typically less than an hour long and designated for spe-cific subject instruction (e.g., history, home economics) or nonacademic activ-ities (e.g., physical education, lunch). The concept of activities is useful for teachers who organize and deliver instruction within the time frame of a class period. An activity is "an organized behavior that the teacher and student engage in for a common purpose" (Emmer et al., 1984, p. 117). Activities take place in a designated location with a discernible beginning and end plus an intended outcome. The pattern of student and teacher participation and inter-action, the interrelationships among students, level of student engagement, and lesson pacing are prescribed by the nature of the activity (Gump, 1974; Ross, 1984). Activities commonly found in the secondary classroom include opening activity, checking classwork or homework, recitation, content devel-opment, discussion, seatwork, small-group work, and closing activity (Emmer et al., 1984). The teacher is advised to select and sequence activities within a class period to enhance attainment of objectives, maintain student involvement, and provide opportunities for student application and practice of lesson content.

Emmer et al. (1984, p. 123) discuss the advantages and disadvantages of two activity sequences for the secondary classroom:

Activity Sequence A	*Activity Sequence B*
Opening Routine	Opening
Checking	Checking
Content Development	First Content Development Activity

Seatwork   First Seatwork Activity
Closing   Checking
                                   Second Content Development Activity
                                     Second Seatwork Activity
                                     Closing

The advantages of Activity Sequence A are the minimal number of transitions, opportunity to check the previous day's work and present new material, and allocated time for student practice or application of lesson content. The disadvantages of the sequence lie in the limitation on content presentation imposed by one content development activity and the demands placed on students' attention spans by the relatively long presentation and practice sessions. Activity Sequence B contains all of the advantages of Sequence A while negating the disadvantages. In addition, Sequence B has distinct advantages for teachers of students with mild disabilities (in regular or special education settings) in that it provides for more teacher-led instructional time, two sessions for active responding, and overall shorter activities that will demand less sustained attention. A decided disadvantage of Sequence B is the greater number of transitions, which encourages off-task behavior and creates opportunities for disruption. Instructionally, Sequence B is more interactive than Sequence A.

Suggestions to increase the effective management of interactive group activities (e.g., content development and recitation) have been offered by Kounin and his colleagues (Gump, 1974; Kounin, 1970; Kounin & Obradovic, 1968). Activity flow, or the "degree to which a lesson proceeds smoothly without digressions, diversions, and interruptions" (Emmer et al., 1984, p. 124), is important to effective management. The teacher's ability to observe and countervene inappropriate behavior before it disrupts the lesson ("withitness"), handle two or more simultaneous events ("overlapping"), maintain a brisk instructional pace ("momentum"), and plan and deliver lessons devoid of jerkiness and digressions ("smoothness") are important management skills.

The intervals between activities are termed *transitions.* Effective management of transitions is important for many reasons. Transitions account for a significant portion of classroom and instructional time (Rieth & Frick, 1982; Rosenshine, 1981). If mismanaged, transitions can erode the available instructional time. Off-task behavior increases markedly during transitions (Arlin, 1979), as does the opportunity for disruptive behavior. Finally, transition time is negatively correlated with student achievement (Arlin, 1979; Larrivee, 1986; Rosenshine & Stevens, 1984). Emmer et al. (1984) offer numerous suggestions for the effective management of transitions. Secondary teachers are urged to pay attention to transitions as many gauge the overall level of classroom management skill in terms of the teacher's ability to handle transitions (Arlin, 1979; Doyle, 1979).

Another important dimension of instructional effectiveness involves the clarity associated with lesson delivery. *Clarity* is the "absence of vagueness, uncertainty, and irrelevant information in presentations" (Zigmond, Sansone,

Miller, Donahoe, & Kohnke, 1986, p. 112). While clarity is important for all instructional exchanges, it is crucial during the presentation of new content or concepts. Lack of clarity in lesson presentations has been associated with reduced student achievement (Land & Smith, 1979). Emmer et al. (1984) have identified sequencing of information, use of sufficient and appropriate illustrations or examples, precision and concreteness of expression, monitoring of student comprehension, and provision of sufficient practice to ensure student mastery as contributing to clarity in instruction.

Considering the importance of clarity for effective instruction, the data of Rieth et al. (1987) are disquieting. They report that the amount of time teachers spend responding to student requests for clarification and assistance (19.5%) nearly equals that devoted to planned explanations. The data do not reflect favorably on instructional practices observed in secondary school resource room programs.

Order is the sequence of content presentation and the emphasis placed on key concepts. Order strategies have been shown to aid student achievement (Rosenshine, 1976; Smith & Sanders, 1981). The "rule-example-rule" presentation strategy, which entails introduction of new concepts, elaboration with examples, and restatement of the concept, is recommended for students with mild disabilities. Repetition of key concepts will also be helpful. Many students benefit from fore knowledge of the lesson's structure (Kallison, 1980). Zigmond et al. (1986) and Emmer et al. (1984) recommend informing students of the direction, intent, and objectives of a lesson at the beginning of the instruction.

Time and Classroom Management. Effective time management conserves the maximal amount of time for instruction while limiting the amount of time devoted to nonacademic or intrusive activities. For students, the level of engagement—that is, the actual amount of time during which students are attending to appropriate academic tasks—is the central concern. The relationship of engagement to achievement is well founded (Borg, 1980; Goodman, 1990); generally, higher levels of engagement are associated with higher levels of achievement (Fisher et al., 1978).

Engagement can be further delineated as active or passive (Hall, Delquadri, Greenwood, & Thurston, 1982). The terms *direct* and *indirect* are often used in place of *active* and *passive* when referring to the nature of reading instructional tasks (Haynes & Jenkins, 1986; Leinhardt & Seewald, 1981). Examples of active engagement are oral or silent reading, calculation of math problems, writing a composition, or responding to a question posed by the teacher. Examples of passive engagement are one student listening to another student read (the listener is passively engaged while the reader is actively engaged), listening to the teacher give directions for an assignment, or watching the teacher or a fellow student writing at the board. The distinction between active and passive engagement is important because the two types of participatory behavior do not yield equal educational results. Greater student achievement gains are associated with active engagement, also termed **active academic responding** (Becker, 1977; Delquadri, Greenwood, Stretton, & Hall, 1983; Fisher et al., 1980; Rosenshine, 1981; Stallings, 1975). The goal, therefore, is to maintain high levels of engagement involving high levels of active student responding.

The levels of engagement and active academic responding observed by Rieth et al. (1987) in secondary-level resource rooms were 76% and 36.7%, respectively. Such a sharp drop from engaged time to active academic responding is characteristic of patterns of time usage (Goodman, 1990). Presently there are no firm guidelines for judging the adequacy of reported levels of engagement or active responding. Based on a review of the relevant literature, Goodman suggests that engagement rates from the mid-70 to mid-80 percentile range are associated with adequate academic performance, while lower engagement rates are often related to less than adequate performance. By this yardstick, the engagement rate reported by Rieth et al. falls within the adequate range. At this time, however, there are insufficient data to formulate any guidelines for evaluating levels of active academic responding. Also, the reader should bear in mind that the data on classroom patterns of time usage are overwhelmingly derived from elementary classrooms. In the absence of a more balanced and representative data base, generalizations to secondary populations should be made with caution.

There are numerous sources that the reader can consult to find strategies for enhancing student engagement. Goodman (1990), for example, has compiled strategies for both the conservation and enhancement of student engagement. Once again, the reader is reminded of the literature's elementary bias. The application of suggested strategies with secondary populations should be approached under the mode of experimental teaching, with the efficacy of specific strategies determined on the basis of student performance data.

An important dimension of time management concerns the distribution of instructional time between teacher-led and independent activities. It is well established that student engagement falls significantly under independent working conditions (Fisher et al., 1978; Good & Beckerman, 1978; Rieth & Frick, 1982; Soar, 1973; Stallings & Kaskowitz, 1974). A drop in student engagement of 15% (from 85% under teacher-led instruction to 70% under independent seatwork) was documented by Fisher et al. in second- and fifth-grade classrooms. In the secondary school resource rooms observed by Rieth et al. (1987), the amount of class time devoted to independent seatwork and teacher-led instruction was 40.7% and 43.9%, respectively. The potential liabilities of seatwork are the drop in levels of student engagement and the lack of interaction between the teacher and students. These data suggest that interactive teaching is not the dominant instructional approach in secondary school resource rooms for students with mild disabilities. There appears to be instead an overreliance on pencil-and-paper seatwork activities.

The distribution of class time across instructional activities offers another perspective on the extent of interactive teaching and related teacher behaviors. The combination of interactive teaching and key instructional behaviors contributes to the overall effectiveness of instruction. Stallings (1981), in a study of effective teaching practices at the secondary level, identified the following distribution of class time across instructional activities:

Instruction-giving examples, explanations, linking to student experience: 16%
Review, discussion of seatwork, and story content: 12%
Drill and practice to help memorization: 4%
Oral reading in small groups: 21%
Silent reading: 9%
Written assignments: 4%

The lion's share of class time is devoted to interactive instructional activities, explanation, discussion, and supervised drill and practice—all of which offer numerous opportunities for active engagement. The amount of time devoted to silent reading and written assignments is limited. Activities of this kind generally entail reduced teacher supervision and may lead to a loss of student engagement. On the other hand, silent reading and written assignments may require active student responding. The exact nature of the task and the level of monitoring will determine the instructional utility of such tasks. On the basis of their observations of more and less effective secondary school teachers, Stallings et al. (1979) recommend that silent reading be limited to less than 15% of class time and that written assignments be limited to less than 20% of class time.

Curricular Integration of Basic Skills.   More rigorous standards of basic skills instruction for all students have been one outcome of the educational reform movements of the 1970s and 1980s. The continuing commitment to basic skills instruction for the student with mild disabilities has already been discussed. Underachievement is one characteristic that cuts across categorical lines and is shared by most, though not necessarily all, students with mild disabilities. A significant discrepancy between actual achievement and expectation for achievement is a basic tenet of the definition of learning disabilities, the most populous group among the mildly disabled.

The prevalence of achievement deficiencies should not lull educators into accepting these same deficiencies. In the academic realm, "the level of accomplishment of nonhandicapped students is the reference point against which the achievement of the mildly handicapped student is judged" (Goodman & Bennett, 1982, p. 259). The effectiveness of basic skills instruction is reflected in the degree to which students who are mildly disabled bridge the social and achievement gaps that separate them from their nondisabled peers.

How does the performance of secondary students with disabilities compare to the performance of the nondisabled? Some important indices of student performance are graduation rates, grade point average (GPA), absenteeism, course failure, grade retention, and performance on minimum competency tests. Regarding graduation rates, approximately 56% of students with disabilities as compared to 79% of the general population graduated from high school (Marder, 1991). The average GPA (1.94) for a national sample of students who were learning disabled does not compare favorably with the GPA for a comparison group of high school seniors (2.85) or the 4-year GPA (2.6) for a sample of sophomores in 1980 (Marder, 1991). Special education students generally achieved higher grades in special rather than regular education courses (GPA 2.2 vs. GPA 1.9) (SRI International, n.d.). Almost one third of students with disabilities had failed at least one course. The average absentee rate among the students with disabilities was 15 days per year. Only 35% of students with disabilities nationwide participated in minimum competency testing; of those who did, 44% passed, 32% passed just part of the test, and 24% did not pass any portion of the test. (The topic of MCT for students who are mildly disabled is discussed in detail in chap. 6.) Collectively, the statistics suggest serious inadequacies in the basic skills instruction provided to those who are mildly disabled.

The growing emphasis on effective instruction is a positive response to the need for improved basic skills instruction. Research is revealing essential teaching competencies and functions in special education settings (Christenson et al., 1989) and for students with disabilities in mainstreamed classrooms (Englert, Tarrant, & Mariage, 1992; Larrivee, 1986). There is a remarkable degree of similarity between the descriptive profiles of effective teaching and teachers in both regular and special education (Larrivee, 1986). A core of teaching competencies seems to be emerging that meets the instructional needs of a large and diverse population of "inefficient learners" (MacMillan, Keogh, & Jones, 1986, p. 71), including those who are mildly disabled, children of low socioeconomic and minority background, and various other at-risk groups. The broad generalizability of core teaching competencies should enhance prospects for effective and integrated education for students with mild disabilities.

A second response to the needs for improved basic skills education is the movement toward integrated academic and vocational instruction. The Carl D. Perkins Vocational Education Act of 1984 specifically mandated an increased emphasis on basic skills instruction in vocational settings and research to identify and develop successful methods of basic skills instruction for vocational education (Weber, Puleo, Kurth, Fisch, & Schaffner, 1988). The integration of basic skills instruction within vocational education enjoys considerable professional support (Greenan & Tucker, 1990; Pickard, 1990; Sarkees-Wircenski & West, 1990; Stevens & Lichtenstein, 1990). Babich and Cassity (1990) discuss three models of integrated academic and vocational instruction. The Pullout Model involves instruction separate from the vocational program to provide academic credit for course work such as math, science, and English or to offer remedial instruction. In the Integrated Model, academic instruction or remediation is provided within the vocational classroom. A successful integrated program involving the provision of applied academic classes by academic teachers in vocational schools has been described in the literature (Weber, 1988). The Combination Model involves variations of the preceding models in order to meet the individual needs of diverse learners.

Within all of the models of integrated instruction, a major issue, and presumably a stumbling block to joint cooperation efforts, is academic credit for course work completed in a vocational setting. Most state regulations tie the issuance of course credit to the delivery of instruction by teachers appropriately certified in specific content areas. Babich and Cassity (1990) propose an alternative that would allow certification of the curriculum, as opposed to certification of teachers, which would thus permit the awarding of academic credit even when a certified academic instructor is not utilized in the classroom. They point to special education as an example of curricular certification in that many school districts allow students with disabilities to attain a high school diploma following completion of an individualized program as outlined in the student's individual education plan (IEP).

The integration of basic skills and vocational education has many potential benefits. Barbieri and Wircenski (1990) point out that the linkage between vocational and basic skills education will help students appreciate the relevance of their academic course work to their future endeavors and provide opportunities for application of academic course content. In addition, the instructional methodology of vocational education lends itself to the concrete, hands-on learning that is appealing and effective for many problem learners. The holding power of vocational education for dropout-prone students is a decided advantage and opportunity that should be fully explored for enhanced basic skills instruction.

In summary, basic skills instruction for students with mild disabilities loses none of its importance as they progress from the elementary to the secondary school. Performance statistics already alluded to indicate that the basic skills instruction provided to such students is lacking at a time when proficiency in basic skills is becoming increasingly important. The transformation in our country's industrial base from a manufacturing to a technological and service economy places a higher demand on basic skills as a prerequisite for job success. Basic skills attainment in high school has already emerged as a strong predictor of employment success in a number of recent follow-up studies of young adults with disabilities (Fardig, Algozzine, Schwartz, Hensel, & Westling, 1985; Fourqurean & LaCourt, 1989; Hasazi et al., 1985). Increasingly, employers are rejecting a "narrow vocationalism" among their workers (Sarkees-Wircenski & West, 1990, p. 6) in preference to workers who possess basic academic skills, problem-solving ability, and decision-making skills as well as specific job skills. Workers of the future will require a broad array of job and job-related skills as well as the ability to adapt to a changing work environment. Basic skills instruction, therefore, must retain a central position in the secondary school curriculum for the student who is mildly disabled, but the definition and delivery of basic skills instruction must change.

❦ ❦ ❦

THE FUNCTIONAL CURRICULUM

Advocates of transitional services consistently stress the importance of a functional curriculum for students with disabilities and the transition process. The functional curriculum has been associated for some time with students who are severely and moderately disabled (Brown, Nietupski, & Hamre-Nietupski, 1976; Snell, 1983). As part of the transition process for students who are mildly disabled, it is a more recent phenomenon (Kerr, Nelson, & Lambert, 1987; Schloss & Sedlak, 1986). Philosophically, the functional curriculum is the same for both groups. It meets individual needs to the greatest extent possible and prepares students for their postschool adult lives. In practical terms, the functional curriculum for the student with mild disabilities is much broader in scope to reflect the wider range of postschool options, vocations, living arrangements, and corresponding responsibilities that those students face as compared to those who are more severely disabled.

The Functional Curriculum versus the Traditional Curriculum

The functional curriculum that is being proposed for the student with mild disabilities differs markedly from the traditional or developmental curriculum. The distinction between the functional and traditional curricular options is important as the selection of one or the other for a particular individual will have far-reaching consequences for school programming and postschool options.

A developmental curriculum denotes the regular school curriculum. At the elementary level, basal programs or other sequential, comprehensive, developmental curricular programs prevail in the major academic areas (e.g., reading, mathematics, language arts). At the secondary level, instruction may become more varied and less dependent on packaged commercial curricula. Many teachers will make an effort to make the subject matter relevant and interesting to the older student, but, with few exceptions, the curriculum essentially conforms to traditional academic and vocational training models and goals (as discussed in chap. 5).

Definitions of functional curriculum abound. Boyer-Stephens and Kearns (1988) define functional curricula as

> curricula in which the students learn functional skills in the most appropriate setting for specific acquisition. It is one which prepares students for adult living and includes independent living, leisure, health and grooming, social skills, communication skills, vocational preparation and skill training, and generalizable skills, as well as community involvement through age appropriate content. (p. 13)

And Wimmer (1981) defines functional skills as "specific, observable, and measurable performance demonstrated by the student and essential in carrying out everyday social, personal, and on the job tasks" (p. 613).

The scope of these definitions for functional curriculum and functional skills clearly encompasses more than preparation for employment. They are consistent with the underlying philosophy of this text, namely that transition for students with mild disabilities must address the multiple facets of adult living in a wide range of environments. The definition places particular emphasis on the development of functional skills in real-life settings, that is, the provision of instruction in functional skills in the actual settings and environments in which students will later need and apply those skills. Boyer-Stephens and Kearns (1988) use this very criterion to distinguish between functional skills and a functional curriculum. They reject so-called functional skills that may be only variations of traditional academics. They repeat these same sentiments by stressing that reading the newspaper or making change in the classroom, for example, do not constitute a functional curriculum. Functional skills become part of a functional curriculum "when those skills are taught *in* their functional contexts" (p. 16).

Valletutti and Bender (1982) hold to this same standard in their discussion of the holistic nature of a functional curriculum. They believe that the functional curriculum must be taught in real situations and contexts, otherwise it remains "mechanical and unidimensional" (p. 3). Others also recommend training in situ as most desirable but do not hold to so stringent a standard (Schloss & Sedlak, 1986).

There are numerous training models available and many that claim to be functional in nature. Wimmer (1981) has compiled a list of the characteristics common to functional training models:

1. They are student centered rather than content centered.
2. They are built around real life experiences rather than artificial, vicarious settings.
3. They are community based, with activities taking place in the community as well as the school.
4. They involve cooperation between students and teachers in the planning of learning experiences.
5. They emphasize process oriented objectives, such as problem solving or provision of services or goods.
6. Activities are centered around small groups and/or individuals rather than a large group, lecture format.
7. The teacher functions as a guide to student learning as well as an information giver.
8. They often involve teams of teachers from various disciplines.
9. Students acquire skills through active participation rather than passive cooperation. (pp. 613–614)

Any given functional curriculum will not necessarily embody all of these characteristics, but it should conform in large measure to the defining characteristics. The list is helpful in that it adds flesh to the bare bones of the preceding definitions.

The need for training on site and in real-life situations is based on the evidence of the limited capability of students with disabilities to generalize and transfer skills and knowledge learned in one setting to other settings or problem situations (Cartwright, Cartwright, & Ward, 1989). The desirability of training in real-life contexts and situations cannot be denied, but the goal may not be easily attained. In fact, the challenge to provide a functional curriculum (one that would satisfy the stringent standards of Boyer-Stephens & Kearns [1988] and Valletutti & Bender [1982]) may pose even greater difficulties for those with mild disabilities than for those who are severely or moderately disabled. The sheer number of students, the scope of the employment and training options, and the much broader social and interpersonal networks engaged in by adults with mild disabilities make the goal of a functional curriculum both more urgent and more difficult at the same time. Fundamental changes in programming and curriculum will have to be instituted if the goal is to be attained. The development of new positions within the educational staff structure may be essential if substantive transitional programs and truly functional curricula are to become a reality.

Postsecondary School Options.   A word of caution is needed at this point. The growing interest in and support for the functional curricular approach for students who are mildly disabled must not lead to the erroneous conclusion that the functional curriculum is appropriate for all such students. Postsecondary school options for young adults with disabilities have been stymied by stereotypical notions of what they were capable of doing and accomplishing. The range of postsecondary school options for these individuals must be broad. Continuation of the more traditional developmental program is the appropriate choice for many students with mild disabilities who aspire to some form of higher academic training. The explosion of higher education programs geared toward the learner with a disability (most notably those who are learning disabled) in colleges, community colleges, and universities is evidence of this fact.

The choice between the developmental and functional curriculum has serious ramifications for the individual student in terms of both school programming and postschool options. Schloss and Sedlak (1986) offer some helpful guidelines for teachers and parents confronting this weighty decision. They recommend that a functional curriculum be adopted if

1.   the learner has significant difficulty learning new skills,
2.   the student has not kept pace with his or her peers in the total number of skills acquired,
3.   the student is actually engaged in instructional activities for a very small portion of the day, or
4.   the student is approaching graduation. (p. 38)

They suggest a developmental curriculum be adopted if

1.   the student acquires new skills fairly efficiently,
2.   the student has kept pace or is only slightly behind the level of his or her peers,

3. the student spends a substantial part of the school day engaged in instruction, or

4. the student will receive a number of years of instruction before graduation. (p. 38)

These guidelines should help distinguish between students whose best interests are served by a functional curriculum and those who can pursue a traditional academic path.

Schloss and Sedlak (1986) also address the essential issue of the process by which functional curriculum and appropriate objectives are developed. They propose an eight-step process:

1. Identify current and future environments in which the learner is expected to participate.
2. Observe others in these settings to determine necessary skills for successful participation.
3. Develop a skills checklist that assesses learner competence in using the skills required by the setting.
4. Apply the checklist to determine skills the student possesses and the skills that are deficient.
5. Determine skills that may be accommodated through prosthetics (e.g., calculators, charts, color codes, amplification).
6. Delineate developmentally sound task sequences that deal with skill deficits not accommodated through prosthetics.
7. Provide educational experiences that promote acquisition of the skill sequence.
8. Assess the learner, using the skills checklist, to determine the effectiveness of instruction and the degree to which the learner is prepared to participate in the target environment. (p. 40)

Valletutti and Bender (1982) provide a second approach to functional curriculum development. For them functional curricular development involves a sequential, detailed process based on a "reality" perspective of adult life. The steps in the process involve developing general and specific objectives, identifying functional contexts, and determining cognitive, psychomotor, and health and safety factors (see Figure 9–1). Valletutti and Bender believe that functional curricular development must address the various roles that the individual student will or may assume as an adult. Therefore, the aforesaid developmental process is applied to the adult living roles of responsive and responsible person, member of household, traveler, learner, worker, participant in leisure activities, consumer of goods and services, and citizen. By applying the developmental framework for functional curricular development in some or all of the adult role areas applicable to a student, the teacher is in a position to develop lesson plans with specific instructional objectives. Instructional objectives at this point conform to the commonly held perception of instructional statements that address the stimulus situation or conditions under which the student is to perform, the behavior or performance to be displayed by the student, and the establishment of performance or mastery criteria. For each of the adult roles, Valletutti and Bender have applied their developmental framework to the point of determining individual instructional objectives that are, in turn, the basis for individual instructional planning. The application of the developmental framework to the student as "learner" is depicted in Figure 9–2.

The work of Valletutti and Bender (1982) and Schloss and Sedlak (1986) regarding the development of a functional curriculum is quite compatible. They have provided a valuable resource for the classroom teacher. Given a framework and process for curricular development, the teacher is in a position to identify the specific skills to teach. Within the functional curricular approach, practical, applied, and real-life-oriented skills will likely take precedence. However, generalizable skills are increasingly being recognized as an important component of the functional curriculum.

Generalizable Skills

Generalizable skills have been defined by Sitlington (1986) as "generic interpersonal and functional academic skills found in a number of occupations and

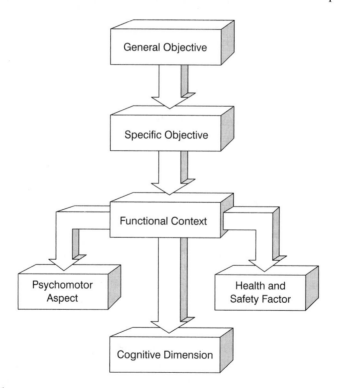

Figure 9–1
Major components of the functional curricular development process
Source: From *Teaching Interpersonal and Community Living Skills: A Model for Handicapped Adolescents and Adults* (p. 6) by P. J. Valletutti and M. Bender, 1982, Baltimore, MD: University Park Press. Adapted by permission.

in vocational education programs which provide specific occupational training" (p. 16). Greenan (1983a, 1983b, 1986) has identified and validated generalizable skills in mathematics, communications, interpersonal relationships, and reasoning. Within each of the four functional/academic areas, specific and relevant skills are listed, 115 skills in all. Each skill is cross-referenced to occupational areas (e.g., agriculture; business, marketing, and management; health;

Specific Objective	1.	The individual responds appropriately to spoken language.
Functional Contexts	a.	When given directions
	b.	Whenever being instructed in a particular skill or task
	c.	Whenever given important information
	d.	Whenever the instructor asks for assistance
	e.	Whenever a colearner asks for assistance that is appropriate to that colearner's program
	f.	Whenever in an emergency situation
Cognitive Dimensions	a.	Comprehension of oral language, including the various precognitive auditory processing skills
	b.	Association of language symbols with their objective reference
	c.	Ability to follow directions in their sequential order
	d.	Judgment of whether to provide assistance to a peer
Psychomotor Aspects	a.	Assisting others to complete tasks
	b.	Carrying out a sequence of motor tasks as part of a particular skill or when following directions involving motor response
Health and Safety Factors		Not applicable

Figure 9–2
Valletutti and Bender's (1982) application of the functional curricular development process
Source: From *Teaching Interpersonal and Community Living Skills: A Model for Handicapped Adolescents and Adults* (p. 174) by P. J. Valletutti and M. Bender, 1982, Baltimore, MD: University Park Press. Adapted by permission.

Specific Objective	2.	The individual communicates orally in such a manner that his or her thoughts, feelings, needs, and wants are readily understood.
Functional Contexts	a.	Whenever he or she wishes to indicate that a task is complete
	b.	Whenever he or she wishes to reinforce colearners socially for attempts and accomplishments
	c.	Whenever he or she needs assistance in completing a task
	d.	Whenever he or she needs to share thoughts and feelings
	e.	Whenever he or she wishes to obtain a desired item
	f.	Whenever he or she wishes to participate in conversations and discussions
	g.	Whenever he or she is in an emergency situation
Cognitive Dimensions	a.	Expression of oral language symbols, including all the various precognitive auditory processing skills and the mechanical aspects of speech (e.g., articulation, pronunciation, and voice production)
	b.	Expression of oral language symbols in the syntactical patterns of his language
Psychomotor Aspects		Not applicable
Health and Safety Factors		Not applicable

Figure 9–2, *continued*

home economics; and industry) and specific vocations within those occupations. Figure 9–3 presents a segment of the generalizable skills curriculum for the area of mathematics. Each of the 115 skills is coded as to its degree of generalizability—high, medium, or low. The skills listing can serve as a resource for both special and vocational education teachers in the development of appropriate instructional programs for individual students and the evaluation of an important dimension of program effectiveness. Student proficiency in the basic generalizable skills can be assessed by student and/or teacher ratings and by performance measures. There is a high degree of consistency among the three measurement approaches (Sitlington, 1986).

Discussion of generalizable skills training is occurring within the context of vocational training, but inspection of the skills quickly reveals that the basic skills are not job specific, though they obviously would enhance a student's performance in many occupational settings. The concept of training in basic generalizable skills is also supported by data on employers' attitudes toward job applicants and job qualifications. Data from a survey of over 5,000 prospective employers in Texas conducted by the Texas Advisory Council on Vocational-Technical Education (1983) reveal that employers place great value on transferable basic skills in addition to occupation-specific skills. Generalizable basic skills are an important determinant in an applicant's getting a job, starting salary, and job retention. Employers cite performance areas in need of improvement among job applicants as writing and speaking effectively, work habits, productivity, dependability, and ability to read and apply printed matter required for the job (cited in Parrish & Colby, 1986).

Elrod (1987) surveyed vocational centers in South Carolina to identify the academic and social skills most important for vocational success. The rationale for such research is to identify the prerequisites for success in vocational education classes in preparation for transition to vocational training. A number of researchers have pursued this avenue of research (Gilgannon & Youshock, 1985; White, Smith, Meers, & Callahan, 1985). Elrod (p. 18) identifies the 11 most frequently cited academic and 10 most frequently cited social skills prerequisites for success in vocational training programs:

Prerequisite Academic Skills:
Basic math skills
Ability to communicate in writing
Linear or volume measurement skills
Basic reading comprehension skills
Read at 10th-grade level
Read at 8th-grade level
Read at 9th-grade level
Read at 7th-grade level
Compute with fractions and decimals
Compute with fractions and mixed numbers
Reasoning ability-logical thinking

Prerequisite Social Skills:
Getting along with others
Taking criticism constructively
Following directions
Working as member of team
Positive attitude
Dependable
Accepts responsibility
Works independently
Honesty
Obeys safety rules

KEY

- High Generalizability ($\bar{x} = 5.01 - 7.00$)
- Medium Generalizability ($\bar{x} = 3.00 - 5.00$)
- Low Generalizability ($\bar{x} = 1.00 - 2.99$)

Columns (Agricultural Occs.): Agricultural Mechanics · Ornamental Horticulture · Agricultural Cooperative Education · Conservation · Cooperative Work Training (CWT) · All Agricultural Occupations Programs

Mathematics Skills

Whole Numbers
1. Read, write, and count single- and multiple-digit whole numbers
2. Add and subtract single- and multiple-digit whole numbers
3. Multiply and divide single- and multiple-digit whole numbers
4. Use addition, subtraction, multiplication, and division to solve word problems with single- and multiple-digit whole numbers
5. Round off single- and multiple-digit whole numbers

Fractions
6. Read and write common fractions
7. Add and subtract common fractions
8. Multiply and divide common fractions
9. Solve word problems with common fractions

Decimals
10. Carry out arithmetic computations involving dollars and cents
11. Read and write decimals in one or more places
12. Round off decimals to one or more places
13. Multiply and divide decimals in one or more places
14. Add and subtract decimals in one or more places
15. Solve word problems with decimals in one or more places

Figure 9–3
Generalizable skills curriculum for math

Source: From *Identification of Generalizable Skills in Secondary Vocational Programs: Executive Summary,* Springfield: Illinois State Board of Education, Department of Adult, Vocational, and Technical Education, 1983. Reprinted by permission.

Vocational Training Areas and Programs

Business, Marketing and Management Occupations

- Advertising Services
- General Merchandise (Sales)
- Personal Services (Sales)
- Marketing Cooperative (D.E.)
- Accounting and Computing Occupations
- Business Data Processing Systems
- Computer Programming
- Filing, Office Machines
- General Office Clerking
- Executive Secretary Science
- Secretarial
- Office Occupations Cooperative Education
- Cooperative Work Training (CWT)
- Word Processing
- Hospitality (Travel and Travel Service)
- Clerical Occupations
- Office Occupations
- **All Bus., Market., And Mgmt. Occupations Programs**

Health Occupations

- Dental Assisting
- Practical Nursing
- Nurse Aide
- Health Care Aide
- Medical Assisting
- Health Aide
- Medical Records
- Health Occupations Cooperative Education
- Cooperative Work Training (CWT)
- Health Occupations
- **All Health Occupations Programs**

KEY

	Generalizability
▢	High Generalizability ($\bar{x} = 5.01 - 7.00$)
▨	Medium Generalizability ($\bar{x} = 3.00 - 5.00$)
▢	Low Generalizability ($\bar{x} = 1.00 - 2.99$)

Home Economics Occs.

Columns:
- Child Care
- Clothing Management, Production, and Service
- Food Management, Production, and Service
- Home Economics Cooperative Education
- Interior Decorating
- Child Development
- Cooperative Work Training (CWT)
- All Home Economics Occupations Programs

Percent

16. Read and write percents
17. Compute percents

Mixed Operations

18. Convert fractions to decimals, percents to fractions, fractions to percents, percents to decimals, decimals to percents, common fractions or mixed numbers to decimal fractions, and decimal fractions to common fractions or mixed numbers
19. Solve word problems by selecting and using correct order of operations
20. Perform written calculations quickly
21. Compute averages

Measurement and Calculation

22. Read numbers or symbols from time, weight, distance, and volume measuring scales
23. Use a measuring device to determine an object's weight, distance, or volume in standard (English) units
24. Use a measuring device to determine an object's weight, distance, or volume in metric units
25. Perform basic metric conversions involving weight, distance, and volume
26. Solve problems involving time, weight, distance, and volume
27. Use a calculator to perform basic arithmetic operations to solve problems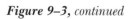

Estimation

28. Determine if a solution to a mathematical problem is reasonable

Figure 9–3, continued

Vocational Training Areas and Programs

Industrial Occupations

Column headers:
- Air Conditioning
- Heating
- Appliance Repair
- Automotive Services
- Body and Fender Repair
- Auto Mechanics
- Aircraft Maintenance
- Commercial Art
- Construction and Building Trades
- Carpentry
- Industrial Maintenance
- Diesel Mechanic
- Drafting
- Electrical Occupations
- Industrial Electrician
- Electronic Occupations
- Radio/Television Repair
- Graphic Arts
- Machine Shop
- Combine Metal Trades
- Welding
- Tool and Die Making
- Cosmetology
- Refrigeration
- Small Engine Repair
- Millwork and Cabinet Making
- Industrial Cooperative Education
- Cooperative Work Training (CWT)
- Truck Driving
- Warehousing
- Home Remodeling and Renovation
- Custodial Maintenance
- Communications and Media Specialist
- **All Industrial Occupations Programs**

KEY

- High Generalizability
  ($\bar{x} = 5.01 - 7.00$)

- Medium Generalizability
  ($\bar{x} = 3.00 - 5.00$)

- Low Generalizability
  ($\bar{x} = 1.00 - 2.99$)

Home Economics Occs.

Columns:
- Child Care
- Clothing Management, Production, and Service
- Food Management, Production, and Service
- Home Economics Cooperative Education
- Interior Decorating
- Child Development
- Cooperative Work Training (CWT)
- All Home Economics Occupations Programs

Whole Numbers

1. Read, write, and count single- and multiple-digit whole numbers
2. Add and subtract single- and multiple-digit whole numbers
3. Multiply and divide single- and multiple-digit whole numbers
4. Use addition, subtraction, multiplication, and division to solve word problems with single- and multiple-digit whole numbers
5. Round off single- and multiple-digit whole numbers

Fractions

6. Read and write common fractions
7. Add and subtract common fractions
8. Multiply and divide common fractions
9. Solve word problems with common fractions

Decimals

10. Carry out arithmetic computations involving dollars and cents
11. Read and write decimals in one or more places
12. Round off decimals to one or more places
13. Multiply and divide decimals in one or more places
14. Add and subtract decimals in one or more places
15. Solve word problems with decimals in one or more places

Figure 9–3, continued

Vocational Training Areas and Programs

Industrial Occupations

Air Conditioning	Heating	Appliance Repair	Automotive Services	Body and Fender Repair	Auto Mechanics	Aircraft Maintenance	Commercial Art	Construction and Building Trades	Carpentry	Industrial Maintenance	Diesel Mechanic	Drafting	Electrical Occupations	Industrial Electrician	Electronic Occupations	Radio/Television Repair	Graphic Arts	Machine Shop	Combine Metal Trades	Welding	Tool and Die Making	Cosmetology	Refrigeration	Small Engine Repair	Millwork and Cabinet Making	Industrial Cooperative Education	Cooperative Work Training (CWT)	Truck Driving	Warehousing	Home Remodeling and Renovation	Custodial Maintenance	Communications and Media Specialist	All Industrial Occupations Programs

219

KEY

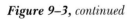

- High Generalizability
  ($\bar{x} = 5.01 - 7.00$)

- Medium Generalizability
  ($\bar{x} = 3.00 - 5.00$)

- Low Generalizability
  ($\bar{x} = 1.00 - 2.99$)

	Agricultural Mechanics	Ornamental Horticulture	Agricultural Cooperative Education	Conservation	Cooperative Work Training (CWT)	All Agricultural Occupations Programs
Percent						
16. Read and write percents						
17. Compute percents						
Mixed Operations						
18. Convert fractions to decimals, percents to fractions, fractions to percents, percents to decimals, decimals to percents, common fractions or mixed numbers to decimal fractions, and decimal fractions to common fractions or mixed numbers						
19. Solve word problems by selecting and using correct order of operations						
20. Perform written calculations quickly						
21. Compute averages						
Measurement and Calculation						
22. Read numbers or symbols from time, weight, distance, and volume measuring scales						
23. Use a measuring device to determine an object's weight, distance, or volume in standard (English) units						
24. Use a measuring device to determine an object's weight, distance, or volume in metric units						
25. Perform basic metric conversions involving weight, distance, and volume						
26. Solve problems involving time, weight, distance, and volume						
27. Use a calculator to perform basic arithmetic operations to solve problems						
Estimation						
28. Determine if a solution to a mathematical problem is reasonable						

Figure 9–3, continued

Vocational Training Areas and Programs

Business, Marketing and Management Occupations	Health Occupations

Business, Marketing and Management Occupations columns:
- Advertising Services
- General Merchandise (Sales)
- Personal Services (Sales)
- Marketing Cooperative (D.E.)
- Accounting and Computing Occupations
- Business Data Processing Systems
- Computer Programming
- Filing, Office Machines
- General Office Clerking
- Executive Secretary Science
- Secretarial
- Office Occupations Cooperative Education
- Cooperative Work Training (CWT)
- Word Processing
- Hospitality (Travel & Travel Service)
- Clerical Occupations
- Office Occupations
- All Bus., Market., And Mgmt. Occupations Programs

Health Occupations columns:
- Dental Assisting
- Practical Nursing
- Nurse Aide
- Health Care Aide
- Medical Assisting
- Health Aide
- Medical Records
- Health Occupations Cooperative Education
- Cooperative Work Training (CWT)
- Health Occupations
- All Health Occupations Programs

The work of Greenan, Elrod, and others highlights the importance of instruction in basic generalizable skills across occupational settings. This body of research is also an important source of curricular goals and objectives for teachers who have major responsibility for the preparation of students for specific vocational training programs during their later secondary school years.

❦ ❦ ❦

SUMMARY

Performance statistics for secondary-age students with mild disabilities must raise questions about the effectiveness of current programming options and approaches. On many important indices of school performance (e.g., GPA, graduation rates, grade retention and failure, minimum competency test scores), these students perform far below their nondisabled peers. In some instances, such as graduation and dropout rates, the magnitude of the difference is substantial. While overall lower levels of school performance for those with disabilities are not unexpected, total rejection of the school experience by large numbers of students with mild disabilities is alarming.

Two themes dominate the literature on secondary programs: (a) instructional effectiveness and (b) curricular directions. The effective schools literature has revealed a generic core of teaching practices with broad applicability across student groups. It appears that effective instruction for students with mild disabilities draws on the same instructional methodology as that for students who are not disabled. Christenson et al. (1989) have summarized essential instructional factors for students who are mildly disabled (see Figure 9–4). Effective teaching is expressed in an active, direct, and interactive teaching style. Under this teaching mode, the teacher and students work toward clear and important instructional goals and objectives. The teacher appreciates the importance of maximizing instructional time and strives to maintain high levels of student engagement and active academic responding. The teacher is sensitive to effective lesson formats and presentation techniques. Questioning strategies, feedback to students, and monitoring of student performance are important aspects of student-teacher interaction. The descriptive phrase "constructively active" (Christenson et al., p. 28) captures the essence of effective instruction for secondary youth with mild disabilities.

Upon entry into the secondary school, if not before, students and their families will be faced with important curricular choices, likely centered on a functional curriculum versus a traditional developmental curriculum. The traditional developmental curriculum is a continuation of the elementary academic program. The outcomes of the traditional program are graduation and, for the majority of nondisabled high school graduates, continuation on to a college or university. The growing concern for the transition of non-college-bound, disadvantaged, and disabled students has raised many questions about the adequacy of the traditional academic curriculum. There is considerable evidence that traditional academic programs do not adequately prepare stu-

---

- The degree to which classroom management is effective and efficient
- The degree to which there is a sense of "positiveness" in the school environment
- The degree to which there is an appropriate instructional match
- The degree to which teaching goals and teacher expectations for student performance and success are stated clearly and are understood by the student
- The degree to which lessons are presented clearly and follow specific instructional procedures
- The degree to which instructional support is provided for the individual student
- The degree to which sufficient time is allocated to academics and instructional time is used efficiently
- The degree to which the student's opportunity to respond is high
- The degree to which the teacher actively monitors student progress and understanding
- The degree to which student performance is evaluated appropriately and frequently

---

Figure 9–4
Instructional factors essential for students with mild disabilities

Source: From "Critical Instructional Factors for Students with Mild Handicaps: An Integrative Review" by S. L. Christenson, J. E. Ysseldyke, and M. L. Thurlow, 1989, *Remedial and Special Education, 10*(5), p. 22. Copyright 1989 by PRO-ED, Inc. Reprinted with permission.

dents who are not going on to higher education for transition to work and other aspects of adult living.

Functional curricular programs are emerging as an alternative. The functional curriculum emphasizes instruction in personal, social, and job-related skills to facilitate the student's entry into the adult world. Vocational preparation is, at this time, the primary focus of functional curricula. For the student with mild disabilities, a too narrow focus on vocational preparation to the exclusion of other important adult roles (e.g., consumer, citizen, spouse, parent) is problematic. Students who are mildly disabled must be prepared for full adult lives.

A rigid dichotomization of curricular options into academic and the functional categories is probably an overstatement. Curricular options vary along two dimensions: (a) restrictiveness, or time spent out of the regular education mainstream, and (b) degree of accommodation of method and materials to meet individual learning needs (Zigmond & Sansone, 1986). Also, there is growing interest in the integration of academic and functional curricula, particularly in the realm of vocational education as seen in innovative teaching arrangements and instruction in "generalizable skills."

The issue of choice between curricular options has implications for the student's future vocational and educational pursuits. Students who attend and graduate from comprehensive academic high schools pursue higher education in far greater numbers than students who pursue more narrow vocational programs, particularly in specialized vocational training centers. However, the emerging conceptualization of transition for students who are mildly disabled envisions a much broader range of postschool options. Ultimately, secondary school programs for them will be judged by the extent to which these programs encourage significant student performance and progress toward the attainment of important instructional goals and objectives.

REFERENCES

Arlin, M. (1979). Teacher transitions can disrupt time flow in classrooms. *American Educational Research Journal*, *16*(1), 42–56.

Babich, A., & Cassity, S. (1990). Integrating academics in vocational programming at the secondary level. *Journal for Vocational Special Needs Education*, *13*(1), 31–34.

Barbieri, J. M., & Wircenski, J. L. (1990). Developing integrated curriculum: Academic and vocational cooperation. *Journal for Vocational Special Needs Education*, *13*(1), 27–29.

Becker, W. C. (1977). Teaching reading and language to the disadvantaged: What we have learned from field research. *Harvard Educational Review*, *47*(4), 518–543.

Bickel, W. E., & Bickel, D. D. (1986). Effective schools, classrooms, and instruction: Implications for special education. *Exceptional Children*, *52*(6), 489–500.

Borg, W. R. (1980). Time and school learning. In C. Denham & A. Lieberman (Eds.), *Time to learn* (pp. 33–72). Washington, DC: National Institutes of Education.

Borich, G. D. (1992). *Effective teaching methods* (2nd ed.). New York: Merrill/Macmillan.

Boyer-Stephens, A., & Kearns, D. (1988). Functional curriculum for transition. *Journal for Vocational Special Needs Education*, *11*(1), 13–18.

Brophy, J. E. (1979). Teacher behavior and its effects. *Journal of Educational Psychology*, *71*, 733–750.

Brophy, J. E., & Good, T. L. (1986). Teacher behavior and student achievement. In M. C. Wittrock (Ed.), *Handbook of research on teaching* (3rd ed., pp. 328–375). New York: Macmillan.

Brown, L., Nietupski, J., & Hamre-Nietupski, S. (1976). The criterion of ultimate functioning and public school services for severely handicapped children. In M. A. Thomas (Ed.), *Hey, don't forget about me!* (pp. 2–15). Reston, VA: Council for Exceptional Children.

Carlson, S. A. (1985). The ethical appropriateness of subject-matter tutoring for learning disabled adolescents. *Learning Disabilities Quarterly*, *8*(4), 310–314.

Carnine, D. W. (1981). High and low implementation of direct instruction teaching techniques. *Education and Treatment of Children*, *4*, 43–51.

Carnine, D., Silbert, J., & Kameenui, E. (1990). *Direct instruction reading* (2nd ed.). New York: Merrill/Macmillan.

Cartwright, G. P., Cartwright, C. A., & Ward, M. E. (1989). *Educating special learners*. Belmont, CA: Wadsworth.

Christenson, S. L., Ysseldyke, J. E., & Thurlow, M. L. (1989). Critical instructional factors for students with mild handicaps: An integrative review. *Remedial and Special Education, 10*(5), 21–31.

Cooley, W. W., & Leinhardt, G. (1980). The instructional dimensions study. *Educational Evaluation and Policy Analysis, 2*(1), 7–25.

Corno, L., & Snow, R. E. (1986). Adapting teaching to individual differences among learners. In M. C. Wittrock (Ed.), *Handbook of research on teaching* (pp. 605–629). New York: Macmillan.

Dalke, C., & Schmitt, S. (1987). Meeting the transition needs of college-bound students with learning disabilities. *Journal of Learning Disabilities, 20*(3), 176–180.

Delquadri, J. C., Greenwood, C. R., Stretton, K., & Hall, R. V. (1983). The peer tutoring program: A classroom procedure for increasing opportunity to respond and spelling performance. *Education and Treatment of Children, 6*(3) 225–239.

Doyle, W. (1979). Classroom tasks and student abilities. In P. Peterson & H. Walberg (Eds.), *Research in teaching: Concepts, findings and implications* (pp. 182–209). Berkeley, CA: McCutchan.

Elrod, G. F. (1987). Academic and social skills pre-requisite to success in vocational training. *Journal for Vocational Special Needs Education, 10*(1), 17–21.

Emmer, E. T., Evertson, C. M., Sanford, J. P., Clements, B. S., & Worsham, M. E. (1984). *Classroom management for secondary teachers.* Englewood Cliffs, NJ: Prentice-Hall.

Engelmann, S., Johnson, G., Hanner, S., Carnine, L., Meyers, L., Osborn, S., Haddox, P., Becker, W., Osborn, J., & Becker, J. (1978). *Corrective reading program.* Chicago: Science Research Associates.

Englert, C. (1984). Effective direct instruction practices in special education settings. *Remedial and Special Education, 5*(2), 38–47.

Englert, C. S., Tarrant, K. L., & Mariage, T. V. (1992). Defining and redefining instructional practice in special education: Perspectives on good teaching. *Teacher and Special Education, 15*(2), 62–86

Evertson, C. M., Emmer, E. T., Clements, B. S., Sanford, J. P., & Worsham, M. E. (1984). *Classroom management for elementary teachers.* Englewood Cliffs, NJ: Prentice-Hall.

Fardig, D. B., Algozzine, R. F., Schwartz, S. E., Hensel, J. W., & Westling, W. L. (1985). Postsecondary vocational adjustment of rural, mildly handicapped students. *Exceptional Children, 52*(2), 115–121.

Fisher, C. W., Berliner, D. C., Filby, N. N., Marliave, R., Cahen, L. S., & Dishaw, M. M. (1980). Teaching behaviors, academic learning time, and student achievement: An overview. In C. Denham & A. Lieberman (Eds.), *Time to learn* (pp. 7–32). Washington, DC: National Institutes of Education.

Fisher, C. W., Filby, N. N., Marliave, R., Cahen, L. S., Dishaw, M. M., Moore, J. E., & Berliner, D. C. (1978). *Teaching behaviors, academic learning time and student achievement: Final report of phase III-B beginning teacher evaluation study, Technical report V-1.* San Francisco: Far West Laboratory for Educational Research and Development. (ERIC Document Reproduction Service No. ED 183 525)

Fourqurean, J. M., & LaCourt, T. (1989). *Perspectives on the transition to young adulthood: A follow-up study of handicapped students (Final report of region IV EHAB Cycle II Discretionary Grant).* Houston, TX: Department of Special Education, Cypress-Fairbanks Independent School District.

Gersten, R. (1985). Direct instruction with special education students: A review of evaluation research. *Journal of Special Education, 19*(1), 41–58.

Gersten, R. M., & Maggs, A. (1982). Teaching the general case to moderately retarded children: Evaluation of a five year project. *Analysis and Intervention in Developmental Disabilities, 2,* 329–343.

Gilgannon, N., & Youshock, J. M. (1985). The holistic approach: Bridging the communication gap between special and vocational educators. *Journal for Vocational Special Needs Education, 8*(1), 23–24, 30.

Good, T., & Beckerman, T. (1978). Time on task: A naturalistic study in sixth-grade classrooms. *Elementary School Journal, 78*(3), 193–201.

Good, T. L., & Brophy, J. E. (1987). *Looking in classrooms* (4th ed.). New York: Harper & Row.

Goodman, L. (1985). The effective schools movement and special education. *Teaching Exceptional Children, 17*(2) 102–105.

Goodman, L. (1990). *Time and learning in the special education classroom.* New York: State University of New York Press.

Goodman, L., & Bennett, R. E. (1982). Use of norm-referenced assessment for the mildly handicapped: Basic issues reconsidered. In T. L. Miller & E. E. Davis (Eds.), *The mildly handicapped student* (pp. 241-262). New York: Grune & Stratton.

Greenan, J. P. (1983a). Identification and validation of generalizable skills in vocational programs. *Journal of Vocational Education Research, 8*(3), 46–71.

Greenan, J. P. (1983b). *Identification of generalizable skills in secondary vocational programs: Executive summary.* Springfield: Illinois State Board of Education, Department of Adult, Vocational, and Technical Education.

Greenan, J. P. (1986). Curriculum and assessment in generalizable skills instruction. *Journal for Vocational Special Needs Education, 9*(1), 3–10.

Greenan, J. P., & Tucker, P. (1990). Integrating science knowledge and skills in vocational education programs. *Journal for Vocational Special Needs Education, 13*(1), 19–22.

Gump, P. V. (1974). Operating environments in schools of open and traditional design. *School Review, 82,* 575–593.

Hall, R. V., Delquadri, J., Greenwood, C. R., & Thurston, L. (1982). The importance of opportunity to respond in children's academic success. In E. B. Edgar, N. C. Haring, J. R. Jenkins, & C. G. Pious (Eds.), *Serving young handicapped children: Issues and research* (pp. 107–140). Baltimore, MD: University Park Press.

Hasazi, S. B., Gordon, L. R., Roe, C. A., Hull, M., Finck, K., & Salembier, G. (1985). A statewide follow-up on post high school employment and residential status of students labeled "mentally retarded." *Education and Training of the Mentally Retarded, 20,* 222–234.

Hawley, W. D., & Rosenholtz, S. J. (1984). Effective teaching. *Peabody Journal of Education, 61*(4), 15–52.

Haynes, M. C., & Jenkins, J. R. (1986). Reading instruction in special education resource rooms. *American Educational Research Journal, 23*(2), 161–190.

Horner, R. H., Jones, D., & Williams, J. A. (1985). Teaching generalized street crossing to individuals with moderate and severe retardation. *Journal of the Association for Persons with Severe Handicaps, 10*(2), 71–78.

Horner, R. H., & McDonald, R. S . (1982). A comparison of single instance and general case instruction in teaching a generalized vocational skill. *Journal of the Association for the Severely Handicapped, 7*, 7–20.

Kallison, J. (1980). *Organization of the lesson as it affects student achievement.* Unpublished doctoral dissertation, University of Texas, Austin.

Kerr, M. M., Nelson, C. M., & Lambert, D. (1987). *Helping adolescents with learning and behavior problems.* New York: Merrill/Macmillan.

Kounin, J. (1970). *Discipline and group management in classrooms.* New York: Holt, Rinehart, & Winston.

Kounin, J., & Obradovic, S. (1968). Managing emotionally disturbed children in regular classrooms: A replication and extension. *Journal of Special Education, 2*, 129–135.

Land, M., & Smith, L. (1979). The effect of low inference teacher clarity inhibitors on student achievement. *Journal of Teacher Education, 31*, 55–57.

Larrivee, B. (1986). Effective teaching for mainstreamed students is effective teaching for all students. *Teacher Education and Special Education, 9*(4), 173–179.

Leinhardt, G., & Seewald, A. M. (1981). Student-level observation of beginning reading. *Journal of Educational Measurement, 18*(3), 171–177.

MacMillan, D. L., Keogh, B. K., & Jones, R. L. (1986). Special educational research on mildly handicapped learners. In M. C. Wittrock (Ed.), *Handbook of research on teaching* (3rd ed., pp. 686–726). New York: Macmillan.

Mangrum, C. T., & Strichart, S. S. (1984). *College and the learning disabled student.* Orlando, FL: Grune & Stratton.

Marder, C. (1991). *How well are youth with disabilities really doing compared with the general population? Findings from the national longitudinal study of special education students.* Menlo Park, CA: SRI International.

Medley, D. M. (1979). The effectiveness of teachers. In P. L. Peterson & H. L. Walberg (Eds.), *Research on teaching: Concepts, findings, and implications* (pp. 11–27). Berkeley, CA: McCutchan.

Parrish, L. H., & Colby, C. R. (1986). Personnel preparation in generalizable skills instruction. *Journal for Vocational Special Needs Education, 9*(1), 34–37.

Pickard, S. (1990). Integrating math skills into vocational education curricula. *Journal for Vocational Special Needs Education, 13*(1), 9–13.

Rieth, H. J., & Frick, T. (1982). *An analysis of academic learning time (ALT) of mildly handicapped students in special education service delivery systems: Initial report on classroom process variables.* Bloomington, IN: Center for Innovation in Teaching the Handicapped.

Rieth, H., Polsgrove, L., Okolo, C., Bahr, C., & Eckert, R. (1987). An analysis of the secondary special education classroom ecology with implications for teacher training. *Teacher Education and Special Education, 10*(3), 113–119.

Rosenshine, B. V. (1976). Recent research on teaching behaviors and student achievement. *Journal of Teacher Education, 27*, 61–64.

Rosenshine, B. V. (1979). Content, time, and direct instruction. In P. L. Peterson & J. H. Walberg (Eds.), *Research on teaching: Concepts, findings, and implications.* Berkeley, CA: McCutchan.

Rosenshine, B. V. (1981). How time is spent in elementary classrooms. *Journal of Classroom Instruction, 17*(1), 16–25.

Rosenshine, B. V. (1983). Teaching functions in instructional programs. *Elementary School Journal, 83*(4), 335–352.

Rosenshine, B. V., & Stevens, R. (1984). Classroom instruction in reading. In P. D. Pearson (Ed.), *Handbook of reading research* (pp. 745–798). New York: Longman.

Ross, R. P. (1984). Classroom segments: The structuring of school time. In L. W. Anderson (Ed.), *Time and school learning* (pp. 69–87). New York: St. Martin's Press.

Sarkees-Wircenski, M. D., & West, L. (1990). Integrating basic academic skills in vocational education programs: A challenge for the future. *Journal for Vocational Special Needs Education, 13*(1), 5–8.

Schloss, P. J., & Sedlak, R. A. (1986). *Instructional methods for students with learning and behavior problems*. Boston: Allyn & Bacon.

Silbert, J., Carnine, D., & Stein, M. (1981). *Direct instruction mathematics*. New York: Merrill/Macmillan.

Sitlington, P. L. (1986). Support services related to generalizable skills instruction. *Journal for Vocational Special Needs Education, 9*(1), 16–19.

Smith, L., & Sanders, K. (1981). The effects on student achievement and student perception of varying structure in social studies content. *Journal of Educational Research, 74* (5), 333–336.

Snell, M. E. (1983). *Systematic instruction of the moderately and severely handicapped* (2nd ed.). New York: Merrill/Macmillan.

Soar, R. (1973). *Follow-through classroom process measures and pupil growth: Final report.* Unpublished manuscript, College of Education, University of Florida, Gainesville.

SRI International. (n.d.). *National Longitudinal Transition Study of Special Education Students: Highlights.* Unpublished manuscript. (Available from SRI International, The National Longitudinal Transition Study, Room BS136, 333 Ravenswood Ave., Menlo Park, CA 94025)

Stallings, J. (1975). Implementation and child effects of teaching practices in follow through classrooms. *Monograph of the Society for Research in Child Development, 40* (7-8, Serial No. 163).

Stallings, J. (1981). *What research has to say to administrators of secondary schools about effective teaching and staff development.* (ERIC Document Reproduction Service No. ED 104 969)

Stallings, J. D., & Kaskowitz, D. H. (1974). *Follow-through classroom observation evaluation, 1972-1973.* Menlo Park, CA: SRI International. (ERIC Document Reproduction Service No. ED 104 969)

Stallings, J., Needels, M., & Stayrook, N. (1979). *The teaching of basic reading skills in secondary schools: Phase II and Phase III.* Menlo Park, CA: SRI International.

Stevens, P., & Lichtenstein, S. (1990). Integrating communication skills into vocational programs. *Journal for Vocational Special Needs Education, 13*(1), 15–18.

Texas Advisory Council on Vocational-Technical Education. (1983). *Qualities employers like, dislike in job applicants: Results of a statewide employer survey.* Austin: Author.

U.S. Department of Education. (1992). *Digest of education statistics* (Report No. 92-660). Washington, DC: U.S. Department of Education, Office of Educational Research and Improvement.

Valletutti, P. J., & Bender, M. (1982). *Teaching interpersonal and community living skills: A model for handicapped adolescents and adults.* Baltimore, MD: University Park Press.

Vitello, S. J. (1988). Handicapped students and competency testing. *Remedial and Special Education, 9*(5), 22–28.

Wagner, M. (1990). *The school programs and school performance of secondary students classified as learning disabled: Findings from the national longitudinal transition study of special education students.* Menlo Park, CA: SRI International.

Weber, J. M. (1988). The relevance of vocational education to dropout prevention. *Vocational Education Journal, 63*(6), 36–38.

Weber, J., Puleo, N., Kurth, P., Fisch, M., & Schaffner, D. (1988). *The dynamics of secondary vocational classrooms.* Columbus: National Center for Research in Vocational Education, Ohio State University. (ERIC Document Reproduction Service No. ED 297 090)

White, S., Smith, H., Meers, G., & Callahan, J. (1985). The key to transition: Merging vocational and special education. *Journal for Vocational Special Needs Education, 8*(1), 15–18.

White, W. J., Alley, G. R., Deshler, D. D., Schumaker, J. B., Warner, M. W., & Clark, F. L. (1982). Are there learning disabilities after high school? *Exceptional Children, 49*(3), 273–274.

Wimmer, D. (1981). Functional learning curricula in the secondary schools. *Exceptional Children, 47*(8), 610–616.

Wong, B. Y. L. (1985). Potential means of enhancing content acquisition in learning-disabled adolescents. *Focus on Exceptional Children, 17*(1), 1–8.

Wong, B. Y. L., Wong, R., Darlington, D., & Jones, W. (1991). Interactive teaching: An effective way to teach revision skills to adolescents with learning disabilities. *Learning Disabilities Research & Practice, 6*(2), 117–127.

Zigmond, N., & Sansone, J. (1986). Designing a program for the learning disabled adolescent. *Remedial and Special Education, 7*(5), 13–17.

Zigmond, N., Sansone, J., Miller, S. E., Donahoe, S. E., & Kohnke, R. (1986). Teaching learning disabled students at the secondary school level: What research says to teachers. *Learning Disabilities Focus, 1*(2), 108–115.

Chapter 10

❦ ❦ ❦

Academic Programming at the Postsecondary Level

I've dealt with psychologists, neurologists, vocational counselors, and they all seem rather unconcerned how to get the help and training I need to succeed. I am currently in college working toward an associate degree in the field of dietetics. After years of frustration I am finally receiving training equal to my intellectual abilities, not just a job. I live with my parents because since I started working at 18 (I'm now 24), I have had 15 jobs all of which required the use of math, knowledge of right and left, and good eye-hand skills which I don't possess. (Smith, 1989, pp. 110–111)

I want to succeed in college, I have a negative view of "I can't do anything but work with my hands (vocational school)." In school I was told I could never go to college. A college degree would mean "I would beat the system; I would show 'them' I could." And I will now that I have help! Through TRC and taped books and tests, extended test time and spelling help, etc., I have a chance. In high school I was told I was retarded by my counselor. (Smith, 1989, p. 106)

S elf-reports of young adults with mild disabilities succeeding in postsecondary settings are beginning to be reported in the literature. The right to participate in postsecondary education for individuals with disabilities was legislated by the Rehabilitation Act of 1973 and its accompanying Section 504 regulations. The need for postsecondary services for this population has already been documented (Bursuck, Rose, Cowen, & Yahaya, 1989; Gajar, 1986, 1992; Mangrum & Strichart, 1984; McGuire, Norlander, & Shaw 1990).

In this chapter we present a discussion of the legal, academic, vocational, and economic foundations for providing programming at the postsecondary level of education for individuals who are mildly disabled. The components of postsecondary programs—admissions, personnel, identification-diagnosis, and service delivery—are then presented. The chapter concludes with a rationale for and examples of unique interventions or methodologies in postsecondary environments, utilized with individuals with mild disabilities.

🌱 🌱 🌱

FOUNDATIONS

Legal

PL 93-112, the Rehabilitation Act of 1973, Section 504, states:

> No otherwise qualified handicapped individual in the United States . . . . shall, solely by reason of his handicap, be excluded from the participation in, be denied the benefits of, or be subjected to discrimination under any activity receiving federal financial assistance.

The regulations issued under this statute (specifically Subpart E) guarantee entrance of qualified students with disabilities into colleges, universities, and trade schools that receive any form of federal assistance including direct financial aid to the students. Under Section 504, postsecondary institutions are obligated to adhere to the following conditions:

1. The institution cannot place a limitation on the number of qualified handicapped* students who can be admitted.
2. Preadmission inquiries as to whether applicants are handicapped or not cannot be conducted.
3. Students cannot be excluded from a course of study solely on the basis of a handicapping condition.
4. Modifications in degree or academic course requirements must be made when such requirements discriminate against qualified students who are handicapped.
5. Rules (such as prohibiting tape recorders in classrooms) must be waived for certain students who are handicapped.
6. Devices or aids which ensure the full participation of students who are handicapped in the classroom cannot be prohibited.
7. Alternative testing and evaluation methods for measuring student achievement may be necessary for students with sensory, manual, or speaking skill impairment. (Exceptions include areas in which these skills are being measured as an indication of achievement.)
8. Faculty members may be requested to adapt teaching techniques and use special devices (such as amplification equipment) for classes in which students who are handicapped are enrolled.
9. It is discriminatory to counsel students who are handicapped toward restrictive careers unless such counseling is justified by the licensing or certification requirements of the profession.
10. Finally, students who are handicapped and feel discriminated against have the right to process complaints through the institution's civil rights channels or to initiate legal proceedings on an individual basis.

The regulations for Section 504 have forced most institutions of higher education to develop policies to accommodate the special needs of students with

---

*In this chapter we will use the word *handicapped* when we are discussing legislation in which that term is used. Otherwise we will use the preferred term *disabled*.

disabilities. The extent of such accommodations required under the law is still debatable and the subject of many lawsuits. The requirement for "reasonable accommodation" has not yet been operationally and consistently defined.

Academic

Based on legislative mandates, an increasing number of adults with disabilities are enrolling in postsecondary college and university programs (Brill, 1987; Gajar, 1989; Mangrum & Strichart, 1984). Students identified as learning disabled (LD) constitute the largest proportion of individuals who are mildly disabled seeking admittance to college and university undergraduate and graduate programs. McGuire et al. (1990) indicate that since 1978 the incidence of learning disabilities among college freshmen has increased tenfold.

In spite of the fact that students who are mildly disabled are succeeding in college and university programs and that applications to postsecondary programs have increased dramatically, a number of authors point out that a dramatic gap still exists between the number of qualified disabled persons who are college students and the number of qualified disabled persons who could be enrolled in a college or university (Killpack & Romero, 1983; Stewart, 1988). Jarrow (1986), in a comparison of disabled and nondisabled students in postsecondary programs, reports that 50% to 65% of students who are not disabled go on to college programs. On the other hand, less than 40% of students with disabilities who have the potential for a college education actually pursue postsecondary education. The discrepancy may be a reflection of tradition, momentum, fear on the part of young adults with disabilities, subtly restrictive policies of higher education, or all of these in combination. The fact that students who are disabled are already being awarded undergraduate and graduate degrees in a number of disciplines demonstrates that such individuals are capable of successfully completing academically oriented postsecondary programs.

Persons with learning disabilities are not the only group of young adults with mild disabilities who are taking advantage of doors newly opened by Section 504. McAfee (1989) and McAfee and Scheeler (1987) investigated community college programs for people with behavioral disorders and mental retardation, respectively. They conclude that colleges (at least community colleges) have begun to serve these two populations as well. In fact, services for students with emotional-behavioral disorders have existed in colleges for decades. These services are usually generic (e.g., personal counseling) and are available to all students. In contrast, services for students with mild mental retardation have more recently emerged and often take the form of special programs for vocational, independent living, or social skills.

Vocational

Postsecondary vocational education for individuals who are mildly disabled is another option in the transitional process. Postsecondary vocational education programs offer specialized training in various occupational areas rather than offering baccalaureate or graduate degrees. Scheiber and Talpers (1987) identify technical institutes, community colleges, and area vocational-technical centers as public vocational education institutions. Private or proprietary programs include trade, technical, and business schools. Scheiber and Talpers state that postsecondary vocational education is available in hundreds of fields, including:

1. *agriculture/agribusiness* (e.g., forestry, horticulture, animal inspection);
2. *marketing and distribution* (e.g., selling, advertising, real estate, food services);
3. *health* (e.g., nursing, medical technology);
4. *business and office* (e.g., secretarial and clerical occupations);
5. *trade and industry* (e.g., carpentry, masonry, automotive service, small engine repair); and
6. *occupational home economics* (e.g., cosmetology, fashion, child care).

Most postsecondary vocational education programs provide a viable alternative to and/or a transitional step toward a college or university program for students who are mildly disabled. The advantages of a postsecondary vocational education for individuals who are mildly disabled include:

1. the absence of stringent admission requirements (in many cases, admission requirements include only proof of age and high school graduation);
2. the availability of vocational education support teams that provide specialized assistance in mastering specific skills and so forth;
3. specialized training in an occupational skill;
4. the provision of individualized job placement services not available in secondary or high school settings; and
5. preparation for transfer to a 4-year institution. Grades and achievement in a community college may negate a poor high school transcript (Scheiber & Talpers, 1987).

Economic

The 1980s experienced an increase in the enrollment of individuals with disabling conditions in postsecondary programs, as well as a rise in funding incentives for model postsecondary programs. Gajar, Rusch, and DeStefano (1989), in a review of models and outcomes of participants served by a number of federally funded projects, report the following:

1. The activities associated with the models were numerous and varied.
2. Major areas of concentration included assessment, participant training, and outreach activities.
3. Most of the models were active in the production and dissemination of project-developed materials.
4. Products and materials were available even for programs for which final reports were missing. The utility of the products disseminated, however, was difficult to determine.

5. Outcome measures varied and, consequently, could not be compared across programs.
6. Problem areas included identification of students, personnel recruitment, scheduling, unrealistic expectations, interagency cooperation, and workshop recruitment.

One of the implications of the research is that the economic position of the postsecondary setting (academic or vocational, public or private) is related to the availability or nonavailability of programs to individuals with disabilities. For many small or private postsecondary institutions, students with disabilities represent a new source of enrollments and an increase in the student base. Thus, they translate into increased financial support (Mangrum & Strichart, 1983a, 1983b). In contrast, major universities with large enrollments may view facilitating access to services for individuals who are disabled as a financial burden that will not be balanced by the increase in tuition revenue. In addition, large universities have many other competing activities that may be more rewarding financially (e.g., research, service contracts with industry, continuing education). Accommodation of persons with mild disabilities may take a back seat.

Federal financial support is a major factor in the delivery of services to students who are mildly disabled in postsecondary settings. Services not specifically mandated by statute or court decision are often curtailed, eliminated, or left undeveloped because of budgetary constraints or when federal money runs out. For example, Gajar (1992) reports that a number of services offered to students in Penn State's model university program for students with learning disabilities have been cut because of budget restrictions.

Cordoni (1982) states that programs designed specifically for students with disabilities can range anywhere from $3,000 to $10,000 per student, per year. Most academic and vocational programs are not able or willing to expend this type of financial support without some kind of governmental assistance. Students with disabilities are often referred to existing generic services available to all students such as university learning centers and career development and placement services. Generic student services and personnel, however, are often ill equipped to handle the unique problems faced by individuals with disabling conditions. In order to provide the necessary services, a number of postsecondary programs charge additional fees or higher tuition (Barbaro, 1982; Mangrum & Strichart, 1983a, 1983b; Ugland & Duane, 1976).

Students with disabilities have a right and a need for postsecondary services. Each postsecondary program must, however, determine whether the monies spent for successful transition are warranted. In addition, each institution must decide how the money that is available can be spent best.

✻ ✻ ✻

POSTSECONDARY PROGRAMS

In a nationwide survey of postsecondary educational services for students with disabilities, Bursuck et al. (1989) found that services varied a great deal from program to program and that postsecondary guides to services were inaccurate and incomplete. Additionally, they found:

- access to programs was a major concern;
- compensatory strategies were found to be important;
- provision of remedial instruction was considered important;
- smaller institutions offered more personalized services;
- the utilization of peer tutoring was an important component; and
- the absence of follow-up data on the rate of graduation, vocational, and life adjustment was formidable.

As an extension of the legal, academic, vocational, and economic foundations for postsecondary education for individuals who are mildly disabled, a number of themes, components, and transitional concerns can be identified. These include concerns over admission requirements, personnel identification, student identification and diagnosis, and service delivery. As illustrated in the following discussion, diverse program components have evolved spontaneously generally in the absence of theoretical justification or an overall guiding model. The fact, however, remains: *a number of students with disabilities are being admitted to and are succeeding in postsecondary programs. Postsecondary institutions are mandated to serve these students.*

Components of Postsecondary Programs

Before discussing postsecondary program components, we remind the reader of the distinction made earlier between postsecondary *academic* and *vocational* programs. Postsecondary academic programs encompass 4-year college or university settings and graduate degree institutions. Postsecondary vocational programs include 2-year community college programs, trade and business schools, and the like. In short, all programs that do not grant postsecondary degrees at the bachelor's level or higher are identified as vocational programs. We recognize that this distinction is somewhat arbitrary and even inaccurate in some cases (e.g., where a community college program is a stepping stone to a 4-year degree at another college); however, the distinction is useful for discussion, and many community college programs are vocational in nature.

Admissions. Scheiber and Talpers (1987) have identified admission requirements and procedures required by various postsecondary programs (see Figure 10–1). Many postsecondary programs (especially institutions that provide academic programs) have not developed specific admission standards for students with disabilities (Bowen, 1986). Often, during the postsecondary admission process, a catch-22 situation develops such as the following:

1. An applicant who is mildly disabled has had difficulty in one or more areas of academic achievement.
2. Admission requirements to the university or college postsecondary setting are based on aspects of achievement including a standardized entrance examination.

Community and Junior Colleges, Public, Two-Year

- Usually open admission
- 18 years or older
- Most require high school diploma or GED for credit courses. GED may be taken during freshman year.

Junior Colleges, Private, Two-Year

- High school diploma or GED
- Usually require some type of entrance exams (SATs, ACTs)
- Usually request grade point average and/or class rank
- Experience and personal qualities usually given consideration

Colleges, Universities, and Technical Schools, Public and Private, Four-Year

Regular Admission

- High school diploma or GED usually required
- Entrance exams (SATs or ACTs)
- Grade point average and/or class rank
- Interview may be required

Special or Provisional Admission

- SATs and ACTs may be waived or lower scores may be accepted.
- Student's potential, goals, interests, commitment, and demonstrated ways of coping with disability are given weight.
- Remedial or study skills classes may be required as basis for admission.

Cooperative Admission
(Special program for students with learning disabilities within college)

- Admission jointly decided by college and special program
- Students *must* disclose disability.
- Usually open admission
- Some schools require high school diploma or GED.
- Some schools or programs require SATs, ACTs, or admissions tests to determine aptitude for the curriculum.

Vocational Education Schools, Public and Private, Two-Year or Less

- Usually open admission
- Some schools require high school diploma or GED.
- Some schools or programs require SATs, ACTs, or admissions tests to determine aptitude for the curriculum.

Figure 10–1

Admission requirements and procedures

Source: From *Unlocking Potential College and Other Choices for Learning Disabled People: A Step-by-Step Guide* (p. 81) by B. Scheiber and J. Talpers, 1987, Bethesda, MD: Adler & Adler. Used by permission.

3. The student experiences difficulty with timed and/or written examinations, so he or she has taken the entrance examination (such as the Scholastic Aptitude Test [SAT]) under nonstandard conditions.
4. This nonstandard administration of the entrance examination has been flagged by the testing service when reporting the results.
5. Because the student has the right to confidentiality and nondiscrimination, the postsecondary program is forbidden to ask preadmission questions concerning the student's disability (including questions about why the test score was obtained under nonstandard conditions).
6. Under mandate, the institution must provide equal access and modified testing and accommodations; however, questions concerning the types of accommodations required by the student are forbidden.

The result is confusion and frustration on the part of both the applicant and the institution.

Personnel. An important phase in the development of postsecondary programs for individuals who are mildly disabled is the identification of key personnel. In college and university programs that assist students with disabilities, the responsibility for contacting and obtaining the support of interested faculty and staff members from various disciplines and administrative services needs to be coordinated by one individual (Vogel, 1982). In postsecondary vocational and/or technical schools, vocational support teams need to be identified and coordinated by a program administrator. The identification of an individual to coordinate a program for university students who are mildly disabled often depends on an individual's interest and willingness to serve in this capacity. Administrators of programs for postsecondary students with mild disabilities are often self-selected and have advocated for their positions. The lack of real commitment on the part of postsecondary educational institutions is reflected in this phenomenon. Furthermore, even after individuals have assumed the position of coordinating services, they may find that they are relatively impotent to effect real change or secure needed resources.

Identification. A consensus on how to identify postsecondary students with disabilities does not exist (Blackburn & Iovacchini, 1982; Cordoni, 1982; Gray, 1981a, 1981b; Hoy & Gregg, 1986). In regard to postsecondary *academic* programs, Nelson and Lignugaris/Kraft (1989) state:

> In some colleges, services are available on request or following student and parent interviews; whereas other programs require lengthy psychoneurological testing or psychoeducational testing to determine if there is a significant discrepancy between aptitude and achievement. (p. 247)

On the other hand, in many *vocational* programs, admissions are open and students can receive services by simply stating that they need them.

To develop effective postsecondary programs for students who are mildly disabled, a decision regarding identification and diagnostic criteria must be reached (especially in academic situations). These criteria will determine whether a student is eligible for services. Universities and degree-granting institutions are required to provide equal access to their programs. The question, however, remains whether these institutions are responsible for providing diagnostic and identification services. Based on current legal interpretation, the answer to this question appears to be no, and many institutions require eligibility verification prior to enrollment.

Gajar (1992) notes that some students (especially students with learning disabilities) may not be identified prior to admission to postsecondary programs. These students achieved average grades or better in high school programs. Their potential, however, exceeded their achievement, and many such students learned to compensate for their disability, or caring teachers provided special, individualized instruction or were willing to overlook their area of disability. Some of these students with mild disabilities are also gifted. Because they were able to use their intellectual abilities to compensate, the gifted students with disabilities were not referred for services. The disability, however, became immediately evident when the student was faced with the rigorous intellectual demands of an academically oriented postsecondary program that strongly stressed independent learning, self-direction, and organization—skills that are often absent. For this reason, early identification is imperative. It permits required services to be provided prior to the development of severe academic problems and failure (Shaywitz & Shaw, 1988).

Service Delivery. Postsecondary service delivery to students who are mildly disabled depends to a large degree on available special funding (Nelson & Lignugaris/Kraft, 1989), as most institutions have been reluctant to set aside a portion of regularly budgeted money for special needs students. In addition, services across programs vary and rely not only on financial backing but also on program objectives.

Academic Education. According to Gajar (1992), academic programs usually provide accommodations such as recorded reading materials, untimed exams, assistance with study skills, and self- and time management. Additional services available to college and university students include mental health counseling, developmental year programs, tutoring, personal or social counseling, academic or program counseling, and career or vocational counseling. Smaller colleges tend to provide more individualized remedial and tutoring services. For example, Barat College and the College of the Ozarks provide intensive individual instruction, while Curry College offers tutoring in groups of two to three students (Vogel & Adelman, 1981).

Vocational Education. A number of postsecondary vocational education programs have developed vocational support teams to work with individuals who are disabled. Scheiber and Talpers (1987) cite California, Colorado, Georgia, Kentucky, Maryland, Missouri, and Wisconsin as states in the forefront of providing services via a team effort. Each of these states employs a specialist in postsecondary vocational education for those who are disabled. This person provides information and counseling regarding the availability and types of postsecondary support programs found in the state. Vocational education team members also give instructional assistance for specific tasks that have proved difficult. Team members may also provide ideas and materials to vocational instructors working with students who are disabled. Finally, team members help individual students find job sites for work experience and eventual job placement.

Counseling. Based on a review of postsecondary programs, Nelson and Lignugaris/Kraft (1989) have determined that counseling services are a major component of programs serving individuals who are disabled. Counseling services typically include (a) personal or social counseling, (b) academic or program counseling, and (c) career or vocational counseling. Gajar (1992) has reviewed these three counseling areas:

1. *Personal counseling.* Students with disabilities often lack the social and interpersonal skills needed to function in a university setting (Mangrum & Strichart, 1984). Difficulties are encountered with time and self-management, communication, and self-advocacy skills. Many academic and vocational programs provide students with mental health and/or psychological counseling services. For example, at Adelphi University social workers provide individual or group counseling (Barbaro, 1982). At the University of Virginia a psychological consultant is available for individual or group counseling sessions (Lefebvre, 1984). These services, however, may not be sufficient. Difficulty with social and personal adjustment often continues to be an obstacle to successful adult functioning. For example, Gajar (1992) reports the difficulty experienced by one student following graduation. The student wrote to inquire about the availability of a group home for adults with learning disabilities. Even though he had graduated with honors, he continued to experience difficulty when interacting with peers, was still living with his parents, and was afraid of not being able to manage within an independent living situation.

The question arises as to whether academic or vocational programs are obligated to provide specialized counseling for students with mild disabilities. The answer to this question must be yes if successful transition from postsecondary to employment and community environments is the intended goal.

2. *Academic counseling.* In a national survey of postsecondary services, Bursuck et al. (1989) found that most institutions surveyed reported arrangements for academic advising, tutoring, advocacy, and progress monitoring for students with learning disabilities. A number of institutions reported the development of Individualized Education Plans (IEPs) and special classes for their students. Academic and vocational programs either emphasized accommodating strategies as intervention objectives or remedial services incorporating basic skill instruction.

In short, it is safe to say that most postsecondary programs emphasize academic counseling and assistance. The extent and nature of these services, however, have not been determined. Research to identify successful intervention techniques for students who are mildly disabled is virtually nonexistent. Finally, the setting demands of the various academic and vocational programs have not been determined (Nelson & Lignugaris/Kraft, 1989). Thus, we are often left with interventions that may be logical but not empirically validated, or we may employ techniques that are "borrowed" from effective practices at the secondary level. Neither of these is a desirable situation. The absence of critical postsecondary methodology inhibits the development and delivery of pertinent and effective services.

3. *Career counseling.* Diverse kinds of career counseling are recommended for students who are mildly disabled, including career awareness, career exploration, job maintenance, and vocational counseling in individual or group sessions (Hoy & Gregg, 1986; Salend, Salend, & Yanok, 1985; Siperstein, 1988; Strichart & Mangrum, 1985). Nelson and Lignugaris/Kraft (1989), however, have found that career counseling is reported to be important by a limited number of surveyed programs (3 out of 14). Again, the question of the need for specialized career counseling and the institution's obligation to provide this type of counseling can be raised. Most academic and vocational programs, however, offer some form of career development and placement service for all of their students, including those who are disabled.

❦ ❦ ❦

POSTSECONDARY METHODOLOGY

Before we discuss techniques or interventions for accommodating students in postsecondary educational settings, the reader must understand the rationale for admitting and serving students who are mildly disabled within postsecondary programs. The beginning of the 1990s experienced a call for "academic excellence" and "a return to the basics" in public education. The call for academic excellence includes the creation of stringent admission and programmatic requirements in academic and vocational postsecondary programs. The call for a return to basics involves an emphasis on basic skill remediation at all levels of education.

We have been conditioned in our society to look for easy answers and to the past for solutions to current problems. We are prone to subscribe to the quick fix. The call for a return to the basics (based on the demand for mastery of basic skills in reading, writing, and arithmetic) as a prerequisite for academic excellence provides an ostensibly fast and simple answer to a complicated problem. However, the needs and rights of students who are disabled are often at odds with these simplistic solutions. In the area of postsecondary education for individuals who are mildly disabled, many people believe that if basic skills are emphasized, literate and creative individuals will evolve. *The fact is that many individuals who are mildly disabled may never master the basic skills of reading, writing, and arithmetic, yet they have the potential for academic excellence.*

If we espouse that academic excellence must be preceded by mastery of basic skills, many students with disabilities will not succeed in postsecondary settings. Basic skill training is important in the early years of education. Later, young adults who are disabled need to use compensating and accommodating strategies to achieve academic independence.

If we bypass the "easy" definition of academic excellence as consisting of the mastery of basic reading, writing, and math skills, we find that broader definitions can apply. For example, *literate* (a component of academic excellence) is defined by the *American Heritage Dictionary* (1976) as "1. Able to read and write. 2. Knowledgeable; educated" (p. 762). Therefore, literacy is something more than just the ability to read and write. It involves knowledge and education. The *Random House Thesaurus* indicates that literacy includes "learning, erudition, scholarship, learnedness, intelligence, enlightenment, edification, culture, intellectuality, a store of knowledge, acquisition, a liberal education." We propose that when provided with adequate interventions, a person who is mildly disabled can achieve literacy in spite of problems with reading and writing.

In a review of the literature pertaining to college students with learning disabilities, Hughes and Smith (1990) found that fewer than one third of approximately 100 articles, published over a 20-year span, were data based and included reports of academic and cognitive performance. Empirical articles dealing with the effectiveness of intervention or treatment approaches are virtually nonexistent. Based on the rationale that academic excellence does not necessarily center on basic skill training, and keeping in mind the paucity of studies identifying successful interventions at the postsecondary level of education, we next present a number of strategies and examples of accommodating techniques that have been developed or used with students who have mild disabilities and are enrolled at Penn State University. These include the PA-A-PA paradigm, a study skills program, the pause procedure, and other suggestions for accommodating students in postsecondary settings. The reader is reminded that these are only a few examples of the unique types of accommodations that potentially can assist postsecondary students who are mildly disabled.

PA-A-PA Paradigm

Most secondary and postsecondary students who are mildly disabled experience problems with time and self-management and identifying the strategies needed for completing a task. The definition of *strategy* (used by these authors when working with postsecondary students) is the response that is taken after alternative actions or options have been identified, presented, or tested; the determination of the probable success of each action is made; and an option is selected. (This definition was related to the authors by Dr. Elizabeth Wiig of Boston College during a visit and presentation at Penn State.) Based on the fact that students who are mildly disabled experience difficulties in identifying pertinent strategies for each task and estimating the time to complete the task, each segment of any activity must be analyzed.

Basically, each task or activity can be divided into three components: the preparatory activity (PA), the activity (A), and the postactivity (PA). This PA-A-PA paradigm is cyclical in that each postactivity begins a new preparatory activity. A simple example involves the activity of brushing one's teeth. The preparatory activity (PA) involves going to the sink, picking up the toothbrush and toothpaste, opening the cap on the toothpaste (some students experience difficulty even with this simple task), and squeezing the paste onto the toothbrush. It may also include purchasing the toothpaste and toothbrush. The activity (A) involves brushing the teeth. The postactivity (PA) involves rinsing, replacing the cap, washing the toothbrush, and returning the brush and toothpaste to the designated area.

If we transfer this paradigm to the secondary or postsecondary setting, the activity may be note taking, studying for an exam, getting information from a text, or using the library. For example, a PA-A-PA paradigm for studying might include preparatory activities such as selecting a study area, deciding on what to study, choosing a strategy for the study session (such as highlighting or recording pertinent details from notes or creating a summary of pertinent information), and finally deciding on the length of time for the study activity. The activity would be the actual study session in which the student applied the selected strategy. Postactivities might include checking to see if the study objectives were met; if not, the student would then evaluate why the objectives were not met and select new objectives or strategies for the next study session. If the objectives were met, then the postactivities would include a new cycle of preparatory activities for the next study session. Figure 10–2 presents a simple example of the cyclical schemata for the PA-A-PA paradigm for a hypothetical study activity. Figure 10–3 illustrates a more complex example of a writing activity that includes a number of PA-A-PA paradigms.

The number of paradigms used and the simplicity or complexity of each paradigm depends on an analysis of a particular student's circumstances and needs. It is hypothesized that any professional working with a postsecondary student who is mildly disabled can develop alternative strategies by developing a pertinent PA-A-PA paradigm. For example, Figure 10–4 illustrates the paradigm as it might be applied to an activity involving career counseling. In this example, the student needs a great deal of direction, and the counselor has created a blueprint for his or her involvement with the student. Each activity may require a separate PA-A-PA for the student to follow.

Postsecondary students with mild disabilities present diverse character-istics. Problems are experienced in a number of areas. Some students experience difficulty in anticipating questions asked in class or on tests. Some students have problems with key words, concepts, relationships. Other students have physical problems: in class they may get the concept but become confused later when the motor activity involved in taking notes interferes with

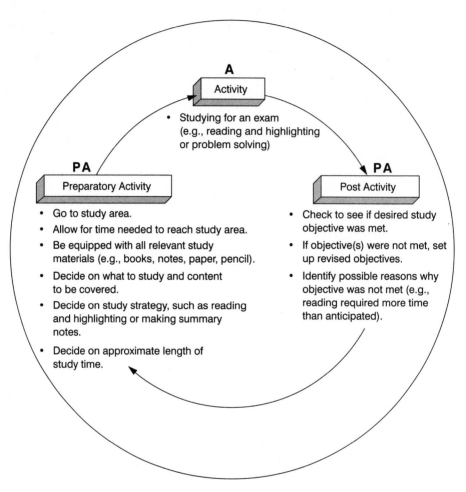

A

Activity

- Studying for an exam (e.g., reading and highlighting or problem solving)

PA

Preparatory Activity

- Go to study area.
- Allow for time needed to reach study area.
- Be equipped with all relevant study materials (e.g., books, notes, paper, pencil).
- Decide on what to study and content to be covered.
- Decide on study strategy, such as reading and highlighting or making summary notes.
- Decide on approximate length of study time.

PA

Post Activity

- Check to see if desired study objective was met.
- If objective(s) were not met, set up revised objectives.
- Identify possible reasons why objective was not met (e.g., reading required more time than anticipated).

Figure 10–2
Cyclical PA-A-PA paradigm for a study activity

their thinking. For these students the preparatory activity for taking notes might involve selecting a strategy such as using a tape recorder or making videotapes (so that body movements can be observed), or note sharing, or word processing. Using the PA-A-PA paradigm, relevant strategies must be determined on an individual basis.

Study Skills Program

In most postsecondary settings (academic and vocational), studying for exams is an important activity involving the extraction of relevant information from lectures and readings. Students who are mildly disabled experience difficulty with identifying and selecting key words, concepts, and relationships from class notes and lectures. Difficulties are encountered in picking appropriate

---

Preparatory Activities

1. Read over the assignment.

2. Clarify assignment with professor.

3. Plan on how information will be collected for assignment.

4. Outline requirements, number of pages, scope, and approach.

5. Collect information and create a PA-A-PA for library activity if appropriate. This would include a PA of:

   a. looking up background information in the encyclopedia, social science index, etc.;

   b. creating a list of sources;

   c. creating a list of key words;

   d. using key words to identify sources through journal abstracts, computer searches, etc. (another PA-A-PA);

   e. locating sources in library;

   f. examining sources for value for written assignment (another PA-A-PA);

   g. photocopying pertinent material; and

   h. taking notes (PA-A-PA).

6. Decide on main points to be made.

7. Arrange important ideas (based on gathered information or notes) under main points and/or themes.

8. Create an outline for the paper and place the main ideas into the outline (may need a PA-A-PA for this activity).

Figure 10–3
Complex PA-A-PA paradigm for a writing activity

strategies for learning the material and for creating hypothetical questions that might be asked during an examination. The following systematic study skills program, created at Penn State, addresses these difficulties.

Overview. The approach to study skills involves the use of sequential strategies for the purpose of (a) selecting relevant information from class notes and assigned readings, (b) organizing selected information, and (c) achieving mastery of the information and/or course content. The program is based on principles of direct instruction and can be used by an individual student or, depending on individual needs and availability of external resources, with teacher, peer, or tutor assistance.

Program Assumptions. The primary assumption of the program is that mastery and application of a series of systematic study skills will result in

9. Plan on time management chart how long it will take to write paper.
10. Plan for a quiet writing area.
11. Prepare work area (paper, notes, outline, utensils, word processor, etc.).

Activity

1. Write according to outline.

Post-Activity

1. Reread for content. Did you cover what you wanted to say?
2. Reread for organization, ways of expression, main idea per paragraph.
3. Cut and paste dependent on above evaluation.
4. Rewrite.
5. Proofread for spelling, grammar, punctuation, style, etc. (Activities 1–5 can be another PA-A-PA labeled "Rewriting Activity.")
6. Give paper to someone else to read and proof.
7. Revise paper according to comments received.
8. Recheck requirements, title page, style, etc.
9. Revise—make additional copy.
10. Reread.
11. Turn paper in on time.
12. Get feedback from instructor.
13. Note instructor's comments for future assignments.

Figure 10–3, continued

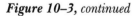

passing grades in any postsecondary academic or vocational course. In other words, the program is geared toward helping the student improve his or her test-taking ability. The program is further based on systematic practices:

1. Study skill tasks are stated in terms that are operational, clear, and precise.
2. Each study skill task has a predetermined objective and a measurable scoring system.
3. Study skill tasks are presented in an *ordered sequence* in line with the logical sequence of learning.
4. Study skill tasks are aimed at attainable goals.

Unique Features. Features of the program that set it apart from other study skill packages include the following:

1. The program can be used with any academic or vocational postsecondary course or program. Its unique structure allows the student to organize

Figure 10–4
PA-A-PA paradigm for career counseling

Preparatory Activities	Activity	Postactivity
• Get input from various teachers about student.	• Advise student on selection of a college for higher education.	• Check on the completion, by the student, of suggested activities (e.g., application materials, interview schedules, and testing schedule or results).
• Get input from student about career goals and preferences.	• Schedule career counseling sessions with the student.	
• Have a list of addresses of colleges of interest to the student or show student how to get this information.		
• If necessary, contact librarian and get him or her to assist student in this search.		
• Have information on admission requirements of selected colleges, options offered, special services, and financial aid information, or show student how to get this from the library.		
• If necessary, include input from parents of student in this decision process.		
• Have a definite strategy by which to advise the student. This should be individualized (e.g., availability of special services is of primary importance).		

and synthesize all available course resources into a compact unit for study. The program is highly specific and helps the student target what needs to be learned for each particular course or subject, and at the same time it has the adaptability and versatility needed to facilitate the learning of very diverse course material. The program does not follow the traditional study skill training approach where study skills are taught and then an attempt is made to generalize the skills to a specific curriculum. The program can be used simultaneously with all courses in which a student needs a structured learning routine.

2.   The contents of the program are based on sound theoretical principles, and program components are conducive to empirical research. The sequence of the study skills is systematic and based on a highly prescribed program of activities that promote academic success through a combination of learning strategies. The program incorporates the principle of repeated practice, a demonstrably effective learning principle. Simply stated, the more correct practice a person has with a skill, the more likely he or she will be to retain and use that skill. The program is data based, molding itself on firm research design and reducing subjectivity. As a result, students can determine at any point how they are progressing. Through a unique coding system that is straightforward and easy to use, the student monitors his or her own progress and, based on discrete evidence, adjusts further study needs and areas of focus. In addition to this self-monitoring, there is also a direct instruction aspect of the program that may be utilized. This provides for a tutor or peer to both facilitate the student's learning and monitor his or her progress. A reliability measure is suggested in which a peer or tutor ensures that the student is following the program accurately and completely.

3.   The time factor is comparable to or less than that traditionally employed. Although it is recognized that this program includes a set of activities that are indeed time-consuming, it is held that the effort required is realistically commensurate with the time necessary for success in a specific course. Furthermore, the process is dovetailed with actual course requirements in contrast to other strategies involving an investment of time outside of course study. The program facilitates the adaptation of study skills to actual course content.

Method.   The specific materials are listed here for clarity but can be varied. The method includes the following steps:

1.   The student takes complete and accurate notes in class.
2.   Immediately after each class the student highlights the class notes using the following method.
    a.   Highlight vocabulary (terms or word definitions) with a yellow marker.
    b.   Highlight concepts (main ideas and supporting details) with a pink marker.
    c.   Highlight concept and term relationships (comparisons and relations between concepts and terms) with a blue marker.

3. After outlining class notes, the student develops an "active file" by daily recording the information from his or her notes into a notebook or binder. The development of an active file involves recording each item of information on separate pages under the appropriate sections labeled "Terms," "Concepts," and "Relationships." (These labels correspond to the three color coding procedures used by the student to highlight.)

4. Each day the student utilizes steps 1 and 2 on assigned readings.

5. The student then records the information from his or her outlined text or assigned readings into the appropriate sections, which correspond to class notes. If readings do not correspond to class notes, then new notebook or binder pages are used for unique terms, concepts, and relationships that have not been addressed in class lectures.

6. The student then composes a question for each item and records this question on the reverse side of the page.

7. (Optional) It is recommended that within the first week of the program a peer/classmate or a tutor follow the same procedures (steps 1–6) as the student with the identical course material. The correspondence between the tutor's and the student's study skill program will indicate the extent to which the student is following the program format. A minimum 90% correspondence is recommended to ensure that the student is taking both accurate and complete notes (steps 1 and 4) and that he or she is recording the information correctly into the study skills notebook.

8. The student then tests him- or herself on all items in the active file, and records a plus or minus (for correct and incorrect responses, respectively) and the date in the columns on the page designated for this purpose.

9. After the student has scored three consecutive plus marks on daily self-quizzing, the items are transferred from the "active file" into the "inactive file" at the back of the notebook or binder.

10. The student periodically tests him- or herself on the items that have been mastered by randomly selecting 30 items from the inactive file. (Optional: It is recommended that a tutor or a peer/classmate conduct this part of the testing on a weekly basis.)

The study skills program has been effective for students with learning disabilities. It provides them with the structure and organization they need to approach complex concepts and chains of concepts.

Pause Procedure

As Ruhl, Hughes, and Gajar (1990) note, few empirically validated strategies have appeared in the literature for faculty to use when lecturing to students who are mildly disabled in postsecondary settings. However, one effective technique for a lecture situation is the pause procedure.

The pause procedure involves 2-minute pauses spaced at logical breaks during a lecture. During a pause, each student and a partner or peer discuss the content of the portion of the lecture just presented. Students are instructed to discuss main ideas and important details. Based on these conversations, students can then utilize the remainder of the pause period to update notes or check them for accuracy. The lecturer does not get involved.

Ruhl et al. (1990) have found that when students with and without learning disabilities were compared on lectures with and without pauses, the pause procedure intervention enhanced the performance of both groups of students on immediate free recall of lecture components and on objective test measures. Long-term free recall, however, was not improved; this is not surprising since transferring information from short-term to long-term memory requires rehearsal, and the students were instructed not to study the material during the research period. On the other hand, the objective test items appeared to have cued student recall. Once the students read the test items, memory for facts was enhanced. In short, given the opportunity to study, students in courses in which the pause procedure is implemented will benefit from its use because they have had the opportunity to take accurate and detailed notes.

The pause procedure possesses many desirable attributes:

1. It is effective for both students who are mildly disabled and those who are not.
2. It alleviates faculty's concern that they are not meeting the classroom needs of students who are mildly disabled.
3. The student, rather than the instructor, has the opportunity to summarize the material and check for the understanding of content, key points, and vocabulary. Thus, it is student centered.
4. Instructor involvement is minimal and simple. The instructor gives up 6 to 8 minutes of lecture time to permit students to discuss the content.
5. The instructor can use the pause time to preview notes on what will be presented next, thereby enhancing the lecture presentation.
6. Finally, a subtle advantage is that it does not require the student to seek outside assistance from the instructor or from a peer, thereby relieving him or her of any personal sense of discomfort or reluctance to do so. In short, the student can adapt without calling attention to him- or herself.

The pause procedure is a strategy instructors can apply in postsecondary settings. Other procedures that have been shown to be useful for postsecondary students with mild disabilities are presented in Figure 10–5. Most of these procedures have been developed for postsecondary students with learning disabilities. However, they are equally applicable to students with mild mental retardation.

❦ ❦ ❦

SUMMARY

The legal foundation for the provision of services for students who are mildly disabled in postsecondary settings has been established by a number of federal

1. Allow untimed testing accommodations.
2. Allow readers for examinations.
3. Allow essay in place of objective examinations.
4. Allow oral or taped examinations.
5. Allow students to clarify exam questions.
6. Allow alternative methods of demonstrating mastery of course objectives.
7. Provide adequate materials, such as lined paper, etc.
8. Allow alternatives to computer exams or computer-scored sheets.
9. In math, allow students to use calculators, etc., and score or analyze the process involved in getting an answer rather than the final solution.
10. Avoid double negatives, questions embedded within questions, etc., when composing essay examinations.

Figure 10–5
Suggestions for modifying evaluation procedures

laws including PL 93-112, the Rehabilitation Act; the 1976, 1983, and 1990 amendments to PL 94-142, the Education for All Handicapped Children Act; and PL 101-336, the Americans with Disabilities Act of 1990 (see chap. 2, "History and Legislation"). Based on these mandates, students are seeking admission to and participation in academic and vocational postsecondary programs. The availability of postsecondary programs to students who are mildly disabled is dependent on the willingness of the institution to provide services and accommodations for this population. Financial considerations often dictate institutional commitment to this population (Gajar, 1992).

Components of postsecondary programs serving students who are mildly disabled include admission, personnel, identification, service delivery, and financial considerations. These diverse components have evolved spontaneously.

Empirically based methodologies for serving postsecondary students who are mildly disabled have not been developed or cited in the literature. The PA-A-PA paradigm, the study skills program, the pause procedure, and recommendations for evaluating students are some methodological suggestions.

REFERENCES

The American Heritage Dictionary of the English Language. (1976). Boston: Houghton Mifflin.

Barbaro, F. (1982). The learning disabled college student: Some considerations in setting objectives. *Journal of Learning Disabilities, 15,* 599–603.

Blackburn, J. C., & Iovacchini, E. V. (1982). Student service responsibilities of institutions to learning disabled students. *College and University, 52,* 208–217.

Bowen, E. (1986, April). Good timers need not apply. *Time*, p. 70.

Brill, J. (1987). *Learning disabled adults in postsecondary education*. Washington, DC: American Council on Education.

Bursuck, W. D., Rose, E., Cowen, S., & Yahaya, M. A. (1989). Nationwide survey of postsecondary education services for students with learning disabilities. *Exceptional Children, 56*, 236–245.

Cordoni, B. K. (1982). Postsecondary education: Where do we go from here? *Journal of Learning Disabilities, 15*, 265–266.

Gajar, A. H. (1986). *Assisting the learning disabled: A program development and service delivery guide for university providers, diagnosticians, tutors, counselors, and learning disabled students*. Columbus, OH: Association on Handicapped Student Service Programs in Postsecondary Education.

Gajar, A. H. (1989). A computer analysis of written language variables and a comparison of compositions written by learning disabled and non learning disabled university students. *Journal of Learning Disabilities, 22*(2), 125–130.

Gajar, A. H. (1992). University based models for students with learning disabilities: The Pennsylvania State University Model. In F. R. Rusch, L. DeStefano, J. Chadsey-Rusch, A. L. Phelps, & E. Szymanski (Eds.), *Transition from school to adult life: Models, linkages, and policy* (pp. 51–70). Sycamore, IL: Sycamore.

Gajar, A. H., Rusch, F. R., & DeStefano, L. (1989). *A descriptive analysis of competition 84.078B postsecondary model programs*. Unpublished manuscript.

Gray, R. (1981a). Serving adults with presumed learning disabilities. *Journal of Developmental and Remedial Education, 4*(2), 3–4, 33.

Gray, R. (1981b). Services for the LD adult. A working paper. *Learning Disability Quarterly, 4*, 426–434.

Hoy, C., & Gregg, N. (1986, Summer). Learning disabled students: An emerging population on college campuses. *Journal of College Admissions, 112*, 10–14.

Hughes, C. A., & Smith, J. O. (1990). Cognitive and academic performance of college students with learning disabilities: A synthesis of the literature. *Learning Disability Quarterly, 13*(1), 66–79.

Jarrow, J. E. (1986). *Integration of individuals with disabilities in higher education*. Washington, DC: DATA Institute, The Catholic University of America.

Killpack, D., & Romero, R. (1983). Enriching the disabled student's experience in seeking higher education. In *Proceedings from the Sixth National Conference of the Association on Handicapped Student Service Programs in Postsecondary Education* (pp. 69–72). Columbus, OH: Association on Handicapped Student Service Programs in Postsecondary Education.

Lefebvre, R. C. (1984). A psychological consultation program for learning-disabled adults. *Journal of College Student Personnel, 25*(4), 361–362.

Mangrum, C. T., & Strichart, S. S. (1983a). College possibilities for the learning disabled: Part one. *Learning Disabilities, 2*(5), 57–68.

Mangrum, C. T., & Strichart, S. S. (1983b). College possibilities for the learning disabled: Part two. *Learning Disabilities, 2*(6), 69–81.

Mangrum, C. T., & Strichart, S. S. (1984). *College and the learning disabled student*. Orlando, FL: Grune & Stratton.

McAfee, J. K. (1989). Community colleges and individuals with emotional disorders. *Behavioral Disorders, 15*(1) 9–15.

McAfee, J. K., & Scheeler, M. C. (1987). Accommodation of adults who are mentally retarded in community colleges: A national study. *Education and Training in Mental Retardation, 22,* 262–267.

McGuire, J. M., Norlander, K. A., & Shaw, S. F. (1990). Postsecondary education for students with learning disabilities: Forecasting challenges for the future. *Learning Disabilities Focus, 5*(2), 69–74.

Nelson, R., & Lignugaris/Kraft, B. (1989). Postsecondary education for students with learning disabilities. *Exceptional Children, 56*(3), 246–265.

Ruhl, K. L., Hughes, C. A., & Gajar, A. H. (1990). Efficacy of the pause procedure for enhancing learning disabled and nondisabled college students' long- and short-term recall of facts presented through lecture. *Learning Disability Quarterly, 13*(1), 55–64.

Salend, S. J., Salend, S. M., & Yanok, J. (1985). Learning disabled students in higher education. *Teacher Education and Special Education, 8,* 49–54.

Scheiber, B., & Talpers, J. (1987). *Unlocking potential college and other choices for learning disabled people: A step-by-step guide.* Bethesda, MD: Adler & Adler.

Shaywitz, S. E., & Shaw, R. (1988). The admissions process: An approach to selecting learning disabled students at the most selective colleges. *Learning Disabilities Focus, 3,* 81–86.

Siperstein, G. N. (1988). Students with learning disabilities in college: The need for a programmatic approach to critical transitions. *Journal of Learning Disabilities, 21,* 431–436.

Smith, J. O. (1989). *Access to rehabilitation services by adults with learning disabilities.* Unpublished doctoral dissertation, Pennsylvania State University, University Park.

Stewart, A. C. (1988). College admissions and handicapped students. In *Support services for LD students in postsecondary education: A compendium of readings* (Vol. 2, pp. 73–80). Columbus, OH: Association on Handicapped Student Service Programs in Postsecondary Education.

Strichart, S. S., & Mangrum, C. T. (1985). Selecting a college for the LD student. *Academic Therapy, 20,* 475–479.

Ugland, R., & Duane, G. (1976). *Serving students with specific learning disabilities in higher education: A demonstration project at three Minnesota community colleges.* Bloomington, MN: Normandale Community College. (ERIC Document Reproduction Service No. ED 135 434)

Vogel, S. A. (1982). On developing LD college programs. *Journal of Learning Disabilities, 15,* 518–528.

Vogel, S. A., & Adelman, P. (1981). Personnel development: College and university programs designed for learning disabled adults. *Illinois Council for Exceptional Children Quarterly, 1,* 12–18.

PART III

✿ ✿ ✿

Vocational Support for Transition

World War II brought changes in the work force as employers discovered the value of hiring women and people with disabilities. For example, Consolidated Vultee trainees in this class in aircraft detail drafting in the early 1940s took a 12-week course then did "a man-sized job" at Vultee plants around the country.

✿ ✿ ✿

❦ *Vignette* ❦

Jerry is a 35-year-old stock clerk in a large general/hardware store in a small town. He is mildly retarded but is more handicapped by his vision and coordination problems, all of which stem from perinatal brain injury due to anoxia. Jerry obtained his current employment on his own after numerous trials in various programs including several years in a sheltered workshop. In the workshop he worked at several jobs, including reclamation of cardboard boxes, construction of wooden shipping pallets, and sorting of small objects such as bolts and nuts. Like most other sheltered workshop clients (U.S. Department of Labor, 1979), Jerry did not progress into competitive employment. In fact, he received neither competitive employment training nor systematic instruction designed to improve the quality and quantity of his production.

The most extensive vocational training program in which he was enrolled involved placement as a grounds maintenance/janitorial worker at a local college. During his months in that job, he received neither instruction nor feedback on his performance by the counselor who visited him on site or by his work supervisor. In spite of many general, positive comments ("hard worker", "nice kid"), he was terminated because he worked too slow. He had never been told how his performance measured up to the expected performance. He had never been told to work faster. He had never received specific instruction on the tasks demanded of him. Jerry and his parents were shocked when the counselor recommended termination.

For a brief time Jerry retreated in anger. He felt betrayed and useless. Gradually, through a friendship and the kind of informal support that exists in a small town, he began to work several hours a week at the hardware store. He learned one task at a time and picked up new responsibilities as he progressed. After 3 years, he still is not working full-time but is getting close. He has found a niche that others believed did not exist. And he is succeeding in the absence of systematic instruction. His employer values his punctuality, loyalty, and intense desire to work. Given the opportunity, Jerry would work 60 or more hours per week. It is how he measures his self-worth.

Jerry's case is one of success in spite of the system. We are left to wonder how successful he might be had he received specific vocational instruction designed to teach him the skills he needed to work at a specific job.

❦ ❦ ❦

OVERVIEW OF PART III

The common element of transitional programs is work. It is hard to imagine a transitional program that does not include vocational training as its focal point. In fact, some experts equate transition and work. Although we feel that this is an oversimplification and devalues other meaningful and challenging elements in the lives of adults, we do believe that work and work training are essential foci of transition.

Vocational training for persons with mild disabilities is a very broad territory. Some persons with mild disabilities may go to college and graduate school and obtain professional positions. Others may attend trade schools and become skilled workers. Yet others may begin at an entry-level position and work their way up the corporate ladder. Sadly, a sizable number may receive little meaningful vocational training. They may attempt and fail at several jobs and eventually end up unemployed or in a sheltered workshop. Although we generally relate sheltered workshops to persons with severe disabilities, current statistics indicate that a sizable number of sheltered work clients have mild disabilities.

This part is devoted to a discussion of training for employment. It is a narrowly focused discussion concerning only the central tasks of jobs (production) and training for those tasks. In Part II we address academic issues including education for academic skills that are critical for employment. In Part IV we discuss extravocational skills including those attendant job-related skills such as punctuality that are critical to job success but are not part of the central job production or service task. It is by conscious design that we have placed vocational support between academic and extravocational support, as it is usual that academic preparation receives early emphasis, followed by an awareness of vocational needs and then other training needs related to transition to adulthood.

We have used the terms ***vocational education*** and ***vocational training*** interchangeably to identify any intervention that is specifically designed to improve an individual's work behavior. This includes specific skills training, general vocational education, career education, vocational rehabilitation, sheltered work, and postsecondary training.

This part is divided into three chapters: chapter 11, "Philosophical and Empirical Foundations of Vocational Training"; chapter 12, "The Technology of Vocational Training"; and chapter 13, "Models and Programs of Vocational Training."

❅ ❅ ❅

CHAPTER 11

In this chapter, we describe the philosophical, theoretical, and research foundations for the current state of vocational training of adolescents and young adults with mild disabilities. Much of the philosophy of vocational training has been influenced by (as it should be) a functional approach (i.e., use what works); therefore, a large part of this chapter addresses research on vocational outcomes, efficacy of vocational training, and research on employers as a means to identify needs, best practices, and current status of knowledge.

✻ ✻ ✻

CHAPTER 12

The technology of vocational training is the focus of this chapter. Our approach has been heavily weighted toward behavioral analytical systems as those appear to be the most effective. We recognize that people more often link behavioral approaches with individuals with severe disabilities. This perception is erroneous as the research literature clearly shows that the techniques are equally effective with persons who are mildly disabled. Furthermore, several behavioral studies in vocational training include a large number of persons with mild disabilities along with more severely disabled subjects, but it is not uncommon for the researcher to describe the subjects as severely disabled in the title.

We have also incorporated counseling and other cognitive approaches that have been used successfully with people who are mildly disabled. These approaches are especially apparent in job awareness, job search, and job acquisition efforts. Chapter 12 also includes discussions of placement and follow-up.

✻ ✻ ✻

CHAPTER 13

In this chapter we integrate and further develop the information presented in the previous two chapters by discussing models and programs of vocational training. Models are those service delivery systems that have enjoyed widespread application across the United States. These include work adjustment, career education, work study, specific skills training, and employment site–based instruction. In the programs section, we describe vocational transitional programs that have been developed at specific sites to meet the needs of adolescents and young adults with mild disabilities.

REFERENCES

U.S. Department of Labor. (1979). *Study of handicapped clients in sheltered workshops.* Washington, DC: Author.

Chapter 11

✿ ✿ ✿

Philosophical and Empirical Foundations of Vocational Training

*I*n this chapter, we describe the bases for the current status of vocational training. First, we discuss philosophical and theoretical foundations. In the second part we describe the research foundations for vocational training: (a) research on vocational outcomes—how do persons with mild disabilities fare when they enter the job market? (b) research that evaluates the effectiveness of several types of vocational training—how good are vocational programs? (c) research about employers—how do employers perceive workers with disabilities? and (d) miscellaneous research. The chapter concludes with a discussion of the implications of the research for vocational training.

✿ ✿ ✿

PHILOSOPHICAL AND THEORETICAL FOUNDATIONS

Students of vocational education would do well to remember that the origins of vocational training are not based in an altruistic desire to help the general population get ahead but rather a need to ensure that business and industry had access to a population that could perform the increasingly complex tasks that industrialization created. Thus, one of the pragmatic underpinnings of vocational training efforts is that it must serve the needs of employers as well as those of trainees. Furthermore, the roots of vocational rehabilitation are also found in economics—a recognition that injured soldiers returning from World War I could be rehabilitated and returned to the work force at a cost lower than that of government "relief."

Unlike intellectual and academic pursuits, which our society views in both functional (leading to employment) and idealistic (knowledge is good) senses, vocational training is viewed primarily as functional. That is, it should lead to employment, and to accomplish that, it must provide employers with workers who have skills that are related to the tasks of production. Astuto (1985) and others have reiterated this obvious tenet: vocational training succeeds when there is a match between employment needs and the skills of exiting students.

Most of the philosophical bases of vocational training are equally pragmatic. Writers and practitioners usually base their philosophical statements on functionality: the desirable attributes of vocational training are those that lead to the best employment in the shortest time for the lowest cost. Perhaps it is fair to say that vocational education does not have a values basis but rather that the values have arisen as a result of empirical evidence. The functionality of vocational training may account for some of its weak track record. Perhaps, because it is utilitarian, vocational education does not receive the same support among the American public as academic education.

Palmer, Velleman, and Shafer (1985) conclude that most of American education is designed to prepare students for the next level of education, not work. The American public values academics over vocational pursuits. This attitude is evident in much of the rhetoric of the excellence in education movement, which stresses academics and mostly ignores efforts to promote vocational competence (Edgar, 1987). Phelps (1985) contends that access to and the quality of vocational programs for youth with disabilities decreased partly as a result of the excellence in education movement.

Even among those who have a direct interest in the lives of persons with disabilities (parents, teachers) it is common to cling inappropriately to an academic curriculum and neglect a functional curriculum far into the high school years. For individuals with learning disabilities, the inclusion of vocational education in secondary programs has occurred only within the past 10 years (Bencomo & Schafer, 1984). In fact, until 1980, individuals with learning disabilities were not eligible for vocational rehabilitation services as their problems were viewed as primarily academic (Gerber, 1981).

A recent change has resulted in renewed attention to vocational education. This change developed from studies such as "The Forgotten Half" in which researchers lamented the neglect of non-college-bound youth. Recognition of the need for education that is functional and prepares students for work and adulthood has come from many quarters, including researchers, employers, and policymakers. These individuals have all realized that the systems to train workers have been inadequate and ineffective (Edgar, 1987). One group of researchers (Palmer et al., 1985), in response to the failure of American vocational education, recommended the development of a new way of evaluating the effectiveness of American schools: a test of students' employability.

Research has led to other changes in philosophy and practice. For example, Ballantyne (1985) notes a shift in secondary programs serving youth with disabilities from one that emphasized academic competence before entering into vocational programs to one that recognizes that delaying vocational development is damaging for many youths with disabilities. This belief and the practices that logically extend from it have been slow to gain widespread application.

In the following sections, we consider philosophical issues more specifically, including considerations for the content and timing of training, service delivery mechanisms, and integration. Discussions of concepts and practices are purposefully brief because most are described in greater detail later in this chapter and in the two chapters following.

Content

What should be included in a vocational training program? Obviously, the answer depends on the age and characteristics of the population to be served, but the trend over the last 20 years has been to expand the content considerably, from a previous concentration on specific occupational skills to the current inclusion of all skills that enable employment. Astuto (1985), for example, states that "vocational program[s] for handicapped adolescents must include exploration, assessment, skill and work adjustment, training, practical experience, supervision, and follow-through" (p. 7). Sitlington (1981) also criticizes the narrow focus of early vocational programs. He believes that skill training without career awareness and exploration is ineffective.

The concept of career education and the people who developed the concept are partially responsible for the increased scope of vocational education in the United States. People who espouse the career education view believe that vocational education and supportive interventions (including those we have labeled extravocational) should be included in the curriculum in the elementary grades and continue into adulthood. They also maintain that career education should be integrated into all other elements of the curriculum, especially for children and adolescents with disabilities (Humes & Hohenshil, 1985). The expansion of vocational education into the elementary school also reflects a perception that the transitional period is longer for youths with disabilities. Vocational training that begins in the 11th grade is too late for most students who are disabled (Sitlington, 1981). Palmer et al. (1985) have determined that youths with disabilities require more time to adjust to the demands of adulthood. Therefore, it is necessary to begin the process earlier and continue it, in many cases, until the individual has reached his or her mid- to late 20s.

Practitioners have also expanded the concept of vocational training to include placement and follow-through (Crimando, 1984). This is an acknowledgment that individuals with disabilities not only need to know how to work but also how to find, secure, and maintain employment.

Service Delivery

The preferred manner in which vocational services are delivered to individuals with disabilities has also changed significantly over the past 10 years. The major change has been to a system in which skills are learned while working. Astuto (1985) declares that vocational training should be delivered in a manner such that work experience complements skill training. Thus, students must be served in programs that provide coincidental skill training and opportunity to practice the skill in a real work environment. This development and others has led to the creation of the concept of job coaching and supported employment.

A second development in vocational training service delivery has been the recognition that effective vocational services are those that are integrated with other services. For those individuals who are receiving vocational training at the secondary level, vocational education should be integrated into the Individual Education Plan (IEP). Failure to fully integrate the vocational aspects into the IEP will result in service delivery that is fragmented and probably ineffective. This belief is the underlying rationale for the relatively new concept of the Individual Transition Plan (ITP). The ITP also makes clear the need for integrated postsecondary services. However, because most postsecondary service providers (e.g., vocational rehabilitation, community colleges, technical schools) do not operate under the same mandates as public education, integration has been somewhat elusive, but few would debate its desirability.

Integration and Adaptation

The extent to which learners with disabilities should be integrated into regular vocational education continues to be debated. According to Astuto (1985), vocational education for adolescents who are disabled should be delivered in the least restrictive environment. Ballantyne (1985) reports that more and more integration of students with disabilities into regular vocational education is taking place across the country. Others have reported that this is not occurring and that when it does, it is often damaging to students who are disabled because the regular vocational education instructors are unprepared and reluctant to adapt to the needs of youth with disabilities. Sitlington (1981) concludes that mainstream vocational education is often much too difficult for students who are disabled and that it is often insensitive to their needs. Edgar (1987) reports that mainstreaming of adolescents with mild disabilities has resulted in greater emphasis on academics at the expense of vocational training.

In order to promote integration, researchers and practitioners have sought to develop instructional techniques that minimize the impact of academic deficiencies. This is a distinct change in values from an earlier time when exclusion was the rule. As an example of this philosophical change, we see how, in 1976, researchers attempted to identify criteria to determine which mentally retarded students should be permitted to enroll in vocational programs and coincidentally which should be excluded (Shill, 1976). More recently, Ballantyne (1985) and Crimando (1984) have described a number of adaptations that have been utilized so that secondary-level students with disabilities could enter and succeed in programs that had been inaccessible because of academic admission requirements. Thus, there is a recognition that effective vocational education can be provided to persons with academic limitations.

Many practitioners and researchers are touting the desirability of providing vocational instruction that is community based (e.g., Gaylord-Ross, Forte, & Gaylord-Ross, 1986). This phenomenon is both philosophical (based on concepts of normalization) and pragmatic (in situ training is more effective). The development of job coaching is one outgrowth of community-based instruction.

Conclusions

The philosophical and theoretical underpinnings of vocational education for youths and adults with mild disabilities are generally pragmatic. During the past 20 years we have witnessed a change in programs. Vocational efforts now include a wider age range, a broader content, and greater efforts to connect them to real jobs in the community.

❦ ❦ ❦

RESEARCH FOUNDATIONS

Many researchers have contributed to our understanding of the vocational training needs of persons with mild disabilities. Following is a discussion of the research that has laid the foundation for the current status of vocational education for adolescents and young adults with mild disabilities. This section is divided into four subsections: general outcomes research, efficacy research, employer research, and miscellaneous research.

In the first subsection we discuss research on the employment status of young adults with mild disabilities. Then we analyze the research on the impacts of various kinds of vocational programs. The third subsection is devoted to research conducted with the employers of people who are mildly disabled. Finally, the fourth section provides an overview of miscellaneous and various studies concerning the vocational status of individuals with mild disabilities.

Outcomes Research

When young adults with mild disabilities leave school, how successful are they at securing employment? What kinds of jobs do they get? How well do they perform? Researchers have investigated these questions and others related to the occupational success of persons with mild disabilities. The following discussion should be interpreted in light of the findings of Wanous, Stumpf, and Bedrosian (1979), who looked at 1,736 newly placed employees in low-wage, blue-collar jobs—the kind of jobs often filled by persons with mild disabilities. Before 1 week of employment was complete, 575 left their jobs. After 7 months, only 27% were still employed in those same jobs. Of those who left their jobs, 42% had quit, 28% were laid off, and 30% were fired. Thus, when we look at some of the dismal statistics on unemployment of persons with mild disabilities, we should recognize that they may be attributable, in part, to the unappealing jobs available to them and not just to the limitations of their skills or the ineffectiveness of the training they have received.

In 1987, the Louis Harris Poll reported that two thirds of all Americans with disabilities aged 16 to 64 were not employed. This is considerably higher than most other reports. Many researchers have attempted to determine the employment rates of young adults with mild disabilities. Walsh (1980) concludes that approximately 60% of young adults with mild disabilities in his sample who participated in some form of secondary vocational education were employed. A lower unemployment rate is reported by Hawkins (1984), who conducted a follow-up of all special education graduates from the Montgomery County, Maryland, public schools. At the time of follow-up, 47% were employed full-time, 25% were in postsecondary education and working full- or part-time, and 12% were in postsecondary education only. Only 13% were unemployed. The former students had been out of school for only 1 year. In another broad-based study, Dalton and Latz (1978) report an employment rate of 75% for 1,395 former clients of a comprehensive rehabilitation center. The highest employment rate (82.55%) was for those classified as mildly retarded, and the lowest was for those classified as emotionally disturbed.

Graduating from high school appears to have a logical and positive effect on employment for persons who are mildly disabled (Levin, Zigmond, & Birch, 1985). Similarly, Fardig, Algozzine, Schwartz, Hensel, and Westling (1985) report that the best predictor of postschool success is the highest grade completed.

Researchers have also reported employment figures for specific categories of people who are mildly disabled. Tobias (1970) determined that 59% of the males and 29% of the females from a large sample ($N = 1,836$) of mildly retarded young adults were employed. An additional 29% of males and females had been employed at some time since leaving high school. Twenty percent had never worked. Crain (1980) also investigated the employment rates of mildly retarded young adults. Her sample included 130 persons, ages 19 to 37. Sixty-eight percent were in the civilian labor force compared to 67% of the entire adult U.S. population. Sixty-nine percent of a sample of mentally retarded young adults had received vocational training in high school, but only 32% were employed 1 to 4 years after leaving school, according to Wehman, Kregel, and Seyfarth (1985). Only 28.6% were employed full-time.

Blalock (1981) reports a high level of unemployment (50%) for a sample of 38 young adults with learning disabilities. Lehtinen and Dumas (1976) found that 67% of a sample of 90 young adults with learning disabilities were employed. In contrast, Cobb and Crump (1984) examined the employment status of 100 young adults (ages 20–24) with learning disabilities. Eighty-seven percent were employed. Humes and Brammer (1985) report a similar high employment rate for young adults with learning disabilities. Of the 24 subjects who had graduated from high school 1 to 6 years before the study, only two were unemployed. Interestingly, only 11 had received vocational training in high school.

Part-time underemployment is also a problem among young adults with learning disabilities, according to Fafard and Haubrich (1981). Of the 15 subjects in their study, 10 were employed part-time, and 1 was unemployed. Similarly, Lehtinen and Dumas (1976) found a high part-time employment rate (40%) among adults with learning disabilities.

Zigmond and Thornton (1985) note the importance of a high school diploma for adults who are learning disabled (LD). They found that 74.1% of the LD graduates in their study were employed, but only 43.8% of the non-graduates were employed. These data become more imposing when one considers that the dropout rate reported for LD adolescents is 54.2%.

Unemployment among young adults with behavioral disorders worsens as their time out of school increases, according to Edgar and Levine (1987). Fifty-two young graduates were interviewed every 6 months for 2 years. At 6 months the employment rate was 55%. At 24 months it was only 49%.

The breadth of jobs held by persons with mild disabilities is the same as that of the general work force. However, the vast majority is concentrated in lower level production and service positions. Walsh (1980) reports that 70% of the employed disabled recipients of secondary vocational education worked at service jobs. An additional 11% were employed in clerical/sales positions. Hawkins (1984) also found a high concentration of individuals with mild disabilities in service jobs. Thirty-five percent were employed in clerical jobs, 23% in food service, and 19% in maintenance or building service.

Only 2.6% of the mildly retarded young adults in a sample studied by Tobias (1970) were employed in skilled occupations. An additional 28% worked at service jobs, and 20% worked at benchwork assembly. Brimer and Rouse (1978) examined the postschool adjustment of 30 mildly retarded young adults who had received vocational training in a cooperative program provided by a school district in South Carolina and the South Carolina Department of Vocational Rehabilitation. These students had received instruction for 4 years in high school. Six hours per week were devoted to general vocational skills, job placement, on-the-job support and counseling. Nine were employed in service jobs, seven were in semiskilled positions, and six were in skilled positions. Dalton and Latz (1978) report that mildly retarded adults were successfully placed into nursing assistant, food service, and building maintenance jobs after receiving vocational training.

Young adults with learning disabilities are also concentrated in lower skill jobs, although more are employed in skilled positions than mentally retarded persons (Butler, 1982; Humes & Brammer 1985; White et al., 1982). Butler found LD workers in 82 different job classifications in Arizona. Most were semiskilled positions. Low-level production jobs were held by a majority of LD young adults studied by Cobb and Crump (1984). Sixty-four percent of the 100 subjects of this study had received an average of 1.25 years of vocational training in 20 different programs. More than 50% had some work experience before they left school, and 50% had not graduated. One graduate was in an executive/management position, 1 in a technical position, 6 in sales, 10 in service, and 37 were in low-level production jobs. Fafard and Haubrich (1981) identify food service, human service, military service, and construction work as the main job classifications of adults with learning disabilities. Thirty-three percent of the LD subjects of a study by Lehtinen and Dumas (1976) held clerical jobs. Another 23.3% were unskilled workers, 13.3% held professional positions, 8.6% were in sales, 6.6% were managers, 6.6% were service workers, 5% were in the military, and 3.3% were skilled craftsmen.

The wages of workers with mild disabilities are generally lower than those of the nondisabled population. The nature and extent of the differences in pay are difficult to specify. It may be that workers who are mildly disabled start lower and receive fewer raises. It may be that they occupy lower level jobs. Lower wages may result from lack of training or a higher rate of school dropout. It is likely that all of these factors and more are at work. Neel, Meadows, Levine, and Edgar (1988) report that twice as many special education graduates as non–special education graduates earned less than $50 per week. Walsh (1980) writes that adults with disabilities who had participated in work experience training earned more than those who had not.

Brimer and Rouse (1978) report that mildly retarded young adults earned hourly wages approximately equal to the statewide average in South Carolina. This finding is uncommon. In a more typical finding, Crain (1980) states that the median income of a sample of mildly retarded graduates was $7,280 compared to $12,392 for other workers in the same area. Peterson and Smith (1960) compared mildly retarded adults to other adults with low socioeconomic status (SES). They found that the low SES males earned 70% more than their mildly retarded counterparts. Low SES females earned 200% more. Wehman, Kregel, and Seyfarth (1985) report that only 17% of employed mentally retarded persons earned more than $500 per month.

Cobb and Crump (1984) determined that two thirds of a sample of 100 LD adults earned less than $10,000. Adults with learning disabilities earned less than other clients of vocational rehabilitation according to Miller, Mulkey, and Kopp (1984). Only 20% of a sample of young adults with behavioral disorders earned minimum wage or better 6 months after they graduated from high school (Edgar & Levine, 1987). After 2 years none was earning more than minimum wage.

Researchers have reported that only a small percentage of young adults who are mildly disabled participate in postsecondary education. Few utilize other postsecondary services. Tobias (1970) reports that less than 40% of mentally retarded adults used postschool vocational rehabilitation (VR) services. Using VR was often a measure of last resort for those who had been unable to secure employment. Brimer and Rouse (1978) determined that only one third of a sample of mildly retarded adults attended postsecondary vocational training programs. Wehman, Kregel, and Seyfarth (1985) state that 75.6% of mentally retarded young adults in their sample received no postsecondary services from their local VR program, 84.6% received no services from local mental retardation services, and 80% received no assistance from the Employment Commission.

Some investigators have looked at the postsecondary educational pursuits of individuals with learning disabilities. Cobb and Crump (1984) found that only 31 of a sample of 100 young adults with learning disabilities had attended postsecondary programs. Fifteen had attended vocational or technical colleges. Only five had completed programs in skilled areas of training. Eleven others attended other kinds of postsecondary vocational training, including beauty college and adult education welding classes. Three received technical training in the military. Not surprisingly, a much higher percentage of the high school graduates attended postsecondary programs than the dropouts. Only 8% of another sample of LD young adults were enrolled in postsecondary education (Humes & Brammer, 1985). Edgar and Levine (1987) report that participation in postsecondary education declined for a sample of new graduates who had been classified as behaviorally disordered. After 2 years only 20% were participating in postsecondary education.

What have researchers discovered about the actual job performance of workers with mild disabilities? Parent and Everson (1986) reviewed a number of studies about the job performance of workers with disabilities. They conclude that workers with disabilities equal nondisabled workers on production rate and accuracy. Workers who are disabled also have fewer absences and lower turnover but require more training. Martin, Rusch, Lagomarcino, and Chadsey-Rusch (1986) conclude that mildly retarded workers lose their jobs more often because of production problems. Few are fired because of social problems, which is a surprising result that may reflect the characteristics (e.g., good social skills) of the specific sample. Or, it may reflect jobs with low social demands or the willingness of the specific employers to tolerate social difficulties. Successful mildly retarded workers have higher production rates than those who are unsuccessful (Chaffin, 1969). Brimer and Rouse (1978) report that none of the mildly retarded subjects in their study had been fired.

Geib, Guzzardi, and Genova (1981) state that workers with learning disabilities are often slow producers who make many errors on simple tasks (e.g., taking phone messages). Employers reported that these workers appeared careless.

How satisfied are workers who are mildly disabled with their jobs and the training they have received? Adults with learning disabilities are not very satisfied with their jobs, according to Fafard and Haubrich (1981), Lehtinen and Dumas (1976), and White et al. (1982). Wehman, Kregel, and Seyfarth (1985) determined that 83% of the retarded workers that they surveyed were satisfied with their employment. Peterson and Smith (1960) conclude that mildly retarded workers were as satisfied with their employment as workers from low SES backgrounds and that both groups expressed high job satisfaction. Talkington and Overbeck (1975) attempted to identify relationships between job satisfaction and other variables. They found that mildly retarded female workers who were rated highly by their employers in efficiency, dependability, interest, helpfulness, carefulness, pleasantness, and responsibility expressed greater job satisfaction. More importantly, those who had shown greater self-direction in obtaining employment were more satisfied and performed better.

Cobb and Crump (1984) report that young adults with learning disabilities rated the vocational training that they had received as helpful or very helpful. In contrast, one third of the behaviorally disordered young adults were dissatisfied with the vocational training and job assistance provided by schools.

Efficacy Research

How effective are vocational programs? Many researchers have attempted to answer this question. Some have taken a general approach, and others have examined specific programs or service delivery systems.

Walsh (1980) reviewed 92 secondary vocational programs for adolescents with disabilities. Data were gathered by on-site visits and interviews with students, former students, and employers. Participants in the programs were predominantly mentally retarded, but there were also some with learning disabilities and behavioral disorders. The costs of the various programs ranged from $44 to $1,664 per student. Walsh indicates that obtaining accurate data was difficult because of poor reporting and monitoring at the state level. Interestingly, 70% of the projects were segregated rather than mainstreamed. Program sites included comprehensive and vocational high schools, institutions, and sheltered workshops. Of the 2,009 students enrolled in the programs, 6% dropped out and only 57% completed the program. Only 48% of the completers were placed in jobs, and only 52% of those placed were placed in areas in which they had received training. As further evidence of the ineffectiveness of the special programs, 33% of those who completed such programs reenrolled in regular vocational education. Surprisingly, 76% of the parents rated the programs as good or excellent, and student ratings were also high.

Walsh (1980) criticizes the overall state of vocational programs for people who are disabled. He reports that in his samples there were no common definitions, complete enrollment and fiscal data did not exist, instruction was primarily theoretical, individualization was absent, and special education students who were served in regular vocational education programs were neglected. The last conclusion is supported by Edgar (1987), who found that the generic vocational services promoted by Will (1984) were not providing the support that students with mild disabilities needed. Unfortunately, Walsh also arrives at a conclusion that is damaging to students who are mildly disabled when he excused the fact that much of the instruction was of the nonskill type because the participants did not have the capacity to participate in skills training. Certainly, research over the past 10 years has indicated that high-level skills can be learned by persons with mild, moderate, and even severe disabilities.

Palmer et al. (1985) reviewed the literature on transition for youth with disabilities. They found that the success of transition often depends on access to information and personal connections. Taggart (1981) concludes that school-based "general employability skills" programs can change attitudes, knowledge, and job-holding and -seeking skills, but they do not improve job success. Only when such programs include work with employers and paid job experience in an area related to eventual employment do we see a major impact of vocational programs. Specifically, Taggart found that using work sites as classrooms with links to unions and employers and specific on-site skills progressions led to higher wages and placement rates.

In contrast to the above, Hasazi, Gordon, and Roe (1985) believe that participation in a high school vocational program is a good predictor of postschool employment. But like most other researchers, they conclude that real work experiences (i.e., those for pay) were more important and more effective than any amount of classroom instruction. There is almost no doubt that the most effective programs are those in which the students learn a job while employed and are subject to all of the conditions and expectations of the employer. Skills trained in the classroom do not generalize well.

Phelps (1980) states that there are two conditions necessary for effective vocational education for disabled persons: extended work experience and instruction in which the work experience is integrated with the skills being taught. There are many ways that adolescents and young adults with disabilities can gain work experience. Summer employment has been an effective means of providing work experience (Hasazi et al., 1985; Taggart, 1981). Summer or part-time employment are better determinants of immediate postschool employment than classroom vocational instruction or unpaid work experience. This is especially true when the employment is also structured as a training site.

Halpern (1978) reviewed 43 federally funded work-study programs and 14 school districts in Oregon. Employment rates and levels were higher for former work-study students than for similar persons with disabilities who had not been in such programs. Although the employment levels were equal to the same-age nonwhite population, they were far below that of same-age whites.

Other researchers have investigated the effectiveness of secondary vocational training. Shanyfelt (1974) describes a program at an occupational high school. Students ($n = 305$ mildly mentally retarded adolescents aged 15–21) in the 5-year program progressed from shop-based training through on-campus work experience to paid part-time jobs. Simultaneously they received instruction in vocational and extravocational skills. At follow-up, 62.5% were employed at the same site since graduation. Eighty-two percent of the males and 67% of the females were employed. These figures are much higher than those reported by other researchers.

The importance of paid employment is further reinforced by Frank, Sitlington, and Carson (1991). These researchers conducted a follow-up study of individuals who were considered to have behavioral disorders in high school. Based on a review of 200 students who had been out of school for 1 year, they drew the following conclusions:

1. Fifty-eight percent of those who graduated were employed (61% for males, 50% for females).
2. Three fourths of the employed graduates held low-status jobs, making a mean hourly wage of $3.94 per hour. These persons were generally employed as laborers or service workers.
3. Three fourths of those employed had obtained jobs through relatives or friends.
4. There was no difference in employment between those who had received vocational training in high school and those who did not.

5. Sixty-one percent of those who had held paid employment while in high school were employed, while only 39% of those without paid employment in high school were employed.
6. Only 30% of those who had dropped out of school were employed. Their wages and jobs were essentially the same as those who had graduated.
7. Few in either the graduate or dropout group had received community assistance in locating a job.

Postsecondary programs have also been targets of research. Neubert, Tilson, and Ianacone (1989) investigated the initial employment success of young adults (ages 18–30) who were mildly disabled and had taken part in a postsecondary transitional program. This was a comprehensive program involving training, placement, and support (job coaching) after a job was secured. (The program is discussed in more detail in chap. 12.) After 6 months, 76% were still employed; after 1 year, 64% were still employed. Seventy-four percent required support from staff during their first month on the job. More of the job difficulties encountered by the trainees were task related (e.g., production rate) rather than work adjustment (e.g., interpersonal).

In another postsecondary study, Neuhaus (1967) employed a form of job coaching long before the term was coined. This vocational rehabilitation project served 29 mildly mentally retarded adults from 17 to 30 years of age. The mentally retarded trainees were integrated with other trainees at the job site where they received instruction. All trainees were provided with on-the-job training in one of two jobs: assembly of electrical wiring harnesses or banking operations. The VR trainer worked at the job site with the trainees. When the trainees reached 50% of the desired production rate, they became part of the regular work force, and supervision and training were transferred to regular company supervisors. Nearly all of the trainees reached acceptable levels of production, and 61% required less than the average (for nondisabled workers) time to reach acceptable production levels. The success of this program can be attributed to two factors: training at a real work site, and close and systematic instruction by a person who was able to adapt instruction and tasks to the needs of the trainees.

Richardson and Hill (1980) evaluate the success of a cooperative vocational rehabilitation program that is part of the federal Projects with Industry (PWI) program in which employers and training organizations work together to secure work for adults with disabilities. Of the 38 individuals (which included those with mental retardation or emotional disorders) who had been placed through the program, 90% were still employed after 1 year, but 47% had been unemployed at some time during the year. Fifty-two percent had jobs related to their previous training, and 32% held jobs they had obtained through PWI.

Finally, Wehman et al. (1985) review the job success of mentally retarded persons in Virginia who received the services of a supported work program over a 5-year period. Forty-one percent of the 167 clients were mildly retarded, and 72 were still working. This success rate might seem low, but many of the trainees had severe disabilities and virtually no competitive employment experience before they were exposed to supported employment. The results of this study should be contrasted with the conclusions of Rusch and Mithaug (1980), who have determined that few persons progress from sheltered work into competitive employment and that those who do generally possess the skills to work competitively before entering the sheltered situation. These individuals are placed quickly.

Employer Research

Several researchers have investigated research questions involving the employers of people who are mildly disabled. These research questions can be stated as follows:

- How do employers rate their workers with mild disabilities?
- How do employers perceive vocational preparation programs?
- To what extent are employers willing to accommodate workers with mild disabilities?

Halloran (1978) surveyed 100 large corporations with workers who are mildly disabled and found that 66 reported that there was no difference in productivity between disabled and nondisabled workers. Twenty-four percent of the respondents reported that workers with disabilities were more productive. Respondents also reported that there was a lower accident rate (57%), a lower turnover rate (83%), and a lower absentee rate (53%) for employees with disabilities. In another study of employers' perceptions of workers who are disabled, Hawkins (1984) found that 80% were satisfied with their employees who had graduated from special education programs. One half of the employers stated that job promotions were possible for their workers with disabilities.

Campbell, Hensel, Hudson, Schwartz, and Sealander (1987) have compared employers' ratings of workers with disabilities (mostly learning disabilities or mild retardation) with the workers' self-ratings. They found that the ratings were essentially the same on the dimensions of learning the tasks, work habits, and work independence.

Employers have been asked to provide their perceptions of the quality and content of vocational programs. Alper (1985) has found that employers and teachers expressed strong agreement about the skills needed for entry-level competitive employment. Both groups were asked to rate the importance of individual skills on a list. Twelve of the skills were rated as important by more than 90% of both groups. An additional 30 skills were rated important by 80% of both groups. The implication of this study is that at least both groups agree on what should be taught in terms of job readiness.

Asche and Vogler (1980) examined the satisfaction of employers with vocational graduates. They conclude that employers prefer vocational graduates and that they specifically prefer cooperative (between the training program and the employer) vocational program graduates. Furthermore, employers rated the vocational skills of vocational graduates superior to those of general academic graduates, but they also ranked the vocational graduates lower on math and reading skills. Hawkins (1984) found that employers, although generally satisfied with their workers who were disabled, stated that there was a critical need to improve job training programs at the secondary level.

Many researchers have examined the willingness of employers to accommodate the special needs of workers with disabilities, but much of this work has been aimed at accommodations for persons with physical disabilities. Emener and McHargue (1978) surveyed 57 employers and found that only 40% understood the role of vocational rehabilitation; most accepted it, however, and were willing to work with VR counselors. Employers expressed some caution about hiring workers who are disabled and stated that they would want to know the exact nature of a disability before they would hire such a worker. They also wanted assurances that the counselor would continue to be available after they hired the person. These researchers concluded that employers needed much more training. Interestingly, the size of the organization did not influence the attitudes of the employer.

In contrast, Combs and Omvig (1986) found that larger companies are more willing to accommodate workers who are disabled than smaller companies. Gruenhagen (1982) surveyed managers of 12 fast-food restaurant chains. The majority of the managers had experience with mentally retarded workers. They believed that mentally retarded persons should be employed, but they were unsure of their own ability and desire to hire and train such employees. Those who had had greater experience with workers with disabilities were more positive about hiring them.

Because the nondiscriminatory regulations of the Americans with Disabilities Act (ADA) went into effect in the summer of 1992, it is too early to determine how employer attitudes have changed as a result of this federal legislation. However, the impact is likely to be profound and lasting.

Miscellaneous Research

In addition to research on general outcomes, efficacy, and employers, there are many studies that address other issues. Phelps (1980) categorizes pre-1980 vocational research as concentrating on mainstreaming and barriers to employment. As further evidence of this, Schneck, Lerwick, and Copa (1980) conducted a broad-based study in Minnesota and conclude that most secondary education students with disabilities were being served in segregated vocational classes. Furthermore, access to postsecondary vocational opportunities was very limited for most adults with mild disabilities.

These conclusions were bolstered by Benz and Halpern (1986), who determined that there was a lack of incentive for vocational educators to serve students with mild disabilities. Based on a survey of administrators, parents, and teachers, they conclude that (a) there was a need to increase vocational opportunities, (b) students with disabilities were often excluded from vocational classes because of academic prerequisites, (c) vocational services were poorly coordinated for learners with mild disabilities, and (d) there was a need for greater collaboration between special education and vocational education. Miller et al. (1984) found that the poor coordination between special and vocational education extends beyond the high school years and that there is poor linkage between educational programs for persons with learning disabilities and vocational rehabilitation programs.

Young adults with learning disabilities have encountered some specific problems in securing postsecondary vocational services even though there have been many federal grant programs to promote postsecondary educational opportunities. Brechim and Kemp (1984) questioned 169 vocational rehabilitation professionals and found that many held misconceptions about persons with learning disabilities. Most thought that learning disabilities affect only academic learning. A large number believed that all LD individuals are hyperactive and lack motivation. With these beliefs, it is easy to understand why postsecondary services are lagging. Newill, Goyette, and Fogarty (1984) conclude that the lack of knowledge of learning disabilities is because of the newness of the concept. They believe that because the first diagnoses of learning disabilities were made in the 1960s, vocational educators are just beginning to face the vocational needs of this group.

Kokaska and Skolnik (1986) asked LD adults about their vocational successes and problems. Nine of their 10 subjects had completed or were enrolled in college. All were optimistic about their potential for career success. One had opened his own contracting business because his reading and writing deficits created barriers in other work environments. These adults also gave advice to other individuals with learning disabilities. They stated that LD adults should (a) select a career that emphasizes strengths, (b) pick jobs that allow adaptations, (c) build strong interpersonal skills, (d) admit that they may have to work harder, and (e) be honest about their shortcomings.

Several researchers have examined the economics of various forms of vocational service delivery. Noble and Conley (1987) state that all forms of supported employment are more cost-effective than postsecondary programs that permit or promote dependence, such as sheltered workshops. Martin, Schneider, Rusch, and Geske (1982) investigated the costs and benefits of several types of training. Extended employment training (sheltered workshops) costs about $500 less than transitional competitive employment training initially. However, after 2 years the earnings of trainees in transitional employment training exceeded the cost of the placement and training. In the 5th year, the excess was $425 per worker. Projections showed that in 10 years the workers would earn $16,153 more than the cost of the training and had that individual remained in a sheltered workshop, the cost would have been $50,280; there would never be a point where the cost would be recaptured through taxes on earnings and so forth. In addition, competitive employment trainees expressed much greater satisfaction with their lives than sheltered employees.

❦ ❦ ❦

SUMMARY

Obviously, the large amount of research and commentary described here leaves us with many unanswered questions, but several consistent findings and interpretations can be made.

First, adjustment to the demands of employment often takes years of trial and error for persons with mild disabilities (Neuhaus, 1967). This may be because of the nature of the disability or the fact that vocational training was ineffective in teaching real work behavior.

Second, postsecondary vocational education providers need to be trained to work with populations who are disabled. Adults with mild disabilities need to be encouraged to take advantage of postsecondary opportunities. Some of their reluctance to do so may be the result of previous unsuccessful and frustrating educational experiences.

Involvement of the private sector is also critical, especially in providing on-site employment training. It makes no sense to train people with mild disabilities for hypothetical jobs. Involvement of employers will ensure targeting jobs that will be available. The job market must be analyzed constantly.

Postschool employment success is related to the level of education completed. Failure to earn a high school diploma makes employment prospects dim. Educators need to find ways to keep mildly disabled students in school. Greater stress on vocational education and employment, with simultaneous deemphasis of academics, appears to provide some motivation to remain in school.

At the same time, schools need to modify vocational programs so that all students have actual on-the-job experience. Shop- or school-based instruction does not spontaneously generalize to the workplace. Students with mild disabilities learn the tasks of work best when they are at work. Presently, it is hard to demonstrate that secondary vocational programs have any real, lasting effect on employability. The emphasis on academics in mainstreamed secondary programs probably hurts many adolescents with mild disabilities who need more functional vocational training. Mainstream vocational education programs have little demonstrable efficacy for students who are mildly disabled. They have not proven to be very adaptable.

In some ways, vocational efforts aimed at persons with moderate and severe disabilities are more sophisticated and focused. To a large degree vocational education for persons with mild disabilities appears to be a "train and hope" proposition. It is rare to see a vocational program for people who are mildly disabled that starts early, provides training in critical job skills in real work environments, and offers placement assistance and long-term follow-through and postsecondary support. Effective models have not received the same kind of attention and acceptance as have the models for persons with moderate or severe disabilities.

There is considerable evidence that the three groups that comprise the mildly disabled have very different vocational needs. Learning disabled and behaviorally disordered children are more likely to drop out of school, yet in general they can be expected to perform higher level jobs. Mentally retarded workers are more satisfied with their employment but have less opportunity for advancement and fewer postsecondary educational services.

Employers are generally pleased with their workers who are mildly disabled. From the worker's perspective, job satisfaction and job performance are in no small part related to the amount of input that the worker with a mild disability had into the choice of jobs. In other words, a person who is mildly disabled and has a job selected for him or her is not likely to be effective or happy.

Where comparative research exists, it indicates that in many ways workers with mild disabilities are much like their nondisabled peers, that is, others from low SES backgrounds with low educational attainment. However, this comparative research shows that workers who are disabled earn less.

Unemployment and underemployment are high among people with mild disabilities, but the causes of unemployment and underemployment are not always easily identified and may include the impact of the disability, economic barriers, employer attitudes, and the dead-end nature of the available jobs. Furthermore, the data that have been provided are often biased by the ages of the subjects, geography, and so on.

The levels of vocational aspiration of adolescents and young adults who are mildly disabled are often not realistic. Frustration and years of failure may lead to underestimation of work potential. Later, the realization that one is "stuck" in a job beneath one's ability may lead to poor performance. For young adults with learning disabilities and behavioral disorders, this may be especially problematic when the individual realizes that his or her potential far outweighs the job or the vocational goals that have been set.

The vocational adjustment of persons with mild disabilities has received a great deal of attention by researchers and practitioners, but more long-term research needs to be conducted. We have a reasonable picture of employment and adjustment in the first few years after leaving school, but we know little of employment success and training when persons with mild disabilities reach their late 20s, 30s, or 40s. Do they return to educational programs for further training? Do their employers provide effective job advancement training? Do they become fully integrated into the work force? Do they advance to higher level jobs?

We have not reached a state wherein we can say that we have developed effective programs that are widely available. Instead, we can identify some effective practices and some practices that should be discontinued. The results of research and field studies now need to be put into practice.

REFERENCES

Alper, S. (1985). Comparing employer and teacher identified entry-level job requisites of service occupations. *Education and Training of the Mentally Retarded, 20,* 89–96.

Asche, F. M., & Vogler, D. E. (1980). Employer satisfaction with secondary vocational education graduates. *Journal of Vocational Education Research*, *5*(4), 53–61.

Astuto, T. A. (1985). *Vocational education programs and services for high school handicapped students*. Bloomington: Indiana University, Council of Administrators of Special Education, Inc.

Ballantyne, D. (1985). *Cooperative programs for transition from school to work*. Washington, DC: U.S. Department of Education, Office of Special Education and Rehabilitation Services, National Institute of Handicapped Research.

Bencomo, A., & Schafer, M. (1984). Remediation and accommodation for clients with learning disabilities [Special issue]. *Journal of Rehabilitation*, 64–67.

Benz, M. R., & Halpern, A. S. (1986). Vocational preparation for high school students with mild disabilities: A statewide study of administrator, teacher and parent perceptions. *Career Development for Exceptional Individuals*, *9*(1), 3–15.

Blalock, J. W. (1981). Persistent problems and concerns of young adults with learning disabilities. In W. M. Cruickshank & A. A. Silver (Eds.), *Bridges to tomorrow: The best of ACLD* (Vol. 2, pp. 35–55). Syracuse, NY: Syracuse University Press.

Brechim, C., & Kemp, W. H. (1984). Misconceptions about learning disabilities. *Journal of Rehabilitation*, *50*(2), 30–33.

Brimer, R. W., & Rouse, S. T. (1978). Post-school adjustment: A follow-up of a cooperative program for the educable mentally retarded. *Journal of Special Educators of the Mentally Retarded*, *14*, 131–137.

Butler, W. D. (1982). *Vocational rehabilitation and the employability of the learning disabled adult in Arizona*. Unpublished doctoral dissertation, University of Arizona, Flagstaff.

Campbell, P., Hensel, J. W., Hudson, P., Schwartz, S. E., & Sealander, K. (1987). The successfully employed worker with a handicap: Employee/employer perceptions of job performance. *Career Development for Exceptional Individuals*, *10*, 85–94.

Chaffin, J. D. (1969). Production rate as a variable in the job success or failure of educable mentally retarded adolescents. *Exceptional Children*, *35*, 533–538.

Cobb, R. M., & Crump, W. D. (1984). *Post-school status of young adults identified as learning disabled while enrolled in public schools: A comparison of those enrolled and not enrolled in learning disabilities programs* (Final Report). Birmingham: University of Alabama, College of Education.

Combs, I. H., & Omvig, C. P. (1986). Accommodation of disabled people into employment: Perceptions of employers. *Journal of Rehabilitation*, *52*(2), 42–45.

Crain, E. J. (1980). Socioeconomic status of educable mentally retarded graduates of special education. *Education and Training of the Mentally Retarded*, *15*, 90–94.

Crimando, W. (1984). A review of placement-related issues for clients with learning disabilities. *Journal of Rehabilitation*, *50*(2), 78–81.

Dalton, R. F., & Latz, A. (1978). Vocational placement: The Pennsylvania Rehabilitation Center. *Rehabilitation Literature*, *39*, 336–339.

Edgar, E. (1987). Secondary programs in special education: Are many of them justifiable? *Exceptional Children*, *53*, 555–561.

Edgar, E., & Levine, P. (1987). *A longitudinal follow-along study of graduates of special education*. Seattle: University of Washington, Experimental Education Unit, Child Development and Mental Retardation Center.

Emener, W. G., & McHargue, J. M. (1978). Employer attitudes toward the employment and placement of the handicapped. *Journal of Applied Rehabilitation Counseling, 9*, 120–125.

Fafard, M. B., & Haubrich, P. A. (1981). Vocational and social adjustment of learning disabled young adults: A follow up survey. *Learning Disabilities Quarterly, 4*, 122–130.

Fardig, D., Algozzine, R., Schwartz, S., Hensel, J., & Westling, D. (1985). Postsecondary vocational adjustment of rural mildly handicapped students. *Exceptional Children, 52*, 115–121.

Frank, A. R., Sitlington, P. L., & Carson, R. (1991). Transition of adolescents with behavioral disorders—is it successful? *Behavioral Disorders, 16*, 180–191.

Gaylord-Ross, C., Forte, J., & Gaylord-Ross, R. (1986). The community classroom: Technological vocational training for students with severe handicaps. *Career Development for Exceptional Individuals, 9*(1), 24–33.

Geib, B. B., Guzzardi, L. R., & Genova, P. M. (1981). Intervention for adults with learning disabilities. *Academic Therapy, 16*, 317–325.

Gerber, P. J. (1981). Learning disabilities and eligibility for vocational rehabilitation services: A chronology of events. *Learning Disabilities Quarterly, 4*, 422–425.

Gruenhagen, K. A. (1982). Attitudes of fast food restaurant managers towards hiring the mentally retarded. *Career Development for Exceptional Individuals, 5*, 98–105.

Halloran, W. D. (1978). Handicapped persons: Who are they? *American Vocational Journal, 53*, 30–31.

Halpern, A. S. (1978). The impact of work/study programs on employment of the mentally retarded: Some findings from two sources. *International Journal of Rehabilitation Research, 1*, 167–178.

Hasazi, S. B., Gordon, L. R., & Roe, C. A. (1985). Factors associated with the employment status of disabled youth exiting from high school from 1979 to 1983. *Exceptional Children, 51*, 455–469.

Hawkins, J. A. (1984). *Follow-up study of special education graduates: Class of 1983.* Rockville, MD: Montgomery County Public Schools.

Humes, C. W., & Brammer, G. (1985). LD career success after high school. *Academic Therapy, 21*, 171–176.

Humes, C. W., & Hohenshil, T. H. (1985). Career development and career education for handicapped students: A reexamination. *Vocational Guidance Quarterly, 34*(1), 31–40.

Kokaska, C., & Skolnik, J. (1986). Employment suggestions from L.D. adults. *Academic Therapy, 21*, 573–577.

Lehtinen, L., & Dumas, L. (1976). *A follow-up study of learning disabled children as adults: A final report.* Evanston, IL: Cove School Research Office. (ERIC Document Reproduction Service No. ED 164 728)

Levin, E., Zigmond, N., & Birch, J. (1985). A follow-up study of 52 learning disabled students. *Journal of Learning Disabilities, 18*, 2–7.

Martin, J. E., Rusch, F. R., Lagomarcino, T., & Chadsey-Rusch, J. (1986). Comparison between nonhandicapped and mentally retarded workers: Why they lose their jobs. *Applied Research in Mental Retardation, 7*, 467–474.

Martin, J. E., Schneider, K. E., Rusch, F. R., & Geske, T. G. (1982). Training mentally retarded individuals for competitive employment: Benefits of transitional employment. *Exceptional Education Quarterly, 33*, 58–66.

Miller, J. H., Mulkey, S. W., & Kopp, K. H. (1984). Public rehabilitation services for individuals with specific learning disabilities. *Journal of Rehabilitation, 50,* 19–29.

Neel, R., Meadows, N., Levine, P., & Edgar, E. (1988). What happens after special education: A statewide follow up study of secondary students who have behavioral disorders. *Behavioral Disorders, 13,* 209–216.

Neubert, D. A., Tilson, G. P., Jr., & Ianacone, R. N. (1989). Postsecondary transition needs and employment patterns of individuals with mild disabilities. *Exceptional Children, 55,* 494–500.

Neuhaus, E. C. (1967). Training the mentally retarded for competitive employment. *Exceptional Children, 33,* 625–628.

Newill, B. H., Goyette, C. H., & Fogarty, T. W. (1984). Diagnosis and assessment of the adult with specific learning disabilities. *Journal of Rehabilitation, 50*(2), 34–39.

Noble, J. H., & Conley, R. W. (1987). Accumulating evidence on the benefits and costs of supported and transitional employment for persons with severe disabilities. *Journal of the Association for Persons with Severe Handicaps, 12,* 163–174.

Palmer, J. T., Velleman, R., & Shafer, D. (1985). *The transition process of disabled youth: Literature review.* Albertson, NY: Human Resources Center.

Parent, W. S., & Everson, J. M. (1986). Competencies of disabled workers in industry: A review of business literature. *Journal of Rehabilitation, 52*(4), 16–23.

Peterson, L., & Smith, L. L. (1960). A comparison of the post-school adjustment of educable mentally retarded adults with that of adults of normal intelligence. *Exceptional Children, 26,* 404–408.

Phelps, L. A. (1980). Research on vocational education programs for special population. In T. L. Wentling (Ed.), *ARRIVE: Annual review of research in vocational education* (Vol. 1, pp. 115–197). Urbana: University of Illinois.

Phelps, L. A. (1985). An agenda for action: Excellence in education. *Journal for Vocational Special Needs Education, 7*(3), 3–6.

Richardson, N. R., & Hill, J. (1980). An evaluation of vocational placement success at a comprehensive rehabilitation center: A third measurement. *Rehabilitation Literature, 41,* 19–22.

Rusch, F. R., & Mithaug, D. E. (1980). *Vocational training for mentally retarded adults. A behavior analytic approach.* Champaign, IL.: Research Press.

Schneck, G. R., Lerwick, L. P., & Copa, G. H. (1980). Assessment of the prevalence and service need requirements of handicapped and disadvantaged students in vocational-technical education programs in Minnesota. In T. L. Wentling (Ed.), *ARRIVE: Annual review of research in vocational education* (Vol. 1, pp. 177–184). Urbana: University of Illinois.

Shanyfelt, P. A. (1974). Occupational preparation of secondary educable students. *The Pointer, 19,* 106–110.

Shill, J. F. (1976). *Development and testing of criteria for the identification of and selection of mentally handicapped students for vocational programs: Project proposal.* Stark: Vocational and Technical Education, Mississippi State University.

Sitlington, P. L. (1981). Vocational and special education in career programming for the mildly handicapped adolescent. *Exceptional Children, 47,* 592–598.

Taggart, R. (1981). *A fisherman's guide: An assessment of training and remediation strategies.*

Kalamazoo, MI: W. E. Upjohn Institute for Employment Research.

Talkington, L. W., & Overbeck, D. B. (1975). Job satisfaction and performance with retarded females. *Mental Retardation, 13*(3), 18–19.

Tobias, J. (1970). Vocational adjustment of young retarded adults. *Mental Retardation, 8*(3), 13–16.

Walsh, J. (1980). An assessment of vocational education programs for the handicapped under the 1968 amendments to the Vocational Education Act: A summary. In T. L. Wentling (Ed.), *ARRIVE: Annual review of research in vocational education* (Vol. 1, pp. 137–161). Urbana: University of Illinois.

Wanous, J. P., Stumpf, S. A., & Bedrosian, H. (1979). Job survival of new employees. *Personnel Psychology, 32*, 651–662.

Wehman, P., Hill, M., Hill, J. W., Brooke, V., Pendleton, P., & Britt, C. (1985). Competitive employment of persons with mental retardation: A follow up six years later. *Mental Retardation, 23*, 274–281.

Wehman, P., Kregel, J., & Seyfarth, J. (1985). Employment outlook for young adults with mental retardation. *Rehabilitation Counseling Bulletin, 29*, 90–99.

White, W. J., Alley, G. R., Deshler, D. D., Schumaker, J. B., Warner, M. M., & Clark, F. L. (1982). Are there learning disabilities after high school? *Exceptional Children, 49*, 273–274.

Will, M. (1984). *Bridges from school to working life.* Washington, DC: Office of Special Education and Rehabilitative Services.

Zigmond, N., & Thornton, H. (1985). Follow up of postsecondary age learning disabled graduates and dropouts. *Learning Disabilities Research, 1*(10), 50–55.

Chapter 12

※ ※ ※

The Technology of Vocational Training

*I*n this chapter we consider the methods and materials utilized to teach work skills to persons with mild disabilities. Our presentation opens with a discussion of curricula then proceeds to an overview of the behavioral approach to instruction including job analysis, task analysis, acquisition of skills, and maintenance and generalization of skills. We also describe some cognitive approaches to vocational training, including counseling and didactic instruction, and job acquisition, job placement, job retention, and follow-through.

※ ※ ※

CURRICULUM

There is no prepackaged appropriate and effective curriculum available for vocational instruction of persons with mild disabilities. Local conditions such as the type of community (rural, suburban, or urban), the local economy and job market (agricultural, manufacturing, or service), the characteristics of the students (e.g., age, disabling conditions, aspirations, level of sophistication), the availability of instructors with the necessary skills, and the availability of the needed resources (e.g., machinery, transportation) are some of the variables that will influence the curricular content. In this section, we will not address specific curricular content but rather the principles and practices that are critical to the development of a comprehensive vocational curriculum for persons with mild disabilities. This curricular development plan is designed for those individuals with mild disabilities who are going to enter the work force soon after graduation, not those who will enter a traditional (albeit adapted) college program.

Continuity

A comprehensive vocational preparation curriculum should provide for continuity of experience from the elementary grades through high school and into postsecondary training opportunities. Vocational activities should become more intense and occupy a greater portion of the student's time as he or she grows older.

Continuity can be developed by ensuring that each experience is a prerequisite for ones yet to come. More importantly, continuity is developed when educators collectively examine the total possible vocational experience of the individual and together agree on roles and assignments. Earlier, in chapter 5, we addressed cooperative agreements. Unfortunately, most cooperative agreements are insufficient and too broad to ensure continuity. What is needed is a more specific analysis of the services and content of all available vocational services within a geographical location. This is a huge undertaking and surely can be accomplished by no one other than a public educator, but it is doubtful that many public school systems are willing to release a person from other responsibilities to conduct such an analysis. However, it should be apparent that without such an analysis, there will be duplication of services and neglected critical services. The end result is inefficient—a curriculum that is incomplete and most likely ineffective. The investment cost of an effective curriculum is high, but an otherwise constructed curriculum, although cheaply constructed, has little effect. The ultimate cost is unemployment and untrained workers.

The focal point for development of vocational curricular continuity should be the secondary school. This is the point at which the most critical vocational decisions are made and when the greatest amount of information about previous curriculum and future possibilities is required. It is also likely that, at the secondary level, the greatest adaptability is possible. Furthermore, postsecondary providers are rarely under the same mandates for comprehensive services as secondary providers. Some postsecondary providers identify a small training niche (e.g., a proprietary auto mechanics training institute) and give little thought to the needs of special populations unless they discover how it can enhance profitability or if they need specific assistance with an enrolled student with special needs. Other postsecondary providers (e.g., community colleges) may have broader missions but limited resources and understanding. We cannot hope that either type of service provider will effectively serve persons with mild disabilities without some leadership and direction from the persons most knowledgeable about the needs of mildly disabled learners/workers—secondary transition specialists.

From the focal point of the secondary transition program, the curricular needs at the elementary level can be developed. Thus, the secondary curriculum developers must base curricular development on what comes after high school, and they must communicate the prerequisites to elementary curriculum specialists.

Listed here are some specific steps to be taken for the development of a curriculum with continuity.

1.   Canvass the geographical area to determine (a) the extent and type of postsecondary vocational training opportunities available and (b) the types of

jobs that are available and are likely to be available in the near future. Postsecondary training opportunities come in many forms, including private and public technical schools, community colleges, vocational rehabilitation programs, other public programs (e.g., those provided by mental retardation and mental health services), specific grant programs, and programs provided by advocacy groups. One type of training that should not be neglected is that provided by major employers. Most large companies offer on-the-job training, and some offer after-work classes. The persons conducting the survey should identify such programs. Chambers of commerce may be able to provide leads for information on both employers and training programs. Another valuable source of information is graduates. Systematic follow-up will provide information about resources discovered by graduates. Follow-up also allows the collection of qualitative information about service providers and employers, namely, which ones are adaptable.

2. Analyze each of the programs and employment opportunities. What are the entry level prerequisites? How stable is the employer or program? It makes no sense to target an employer who is about to go out of business or an industry that is obsolete. To what extent are the employers and program managers willing to adapt to persons with mild disabilities?

3. Plan support services to help employers and vocational training providers adapt.

4. Identify missing and needed services. Can existing service providers expand or modify services so that the needs can be met? Can the needs be met in secondary vocational programs?

5. Develop curricular content at the secondary level so that participants have the opportunity to receive instruction targeted to specific outcomes. Transition specialists should recognize that local conditions change, often drastically and with little warning. A well-designed curriculum based on available postsecondary opportunities does not ensure successful employment. Such a curriculum does, however, significantly improve the odds for job success.

6. Build into the curriculum opportunities for both the students and parents to learn that as the student progresses through the curriculum, decision windows become narrower. Each time a student and/or parent makes a choice to follow a specific branch of the curriculum (e.g., college prep vs. vocational, auto mechanics vs. carpentry), it becomes increasingly difficult to change a decision. This does not mean that decisions are irrevocable, but the decision makers should be aware of the consequences of the decision and the subsequent effort that will be required to undo a decision. Avoiding decisions should not be permitted. Decision points should be specified in the cur-

riculum. These decision points may be time based (e.g., in the freshman or sophomore years) or competency based (i.e., when the student has attained competency on specific goals).

7. After the secondary curriculum has been elaborated, elementary prerequisites and experiences should be specified. These should be developed jointly by elementary and secondary educators. These prerequisites and experiences should be limited. They should include only those that lead to the attainment of competence required to progress to the secondary curriculum.

8. Build the role of the Individual Education Plan (IEP) into the curriculum. Early on the IEP should address the most likely future environments for the child and an overall plan for how he or she will be enabled to arrive at that environment and succeed. This may require an early abandonment of a strictly developmental curriculum for one that is functional.

Functionality

Vocational curricula must have utility. Goals and objectives should be keyed to foster skills that are useful in the workplace and to gain entrance into the workplace. A functional curriculum is parsimonious; that is, it should include all of the elements necessary for vocational success and exclude those that are not necessary (Bownas, Bosshardt, & Donnelly, 1985). The functionality of a curriculum can be established only by an analysis of the job market and specific jobs. There are no commercially available *functional* curricula, although commercially available curricula may be used to construct a functional curriculum. A functional curriculum is developed by analyzing how employers select employees and studying job requirements and expectations. Both of these items are addressed in detail in subsequent sections of this chapter.

Integration

An effective vocational curriculum for people who are mildly disabled must be integrated in several ways: (a) between special education and vocational education, (b) between special education and regular education, and (c) between academic education and vocational education. Generally, for individuals this is accomplished by means of the IEP and Individual Transition Plan (ITP). However, there should also be agreement among these parties (regular education, special education, vocational education, academic departments) that establishes relative priorities at various ages. For example, Wehman (1983) believes that vocational activities should occupy approximately 1 hour per week in the early elementary grades. In the last years of high school they should occupy 80% to 90% of the student's day.

Unfortunately, analyses show that vocational objectives occupy a minor place in the IEPs of students who are mildly disabled (McBride & Forgnone, 1985). The IEPs of the 90 students who were reviewed and had mild disabilities contained 453 academic objectives, 90 sociobehavioral objectives, 43 self-help objectives, but only 7 career-vocational objectives. Cobb and Phelps (1983) also identify some problems with the IEPs of students with mild disabilities. They found that mildly retarded students were more likely to have vocational goals in their IEPs than students with learning disabilities (64.6% vs. 27.3%). They also found that 51.5% of the goals were to be addressed in special vocational classes, 30.3% in work study, and only 16.2% in regular vocational classes. As further testimony to the inadequacy of the IEPs, they report that only one third contained vocational assessment information, and very few were constructed with the input of a vocational educator. Greenwood and Morley (1980) report that 70.8% of the vocational education teachers in Iowa had no training with special needs populations. More than half had no experience with such students. Halpern and Benz (1987) write that vocational teachers have access to few supports when they serve students with disabilities in the mainstream of vocational education. With such data in mind, it is easy to see why effective integration has been elusive. We may hope that with the new emphasis on transition and the requirement for ITPs, the distribution has already shifted so that vocational objectives become predominant in the secondary years.

Progression

The progression of a curriculum refers to the manner in which the students are led to independence and competence. Thus, as the student progresses through the vocational curriculum, the demands placed on him or her should become increasingly sophisticated. In the elementary years, teachers and parents will make most of the decisions about what the student will learn. In the final years of high school, the student should be exercising most of the choice. Without this systematic progression, how can we expect the student suddenly to make mature choices in an adult world? Thus, the curriculum needs to provide opportunities to become self-directed and deal with the consequences of decisions. In addition, a progressive curriculum is one in which skills learned early are simple. Those that come later are more complex and incorporate the earlier skills. If a skill is not required in order to perform a later skill or skill sequence, it should not be included. For example, finger painting, although an effective motor control exercise, has no vocational relevance. It is not a skill on which to build the motor control required for vocational tasks, but other forms of painting that are encountered in jobs are vocationally relevant and could be incorporated.

The progression of the curriculum should also include increased demands for speed. Speed should be relatively unimportant in the elementary years and at the initial stages of learning a new task. As the student progresses into the curriculum, speed demands should increase. In contrast, when the student is learning a new task, speed demands should be limited. As the student demonstrates acquisition, speed demands should be incorporated and gradually approach those on the job.

A progressive curriculum is one in which repetition of training is minimized. Thus, aspects of linear measurement taught in elementary school should not be in the curriculum again in the secondary school. Rather, those linear measurement skills should be maintained by incorporating them into higher order tasks with sufficient but gradually decreasing frequency until those skills are used at about the same rate as they are on the job.

The time spent in learning should reflect the importance of the component (Bownas et al., 1985) The question to be asked is, Can the student work effectively without this skill? If the skill is absolutely critical to success, then time should be devoted to it. If an adaptation can be made that eliminates or reduces the importance of the skill, then the time allotted should be reduced or eliminated if the adaptation is acceptable to employers.

Finally, the curriculum should gradually increase the student's exposure to occupational variety. This exposure should begin early so that by the time the student needs to begin to make choices, he or she has a comprehensive understanding of many possible career paths.

Wehman (1983) has identified a progression for students with severe disabilities that has equal applicability for those with mild disabilities, and indeed some of the students who have been served in programs designed by Wehman were mildly disabled (see Figure 12–1).

Figure 12–1

Curricular content in elementary, middle, and secondary programs

Elementary

1. Job sampling
2. Work concepts—employer, pay, and so forth
3. Development of expectations
4. Analysis of probable later environments

Middle

1. Work habits–work support skills
2. Specific vocational skills
3. Vocational paths and decision making

Secondary

1. Increase in production rates
2. Improvement of quality
3. Improvement of endurance
4. Real job experiences
5. Transition to postsecondary environments

Adaptability

Vocational curricula for persons with mild disabilities must be adaptable. Those who build the curricula must ask, How can we adapt the instruction, tasks, and so forth so that we can include students with distinctive learning needs? Ballantyne (1985) describes several examples of such adaptability. Vocational programs in Michigan, Missouri, California, and Oklahoma have adopted an open entry/open exit competency-based system that permits vocational-technical schools to increase the enrollment of students with mild disabilities. Students are not assigned to vocational classes on a time basis (i.e., one semester) but rather until they reach a prespecified level of competency. Therefore, a student who is mildly disabled may take longer to complete a course but can finish it instead of receiving a failing grade. Students receive certificates for different levels of proficiency in the specific area. Each of these levels is matched to real jobs. Thus, a student might enroll in masonry training and progress to the level of skill where he or she could enter the work force as a skilled bricklayer. Alternately, the student might only progress to the level of masonry laborer. In either case, the student receives a certificate that is related to a real job. In a traditional program, the latter student would probably receive a poor or failing grade, plus insufficient learning to be employable.

Ballantyne (1985) also describes accommodations developed in Illinois and North Dakota, where special educators and vocational educators have worked together to adapt vocational offerings by changing methods and materials. They put vocational textbooks on audiotape for poor readers. They permit longer test times and revised test instruments so that they required less reading. They also permit oral administration of the tests.

The Vocational Studies Center at the University of Wisconsin–Madison has produced a handbook for modifying secondary and postsecondary vocational education for students with disabilities (*Puzzled*, n.d.). This guide provides information on resources for teachers, interagency linkages, assessment modifications, and modification of service delivery.

Experience

Vocational curricula must be experiential; students cannot learn about work effectively from a text. The best experience is that which is identical to the conditions existing in real jobs. Many researchers support the move to community-based education for students with moderate to severe disabilities. Similar activities are imperative for students with mild disabilities, especially in the area of vocational education. All students should experience real paid employment as part of their vocational training. There are several advantages to experiential vocational education:

1. It provides the learner with the opportunity to practice skills learned in a school-based environment under the real conditions of work while simultaneously providing the support of the vocational staff.

2. Students work under the conflicting demands of the real job: multiple supervisors, distractions in the workplace, and formal and informal work rules.
3. Skills will generalize better from one real work environment to another than from a simulated environment to a real environment.
4. Real work experience promotes independence, problem solving, and decision making. Simulation cannot accomplish this to the same degree.
5. Experiential episodes can lead to later permanent employment.
6. Experiential placements in real jobs reduce the investment cost for special equipment and materials required for training.

Several modes of delivering job experience are being used around the country. *Work study* is one of the most common examples (Greenwood & Morley, 1980). Students operating under this model (which is discussed more fully in chap. 13) attend classes for part of the day and work for part of the day. Work study often has limited effectiveness as the work is usually unpaid employment in "made-up" jobs. This does not give the student the opportunity to work under real conditions. Furthermore, it is common that the job assignment does not represent any real job that is available in the community. Work and study assignments may not be integrated (Walsh, 1980), and the student ends up with two programs rather than a single integrated one. This criticism is leveled not at the model but rather the manner in which the model is often implemented.

Another means by which structured job experience can be gained is through *work stations* in business and industry (Materials Development Center, 1988b). In this system, students rotate through actual work stations in real businesses. Time at each station is brief and not generally viewed as a job. This system is most effective for career counseling rather than actual job training, especially when the experiences at each station are brief. At the least, students can gain a firsthand glimpse of a possible career.

Summer youth employment programs were part of the programs of 35% of the students studied by Greenwood and Morley (1980). Given the research that indicates that students with mild disabilities who held summer jobs are more successful as adult workers, summer employment has and should continue to grow as a means of providing job experience. Summer Youth Employment Development Projects are one means to accomplish this (Ballantyne, 1985).

Community-based instruction is another means to provide job experience to students, at least in terms of exposure to various careers. Although we know that community-based instruction is effective, few teachers (7%) of students with mild disabilities utilize it (Halpern & Benz, 1987).

Conclusion

Vocational curricula can take many forms, and most include continuity, functionality, integration, progression, adaptability, and experience. Vocational curricula should be subject to an evaluation in which the outcomes of the curriculum (e.g., student employment rates, congruence between skills taught and the skills demanded by employers) are compared to the goals. This process should be ongoing and annual. Good follow-up studies of students and surveys of employers should be the major sources of evaluative data.

❦ ❦ ❦

BEHAVIORAL APPROACH TO VOCATIONAL TRAINING

The behavioral approach to vocational training is systematic and precise, with a proven record of success. It is also time-consuming (but not inefficient) and demanding. Vocational educators who would like to use a behavioral approach should recognize that it requires a tremendous initial investment in planning. The behavioral approach should be used when a less structured, more traditional "tell and show" didactic approach has not or is not likely to work with an individual student.

How can educators make this determination? The best predictor of future behavior is past behavior. Thus, if a student has been unsuccessful in learning with a didactic approach, that student is likely to continue to be unsuccessful with that strategy, and a more structured analytical behavioral approach should be employed.

What is the behavioral approach? It is a model for learning and instruction in which specific learning outcomes (objectives) are enumerated, and the conditions (antecedents and consequences) are structured to bring about the desired outcomes. In the following subsections we will describe (a) how functional objectives are developed, (b) how jobs are analyzed, and (c) how conditions are designed to enhance acquisition, fluency, maintenance, and generalization of skills.

Development of Performance Objectives

Vocational performance objectives are statements of the outcome expectations for a learner. They answer the question, What will the learner be able to do at the end of instruction? There are three parts to a performance objective: (a) specification of the expected outcome, (b) specification of the conditions under which the outcome is to occur, and (c) specification of the criterion for evaluating attainment of the objective. Several examples of vocationally relevant objectives are analyzed in Figure 12–2.

Vocationally relevant objectives can be developed after answers to the following questions are obtained:

1. What skills/behaviors are likely to be required or expected of all or most workers no matter what job they work at?
2. What special skills/behaviors are likely to be required or expected of workers in the classes of jobs in which the specific student is likely to work?
3. What special skills/behaviors are required by the employer for whom the student is working or training to work?

Performance Objective 1—Drywaller

Given a power drywall screwdriver, 1 3/4-inch drywall screws, a 4- x 8-foot sheet of drywall, and a studded interior wall, Stewart will attach the drywall to the studs *within 2 minutes. The drywall will be attached so that the perpendicular edges are plumb and centered on the studs. The drywall screws will be spaced at 8-inch to 1-foot vertical intervals and will be applied to each and every stud covered by the drywall sheet.*

Performance Objective 2—Postal clerk

Given packages of more than 3 pounds, a postal scale, and a postal rate chart, Mary will determine the correct postage to mail the package and write the correct amount on the upper right corner of the top of the package *for three packages within 2 minutes.*

Key: regular typeface = the expected outcome; **bold typeface** = **conditions**; *italic typeface* = *evaluation criteria.*

Figure 12–2
Analysis of vocational performance objectives

These three questions represent a progression from the most general work skills and behaviors to the most specific. Responses to the first question represent a large set of skills/behaviors that are commonly expected by most employers. Many of these skills and behaviors would fall into those we have classified as *extravocational* (e.g., punching a time clock, getting to work, accepting supervision). These skills are those on which focus falls early in the student's vocational training (beginning in elementary school and progressing through middle school). These skills should be firmly established in the student's repertoire by the time real work experience begins. This does not mean that they will not continue to be important but rather that the student should be able to perform the components of the skill prior to paid placement, which then provides the opportunity for real-life practice. For some students these skills will not be fully maintained or may not be generalized to the specific workplace. Thus, the skill may remain an important part of in situ training.

There are numerous sources for general vocational objectives, and this area constitutes one of the few in which "prepackaged" curricular content can be used to great effect. Such curricula should be augmented with locally developed objectives and content that reflect local conditions and the specific needs and characteristics of the student. (The reader is directed to later discussions of specific programs and models in chap. 13 and to the section on extravocational skills in chaps. 14, 15, and 16 for sources of such curricular content.)

Rusch, Schutz, and Agran (1982) identify seven vocational skills that were selected as important skills for entry-level workers by 90% of a sample of employers from food service and janitorial service businesses. These skills are part of the response to the first question posed earlier; that is, it is likely that these skills are also important to most employers of entry-level workers. The seven skills are

1. completing repetitive tasks within 25% of the average rate,
2. moving about the workplace safely,
3. understanding work routines and schedule changes,
4. obeying safety rules,
5. continuously working for 30- to 60-minute intervals,
6. learning new tasks by observing coworkers and supervisors, and
7. correcting work after the supervisor gives directions.

Responses to the second question constitute a set of skills or behaviors that are important and expected by employers of specific categories of workers (e.g., construction workers, including carpenters, electricians, plumbers, masons, etc.; clerical workers, including typists, filers, receptionists, data entry clerks, etc.). These skills may include the ability to recognize and utilize basic tools of the job category (e.g., for construction workers: hand and power tools such as hammers, saws, layout and measurement devices; for clerical workers: typewriters, copiers, telephones). Objectives that fall into this second category generally begin to appear in the student's IEP/ITP during the middle school years.

Objectives in this second category can be subgrouped as either *exploratory* or *skill training*. The objectives progress from exploratory (i.e., gaining an understanding of the job through exposure and experience with the tasks and materials) to skill training (e.g., learning to use a tool in a way that is related to a specific job type in which the student has expressed interest). The purpose of the objective (exploratory vs. training) depends on how far along the decision line the student has progressed. Students are expected to accomplish many exploratory objectives before they begin work on training objectives. As the student makes choices to follow narrower career paths, skill training objectives become predominant. Most students who are not going on to 4-year college programs should be expected to begin to make these choices early in the high school years and to have a relatively narrowed focus by the middle of the next to last year of high school or when the student is old enough to begin actual paid work. For many students, paid work experience in actual jobs is the point at which career choices become more sharply defined (e.g., the experience confirms or disconfirms the student's interest).

Objectives and curricular content for the exploratory and skill training categories can also be obtained from available curricula. At the least, available job exploration curricula can be used on which to build a locally valid curriculum and objectives. Again, such curricula should be augmented with locally developed content and objectives based on local conditions and specific student needs and characteristics. Skill training objectives and curricula are likely to represent local conditions more than exploratory objectives and curricula, although again, preexisting curricula can be used as a core for many job categories. However, the most important source for objectives and content is local employers. Objectives and content are developed from specific job analysis. Such analysis may be time-consuming, but it ensures that objectives will be related to real jobs and that they will be parsimonious (i.e., they will exclude skills that are unimportant to local employers).

Responses to the third question provide the content for objectives related to training for *specific* available employment. These objectives reflect the work demands of a specific employer for a specific worker (e.g., the Ace Construction Company expects its laborers to be able to assist in the construction of a truss roof). Objectives in this category are likely to become increasingly important as the student nears graduation from high school. They are also important when the student is enrolled in postsecondary programs such as those based in community colleges, in proprietary vocational training schools, or on the job. These objectives are determined solely by the demands of a particular job through a specific job analysis.

Job Analysis

A *job analysis* is a systematic description and breakdown of a job. A good job analysis is based on observation of job incumbents over sufficient time to note all of the aspects of a job. There are numerous sources for job analysis and job analysis systems. Available job analyses based on fictitious or representative jobs are not appropriate for training persons with mild disabilities. Such analyses do not identify important local conditions and expectations. They may lead to training of skills that are not critical to a real job or to neglect of those that are. Such analyses, however, can be useful as formats and may make it easier to complete an analysis for an actual job.

Banks, Jackson, Stafford, and Warr (1983) describe a process and an inventory for analyzing jobs requiring limited skill. There are five categories of analysis in the inventory: (a) tools and equipment, (b) physical and perceptual requirements, (c) math requirements, (d) communication requirements, and (e) decision-making/responsibility requirements. Figure 12–3 provides a more detailed format for conducting a job analysis.

Job analyses should be validated by direct observation of workers in the same position in the same organization. A job analysis is valid if a comparison of the specifications in the job analysis demonstrates agreement with those obtained by observation of workers in the job. In some cases, employers may permit adaptation of jobs so that applicants who are mildly disabled and have specific deficits (e.g., lower reading achievement than that normally required) can still work at the job effectively. In these cases an adapted job analysis should be prepared. Adapted jobs should generally be used as a last resort. It is often better to improve the capacity of the individual to meet the usual demands of the job for several reasons, such as possible negative reactions of coworkers who may feel that the worker with mild disabilities is receiving special treatment. Adapting the job also may allow the individual to work at

I. Organization Description
   A. Name
   B. Location
   C. Name of personnel manager, other contact persons
   D. Number of employees
   E. Nature of business
   F. Organizational characteristics
      1. Work seasonality
      2. Union presence
      3. Other
II. Job Information
   A. Position title
   B. General job description
   C. Job tasks performed
   D. Stability of job tasks performed
   E. Entry-level requirements
      1. Training
      2. Experience
      3. Special requirements
   F. Equipment operated
   G. Physical requirements
      1. Speed
      2. Strength
      3. Endurance
      4. Sensory acuity
      5. Tolerance of extreme conditions
         a. Noise
         b. Heat
         c. Other
   H. Task monitoring
      1. Quality control

Figure 12–3
Job analysis format

    2. Quantity control

    3. Supervision received

       a. From whom?

       b. How?

       c. How often?

I. Social requirements

    1. Coworkers

       a. Number

       b. Job classifications

       c. Proximity

       d. Relationship to incumbent

    2. Persons outside the organization

       a. Customers

       b. Public

       c. Representatives of other organizations

    3. Communication requirements

       a. Written

       b. Oral

J. Other requirements/conditions

    1. Uniforms or special clothing

    2. Transportation

    3. Normal workday

       a. Shifts

       b. Breaks and meals

    4. Decision-making requirements

    5. Compensation

       a. Pay

       b. Benefits

    6. Career ladder

    7. Organizational training

    8. Other

Figure 12–3, continued

this specific job but may hinder his or her ability to move on to another job within the organization or at a new workplace.

Structuring Instruction

The discussion here is limited to central work tasks—those that lead to the production of the product or the service of the organization. Discussion of other job-related skills (e.g., social skills, work adjustment skills) is provided in chapters 14 and 15.

When a student learns a task, he or she proceeds through several stages:

1. Acquisition
2. Fluency
3. Maintenance
4. Generalization

Each stage will be discussed separately in the following sections.

Acquisition. ***Acquisition*** is the achievement of the ability to perform the task consistently. Generally, acquisition is accomplished when the student performs the task steps correctly in the correct sequence for three or more consecutive trials. The selection of three consecutive trials as a criterion is somewhat arbitrary but is usually sufficient to demonstrate that the correct performance is more than accidental.

Determining a Performance Objective. Skill acquisition begins with a specification of a *performance objective* such as those appearing in Figure 12–2. These performance objectives are determined by a job analysis and the minimal performance standards set by the employer for the task. Performance standards should be validated by direct observation of the employees in the targeted job. The person making this observation should determine the average performance of employees in the targeted job on dimensions such as speed and accuracy and the range of performance (i.e., the highs and lows). The range provides an estimate of the acceptable levels of performance, but the average provides a target level for a trainee.

Devising a Task Analysis. The next step in the process of structuring instruction is to develop a task analysis. A ***task analysis*** is a sequentially ordered listing of the behavioral steps required to accomplish a performance objective. Task analyses for the performance objectives stated in Figure 12–2, for example, are enumerated in Figure 12–4.

Task analyses can and should be developed by observing workers performing the job task. More than one worker should be monitored to determine if the task can be accomplished with *equifinality*—through two or more different sequences that lead to the same result. The task analysis provides both the student and the instructor with a means of continuous evaluation (i.e., how many steps in the task sequence have been learned) and

---

Task Analysis 1: Full-sheet drywall installation

Start conditions

The student will have a tool belt with a fully charged cordless drywall screwdriver, a belt pocket full of 1³/₄-inch drywall screws, a drywall lift jig, and a 4- × 8-foot sheet of ¹/₂-inch drywall propped against a fully studded wall.

Task steps

Stud centers will be determined from left corner (inside corner).

1. Insert drywall lift jig under drywall.
2. Push drywall flat against wall.
3. Push drywall flush even with left corner.
4. Lift drywall off subflooring by stepping on drywall lift lever until board is flush with ceiling panel.
5. Check alignment with corner.
6. Realign if necessary.
7. Check plumb with level.
8. Set first drywall screw in upper left corner into leftmost stud approximately 2 inches from ceiling board.
9. Set second drywall screw into upper right corner into stud approximately 2 inches from ceiling board.
10. Mark plumb lines in the center of each stud.
11. Set remaining screws in horizontal rows beginning with top row, and working to bottom. Maintain 8- to 12-inch vertical spacing between screws.

Figure 12–4
Task analyses

smaller steps in a complex task that can be learned more quickly than the whole task. Most learners, when faced with a complex task, attempt to break the task down into a series of manageable chunks. For instance, learners generally study several words at a time when preparing for a vocabulary test of 100 words. They dismantle and assemble one component from an automobile before they take apart an entire car engine. These are informal attempts to impose the same conditions on learning that task analysis accomplishes (i.e., breaking the task down into manageable components).

When deciding on the specific elements of a task analysis, the instructor should ask several questions:

1. How fine should the steps be?
2. How many step paths are there to the final result (equifinality)?
3. Can the task be adapted through the use of specially designed equipment and assistive material?

Task Analysis 2: Determining postage for packages of more than 3 pounds (manual operation)

Start conditions

The student will have several packages, a postal scale, a rate sheet, and a marker.

Task steps

1. Select one package.
2. Check package for proper wrapping.
   a. No string wrapping
   b. Package tape at all seams
   c. No tears in package
   d. No protuberances
   e. Not oversize
3. Place package on scale.
4. Note weight to next higher pound.
5. Note postal zone.
6. Locate postage amount required on rate chart at intersection of column with correct zone and row with correct weight.
7. Write postage amount required in upper right corner of address surface of package using marker.
8. Repeat steps 1–7 for remaining packages.

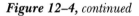

Figure 12–4, *continued*

The answers to these three questions are usually determined by the character-istics of the learner, the learner's familiarity with similar tasks, and observation of job incumbents. The number and size of steps in a task analysis is a function of the complexity of the task and the size of each step that the learner can be expected to learn quickly. For students who are encountering difficulty learning a task, the instructor should consider breaking the task down into finer steps. Each step should represent a discrete change in behavior from the preceding one.

There may be more than one way in which a task can be accomplished. For the first task analysis in Figure 12–4, for example, the drywall sheet can be held in place by a coworker, a jig, or wedges while the worker is setting the drywall screws. Drywall screws can be set in two orders: the top row, then the next row, and so forth, or the top two corners, then the left stud, then the next stud, and so forth. The choice of task path may be arbitrary (does it really matter if drywall screws are set from left to right, vertically or horizontally?), or the choice may have real significance for the learner (perhaps a jig used by some drywallers will help the learner achieve perpendicularity with more consistency than using wedges or holding the panel by hand).

Before the final question can be answered, several more specific questions must be addressed:

1. Is the proposed adaptation one that might bring social ridicule to the learner?
2. Is there an adaptation that can be used by the learner that is used by others performing the task?
3. Will the adaptation have a negative impact on the learner's ability to progress in the target job or move into a new job?
4. Is the adaptation acceptable to the employer?

In some cases, it might not be necessary to perform a written task analysis. Videotapes of workers performing the task can serve as audiovisual task analyses, especially if instructional voice-over or written step captions are also provided. Such video can provide the learner with a model to imitate and spoken and/or written task instructions to explain the actions of the model. However, the action in some videos may occur too quickly for the learner, which makes imitation difficult. In those cases, a more formal task analysis will be required.

Choosing Sequencing Strategies. In addition to specifying objectives and developing task analyses, how can an instructor control conditions so that acquisition occurs in the least amount of time? One way is by utilizing an effective *sequencing strategy.* There are three types of instructional sequencing:

1. **Forward chaining** is the learning of the task chain (sequence) in the order in which the task steps occur. That is, the first step in the task chain is targeted for instruction until it is performed to criterion before the student goes on to the second step. The student then practices the first step, and the second step is targeted for instruction before going on to the third step. In other words, the student will perform the first step (which has been acquired) and then receive instruction on the second step immediately after performing the first step. This sequence is repeated until acquisition is demonstrated for the first *two* steps in sequence. The process is then repeated for the third and subsequent steps until all steps are acquired in their proper sequence.

2. **Backward chaining** is the learning of the task chain in the reverse order in which the task steps occur. This does not mean that the student performs the task in reverse, only that he or she first learns the last step, then the last two steps (performed in their correct order), then the last three steps, and so forth, until all the steps are demonstrated in their correct order. In both forward chaining and backward chaining, only a single task step of the task

analysis is targeted at one time, and a new task step is targeted only when all previously instructed steps are performed to criterion in the correct sequence.

3. ***Whole task instruction*** is significantly different from both forward chaining and backward chaining. In whole task instruction, the student attempts to perform each and every step in the chain in the correct sequence on every trial. When the student encounters a step that he or she is unable to perform, the instructor provides further assistance for that step.

For most tasks and for most students with mild disabilities, whole task instruction is probably the most appropriate type of instructional sequencing for several reasons:

1. It allows the learner to practice all skills at each trial in the correct sequence.
2. It lets the learner see how each step is related to the others.
3. It results in the desired final outcome of the task (e.g., fastening the wallboard to the studs). Task completion is a reinforcing event by providing the learner with a sense of accomplishment that probably would not occur if backward or forward chaining were used.
4. It is the sequencing system most often used in business, industry, and regular vocational training programs (without, perhaps, a formal task analysis). Therefore, this system is more normalizing, and learning in this way may make future learning easier.

If a student appears overwhelmed by the whole task—if he or she is confused about the sequence or makes errors of inconsistency—then the instructor should consider two alternatives: (a) breaking the task into two shorter behavioral chains and teaching first one chain and then the other or (b) initiating forward or backward chaining.

Using Cues and Prompts. The task-sequencing approaches discussed here are one way to improve the prospect that learning will occur efficiently. Another condition that can be utilized to enhance learning is the presentation of assistive stimuli, or ***cues and prompts.***

Cues and prompts can be classified in several ways. One is to group them by the sense used by the learner to detect the cue. In this classification scheme there are three types of cues and prompts: *auditory, visual,* and *tactile.* The most common form of auditory prompt is a verbal message delivered aloud by the instructor (spoken directions); other kinds of sound signals can also be used (buzzers, bells, etc.). Some such signals may be used to signal when to stop or start a task. Other auditory signals may be more natural such as the sound of an electric drill motor when it is overloaded.

Visual cues are those that the learner receives through seeing. These include written verbal directions and signals, modeling, gesturing, pictures, and color coding. In each case, seeing the prompt or cue is supposed to bring about the correct behavior on the part of the learner. Many forms of visual prompting have been used successfully with learners who are mildly disabled. Among the most commonly used are modeling (with both live and filmed models) and verbal directions (e.g., written instructions for the steps in an assembly process).

Tactile prompting, also known as *physical guidance,* is used less frequently with learners who are mildly disabled, although it is appropriate in some instances with tasks that involve a specific and precise movement or position such as the locating of one's fingers on a computer keyboard to begin typing. The instructor may guide the learner's body (or body part) through the movement by touching that part and moving it.

How should an instructor decide what kinds of prompts to use? There are several rules of thumb:

1. Begin by using the natural prompts/cues. The instructor should look for natural prompts and identify them to the learner. In any task chain, each step is a naturally occurring cue for the step that follows. These natural cues can be enhanced by the process of verbal rehearsal. For example, for the drywall task analysis enumerated in Figure 12–4, the learner might begin by saying to him- or herself, "First, I insert the lifter under the drywall," as he or she does the task step. As the first step is being completed the learner says, "Then I push the drywall flat against the wall." This process allows the learner to use both natural visual cues (the position of the drywall, the presence of the lifting jig) and auditory cues (the verbal rehearsal to accomplish the task chain).

Natural cues are preferable to others because they allow the learner with disabilities to learn in the way that most other learners do. Other more intrusive kinds of prompts may bring unnecessary attention to the learner's condition making it harder to gain coworker acceptance.

2. Use prompts that can be easily faded as the learner gains mastery over the task chain. For example, perhaps the learner of the drywalling sequence inconsistently forgets to start the screw setting at the top of the panel. An "X" can be drawn in pencil in the upper left corner and gradually made less distinct as consistency is demonstrated.

3. Use prompts that are likely to be acceptable and usable in the work-place. For example, a pocket-size card with the drywall task steps enumerated could be easily accessed by the learner while on the job. Coworkers are not likely to notice or object. The instructor could also teach the task using an audiotape for prompting, but such a prompting mechanism is not likely to be accepted even if the learner/worker uses a personal cassette recorder and ear-phones. The earphones would also prohibit the worker from hearing orders and other remarks from supervisors and coworkers.

Prompts and cues are used to enhance performance and to speed the acquisition of a skill or skill chain. Correct application of prompts and cues requires a sensitive balance of what will allow the learner to acquire the skills quickly with what will allow the learner to continue to perform the task in as normal a fashion as possible after the instruction is completed.

Providing Consequences.   Good performance objectives and task analyses are antecedents to student skill practice and acquisition. Effective cues and prompts are concurrent with student skill practice and acquisition. Instructors can also utilize ***consequences***—conditions that exist after a student's practice/trial—to foster learning efficiency. Consequences enhance learning when they provide feedback to the learner about his or her performance and reinforcement for correct performance. Most students who are attempting to acquire a vocational skill are adolescents and young adults. Effective utilization of consequences for students of this age involves the use of age-appropriate and/or naturally occurring consequences such as the following:

- Praise for completion or mastery of a task. Praise from coworkers or real work supervisors is more valued by adolescents and young adults than praise from instructors (especially secondary-level instructors).
- Feedback about the correctness of a performance. It is unfair and ineffi- cient to provide a learner with general positive feedback. Positive feedback works better than negative feedback (e.g., "That's wrong"), but it must be specific and honest. Learners must know how they are performing. Saying to a learner "Good the wallboard is snug against the ceiling board but it's not plumb" is effective feedback; saying "You did better than yesterday" is not.
- Pay.
- A visual display of advancement toward a long-term goal, such as a graph or chart.
- Task completion itself. There is ample evidence that humans are rein- forced by success. Thus, instructors can enhance reinforcement by struc- turing the task and the learning environment to raise the likelihood of success. Instructors should, however, avoid structuring so that every attempt becomes a success as successes too easily gained have less value. Success rates should be high early in an instructional sequence and grad- ually more difficult to attain.
- Increased autonomy and decision-making input for the learner. This con- sequence enhances self-worth. All of us want to believe that we have some control over our own lives. In general, the more we feel this, the more we feel reinforced for our performance. Providing increased opportunity to make decisions or to work with less continuous supervision is reinforcing to most workers.

None of these consequences will enhance learning for all learners. Some learners may reject autonomy. Others may be embarrassed by a visual display that others can see but might like a private display. For some a pay raise might be strong reinforcement. Others might not care and would rather receive praise from coworkers (or just more coworker interaction). There are several ways to determine what influence consequences have on the performance of the learner (both positive and negative). The most obvious is simply to ask the learner, "What's important to you?" Another is to observe what the learner does when given a choice of activities. Yet another approach is to develop a menu of choices from which the learner can select a consequence for achieving an important goal.

Perhaps the most important principle to guide the selection of consequences is that the consequence should be as much like those that are attained by other workers in similar jobs as possible. Artificial and inflated consequences do little to teach the learner about the real world of work. In real jobs people get paid; they receive praise from coworkers, supervisors, and customers; and they also receive reprimands, suspensions, and other punishments for poor work. Naturally occurring consequences should be built into the training program. They should be garnered through observation of workers in jobs. What are the positive consequences of good performance? What are the negative consequences of poor performance? Open discussion of natural consequences should occur so that learners understand how their behaviors are related to the reinforcers, punishers, and reactions they receive.

Evaluating Progress.   The final element of a behavioral approach to skill acquisition is measurement of progress. Direct, daily recording of performance is imperative. Unit tests and paper-and-pencil exercises are inefficient, and they may highlight the student's deficiencies in academics and underestimate true performance. Direct daily measurement in the form of graphing or charting provides direct feedback to the instructor and the student on the student's performance on the target skills. It allows direct identification of weaknesses and successes. Instructors should utilize such measures to discuss the student's progress with the student, the student's parents, and the employer or potential employer.

Skill Acquisition Research.   Many researchers have examined skill acquisition in both simulated and in situ training. Most of this research has been conducted with mentally retarded learners. Gaylord-Ross, Forte, Storey, Gaylord-Ross, and Jameson (1987) have utilized systematic behavioral instruction to teach 12 learners with disabilities to do three chemical tasks at Chevron Labs. Instruction included task analysis, modeling, reinforcement, and direct daily measurement of performance. Students were supervised at the lab by a community classroom teacher. After 4.5 months of training, four subjects had reached skill acquisition on all three tasks, three had reached skill acquisition on two tasks, and three had reached acquisition on one task.

Gold and Barclay (1973) have demonstrated a principle of skill acquisition that endures: learners should master simple tasks before advancing to more complex tasks. They determined that mentally retarded learners could make very fine discriminations (e.g., differentiating 1- and 7/8-inch screws) if they first learned to make easier discriminations (e.g., differentiating 3/4- and 1 1/4-inch screws). There are a number of explanations for this phenomenon. First, early success breeds continued effort, and early failure breeds hopelessness. Second, the approach that the human mind takes to all new situations is generally to sense gross features and slowly to notice more and more detail and complexity.

Agran, Fodor-Davis, and Moore (1986) evaluated a self-instructional training approach with four mentally retarded learners, three of whom had mild disabilities. These students were enrolled in a hospital work skill training program and had encountered difficulty in performing the task steps in sequence. The training approach included (a) modeling—the students imitated the performance of the instructor, (b) behavioral rehearsal—the students rehearsed the performance repeatedly in simulated conditions with instructor assistance to limit errors of sequence prior to in situ practice, (c) verbal rehearsal—the students talked themselves through the task by stating what they had just finished doing and what they needed to do next, and (d) corrective feedback and praise. All of the students improved their sequencing markedly, and three improved to a level of near 100% accuracy.

Autonomy and self–goal setting have an influence on skill acquisition. In a study by Warner and Mills (1980), a sample of mentally retarded learners demonstrated accelerated skill acquisition when they were permitted to set their own goals. Previously, they had received performance feedback from the instructor based on a comparison of their performance to an external standard.

Prompting for skill acquisition in complex assembly tasks was investigated by Walls, Ellis, Zane, and Vanderpoel (1979). These researchers compared the efficiency of four different prompting conditions: tactile; auditory; visual; and a combination of auditory, tactile, and visual. Tactile prompting was provided by hand-on-hand guidance. Auditory prompting was delivered by verbal instructions, and visual prompting took the form of modeling correct behaviors. The learners were 18 to 50 years old and ranged from severely to mildly disabled. Auditory prompting was related to more errors and more time required to reach criterion than any of the other prompt conditions. Combination prompting was slightly better than tactile prompting, which was also better than visual prompting. Combination prompting produced more stability across subjects than other prompt forms (i.e., combination prompting was consistently effective across learners and tasks, whereas the other forms were effective for some and not for others).

On first glance, this result appears to contradict the previous discussion about utilizing prompts that are most like those used in the workplace (heavily auditory/verbal). However, several considerations make this conclusion suspect. First, some of the subjects in the Walls et al. (1979) study had severely limited language. It is predictable that these individuals would not respond well to spoken prompts. Second, although auditory/verbal prompts may not be as efficient in the short term, we still must believe that utilizing a prompt system that is a close approximation to that used in a real job training system will in the long run produce a worker who is more likely to succeed and advance.

Connis (1979) has demonstrated the effectiveness of sequential photos as prompts for mentally retarded students learning a job task. As students completed one component of a job, they went to look at a photo of the next part. The students also recorded their own performance below the photo. All of the students progressed to near 100% sequence accuracy with the photo prompts.

Isometric assembly drawings proved to be effective prompts for a sample of 537 mentally retarded learners (Fisher, 1984). The 15- to 20-year-old students learned a series of simple and complex assemblies.

The temporal placement of prompts appears to have an effect on the acquisition of skills (Haught, Walls, & Crist, 1984). In this study, mildly and moderately mentally retarded learners produced fewer errors while in training when they were given preresponse prompting (i.e., telling the learner what the expected behavior is before he or she has a chance to respond). However, error correction prompts (when the instructor waited for the learner to attempt a task and then prompted the student to correct an error) were related to fewer errors during posttraining probes (i.e., once students had acquired the skill, they made fewer errors if they had learned the skill under error correction prompts). This study highlights one of the complexities of prompting: what is most effective in the short run may not be most effective for maintenance and generalization.

Schutz, Jostes, Rusch, and Lamson (1980) demonstrated the validity of a behaviorally produced skill acquisition by asking job incumbents to rate the performance/output of mentally retarded trainees who learned janitorial tasks through a behavioral approach. The incumbents rated the work of the trainees equal to that of workers in those jobs.

There is little doubt that behavioral approaches work, but the complexity of the approach produces many questions. Techniques that are successful in the short term may not provide long-term success. The planning that is required for behavioral interventions is substantial.

How can an instructor make a decision about how closely instruction should approximate the requisite structure and precision of the behavioral approach? The starting point is that used in the organization for which the student is being trained. The instructor should begin by paralleling the instruction that job incumbents received. When the student encounters difficulty, the instructor should adopt more structure and greater precision and pay more attention to setting the conditions for acquisition.

Fluency.   *Fluency* refers to the development of acceptable levels of speed and quality in the performance of a task. Nearly all jobs have some demand for speed and accuracy, and the research reviewed previously reveals that persons with mild disabilities often encounter difficulty meeting production rate demands at an acceptable quality level.

The primary means by which quality and quantity of production are improved involves systematic and incremental changes in goal setting. Other quality and quantity improvement techniques include prompting (e.g., directing an individual to speed up), systematic feedback (e.g., showing an individual how his or her performance compares with a target level of performance), several variations on self-monitoring (including verbal rehearsal for self-prompting and self-charting of performance), and combinations of these techniques.

For many learners with mild disabilities, the most appropriate way to bring about improvements in quality and/or quantity of production is to identify to the learner the discrepancy between the level at which the learner is currently producing and the level at which he or she must produce in order to gain or retain employment. This technique is representative of the means by which most workers are informed about their production deficiencies. Again, the first approach to utilize is that which mirrors practice in the employing organization. The target levels should be determined by asking the employer or potential employer then validated by looking at the levels of performance of job incumbents.

Simply identifying the discrepancy should produce the needed improvements in the production of many learners with mild disabilities. However, for those for whom this informal technique is ineffective, a more systematic behavior analytic approach is warranted. To do this the instructor should determine the answers to several questions:

1. Is there something in the way the task has been structured that is hindering production?
2. Has the student failed to acquire one or more of the necessary component skills?
3. Are there natural prompts that have been neglected?

If the answer to these questions is no, then the instructor should proceed to a more systematic approach, which can take several different forms singularly or in combination:

1.   A changing criterion approach can be utilized (Bates, Renzaglia, & Clees, 1980). The final quantity rate or quality specification is identified. The current quantity or quality of the trainee is established through daily observation and recording to determine the baseline. Enough measurements (usually over 5-10 days) should be made to ensure that the baseline is representative of the trainee's typical performance. Incremental improvements in production are targeted as short-term objectives. Each time the trainee meets the new incremental increase with some consistency (generally three or more consecutive trials), a new incremental increase becomes the objective. In most cases, some positive reinforcement is provided for reaching the new increment. For many students with mild disabilities, the progress toward the goal will be sufficient. For others, praise combined with other reinforcers will

be necessary. However, any extrinsic reinforcement (i.e., reinforcement that is not natural to the situation) will have to be gradually faded after the final goal is reached.

2.   Self-determination of goals has also been an effective means of improving production rates and consistency of quality (Warner & Mills, 1980). Learners are asked to identify a production rate or quality level at which they will produce for a given period of time.

3.   Self-monitoring of productivity allows learners a measure of autonomy and maturity. It is also more desirable than external monitoring as it provides the learner with a means to adapt to many jobs in which levels and frequency of monitoring may vary.

In the following subsection we describe the research that has been conducted with some of these practices.

Fluency Research.   Research on vocational skill fluency is relatively common. Bates, Renzaglia, and Clees (1980) describe the development, application, and evaluation of several forms of a changing criterion design. In their study systematic changing criteria for both quantity and quality of production were utilized to improve the performance of three mentally retarded young adults. In all cases, the application of the changing criteria through very small increments led to production rates and quality that met the target criteria.

Goal setting has been the focus of some vocational research. Mentally retarded individuals have successfully set their own goals for increased production, as shown by Warner and Mills (1980). All of the subjects of this study had received training on the target tasks, but performance was inconsistent. Feedback from the trainer increased performance, but feedback and goal setting for short work periods produced even greater gains for all subjects.

Flexer, Newbery, and Martin (1979) utilized three variations of goal setting, all of which resulted in increased production rates. The three variations were (a) setting a long-range production goal and receiving monetary reinforcement for accomplishing increments of the goal; (b) setting a long-range goal, receiving monetary reinforcement, setting production goals for each work/training session, and getting contingent praise for reaching session goals; and (c) setting a long-range goal, a session goal, receiving monetary reinforcement, and earning monetary bonuses contingent on surpassing session goals. Interestingly, the contingent bonus group had the smallest gain in production. The greatest gain was evinced by the group that received contingent praise for reaching session goals. Chaffin's (1969) work also demonstrates the effectiveness of daily goal setting and social reinforcement.

In their study Ackerman and Shapiro (1984) replaced contingent praise and prompts with self-monitoring of production for a group of mentally retarded adults. Trainees recorded their own production on daily production charts. Crouch, Rusch, and Karlan (1984) trained three mentally retarded persons to use self-generated cues to enhance consistent production. These individuals had difficulty in beginning and ending tasks on time. During the training period, the trainees were reinforced for making job-related time statements to decrease the amount of time spent on tasks. Wristwatches and coworker prompts were also employed. Trainees were taught to state when they should begin and end each task. All gained verbal self-control over task completion and hence more consistency of production.

Maintenance.   Training a person with mild disabilities to perform a task is useless if the individual does not maintain the performance after employment. Skill maintenance is enhanced by a number of practices:

- systematic withdrawal of prompts and other instructional assistance after acquisition and fluency are demonstrated,
- using naturally occurring cues during training (Rusch, Martin, & White, 1985; Wacker & Berg, 1986),
- using self-monitoring, recording, and/or reinforcement (Rusch et al., 1985; Wacker & Berg, 1986),
- gradually reducing artificial reinforcement,
- using naturally occurring reinforcers during acquisition and fluency,
- using training cues that are transportable to the workplace, and
- using intermittent, variable reinforcement during training (Rusch et al., 1985; Wacker & Berg, 1986).

Obviously, maintenance is always enhanced when the skills that are taught during training are the ones important in work settings.

Maintenance Research.   Maintenance of acquired vocational skills is the subject of much research. Rusch, Connis, and Sowers (1978) successfully utilized sequential withdrawal of various training components (e.g., prompts) to enhance maintenance of the vocational skills of a mildly retarded woman. Withdrawal of each component was followed by an evaluation of maintenance. Further component withdrawal was contingent upon skill maintenance at each stage of withdrawal.

Gaylord-Ross et al. (1987) utilized "booster training trials" to enhance maintenance when performance fell below 80%. Booster trials were quick retraining episodes.

Agran et al. (1986), Connis (1979), and Crouch et al. (1984) used self-regulation to enhance maintenance. Connis found that self-recording and self-prompting using pictorial cues resulted in high levels of maintenance, while Agran et al. determined that self-generated verbal cues resulted in near 100% maintenance 3 months after instruction ceased. Crouch et al. utilized a program similar to that of Agran et al. and arrived at similar results.

Flexer et al. (1979) found that self-set goals were an effective means to reverse a trend toward lower production on repetitive tasks.

Generalization. ***Generalization*** refers to the performance of a skill under conditions different from those under which it was trained. Vocational skills should be taught in a way that they are likely to be generalized from training conditions to work conditions and from one set of work conditions to another set of work conditions. There are several procedures that increase the probability that appropriate generalization will occur:

1. Identify the conditions under which a task is performed in the target job and train under the same conditions (Stokes & Baer, 1977).
2. Observe the performance of a job in several different employing organizations, identify common conditions across the organizations, and train under those conditions (Sprague & Horner, 1984).
3. Train skills under various conditions, in various settings, with various trainers (Stokes & Baer, 1977).
4. Teach the trainee to identify environmental conditions under which specific behaviors or behavior chains should occur.
5. Train skills that have wide applicability across many settings and task chains.

For individuals with mild disabilities, generalization is often the most difficult aspect of acquiring vocational competence. In a behavioral approach, skills are usually taught by means of consistent, specific, and often unchanging conditions. Yet, in real work, skills must be demonstrated under constantly changing conditions—new supervisors, a different work site, varied equipment, and so forth. Training procedures must include opportunities to develop adaptability and problem solving. Initial acquisition is enhanced by consistent environmental conditions, but generalization is enhanced by changing conditions. As it is likely that most competitive employment situations will involve varying conditions, it is important that training conditions differ enough so that the learner with a mild disability does not adopt a rigid response pattern or cue regulation. For most persons with mild disabilities, it is probably wise to begin with consistent conditions and gradually introduce variations garnered from actual on-the-job practice.

Generalization Research. Agran, Martin, and Mithaug (1989) state that persons with learning problems have difficulty responding to change in their work because they have been denied autonomy. It is not uncommon that persons with mild disabilities are overprotected by their parents, teachers, and others. Risk is minimized, and therefore they do not learn how to make choices. Agran et al. believe that self-management, self-instruction, goal setting, picture cues, self-evaluation of work, and self-reinforcement provide some of the skills that learners with disabilities need in order to adapt to changes in work environments. Not only should these procedures be used by instructors, but persons with mild disabilities should learn how to develop their own self-management, cueing, and other procedures to be applied to novel tasks and situations. In short, they should learn how to learn.

Gaylord-Ross, Forte, and Gaylord-Ross (1986) conclude that generalization occurs more efficiently when instruction takes place in the real world outside of the classroom. This is the basis for community-based instruction. Instruction that occurs in the community (e.g., at work sites) is more effective because the conditions are more representative of the eventual work conditions. Gaylord-Ross et al. (1987) believe that students with a variety of vocational experiences at real work sites are better able to generalize to new jobs and sites. Generalization is also enhanced by varying the difficulty of the tasks performed.

Wacker and Berg (1983) have found that picture prompts enhanced generalization of skills to untaught tasks. Trainees in their study who learned one complex task using picture prompts were able to learn new tasks more efficiently using new picture prompts.

Finally, Walls, Sienicki, and Crist (1981) describe and apply operations training to generalization. *Operations training* is the training of a response chain that is applicable to more than one task environment. Walls et al. successfully applied operations training to two sets of vocational tasks: a mechanical task and a woodworking task. The trained mechanical task was checking generator wires for continuity; the generalized mechanical task was checking lawn mower wires for continuity. The trained woodworking task was miter cutting a chair slat at an angle; the untrained woodworking task was miter cutting molding for a clock at an angle. Students were taught several operations under the trained conditions. For example, for the mechanical task (generator) they were taught to use a ratchet and socket to remove a cover to expose wires, a screwdriver to tighten wires on terminals, and a meter to check wires for continuity. Under untrained conditions the students were expected to utilize the same operations for a different set of task conditions—for example, use the ratchet and socket to remove the magneto cover on the lawn mower, use the screwdriver to tighten wires on terminals, use the meter to check those wires for continuity. Trainees learned to apply the operations to the second set of task conditions in much less time than it had taken to learn the first task. They had learned to generalize an operation to a new task. The importance of this result is that the learners were on their way to becoming more adaptable employees. They were no longer just "generator continuity checkers"; they were becoming "continuity checkers." According to Walls et al., operations training produces workers who are more adaptable to changing jobs and tasks and have more marketable skills. This is the goal of generalization training.

❦   ❦   ❦

COGNITIVE APPROACHES TO VOCATIONAL TRAINING

Not all training approaches for persons with mild disabilities should be behavioral. In chapters 6 through 10 we discuss effective instructional techniques that are more cognitive and traditional. These techniques are equally applicable to vocational instruction at both secondary and postsecondary levels.

The cognitive techniques that are most often used in vocational preparation of persons with mild disabilities are (a) role playing; (b) individual, group, and peer counseling; (c) direct instruction; and (d) planning and goal setting. These techniques have been applied to (a) job search, interview, and attainment skills, (b) attribution of responsibility, (c) interest identification, (d) development of vocational realism, (e) decision making and problem solving, and (f) vocational planning.

Kuhn (1966) has found that mildly retarded junior high school students have a lower level of understanding of occupations than chronologically and mentally age-matched nondisabled peers. This low level of understanding has been blamed for inappropriate career aspirations. Without an understanding of occupations, adolescents with mild disabilities could be expected to aspire to occupations that are beyond or below their ability. Indeed, Plata (1981) has determined that the occupational aspirations of adolescents with behavioral disorders are low, as well as inconsistent and unpredictable.

Career aspirations can be directly influenced by knowledge and direct instruction about careers. Gill and Langone (1982) state that the IEPs of adolescents should include an assessment of their career knowledge maturity including their interests, experiences, and aptitudes. (Further information on career development and knowledge appears in chap. 13.)

Role playing has proven its worth in numerous situations. Learning disabled secondary students utilized role playing to enhance employment interview skills (McGee, 1981). Students role-played interviews that were videotaped and played back for their analysis and critique. Ten of the 15 participants were able to secure their own employment after training. Azrin and Philip (1979) used role playing successfully with 154 individuals, many with mild disabilities, who were experiencing difficulty obtaining a job. Practice scripts were developed for participants when making employment inquiry calls. After 6 months more than 90% were employed.

Various forms of counseling have been used with mildly disabled persons. Zoeller, Mahoney, and Weiner (1983) employed a sort of counseling to address the motivational problems of mildly retarded adults. Mildly retarded adults are often thought to have an external locus of control; that is, they believe that they have little control over the things that happen to them. Zoeller et al. used counseling and other instructional procedures to bring about changes in the attribution of success and failure. The 36 subjects had been selected because of motivational problems. Their performance was not commensurate with their ability. When they failed, they were told that the failure was due to their lack of effort; when they succeeded, they were told that their success was due to their effort. Their performance improved noticeably as a result of the counseling.

Azrin and Philip (1979) utilized a form of peer support to assist job seekers. Each job seeker was assigned another job-searching "buddy" from whom they received support for and reaction to their job-seeking activities. Buddies were expected to react to specific job-seeking behaviors. They also assisted each other in finding job leads. The success of the program would lead to the conclusion that peer counseling and support increases the capacity of the individual to manage the demands of the search.

Hershenson (1984) describes vocational counseling with learning disabled adults. Such counseling should target (a) the development of a self-concept as a worker, (b) development of work goals, (c) identification of realistic and sufficiently challenging aspirations, (d) development of organizational skills, and (e) career planning.

Bolles (1972) has developed a unique job-seeking technique that has applicability for all job seekers with mild disabilities. Job seekers conduct interviews of job incumbents to find out about the job requirements, interviews, and application procedures. The job seeker can then determine if the job is desirable and realistic.

❦ ❦ ❦

JOB ACQUISITION

The process of getting a job begins long before a person goes for an interview. It starts in elementary school and may continue far into adulthood as the individual leaves one job and seeks another. For persons with mild disabilities the process involves

- learning about occupations,
- locating jobs,
- applying for specific jobs, and
- receiving placement and follow-up.

In the rest of this chapter we discuss each of these stages and conclude with a brief review of research on job acquisition and persons with mild disabilities.

Learning about Occupations

We cannot expect adolescents or young adults with mild disabilities to make the right decisions about going to work if they have little knowledge about occupations. There are many sources of information about jobs. Foremost is the *Dictionary of Occupational Titles (DOT)*, a periodic publication of the U.S. Department of Labor in which occupations are listed, described, and analyzed. Other resource publications include the *Occupational Outlook Handbook* published every 2 years by the Department of Labor. This publication contains descriptions of 200 jobs in 19 clusters, citing required skills, work conditions, opportunities, training requirements, and projected earnings. The *Occupational Digest* contains descriptions of 400 occupations including wages, the method of entry, and worker comments about the occupation. *Career Resources*, published by the Vocational Studies Center at the University of Wisconsin–Madison, is a reference manual with 400 sources on occupations and job hunting. This publication can be most helpful to vocational, special, or regular education teachers who are engaged in career awareness training.

After students learn about occupational possibilities, they should begin to develop occupational plans, explore options, and select possible jobs (Crimando, 1984). Palmer, Velleman, and Shafer (1985) have determined that many of the job acquisition problems of youth with disabilities result from the lack of awareness of opportunities. Richter-Stein and Stodden (1981) echo the conclusions of Palmer et al., stating that special needs students have limited experiences with jobs. This makes the use of interest inventories meaningless. These writers suggest a structured occupational exploration during junior high school that uses simulated job samples representing the tasks and conditions in job roles. We believe that job exploration and awareness should begin early in the elementary years through numerous activities including simulation, work visitors (classroom presentations by workers), and more traditional occupational exploration material.

Locating Jobs

Students may make career choices and train for specific types of jobs, but if they do not know how to locate positions for which they can apply, they will remain unemployed.

Job search behaviors are usually obtained through counseling and cognitive instruction (Crimando, 1984). The Vocational Studies Center at the University of Wisconsin–Madison and the Materials Development Center (1988a) at the University of Wisconsin–Stout have developed many instructional materials for job search activities, including the following sources:

1. *Going to Work*—a workbook for high school students with activities designed to improve job search strategies. Among the activities are locating classified and want ads; understanding abbreviations in classifieds; and using placement services, friends, and relatives as job sources.
2. *Job Hunt: Staying on Track*—a video that illustrates the activities of job searching for high school students and adults. In the video, job seekers are followed as they pursue job leads. The video also provides information on staying motivated in the face of unfruitful efforts.
3. *How to Get the Job You Want*—a video that presents effective job search techniques, including stating job objectives, developing a daily job search plan, and arranging at least two interviews a day. The information is provided by a presenter working with a group of job seekers.
4. *Job Seeking Skills Course*—an instructor's manual and student workbook containing activities such as goal setting, job location, job search planning, and contacting employers.

Activities for locating jobs should begin early in high school with opportunities and instruction in using job search resources. Students should be taught how to locate and decode classified ads. They should also learn how to develop a job search network of friends and family. Finally, they should learn about both private (i.e., employment agencies) and public (e.g., vocational rehabilitation) job search support systems.

Applying for Specific Jobs

In addition to learning how to locate job openings, learners who are mildly disabled must develop application skills. These skills include (a) making inquiry calls to employers, (b) composing a resumé, (c) completing applications, (d) scheduling interviews, (e) interviewing, and (f) following up.

Inquiry Calls. Telephone skills are often critical for a successful job search. Many employers will not permit unscheduled application processing. Persons with mild disabilities should practice telephone inquiry skills. Two effective means of developing such skills are (a) scripting—writing out a series of questions for the caller to ask and then recording the responses of the employer— and (b) role playing—practicing phone calls under simulated conditions. The Materials Development Center at the University of Wisconsin–Stout includes contacting employers in its *Job Seeking Skills Course.*

Resumés. A clean, well-organized resumé can open doors to employment. Students with mild disabilities should learn to construct and update a resumé while they are in high school. There are numerous sources for effective resumé development.

Applications. Completing applications requires many skills, including reading, recalling information, and writing clearly (both penmanship and expression). Instructors of adolescents with mild disabilities should employ a functional approach to reading that includes reading and understanding job application forms. Students with mild disabilities who have difficulty recalling the information that is requested on application forms (e.g., dates of previous employment, names of previous employers) should be taught to develop and maintain an information card that they can take with them when they are to complete an application. An accurate and neat application creates a good first impression.

Job application forms may present many obstacles to persons with mild disabilities who have limited reading and writing skills. Smith and Schloss (1986) identify these problems as defining terms, comprehending questions, and writing clear responses. In response to these problems they have developed a "superform" for training. Utilizing 200 application forms from employers, they analyzed the content by calculating the percentage of forms on which specific questions were asked or specific information was requested. They also analyzed the vocabulary used on the forms. The result was a superform containing all of the items that appeared on 20% or more of the forms analyzed. The final superform comprised 96 items.

Interviews.   The interview process has been addressed by a number of individuals interested in the employment success of persons with mild disabilities. Again the Vocational Studies Center at the University of Wisconsin–Madison has produced and/or distributes instructional materials designed to improve the interview skills of adolescents and adults. *Job Interviews: Tipping the Odds* is a video on preparation for job interviews that identifies the specific interview skills needed to enhance the probability of being hired. *Effective Answers to Interview Questions* covers appearance, reliability, and experience and how the applicant can communicate his or her positive attributes to the interviewer. Another video, *The Seven Phases of a Job Interview*, is presented using humorous scenarios concerning (a) preparation for the interview, (b) openings, (c) the interview body, (d) closing the interview, (e) follow-up, (f) negotiation, and (g) making a decision.

None of these materials can be effective without the opportunity to practice the skills taught. The most common mode of practice is simulation (role playing). Role playing is effective but limited. Job seekers who are mildly disabled may need extensive real interview experience with feedback. This can occur in two ways. First, the instructor may enlist the aid of local employers to conduct interviews with trainees for actual job openings. These may be done regardless of whether the trainee is an actual applicant. At the conclusion of the mock interview, employers should indicate if they would have hired the trainee. Together, the employer and the instructor should give the trainee feedback on his or her performance. The trainee and the instructor should then formulate and implement plans for bettering performance. After performance improves in a simulated situation, the trainee should repeat the experience with a different employer.

The second (but less efficient and perhaps destructive) way is to use only simulation until the trainee is ready to begin the actual job search/interview process. This requires the trainee to generalize skills learned under simulation to actual interview conditions. Some may succeed; many will probably fail.

In all cases, "postmortems" should be conducted on all application/interview episodes. The instructor and trainee should together analyze and identify weaknesses and undertake efforts to improve the identified weak skills.

Trainees should also learn how to follow up with the employer. Making contact after the interview to indicate continued interest is appropriate and may place the trainee in an advantageous position if the contact is made at a time when the employer is about to make a choice. In contrast, the trainee should be taught to refrain from making numerous follow-up phone calls to the employer. Such activity may negate the effects of a positive interview.

Placement and Follow-up.   In many programs, transition specialists provide greater placement assistance than merely instructing people who are mildly disabled in the skills of job acquisition. When trainees are in need of extra assistance, transition specialists may work with employers to find appropriate openings, cultivate new jobs, and help employers make adaptations to accommodate the needs of workers with mild disabilities.

Brody-Hasazi, Salembier, and Finch (1983) state that transition teachers need to have flexible teaching schedules and responsibilities so that they can go into the community, develop placements, educate employers, and monitor placements already made. Systematic follow-up permitting analysis of successes and failures promotes refinement of programs and greater effectiveness.

Several researchers and practitioners have written of the roles and activities of vocational training personnel who assist in securing placement. Among the roles discussed are

- job development—working with employers, chambers of commerce, and business associations to identify employment opportunities (Crimando, 1984; Martin, 1986);
- job restructuring—working with employers to rearrange job tasks, remove nonessential elements, develop adaptive approaches, and so forth, so that mildly disabled learners have access to a wider array of employment opportunities (Brown, 1984; Crimando, 1984);
- employer development—nurturing a sense of responsibility for and willingness to hire persons with disabilities. This entails education about the characteristics of such employees, the benefits of working with them, and identification of "success stories" for employers to emulate (Goodall, Wehman, & Cleveland, 1983); and
- public relations—initiating efforts to ensure that effective employers of people with disabilities receive positive media coverage and developing similar coverage for training programs and successes.

Martin (1986) describes a nine-step placement process that is an effective model for use by transition specialists:

1. *Identify placements.* Look at entry-level jobs and consider using a community-based committee to broaden the base of identification.
2. *Survey* potential employers. Explain the benefits of hiring disabled workers, and analyze employer response.
3. *Evaluate opportunities.* Conduct job analyses to screen out unacceptable jobs.
4. *Match candidates* to specific job opportunities.
5. *Plan adaptations* in jobs with employers.
6. *Communicate.* Work with employers to operationalize expectations and roles.
7. *Involve parents.*
8. *Train applicants* for interviews.
9. *Evaluate placements* to be used to modify procedures and so forth.

Martin's publication includes numerous sample forms that can be used to manage this process.

Long-term follow-up serves many purposes (Rusch, 1986). It may prevent terminations, allow validation of training procedures, and permit evaluation of adjustment. Follow-up permits verification that written job performance standards are congruent with actual on-the-job supervisor expectation. It also provides an opportunity for observing coworker interactions and intervening when those interactions are negative.

According to Rusch (1986), follow-up should be gradually faded to promote independence and local work site supervision. Staff should be withdrawn systematically while the performance of the trainee is monitored. Supervisory control should be transferred gradually to the on-site organization supervisor. Withdrawal should include instruction for the on-site supervisor in working with the employee (e.g., giving instructions, providing critical feedback). The individual conducting follow-up activities should also ensure that the employer is not using more stringent criteria for the worker who is disabled than for the one who is not.

Systematic placement assistance and follow-up are vital to transitional program success. Persons with mild disabilities require assistance with all aspects of transition. It makes little sense to train people with mild disabilities to work and then fail to provide them with the resources needed to secure employment and, perhaps more importantly, retain employment. If there is a single most deficient area in transition practices, it is probably that of long-term follow-up and access to assistance.

Few researchers describe follow-up and assistance that is available to individuals who are mildly disabled and in their late 20s, 30s, or 40s. Yet, our research base indicates that problems persist. Often a small problem grows until the individual is no longer employable. Consistent follow-up would allow short-term remedial intervention—intervention that is probably more cost-effective.

Job Acquisition Research

Much of the research on job acquisition has been discussed in chapter 11. Here, we will discuss other studies related to specific job acquisition training practices.

Doane (1973) and Salomone, Lehmann, and Green (1973) conclude that people with disabilities who participate in occupational exploration experiences are more vocationally sophisticated. In Doane's study participants were twice as likely as nonparticipants to secure a job. Job-seeking skills training, including interview practice and training and resumé preparation, have been related to higher employment rates (Stude & Pauls, 1977).

McGee (1981) specifically investigated the abilities of high school students with learning disabilities to complete application forms and decode classified ads. Prior to training, none of the students were able to complete a standard application, and their scores on a classified ads vocabulary test averaged less than 20%. Students were taught to complete progressively longer, more difficult applications. As a result of this instruction, 70% were able to acquire jobs on their own. Clark, Boyd, and Macrae (1975) used modeling, feedback, and reinforcement to teach mentally retarded adolescents how to complete application forms. Although their performance on the trained forms improved, the skills did not generalize to other forms.

❦ ❦ ❦

SUMMARY

Vocational training of persons with mild disabilities is a complex process that should be initiated in the elementary years and progressively expand through the secondary years. There is little doubt that systematic training will enhance the probability that individuals with mild disabilities will acquire and retain meaningful jobs. The characteristics of vocational training that appear to be the most critical to success are as follows:

1. *Early exposure.* Students who are mildly disabled should begin to learn about work and jobs in elementary school.
2. *Systematic instruction.* Instruction should be delivered so that goals and objectives are specific. Corrective feedback should be provided often and as quickly after performance as possible. A behavioral approach offers the most systematic means for providing efficient and effective instruction. However, vocational educators must guard against using a behavioral approach that promotes dependence (e.g., utilizing too many artificial cues) or immaturity (e.g., providing childish reinforcement).
3. *Community instruction.* Training must be provided in environments that are most like the environments in which real work occurs.
4. *Experiential instruction.* Training should be heavily weighted toward experience as opposed to didactic learning in the classroom.
5. *Comprehensive instruction.* Instruction should include not only specific work skills training but also training in the skills necessary to find and obtain employment.
6. *Opportunity development.* Vocational educators and special educators must develop the capacity of employers to hire persons with mild disabilities.

If these characteristics form the basis for a comprehensive program, young adults with mild disabilities will gradually improve their status in the working world.

REFERENCES

Ackerman, A. M., & Shapiro, E. S. (1984). Self-monitoring and work productivity with mentally retarded adults. *Journal of Applied Behavior Analysis, 17*, 403–407.

Agran, M., Fodor-Davis, J., & Moore, S. (1986). The effects of self instructional training on job task sequencing: Suggesting a problem-solving strategy. *Education and Training of the Mentally Retarded, 21*, 273–281.

Agran, M., Martin, J. E., & Mithaug, D. E. (1989). Achieving transition through adaptability instruction. *Teaching Exceptional Children, 21*(2), 4–7.

Azrin, N. H., & Philip, R. A. (1979). The job club method for the job handicapped: A comparative outcome study. *Rehabilitation Counseling Bulletin, 23*, 144–155.

Ballantyne, D. (1985). *Cooperative programs for transition from school to work*. Washington, DC: U.S. Department of Education, Office of Special Education and Rehabilitation Services, National Institute of Handicapped Research.

Banks, M. H., Jackson, P. R., Stafford, E. M., & Warr, P. B. (1983). The job components inventory and the analysis of jobs requiring limited skill. *Personnel Psychology, 36*, 57–66.

Bates, P., Renzaglia, A., & Clees, T. (1980). Improving the work performance of severely/profoundly retarded young adults: The use of a changing criterion procedural design. *Education and Training of the Mentally Retarded, 15*, 95–104.

Bolles, R. N. (1972). *What color is your parachute?* Berkeley, CA: Ten Speed Press.

Bownas, D. A., Bosshardt, M. J., & Donnelly, L. F. (1985). A quantitative approach to evaluating training curriculum content sampling adequacy. *Personnel Psychology, 38*, 117–131.

Brody-Hasazi, S., Salembier, G., & Finch, K. (1983). Vocational preparation for secondary mildly handicapped students. *Teaching Exceptional Children, 15*, 206–209.

Brown, D. (1984). Employment considerations for learning disabled adults. *Journal of Rehabilitation, 50*(2), 74–78.

Chaffin, J. D. (1969). Production rate as a variable in the job success or failure of educable mentally retarded adolescents. *Exceptional Children, 35*, 533–538.

Clark, H., Boyd, B., & Macrae, J. (1975). A classroom program teaching disadvantaged youth to write biographic information. *Journal of Applied Behavior Analysis, 8*, 67–75.

Cobb, R. B., & Phelps, L. A. (1983). Analyzing individualized education programs for vocational components: An exploratory study. *Exceptional Children, 50*, 62–64.

Connis, R. T. (1979). The effects of sequential pictorial cues, self recording, and praise on the job task sequencing of retarded adults. *Journal of Applied Behavior Analysis, 12*, 355–361.

Crimando, W. (1984). A review of placement-related issues for clients with learning disabilities. *Journal of Rehabilitation, 50*(2), 78–81.

Crouch, K. P., Rusch, F. R., & Karlan, G. R. (1984). Competitive employment: Utilizing the correspondence training paradigm to enhance productivity. *Education and Training of the Mentally Retarded, 19*, 268–275.

Doane, C. J. (1973). Job personalization and the Vocational Exploration Group. *Journal of Employment Counseling, 10*(1), 3–10.

Fisher, M. K. (1984). Vocational assembly skills using isometric projection exploded view assembly drawings for mentally handicapped students. *Education and Training of the Mentally Retarded, 19*, 285–290.

Flexer, R. W., Newbery, J. F., & Martin, A. S. (1979). Use of goal setting procedures in increasing task assembly rate of severely retarded workers. *Education and Training of the Mentally Retarded, 14*, 177–184.

Gaylord-Ross, C., Forte, J., & Gaylord-Ross, R. (1986). The community classroom: Technological vocational training for students with severe handicaps. *Career Development for Exceptional Individuals, 9*(1), 24–33.

Gaylord-Ross, R., Forte, J., Storey, K., Gaylord-Ross, C., & Jameson, D. (1987). Community referenced instruction in technological work settings. *Exceptional Children, 54*, 112–120.

Gill, D. H., & Langone, J. (1982). Enhancing the effectiveness of the IEP. *Journal for Vocational Special Needs Education, 4*, 9–11.

Gold, M. W., & Barclay, C. R. (1973). The learning of difficult visual discriminations by the moderately and severely retarded. *Mental Retardation, 11*, 9–11.

Goodall, P. A., Wehman, P., & Cleveland, P. (1983). Job placement for mentally retarded individuals. *Education and Training of the Mentally Retarded, 18*, 271–278.

Greenwood, C. S., & Morley, R. E. (1980). Iowa vocational education special needs assessment survey. In T. L. Wentling (Ed.), *ARRIVE: Annual review of research in vocational education* (Vol. 1, pp. 163–176). Urbana: University of Illinois.

Halpern, A. S., & Benz, M. R. (1987). A statewide examination of secondary special education for students with mild disabilities. Implications for the high school curriculum. *Exceptional Children, 54*, 122–129.

Haught, P., Walls, R. T., & Crist, K. (1984). Placement of prompts, length of task, and level of retardation in learning complex assembly tasks. *American Journal of Mental Deficiency, 89*, 60–66.

Hershenson, D. B. (1984). Vocational counseling with learning disabled adults. *Journal of Rehabilitation, 50*(2), 40-44.

Kuhn, E. (1966). A comparative analysis of the nature of EMR adolescents' expressed level of understanding of selected occupations. *Dissertation Abstracts, 27*, 1204.

Martin, J. E. (1986). Identifying potential jobs. In F. R. Rusch (Ed.), *Competitive employment issues and strategies* (pp. 165–174). Baltimore, MD: Brookes.

Materials Development Center. (1988a). *Transitional employment and supported work. An annotated bibliography*. Menomonie: School of Education and Human Services, University of Wisconsin–Stout.

Materials Development Center. (1988b). *Job seeking skills course*. Menomonie: School of Education and Human Services, University of Wisconsin–Stout.

McBride, J. W., & Forgnone, C. (1985). Emphasis of instruction provided LD, EH and EMR students in categorical and cross-categorical resource programs. *Journal of Research and Development in Education, 18*, 50–54.

McGee, D. W. (1981). Sharpen students' job seeking skills with employment applications and role played interviews. *Teaching Exceptional Children, 13*, 152–155.

Palmer, J. T., Velleman, R., & Shafer, D. (1985). *The transition process of disabled youth: Literature review*. Albertson, NY: Human Resources Center.

Plata, M. (1981). Occupational aspirations of normal and emotionally disturbed adolescents: A comparative study. *Vocational Guidance Quarterly, 30*, 130–138.

Puzzled about educating special needs students? A handbook on modifying vocational curricula for handicapped students. (n.d.). Madison: Vocational Studies Center, School of Education, University of Wisconsin.

Richter-Stein, C., & Stodden, R. A. (1981). Simulated job samples: A student centered approach to vocational exploration and evaluation. *Teaching Exceptional Children, 14*, 116–119.

Rusch, F. R. (1986). Developing a long term follow-up program. In F. R. Rusch (Ed.), *Competitive employment: Issues and strategies* (pp. 225–232). Baltimore, MD: Brookes.

Rusch, F. R., Connis, R. T., & Sowers, J. (1978). The modification and maintenance of time spent attending to task using social reinforcement, token reinforcement and response cost in an applied restaurant setting. *Journal of Special Education Technology*, 2, 18–26.

Rusch, F. R., Martin, J. E., & White, D. M. (1985). Competitive employment: Teaching mentally retarded employees to maintain their work behavior. *Education and Training of the Mentally Retarded, 20*, 182–189.

Rusch, F. R., Schutz, R. P., & Agran, M. (1982). Validating entry-level survival skills for service occupations: Implications for curriculum development. *Journal of the Association for Persons with Severe Handicaps, 7*(3), 32–41.

Salomone, P. R., Lehmann, E., & Green, A. J. (1973). Occupational exploration practices: A pilot study to increase the vocational sophistication of slow learners. *Mental Retardation, 11*(4), 3–7.

Schutz, R. P., Jostes, K. F., Rusch, F. R., & Lamson, D. S. (1980). Acquisition, transfer, and social validation of two vocational skills in a competitive employment setting. *Education and Training of the Mentally Retarded, 15*, 306–310.

Smith, M. A., & Schloss, P. J. (1986). A superform for enhancing competence in completing employment applications. *Teaching Exceptional Children, 18*, 277–280.

Sprague, J., & Horner, R. D. (1984). Multiple instance and general case training on generalized vending machine use by moderately and severely handicapped students. *Journal of Applied Behavior Analysis, 17*, 273–278.

Stokes, T., & Baer, D. (1977). An implicit technology of generalization. *Journal of Applied Behavior Analysis, 10*, 349–367.

Stude, E. W., & Pauls, T. (1977). The use of a job seeking skills group in developing placement readiness. *Journal of Applied Rehabilitation Counseling, 8*(2), 115–120.

Wacker, D. P., & Berg, W. K. (1983). Effects of picture prompts on the acquisition of complex vocational tasks by mentally retarded adolescents. *Journal of Applied Behavior Analysis, 16*, 417–433.

Wacker, D. P., & Berg, W. K. (1986). Generalizing and maintaining work behavior. In F. R. Rusch (Ed.), *Competitive employment issues and strategies* (pp. 129–140). Baltimore, MD: Brookes.

Walls, R. T., Ellis, W. D., Zane, T., & Vanderpoel, S. J. (1979). Tactile, auditory and visual prompting in teaching complex assembly tasks. *Education and Training of the Mentally Retarded, 14*, 120–130.

Walls, R. T., Sienicki, D. A., & Crist, K. (1981). Operations training in vocational skills. *American Journal of Mental Deficiency, 86*, 357–367.

Walsh, J. (1980). An assessment of vocational education programs for the handicapped under the 1968 amendments to the vocational education act: A summary. In T. L. Wentling (Ed.), *ARRIVE: Annual review of research in vocational education* (Vol. 1, pp. 137–161). Urbana: University of Illinois.

Warner, D. A., & Mills, W. D. (1980). The effects of goal setting on the manual performance rates of moderately retarded adolescents. *Education and Training of the Mentally Retarded, 15*, 143–147.

Wehman, P. (1983). Toward the employability of severely handicapped children and youth. *Teaching Exceptional Children, 15*, 220–225.

Zoeller, C., Mahoney, G., & Weiner, B. (1983). Effects of attribution training on the assembly task performance of mentally retarded adults. *American Journal of Mental Deficiency, 88*, 109–112.

Chapter 13

❦ ❦ ❦

Models and Programs
of Vocational Training

*T*here are many means through which vocational instruction can be
delivered. In this chapter we describe some of these options. We begin with
a discussion of secondary and postsecondary possibilities, then describe some of
the various models of vocational education that have developed, including work
adjustment, career education, work experience, work study, generalizable vocational skills training, specific skills training, and employment-site-based
instruction. This chapter also includes a brief description of some of the roles of
persons and providers in vocational instruction. We conclude the chapter with
brief descriptions of some specific programs that have been developed to serve
youth and adults with mild disabilities.

❦ ❦ ❦

SECONDARY AND POSTSECONDARY SERVICE DELIVERY

Individuals with mild disabilities participate in vocational training programs at
both the secondary and postsecondary levels. Is there a difference in the impact
of the vocational program that is in some way related to whether it is delivered
at a secondary or postsecondary level? There is virtually no research in which
postsecondary and secondary vocational programs for persons with mild disabilities are compared in a meaningful and valid way. However, there are characteristics of postsecondary education that would logically lead to the conclusion that the impact would be somewhat different than secondary programs:

1.   Students in postsecondary programs are older; therefore, they are
likely to be more mature about their aspirations and the efforts they need to
put forth to achieve.

2.   Students in postsecondary education participate in such programs vol-
untarily (although they may still be heavily influenced by parents and others).
This willingness must have an impact on their attitudes toward the program.

3.   Expectations in postsecondary programs are generally higher. Expectations are especially high (when compared to the expectations in high school) when the program is a generic rather than a special or adapted program.

4.   Postsecondary programs are often not free of cost. Students pay tuition, and programs compete for students on the dimensions of both quantity and quality. Students will usually drop out if they are not being adequately served. Given the data on high school dropout rates for persons with mild disabilities, it would appear that this is a problem at both levels. It is likely, however, that the postsecondary population is comprised of those who were more successful in high school and at least believed that they could benefit from further education.

5.   Postsecondary programs may be free of some of the constraints placed on secondary programs. They usually do not exist in the same political climate as secondary programs (i.e., the demands of local taxpayers, school boards, state and federal regulation). As such they are probably freer to experiment. In contrast, secondary providers are under a mandate to coordinate and link services with other agencies.

6.   Many postsecondary providers will include adapted services only when they can get special funds to do so (McAfee, 1989; McAfee & Scheeler, 1987).

7.   Postsecondary providers often specialize—either as providers of services to a particular clientele (e.g., persons with learning disabilities) or in the content of their instruction (e.g., auto mechanics). Public secondary schools do not enjoy this luxury.

8.   Students in postsecondary programs are likely to be from a broader age range. This may make teenage peer pressure motivations less potent.

9.   Some postsecondary training carries special motivational aspects that cannot be duplicated at the secondary level. This would include the training programs provided by the military that appear to be successful for learners who are mildly disabled insofar as we have data. It would also include the training programs provided by employers that may carry the motivations of job retention and advancement.

10.   Postsecondary educators rarely have specific and extensive training in special education. However, secondary-level vocational educators may not have much more training. The U.S. Office of Education (1979) has determined that only 3% of secondary vocational teachers have completed special education courses. As a result, they are reluctant to accept students with dis-

abilities in their classes. Minner (1982) examined the expectations of regular vocational education teachers. Only eight of the teachers had taken one or more courses in special education. Using both positive and negative vignettes of students who were labeled learning disabled (LD), mildly mentally retarded, or not labeled, the researcher determined that the presence of a label led to lowered vocational and behavioral expectations. Interestingly, the teachers held the same expectations of labeled LD students regardless of the content of the vignette.

Several researchers have attempted to identify the extent of postsecondary involvement of persons with mild disabilities (Hippolitus, 1986; McAfee, 1989; McAfee & Scheeler, 1987). Unfortunately, these studies do not give us a clear indication of the extent of vocational as opposed to academic involvement. Hippolitus found that 7.4% of college freshmen reported a personal disability. Only 2.4% of the freshmen with disabilities were enrolled in vocational certificate programs. Slightly more than 1% of the freshmen reported themselves as having a learning disability. The most common fields of study were business (22.7%), professional (12.7%), and arts and humanities (10.3%). This survey included all disability categories, and physical and sensory disabilities were heavily represented. McAfee and McAfee and Scheeler surveyed community colleges regarding services for students with emotional disorders and mental retardation, respectively. Special programs (including adaptations of generic programs) for students with mental retardation were related to earmarked funding. In other words, few community colleges provided programs for persons with mental retardation unless the college had received special grant funds to do so. Services for students with emotional disorders were more widespread and had been worked into the fabric of the counseling system in most colleges.

Research on postsecondary programs has quickened over the past 5 to 10 years. This is partly the result of changes in the vocational rehabilitation (VR) regulations at the federal and state levels in which learning disabilities were recognized as a vocational as well as academic disability (Gray, 1981). In the early 1980s, postsecondary agencies began to develop programs and services for students with learning disabilities. Butler (1984) identifies many other barriers to the successful deployment of postsecondary vocational services to people with learning disabilities:

- A lack of a research base on the vocational problems of adults with learning disabilities. Although researchers have begun to address this deficiency, the research base is still very limited.
- Difficulty understanding what a learning disability is. Vocational rehabilitation counselors have little experience in learning disabilities. The training that they received often occurred before learning disabilities were recognized by VR professionals. For many, learning disabilities remain an abstract and confusing concept. Indeed, of all the disability categories it is undoubtedly the most difficult to define. There is great variability in the

LD population in terms of specific deficits. Counselors who expect to meet an LD adult with deficiencies in reading and writing are often surprised by more severe deficiencies in social skills and basic vocational skills.

- Job-seeking deficits. Vocational rehabilitation counselors may provide specific skills training only to discover that the LD client does not know where to begin to look for a job.

- A lack of on-the-job training opportunities. Learning disabled (and mentally retarded and emotionally disturbed) trainees must experience the conditions of employment in order to learn the subtle aspects of effective work behavior. On-the-job opportunities may be more difficult to secure at the postsecondary training level.

- A mismatch between clients' skills and the jobs they are offered. Employers may perceive that an applicant is less competent than he or she really is because of prejudice, social immaturity, or other characteristics. The applicant may not be considered for a more demanding position for which the applicant was trained.

- Academic entrance requirements. Entrance into many postsecondary vocational programs may be difficult for applicants with mild disabilities who have not completed required high school courses or who may perform poorly on standard tests of admission, both national (e.g., SATs) or local (e.g., a test of mechanical aptitude). Lax admissions policies are also a disservice to applicants with mild disabilities who may be accepted into a program only to fail.

- A history of failure. Most people with mild disabilities have experienced significant and repeated failure in their school careers. This creates anxiety when they enter the postsecondary educational environment.

Butler (1984) describes several specific practices to enhance the probability of postsecondary vocational training success for persons with mild disabilities. First, postsecondary vocational education providers must be given opportunities to learn the characteristics, needs, and potential of individuals with mild disabilities. Second, applicants and counselors should be honest in identifying specific needs and problems and in suggesting compensatory practices and adaptations. These needs must then be communicated to instructors. Third, counselors and others should provide anxious applicants to postsecondary programs with systematic desensitization. This could include touring the campus and facilities, previewing curricula, receiving group counseling, and practicing skills such as traveling to and about the campus.

❦ ❦ ❦

MODELS OF VOCATIONAL SERVICES

Vocational education and training can take many different forms, most of which are not mutually exclusive. We describe some of the most common models of vocational education here.

Work Adjustment Training

This form of vocational education is targeted toward prevocational and extravocational skills. Work adjustment students are taught work behaviors that are common to most jobs, such as punctuality and acceptance of supervision. Most often, work adjustment training occurs in a classroom, school shop, or sheltered work situation. Training may involve simulation but not usually paid, real employment. That is the major weakness of work adjustment training—generalization is not promoted because the training environment and the employment environment are too dissimilar. The usual content of work adjustment training can be provided in real work situations such as summer or part-time employment. In those instances, it would be a more effective way of imparting prevocational and extravocational skills.

Career Education

This conception of vocational education has been in existence for 20 years. It is not so much a specific way or content of training as it is a way of formulating the entire set of experiences that an individual needs to become an effective adult.

Brolin (1983) describes the major tenets of career education as follows:

- *Infusion.* Career education and vocational experiences should be integrated into all aspects of education. This should begin early (in elementary school) and continue and intensify through the secondary years and into adulthood. Career education includes not just jobs and working but all of the elements of education that influence and contribute to the meaningfulness of adult life. Thus, career educators have adopted the same approach that we have adopted for transition. That is, transition is more than jobs; it is adult participation in a wide array of opportunities.
- *Stage development.* Brolin believes that career education activities should be reflective of the developmental stages of children and youth. Career education should start with simple activities and understanding of work and adult roles and progress to more complex, abstract, and subtle requirements.
- *Systemwide involvement.* All personnel, at all levels, should be involved in career education. Turning out productive and effective adults should be the primary goal of education.
- *Experientiality.* Career education activities should include hands-on experiences. Children and adults learn best by doing, whereas lecture and classroom activities have limited utility.
- *Family/community liaison.* Career education cannot be fully effective if the family and community are not involved. The influence of the family is so powerful that if the parents and the school are at cross purposes, the student will be unable to function. Furthermore, the student will eventually have to perform outside of the school in the community. Career educators had better determine what the community expects.

Brolin (1982) has written extensively on career education and developed the Life-centered Career Education Model (LCCE). This competency-based model has work at the center but includes other roles (e.g., avocational, familial, civic). Brolin's model includes learning outside of school. All learning should be functional and related to careers. According to Brolin, career education should lead to sellable work skills. This requires a redirection of traditional education. Brolin is not viewing career education as an element of education but rather as a new core of education. He believes that career education has been slow to develop because comprehensive curricula were not available for educators to use to plan appropriate Individual Education Plan (IEP) goals. The LCCE model includes 22 major competencies in three areas with 102 subcompetencies. These competencies were gleaned from research and validated by other educators.

Brolin (1982) identifies five stages of career development: (a) awareness, (b) exploration, (c) preparation, (d) placement/follow-up, and (d) continuing education. Awareness begins in the elementary school and continues through the secondary years. It includes learning about work and developing attitudes toward work. Exploration begins in junior high school and continues through high school. It entails hands-on experiences in elements of occupations and leisure activities. Formal vocational evaluation should begin at this time. Preparation is experiential and involves the heavy use of community resources such as businesses. Job experiences are an integral part of preparation activities. Placement and follow-up is, according to Brolin, the most neglected area of career education. It should extend into adulthood. Continuing education is the means by which individuals maintain and extend their skills. This area has also been neglected.

In order to enact career education effectively, special education teachers should serve as consultants, coordinators, and resources to regular educators, vocational educators, parents, and other agencies. Brolin (1982) believes that competencies can be developed using a variety of techniques including role playing, simulation, field trips, occupational games, work samples, and work experiences.

Humes and Hohenshil (1985) identify some needs that must be met for career education to be as effective as it should be. Career education needs to be evaluated. Research on its effectiveness is limited. Career education requires greater parent involvement than that currently experienced in most schools. It also demands substantial staff development. Contact with persons in postschool settings must increase. Educators must get away from the notion that career education begins in the secondary years. Finally, career educators need to do a better job of disseminating information. Successes and failures must be shared.

Work Experience

When students perform work at actual work sites, they are receiving work experience. Work experience, a common element of career exploration, provides students with some experience in a job in order to help them make a judgment about the desirability and suitability of that vocational area. The work experience student is generally not paid. Work experience may be integrated into other vocational efforts such as specific skill training or career education. However, more often it stands alone, with more global and/or extravocational objectives. In many cases, the work experience is in a "made up" job that does not represent any real job. Work experience is a necessary component of effective training, but it is only effective if it is conducted with specific training goals in mind and integrated with the other elements of the program.

Work Study

Work study takes two forms. In the first form, participants attend classes and perform paid work outside of class. The purpose of the work is to provide the participant with income so that he or she can remain in the educational program. Usually, this work is performed for the same agency that is providing the educational program, and the work may or may not be related to the area of study. It is a financial assistance program more than a training program. This type of work study is often encountered in postsecondary programs such as colleges and community colleges.

In the second form of work study, the participant's day is divided into a study period (classes) and a paid work period. The purpose of the paid work period is to provide simultaneous vocational education and paid work experience. Work-study programs of this type can be an effective means of vocational training if the work experience is not a made-up job and if the work experience is closely related to the area of vocational training. Work-study programs are used at both the secondary and postsecondary levels. Secondary work study programs do not usually have financial support as a purpose. Postsecondary programs may be designed for both financial and training reasons.

Generalized Skills Training

Participants in this type of training learn specific skills that are applicable to a number of occupations. For example, students may participate in "tools training" in which they would learn to use a broad array of hand and/or power tools that are used in several occupations such as plumbing, carpentry, and auto mechanics. Other students might participate in an office procedures course in which they learn to operate office equipment, basic accounting, and business law. Neither of these courses is tied to a specific occupation. The purposes of the training are to provide exposure to possible occupational areas, and hence increase occupational awareness, and to provide some basic and generalizable work skills.

Generalized work skills training is effective as an occupational awareness and exploration activity. It is much less effective as an activity that leads to employment. It cannot stand on its own but must be supplemented by more specific training. This type of activity is appropriate to the junior high school and early high school years.

Specific Skills Training

Participants in this type of vocational training are taught specific skills that are required for specific types of jobs such as bookkeeping, carpentry, medical technology, and building maintenance. Specific skills training is not usually designed for employment with a specific employer but rather for employment in a job category with a number of possible employers. Specific skills training is usually delivered in a traditional vocational training classroom setting at either a secondary or postsecondary level. Specific skills training can be effective if it is combined with related work experience during training and job placement support that enables the new employee to apply the skills to the specific work environment. The employment environment may require the trainee to modify his or her approach to tasks from the way in which it was taught in specific skills training. Persons with mild disabilities may have difficulty making these adaptations.

Employment Site Instruction

This form of vocational instruction occurs on the job. Its purpose may be traditional on-the-job training provided by employers for workers to update and improve their skills in their specific jobs. It may also take the form of a formal or informal apprenticeship for a new employee to learn a job. A third form, a more recent development, involves training provided by vocational educators and special educators to persons who are not likely to learn a job through the traditional approaches used by employers. Job coaching and other forms of supported employment are included in this category. (We will discuss specific forms of this kind of instruction later in this chapter in the section "A Review of Some Specific Vocational Programs.") The Materials Development Center (1988) at the University of Wisconsin–Stout has developed a guide for industry-based training with instructions and guidelines for developing such programs.

Stainback, Stainback, Nietupski, and Hamre-Nietupski (1986) cite several advantages of employment site instruction: (a) trainees will learn vocational survival skills that are functional, (b) trainees will learn social interaction skills, (c) trainees will learn ancillary survival skills (e.g., time management), (d) coworkers can serve as effective and realistic models, (e) coworkers will have the opportunity to interact with people with disabilities in a real-life environment, (f) trainers can gather information about real work that can be included in the curriculum, (g) trainees with disabilities and coworkers will have opportunities for interdependence, (h) generalization is promoted, (i) the environment is more normalizing, (j) successes can be used to counteract the low expectations of the community, and (k) it is more likely to lead to consistent competitive employment.

❦ ❦ ❦

PERSONS, PROVIDERS, AND ENVIRONMENTS

Effective vocational training requires the services of many people in many roles in various environments. Ellington (1983) enumerates several of these roles:

1. The **guidance counselor** is primarily responsible for career awareness, career planning, and inclusion of the family. The guidance counselor usually provides these services in the secondary school environment, although similar counselors may work in some traditional postsecondary settings such as community colleges.

2. The **occupational specialist** works with students to increase self-awareness, job exploration, and decision-making and employability skills. In some cases, the occupational specialist may provide liaison services among the school, the community, and businesses. The occupational specialist may also serve as a resource to the classroom teacher. Occupational specialists are usually employed by secondary schools and occasionally by postsecondary educational programs.

3. The **work evaluator** provides hands-on experiences to students for the purpose of making decisions about careers, identifying capabilities, and specifying the content of training needed to correct deficiencies. Work evaluators are evident in educational programs from junior high school to postsecondary environments.

4. The **work experience teacher** provides academic and remedial job-related instruction and arranges work experiences for the purpose of trying out the world of work. Work experience teachers most often work in high schools.

5. **Rehabilitation specialists** perform numerous tasks related to the immediate entry into the world of work. These tasks include career counseling, interest and skill evaluation, placement, and referral for further training or services (e.g., physical therapy, medical intervention, psychological counseling). Rehabilitation specialists provide their services most often to postsecondary-age individuals; however, because of the new mandates for integrated and smooth transitional services, rehabilitation specialists have begun to provide more services to high school students. In 1983 less than 5% of VR counselors reported that they had participated in planning vocational services for high school students (Miller, Mulkey, & Kopp, 1984).

329

6. The *special education teacher* may provide leadership and coordination for all vocational services to elementary and secondary students. The special education teacher may also offer similar services to students who have recently left a secondary program and who are on a follow-along status. This role is very different from the traditional self-contained or resource room role. It necessitates leadership and consultation skills, plus the time outside of the usual classroom duties to conduct the coordination activities.

Ellington's (1983) list of responsibilities should not be seen as complete. Events of the past decade have combined to produce new roles for existing positions, and the demand for new services has led to the creation of new positions. One such role that has become widespread and critical to the vocational success of persons with disabilities, including those with mild disabilities, is the *job coach.* Job coaching may take many forms. Wehman and Melia (1985) identify the roles of the job coach as (a) travel trainer, (b) parent educator, (c) job-client matchmaker, (d) on-site vocational trainer, (e) vocational counselor, and (f) evaluator. In essence, the job coach is the person who helps an individual obtain and retain a job on an ongoing basis. Probably the most important aspect of job coaching is the method with which it is provided. Job coaches provide ongoing support to workers with disabilities while they are working. For some workers this might include daily instruction and supervision. For others who are more independent, it might include periodic checks and assistance with specific problems that are preventing them from performing to their maximum potential.

Most often, job coaches are secondary special education teachers who have been released from classroom duty or have been hired for a postsecondary program. Cobb, Hasazi, Collins, and Salembier (1988) note the great need to increase the numbers and improve the training of special education employment training specialists, some of whom would assume the role of job coach. This need is a direct result of the increased emphasis on transition and the recognition that old systems and regular secondary vocational education had been ineffective for most students with disabilities.

In spite of this ineffectiveness, regular vocational education teachers continue to provide services to students with mild disabilities in both secondary and postsecondary programs. McDaniel (1982) found that part of the reason for this ineffectiveness was the negative attitude toward students with disabilities held by vocational education teachers. McDaniel also determined that the most effective ways to change these negative attitudes were undergraduate special needs vocational education courses and in-service special needs workshops. The least effective way was to include special needs information in regular vocational education courses. It appears that regular education teacher-trainers were not as effective at communicating information about special needs students as were special education teacher-trainers.

Vocational rehabilitation services are provided under a joint program of the states and the federal government. All states have VR departments or offices that obtain much of their funding through federal legislation and the Office of

Special Education and Rehabilitation Services (OSERS). The purpose of VR is to help people become more employable. Persons who are eligible for VR services are provided an Individual Written Rehabilitation Plan (IWRP). The IWRP serves much the same function as an IEP or Individual Transition Plan (ITP).

Vocational rehabilitation agencies are authorized to provide or fund (a) medical examinations; (b) medical intervention to reduce or remove a disability; (c) job training or funds for job training at trade schools or rehabilitation centers; (d) educational tuition assistance; (e) financial assistance during rehabilitation for room, board, transportation, and so forth; (f) referral and job placement; and (g) on-the-job assistance. It is apparent that VR agencies offer a wide array of services to persons with disabilities, including those who are mildly disabled. Walls, Tseng, and Zarin (1976), however, describe a limitation to VR services; the tendency to close cases quickly after job placement, often within 30 days. Early case closure is problematic to many persons with mild disabilities who need more extensive follow-along services. It remains to be seen if changes in approaches to transition will be associated with increased VR follow-along.

Interestingly, VR utilizes quite different definitions than does education. Miller et al. (1984) found that 35 of 36 reporting state VR agencies considered clients with learning disabilities to be severely disabled. Furthermore, the majority of VR cases involving persons with learning disabilities were closed without a successful outcome. In other words, these individuals were considered to be unemployable. Another disturbing observation made by Miller et al. was that VR workers had received training in identification and evaluation of learning disabilities but not in remediation or vocational training. This may account for the large number of unsuccessful cases as it is hard to see how an evaluation can be helpful if no plan for services is developed. This observation is further supported by the fact that after evaluation, the most common service provided was remediation of academic deficiencies (60%). Fewer than 20% of the VR clients with learning disabilities were referred to rehabilitation centers for work adjustment training, fewer than 5% were provided on-the-job training, and fewer than 1% received specific employer assistance. Miller et al. stated that VR counselors were most in need of information on how to provide appropriate vocational training and job placement.

Other providers of vocational education services for individuals with mild disabilities include trade schools, community colleges, and private postsecondary special needs programs. Unfortunately, little meaningful literature has been published that would provide insight into the means by which these services are provided or their effectiveness. We know nothing of the capability of the teachers in trade schools, the faculty in community colleges, or the personnel in private postsecondary special programs to provide functional services.

A Review of Some Specific Vocational Programs

In this section, we consider only those programs for people with mild disabilities for which evaluative data are available, to avoid describing programs with no demonstrable efficacy.

Stodden and Browder's Community-based Employment.   Stodden and Browder (1986) developed and evaluated a postsecondary vocational training program for 44 mentally retarded and 9 LD adults aged 18 to 59. The goal of the program was competitive employment. Stodden and Browder used community-based training and behavioral principles to teach work skills in a real work environment. At the beginning of the project, 23 of the trainees had some competitive work experience, and 16 had only prevocational training. The program included five major activities:

1. *Assessment.*   Trainee work behaviors were assessed in a variety of work situations in a sheltered workshop. These assessments were not used to make predictions about who would be successful in which jobs but rather what skills individuals possessed and what skills needed to be taught.
2. *Preemployment training.*   This training was aimed at work adjustment skills. It occurred in small classes.
3. *Work experience.*   Trainees were provided volunteer work experiences in community jobs, mostly in nonprofit organizations, for 2 to 4 months. Training during work experience was individualized and provided by job coaches.
4. *On-site competitive work training.*   Trainees were placed with local employers in entry-level jobs. Job coaches assisted both trainees and employers.
5. *Supported employment.*   For a period of 1 year from the date the trainee started competitive employment, assistance in the form of job coaching was provided.

Of the 53 trainees, 28 were successfully placed in competitive employment. Their wages ranged from $3.35 to $5.50 per hour, with a work week ranging from 10 to 40 hours. They received universally high ratings from their employers. Stodden and Browder (1986) concluded that the greatest needs of the trainees were increased speed, greater consistency, ability to handle pressure, and better judgment.

Rusch's Supported Employment.   Rusch and others have developed several variations of supported employment (Rusch, 1990). They have used three approaches:

1. *Enclaves.*   Small groups of workers with disabilities are placed in a business together. Ongoing support is provided at the job site by a job training specialist.
2. *Individual.*   A job coach provides training to a single individual at a job site, with his or her presence gradually reduced over time.
3. *Mobile work crew.*   A crew of individuals with disabilities is employed through contract work. The crew and the trainer/supervisor move from site to site. Work at specific job sites may be short and cyclical (e.g., 1/2 day per week every week) or longer and for a single episode (e.g., one 2-week job contract).

Among the benefits to supported employment identified by Rusch (1990) are (a) integration with nondisabled workers, (b) real work, (c) real wages, and (d) continued support that enhances job retention and skills maintenance. The specific successes of Rusch's approach have been documented elsewhere in this text.

Brickey's Competitive Employment Training. Brickey and Campbell (1981), Brickey, Browning, and Campbell (1982), and Brickey, Campbell, and Browning (1985) describe their approach to competitive employment training for individuals with moderate or mild mental retardation. The original program developed by Brickey and Campbell was known as the McDonald's Project. This project occurred in Columbus, Ohio, and involved 27 mentally retarded adults between 21 and 52 years of age. Seventeen job placements were made in 15 different McDonald's restaurants. The trainers met with the employers prior to placements and discussed expectations and training approaches. McDonald's managers met with employees to prepare them for the new mentally retarded employees. Trainers provided on-site instruction and supervision for the new employees. After 1 year, 10 of the trainees were still employed, and 3 had left to work elsewhere. Acceptance of the mentally retarded workers by their coworkers was good. The mentally retarded workers had a much lower turnover rate than their coworkers; however, they averaged only 20 to 25 hours per week, and some actually had lower income as a result of the work (e.g., lost supplementary security income).

Brickey et al. (1982) analyzed the success of mentally retarded trainees who had been served in Projects with Industry (PWI) or other competitive employment training over a 30-month period. Of the 73 trainees, 33 were mildly mentally retarded. A number of those included in this study were from the McDonald's Project. The PWI placements differed from the competitive placements in that they were short-term positions. The clients in PWI were placed in PWI because their parents objected to competitive placement, no competitive placement was available, or the employer needed a large number of temporary employees. Of the 27 placed in PWI positions, 13 were later placed in permanent competitive jobs. Sixty percent of those placed in competitive employment retained their jobs or acquired other jobs. The variety of jobs included food service, housekeeping, and factory work. The most common reasons for a job separation was lack of speed, followed by absenteeism and tardiness. Thus, both vocational and extravocational skills were problematic. Turnover rates were comparable to or better than those for similar groups of people in similar jobs. Female trainees were more successful than male trainees, but age, IQ, and previous work experience were not related to success. The McDonald's placements were the most effective because the trainers knew those jobs well and were better able to prepare the candidates, there were more positions available, McDonald's commitment was very high, and McDonald's had very specific job descriptions on which to base training.

Brickey et al. (1985) conducted a follow-up of those same trainees. Their original optimism was unsupported as only 34% were still competitively employed. This result highlights the need for continued and long-term follow-along and support.

Neubert, Tilson, and Ianacone's Postsecondary Project.   Neubert, Tilson, and Ianacone (1989) describe a federally funded transition program for young adults (ages 18–30) in Maryland. This program served 66 LD and educable mentally retarded students who were referred by teachers, VR counselors, and family members. The program included seven activities: (a) intake; (b) an 8-week employability course including vocational assessment, community-based career exploration, and job-seeking skills; (c) job tryouts at community employment sites; (d) job search support; (e) competitive placement and follow-up; (f) a job club; and (g) job change and advancement support. Fifty-nine percent of the trainees were female, and 44% had a learning disability. Prior to placement, trainees were encouraged to be as independent as possible in job searches, but all received some assistance with tasks such as identifying job leads, arranging interviews, or completing applications. After placement, trainees were given an orientation and on-site support during their first week of employment. In addition, some were taught how to modify their work stations to suit their needs. Others received clarification of company policies and procedures or encouragement of appropriate social behavior. During the first month, all trainees received at least one follow-up visit per week. After the first month, follow-up and data collection were accomplished through quarterly surveys and biweekly visits or phone contacts.

Neubert et al. (1989) report extensive evaluative data. Forty-eight percent of those who acquired jobs worked in clerical or sales positions, 25% worked in service positions. Fifty percent of the initial appointments were part-time. The average hourly wage was $4.40, with few nonwage benefits. Seventy-four percent required staff support during their first month of employment. Support during the first week ranged from 1 hour to 12.5 hours, with a mean of 4.7 hours. During week 2, the mean amount of staff support was 2.7 hours, and in week 4 it declined to 47 minutes. Ninety-two percent of the trainees experienced task-related problems such as lower than acceptable productivity. Seventy-one percent had work adjustment problems such as interpersonal conflict. Only 12% underwent health problems that affected their work. Seventy-six percent of the trainees were still employed after 6 months, 64% after 1 year. Thirteen of those had changed their jobs because of layoffs (4), firings (5), or better pay (4).

Weber's Program for Delinquent Youth.   In 1986, Weber reported the results of a job training/career awareness program for emotionally disturbed juvenile delinquent youths. These youths were served in a community-based, self-contained program staffed by teachers, a social worker, and a job training specialist. They received instruction in academics, career development, and job-appropriate behaviors. The behaviorally based program allowed the students to earn points toward reintegration into regular education. Earlier efforts with these students had been unsuccessful, and the program was modified to include more job training. The goals of the program were improved appropriate work habits, increased career awareness, at least one successful pregraduation job experience, and postschool employment. The program had four components:

1. *Individual assessment.* Students were evaluated for vocational interests, awareness, and skills.
2. *Job responsibilities.* This component included instruction in extravocational skills such as communication, peer interactions, and hygiene. Students established their own goals in this area.
3. *Job stations.* For this component, students worked at jobs in the school district 1 hour a day, 2 to 3 days per week. Performance was managed by a behavioral incentive system. As performance improved, job station time was expanded.
4. *Community job placement.* Students were placed in jobs at which they earned minimum wage or more. Employers were provided with support through the Job Training Partnership Act. A job training instructor provided job coaching, and employers conducted weekly evaluations. If the students committed criminal acts on the job, they were required to make monetary restitution from their pay.

Of the 44 participants, 8 graduated, another earned a GED, and 3 withdrew; the remainder were still in the program at the time the study was published. The 12 who left the program entered the job market, and 11 were employed or pursued postsecondary education. Employers expressed high levels of satisfaction with graduates, and three participants were being considered for promotion.

Siegel's Career Ladder Program. The career ladder program (Siegel, 1988) is a demonstration project operated under collaboration by the San Francisco Public Schools, San Francisco State University, the California Department of Rehabilitation, and local employers. High school seniors with mild disabilities are recruited to participate in the program that includes half-day placement in a real work setting. Vocational instructors are present during the work placement. Participants are viewed as interns and receive academic credit and minimum wage for their work. At the beginning of placement, supervision is provided mostly by vocational instructors then gradually shifts to work site supervisors. All participants attend employment skills workshops designed to promote responsibility and the acquisition of work-related skills. The workshops also include instruction in job keeping and social and job-seeking skills. A student who completes the training receives a lifetime commitment of career development support from program staff. A transition specialist maintains quarterly contact with graduates. Ninety percent of the graduates are employed or enrolled in school, compared to a rate of 60% to 65% for similar individuals not in the program. The major emphasis of the program is on helping individuals obtain and retain specific jobs rather than on general job training. Therefore, the transition specialists work closely with employers and trainees at the job site.

Project WORTH. Vautour, Stocks, and Kolek (1983) cite a junior and senior high school project in Connecticut that was designed to prepare students with mild disabilities for employment. Project WORTH included career awareness and specific skill training with an end goal of postschool employment or education. The program involved coordination of regular education, special education, vocational education, and counseling. A community liaison teacher provided a link with employers and the community at large. The curriculum included four phases: self-awareness, careers, work preparation, and work experience. Fiscal and plant limitations precluded development of a school-based training facility; therefore, community job sites were used as training sites and employers were used as trainers.

Initially, employers expressed stereotypical views of people with disabilities. Project staff conducted a public relations campaign to alter stereotypes, emphasizing that employees with disabilities are good employees. Public relations efforts included a mailing to all possible employers in which the project was described. This was followed by phone calls and visits.

Vautour et al. (1983) found that prior to training the students had an unrealistic appraisal of their vocational strengths and weaknesses and little awareness of the variety of jobs. They were unfamiliar with work-related terms such as those found on job applications. They demonstrated poor work behavior such as tardiness. All of the 18 graduates of the program were in competitive employment at the time of the study, and 6 were in postsecondary vocational training. Another was enrolled in a regular college program.

❦ ❦ ❦

SUMMARY

There are many examples of effective practice, models, and programs across the country. We now know a great deal about what works and what does not. Unfortunately, effective practices are not in place for all persons with mild disabilities. Effective practice requires tremendous coordination among regular education, special education, vocational rehabilitation, social services agencies, families, employers, postsecondary providers, and the students and clients who receive the services. The common elements of the successful practices, models, and programs are real job experience, on-the-job training and assistance, long-term follow-along, and opportunities for students to learn self-responsibility. All of this must be translated into local practice.

REFERENCES

Brickey, M., Browning, L., & Campbell, K. (1982). Vocational histories of sheltered workshop employees placed in projects with industry and competitive jobs. *Mental Retardation, 20*, 52–57.

Brickey, M., & Campbell, K. (1981). Fast food employment for moderately and mildly mentally retarded adults: The McDonald's project. *Mental Retardation, 19*, 113–116.

Brickey, M. P., Campbell, K. M., & Browning, L. J. (1985). A five year follow up of sheltered workshop employees placed in competitive jobs. *Mental Retardation, 23*, 67–73.

Brolin, D. E. (1982). Life-centered career education for exceptional children. *Focus on Exceptional Children, 14*(7), 1–15.

Brolin, D. E. (1983). Career education: Where do we go from here? *Career Development for Exceptional Individuals, 8*, 3–14.

Butler, W. D. (1984). The learning disabled client's rehabilitation program: Issues in training. *Journal of Rehabilitation, 50*(2), 68–73.

Cobb, R. B., Hasazi, S. B., Collins, C. M., & Salembier, G. (1988). Preparing school-based employment specialists. *Teacher Education and Special Education, 11*(2), 64–71.

Ellington, C. (1983). Career education: People and programs working together. *Teaching Exceptional Children, 15*, 210–214.

Gray, R. A. (1981). Services for the LD adult: A working paper. *Learning Disabilities Quarterly, 4*, 426–434.

Hippolitus, P. (1986). *College freshmen with disabilities: Preparing for employment.* Washington, DC: President's Committee on Employment of the Handicapped.

Humes, C. W., & Hohenshil, T. H. (1985). Career development and career education for handicapped students: A reexamination. *Vocational Guidance Quarterly, 34*(1), 31–40.

Materials Development Center. (1988). *Job coaching in supported work settings.* Menomonie: School of Education & Human Services, University of Wisconsin–Stout.

McAfee, J. K. (1989). Community colleges and individuals with emotional disorders. *Behavior Disorders, 15*(1), 9–15.

McAfee, J. K., & Scheeler, M. C. (1987). Accommodation of mentally retarded adults in community colleges: A national study. *Education and Training of the Mentally Retarded, 22*, 262–267.

McDaniel, L. (1982). Changing the vocational teachers' attitudes toward the handicapped. *Exceptional Children, 48*, 377–378.

Miller, J. H., Mulkey, S. W., & Kopp, K. H. (1984). Public rehabilitation services for individuals with specific learning disabilities. *Journal of Rehabilitation, 50*(2), 19–29.

Minner, S. (1982). Expectations of vocational teachers for handicapped students. *Exceptional Children, 48*, 451–453.

Neubert, D. A., Tilson, G. P., Jr., & Ianacone, R. N. (1989). Postsecondary transition needs and employment patterns of individuals with mild disabilities. *Exceptional Children, 55*, 494–500.

Rusch, F. R. (1990). *Supported employment: Models, methods, and issues.* Sycamore, IL: Sycamore.

Siegel, S. (1988). The career leader program: Implementing RE-ED principles in vocational settings. *Behavior Disorders, 14,* 16–26.

Stainback, W., Stainback, S., Nietupski, J., & Hamre-Nietupski, S. (1986). Establishing effective community-based training stations. In F. R. Rusch (Ed.), *Competitive employment issues and strategies* (pp. 103–113). Baltimore, MD: Brookes.

Stodden, R. A., & Browder, P. M. (1986). Community based competitive employment preparation of developmentally disabled persons: A program description and evaluation. *Education and Training of the Mentally Retarded, 21,* 43–53.

U.S. Office of Education, Department of Health, Education and Welfare. (1979). *Progress toward a free appropriate public education. A report to Congress on the implementation of PL 94-142: The Education for All Handicapped Children Act*. Washington, DC: U.S. Government Printing Office.

Vautour, J. A. C., Stocks, C., & Kolek, M. M. (1983). Preparing mildly handicapped students for employment. *Teaching Exceptional Children, 16,* 54–58.

Walls, R. T., Tseng, M. S., & Zarin, H. N. (1976). Time and money for vocational rehabilitation of clients with mild, moderate and severe mental retardation. *American Journal of Mental Deficiency, 80,* 595–601.

Weber, M. (1986). Job training/career awareness partnership program for emotionally disturbed juvenile delinquent youth. *Teaching Behaviorally Disordered Youth, 2,* 20–25.

Wehman, P., & Melia, R. (1985). The job coach: Function in transitional and supported employment. *American Rehabilitation, 11,* 4–7.

PART IV

❧ ❧ ❧

Extravocational Support for Transition

College life is not all books and studying, as demonstrated in this photo of a 1912 pushball contest at Penn State. Similarly, transition to adult life is more than simply preparation for work.

❦ *Vignettes* ❦

(a) Jerome Bowden was executed for murder by the state of Georgia in 1986. He had confessed to the crime. When he was 14, a psychologist determined that his IQ was 59. His psychological report stated that "his potential was so limited that he wasn't worth wasting time on" (Smith, 1986, p. 36). Jerome had an accomplice in the crime who was not retarded but had implicated Jerome. His accomplice was sentenced to life imprisonment. There was no evidence tying Jerome to the crime, just the confession that he claims he signed after a detective told him he would help him if he signed it.

Jerome had been arrested several times before the murder charge arose, mostly for petty theft, which was common where he lived. Before he was arrested for the murder, he had lived on the streets for 3 months. There is reason to believe that he welcomed a stay in jail when he was arrested for the murder because he knew he could eat and watch television. Jerome maintained his innocence until his execution (Smith, 1986).

(b) At 35, Sue has just voted for the first time. She had never thought much about elections and politics until she started taking courses at the community college. Although she had learned about American history and government in high school, somehow it did not seem important then. After all, neither of her parents had ever voted.

Sue had never belonged to any organizations until her coworkers organized the food drive last Thanksgiving. Working on that project made her feel good. Now, she spends at least 1 day a month at her church, collecting or distributing clothing or food. She is not sure why, but for the first time, she feels that she is truly an adult. People seem to talk to her differently. She is very happy with her new maturity and sense of responsibility.

Sue and Jerome are a study in contrasts. Jerome carried his problems with him into his adult life. He never had an opportunity to grow, to learn, to become a responsible adult. Sue has suddenly become a more complete person. Both have been heavily influenced by their peers. Sue has learned that service to others enhances self-worth. Jerome learned how to steal and perhaps to murder.

❦ ❦ ❦

WHAT ARE EXTRAVOCATIONAL SKILLS?

Successful transition involves much more than attainment of vocational adequacy. Dearden noted in 1952 that mentally retarded people who had obtained jobs and achieved vocational competence as a result of the need for workers during World War II were displaced from their jobs by returning veterans. Although these workers had been effective during the war years, they were less valued members of our society, and when work force reductions were necessary, they were the first to be dismissed. This devaluation resulted from a public perception that individuals who were retarded, even those with mild disabilities, were limited in all areas of life; their lives were less fulfilling; they were societal burdens, severely deficient in managing their own affairs; and they were incapable of contributing significantly to the overall good. Although the work success of people with disabilities eventually provided impetus for profound changes in education and rehabilitation, work success alone was insufficient to bring about the extent of the integration effort that is apparent today.

Although it is almost obvious that people with severe disabilities will experience difficulties in areas such as independent living, social skills, citizenship, and sexuality, research reveals that people with mild disabilities have similar (and in some cases more extensive) problems adjusting to the independence and expectations of adulthood. The extent of the problem for people with mild disabilities is not as well documented as it is for people with severe disabilities, but it is firmly established and logical. Expectations for adult success are higher for people with mild disabilities. In fact, it is not uncommon for parents and the mildly disabled themselves to expect that a disability will more or less disappear after high school. It is also likely that because deficiencies in living and social skills may not be so obvious, adolescents with mild disabilities may not receive the kind of transitional training that they need but will be expected to sink or swim in routine vocational or college prep programs. Finally, young adults with mild disabilities are more likely to be exposed to more different environments, requiring greater adaptation than persons with severe disabilities. For these reasons, and others that are enumerated throughout Part IV, it is critical that transition planners for people with mild disabilities consider the breadth of adult experiences that these individuals are likely to face.

There are many people who have high-paying or prestigious jobs who are unhappy, have few friends, abuse alcohol or drugs, or face family disintegration. Although the prestige of a job is the principal way by which adults gain status in our society, it is folly to focus solely on jobs and vocational training when there are so many other important elements of life adjustment and success. Although vocational success and extravocational skills are highly interactive, many individuals with mild disabilities obtain adequate employment but are otherwise unsuccessful and poorly adjusted.

Extravocational skills are those skills that do not involve actual job task performance but are important for (a) job success (e.g., getting along with others), (b) living independence (e.g., money management), (c) health maintenance (e.g., absence of substance abuse), (d) family living (e.g., child rearing), (e) recreation and leisure, and (f) civic participation (e.g., voting). Table 1 provides an analysis of extravocational skill areas.

Three major extravocational skill areas are described and analyzed in detail in this part: work support skills (chap. 14), independent living skills (chap. 15), and citizenship skills (chap. 16). Chapters are divided into two major sections: (a) background research on the status of individuals with mild disabilities in that area and (b) a description of programs and practices designed to improve the functioning of individuals with mild disabilities in each extravocational area.

Table 1

Extravocational Skill Areas

Skill Areas	Skill Subareas	Skill Examples
I. Work support	A. Transportation	1. Driving 2. Using public transportation
	B. Work responsibility	1. Self-management 2. Finishing work 3. Understanding the work schedule
	C. Social skills	1. Getting along with peers 2. Accepting supervision 3. Handling stress
II. Personal management	A. Consumer skills	1. Budgeting 2. Banking 3. Buying 4. Using credit 5. Shopping 6. Using insurance
	B. Household management	1. Housecleaning 2. Maintaining home
III. Personal health	A. Preventive health maintenance	1. Resisting substance abuse 2. Scheduling physical exams 3. Personal hygiene
	B. Health support	1. Understanding insurance
IV. Family living	A. Sexuality	1. Dating 2. Having sexual knowledge 3. Understanding sexual abuse
	B. Family skills	1. Rearing children
V. Leisure	A. Recreational skills	1. Knowing about recreational opportunities 2. Knowing game rules
	B. Friendship	1. Sharing 2. Having conversation skills
VI. Citizenship	A. Civic participation	1. Voting 2. Participating in community activities
	B. Law	1. Having legal knowledge 2. Resisting criminal activity

❦ ❦ ❦

THE VALUES BASIS FOR EXTRAVOCATIONAL TRAINING

In our society, we believe that meaningful work is a right of all individuals who desire to work. The development of sheltered workshops was one way in which we sought to provide work for people with disabilities. In the early history of sheltered employment, the majority of clients had mild disabilities. Now, many experts question the value and normality of sheltered employment for many individuals with severe disabilities. It has become apparent that sheltered employment does not provide the same prestige, perceived worth, habilitation, or integration that competitive employment does, just as institutionalization does not offer opportunities for independence, and segregated classes do not provide exposure to the full spectrum of human experience (yet it is still common to read about people with mild disabilities who are institutionalized or taught in segregated classes). In the 1980s, special educators attempted to broaden work opportunities for people with disabilities. This trend may be viewed in the broader context of the normalization and mainstreaming movements of the past 25 years.

If we extend this argument and accept the values of normalization (that every person is entitled to a life that is as close to normal as possible), then it would be inconsistent to train individuals with mild disabilities to work effectively without simultaneously providing training that enables them to live independently, be healthy, raise a family, participate in the civic process, and enjoy off-work hours. A value inherently expressed in this book is that people with mild disabilities must be provided with the opportunity, knowledge, and skills to be valued and effective people, as well as valued workers.

❦ ❦ ❦

THE RESEARCH BASIS FOR EXTRAVOCATIONAL TRAINING

Nearly every large-scale study of people with mild disabilities provides evidence that the majority of people with mild disabilities encounter difficulty with independent functioning in one or more of life's major activities. According to Knowles (1978), among the most common problems encountered by young adults are (a) preparing to vote, (b) learning how to exert influence, (c) developing leadership skills, (d) keeping up with the world, (e) taking action in the community, and (f) organizing community activities. These difficulties spread into the workplace and adversely affect the work performance of people with mild disabilities who otherwise possess adequate job skills. Many researchers and practitioners believe that these people are more likely to lose their jobs because of poor social skills than because of poor job skills. This belief provides the support for a strong extravocational element in any transitional program.

Consider the following conclusions about extravocational adjustment:

1. More people with mild disabilities lose their jobs because of social inadequacy than for vocational inadequacy (McAfee & Mann, 1982).

2. Individuals with mild disabilities often misunderstand formal and informal work rules (McAfee & Mann, 1981).
3. Workers with mild disabilities often have difficulties with transportation to work (McAfee & Mann, 1981).
4. Adults with mild disabilities have difficulty with money management. They do not use credit wisely, nor do they shop wisely (Clark, Kivitz, & Rosen, 1968).
5. Adults with mild disabilities may have difficulty in obtaining housing (McAfee & Mann, 1981).
6. Adults with mild disabilities abuse alcohol and drugs at a rate at least equal to that of the general population, but they have greater difficulty obtaining help for their abuse problems (Krishef & DiNitto, 1981).
7. Adults with mild disabilities are less health conscious and physically fit than the general population (McAfee & Mann, 1981).
8. Adults with mild disabilities are less knowledgeable about human sexuality than adults without disabilities (Andron & Strum, 1973).
9. Adults with mild disabilities have difficulties raising children (Andron & Strum, 1973).
10. Adults with mild disabilities have poor knowledge of political issues and vote at a low rate (Warren & Gardner, 1973; Olley & Ramey, 1978).
11. Adults with mild disabilities rarely participate in activities for community good (Kregel, Wehman, Seyfarth, & Marshall, 1986).
12. Adults with mild disabilities are involved in criminal activity at least as much as the general population, but they are more likely to go to jail. They have poor knowledge of the legal system (Reichard, Spencer, & Spooner, 1980).
13. Adults with mild disabilities have a limited repertoire of recreational interests (Redding, 1979).
14. Adults with mild disabilities have fewer close friends than nondisabled adults (Scott, Williams, Stout, & Decker, 1980).

Obviously, these conclusions are generalizations. Many adults with mild disabilities do not encounter the difficulties described. However, the research is fairly conclusive that the majority of individuals with mild disabilities encounter one or more adjustment problems when they leave the security provided by schools and face the challenge of making choices and accepting responsibility. It is also safe to say that many secondary educational programs do not prepare students with mild disabilities for the challenges they will face.

REFERENCES

Andron, L., & Strum, M. L. (1973). Is "I do" in the repertoire of the retarded? A study of the functioning of married retarded couples. *Mental Retardation, 11,* 31–34.

Clark, G. R., Kivitz, M. S., & Rosen, M. (1968). *A four year project: Vocational training, rehabilitation and follow up* (Report No. RD1275P). Washington, DC: Department of Health, Education, and Welfare.

Dearden, H. (1952). The efforts of residential institutions to meet the problem of job finding and employment. *American Journal of Mental Deficiency, 80*, 295–307.

Knowles, M. (1978). *The adult learner: A neglected species* (2nd ed.). Houston, TX: Gulf.

Kregel, J., Wehman, P., Seyfarth, J., & Marshall, K. (1986). Community integration of young adults with mental retardation: Transition from school to adulthood. *Education and Training of the Mentally Retarded, 21*, 35–42.

Krishef, C. H., & DiNitto, D. M. (1981). Alcohol abuse among mentally retarded individuals. *Mental Retardation, 19*, 151–155.

McAfee, J. K., & Mann, L., (1982). The prognosis for mildly handicapped students. In T. Miller (Ed.), *The mildly handicapped student* (pp. 461–496). New York: Grune & Stratton.

Olley, J. G., & Ramey, G. (1978). Voter participation of retarded citizens in the 1976 presidential election. *Mental Retardation, 16*, 255–258.

Redding, S. F. (1979). Life adjustment patterns of retarded and non-retarded low functioning students. *Exceptional Children, 45*, 367–368.

Reichard, C. L., Spencer, J., & Spooner, F. (1980). The mentally retarded defendant-offender. *Journal of Special Education, 14*, 113–119.

Scott, A. J., Williams, J. M., Stout, J. K., & Decker, T. W. (1980). *Field investigation of learning disabilities*. Scranton, PA: University of Scranton Press.

Smith, P. (1986, June 28). The execution of Jerome Bowden: Bringing to light something wrong. *The Atlanta Constitution*, p. 36.

Warren, S. A., & Gardner, D. C. (1973). Voting knowledge of the mildly retarded. *Exceptional Children, 40*, 215–216.

Chapter 14

❧ ❧ ❧

Work Support Skills

*P*eople with mild disabilities often encounter difficulties in the workplace because they possess inadequate work support, or work adjustment, skills (see Figure 14–1). These skills are not directly related to the central production or service tasks (e.g., assembling an electrical switch, filing correspondence, cooking french fries) but are essential to the smooth operation of the workplace (e.g., being on time, accepting supervision). According to Salzberg, Agran, and Lignugaris/Kraft (1986), true vocational competence is the product of job responsibility, task production competence, and social competence. This chapter describes the non–task production skills that are necessary for employment in competitive settings. We call these skills *work support skills.*

In general, work support skills are more difficult to teach and learn than central task skills because the discriminative stimuli that should cue the behavior are more subtle (e.g., a look of disapproval from a coworker). The range of acceptable responses is much broader than central task skills. For example, the procedure for cooking french fries in a fast food restaurant may involve 10 or 12 simple and unchanging steps, but an appropriate response to an insult from a coworker could range from ignoring the insult to reporting it to a supervisor. In addition, coworker behavior can take many forms, and an insult may be a reflection of the culture in that workplace. Differentiating between a caustic insult and good-natured kidding may be very difficult for people with mild disabilities. Thus, work support skills often require judgment about the correctness of possible responses.

Also, work support skills often require incidental learning—watching the norms in the workplace and testing one's own behavior against those norms. Many people with mild disabilities have difficulty learning in this manner. Most employers provide on-the-job training in central task skills, but they expect new employees to have adequate work support skills when they are hired. Therefore, professionals involved in transition training must make work support skills a major element of the program. .

1. Transportation/mobility
   a. Using public transportation
   b. Traveling about community
   c. Operating a motor vehicle
2. Job responsibility
   a. Reporting to work on time
   b. Having satisfactory work attendance
   c. Performing tasks in allotted time
   d. Organizing work area
   e. Organizing work time
   f. Complying with supervisor's instructions
   g. Working without constant supervision
   h. Exhibiting initiative
3. Social skills
   a. Communicatiing effectively
   b. Handling teasing
   c. Assisting coworkers
   d. Maintaining personal appearance
   e. Accepting criticism
   f. Giving criticism
   g. Accepting praise
   h. Giving praise
   i. Negotiating conflict
   j. Refraining from aggression
   k. Refraining from bizarre behavior
   l. Resisting peer pressure
   m. Following conversations
   n. Initiating conversations

Figure 14–1
Work support skills

❦ ❦ ❦

RESEARCH ON WORK SUPPORT SKILLS

What have researchers discovered about the adequacy of work support skills in persons with mild disabilities? Many researchers have investigated why people with disabilities fail to obtain or keep jobs. Wilson and Rasch (1982) have found that there is no relationship between educational level and placement success for individuals with a history of emotional disorders. Also, physical strength and other physical attributes were not related to job acquisition. Hill, Wehman, Hill, and Goodall (1986) investigated the reasons why people with mental retardation lost their jobs. For a sample of 165, there were 107 separations over a 6-year span. They found that subjects with higher IQs lost their jobs because of their own actions, whereas those with lower IQs were more often dismissed because of environmental reasons (e.g., economic downturn). The most frequent reason for leaving was attitude problems (e.g., "does not try"); the second most frequent cause was negative social reactions to the employee (e.g., coworkers were uncomfortable with the employee). Actual job skill deficits accounted for less than 15% of the separations, and insubordination, aggressiveness, and aberrant behavior, 10%. Persons with milder disabilities were more likely to be dismissed for poor job responsibility such as poor attendance. Hill et al. suggest that poor work habits in people with mild retardation may be because of their knowledge of disincentives to work (e.g., disability payments). Also, they believe that mildly retarded individuals may not receive specific transition instruction but rather a watered-down academic curriculum. Therefore, they may not have had the opportunity to learn specific work support skills.

Agran, Martin, and Mithaug (1989) contend that people with learning and behavioral problems have difficulty responding to changes in the work environment. They are able to perform adequately under conditions that are very similar to those under which they were trained, but they do not adapt easily to different conditions. Some of this deficiency may result from the lack of opportunity to behave autonomously. Decisions have been made for them; they have not had to make choices and deal with consequences.

In the following sections we will take a closer look at problems encountered by individuals with mild disabilities in the specific areas of transportation/mobility, job responsibility, and social skills. We shall see how deficits in these areas create problems in the workplace, then present suggestions for skills training to overcome these problems.

Transportation/Mobility

Lack of adequate transportation or mobility skills presents an additional barrier for adults with mild disabilities who are seeking to obtain or maintain employment. In 1975 approximately 100,000 people with disabilities were unable to work because of inadequate transportation (D'Alonzo & Drower, 1984). In rural and suburban areas, public transportation is scarce. Individuals with mild disabilities may not learn to drive at the same rate as their nondisabled peers. Finally, learning to use available transportation may be difficult for some individuals with reading disabilities.

Researchers have determined that individuals with mild disabilities do not learn to drive as early or at the same rate as others. Bell (1976) reports that only 10% of a group of mildly retarded persons who had been residents of a state school obtained driver's licenses. Transportation was one of the three problems most frequently encountered in their attempts to live independently, and it was a barrier to employment and normal social lives. Likewise, Kregel, Wehman, Seyfarth, and Marshall (1986) found that only 33% of a group of young mildly retarded adults drove cars and 30% used public transportation. Lack of transportation was cited as one of the two main problems in their lives. In another study, only 50% of a group of adults with learning disabilities had driver's licenses (Fafard & Haubrich, 1981). However, all were able to secure and maintain employment. Getting around in the community was cited as a major problem by a group of adults aged 17 to 37 with learning disabilities (Blalock, 1981). Only 50% of this sample was self-supporting.

Learning to drive is a rite of passage to adulthood for most adolescents, but traditional driver training programs may not be adequate for people with mild disabilities (Kubaiko & Kokaska, 1969). Bologna, Kettering, Mullin, and Strickler (1971) found that persons with mild mental retardation in their study were less likely to participate in driver training programs, but those who did were less likely to have accidents than those who did not—an indication that training is helpful. People with mild disabilities also scored lower on the Pennsylvania driver's manual test. D'Alonzo and Drower (1984) also investigated the adequacy of driver training for people with mild disabilities. They found that few programs were available and that qualified instructors who could teach driving to individuals with mild disabilities were rare. These problems were exacerbated by a lack of research on the needs of driver trainees with mild disabilities and the performance of drivers with mild disabilities.

Wirths and Leonard (1982) have arrived at similar conclusions. They surveyed state supervisors of driver training and found that options for people with learning disabilities were few, especially for those with limited reading skills. They also concluded that many nonreaders avoid the tests and drive illegally even though tests can be administered orally.

People with mild disabilities seem to have worse driving records than others, although the research is sparse and dated (Egan, 1967; Gutshall, Harper, & Burke, 1968). Egan reviewed the driving records of persons with mild retardation and concluded that they had difficulty applying rules and techniques to driving conditions. People with mild disabilities acquire more points against their driving records for violations other than speeding. This also is an indication of problems in judgment. However, considering that driving is a complex set of skills and people with mild disabilities are less likely to enter formal driver training, it is understandable that they would encounter difficulty. Again, the deficiency arises not because of the disability but because of inadequate skill training and insufficient opportunity to practice under controlled conditions.

Job Responsibility

Employers want employees who will complete tasks without constant supervision, comply with instructions without constant reminders, exhibit initiative, come to work on time, and organize their work for efficiency. In short, employers want workers who are responsible.

Many researchers have documented the difficulties that people with mild disabilities have with job responsibility. As in other areas, it is difficult to determine if the problems are because of the impact of the disability, lack of opportunity to learn the skills, or overprotection. Most likely, they are the result of the interaction of all three explanations.

Floor and Rosen (1975) have examined the problem of helplessness in mentally retarded adults and found that mentally retarded people were more likely than people who were not retarded to act helpless when faced with a new or unstructured problem. Blalock (1981) cites the appearance of lack of initiative as a principal work problem for workers with learning disabilities. Obviously, people with mild disabilities have deficiencies in problem-solving skills and look to others to help them. This response pattern may be habitual and is likely reinforced by teachers, parents, and other caregivers who "jump in" too quickly. Such helplessness is definitely a liability at work where employers are looking for workers to take initiative. Indeed, Cheney and Foss (1984) and Foss and Peterson (1981) conclude that working without constant and direct supervision is one of the skills related to maintaining employment for people with mental retardation. Ironically, requesting assistance is also a critical skill. Obviously, the really important element is knowing when to request assistance and keeping requests at a reasonable level. These are skills that require subtle judgments that may not be taught easily.

After reviewing the literature on social competence and adjustment, Walker and Calkins (1986) conclude that compliance with employers' expectations is a determinant of perceived competence. Foss and Peterson (1981) have interviewed job placement personnel and found that complying with instructions is the most important skill related to job tenure. Schumaker, Hazel, Sherman, and Sheldon (1982) have determined that adolescents with learning disabilities experience greater difficulty complying with instructions than students who are not learning disabled.

Punctuality, attendance, and compliance with work schedules are skills employers demand. The research on these skills and people with mild disabilities is mixed. Martin, Rusch, Tines, Brulle, and White (1985) have found that mentally retarded employees have attendance records every bit as good as employees who are not retarded. There were no differences in unexcused absences, excused absences, and sick leave in their study. Nondisabled workers did work more overtime, but they also took more vacation time. Martin et al. conclude that based on this study and a review of others, absenteeism and tardiness are not major problems for mentally retarded workers.

This represents a departure from the conclusion of Wehman (1981), who found that attendance and punctuality are problems that arise because of transportation, lack of time concepts, and lack of knowledge of contingencies. Pothoff (1979) also has determined that tardiness is a chronic and pervasive problem for secondary-level students with learning disabilities and that it has a profound effect on obtaining and maintaining a job. Shields and Heron (1989) have arrived at similar conclusions.

Finally, responsibility on the job includes the ability to organize tasks, complete them in a systematic and efficient way, and make smooth transitions from one task to another without wasting time. Foss and Peterson (1981) have interviewed job placement personnel and conclude that such skills are held in high regard by employers. Researchers have concluded that competence in this area is elusive for many persons with mild disabilities. Adolescents with learning disabilities often exhibit deficient organizational skills (Shields & Heron, 1989). These deficiencies extend to the organization of materials, tasks, and time. They do not know how to plan and adhere to a schedule. Others have made similar observations for people with mental retardation or emotional disorders. Tollefson, Tracy, Johnsen, Farmer, and Buenning (1984) attribute some of this difficulty to an inability to set realistic goals and then organize efforts around these goals. These researchers believe that adolescents with mild disabilities set unrealistic goals for themselves and then blame their disabilities for their failures. They do not see the relationship between their efforts and achievement. Again, this may be the result of a system (educational and social) that does not teach or expect responsible behavior from people with mild disabilities.

Social Skills

Among the most common observations about people with mild disabilities is that they often lack the social skills to get along on the job, deal with coworkers and supervisors, and become integrated into the work force (Rusch, 1979). Importantly, employers perceive social competence as more critical than task competence (Goldstein, 1972). According to Hazel, Schumaker, Sherman, and Sheldon-Wildgen (1983),

> a socially skilled person is able to perceive which situations require the use of social skills, discriminate which social skills would be appropriate to use, and then perform the skills in a manner that increases the likelihood that the behavior will result in positive consequences. (p. 118)

Social competence is a set of skills, and simply mainstreaming people with mild disabilities does little to enhance the skills; rather, direct skill instruction is needed (Gresham, 1982).

Greenspan and Shoultz (1981) have found that persons with mental retardation are four times more likely to lose their jobs for social skill deficiencies than for production deficiencies. These authors characterize these deficiencies as problems of temperament, character, and social awareness. In nearly all of the research they reviewed, interpersonal ineptness is the major difficulty. Often, people with mild disabilities fail to see the probable consequences of their social actions. The relationship between similar social skill deficits and employment problems has also been demonstrated for individuals with learning disabilities (Mathews, Whang, & Fawcett, 1982) and emotional disorders (Hazel et al., 1983).

The social skill problems experienced by people with mild disabilities fall into five areas: (a) acceptance of supervision, (b) interpersonal skills with coworkers, (c) physical appearance, (d) bizarre behavior, and (e) aggressive behavior. Schumaker et al. (1982) have found that youths with learning disabilities do not accept criticism from persons in authority as well as those without learning disabilities. They also have more difficulty following instructions. Hazel et al. (1983) conclude that students with behavioral disorders have similar problems. They are more likely to respond to instruction and criticism by becoming aggressive. Accepting criticism and correction from supervisors appears to be the most common social skills problem exhibited by mentally retarded workers (Cheney & Foss, 1984; Foss & Peterson, 1981). Mentally retarded workers also have difficulty following supervisors' instructions and accepting new supervision.

Interpersonal problems with coworkers are described by many researchers. Foss and Bostwick (1981) and Niziol and DeBlassie (1972) conclude that interpersonal problems are the most common work problem for people with mental retardation. Hazel et al. (1983) have found that deficient interaction skills create numerous difficulties for young people with learning disabilities, mental retardation, or behavioral disorders. These individuals do not know the skills necessary to avoid and negotiate conflict. They are more likely to become unnecessarily aggressive because they do not know how to be realistically assertive and so overreact. They have difficulty giving positive or negative feedback, resisting peer pressure, and even following conversations (Blalock, 1981; Peckham, 1951; Schumaker et al., 1982).

They also have trouble adapting to new social situations. Peckham (1951) and Cheney and Foss (1984) have found that mildly retarded workers are not easily accepted by their coworkers and are often ridiculed. One third of the problems that mentally retarded workers have on the job are related to interpersonal difficulties with colleagues. Cheney and Foss also conclude that mildly retarded workers are often in conflict with their coworkers over the division of tasks. Vaughn (1985) describes some of the specific interpersonal skill deficiencies of adolescents with learning disabilities. They are more likely to make competitive, nasty, and self-statements. They are less able to take the perspective of others or adapt to others in conversations, and they spend less time making eye contact or smiling at others while in conversation.

Absence of bizarre or aberrant behavior is one of the characteristics mentioned most frequently by job placement personnel as related to job tenure (Foss & Peterson, 1981), and, indeed, disruptive behavior (e.g., inappropriate or excessive laughing or talking, loudness, overpersonal conversation) has been identified as a frequent problem (Cheney & Foss, 1984; Peckham, 1951). Researchers have also identified inappropriate or slovenly appearance and dress as problems that lead to work problems and dismissal (Foss & Peterson, 1981; Peckham, 1951; Vaughn, 1985). Finally, job placement personnel report that excessive aggression is a problem that leads to dismissal for a substantial number of persons with mild disabilities (Foss & Peterson, 1981). Hazel et al. (1983) and Freedman, Donahoe, Rosenthal, and Schlundt (1978) conclude that resisting the urge to become aggressive and responding to provocation in a nonaggressive manner were skill sets that had not been learned by a sizeable number of youths with learning disabilities, mental retardation, or behavioral disorders.

❦　❦　❦

IMPROVING WORK SUPPORT SKILLS

Because work support skills present a common problem to people with mild disabilities, practitioners and researchers have developed many interventions. The content and process of those interventions are discussed next.

Davies and Rogers (1985) have reviewed the literature on social skills training and conclude that such training is effective in teaching the motor, verbal, and cognitive social skills. Schloss, Schloss, Wood, and Kiehl (1986) have determined that although such training is effective in teaching the specific skills, training priorities often do not match the real needs of students, generalization from classrooms to other setting and times is not programmed effectively, and there is a lack of research on the impact of the training on adult adjustment in the community.

Social skills maintenance and generalization are especially difficult for people with behavioral disorders (Kiburz, Miller, & Morrow, 1985). Procedures such as self-monitoring have been effective means to promote maintenance. Wacker and Berg (1986) describe a number of procedures to enhance generalization and maintenance of work behavior. They believe that because most training relies on a task-analytic approach, which involves specific responses to specific environmental cues, problems arise when a person with a mild disability changes jobs or the conditions in the job environment change. Trainees must be able to perform across settings, supervisors, and materials and over time. (The procedures designed to promote generalization and adaptability are described in chap. 12.)

As in all other areas of skill training, work support skill training must adhere to a few guidelines:

1. Training should occur in real situations. If simulation is used, generalization to real contexts must be programmed.
2. Training should concentrate on acquisition of specific skills. It should be behavioral, and specific rather than dogmatic and cognitive.
3. Training should be based on the situations that the trainee is likely to encounter in the available work environments. Job descriptions and analyses should be used to determine content.
4. Wherever possible, skills taught should be those that are likely to be maintained by naturally occurring reinforcement. Skills should be transferable from one environment to another. Trainees should be taught how to recognize contextual clues, especially for interpersonal situations.

Let us see how training in the three specific areas we are considering—transportation/mobility, job responsibility, and social skills—can be developed to improve the performance of people with disabilities.

Transportation/Mobility Training

The transportation/mobility skills that should be taught to people with mild disabilities fall into three main categories: (a) operating a motor vehicle, (b) using public transportation, and (c) getting around in the community.

Learning to Drive. Several writers have described driver training programs for adolescents and young adults with mild disabilities. D'Alonzo and Drower (1984) detail a program used in Mesa, Arizona, that includes classroom instruction, simulator training, multimedia instruction, driver's education range training, behind-the-wheel training, and parent involvement. Of 27 participants with mild disabilities who had completed the training at the time of publication of D'Alonzo and Drower's article, 7 obtained their licenses and another 14 received permits. Depending on participants' reading ability and specific disabilities, they were mainstreamed into regular driver's ed classes, enrolled in adapted classroom instruction with mainstreamed road work, or placed in a special adapted classroom and adapted road instruction. McCune (1970) recommends role-playing the written and road test situations with persons who are mildly disabled because research has shown that they are likely to fail the test repeatedly. Match and Miller (1969) have also found that people with mild disabilities are likely to fail the driving test repeatedly, but they also conclude that those who participate in driver's education and finally pass are able to drive without serious violations or accidents.

Most special driver training programs have targeted persons with mild retardation. Wirths and Leonard (1982) describe three programs designed for people with learning disabilities. These programs utilize low-reading-level manuals, and one, in Florida, uses audiotapes. All are successful and can be replicated easily.

Learning to Use Public Transportation and Get Around the Community. Most special programs designed to teach public transportation and community mobility skills have been applied to persons with more severe disabilities. Evidently, students with mild disabilities have been able to learn to use public transportation and mobility skills through generic programs or through everyday experience. Indeed, Martin, Rusch, and Heal (1982) conclude that persons with moderate/severe disabilities require in situ training for travel skills, but people with mild disabilities are often able to learn the skills by simulation. In contrast, Marchetti, McCartney, Drain, Hooper, and Dix (1983) state that real-world training is more effective for teaching the skills needed to get around in the community, primarily pedestrian skills. The real world presents opportunities for learning, generalization, and adaptation that can never be replicated in the classroom. Thus, it is always the preferred environment for such skills training.

Daily living skills curricula such as *Learning Skills for Daily Living* (1978) and Brolin's (1989) *Life-centered Career Education* provide skill clusters and methods of instruction for skills such as reading a bus schedule. These curricula should be consulted by the reader who wishes to learn more about mobility instruction.

Job Responsibility Training

Teaching job responsibility skills to people with mild disabilities is often difficult, but researchers and practitioners have succeeded in teaching punctuality and attendance skills, goal-setting and initiative skills that help people stay on task and look busy, and self-management skills in which people with mild disabilities learn to be responsible for their own behavior.

Peck, Fasbender, Cooke, and Apolloni (1982) taught promptness skills to three mildly retarded adolescents who were tardy more than 50% of the time. The instruction involved a three-step process. First, students were taught the desired behavior and the reason for the behavior. Then they were taught the steps to self-evaluation. Finally, they received praise if their self-evaluations were correct. Promptness improved to near 100%. Pothoff (1979) used a similar procedure to reduce the tardiness of adolescents with learning disabilities. However, in this case, self-evaluation was replaced by teacher-managed reinforcement. It is unlikely that such a procedure would generalize to the work environment without specific generalization intervention.

Shields and Heron (1989) present strategies to teach people with learning disabilities how to organize their materials, tasks, and time. The strategies include color-coded charts to keep track of multiple tasks, timers to manage the time allotted to various tasks, performance feedback, and self-management training so that students can apply the skills to other situations and times and succeed without constant supervision. Sowers, Rusch, Connis, and Cummings (1980) describe a procedure for work time management that was successfully applied to people with moderate retardation and might be useful for some people with mild disabilities who have limited time-telling skills or who do not follow schedules well. Sowers et al. used cards with clock faces set at times for breaks, tasks, and so forth, that the subject could carry and match with times on clocks at the workplace. After this procedure was applied, subjects exhibited better than 90% on-time behavior.

Self-management skills have been used successfully with persons with mild disabilities who have emotional disorders, mental retardation, or learning disabilities. If adolescents and young adults with mild disabilities learn the skills of self-management and apply them to situations in the workplace, employers are likely to perceive them as more independent and more competent—that is, more responsible. Clark and McKenzie (1989) taught students with behavioral disorders how to evaluate their own behavior and rule following. Students attempted to match their behaviors to posted rules and expectations and make judgments about their performance. In addition to a huge increase in production and desirable behavior, the procedure was associated with generalized improvements in other environments. Birkimer and Brown (1979) used a similar procedure and conclude that improvements were greater under self-management than under teacher management. In addition, behavior changes were maintained. Peck et al. (1982) demonstrated that self-evaluation can be used to help adolescents with mild disabilities show initiative in their work. Prior to the intervention, the subjects of this study did not initiate new activities when they completed a task. After self-management training, initiation rose to 80%.

Montague (1987) and Hughes, Ruhl, and Peterson (1988) provide comprehensive reviews of the methodology of self-management, which Hughes et al. define as "the ability to regulate ones own behavior" (p. 70). Self-management can involve *self-instruction,* in which an individual gives him- or herself instructions for a task. This procedure involves (a) devising a task analysis, (b) composing a set of instructions based on the task analysis, (c) modeling self-instructions, (d) role-playing, (e) receiving feedback from an observer, and (f) practicing in a natural setting. *Self-questioning* includes a series of queries to guide task completion (e.g., After I sweep the floor what do I do next?). *Self-monitoring* involves self-observation and self-assessment (e.g., Did I maintain eye contact during the interview? Did I complete my job in the fastest time possible?). *Self-reinforcement* entails (a) setting goals (e.g., producing the company's product at a rate equal to the average worker's production), (b) deciding how to reinforce oneself (e.g., I'll treat myself to a movie), and (c) evaluating performance.

Goal setting is part of the procedure for self-reinforcement. Tollefson et al. (1984) have found that people with mild disabilities can be taught to set and achieve realistic goals and that when they do, they learn to accept responsibility for the outcomes. Lyman (1984) concludes that students with behavioral disorders who set their own goals are more likely to achieve them. Self-management strategies have also been applied to interpersonal skills (Kiburz et al., 1985; Schloss, 1987).

Certainly employers want workers with initiative, who can assume some measure of autonomy, and who do not require constant supervision. Self-management strategies, goal setting, and time and organizational skills can help persons with mild disabilities become more autonomous workers and students.

Social Skills Training

Probably no other area of transition has received as much attention during the past decade as social skills training. This is the obvious result of the research that has demonstrated over and over that people with mild disabilities exhibit ineffective social skills. In this section, we will describe which and how social skills have been taught.

One very important set of social skills revolves around supervision. Good workers accept supervision and changes in supervision. The specific social skills related to supervision that have been taught to persons with mild disabilities include (a) complying with instructions, (b) asking a supervisor for assistance, (c) responding to criticism and suggestions, (d) getting information about a task, (e) communicating feelings to supervisor, and (f) conversing with a supervisor (Bates, 1980; Bullis & Foss, 1986; Chadsey-Rusch, 1985; Hazel et al., 1981, 1983; Warrenfeltz et al., 1981; Weisgerber & Rubin, 1985; Whang, Fawcett, & Mathews, 1984).

Interpersonal skills, especially those involving coworkers, comprise the second set of important social skills. These skills are (a) offering to help coworkers, (b) responding to criticism and suggestions, (c) conversing, (d) expressing feelings, (e) developing close relationships, (f) contributing to the group, (g) respecting the rights of others, (h) showing honesty and fairness, (i) negotiating conflict, (j) giving and receiving positive feedback, (k) giving and receiving negative feedback, (l) resisting peer pressure, (m) accepting assistance, and (n) handling teasing and provocation (Bates, 1980; Bullis & Foss, 1986; Chadsey-Rusch, 1985; Hazel et al., 1981; Weisgerber & Rubin, 1985).

Other social skills that have received considerable attention include (a) reducing aggression (Lee, Hallberg, & Hassard, 1979), (b) improving assertiveness (Gentile & Jenkins, 1980), (c) reducing inappropriate or bizarre behaviors (Gentile & Jenkins, 1980), and (d) improving personal appearance.

Because of the interdependence and generalizability of many social skills, we will not attempt to describe interventions for each of the skills or skill clusters just mentioned. (Such an effort would require hundreds of pages!) Instead, we will describe some of the comprehensive social skills programs and some of the specifically targeted interventions. Many of the procedures are adaptable for a wide range of skills.

Chadsey-Rusch (1985) states that a social skills training program should include three types of social skills: (a) social decoding skills—What's going on? (b) social decision skills—What are my choices? and (c) social performance skills—What is the best choice? Similarly, Weisgerber and Rubin (1985) describe a social skills training approach that involves explanation of the concept, steps to the skill, practice responses, and follow-up exercises. Role playing is used extensively, and understanding of the rationale behind the skill acquisition is emphasized.

Hazel et al. (1983) taught social skills to court-adjudicated adolescents and views social skills as an appropriate means to obtain rewards. Social competence will determine how well a person will be treated by others. Training involved eight stages: (a) explaining the skill to be learned, (b) explaining the reason for the skill, (c) describing example situations, (d) enumerating the behavioral steps, (e) modeling, (f) using verbal rehearsal, (g) using behavioral rehearsal, and (h) giving home assignments. The program resulted in lower recidivism after 1 year, although a critical element—in situ training—appears to be missing.

Warrenfeltz et al. (1982) have found that social skills training that is didactic results in changes in relationships with supervisors but no change in interpersonal behavior. After adding role playing and self-monitoring, generalized improvements in social skills were recorded in their study. Targeted skills included response to critical feedback and conversational initiatives. Bates (1980) concludes that classroom-based interpersonal skills training that involves role playing, feedback, and reinforcement does not result in generalization to natural settings. Long and Sherer (1984) have found that structured social skills training is more effective than discussion in teaching social skills to adolescents with more frequent offenses. Thus, in situ training that includes specific skill development and generalization training has been established as the cornerstone of effective social skills training.

Whang et al. (1984) were successful in teaching social skills to two adolescents with learning disabilities. They used role playing and on-the-job training that resulted in 100% improvements in accepting criticism, providing criticism, explaining a problem, accepting an instruction, giving a compliment, and accepting a compliment. Improvements were noted in both classroom and job situations.

Rusch and Menchetti (1981) taught a mentally retarded kitchen worker appropriate responses to requests for help from coworkers. The subject was taught to practice the skills, and then natural consequences were applied if he failed to perform appropriately (i.e., he was suspended from his job). Application of natural consequences would probably not have been successful without providing the training in appropriate responses.

Bullis and Foss (1986) have developed the "Test of Interpersonal Competence for Employment" based on information provided by production supervisors and mentally retarded trainees in vocational programs. They were able to construct 246 discrete problem situations that could form the basis of training.

Some researchers are concerned that skills training is effective for teaching individuals responses to specific situations but ineffective for teaching adaptability. Mithaug, Martin, and Agran (1987) have determined that adaptability instruction is a major component of transitional training. Adaptability instruction revolves around problem-solving skills to apply to a variety of situations. Mithaug et al. advocate a six-stage procedure:

1. Identify the problem.
2. Define alternate solutions.
3. Determine action.
4. Take action.
5. Evaluate consequences.
6. Determine the need for adjustment.

This model promotes decision making, independent performance, self-evaluation, and adjustment. Similarly, Sarason and Sarason (1981) used modeling and role playing to teach individuals with behavioral disorders how to think of more adaptive solutions. These students were able to perform more effectively in job interviews, and they had fewer on-the-job behavioral problems. Friedman, Quick, Mayo, and Palmer (1983) taught broad problem-solving skills to emotionally disturbed adolescents. Skills were taught in the classroom and practiced in real situations throughout the day. Major decreases in interpersonal conflict resulted, and long-term follow-up revealed that fewer psychiatric placements and less delinquency resulted from the program, which taught fair fighting and negotiation.

Problem-solving approaches have also been used by Foss, Auty, and Irvin (1989), Goldstein (1988), and Vaughn, Ridley, and Cox (1983). Foss et al. conducted a 2-year study to compare the effectiveness of four methods to teach employment-related social skills to adolescents with mild retardation. They determined that all four methods were successful but that problem solving was more effective than either rehearsal or teacher modeling. Stowitschek and

Salzberg (1987) have used a unique procedure to teach adaptability. First, they taught general social skills, then the application of those skills to five different jobs.

❧ ❧ ❧

SUMMARY

Vernon, Hazel, and Schumaker (1988) discuss six considerations for social skills training that can be applied to all training in work support skills:

1. Does the curriculum promote social competence?
2. Does the curriculum accommodate the learning characteristics of students with disabilities?
3. Does the curriculum target the social skill deficits of students with disabilities?
4. Does the curriculum provide training in situations as well as skills?
5. Does the curriculum incorporate instructional methodology found effective with students with disabilities?
6. Does the curriculum include a method for measuring student progress? (pp. 1–2)

To these we would add a few more:

7. Is it normalizing?
8. Does it promote generalization and adaptability?
9. Does it involve in situ training?

There is no doubt that work support skills will occupy a position of importance in transitional training. The only questions that remain are how effective can such training become, and how can it be made as applicable to real-life situations as possible?

REFERENCES

Agran, M., Martin, J. E., & Mithaug, D. E. (1989). Achieving transition through adaptability instruction. *Teaching Exceptional Children, 21*(2), 4–7.

Bates, P. (1980). The effectiveness of interpersonal skills training on the social skill acquisition of moderately and mildly retarded adults. *Journal of Applied Behavior Analysis, 13*, 237–248.

Bell, N. J. (1976). IQ as a factor in community lifestyle of previously institutionalized retardates. *Mental Retardation, 14*, 29–33.

Birkimer, J. C., & Brown, J. H. (1979). The effects of student self control on the reduction of children's problem behaviors. *Behavioral Disorders, 4*, 131–136.

Blalock, J. W. (1981). Persistent problems of young adults with learning disabilities. In W. M. Cruickshank and A. A. Silver (Eds.), *Bridges to tomorrow: The best of ACLD* (Vol. 2, pp. 35–55). Syracuse, NY: Syracuse University Press.

Bologna, J. F., Kettering, W. R., Mullin, R. C., & Strickler, D. J. (1971). *The measurement and comparison of variables related to driver and highway safety between educable mentally retarded and normal high school students in Pennsylvania.* Millersville, PA: Millersville State College.

Brolin, D. (1989). *Life-centered career education: A competency-based approach*. 3rd ed. Reston, VA: Council for Exceptional Children.

Bullis, M., & Foss, G. (1986). Assessing the employment related interpersonal competence of mildly retarded workers. *American Journal of Mental Deficiency, 91*, 43–50.

Chadsey-Rusch, J. (1985). Identifying and teaching valued social behaviors. In F. R. Rusch (Ed.), *Competitive employment issues and strategies* (pp. 273–287). Baltimore, MD: Brookes.

Cheney, D., & Foss, G. (1984). An examination of the social behavior of mentally retarded workers. *Education and Training of the Mentally Retarded, 19*, 216–221.

Clark, L. A., & McKenzie, H. S. (1989). Effects of self-evaluation training of seriously emotionally disturbed children on the generalization of their classroom rule following and work behaviors across settings and teachers. *Behavioral Disorders, 14*(2), 89–98.

D'Alonzo, B. J., & Drower, I. S. (1984). Driver education for the mildly handicapped adolescent. *Teaching Exceptional Children, 19*, 10–17.

Davies, R. R., & Rogers, E. S. (1985). Social skills training with persons who are mentally retarded. *Mental Retardation, 23*, 186–196.

Egan, R. (1967). Should the educable mentally retarded receive driver education? *Exceptional Children, 33*, 323.

Fafard, M., & Haubrich, P. A. (1981). Vocational and social development of learning disabled young adults: A follow up study. *Learning Disabilities Quarterly, 4*, 122–130.

Floor, L., & Rosen, M. (1975). Investigating the phenomenon of helplessness in mentally retarded adults. *American Journal of Mental Deficiency, 79*, 565–572.

Foss, G., Auty, W. P., & Irvin, L. K. (1989). A comparative evaluation of modeling, problem-solving, and behavior rehearsal for teaching employment-related interpersonal skills to secondary students with mental retardation. *Education and Training of the Mentally Retarded, 24*, 17–27.

Foss, G., & Bostwick, P. (1981). Problems of mentally retarded adults: A study of rehabilitation service consumers and providers. *Rehabilitation Counseling Bulletin, 25*, 66–73.

Foss, G., & Peterson, S. L. (1981). Social-interpersonal skills relevant to job tenure for mentally retarded adults. *Mental Retardation, 19*(3), 103–106.

Freedman, B. J., Donahoe, C. P., Jr., Rosenthal, L., & Schlundt, D. G. (1978). A social-behavioral analysis of skill deficits in delinquent and nondelinquent adolescent boys. *Journal of Consulting and Clinical Psychology, 46*(6), 1448–1462.

Friedman, R. M., Quick, J., Mayo, J., & Palmer, J. (1983). Social skills training with adolescents: A review. In C. W. LeCroy (Ed.), *Social skills training for children and youth* (pp. 139–152). New York: Haworth.

Gentile, C., & Jenkins, J. O. (1980). Assertive training with mildly mentally retarded persons. *Mental Retardation, 18*, 315–317.

Goldstein, A. P. (1988). *The Prepare Curriculum: Teaching prosocial competencies*. Champaign, IL: Research Press.

Goldstein, H. (1972). Construction of a social learning curriculum. In E. L. Meyen, G. A. Vergason, & R. J. Whelan (Eds.), *Strategies for teaching exceptional children* (pp. 102–132). Denver: Love.

Greenspan, S., & Shoultz, B. (1981). Why mentally retarded adults lose their jobs: Social competence as a factor in work adjustment. *Applied Research in Mental Retardation, 2*, 23–38.

Gresham, F. M. (1982). Misguided mainstreaming: The case for social skills training with handicapped children. *Exceptional Children, 49,* 422–433.

Gutshall, R. W., Harper, C., & Burke, D. (1968). An exploratory study of the interrelations among driving ability, driving exposure and sociometric status of low, average and high intelligence males. *Exceptional Children, 35,* 43–45.

Hazel, J. S., Schumaker, J. B., Sherman, J. A., & Sheldon-Wildgen, J. (1981). *Asset: A social skills program for adolescents.* Champaign, IL: Research Press.

Hazel, J. S., Schumaker, J. B., Sherman, J. A., & Sheldon-Wildgen, J. (1983). Social skills training with court-adjudicated youths. In C. W. Lecroy (Ed.), *Social skills training for children and youth* (pp. 117–137). New York: Haworth.

Hill, J. W., Wehman, P., Hill, M., & Goodall, P. (1986). Differential reasons for job separation of previously employed persons with mental retardation. *Mental Retardation, 24,* 347–351.

Hughes, C. A., Ruhl, K. L., & Peterson, S. K. (1988). Teaching self management skills. *Teaching Exceptional Children, 20*(2), 70–72.

Kiburz, C. S., Miller, S. R., & Morrow, L. W. (1985). Structured learning using self monitoring to promote maintenance and generalization of social skills across settings for a behaviorally disordered adolescent. *Behavioral Disorders, 10,* 47–55.

Kregel, J., Wehman, P., Seyfarth, J., & Marshall, K. (1986). Community integration of young adults with mental retardation: Transition from school to adulthood. *Education and Training of the Mentally Retarded, 21,* 35–42.

Kubaiko, J. H., & Kokaska, C. J. (1969). Driver education for the educable mentally retarded: Is our instruction adequate? *Training School Bulletin, 66,* 111–114.

Learning skills for daily living. (1978). Baltimore: Hampden.

Lee, D. Y., Hallberg, E. T., & Hassard, H. (1979). Effects of assertion training on aggressive behavior of adolescents. *Journal of Counseling Psychology, 26,* 459–461.

Long, S. J., & Sherer, M. (1984). Social skills training with juvenile offenders. *Child & Family Behavior Therapy, 6*(4), 1–11.

Lyman, R. D. (1984). The effect of private and public goal setting on the classroom on-task behavior of emotionally disturbed children. *Behavior Therapy, 15,* 395–402.

Marchetti, A. G., McCartney, J. R., Drain, S., Hooper, M., & Dix, J. (1983). Pedestrian skills training for mentally retarded adults: Comparison of training in two settings. *Mental Retardation, 21,* 107–110.

Martin, J. E., Rusch, F. R., & Heal, L. W. (1982). Teaching community survival skills to mentally retarded adults: A review and analysis. *Journal of Special Education, 16*(3), 243–267.

Martin, J. E., Rusch, F. R., Tines, J. J., Brulle, A. R., & White, D. M. (1985). Work attendance in competitive employment: Comparison between employees who are not handicapped and those who are mentally retarded. *Mental Retardation, 22,* 142–147.

Match, E., & Miller, A. W. (1969). Two driver education programs for the physically and mentally handicapped. *Exceptional Children, 35,* 563–564.

Mathews, R. M., Whang, P. L., & Fawcett, S. B. (1982). Behavioral assessment of occupational skills in learning disabled adolescents. *Journal of Learning Disabilities, 15,* 38–41.

McCune, J. W. (1970). Including driver education in the special class curriculum. *Teaching Exceptional Children, 13,* 106–112.

Mithaug, D. E., Martin, J. E., & Agran, M. (1987). Adaptability instruction: The goal of transition programming. *Exceptional Children, 53*, 500–505.

Montague, M. (1987). Self management strategies for job success. *Teaching Exceptional Children, 19*(2), 74–76.

Niziol, U. M., & DeBlassie, R. R. (1972). Work adjustment and the educable mentally retarded adolescent. *Journal of Employment Counseling, 9*,150–167.

Peck, C. A., Fasbender, T. B., Cooke, T. P., & Apolloni, T. (1982). Teaching prevocational skills to EMR adolescents. *Adolescence, 17*, 872–880.

Peckham, R. A. (1951). Problems in job adjustment of the mentally retarded. *American Journal of Mental Deficiency, 56*, 448–453.

Pothoff, J. (1979). Late again? Three techniques to reduce tardiness in secondary level learning handicapped students. *Teaching Exceptional Children, 11*(4) 146–148.

Rusch, F. (1979). Toward the validation of social vocational survival skills. *Mental Retardation, 17*, 143–144.

Rusch, F., & Menchetti, B. M. (1981). Increasing compliant work behaviors in a non-sheltered work setting. *Mental Retardation, 19*, 107–111.

Salzberg, C. L., Agran, M., & Lignugaris/Kraft, B. (1986). Behaviors that contribute to entry-level employment: A profile of five jobs. *Applied Research in Mental Retardation, 7*, 299–314.

Sarason, I. G., & Sarason, B. R. (1981). Teaching cognitive and social skills to high school students. *Journal of Consulting and Clinical Psychology, 49*, 908–918.

Schloss, P. J. (1987). Self management strategies for adolescents entering the work force. *Teaching Exceptional Children, 19*, 39–43.

Schloss, P. J., Schloss, C. N., Wood, C. E., & Kiehl, W. S. (1986). A critical review of social skills research with behaviorally disordered students. *Behavior Disorders, 12*, 1–14.

Schumaker, J. B., Hazel, J. S., Sherman, J. A., & Sheldon, J. (1982). Social skill performance of learning disabled, non–learning disabled and delinquent adolescents. *Learning Disabilities Quarterly, 5*, 388–397.

Shields, J. M., & Heron, T. E. (1989). Teaching organizational skills to students with learning disabilities. *Teaching Exceptional Children, 21*(2), 8–13.

Sowers, J., Rusch, F. R., Connis, R. T., & Cummings, L. E. (1980). Teaching mentally retarded adults to time manage in a vocational setting. *Journal of Applied Behavior Analysis, 13*, 119–128.

Stowitschek, J., & Salzberg, C. (1987). *Job success for handicapped youth: A social protocol curriculum*. Reston, VA: Council for Exceptional Children.

Tollefson, N., Tracy, D. B., Johnsen, E. P., Farmer, A. W., & Buenning, M. (1984). Goal setting and personal responsibility training for LD adolescents. *Psychology in the Schools, 21*, 224–233.

Vaughn, S. (1985). Why teach social skills to learning disabled students? *Journal of Learning Disabilities, 18*, 588–591.

Vaughn, S. R., Ridley, C. A., & Cox, J. (1983). Evaluating the efficacy of an interpersonal skills training program with children who are mentally retarded. *Education and Training of the Mentally Retarded, 18*, 191–196.

Vernon, S., Hazel, S., & Schumaker, J. (1988). Now that the door is open: Social skills instruction in the classroom. *PRISE Reporter, 20*, 1–2.

Wacker, D. P., & Berg, W. K. (1986). Generalizing and maintaining work behavior. In F. R. Rusch (Ed.), *Competitive employment issues and strategies* (pp. 129–140). Baltimore: Brookes.

Walker, H. M., & Calkins, C. F. (1986). The role of social competence in the community adjustment of persons with developmental disabilities: Processes and outcomes. *Remedial and Special Education, 7*(6), 46–53.

Warrenfeltz, R. B., Kelly, W. J., Salzberg, C. L., Beegle, C. P., Levy, S. M., Adams, T. A., & Crouse, T. R. (1981). Social skills training of behavior disordered adolescents with self-monitoring to promote generalization to a vocational setting. *Behavioral Disorders, 7*(1), 18–27.

Wehman, P. (1981). *Competitive employment: New horizons for severely disabled individuals.* Baltimore: Brookes.

Weisgerber, R. A., & Rubin, D. (1985). *Social solutions for school-to-work transition.* Palo Alto, CA: American Institutes for Research in the Behavioral Sciences.

Whang, P. L., Fawcett, S. B., & Mathews, R. M. (1984). Teaching job-related social skills to learning disabled adolescents. *Analysis and Intervention in Developmental Disabilities, 4*(1), 29–38.

Wilson, R. J., & Rasch, J. D. (1982). The relationship of job characteristics to successful placements for psychiatrically handicapped individuals. *Journal of Applied Rehabilitation Counseling, 13*(2), 30–33.

Wirths, C. G., & Leonard, S. (1982). Driver education and the learning disabled. *Journal of Learning Disabilities, 15*, 236–237.

Chapter 15

❧ ❧ ❧

Independent Living Skills

S ucceeding as an adult requires many skills in addition to those needed to work, and numerous researchers have concluded that people with mild disabilities experience considerable difficulty when they face the demands of independent living. At least one researcher (Bell, 1976) believes that increasing complexity in society may make it more difficult for people with disabilities to live independently. In this chapter, we will describe what researchers have uncovered regarding the problems that independent living presents to people with mild disabilities in (a) personal management, (b) housing and household maintenance, (c) health maintenance, (d) sexuality and family living, (e) friendships, and (f) leisure and recreation. The chapter will conclude with a discussion of interventions designed to improve functioning in independent living skills.

❧ ❧ ❧

THE INDEPENDENT LIVING STATUS OF ADULTS WITH MILD DISABILITIES

Scores of researchers have investigated how well people with disabilities adjust to the demands of adult life. These same researchers have attempted to identify important variables in the subjects' personalities, intellects, families, and training that are associated with independent living success. After more than 40 years of work, many questions remain, but there are some recurring patterns in the literature. In some cases, the literature is difficult to interpret because the subjects of the study represent the spectrum of disability from mild to profound. In other cases, the subjects are inadequately described.

Finally, we must recognize that a broad array of skills, abilities, and backgrounds are evident among people with mild disabilities. For example, some young adults with mild disabilities graduate from high school and go to college. For them this may be their first adventure in independent living. Other people with mild disabilities may experience independent living for the first time when they leave a residential facility. This latter point is important to emphasize because although we associate deinstitutionalization with people with severe disabilities, the literature shows that many of the people leaving residential programs are mildly retarded, emotionally disturbed, or even learning disabled.

Several researchers have provided a general view of the adult independent living adjustment of people with mild disabilities. Sutter, Mayeda, Call, Yenagi, and Yee (1980) conclude that successful adjustment is inversely related to the frequency and severity of maladaptive behavior. Mildly retarded adults in their study who were less successful had lower levels of self-sufficiency and social responsibility. Ironically, people whose retardation was the least severe often exhibited greater difficulty. These researchers and others who have encountered the same phenomenon believe that this may be the result of higher expectations and exposure to greater risk without support.

Other researchers found that independent living success is related to the atmosphere in the individual's childhood home (Zetlin, Turner, & Wenik, 1987). Individuals with mild disabilities who adjust well to the demands of independence come from homes in which parents were supportive and developed the individual's self-confidence. They allowed the individual to take risks and assume responsibility. Poorly adjusted individuals with mild disabilities come from homes that reinforced dependence and compliance. Seltzer (1981) supports these findings and concludes that young adults with mild disabilities are more likely to learn the skills needed for independent living if they grew up in homes that were normalized, in which they were required to assume increasing responsibility and were granted greater autonomy, and in which expectations were clearly communicated. A. C. Campbell (1971) also has found that lack of independent living skills is related to lack of opportunity to learn and overprotection in adolescence.

Schalock, Harper, and Genung (1981) and Hull and Thompson (1980) have reviewed the progress of large samples of individuals with disabilities. Unfortunately, the samples included people with severe disabilities as well as those with mild ones. In spite of this, their findings are useful. They conclude that IQ and severity of behavioral maladaptation are related to the degree of independence shown and that age-appropriate training, culturally normative environments, and long-term preindependence training to acquire autonomy are all related to becoming a successful, independent adult. Furthermore, Shalock et al. conclude that the degree of independence achieved is related to language skills. This is not surprising, as a person who can communicate well will obviously succeed better in a world of interdependence.

Personal Management

Individuals who want to live independently must be able to care for their personal needs. They must be able to handle money and bank accounts, shop for food and clothing, purchase insurance, use credit, and care for clothing. Researchers have concluded that people with mild disabilities often exhibit deficits in personal management. These deficits then make it more difficult for the individual to attend to and succeed in the more complex demands of independence.

For example, Schalock, Harper, and Carver (1981) determined that personal maintenance was related to the independent living success of 69 adults with an average IQ of 66. Competence in clothing care and food preparation were two specific areas related to the ability to adjust to independence. Kregel, Wehman, Seyfarth, and Marshall (1986) reviewed the independent living status of 183 mildly retarded young adults. They conclude that only 11% lived independently, although 98% were independent in basic self-care (dressing, feeding, etc.), 87% could prepare basic meals, 54% could take care of laundry, 34% could mend clothes, 37% used banks, 95% made their own purchases, 77% could make change, 24% could write checks, 21% managed savings, and 16% balanced their own checkbooks. Ewing and Williams (1981) found that 11 mildly retarded adults had very poor shopping skills. When told to purchase eight items, the subjects rarely examined all of the brands available. They tended to purchase the first item seen or the one with the most prominent display. Most chose an item because of its packaging appearance. Even when the subjects indicated that they had searched for the cheapest item, it often was not. McGee (1982) discovered that 15- to 18-year-old students with learning disabilities were severely deficient in banking skills. None of the 12 subjects were able to complete a deposit/withdrawal slip. Finally, Thompson, Broam, and Fuqua (1982) determined that a group of mildly to moderately retarded adolescents and young adults had mastered few of the steps needed to successfully wash and dry clothing at a public laundromat.

Obviously the research described in the preceding paragraph is not a thorough review of personal management skills. There are dozens of studies that describe the deficiencies of people with mild disabilities in this area. The purpose of this brief discussion is to show that these skills must be taught and to spotlight the error in assuming that people with mild disabilities will acquire these skills on their own. The literature seems to indicate that the deficiencies exist not because of any learning problem but because of a lack of opportunity to learn resulting from overprotection or incomplete curricula.

Housing and Household Maintenance

Obtaining and maintaining a household are major reflections of independence, yet very little research has been done in these areas. Hull and Thompson (1980) have found that a culturally normative residence is important to the adult adaptation of mildly retarded people. That is, it is important for mildly retarded individuals to live in residences that look like those of their nondisabled peers. Hull and Thompson also conclude that IQ is related to the efficiency with which a household is maintained (e.g., cleanliness, repair, and organization).

Salend, Michael, Veraja, and Noto (1983) and Salend and Giek (1987) have investigated how landlords reacted to mentally retarded tenants. They found that landlords received little help from transition agencies after the rental was obtained. Furthermore, 82% said they would rent to people with retardation, and those landlords with prior experience were more likely to be favorable.

Five years after independent living placements, 80% of a group of 69 young adults, most of whom were mildly retarded, were still living in their original housing (Schalock, Harper, & Carver, 1981). Many of those who had been unsuccessful had inadequately maintained their households.

Maintenance of a household has been investigated by Kregel et al. (1986), who conclude that young adults with mild retardation in their sample were somewhat deficient in this area as only 85% routinely cleaned their own rooms. Only 67% did household chores. Perhaps this is an example of lack of opportunity having a negative effect on learning.

Health Maintenance

Numerous researchers have concluded that individuals with mild disabilities have more health problems than nondisabled people. For example, Fox and Rotatori (1982) have found that the prevalence of obesity is higher among people with mild retardation, and Scott, Williams, Stout, and Decker (1980) have determined that 26% of people with learning disorders have significant medical problems.

Even if health problems were not more prevalent among people with mild disabilities, the impact would be more severe because these individuals have less capacity for dealing with health problems. Eagle (1967) found that health problems accounted for a quarter of the cases of reinstitutionalization for a group that contained a significant proportion of people with mild disabilities. Health problems among people with mild disabilities are exacerbated by lack of knowledge, poor hygiene, inadequate access to medical care, and lower support from medical insurance.

What are some of the specific health problems encountered by individuals with mild disabilities, and how do those problems affect transition? Miller (1965) found that the mortality rate for people with mild retardation was twice that of people who were not retarded. Much of the difference was associated with a high rate of accidental death. This suggests deficiencies in training—for example, recognizing danger and responding to emergencies. Another finding that implies weaknesses in training is that people with mild mental retardation are less physically fit than able individuals (J. Campbell, 1973). Aninger, Growick, and Bolinsky (1979) followed 18 retarded adults through independent transitional training. The median IQ of this group was 66. Overeating was a major problem for seven of the subjects, and poor nutrition was the third most common problem experienced in trying to adapt to independent living.

Other problems that are mentioned in the literature are depression (Balow & Bloomquist, 1965; Sovner, Hurley, DesNoyes, & LaBue, 1982) and alcohol and drug abuse (Edgerton, 1986; Krishef & DiNitto, 1981; Robins,

1966; White, Schumaker, Warner, Alley, & Deshler, 1980). Substance abuse is especially problematic for people with mild disabilities, not because it is more prevalent but because treatment programs are ill equipped to deal with the interaction of the disability and the abuse.

Most of the literature indicates that people with mild disabilities abuse alcohol and drugs at a rate no higher than the general population. Edgerton (1986) examined alcohol and drug use among mentally retarded adults in a variety of community settings. He found that they used alcohol and drugs less often than their parents, siblings, spouses, and friends. Subjects were also less likely to engage in alcohol-related crime. Three reasons are advanced for the lower use: (a) expense—subjects had low incomes and could not afford to purchase alcohol and drugs, (b) negative role models—subjects had seen the damaging effects of substance abuse on others, and (c) socialization—subjects had been repeatedly warned by parents about the dangers.

Krishef and DiNitto (1981) present a slightly less positive view of alcohol abuse among mentally retarded individuals. They conclude that alcohol abuse is related to job absenteeism for a significant number of mildly retarded adults as well as to arrest frequency. Similarly, Robins (1966) reports that excessive drinking was a major problem for 48% of a group of individuals who had experienced emotional disorders as children. Finally, White et al. (1980) conclude that young adults with learning disabilities use alcohol and drugs at a rate equal to their peers who are not learning disabled.

Sexuality and Family Living

Young adults and adolescents with mild disabilities face many challenges, not the least of which is learning to accept sexual and family responsibilities. Many researchers have determined that people with mild disabilities are often unprepared to deal with these aspects of their lives because of lack of training and overprotection, yet sex and marriage are consistently listed among the top five concerns of young adults with mild disabilities (Aninger et al., 1979; Bell, 1976). Most of the research in this area has been conducted with people who are mildly retarded. There is virtually no research on sexuality and people with learning disabilities and very little on people with emotional disorders.

Hall and Morris (1976) found that fewer than half of a group of mildly retarded adolescents were knowledgeable about venereal diseases and sterilization, a finding that is supported by Hall, Morris, and Barker (1973). Kalma (1976) encountered similar ignorance among emotionally disturbed adolescents. Their responses often expressed fear, resentment, and anger about sexuality. They tended to personalize biological discussions. Brantlinger (1985) examined the sexual information and attitudes maintained by mildly retarded adolescents. None were well informed. Many held the opinion that talking about sex was wrong. Nearly one third had almost no correct knowledge about human sexuality. They were confused about birth control, puberty, abortion, body parts, and rape. More than three fourths expressed a desire to marry, and most wanted children although they did not understand the reproductive process. They wanted more information on sexuality in spite of the fact that they had received little information from their parents. Hall et al. conclude that parents provided poor estimates of the sexual knowledge of their mildly retarded adolescent offspring. Perhaps the most alarming finding was that 62% of the adolescents supported premarital sex even in the face of their ignorance (Brantlinger, 1985). This liberal attitude was also encountered by Hall et al. (1973).

Russell and Hardin (1980) state that limited knowledge of sexuality makes people with disabilities more likely objects of sexual exploitation. These researchers have found that mentally retarded adolescents have great difficulty talking to their parents about sex, and their parents make little effort to give them sexual instruction despite their anxiety over the danger. Interestingly, Gebhard (1974) concludes that mentally retarded adults derive most of their sexual knowledge from their peers, a very unreliable source. This is especially troublesome when considered in the light of Bell's (1976) findings that contacts with the opposite sex are usually related to the amount of independence allowed to the individual at work and in living arrangements. Therefore, there is usually little opportunity to practice dating skills until the person leaves the protection of family and school.

Most mentally retarded adults express a desire for sexual contact when they begin to live independent lives (Heshusius, 1982). They also express a fear of contact, which is the result of sexual ignorance and familial and societal attitudes that would attempt to keep the sexual relations of mentally retarded individuals at a preadolescent level. The sexuality of adolescents and young adults with mild disabilities makes parents, professionals, and the public uncomfortable.

People with mild disabilities do marry. How well do these marriages work? Gebhard (1974) found that three fifths of the marriages of individuals with mild mental retardation ended in divorce or separation. The uniqueness of Gebhard's sample may account for this dismal finding, as many subjects were serving time in prison, certainly not a representative group of mildly retarded adults. Other researchers conclude that the marriages of people with mild disabilities suffer from greater stress than those of the nondisabled, and they are more likely to separate or divorce but not at the rate suggested by Gebhard. Andron and Strum (1973) examined the marriages of 12 couples with at least one partner who was mentally retarded. All of the marriages were intact, but only 50% had no major marital problems. Floor, Baxter, Rosen, and Zisfein (1975) investigated the marriages of 80 adults, most of whom had mild retardation. Like Andron and Strum, they concluded that only one third had satisfactory partnerships. Fifteen percent had divorced because of health, money, or legal problems. This finding reflects the importance and interdependence of independent living skills. Skill deficits in one area (e.g., money management) are likely to create problems in other areas.

Robins and O'Neal (1959) provide one of the few insights into the marriages of people who were considered emotionally disturbed as children. Their prognosis for this group is more dismal than the prognosis for people with mild retardation. More than 50% of their subjects had experienced marriages that ended in divorce. This high figure must be interpreted in the context of the year in which it was identified. Indeed, today nearly half of marriages end in divorce, but in 1959 such a figure was very unusual.

Only a single study on the quality of the marriages of people with learning disabilities was encountered in a search of the literature. This may result from the difficulty in locating adult subjects with learning disabilities who are willing to provide this personal information. It may also reflect the newness of the field. Research on the social aspects of mental retardation and emotional disorders has been conducted for more than 100 years. Research in social aspects of learning disabilities is recent, and researchers have not had the opportunity to probe deeply into the issues. Whatever the reason, Balow and Bloomquist (1965) found that only 3 of 32 young adults with learning disabilities were married and that their lives were characterized by a generally negative attitude about their status.

People with mild disabilities become parents. Bass (1975) and others conclude that people with mental retardation have no more children than those who are not retarded. However, Shaw and Wright (1966) and Scally (1974) have determined that mentally retarded parents with more than one or two children were likely to be overwhelmed by the responsibility. Scally also concludes that the vast majority of mentally retarded mothers need help caring for their children. Still, Floor et al. (1975) encountered only a single instance in which a child was removed from the home of mentally retarded parents because of neglect.

Lenkowsky and Saposnek (1978) provide one of the few insights into the impact of a parent's learning disability on offspring. Admittedly, this case study is limited because it includes only a single case, but it does document the problem that may exist because of a lack of adequate pretransitional training. The dyslexia of the father in this case study appeared to be related to poor interaction with the children in the family. The result of the father's knowledge and skill deficits were poor grades, drug abuse, and promiscuity among his teenage children. Certainly, no one can determine that the father's disability was the cause of the problems, but his helplessness and ineffectiveness point to the need to provide direct instruction for individuals who are not likely to acquire parenting skills through incidental learning.

Friendships

It is difficult to conceive of a person living an independent and fulfilling adult life without close friends. The literature indicates that friendship is problematic for people with mild disabilities. Madden and Slavin (1983) conclude that children with mild disabilities have fewer friends and were more often rejected than their nondisabled peers. White et al. (1980) arrived at a slightly different conclusion when they conducted a follow-up study of young adults with learning disabilities. The subjects of this study had the same number of close friends as their nondisabled peers but fewer "social" friends. After conducting a series of studies, Bryan (1978) states that adolescents with learning disorders have difficulties making friends because they are less able to understand nonverbal clues and hence do not elicit positive responses from others.

Children with behavioral disorders are also rated lower on sociometric scales by their nondisabled peers (Sabornie & Kauffman, 1985). Interestingly, adolescents with behavioral disorders rated others with behavioral disorders higher than they were rated by peers without behavioral disorders.

Not surprisingly, Reiter and Levi (1980) have found that mentally retarded adults who had better social skills were more likely to have friends who were not retarded. Kingsley, Viggiano, and Tout (1981) provide even more specific information on the friendship patterns of mildly retarded people. They have determined that mildly retarded boys are more egocentric in their friendships than boys who are not retarded (e.g., What's in the friendship for me?). Mildly retarded boys also tend to play with other boys who were mildly retarded, a finding echoed by Landesman-Dwyer, Berkson, and Romer (1979). More importantly, they prefer passive solitary activities that are unlikely to lead to development of the skills required to make and maintain friendships. Furthermore, deficiencies in friendship skills are related to deficiencies in language. Likewise, Landesman-Dwyer et al. found that people with mental retardation are likely to have friends with similar language abilities.

Mentally retarded young adults usually have a small social circle that rarely extends beyond the friendships they have made at work or through special recreational programs (Schalock, Harper, & Carver, 1981; Stanfield, 1973). This may be a reflection of separation while in nonmainstreamed school settings, a lack of opportunity to learn how to make friends with schoolmates who are not disabled, or a generally overprotected childhood. In any case, researchers have consistently shown that mainstreaming by itself does not lead to increased acceptance of people with mild disabilities or increased friendships between people with mild disabilities and those without. However, such friendships are virtually impossible without the contact promoted by mainstreaming. In addition, Kregel et al. (1986) have found that more mildly retarded adults spend a majority of their free time with their families than with friends, an indication that independence is a step not easily taken.

Leisure

Unlike work activities, which involve little choice, leisure activities generally reflect the preferences of the participants. People with mild disabilities participate in a narrower range of leisure activities, on the average, than people without disabilities. To some extent, this may reflect a lack of experience in a wide range of activities as children or a continuing isolation into adulthood. For example, White et al. (1980) conclude that young adults with learning disabilities were less involved in social, fraternal, and group recreational activities than their nondisabled peers. Dinger (1961) arrived at similar conclusions for a group of mildly retarded young adults. Seventy-five percent did not belong to any socializing activity (team, club, etc.), and most of their recreational activities were undertaken with their parental families. Passive activities such as watching television or movies are mentioned frequently in the literature concerning leisure and people with mild disabilities (Heimark & McKinnon, 1979; Luckey & Shapiro, 1974; Reiter & Levi, 1980; Salzberg & Langford, 1981). People who were classified as emotionally disturbed as children are likely to participate in no formal group social activities as adults (Robins, 1966).

Birenbaum and Re (1979) and Salzberg and Langford (1981) suggest that because people with mild disabilities often participate in special, separate activities when they are children, they do not learn to integrate themselves into normal adult recreational opportunities when they gain autonomy as adults. Luckey and Shapiro (1974) believe that many mildly retarded adults are not even aware of the generic resources that are available to them.

Appropriate use of leisure time is one of the problems most frequently faced by newly independent young adults with mild disabilities (Bell, 1976). In Bell's study the only adjustment problem that occurred with more frequency was managing money.

In spite of the vast research that seems to indicate many problems and limitations, it is very important to note that many young adults with mild disabilities do participate in a wide range of activities. This is further evidence that it is not the presence of the disability that leads to passivity but the lack of training and opportunity and overprotection. The study of Kregel et al. (1986) shows that of 183 mildly retarded adults, 28% spent time in outdoor recreation, 21% jogged, 22% swam, 27% cycled, 47% attended sporting events, 13% attended concerts, 50% attended movies, and 17% participated in church activities.

Conclusions

The above discussions make it obvious that people with mild disabilities encounter many difficulties in their attempts to become independent. These difficulties go far beyond gaining and maintaining employment. In fact, nearly every aspect of their lives during transition presents special difficulties. Much of this difficulty is due to a lack of opportunity to learn the skills needed to be an autonomous individual. Overprotection and inefficient or neglected curricula and methodology are responsible for many problems. There is no research that indicates that the problems cannot be overcome with systematic, direct instruction in the skills needed to manage one's personal life, maintain a household, live healthily, marry and raise a family, make and maintain friendships, and participate in meaningful and life-enhancing recreation.

❦ ❦ ❦

IMPROVING INDEPENDENT LIVING SKILLS

There are numerous curricula describing the content and methodology for teaching independent living skills to people with mild disabilities. Regardless which, if any, are used to form the basis of instruction, there are several critical guidelines applicable to any program:

1. Instruction in independent living skills should begin long before the transition to independence is made.
2. Skills should be taught and practiced in the natural environment. Researchers have demonstrated that when such skills are taught in the classroom, they do not generalize to the natural environment unless generalization and maintenance activities are part of the training.
3. Risk should be recognized as a part of the transition process. It is impossible to learn the skills required to be independent without assuming the attendant risk to try them out.
4. Parental involvement is an absolute necessity. The literature reflects the dampening effects of parental overprotection or nonparticipation. There is no doubt that children with mild disabilities who become independently functioning adults were given the opportunity to assume independence gradually by their parents. Professionals must persuade parents to encourage their children to accept responsibility and to learn the skills for independent functioning.
5. When independent living is viewed as a set of skills that can be learned rather than simple maturation or overcoming a disability, the chance for success is greater. Expectations for skill performance should be clear.
6. Many people with mild disabilities will require the independent living equivalent of a job coach in order to learn the skills needed. After all, transition to independence is a process, not an event. It requires repeated practice of the skills and feedback regarding performance. For most people the independent living coach will be a parent, but even parents will need training.
7. Skills should be taught in the most normalized setting possible (e.g., regular home ec classes rather than special classes).

Personal Management Skills

Many of the skills involved in personal management are included in traditional secondary curricula (see Figure 15–1). Among the specific curricula available for adolescents and young adults with mild disabilities are *Learning Skills for Daily Living* (1978) and *Becoming Independent: A Living Skills System* (1978), which are high-interest, low-vocabulary programs that include instruction in skills such as using a telephone and credit cards to buying from catalogs. Brolin (1989) describes a comprehensive career education curriculum that includes competencies in activities of daily living such as managing finances, buying and preparing food, and purchasing and caring for clothing. The curriculum also includes a competency rating scale for assessment purposes. There is no dearth of curricula in this area that can be used to determine content.

Researchers have demonstrated that personal management skills can be learned and maintained by people with mild disabilities. For example,

Figure 15–1
Personal management skill clusters

1. Money management
   a. Banking
   b. Credit
2. Communications
   a. Using the telephone
   b. Responding to mail
   c. Using newspapers
3. Consumer skills
   a. Purchasing
   b. Determining product value
4. Personal care
   a. Doing laundry
   b. Selecting and caring for clothing
5. Food preparation/cooking

Bourbeau, Sowers, and Close (1986), McGee (1982), and Shafer, Inge, and Hill (1986) evaluated the instruction of banking skills. Bourbeau et al. describe a program in which simulation was used to teach deposit, withdrawal, checking, and saving skills to four mildly retarded persons. Initial training occurred in the classroom. Training was then generalized to a real bank that had been used to design the simulated classroom bank. Finally, training was extended to another bank to promote generalization. All of the subjects mastered all of the skills that resulted from a task analysis. The skills were generalized to other banks in the community although in situ training was sometimes necessary. Subjects also retained the skills over time. In a similar vein, McGee demonstrated that in-class training in the skills required for managing a savings account could be taught to and generalized by 12 learning disabled adolescents. Prior to instruction, none of the students was able to complete a deposit/withdrawal form accurately. In addition, few understood the reasons for saving or how the system worked. After instruction, all students were able to perform the required skills with at least 90% accuracy. Seven of the students opened and maintained savings accounts, a testament to generalization.

Researchers have also demonstrated that laundry skills can be learned easily through a system involving task analysis, modeling, graduated guidance, chaining, and generalization training (Cuvo, Jacobi, & Sipko, 1981; Thompson et al., 1982). The procedures used in these two studies closely parallel those employed in the banking skills studies just described. In the Thompson et al. study, students were able to generalize the skills to public laundromats after instruction in a home economics class. Tasks included sorting, washing, and drying. Prior to instruction none of the subjects was able to complete more than 18% of the task correctly.

There are dozens of studies, curricula, and instructional packages for teaching personal management skills to people with mild disabilities. The research cited here is representative of the procedures used in nearly all of the variations available.

Housing and Household Maintenance Skills

Brolin (1989) includes selecting and managing a household as one of the major competency clusters in his discussion of career education. Among the specific skill areas included in this competency cluster are (a) selecting a place to live; (b) caring for a home, furniture, and appliances; and (c) understanding basic electricity and plumbing. There is little or no research on teaching people with mild disabilities how to perform these skills. It is likely that they could be taught successfully using the guidelines presented at the beginning of this section (i.e., task analysis, in situ training, modeling, etc.) and generic home economics curricula.

The skills required to maintain a home can and should be taught while the student is still living in his or her parents' house. Instruction should involve gradual increases in quantity and difficulty. Obviously, such a program requires the cooperation of parents. Although there are numerous examples of instruction in housekeeping skills (i.e., cleaning), one particular study provides some important insight in promoting independence in this skill cluster. Bauman and Iwata (1977) taught 21 skill clusters to two mildly retarded adults. The instruction was typical in that it involved task analysis and so forth; however, the important novelty of the instruction was the manner in which it was designed to promote independence. The subjects prepared the schedule for practicing and maintaining the skills, and they used self-recording to assess their performance. Maintenance was thus produced because the subjects did not rely on a trainer to ensure compliance. This point is critical. Any time that a person with mild disabilities can be taught to manage an aspect of his or her life independently, scarce resources become more available for other troublesome areas.

Health Maintenance Skills

Much has been written about the development of health maintenance skills for people with mild disabilities (see Figure 15–2). Skills for personal fitness are included in Brolin's (1989) work on career education.

Some health maintenance skills can be learned in vivo. Others require simulation as it is inappropriate to await a medical emergency to teach skills such as first aid. However, students can practice healthy lifestyle skills as part of their everyday life.

Weight loss, nutrition, and exercise programs have been successfully applied to people with mild disabilities. Norvell and Ahern (1987) used a behaviorally based approach to help a group of adults with mild disabilities adopt a healthier lifestyle. Subjects were taught how to select foods for nutritional value and how to develop effective personal exercise programs. Based on the tenets of self-management, the program resulted in significant weight

Figure 15–2
Health maintenance skill clusters

1. Healthy lifestyle
    a. Nutrition
    b. Exercise
2. Use of health services
    a. Clinics
    b. Private physicians
    c. Other health providers
3. Use of medications
4. Harmful substances
    a. Poisons/toxins
    b. Drugs
    c. Alcohol and tobacco
5. First aid
6. Emergency procedures

loss and improvements in fitness. Rotatori et al. (1980) used a similar program with comparable results. Halle, Silverman, and Regan (1983) concentrated only on cardiovascular fitness. Using a program of daily walk/run sessions, their subjects exhibited improvement in overall fitness. Interestingly, Evans, Evans, Schmid, and Pennypacker (1985) found that exercise had a positive effect on the amount of work completed by adolescents with behavioral disorders and the frequency of their talkouts.

Brickey (1978) describes a program in which mildly retarded adults were taught the skills for self-medication. Utilizing a task-analytical approach, all of the subjects were able to assume complete responsibility for self-medication within 10 days. Later follow-up revealed that the skills had been maintained. Other researchers have been successful in teaching emergency skills to mildly retarded adults. The subjects in a study by Risley and Cuvo (1980) were taught to respond appropriately to 18 emergency situations. The skills were broken down into four major steps: (a) deciding when to call an emergency number, (b) finding the correct emergency number, (c) dialing, and (d) providing the correct information. The subjects learned the skills and were able to generalize them to untaught situations.

Although the literature reveals that people with mild disabilities are susceptible to substance abuse, there is no literature describing successful preventive or interventional instruction. Perhaps generic substance abuse programs are sufficient, but a secondary or postsecondary transition program must include instruction in this area. *Prevention Plus: Involving Parents and the Community in Alcohol and Drug Education,* a publication of the National Institute on Alcohol Abuse and Alcoholism (NIAAA, 1984), can be used to form the basis for an instructional program.

Sexuality and Family Living Skills

According to Fisher and Krajieck (1974), individuals with mild disabilities are capable of learning societal expectations regarding sexual activities. There are many curricular guides and some research on the effectiveness of instruction. Brolin's (1989) curriculum contains many of the clusters listed in Figure 15–3 and is specifically designed for people with mild disabilities.

Kempton and Hanson (1976) have developed a slide-based program for teaching sexuality to people with mild retardation. Included in the program are slides, scripts, and teacher guides in seven clusters: body parts, male puberty, female puberty, social behavior, reproduction, fertility regulation and venereal diseases, and marriage and parenting. Role playing and discussion activities also appear.

Another curriculum is *EASE* (1976), an empirically validated curriculum. This curriculum, designed for adolescents and adults, includes four units broken into 23 lessons: (a) biology, (b) sexual behavior, (c) health, and (d) social relationships. Each unit includes objectives, content, teaching sequences,

Figure 15–3
Sexuality and family living skill clusters

1. Biology of reproduction
2. Exploitation and abuse
   a. Rape
   b. Abuse
   c. Prostitution
3. Appropriate sexual relationships
   a. Privacy
   b. Appropriate touching
   c. Sharing feelings
   d. Dating
4. Contraception
5. Venereal diseases
6. Marriage
   a. The marriage contract
   b. Marital responsibilities
   c. Divorce and separation
7. Parenting
   a. Child care
   b. Child development
   c. Child abuse and neglect

visual aids, worksheets, and discussion items. Diagnostic materials are also included.

McClennen (1988) and McNab (1978) believe that most unacceptable sexual behavior expressed by people with disabilities is attributable to lack of instruction of acceptable behaviors. McNab states that in addition to lacking formal sexuality training, people with disabilities do not know how to use the resources that are available to others such as clinics, books, and library materials. Furthermore, McClennen believes that the most critical element of sexuality instruction is appropriate modeling in normal interactions. Money (1974) agrees with McClennen's analysis but describes the difficulty in teaching sexuality to individuals such as those with mild disabilities who require concrete images. Such instruction could be viewed as pornographic in some communities.

Any program of instruction in sexuality must include at least the sanction of the parents of the learner. Active involvement is preferable, but any instruction will be undone if it is done without parental support (McNab, 1978). Brantlinger (1985) and Kalma (1976) describe a second problem that may negatively affect sexuality instruction. Students in their studies (emotionally disturbed and mildly retarded) revealed strong affective responses to discussions of sexuality. Attempts to discuss sex in a factual manner were often met by anger, fear, and personalization. Thus, any instructor must be skilled in dealing with the strong feelings created by the topic. Weisgerber and Rubin (1989) have developed a curriculum that can be used by teachers who must deal with such feelings. Although the curriculum was not specifically designed for discussion of sexuality, the methodology employed is applicable. Utilizing skill instruction, practice responses, and follow-up exercises, students learn how to handle stress, take responsibility, communicate feelings, develop close relationships, touch in the right way, and respect the rights of others. Brolin's (1985) curriculum also includes competencies in the affective domain of sexuality.

Unlike the other skill areas for independent living, it is not possible merely to use task analysis for many of the elements of sexuality and family living instruction. Obviously, in situ instruction cannot occur for many of the behaviors (e.g., using contraception), and some of the instruction is knowledge based rather than skill based. This knowledge must be stored until it is needed. Simulation, visual aids, and other methods and materials are often substituted, but nothing can replace normal development of sexual interest and activity and the opportunities it provides for instruction.

In addition to sexuality instruction, adolescents and young adults with mild disabilities need to receive direct instruction in marriage and parenting skills. Most young adults have learned parenting by observing their parents; however, with deficits in incidental learning it is less likely that people with mild disabilities will learn these skills in this way, nor is it likely that they will be able to judge the goodness of the behaviors they have observed.

Walker (1977) describes premarital counseling for people who are mildly retarded. The five-pronged program includes (a) "knowledge of budget, social behavior and sex, (b) what their mutual attraction was . . ., (c) role identification and expectation as a family unit, (d) individual ego strengths, and (e) involvement of prospective in laws, and possible areas of conflict with extended family members" (p. 478). Although these areas are not skill clusters per se, Walker taught problem-solving skills that were applied to specific conflicts and conditions. Participants were successful in applying the skills to their own situations.

Parenting classes can be skill oriented and concrete. Madsen (1979) used a modified form of the Red Cross babysitters' course to instruct mentally retarded parents how to care for their children. This class is an example of how generic programs can be adapted for learners with special needs. The 5-week course was offered at the University of Wisconsin–Milwaukee by the School of Nursing. As evidence that the class was necessary, Madsen states that 50% of the students had parents who had been abusive or neglectful. Certainly modeling would have been inappropriate in many cases. Topics included (a) handling small infants, diapering, washing, dressing, and treating common illnesses; (b) child growth and development; (c) food, recreation, discipline, toys, and positive parent-child interactions; (d) hazards, safety measures, emergencies, and first aid; and (e) use of community health resources. Although this content is appropriate, the fact that the course was limited to 5 weeks and no maintenance was described leaves questions as to its effectiveness.

Friendship Skills

Although we may not teach people to be friends, we can teach people the behaviors that are likely to lead to friendship (see Figure 15–4). Many researchers have attempted to teach friendship skills to people with mild disabilities. Given the deficits exhibited in this area and the impact that friendships have on adult adjustment, these skills (which have been specifically identified and verified) are critical and overlap other skill clusters that we have discussed (e.g., social skills for work, sexuality, and family life).

Figure 15–4
Friendship skill clusters

1. Understanding nonverbal behavior
2. Eliciting positive responses from others
3. Emitting positive responses
4. Assuming leadership
5. Establishing areas of compatibility
6. Taking the perspective of others
7. Providing support for others
8. Resolving conflict
9. Initiating and maintaining conversations

The methodology for teaching friendship skills is similar to that employed in other areas of independent living; that is, direct instruction of the skills is essential to success. For example, Madden and Slavin (1983) have found that cooperative learning leads to lower rejection of people with mild disabilities but not to more friendships. Stainback and Stainback (1987) list systematic reinforcement, teacher/peer counseling, role playing, and modeling as the methods that have been effective. Practice in daily situations, follow-up, and feedback are also necessary. Schumaker, Hazel, and Pederson (1988) utilized workbooks, comic books, peer practice, and game simulation as the methodology in their curriculum for conversation, friendship, and skills for getting along with others. Their curriculum also includes situations for practice and procedures for generalization.

Leisure and Recreation Skills

Researchers and practitioners have developed many curricula and methods for teaching leisure skills to individuals with mild disabilities. Brolin (1989) describes leisure competencies for people with mild disabilities. Hebeler and Lance (1976) believe that development of leisure skills depends on the opportunity to learn and practice on five different tiers: (a) active socialization, (b) hobbies, (c) games, (d) passive leisure, and (e) action on play materials. Researchers have shown that people with mild disabilities can learn and apply the skills necessary to play competitive sports (Levine & Langness, 1983), change from passive leisure to active leisure (Johnson & Bailey, 1977), generalize leisure skills to untrained areas (Ashcroft, 1987), and use public recreational facilities (Corcoran & French, 1977).

Schloss, Smith, and Kiehl (1986) describe a comprehensive program designed to teach leisure skills to mildly retarded young adults. In addition to learning the individual skills, participants were taught how to use available community resources. The Rec Club approach, as it was called, was designed to foster independent recreational functioning under a philosophy of normalization and age appropriateness. All activities were available in the community to any citizen. Training targeted specific skills needed for participation in client-selected activities. Minimum assistance was provided and then reduced over time. Acceptance of risk was also central. Participants were successful in learning to manage themselves as they increased the frequency and variety of their activities. The program involved six stages:

1. Recreational opportunities in the community were identified.
2. A skills checklist was developed for each activity.
3. Participants were observed at the activity.
4. Prosthetics were used wherever possible (e.g., calculators, special transit maps).
5. Specific skills were taught to participants.
6. Posttest observations were made.

The Rec Club program contains all of the elements that are necessary for success in training independent living skills. It is normalizing and hence likely to be reinforced by others. It is skill based and concrete. It occurs in the natural environment. It promotes responsibility and assumption of risk. It involves coaching rather than direct and continuous management.

❦ ❦ ❦

SUMMARY

People with mild disabilities who acquire independent living skills are proud of doing for themselves (Schalock, Harper, & Carver, 1981; Schalock, Harper, & Genung, 1981). In many cases they are at a disadvantage not because of their disabilities but because of the low expectations of their parents, teachers, and peers. The literature reviewed here and the many testaments to success indicate that the worst enemy of independence is the lack of opportunities to learn and practice the skills.

REFERENCES

Andron, L., & Strum, M. L. (1973). Is "I do" in the repertoire of the retarded? *Mental Retardation, 11,* 31–35.

Aninger, M., Growick, B., & Bolinsky, K. (1979). Individual community placement of deinstitutionalized mentally retarded adults: Some personal concerns. *Mental Retardation, 15,* 307–308.

Ashcroft, R. (1987). A conceptual model for assessing levels of interpersonal skill. *Teaching Behaviorally Disordered Youth, 3,* 28–32.

Balow, B., & Bloomquist, M. (1965). Young adults ten to fifteen years after severe reading disability. *Elementary School Journal, 66,* 44–48.

Bass, M. S. (1975). *Marriage and parenthood: Proceedings of the White House Conference on the Sexual Rights and Responsibilities of the Mentally Retarded.* Washington, DC: SIECUS.

Bauman, K. E., & Iwata, B. A. (1977). Maintenance of independent housekeeping skills using scheduling plus self recording procedures. *Behavior Therapy, 8,* 554–560.

Becoming independent: A living skills system. (1978). Bellevue, WA: Edmark.

Bell, N. J. (1976). IQ as a factor in community lifestyle of previously institutionalized retardates. *Mental Retardation, 14,* 29–33.

Birenbaum, A., & Re, M. (1979). Resettling mentally retarded adults in the community-Almost 4 years later. *American Journal of Mental Deficiency, 83,* 323–329.

Bourbeau, P. E., Sowers, J., & Close, D. W. (1986). An experimental analysis of generalization of banking skills from classroom to bank settings in the community. *Education and Training of the Mentally Retarded, 21,* 98–107.

Brantlinger, E. A. (1985). Mildly mentally retarded secondary students' information about and attitudes toward sexuality and sexuality education. *Education and Training of the Mentally Retarded, 20,* 99–108.

Brickey, M. (1978). A behavioral procedure for teaching self medication. *Mental Retardation, 16,* 29–32.

Brolin, D. E. (Ed.). (1989). *Life-centered career education: A competency-based approach* (3rd ed.). Reston, VA: Council for Exceptional Children.

Bryan, T. (1978). Social relationships and verbal interactions of learning disabled children. *Journal of Learning Disabilities, 11,* 58–66.

Campbell, A. C. (1971). Aspects of personal independence of mentally subnormal and severely subnormal adults in hospital and in local authority hostels. *International Journal of Social Psychology, 17,* 305–310.

Campbell, J. (1973). Physical fitness and the mentally retarded: A review of research. *Mental Retardation, 11,* 26–29.

Corcoran, E. L., & French, F. W. (1977). Leisure activity for the retarded adult in the community. *Mental Retardation, 15*(1), 21–23.

Cuvo, A. J., Jacobi, L., & Sipko, R. (1981). Teaching laundry skills to mentally retarded students. *Education and Training of the Mentally Retarded, 16,* 54–64.

Dinger, J. (1961). Post-school adjustment of former educable retarded pupils. *Exceptional Children, 27,* 353–386.

Eagle, E. (1967). Prognosis and outcome of community placement of institutionalized retardates. *American Journal of Mental Deficiency, 72,* 232–243.

EASE: The first empirically validated sex education curriculum for the mentally handicapped. (1976). Pasadena, CA: Stanfield.

Edgerton, R. B. (1986) Alcohol and drug use by mentally retarded adults. *American Journal of Mental Deficiency, 90,* 602–609.

Evans, W. H., Evans, S. S., Schmid, R. E., & Pennypacker, H. S. (1985). The effects of exercise on selected classroom behaviors of behaviorally disordered adolescents. *Behavioral Disorders, 7,* 42–51.

Ewing, S., & Williams, R. D. (1981). Consumer roulette: The shopping patterns of mentally retarded persons. *Mental Retardation, 19,* 145–149.

Fisher, H. L., & Krajieck, M. J. (1974). Sexual development of the moderately retarded child. *Clinical Pediatrics, 13,* 78–83.

Floor, L., Baxter, D., Rosen, M., & Zisfein, L. (1975). A survey of marriages among previously institutionalized retardates. *Mental Retardation, 13,* 33–37.

Fox, R., & Rotatori, A. F. (1982). Prevalence of obesity among mentally retarded adults. *American Journal of Mental Deficiency, 87,* 228–230.

Gebhard, P. H. (1974). Sexual behavior of the mentally retarded. In F. F. de la Cruz & G. D. Laveck (Eds.), *Human sexuality and the mentally retarded* (pp. 29–49). Baltimore: Penguin.

Hall, J. E., & Morris, H. L. (1976). Sexual knowledge and attitudes of institutionalized and noninstitutionalized retarded adolescents. *American Journal of Mental Deficiency, 80,* 382–387.

Hall, J. E., Morris, H. L., & Barker, H. R. (1973). Sexual knowledge and attitudes of mentally retarded adolescents. *American Journal of Mental Deficiency, 77,* 706–709.

Halle, J. W., Silverman, N. A., & Regan, L. (1983). The effects of a data-based exercise program on physical fitness of retarded children. *Education and Training of the Mentally Retarded, 18,* 221–225.

Hebeler, J. R., & Lance, W. D. (1976). A leisure time activities curriculum for the developmentally disabled. *Classroom Techniques, 11,* 309–313.

Heimark, R., & McKinnon, R. (1979). Leisure preferences of mentally retarded graduates of a residential training program. *Therapeutic Recreation Journal, 5,* 67–68.

Heshusius, L. (1982). Sexuality, intimacy, and persons we label mentally retarded: What they think-what we think. *Mental Retardation, 20,* 164–168.

Hull, J. T., & Thompson, J. C. (1980). Predicting adaptive functioning of mentally retarded persons in community settings. *American Journal of Mental Deficiency, 85,* 253–261.

Johnson, M. S., & Bailey, J. S. (1977). Leisure training in a halfway house. *Journal of Applied Behavior Analysis, 10,* 273–282.

Kalma, S. H. (1976). Sex education within biology classes for hospitalized disturbed adolescents. *Exceptional Children, 42,* 451–455.

Kempton, W., & Hanson, G. (1976). Sexuality and the mentally handicapped. Pasadena, CA: Stanfield.

Kingsley, R. F., Viggiano, R. A., & Tout, L. (1981). Social perception of friendship, leadership and game playing among EMR special and regular class boys. *Education and Training of the Mentally Retarded, 16,* 201–206.

Kregel, J., Wehman, P., Seyfarth, J., & Marshall, K. (1986). Community integration of young adults with mental retardation: Transition from school to adulthood. *Education and Training of the Mentally Retarded, 21,* 35–42.

Krishef, C. H., & DiNitto, D. M. (1981). Alcohol abuse among mentally retarded individuals. *Mental Retardation, 19,* 151–155.

Landesman-Dwyer, S., Berkson, G., & Romer, D. (1979). Affiliation and friendship of mentally retarded residents in group homes. *American Journal of Mental Deficiency, 83,* 571–580.

Learning skills for daily living. (1978). Baltimore: Hampden.

Lenkowsky, L. K., & Saposnek, D. T. (1978). Family consequences of parental dyslexia. *Journal of Learning Disabilities, 11,* 47–53.

Levine, H. G., & Langness, L. L. (1983). Context, ability and performance: Comparison of competitive athletics among mildly mentally retarded and nonretarded adults. *American Journal of Mental Deficiency, 87,* 528–538.

Luckey, R. E., & Shapiro, I. F. (1974). Recreation: An essential aspect of habilitative programming. *Mental Retardation, 12,* 33–35.

Madden, N. A., & Slavin, R. E. (1983). Effects of cooperative learning on the social acceptance of mainstreamed academically handicapped students. *Journal of Special Education, 17,* 171–182.

Madsen, M. K. (1979). Parenting classes for the mentally retarded. *Mental Retardation, 17,* 195–199.

McClennen, S. (1988). Sexuality and students with mental retardation. *Teaching Exceptional Children, 20*(4) 59–61.

McGee, D. W. (1982). An introduction to savings accounts for learning disabled adolescents. *Teaching Exceptional Children, 15,* 113–116.

McNab, W. L. (1978). The sexual needs of the handicapped. *Journal of School Health, 48,* 301–306.

Miller, E. L. (1965). Ability and social adjustment at midlife of persons earlier judged mentally deficient. *Genetic Psychology Monographs, 72,* 139–198.

Money, J. W. (1974). Some thoughts on sexual taboos and the rights of the retarded. In F. F. de la Cruz & G. D. Laveck (Eds.), *Human sexuality and the mentally retarded* (pp. 3–11). Baltimore: Penguin.

National Institute on Alcohol Abuse and Alcoholism. (1984). *Prevention plus: Involving schools, parents and community in alcohol and drug education*. Rockville, MD: U.S. Department of Health and Human Services.

Norvell, N. K., & Ahern, D. K. (1987). Worksite weight-loss intervention for individuals with mental retardation: A pilot study. *Education and Training of the Mentally Retarded, 22*, 85–90.

Reiter, S., & Levi, A. M. (1980). Factors affecting social integration of noninstitutionalized mentally retarded adults. *American Journal of Mental Deficiency, 85*, 25–30.

Risley, R., & Cuvo, A. J. (1980). Training mentally retarded adults to make emergency phone calls. *Behavior Modification, 4*, 513–525.

Robins, L. (1966). *Deviant children grown up*. Baltimore: Williams & Williams.

Robins, L. N., & O'Neal, P. (1959). The adult prognosis for runaway children. *American Journal of Orthopsychiatry, 29*, 752–761.

Rotatori, A. F., Fox, R., & Switzky, H. (1980). A multicomponent behavioral program for achieving weight loss in the adult mentally retarded person. *Mental Retardation, 18*, 31–33.

Russell, T., & Hardin, P. (1980). Sex education for the mentally retarded. *Education and Training of the Mentally Retarded, 15*, 312–314.

Sabornie, E. J., & Kauffman, J. M. (1985). Regular classroom sociometric status of behaviorally disordered adolescents. *Behavior Disorders, 10*, 268–274.

Salend, S. J., & Giek, K. A. (1987). The availability of follow up services to landlords renting to individuals who are retarded. *Education and Training of the Mentally Retarded, 22*, 91–97.

Salend, S. J., Michael, R. J., Veraja, M., & Noto, J. (1983). Landlords' perceptions of retarded individuals as tenants. *Education and Training of the Mentally Retarded, 18*, 232–234.

Salzberg, C. L., & Langford, C. A. (1981). Community integration of mentally retarded adults through leisure activity. *Mental Retardation, 19*, 127–131.

Scally, B. G. (1974). Marriage and mental handicap: Some observations in Northern Ireland. In F. F. de la Cruz & G. D. Laveck (Eds.), *Human sexuality and the mentally retarded* (pp. 186–194). Baltimore: Penguin.

Schalock, R. L., Harper, R. S., & Carver, G. (1981) Independent living placement: Five years later. *American Journal of Mental Deficiency, 86*, 170–177.

Schalock, R. L., Harper, R. S., & Genung, T. (1981). Community integration of mentally retarded adults: Community placement and program success. *American Journal of Mental Deficiency, 85*, 478–488.

Schloss, P. J., Smith, M. A., & Kiehl, W. (1986). Rec Club: A community centered approach to recreational development for adults with mild to moderate retardation. *Education and Training of the Mentally Retarded, 21*, 282–288.

Schumaker, J. B., Hazel, J. S., & Pederson, C. (1988). *Social skills for daily living*. Circle Pines, MN: American Guidance Service.

Scott, A. J., Williams, J. M., Stout, J. K., & Decker, T. W. (1980). *Field investigation and evaluation of learning disabilities*. Scranton, PA: University of Scranton Press.

Seltzer, G. B. (1981). Community residential adjustment: The relationship among environment, performance and satisfaction. *American Journal of Mental Deficiency, 85*, 624–630.

Shafer, M. S., Inge, K. J., & Hill, J. (1986). Acquisition, generalization and maintenance of automated banking skills. *Education and Training of the Mentally Retarded, 21*, 265–272.

Shaw, C. H., & Wright, C. H. (1966). The married mental defective: A follow up study. *Lancet*, 273–274.

Sovner, R., Hurley, A., DesNoyes, A., & LaBue, R. (1982). Diagnosing depression in the mentally retarded. *Psychiatric Aspects of Mental Retardation Newsletter, 1*, 1–3.

Stainback, W., & Stainback, S. (1987). Facilitating friendships. *Education and Training of the Mentally Retarded, 22*, 18–25.

Stanfield, J. S. (1973). Graduation: What happens to the retarded child when he grows up? *Exceptional Children, 39*, 548–552.

Sutter, P., Mayeda, T., Call, T., Yenagi, G., & Yee, S. (1980). Comparison of successful and unsuccessful community placed mentally retarded persons. *American Journal of Mental Deficiency, 85*, 262–267.

Thompson, T. J., Broam, S. J., & Fuqua, R. W. (1982). Training and generalization of laundry skills: A multiple probe evaluation with handicapped persons. *Journal of Applied Behavior Analysis, 15*, 177–182.

Walker, P. W. (1977). Premarital counseling for the developmentally disabled. *Social Casework, 58*(8), 475–479.

Weisgerber, R. A., & Rubin, D. (1985). *Social solutions for school-to-work transition*. Palo Alto, CA: American Institutes for Research in the Behavioral Sciences.

White, W. J., Schumaker, J. B., Warner, M. M., Alley, G. R., & Deshler, D. D. (1980). *The current status of young adults identified as learning disabled during their school career*. Lawrence, Institute for Research in Learning Disabilities: University of Kansas.

Zetlin, A. G., Turner, J., & Wenik, L. (1987). Socialization effects on the community adaptation of adults who have mild mental retardation. In S. Landesman & P. Vietze (Eds.), *Living environments and mental retardation* (pp. 293–313). Washington, DC: American Association on Mental Retardation.

Chapter 16

❦ ❦ ❦

Citizenship Skills

*I*ndividuals with mild disabilities can be expected to become productive participants in the civic process. Integration as citizens requires direct instruction of citizenship skills and the opportunity to practice these skills. This chapter is divided into two main sections: research that describes how persons with mild disabilities fare as citizens, and methods and materials that can be used to teach and enhance citizenship skills. Good citizenship is based on an understanding of socially acceptable morality; therefore, that is the point of departure for the ensuing discussion in each of the main sections.

❦ ❦ ❦

THE CITIZENSHIP STATUS OF ADOLESCENTS AND ADULTS WITH MILD DISABILITIES

Citizenship includes (a) mature moral reasoning and decision making; (b) knowledge of government and participation in the political process; (c) knowledge of law, absence of criminal behavior, and resistance to victimization; and (d) service to the nation, state, and community. According to many researchers, adolescents and young adults with mild disabilities often experience problems in attaining full participation and in accepting full responsibility as citizens. This difficulty stems from the limitations imposed by their disabilities on the acquisition of citizenship skills and knowledge, the lack of opportunity to observe and practice citizenship skills, and a perception (as evidenced by neglect in many curricula for adolescents with mild disabilities) that citizenship skills are unimportant.

Moral Reasoning and Decision Making

Kohlberg and others have postulated theories and models of moral development; a condensation of Kohlberg's (1981) model is presented in Figure 16–1. According to Kohlberg, Levine, and Hewer (1983), children progress

---

Level I — Preconventional Morality

Stage 1. Obedience to avoid punishment

Stage 2. Doing what is best for one's own needs, making deals of equal exchange

Level II — Conventional Morality

Stage 3. Conforming to peer group expectations

Stage 4. Upholding the social order

Level III — Postconventional Morality

Stage 5. Awareness of the rights on which a society is based

Stage 6. Development of universal ethical principles

Figure 16–1
Kohlberg's stages of moral development

through moral stages as a result of cognitive conflict; that is, as they begin to comprehend greater complexity in moral dilemmas, their simple egocentric view can no longer account for human behavior. This conflict prompts children to adopt more sophisticated structures and reasoning. Generally, this growth includes the ability to view a moral issue through the eyes of another person (Lickona, 1988).

Researchers have determined that children, adolescents, and adults with mild disabilities often exhibit chronologically immature moral reasoning and decision-making skills. Thus, mildly disabled people do not acquire sophisticated moral reasoning skills as early or as easily as nondisabled persons. In many cases, unless direct intervention is present, adults with mild disabilities continue to approach moral dilemmas with very immature reasoning. This phenomenon occurs, at least in part, because persons with mild disabilities do not acquire skills and knowledge through incidental learning with the same efficiency as nondisabled learners.

Gibbs (1987) has investigated the moral reasoning of behaviorally disordered/emotionally disabled individuals and concludes that they evidence deficits in the development of empathy. They tend to view others as things that get in their way or as things to be used to gain a personal advantage. Swarthout's (1988) research supports Gibbs's conclusions. He has determined that the moral development of behaviorally disordered/emotionally disabled individuals is immature, antisocial, egocentric, and unconcerned with violating the rights of others.

People with mental retardation also demonstrate moral immaturity (Ford, Dineen, & Hall, 1984). This immaturity results from lack of experience in making decisions (partly because of parental and professional overprotectiveness) and incidental learning deficits. Some moral maturation occurs in adulthood as a result of increased demand and opportunity for decision making; however, the consequences of failure are often severe (e.g., jail, lack of friends).

Several researchers have investigated the moral maturity of individuals with learning disabilities. Bryan, Werner, and Pearl (1981) have found that persons with learning disabilities are more likely than nondisabled persons to succumb to peer pressure, less likely to consider moral issues on a broader basis, and less likely to adopt principles of moral reasoning that involve consideration of the impact of decisions on others. This results in a high rate of antisocial acts. Derr (1986) concurs with these conclusions. The 25 adolescents with learning disabilities in Derr's study were insensitive to the social aspects of a verbal encounter. They reasoned at a significantly lower level (on Kohlberg's model). The non–learning disabled youths were concerned with norms and community and societal values, but those who were learning disabled utilized egocentric judgments and attempted to promote their own needs and desires. They would follow rules only when doing so was in their self-interest. Youths with learning disabilities were less able to understand conventional group processes such as negotiation and compromise.

Based on these studies, it is obvious that individuals with mild disabilities encounter many difficulties in making moral decisions. As we shall see, these problems have a profound effect on their attempts to become fully participating, responsible citizens.

Knowledge of Government and the Political Process

Adolescents and adults with mild disabilities are deficient in their knowledge of government and politics because of lack of exposure and training, inadequate abstract reasoning, and the low priority placed on this area in special education programs (Gozali & Gonwa, 1973). Kokaska (1972) states that voting is limited among individuals who are mildly retarded because of legal constraints (which have been mostly removed since 1972), lack of knowledge, and lack of exposure and support in special education classes. Obviously, training for employment is more important than training in the functions of government for adolescents with mild disabilities. However, researchers have concluded that mildly disabled adults who have succeeded vocationally begin to recognize other deficiencies in their lives as they enter their 30s and 40s, which leads to dissatisfaction. Among the complaints expressed frequently is a belief that they are missing a large part of life because they have not learned how to participate in the political process. This promotes a heightened awareness of "difference" and general dissatisfaction.

Green and Klein (1980) have investigated the political values of mentally retarded adults. By comparing mentally retarded adults who resided in public and private residential facilities, mentally retarded adults who lived at home, urban college freshmen, and fifth- and eighth-grade children, they produced an interesting picture of political values. Utilizing a 40-item questionnaire, they concluded that (a) there was a high degree of similarity among all four groups, (b) values of the mentally retarded individuals who lived at home were most similar to the values of same-age college students, (c) the values of mentally retarded individuals who resided in residential facilities were most similar to the values of the children, and (d) the values of the mentally retarded in residential facilities were least like those of college freshmen. Several reasons for these findings are possible:

1. Mentally retarded adults are affected by political socialization just as the nonretarded. Those who lived in the community were exposed to more political socialization. Political socialization is affected more by experience than by intellectual limitations.
2. Mentally retarded adults who resided in the community were better educated than those in residential facilities. Previous research indicates that more highly educated people tend to adopt dominant political values (Green & Klein, 1980).
3. Public education emphasizes political socialization, whereas residential education does not.
4. Other differences in the backgrounds of the residential and nonresidential groups account for the differences in values (the groups did not differ significantly in intelligence).

Warren and Gardner (1973) have investigated the voting knowledge of 119 educable mentally retarded (EMR) young adults. Even after receiving instruction, the group performed very poorly on a multiple-choice test of political knowledge. Their average score on an 18-item test was 7.5. The test was administered 2 weeks before the 1972 election and included questions about the identity of the candidates and voter registration. Another group of EMR adults had virtually no knowledge of politics, government functions, and American history (Gozali, 1971). These 68 young adults were unable to identify the three branches of government or the highest court.

Gerard (1974) presents more favorable data. As part of an effort to ascertain the voting rights of institutionalized retarded persons in California, a county legal counsel was asked to render an opinion. The counsel determined that those persons who could demonstrate understanding of the purpose of elections were eligible to vote. Understanding was determined by the answers to four questions: (a) What is your name? (b) What is an election? (c) Who is running? and (d) Do you prefer one candidate to another? Of the 111 individuals who expressed an interest in voting, 41 passed the test, which was administered by local voting registrars.

Several researchers have investigated the support or resistance that local, state, and federal government agencies provide to voters with disabilities. Olley and Fremouw (1974) surveyed states after the 1972 election. They found that only 5 of 47 responding states had promoted voting among the mildly retarded, and only 5 had known mentally retarded voter participation. Olley and Ramey (1978) repeated the state survey after the 1976 election and also investigated state laws concerning voting rights of mentally retarded citizens. Seven states had no restrictions on voting by persons with mental retardation;

21 states denied the vote to those adjudicated incompetent. Thirty-two states had specific efforts to promote voting of persons with mental retardation who resided in institutions, and 30 had efforts to promote voting among persons with mental retardation who lived in the community.

All of the research on voting behavior of persons with mild disabilities indicates that their voting rates are lower than those of the general population. Kandel, Raveis, and Kandel (1984) followed former school absentees (truants, etc.). They found that 62% of the males were registered to vote compared to 74% of nonabsentee males. For the females, the rates were 67% and 72%, respectively. Clark, Kivitz, and Rosen (1968) found that only 6% of a group of retarded individuals who had participated in a deinstitutionalization program had voted and less than 8% were registered. Dinger (1961) presents much higher rates for a group of mildly retarded individuals who had been educated in public schools. Of the 100 subjects interviewed, 34 had voted in the last election. This was approximately half the rate of the general public at that time but much higher than the rate reported by Clark et al. Comparison of the Clark et al. study with the Dinger study provides evidence that institutionalization has a negative influence on political socialization. In a study of a sample of mentally retarded individuals who had been out of school for approximately 15 years, it was determined that 86% had voted compared to 98% of a control group (Kennedy, 1962). Several researchers have determined that not one member of their samples, all mentally retarded, had ever voted (Edgerton, 1967; Gozali, 1971; Kokaska, 1966). Other researchers report voting rates ranging from 34% (Cassidy & Phelps, 1955) to 50% (Miller, 1965) to 64% (Bobroff, 1956).

Little research has been conducted on voting patterns of adults who are learning disabled. White, Schumaker, Warner, Alley, and Deshler (1980) conclude that political involvement was low for a group of young adults with learning disabilities, but the rate was similar to a sex- and age-matched comparison group.

Many factors influence the voting rates of mildly disabled adults. The extent to which youths with mild disabilities are educated in the mainstream appears to exert a strong influence (Bobroff, 1956; Clark et al., 1968; State Board of Public Instruction, 1969). Older individuals with mild disabilities tend to vote at higher rates than young adults with mild disabilities (Kennedy, 1962; Miller, 1965). Voting behavior is directly related to educational achievement (Levin, Guthrie, Kleindorfer, & Stout, 1971; Peterson & Smith, 1960) and socioeconomic status (Peterson & Smith, 1960).

Knowledge of Law, Criminal Behavior, and Victimization

Many researchers have concluded that adolescents and adults with mild disabilities are more likely to commit crimes than nondisabled adolescents and adults. Teachers in Illinois have estimated that 7.7% of special education students are violent offenders and 18.5% are property offenders (Lang & Kahn, 1986).

Kandel et al. (1984) report that 28% of a sample of 229 young adult males (who were considered behaviorally disordered as children) had been arrested. Only 23% of a nondisabled comparison group had been arrested. For females, the rates were 6% and 5%, respectively.

After having examined the records of a group of young adults with more severe behavioral disorders, Robins (1966) concludes that 75% of the men and 40% of the women had been arrested for offenses other than traffic violations. Fifty percent of the males had been arrested three times or more. These high rates of criminal behavior are not surprising given the fact that these individuals had been referred as children because of antisocial behavior. Robins also examined the crime patterns of young adults who were considered behaviorally disordered as children but who were not antisocial. These individuals committed crimes at a rate far below that of the antisocial group but above the general population's. In addition, members of the antisocial group were arrested frequently for crimes against persons and property. Members of the nonantisocial group were arrested for property crimes and drunkenness. Females in both groups were most often arrested for prostitution, drunkenness, and vagrancy. In another study of crime rates of persons who had been identified as behaviorally disordered as children, Phillips (1978) determined that 8% were in prison at the time of follow-up (young adulthood). This rate is far above the national rate.

Researchers have also examined the rate of criminal behavior among individuals with learning disabilities. Satterfield, Hoppe, and Schell (1982) compared 110 adolescent boys with attention deficit disorders (ADD) to 88 nondisabled boys. Both groups were followed over 8 years. The ADD group had an arrest rate seven times that of the comparison group. Multiple arrests were 16 times that of the comparison group. White et al. (1982) also conclude that the criminal conviction rate for young adults with learning disabilities was much higher than that of adults without learning disabilities.

There are dozens of studies documenting a higher crime rate among persons with mental retardation. Nearly all lead to the conclusion that a high percentage of mentally retarded adolescents and adults are arrested, convicted, and go to jail. Reichard, Spencer, and Spooner (1980) have determined that approximately 10% of the prison population is mentally retarded. This is far above the less than 3% that would be expected based on the generally accepted prevalence of mental retardation in the population of the United States.

Why is criminal behavior elevated among persons with mild disabilities? Researchers believe that the causes are many and complex. Persons with mild disabilities are likely to be exploited and enticed to commit crimes by others because of their cognitive deficits (Balkin, 1981). Weak appearances, submissiveness, physical abnormality, and social immaturity are characteristics that appear in mildly disabled persons more often than in the nondisabled population. These characteristics have been related to criminal exploitation (Balkin, 1981). People with mild disabilities often lack the insight to identify risk situations and may unquestioningly follow others into crime. Lang and Kahn (1986) have found that mildly retarded persons were often solicited to commit crimes even in small communities. The aforementioned moral reasoning deficiencies also impinge on criminal activity.

Walberg (1972) relates poor verbal ability to higher crime rates among mildly disabled people who were unable to talk their way out of dangerous and exploitative situations. Other researchers believe that the high crime rate among adults and adolescents with mild disabilities is because of a lack of training in law and criminal procedures. Reichard et al. (1980) have found that mentally retarded persons are disadvantaged because they do not know how to defend themselves from charges. Brown and Courtless (1971) also believe that ignorance is a major reason that mentally retarded persons more frequently go to jail. They have ascertained that mentally retarded defendants plead guilty more often than nonretarded defendants, are unsuccessful in gaining parole, and often confess. Brown and Courtless deem that mentally retarded persons place themselves at jeopardy because they do not know how the system works and they trust others to look out for them.

Another reason advanced for higher crime rates among populations with mild disabilities is the lack of crime prevention training offered to children and youth who are mildly disabled. Child care workers are not adequately trained to teach mildly disabled children to avoid exploitation (Schilling, Kirkham, & Schinke, 1986). Law enforcement agencies often overlook the needs of individuals with disabilities when they plan crime prevention activities (Lang & Kahn, 1986). In addition, there is a lack of research and validated intervention for mildly disabled populations by law enforcement authorities (Lang, 1987).

Individuals with mild disabilities are also frequent victims of crimes. Longo and Gochenour (1981) have found that retarded persons in institutions are frequently sexually exploited and assaulted. Later crime victimization often begins with early child abuse (Sandgrund, Gaines, & Green, 1974), and mentally retarded persons are at high risk of abuse as children (Frodi, 1981). Balkin (1981) concludes that mentally retarded persons do not know how to respond to victimization; therefore, it is often repeated. Mentally retarded children, adolescents, and adults do not effectively identify situations in which they are at risk of being victimized; they have difficulty identifying people and places that are dangerous. When they do sense danger, they are unable to act defensively in time to prevent victimization.

Community Service

Our society values community service. We believe that citizens should engage in activities for the general good. Activities such as charity work, participation in civic or service organizations, and formal service to the nation (e.g., military service, work in the Peace Corps) are recognized as measures of a person's goodness and worthiness. It appears that individuals with mild disabilities do not engage in these activities to the extent of nondisabled people, or at least activity in this area goes unrecorded. Perhaps professionals who work with individuals who are mildly disabled have so concentrated on ensuring the provision of services to people with disabilities that they have neglected to teach, encourage, and provide opportunities for service. In all the reference material reviewed for this chapter, only two writers discussed the importance of community service training in special education secondary curricula (Browder, 1987; Wimmer, 1981). Browder states that transition to adulthood involves transition to responsible citizenship. Wimmer is more specific when she concludes that a functional curriculum should include real-life service experiences.

Very few researchers have investigated the extent and kinds of community service performed by persons with mild disabilities. Robins (1966) followed individuals with behavioral/emotional disorders into adulthood. She found that none had engaged in civic or charitable activities. Others report similar dismal figures. Kregel, Wehman, Seyfarth, and Marshall (1986) determined that the least frequently reported activity of 300 mentally retarded graduates of public special education programs in Virginia was involvement in clubs, church work, and other socially responsible undertakings. In two studies of adults with learning disabilities, Scott, Williams, Stout, and Decker (1980) and White et al. (1982) state that they are much less active in community service clubs and fraternal organizations than age- and sex-matched nondisabled peers. The only study that contradicts these conclusions is Dinger's (1961). He found that 22% of a sample of mildly retarded adults were active in community projects.

One area of service that has been examined repeatedly is the military service of persons with mild disabilities. McAfee (1988) writes that most of the extensive research on the military service of persons with mental retardation was done during or immediately after World War II. That research is of little value today because of the changes in the armed forces and special education. However, it is important to note that mildly retarded persons did serve adequately and in some cases with distinction.

Chaffin, Spellman, Regan, and Davison (1971) reviewed the status of a group of 30 former work-study students 2 to 5 years after they left school. Two of the students were in the military at follow-up.

Dinger's (1961) investigation of mildly retarded adults reveals that 65% of the eligible males served. Their service records were generally satisfactory, and they received promotions at approximately the average rate. However, research done by Lee, Hegge, and Voelker (1959) contradicts Dinger's conclusions. Lee et al. found that mentally retarded adults had poorer military records than nonretarded adults.

Robins (1966) reviewed the military service records of adults who had behavioral/emotional disorders as children. She determined that they had a much higher rate of rejection from service, a high rate of problems while in the military, and many less than honorable and psychiatric discharges. They also exhibited a high rate of desertion and going absent without leave. Yet, 40% finished their service at the rank of sergeant or above. The rate for the control group was 72%. Only one other study was found in which mention was made of the military service of adults who had been considered behaviorally disordered (Neel, Meadows, Levine, & Edgar, 1988). In this study, only 6 of 96 subjects (6.25%) who had been out of school for 2 to 10 years had been in the military service compared to 38 of 398 control subjects (9.5%).

Hasazi, Gordon, and Roe (1985) have conducted a follow-up study of 301 adults who had left public special education programs in Vermont between 1979 and 1983. The sample comprised mildly disabled persons who had been considered learning disabled, mentally retarded, or behaviorally disordered. Only eight (2.7%) had been in the military.

✻ ✻ ✻

IMPROVING CITIZENSHIP SKILLS

More has been written about the poor citizenship status of persons with mild disabilities than about improving their status. However, while much of the research on citizenship skills of people who are mildly disabled is old (and perhaps no longer accurate or applicable), the research that is available on improving citizenship functioning is fairly current. Although in many areas specific curriculum content and methodology are undeveloped, sufficient knowledge exists for educators to begin the task of improving skills and participation.

The William T. Grant Foundation Commission on Work, Family, and Citizenship (1988) concludes that the key to civic integration of non-college-bound youth is the development of alternative forms of lifelong learning. Current emphasis on standardized curricula hurts non-college-bound youth, such as the majority of young adults with mild disabilities. These youths frequently drop out of school without sufficient socializing experiences. As a result, a high percentage of young adults do not undergo a successful transition to adult citizenship. In order to prevent this, educators must include participation in normative citizenship activities as part of the secondary and postsecondary experience (Browder, 1987). Educators must also provide incentives for completion of secondary and postsecondary education (William T. Grant Foundation, 1988). Curricula should be functional and experiential. Classroom time should be minimized, and time practicing adult citizenship skills in the community should be maximized (Wimmer, 1981). Professionals must develop systems that provide continued citizenship support to newly emancipated, young adults with mild disabilities. Secondary and postsecondary citizenship training should begin with the development of values rooted in the real-life, everyday experiences of the learner who is mildly disabled (Clark, 1979; Wircenski, 1982).

Wehman, Moon, Everson, Wood, and Barcus (1988) state, "The successful adult adjustment of special education graduates is undoubtedly a reflection of how effective a special education program is in preparing students" (p. 31). Following are descriptions of educational practices designed to enhance moral reasoning and decision making; increase informed political involvement; decrease criminal involvement and victimization; and increase service to the community, state, and nation. The ultimate measure of the effectiveness of these practices and the educators who use them lies in the extent to which today's young adults with mild disabilities are more effective citizens than their predecessors.

Improving Moral Reasoning and Decision Making

Many educators, including special educators, have developed effective curricula and procedures for developing moral maturity in adolescents and young adults. Figure 16–2 provides an outline of the essential elements of a comprehensive program of moral development. Educators and others can use this program as the basis for developing citizenship skills, since the foundation of effective citizenship lies in adoption of prosocial values.

Moral education is a part of the school curriculum whether intentional or not (Benninga, 1988). In most schools it is part of the hidden curriculum. Basically, there are two approaches to moral education: direct and indirect. The direct approach is telling students what is acceptable and enforcing acceptability. The indirect approach involves encouraging students to develop their own value and moral systems (Benninga, 1988). Wircenski (1982) concludes that development of values clarification skills is an essential part of career education. Students should explore values such as (a) pride in oneself, (b) responsibility, (c) dependability, (d) acceptance of just criticism, (e) assertiveness, and (f) honesty.

Swarthout (1988) has reviewed moral development training as it relates to persons with behavioral or emotional disorders, and his conclusions and observations are applicable to other persons with mild disabilities. Moral education involves teaching and learning rules for making decisions about conflicts between two or more people. Although educators may succeed in changing moral reasoning, these changes may not be accompanied by changes in behavior unless there is opportunity for guided practice in day-to-day situations (Berkowitz & Gibbs, 1983; Kohlberg & Higgins, 1987; Murphy, 1988; Swarthout, 1988).

Among the successful techniques for improving moral reasoning and moral behavior are peer discussion groups (Arbuthnot & Gordon, 1986; Berkowitz & Gibbs, 1983; Blatt & Kohlberg, 1975; Derr, 1986), role playing (Brion-Meisels, Lowenheim, & Rendeiro, 1983; Derr, 1986), and participatory decision making (Lickona, 1988). Blatt and Kohlberg (1975) conclude that moral judgment could be improved significantly by discussion of everyday moral dilemmas from the lives of the students. One of the critical elements of these discussions is the presence of an adult facilitator who can advance discussion, expose students to higher levels of reasoning, and ask probing questions. Derr (1986) suggests similar tactics to improve the moral judgment of

I. Content
   A. Identifying values
      1. Acceptable human values
      2. Desirable human values
      3. Socially dominant values/norms
   B. Moral dilemmas
      1. The nature of human conflict
      2. The impact of egocentrism
   C. Procedures for enforcement of human values in social interchange
      1. Peer pressure and acceptance
      2. Official sanctions
         a. regulations
         b. laws and punishments
      3. Other consequences
II. Processes
   A. Direct instruction of moral acceptability
   B. Discussion
      1. Moral aspects of day's events
      2. Moral aspects of content of subject curricula
      3. Moral aspects of news events
   C. Role playing
      1. Taking another's view
      2. Projecting the consequences of moral decisions into the future
      3. Practicing mature reasoning and decision making
   D. Group problem solving
      1. Exploration of multiple viewpoints
      2. Development of group norms
      3. Exposure to higher levels of reasoning from peers
         a. negotiation
         b. compromise
         c. arbitration
   E. Daily practice
      1. Student-directed development of a moral system in the classroom and school
      2. Generalization to out-of-school activity

Figure 16–2
A program for developing moral reasoning

adolescents with learning disabilities. Peer discussion groups have been used successfully to decrease the frequency of transgressions of adolescents with behavioral disorders (Arbuthnot & Gordon, 1986).

Keeping in mind Gibbs's (1987) observation that individuals with behavioral disorders often lack empathy, the technique of transactive discussion espoused by Berkowitz and Gibbs (1983) appears to be highly appropriate. In that process, students are taught to reason about another's moral reasoning and decisions in order to develop an understanding of the motives of others.

Keller and Reuss (1985) describe the goal of moral training as development and maintenance of cooperative relationships based on negotiation and problem solving. Another goal of moral training is learning the rules and roles governing relationships in the social process (Swarthout, 1988). This is accomplished best through normative experiences (i.e., those experiences that are experienced by the majority of people of the same age and social set). Thus, secondary and postsecondary teachers must ensure that youths with mild disabilities have the same experiences as their nondisabled peers (e.g., registering to vote, registering for the selective service, participating in school-based fund-raising and charitable events). Failure to include such activities almost ensures that mildly disabled persons will not learn adult moral values and responsibility.

Several writers and researchers have developed classroom systems in which students became increasingly responsible for their own moral standards and enforcement of codes of conduct. The Just Community approach (Kohlberg & Higgins, 1987; Murphy, 1988) is a system that has great applicability to special education because it is experiential rather than didactic. Students are given responsibility for the "quality of life in their school community" (Murphy, 1988, p. 427). Classrooms become participatory democracies, with governance based on reasoning rather than authority. Students have the opportunity to make decisions and accept responsibility for their actions before they face the more dangerous world outside of school. Each class conducts "circle meetings" in which each student has an opportunity to speak. Decisions about specific actions are reached by consensus. Outcomes of decisions and actions are discussed as they occur. The Just Community approach promotes ownership and participation, two qualities that are often missing in the moral lives of many adults with mild disabilities.

Any attempt at moral education for persons with mild disabilities should include the following elements (Swarthout, 1988):

1. Teachers should analyze the hidden curriculum of the school and the values of the community.
2. Teachers should function as more mature moral role models.
3. Regular curriculum content (e.g., reading assignments) should be used to illustrate moral dilemmas.
4. Explicit moral education should be added to the curriculum. This is especially important for adolescents with mild disabilities who are likely to miss subtleties in everyday situations unless they are highlighted.

5. Teachers should conduct moral discussions and help students analyze their own moral decisions and those of others.
6. Teachers should educate students to think for themselves and develop their own codes so that they can resist undue and harmful peer pressure.
7. Teachers should conduct regular classroom meetings to discuss moral issues that emerge. Students should discuss rationale for rules.

Enhancing Political Socialization

Obviously, for many adolescents and adults with mild disabilities, complete political socialization (e.g., voting, knowledge of current events, knowledge of political issues) is an unrealistic goal. The reading deficits that are characteristic of a large segment of the mildly disabled population have a negative impact on their ability to remain abreast of current events and issues. Teachers can help students with mild disabilities overcome that problem by directing their attention to electronic media because reading failures experienced by many learners who are mildly disabled make it unlikely that they will devote much of their time to an activity with such unpleasant memories. Teachers who would enhance the political knowledge of learners with mild disabilities must be willing to utilize effective media early if they wish their students to develop a habit of remaining informed.

At the secondary and postsecondary levels, political education for individuals with mild disabilities must be functional, basic, and practical. Except in cases where students are planning to attend a postsecondary educational program, they are unlikely to benefit from extensive instruction in the workings of government and American history because much of their time and attention will be directed to the more important tasks related to obtaining employment. However, they should be taught how to register to vote; if they are 18, registration could be a school-sponsored activity. Students should learn whom to contact for registration and voting assistance. (The Voting Rights Act of 1982 allows persons with reading difficulty to have assistance in the booth.) Teachers can conduct mock registrations and elections so that students can practice their skills and discuss political issues. Teachers should also inform students about restrictions on voting that might affect the voting rights of some individuals with disabilities (i.e., adjudicated incompetence). Finally, students should learn how to obtain information about candidates and issues through organizations such as the League of Women Voters.

Improving Legal Knowledge and Developing Resistance to Crime and Victimization

Just as teaching people how to vote will not ensure their presence at the polling place on election day, teaching people about criminal law, their rights, and the consequences of violating the law will not ensure that they will be law-abiding citizens. However, ignorance of the voting process or law and individual rights will ensure that they will not vote and that they will encounter legal difficulties.

A program in legal education for adolescents and adults with mild disabilities should include three major goals: (a) basic understanding of the legal system and individual rights when a criminal charge has been made, (b) development of skills and behaviors to recognize and resist criminal behavior and criminal exploitation, and (c) development of skills to reduce the risk of criminal victimization.

Brown and Courtless (1971) and others have observed that persons who are mentally retarded or otherwise disabled are less likely than able persons to understand criminal processing procedures. For many adolescents, the only sources of legal knowledge are the popular media. Much of what is dramatized in the media is incomplete, inaccurate, and misleading. Furthermore, given the deficits in incidental learning that characterize much of the mildly disabled population, it is unlikely that mere observation is sufficient. Direct instruction is essential. Using actual observation of criminal processing, teachers can illustrate the concepts of culpability (responsibility for crimes) and competence (ability to participate in one's defense) and tie these lessons to discussions of morality. Competence can be taught to persons with disabilities. Although it might appear that developing competence exposes persons with disabilities to greater risk of a prison sentence (because incompetent defendants may not be prosecuted), research (McAfee & Gural, 1988) demonstrates that legal incompetence places people with disabilities in jeopardy of longer and more frequent incarceration.

Units for instruction in law should include (a) a basic definition of criminal behavior; (b) an analysis of the authority of the government to prosecute; (c) a description of criminal processing including arrest, arraignment, and trial; (d) an analysis of the rights of a defendant/offender (e.g., right to an attorney, right to remain silent); and (e) an analysis of the consequences of certain defendant actions (e.g., confessing, pleading incompetence). Teachers can use classroom trials for infractions of rules to illustrate points of law and to provide actual experience. News events are also valuable sources of examples of legal points and procedures. The ultimate goals of such a program are not to help people with mild disabilities become experts in law but to teach them how to obtain effective assistance and ensure their rights.

Prevention of criminal behavior should be included in both elementary and secondary curricula. The first step in lowering crime rates among persons with mild disabilities is to involve criminal justice personnel. Lang (1987) concludes that most people involved in criminal justice have poor knowledge of the characteristics of individuals with mild disabilities. Furthermore, crime prevention programs developed by criminal justice personnel neglect the needs of learners with disabilities. Special educators should discuss their needs with local officials. Together they can determine what programs are available and how they can be adapted for learners with disabilities. Specific elements of a prevention program include (a) instruction in identifying dangerous and exploitive situations and relationships, (b) development of behaviors that reduce the risk of exploitation (e.g., appearance of confidence, resistance to peer pressure, avoidance of exploitive people), (c) development of empathy for potential victims, (d) assertiveness, (e) procedures to report criminal enticement, and (f) training of professionals and parents to recognize exploitation.

Persons with mild disabilities are more likely to be victims of crimes. Professionals can provide instruction to reduce the risk of victimization by training these individuals how to (a) identify victimization, (b) report victimization, (c) identify the characteristics of high-risk situations, and (d) promote an image that reduces the perception of easy victimization. Professionals who work with people with disabilities should be taught how to identify victimization and how to obtain help for people with mild disabilities who have been victimized.

It would be naive to believe that such interventions could eliminate the problems of crime for persons with mild disabilities, but many of the problems stem from phenomena that are beyond the scope of educators (e.g., the living situation of Jerome Bowden described in Smith [1986]). Ample evidence exists, however, that criminal behavior, exploitation, and victimization can be reduced.

Increasing Service Opportunity and Performance

Improving the service performance of adolescents and adults with mild disabilities requires presentation of opportunities while these individuals are still in school. Service should become a habit. Wimmer (1981) believes that community service projects should be part of the high school curriculum. Pereira (1988) states that such projects enable adolescents to gain a better perspective on citizenship and responsibility. This may be especially important to persons with mild disabilities for whom service expectations are low. Without planned opportunities to provide service, individuals with mild disabilities are likely to view the relationship between themselves and society as one way in which people who are mildly disabled are the receivers of service but are not expected to reciprocate.

Teachers should also present the opportunity for military service to adolescents with mild disabilities. The William T. Grant Foundation (1988) concludes that training while in the armed forces is one way that non-college-bound youth can receive meaningful postsecondary education. Service in the military may also provide concrete lessons in the reciprocal relationship between individuals and society.

❦ ❦ ❦

SUMMARY

From the preceding discussion, readers should have learned that persons with mild disabilities are often limited as citizens, for many reasons. Some limitations stem from an individual's disabilities (e.g., deficits in incidental learning). Others result from a failure to practice necessary skills (e.g., service to the community), and others are attributable to the limitations of social systems that are designed for nondisabled individuals. All of these deficiencies can be improved. Researchers have demonstrated that persons with mild disabilities can be effective citizens if they are given the necessary opportunity and training.

REFERENCES

Arbuthnot, J., & Gordon, D. A. (1986). Behavioral and cognitive effects of a moral reasoning development intervention with high-risk behavior disordered adolescents. *Journal of Clinical and Consulting Psychology, 54*, 208–216.

Balkin, S. (1981). Toward victimization research on the mentally retarded. *Victimology, 6*, 331–337.

Benninga, J. S. (1988). An emerging synthesis in moral education. *Phi Delta Kappan, 69*, 415–418.

Berkowitz, M., & Gibbs, J. (1983). Measuring the developmental features of moral discussion. *Merrill-Palmer Quarterly, 29*, 399–410.

Blatt, M., & Kohlberg, L. (1975). The effects of classroom discussion upon children's level of moral judgment. *Journal of Moral Education, 4*, 129–161.

Bobroff, A. (1956). A survey of social and civic participation of adults formerly in classes for the mentally retarded. *American Journal of Mental Deficiency, 61*, 127–135.

Brion-Meisels, S., Lowenheim, G., & Rendeiro, B. (1983). Student decision making: Improving the school climate for all students. In S. Braaten, R. B. Rutherford, Jr., & C. A. Kardash (Eds.), *Programming for adolescents with behavioral disorders* (Vol. 1, pp. 117–130). Reston, VA: Council for Children with Behavioral Disorders.

Browder, P. M. (1987). Transition services for early adult age individuals with mild mental retardation. In R. N. Ianacone & R. A. Stoddard (Eds.). *Transition issues and directions* (pp. 77-90). Reston, VA: Division on Mental Retardation, Council for Exceptional Children.

Brown, B. S., & Courtless, T. F. (1971). *The mentally retarded offender*. Rockville, MD: National Institute of Mental Health.

Bryan, T., Werner, M., & Pearl, R. (1981). Learning disabled students' conformity responses to prosocial and antisocial situations. *Learning Disability Quarterly, 5*, 344–352.

Cassidy, V. M., & Phelps, H. R. (1955). *Post-school adjustment of slow learning children*. Columbus: Ohio State University.

Chaffin, J. D., Spellman, C. R., Regan, C. E., & Davison, R. (1971). Two follow up studies of former educable mentally retarded students from the Kansas Work-Study Project. *Exceptional Children, 37*, 733–738.

Clark, G. M. (1979). *Career education for the handicapped child in the elementary classroom*. Denver: Love.

Clark, G. R., Kivitz, M. S., & Rosen, M. (1968). *A four year project: Vocational training, rehabilitation, and follow-up* (Report No. RD1275P). Washington, DC: Department of Health, Education, and Welfare.

Derr, A. M. (1986). How learning disabled adolescent boys make moral judgments. *Journal of Learning Disabilities, 19*, 160–164.

Dinger, J. C. (1961). Post-school adjustment of former educable mentally retarded pupils. *Exceptional Children, 63,* 353–386.

Edgerton, R. B. (1967). *The cloak of competence: Stigma in the lives of the mentally retarded.* Berkeley: University of California Press.

Ford, L., Dineen, J., & Hall, J. (1984). Is there life after placement? *Education and Training of the Mentally Retarded, 19,* 291–296.

Frodi, A. M. (1981). Contribution of infant characteristics to child abuse. *American Journal of Mental Deficiency, 85,* 341–349.

Gerard, E. O. (1974). Exercise of voting rights by the mentally retarded. *Mental Retardation, 12,* 45–47.

Gibbs, J. (1987). Social processes in delinquency: The need to facilitate empathy as well as sociomoral reasoning. In W. Kurtines & J. Gerwitz (Eds.), *Moral development through social interaction* (pp. 101–118). New York: Wiley.

Gozali, J. (1971). Citizenship and voting behavior of mildly retarded adults: A pilot study. *American Journal of Mental Deficiency, 75,* 640–641.

Gozali, J., & Gonwa, J. (1973). Citizenship training for the EMR: A case of educational neglect. *Mental Retardation, 11,* 49–50.

Green, B. B., & Klein, N. K. (1980). The political values of mentally retarded citizens. *Mental Retardation, 18*(1), 35–38.

Hasazi, S. B., Gordon, L. R., & Roe, C. A. (1985). Factors associated with the employment status of handicapped youth exiting high school from 1979 to 1983. *Exceptional Children, 51,* 455–469.

Kandel, D. B., Raveis, V. H., & Kandel, P. I. (1984). Continuity in discontinuities: Adjustment in young adulthood of former school absentees. *Youth and Society, 15,* 325–352.

Keller, M., & Reuss, S. (1985). The process of moral decision making: Normative and empirical conditions of participation in moral discourse. In M. Berkowitz & F. Oser (Eds.), *Moral education: Theory and application* (pp. 87–108). Hillsdale, NJ: Erlbaum.

Kennedy, R. J. (1962). *A Connecticut community revisited: A study of the social adjustment of a group of mentally deficient adults in 1948 and 1960* (Report No. 655). Washington, DC: Department of Health, Education, and Welfare, Office of Vocational Rehabilitation.

Kohlberg, L. (1981). *Essays on moral development. Vol. I: The philosophy of moral development.* San Francisco: Harper & Row.

Kohlberg, L., & Higgins, A. (1987). School democracy and social interaction. In W. Kurtines & J. Gerwitz (Eds.), *Moral development through social interaction* (pp. 202–250). New York: Wiley.

Kohlberg, L., Levine, C., & Hewer, A. (1983). *Moral stages: A current formulation and a response to critics.* New York: Wiley.

Kokaska, C. J. (1966). The mentally retarded and the ballot box. *The Digest of the Mentally Retarded, 3,* 124–125, 132.

Kokaska, C. J. (1972). Voter participation of the EMR: A review of the literature. *Mental Retardation, 10*(5), 6–8.

Kregel, J., Wehman, P., Seyfarth, J., & Marshall, K. (1986). Community integration of young adults with mental retardation: Transition from school to adulthood. *Education and Training of the Mentally Retarded, 21,* 35–42.

Lang, R. E. (1987). Police generated safety programs for handicapped children: A school centered, community-based model. *The Illinois Policeman, 19,* 19–34.

Lang, R. E., & Kahn, J. V. (1986). Teacher estimates of handicapped student victimization and delinquency. *The Journal of Special Education, 20,* 359–365.

Lee, J. L., Hegge, T. R., & Voelker, D. H. (1959). *A study of social adequacy and of social failure of mentally retarded youth in Wayne County.* Detroit: Wayne State University.

Levin, H. M., Guthrie, J. W., Kleindorfer, G. B., & Stout, R. T. (1971). School achievement and postsecondary success: A review. *Review of Educational Research, 41,* 1–16.

Lickona, T. (1988). Four strategies for fostering character development in children. *Phi Delta Kappan, 69,* 419–423.

Longo, R., & Gochenour, C. (1981). Sexual assault of handicapped individuals. *Journal of Rehabilitation, 47,* 24–27.

McAfee, J. K. (1988). Adult adjustment of individuals with mental retardation. In P. J. Schloss, C. A. Hughes, & M. A. Smith (Eds.), *Mental retardation: Community transition* (pp. 115–162). Boston: College-Hill.

McAfee, J. K., & Gural, M. (1988). Individuals with mental retardation in the criminal justice system: The view from states' attorneys general. *Mental Retardation, 26,* 5–12.

Miller, E. L. (1965). Ability and social adjustment at midlife of persons earlier judged mentally deficient. *Genetic Psychology Monographs, 72,* 139–198.

Murphy, D. F. (1988). The Just Community at Birch Meadow Elementary School. *Phi Delta Kappan, 69,* 427–428.

Neel, R. S., Meadows, N., Levine, P., & Edgar, E. B. (1988). What happens after special education: A statewide follow-up study of secondary students who have behavioral disorders. *Behavioral Disorders, 13,* 209–216.

Olley, J. G., & Fremouw, W. J. (1974). The voting rights of the mentally retarded: A survey of state laws. *Mental Retardation, 12*(1), 14–16.

Olley, J. G., & Ramey, G. (1978). Voter participation of retarded citizens in the 1976 presidential election. *Mental Retardation, 16,* 255–258.

Pereira, C. (1988). Educating for citizenship in the elementary grades. *Phi Delta Kappan, 69,* 429–431.

Peterson, L., & Smith, L. A. (1960). A comparison of postschool adjustment of educable mentally retarded adults with adults of normal intelligence. *Exceptional Children, 26,* 404–412.

Phillips, G. (1978). The turned off revisited. *Today's Education, 67,* 88–91.

Reichard, C., Spencer, J., & Spooner, F. (1980). The mentally retarded defendant-offender. *Journal of Special Education, 14,* 113–119.

Robins, L. N. (1966). *Deviant children grown up.* Baltimore: Williams & Wilkins.

Sandgrund, A., Gaines, R. W., & Green, A. H. (1974). Child abuse and mental retardation: A problem of cause and effects. *American Journal of Mental Deficiency, 79,* 327–330.

Satterfield, J. H., Hoppe, C. M., & Schell, A. M. (1982). A prospective study of delinquency in 110 adolescent boys with attention deficit disorder and 88 normal adolescent boys. *The American Journal of Psychiatry, 139,* 795–798.

Schilling, R. F., Kirkham, M. A., & Schinke, S. P. (1986). Do child protection services neglect developmentally disabled children? *Education and Training of the Mentally Retarded, 21,* 21–26.

Scott, A. J., Williams, J. M., Stout, J. K., & Decker, T. W. (1980). *Field investigation of learning disabilities.* Scranton, PA: University of Scranton Press.

Smith, P. (1986, June 28). The execution of Jerome Bowden: "Bringing to light something wrong." *The Atlanta Constitution,* p. 36.

State Board of Public Instruction. (1969). *Post high school adjustment of the educable mentally retarded.* Des Moines, IA: Author.

Swarthout, D. W. (1988). Enhancing the moral development of behaviorally/emotionally handicapped students. *Behavioral Disorders, 14*(1), 57–68.

Walberg, H. J. (1972). Urban schooling and delinquency: Toward an integrative theory. *American Educational Research Journal, 9,* 285–299.

Warren, S. A., & Gardner, D. C. (1973). Voting knowledge of the mildly retarded. *Exceptional Children, 40,* 215–216.

Wehman, P., Moon, M. S., Everson, J. M., Wood, W., & Barcus, J. M. (1988). *Transition from school to work: New challenges for youth with severe disabilities.* Baltimore: Brookes.

White, W. J., Alley, G. R., Deshler, D. D., Schumaker, J. B., Warner, M. M., & Clark, F. L. (1982). Are there learning disabilities after high school? *Exceptional Children, 49,* 273–274.

White, W. J., Schumaker, J. B., Warner, M. M., Alley, G. R., & Deshler, D. D. (1980). *The current status of young adults identified as learning disabled during their school career.* Lawrence: University of Kansas.

William T. Grant Foundation Commission on Work, Family and Citizenship. (1988). *The forgotten half: Non-college-bound youth in America.* Washington, DC: Author.

Wimmer, D. (1981). Functional learning curricula in the secondary schools. *Exceptional Children, 47,* 610–616.

Wircenski, J. L. (1982). *Employability skills for the special needs learner.* Rockville, MD: Aspen.

PART V

𝓍 𝓍 𝓍

Issues in Transition

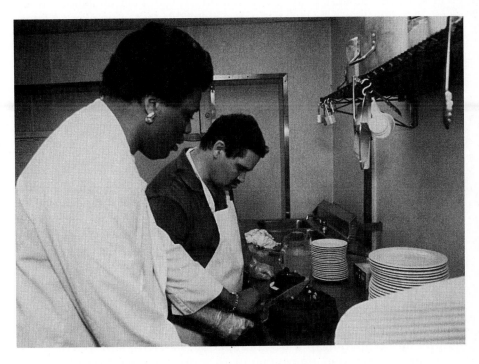

With defined goals, effective methods, and a facilitator, the future of transition for people with mild disabilities can be a successful one.

I ssues in transition are presented in two chapters. In chapter 17 we discuss current and future research trends and needs, and in chapter 18 we consider the future of transition, including issues, goals, and trends.

❦ ❦ ❦

CHAPTER 17

Legislation, advocacy, and social commitment to transition and adult literacy have provided the basis for a growing interest in the provision of transitional services to adolescents and adults with mild disabilities. A number of authors have indicated that the transition literature is often heavily weighted toward individuals with severe disabilities to the near exclusion of other disabling conditions (Knowlton & Clark, 1987; White, Schumaker, Warner, Alley, & Deshler, 1980). In this chapter, we present an overview of the current status of the transition research literature dealing with individuals with mild disabilities. Based on the literature we have reviewed throughout this text, a number of future research issues and needs are identified. Specific research issues and needs are described in the three realms of transition: (a) academic, (b) vocational, and (c) extravocational. This discussion is followed by an analysis of research issues and needs that cut across more than one realm. Finally, we present a very brief description and comparison of various research methodologies that can be and have been utilized by transition researchers and practitioners.

Some of the more important research issues addressed in this chapter include the need to

- develop identification and service delivery assessments for a heterogeneous population;
- identify, catalog, and disseminate successful intervention techniques within the academic, vocational, and extravocational realms, and the need to validate those techniques with persons who have differing attributes; and
- conduct research in different environments and across the life span with the resources that are commonly available in the community. The critical environments include the community, work sites, postsecondary sites, and family settings. Critical periods during an individual's life span include movement from high school to employment, high school to postsecondary education, employment to postsecondary education (and vice versa), present occupation to a new occupation, current employer to a new employer, present employment to more advanced employment, employment to retirement, and retirement to leisure or community service.

❦ ❦ ❦

CHAPTER 18

In this chapter, we project the evolution of transition theory and practice. We begin with a brief discussion of the need for broader theory development in transition. Theories that have been related to transition are described in some detail. We then consider how those theories might be useful in the future. The discussion evolves into an analysis of specific issues within the systems framework described in chapter 5.

At all points in this chapter, our discussion is guided by the observation of Johnson, Bruininks, and Thurlow (1987):

> Effective transition service planning and coordination can be accomplished only by (a) developing consistent policy goals at all levels; (b) formulating more effective management strategies to interpret and articulate policy goals and objectives, using proven planning models in organizing and coordinating services; (c) collecting reliable and valid information to guide decision making; and (d) using systematic evaluations of participant outcomes and the costs and benefits of services. (p. 326)

❦ *Vignette* ❦

Bernie is a 33-year-old father of two who has worked for a large communications company for 8 years. He began as an unskilled worker and has impressed his employer with his hands-on approach to solving problems. His hard work and dedication to his job have made him a highly valued employee who now works in one of the laboratories doing quality control.

Bernie has not always been successful. He graduated from high school mostly because of social promotions (i.e., promotions due to chronological age rather than achievement) and sympathetic teachers who admired his motivation but were unable to remediate his severe reading disability. His grades were dismal, but he was a hard worker, never made waves, and came to school every day. Now, his history is about to catch up with him. He was recommended for a promotion to a first-line supervisory position. His initial excitement turned to fear and then to anger when he took and failed the required written test for the position. Company policy allows only one retake of the test. Bernie's failure is likely a result of his slow reading rate and comprehension deficits. Although the supervisory position requires minimal reading, Bernie will probably not get the promotion. There is no doubt that he possesses the other skills; his work is thorough and accurate, and his peers respect him.

Much time and energy was devoted to the development of the supervisory test, and although sympathetic, company "brass" is reluctant to abandon the system to meet the needs of one man. Bernie wants the job, he has bought a new house, he has been a loyal employee, and he is trying to suppress his feelings of anger and abandonment.

Bernie's situation illustrates a phenomenon that is just now becoming apparent with improved and extended follow-up studies. A person with a disability appears to have made a successful transition; he or she has obtained steady employment, is integrated into the community, and has a successful family life. Others get promoted, however, and the person with the disability finds that the impact of the disability becomes prominent again. There is a new transition to be faced, perhaps a need to return to school to upgrade skills in a technologically changing job. But school has been the scene of the greatest failures. In addition, the services and assistance that were available when Bernie and others like him were 21 are harder to find at 33.

Our society is one that demands constant updating and retraining. People like Bernie are decidedly disadvantaged by their disabilities and a conceptualization that transition ends at a specific age or when the individual begins to exhibit success. Transitions present problems for persons with mild disabilities at all stages of life. One of the characteristics commonly associated with persons with mild disabilities is an inability to adapt. But, society requires constant and sometimes abrupt adaptation. It is insufficient to help Bernie make an initial successful transition to adult life without also helping him acquire the skills and identify the resources he needs to continue to make adaptations.

Part V is devoted to a discussion of the "unfinished business" of transition including issues such as those confronting Bernie.

REFERENCES

Johnson, D. R., Bruininks, R. H., & Thurlow, M. L. (1987). Meeting the challenge of transition service planning through improved interagency cooperation. *Exceptional Children, 53*, 522–530.

Knowlton, H. E., & Clark, G. M. (1987). Transition issues for the 1990s. *Exceptional Children, 53*, 562–563.

White, W., Schumaker, J., Warner, M., Alley, G., & Deshler, D. (1980). *The current status of young adults identified as learning disabled during their school career* (Research Report No. 21). Lawrence: University of Kansas Institute for Research in Learning Disabilities.

Chapter 17

❦ ❦ ❦

Current and Future Research Priorities

Social and legal changes have provided the basis for changes in services to persons with mild disabilities. Many of the social and legal changes have occurred because of research findings. For example, researchers have determined that infant stimulation programs are effective in reducing the impact of disabilities. This resulted in legislation at the federal level to support such programs (PL 99-457). Researchers have also determined that persons with disabilities encounter great difficulty in making the transition from school to adult life. The abrupt reduction in support services at that stage often results in inactivity, frustration, and poverty. Researchers have also determined that proper planning and sequenced reduction of support enhances the prospect for transition success. Thus, research has led to changes in funding and expectations for our schools and other agencies. The phenomenon is iterative: research leads to changes in practice, and changes in practice provide new opportunities for research. Because of this relationship, practitioners and researchers must collaborate to design and implement effective, research-based intervention programs for this population.

In this chapter we briefly describe the kinds of research related to transition for persons with mild disabilities that have appeared in recent literature. We then describe what we believe are the research priorities in the academic, vocational, and extravocational realms. This is followed by a discussion of research needs that cut across the three realms. Finally, we present a description and comparison of various research methodologies that may be and have been used in transition research.

❦ ❦ ❦

RESEARCH TRENDS

Throughout this text we have described hundreds of references related to the transition of persons with mild disabilities from secondary schools to postsecondary pursuits. Broadly, studies have fallen into one or more of the following realms: (a) academics (both secondary and postsecondary), (b) vocational (work and employment), and (c) extravocational (social and community integration). A brief analysis of trends in transition research, most of which has occurred since the mid-1960s, is presented here.

Longitudinal Studies

Longitudinal research with persons who have disabilities dates to the late 19th century when researchers began to investigate the pervasive influence of disabilities on families. Much of this early research was directed at identifying an immutable influence of genetics, especially in cases of mental retardation and mental illness. Even though this research was more emotionally charged than it was scientific, it did demonstrate the lifelong impact of disabilities.

In the early part of the 20th century, researchers such as Baller (1936) conducted longitudinal research for the sole purpose of determining adjustment patterns across the life span. Specifically, they sought to determine whether people with mental retardation became integrated into society and adjusted to life's demands after they left the relative security of school. For the most part, these studies revealed that the road through adulthood was rocky but that some persons made remarkable adjustments and were very successful, fully participating members of society. Longitudinal research continues as an important element of the transition literature.

What have we learned from longitudinal research? We know that the impacts of mild disabilities persist into adulthood. They do not go away, nor are they "outgrown." Persons with mild disabilities often lead marginal adult lives on the edge of poverty, in low-paying jobs, without participation in the meaningful activities of adult life. Some persons with mild disabilities lead very successful and well-adjusted adult lives. Research has failed to yield any consistent factors for accurate long-term discriminating predictions except that more successful adults with mild disabilities come from families of higher socioeconomic status, have earlier and more extensive work and social experiences, and develop skills of independence at an earlier age. The latter conclusion provides us with some important implications for transition practice: Persons with mild disabilities must be provided with graduated opportunities for independent work and social experience.

Predictive Studies

Closely associated with longitudinal research is predictive research. In predictive research, the investigator attempts to identify and measure relationships between childhood characteristics and adult adjustment. Predictive studies have occurred with relative frequency (see, e.g., Balow & Bloomquist, 1965; Silver, 1969). Although these studies have provided some interesting data, they have not been especially useful in terms of providing information about improving education and training practices that enhance the likelihood that a person with a mild disability will make a successful transition into adult life. Predictive research has led us to the conclusion that the more severe a disability is, the more pervasive its impact will be on adult adjustment. It has also indicated that mildly disabled children who evidence antisocial behaviors will encounter greater difficulty in adult life than those whose disabilities are more cognitive. Most importantly, however, predictive research has shown that people with very severe antisocial symptoms in childhood can and have made successful transitions, and people with very mild symptoms have encountered great difficulty. Thus, although childhood characteristics are important, other variables may overshadow and ameliorate their impact.

Effective Practices Research

More recently, researchers have focused on effective practices. The practices we have described in chapters 6 through 16 (academic, vocational, and extra-vocational) have emerged as a direct result of specific research in areas such as direct instruction, time and learning, job coaching, in situ vocational training, graduated independence, and social skills training. Unfortunately, most of the effective practices research for persons with mild disabilities has been limited to academic instruction. Some of the social skills research has been conducted with persons with mild disabilities, but the majority of the recent research on effective vocational training has been aimed at moderately and severely disabled populations. This is indeed problematic as there is every reason to believe that persons with mild disabilities can benefit significantly from the emerging practices in vocational and community-based instruction. Indeed, as we have stated previously, much of the research in vocational and extravocational practices has included people with mild disabilities even though the titles of such studies would lead the casual reader to believe that the sample used was solely moderately to severely disabled. Unfortunately, this phenomenon and its implications have not been adequately analyzed.

Transition Conceptualization Research

Many researchers have attempted to define the perimeter of transition; that is, they have sought to answer the question, What are the important elements of transition? In earlier research, it is evident that work and employment were the primary foci. As we have stated repeatedly in this text, the notion that employment training can be separated from other elements of adult life is indefensible. Research of the past 20 years has shown us that work skills, social skills, academic skills, civic responsibility, and leisure are interactive in determining the adequacy of adult adjustment. Yet we find that such broad research with persons with mild disabilities is relatively scarce.

For example, there are few studies of the community adjustment of persons with learning disabilities and even fewer that include multiple elements of adjustment in the academic, vocational, and extravocational realms. Most studies deal solely with employment or postsecondary education. The research that is available tends to be descriptive (e.g., Fafard & Haubrich,

1981; White, Schumaker, Warner, Alley, & Deshler, 1980)—it describes the social and adjustment problems encountered by adults who are learning disabled but provides little information on intervention and successful practices. Thus, we are left with an incomplete and perhaps oversimplified picture. The situation is similar for people with emotional disorders. Research on transition for such persons tends to be targeted toward the persistence of the emotional problems in adulthood. Researchers seem to neglect vocational research and academic research for this population.

The picture is somewhat more complete for individuals who are mildly retarded. This may be the result of a belief that mental retardation is a broader disability, that is, that it affects all activities, whereas learning disabilities have been viewed until recently as having an academic influence only and emotional disorders as having a social influence only. Of course, we know that this is a gross oversimplification and that all three disabilities have a more extensive impact on transition. Thus, we are beginning to see more extensive studies of persons in these two categories who are experiencing transition.

Research in Behavioral/Emotional Disorders

Research on the transition needs of people with emotional/behavioral disorders is also scarce. There are few studies in which exemplary vocational training practices for this population are described and evaluated. This research is emerging as the evidence begins to mount that this disability has been the most impervious to intervention. The effect of serious behavioral problems in our schools has not gone unnoticed as administrators and teachers note the escalation of violence, crime, and disruption. Researchers have concluded that without successful intervention leading to secure and meaningful employment, the patterns persist into adulthood. As a result, we are beginning to witness research that addresses the entire range of the emotionally disordered student's needs, including vocational training. In fact, there is evidence that effective academic and vocational programs bring about a concomitant improvement in social behavior.

Categorical Research

In this text we have addressed the transition needs of persons who are learning disabled, mentally retarded, or emotionally disturbed. We believe that persons who fall within these three categories share characteristics and needs. Yet, research leads us to conclude that categorically different needs also exist. The transition needs of young adults with learning disabilities are likely to be somewhat different from those with mild retardation, whose needs are likely to be somewhat different from those with emotional/behavioral disorders. These differences may be artificially enhanced by the emphases of the research that is available: academic and postsecondary education research for young adults with learning disabilities, social skills research for young adults with behavioral disorders, and employment research for young adults with mild mental retardation.

The research of the last 15 years indicates that it is not the content of transition programs that should differ for the three groups but the relative emphasis given to the three realms. Persons with learning disabilities need extravocational and vocational training, but, because of their cognitive abilities and needs, academic training may be more heavily stressed. Individuals with emotional disorders need extravocational training to address their primary deficits, but they also require academic and vocational support. People with mental retardation obviously need support in all three areas.

It is apparent that much work remains to be done in order to improve the empirical basis of transition practices. Research has not generated a comprehensive, effective overall approach to or even a foundation for transition for persons with mild disabilities. However, research has provided us with many effective practices for improving specific skills. It appears that this is the manner in which effective transition programs will be built—step by step.

❦ ❦ ❦

RESEARCH PRIORITIES FOR THE 1990s

Review of the literature utilized to write this text leads to many inescapable conclusions about what should constitute the research priorities for the next 10 years. These priorities include items that have been specifically identified as a result of previous research (e.g., to what extent do the vocational training procedures developed for the severely disabled apply to people with mild disabilities?) and items that have been neglected by researchers (e.g., how should transitional practices reflect the multicultural society that we have become?).

In the following subsections, we identify some of the primary research needs in the academic, vocational, and extravocational realms, then conclude by discussing research needs that incorporate more than one realm.

Academic Research Needs

Our exploration of secondary programming in relation to the transition of students with mild disabilities has brought to light a challenging research agenda. The foremost challenge in secondary education is to develop validated systems to keep students with mild disabilities in school to graduation or to successful completion of a transition program. Approximately one quarter of the general student population drops out. Dropout rates for students with disabilities are much higher and have reached truly alarming proportions for certain subgroups of at-risk students (e.g., students who are emotionally disturbed, Latino, or African-American).

To date, research on the dropout phenomenon has followed two major lines of inquiry: research on student characteristics and, more recently, research on structural and organizational characteristics of schools as they relate to school termination. These two research thrusts are essential for the third and most important: dropout prevention. Research that leads to the development of schools with "holding power" is most critical. Program development, implementation, and evaluation will be important interrelated issues. Diverse programs are likely to emerge to address the needs of subsets of students at risk of dropping out.

A second challenge involves collaboration and cooperation among the various programs and service providers who contribute to the transition success, or failure, of students with mild disabilities. Secondary programs are characterized by departmentalization and separation (e.g., special education vs. regular education, special education vs. vocational education, secondary schools vs. postsecondary schools). It has become abundantly clear that the transition needs of persons with mild disabilities cut across lines and barriers that stand between programs and service providers. It is also clear that most persons with mild disabilities have been ineffective in coordinating these services for themselves. Collaboration, cooperation, and consultation are key elements in effective service delivery. Research on collaborative and consultative models and methods is needed to enhance the effectiveness of personnel, services, and programs. Researchers must identify the motivational elements for collaboration so that those elements can be manipulated to reduce territoriality and resolve other problems.

A third challenge for researchers involves the continued growth and implementation of transition programs tied to secondary schools. Transition programs are in their infancy. Research is needed to guide development along sound theoretical lines, cull ineffective methods while highlighting effective ones, and match program variables and components to the needs of individuals and groups of students. The ultimate question is, What works, and for whom? Once again, diversity within the population and the need to respond to individual needs argues against a blanket approach.

The growth of transition programs raises an equity issue that must be addressed. The descriptive studies reveal that availability of and accessibility to transitional services and programs is tied to school characteristics such as district size and wealth. It appears that the endemic/systemic inequality that characterizes the public school system will impact on transitional services. It is also true that transitional services are more critical in the districts in which they are most likely to be underfunded (i.e., large urban districts and small rural districts) because the community is economically depressed. Research is needed to further document this effect or trend as a basis for exploring ways to mitigate the social and economic factors that prevent all students from obtaining the services they need.

A final challenge involves the imperative of follow-up research on programmatic and instructional effects. Such research is needed to determine

• the effects of secondary school curricular choices on postsecondary pursuits and success;

- the effects of traditional and nontraditional transitional services and models across diverse student populations, economic levels, and geographic regions;
- the effects of newly defined "basic skill" instruction on the school success of persons with mild disabilities;
- the effects of collaborative approaches on interdisciplinary cooperation and ultimately on student performance; and
- the effects of emergent approaches to assessment on students' school performance.

The ultimate value of follow-up research lies not in the immediate data but rather in the use of the data for program and service development through evaluation, modification, and improvement.

Vocational Research Needs

The needs for vocational research are several, some less obvious than others. The most straightforward of the research needs in the vocational realm is the development of validated training technology. As we have stated, much of the technology in special vocational education has been borrowed from the literature on training persons with moderate to severe disabilities. There is ample evidence that this technology is effective for people with mild disabilities, but we are still in need of more extensive evaluation of specific procedures. We also need to evaluate the social appropriateness of techniques that may be viewed as condescending. Yet, it is apparent that regular vocational education that relies heavily on cognitive approaches to learning skills has not been terribly effective for learners with mild disabilities, and there appears to be a reluctance to adapt behavioral techniques to vocational education. The adaptation of these techniques must occur with respect for what employers will tolerate in the workplace. Thus, researchers need to develop and validate behavioral vocational procedures that do not highlight the differences between those with mild disabilities and those without.

A second critical need in the vocational realm is developing the mildly disabled individual's capacity to seek and obtain job advancement. Few employees are content to remain in one job without prospect for promotion for a lifetime; yet, we seem to have totally neglected the need of people with disabilities for advancement. Our concepts of transition often end at the point at which the individual has held a job for 6 months. Researchers have not addressed the need to build into the individual's repertoire the means to seek advancement. It is almost as though we are telling people with disabilities that merely having a job is enough. There is research that shows that job satisfaction and performance decline for people with disabilities when they perceive their jobs as dead ends. An attendant need in this area is to evaluate the practices of employers that enhance or reduce job advancement for persons with mild disabilities.

Related to the issue of job advancement is the need for lifelong vocational education opportunities. Technology is changing so rapidly that the person who does not take advantage of continuing education is likely to become unemployed because of obsolescence. Researchers must develop systems for lifelong learning that can accommodate persons with mild disabilities. Also, they must develop the individual's knowledge of and motivation to use continuing education. Otherwise, the efforts put into transition may result in short-term gain only.

An issue that was addressed in the preceding subsection must also be discussed here: integration of effort and services. Secondary vocational education, postsecondary vocational education, vocational rehabilitation, colleges and universities, and proprietary vocational/technical schools must develop integrated systems through collaboration and cooperation. Researchers should evaluate collaborative practices with the ultimate criterion being the degree of successful transition.

Research targeted toward improving the capacity of postsecondary systems to deliver vocational education (including education for professions at colleges and universities) to persons with mild disabilities is almost nonexistent. There is a smattering of special programs focused primarily on those who are learning disabled, but the entire postsecondary industry (including barber and beauty colleges, auto mechanics schools, paralegal institutes, etc.) must begin to serve the population that has mild disabilities. Before this can happen, researchers need to develop and implement effective accommodation practices that can be utilized and evaluated in those environments.

Finally, researchers must continue to analyze the job market, educate employers, and assist organizations that must meet the requirements of the Americans with Disabilities Act. It is insufficient that special educators and other advocates have succeeded in convincing Congress to enact this legislation. Researchers must show practitioners that accommodation makes sense and is achievable. Failure to do so will result in a backlash that will surely make the employment situation worse for persons with disabilities.

Extravocational Research Needs

It is the extravocational realm that provides the broadest opportunities for research. The needs here are enormous, and the current knowledge is very limited. For that reason, we have restricted our discussion to four of the most pressing needs.

There is no doubt that social integration is one of the goals of transition efforts for persons with mild disabilities. Yet, we have little research describing the social integration status of people with mild disabilities beyond the age of 21. We need some simple descriptive research that analyzes phenomena such as friendship patterns, use of recreational opportunities, and employment related social networks. After researchers have determined the extent and nature of social integration, they must begin to identify and evaluate practices that can be implemented in school that will enhance integration.

Associated with integration is the issue of personal responsibility. Researchers have concluded that many persons with mild disabilities are over-protected by their families and the professionals charged with developing their capacities (i.e., teachers, counselors, etc.). This overprotection creates individuals who are unable to make decisions and accept the responsibility for the consequences. Thus, persons with mild disabilities are presented with a two-pronged dilemma: their disabilities make it more difficult for them to assume responsibility, predict consequences, and plan accordingly, and those who are closest to them often deny them the experiences they need to learn the skills of responsibility. Successful transitions will never occur unless researchers develop programs of graduated risk taking and responsibility. Sooner or later a "driver in training" must get behind the wheel, and people with mild disabilities must learn to make and accept decisions. Researchers need to determine how and when measures of independence are best granted.

Along with research on responsibility comes the need for research on family and parenting. For most persons, the transition to adult life includes marriage and responsibility for a family. Researchers have begun to provide some descriptive research on family life for people with disabilities, but they have yet to develop and evaluate programs to help individuals with mild disabilities cope with the demands. There are some programs available but little evaluative data.

Finally, an issue that has become increasingly important and difficult in our society is that of alcohol and substance abuse. Researchers have deter-mined that people with mild disabilities are at greater risk for substance abuse than nondisabled persons. There are a host of reasons for this: low self-esteem, susceptibility to peer pressure, and the drug treatment that many receive as therapy. Whatever the reasons, we know little about the impact of substance abuse on their lives and even less about effective treatment. These two areas must be addressed quickly, especially if the goals of transition for mildly disabled people are to gain independence and become integrated into the community.

Broader Research Needs

In addition to the research needs outlined so far in the three specific realms, there are a number of needs that cut across more than one realm. Again, a complete analysis of the research issues is beyond the scope of this text. Therefore, we limit our discussion to a few of the more important issues.

Researchers need to expand efforts to provide more extensive information about unstudied or understudied groups. Most transition research involves very young adults only (under age 22). This is because federal funding requirements target school-age populations. This allows a truncated view of transition. We need to know more about long-range adjustment so that we can improve practices that have an impact across the life span.

As mentioned previously, transition research has been differentially targeted for subgroups of persons with disabilities. The research base is much greater for those with mild retardation than for those with learning disabilities or behavioral disorders. Researchers must continue to expand knowledge about adults who are learning disabled in areas such as specific vocational training practices, community integration, and amelioration of the isolation so often reported by them. Researchers must also investigate job training practices for young adults with behavioral disorders. We know that effective academic programs have concomitant positive influences on the social behavior of behaviorally disordered children. Do effective vocational programs lead to similar concomitants?

Researchers should continue to expand the catalog of specific effective practices across the academic, vocational, and extravocational domains. The effectiveness of these practices should be established for subjects with specific characteristics across a variety of environments and across the life span. Practices employed in one domain should be exported to and evaluated in the others.

Researchers should take a critical look at generic services and their effectiveness for persons with mild disabilities. Throughout this text, we have encountered research and testimony that indicate that people with mild disabilities are inadequately served in generic transition programs—colleges, high school vocational programs, and so forth. It appears that those who operate generic programs are convinced of their responsibility to serve persons with mild disabilities only when they are provided with special funds from the federal government, and then their efforts are often ineffective because they try to force the person who is mildly disabled to "fit" rather than to accommodate his or her uniqueness. Perhaps the Americans with Disabilities Act will provide some much needed impetus for service providers to take an inclusive rather than exclusive approach. In any case, there are some generic programs that are effective. What is it that makes them so?

Much of the research in transition is piecemeal. The development of some complex statistical models of transition would begin to provide some unifying influence over what is often a fractionated field. Multivariate, large-sample studies are needed. Such studies can also aid the development of more elaborate theory.

Researchers must continuously evaluate the impact of instructional programs. There is a growing chorus of negative feelings about the persistent entrenched emphasis on basic skills. Advocacy for alternatives is growing, including vocational competence and functional curricula. Simultaneously, there is a reaffirmation of the importance of basic skills as generalizable skills and the integration of academic skills into vocational education (Cobb & Neubert, 1992). Researchers must redefine what constitutes basic skills for persons with mild disabilities. This redefinition must be based on a backward-looking approach—which skills are necessary in the postschool environment most likely for that child.

At this point it should be obvious that there are many critical research topics in the area of transition. We have made no attempt to be exhaustive; however, we believe that the issues enumerated are the most critical. In the next section, we describe some of the research methodology that can and should be applied to the research questions.

❦ ❦ ❦

RESEARCH METHODOLOGY

In order to determine the current status of adults with learning disabilities, a number of descriptive, experimental, and correlational studies have been conducted with individuals and small and large groups. We discuss next the purposes, strengths, and weaknesses of descriptive/group designs, single-subject designs, and qualitative research. A comparison of single-subject and group designs is presented.

Group Research

Group research takes many forms. At its simplest, researchers can employ the methods of ***descriptive research*** to convey only the current status of the group studied on some variable or variables. For example, a researcher might interview a group of persons who are learning disabled to determine the extent to which they consume alcohol. Another form of descriptive research is developmental research. In a developmental study the researcher might obtain information about how people with mild disabilities make decisions at various stages of their lives.

    Correlational studies describe relationships between phenomena. A researcher conducting correlational research might investigate the relationship between the amount of alcohol persons with mild disabilities consume and other variables such as the number of friends they have, their access to an automobile, and their exposure to alcohol education.

    Researchers conducting ***causal-comparative research*** draw cause-and-effect relationships between phenomena. These cause-and-effect relationships are very tentative because the researcher has been unable to exercise the degree of control over the variables that is necessary to be more conclusive. A researcher conducting a causal-comparative study might, for example, attempt to link parental attitudes with the disabled person's degree of transition success. As the researcher is not really able to manipulate the parents' attitudes to determine if they influence success, he or she can only suggest that there is a possible causal link between the two.

    The most complex and best controlled group research is ***experimental research.*** In experimental research, the researcher compares the performance of two groups that have been randomly assigned. This comparison is made on the basis of some variable of interest to the researcher. The comparison is made after each group receives some different treatment. For example, a transition researcher might assign students to two different forms of vocational training and then compare their productivity. If the study was adequately controlled, it would be considered an experimental study.

Single-Subject Research

Intrasubject replication designs, also referred to as *single-subject research,* replicate treatment effects within a subject to support the internal validity of the approach (i.e., extent to which behavioral change can be attributed to the treatment procedure). These designs are relevant in identifying successful intervention techniques for individual subjects.

The adult population with mild disabilities has been identified as a heterogeneous one. Single-subject designs are especially useful with such populations because they allow the researcher to make precise and valid statements regarding the effectiveness of specific procedures with specific subjects when homogeneous groups are not available. Single-subject designs are appropriate for monitoring the progress and effectiveness of interventions in vocational, social, academic, personal, and citizenship skills.

Qualitative Research

Because of the heterogeneous nature of the mildly disabled population, a number of researchers (Eldredge, 1988; Geib, Guzzardi, & Genova, 1981; Simpson & Umback, 1989; Temple, 1988) have either utilized or suggested the use of case studies or qualitative research as an alternative to group or single-subject investigations. *Qualitative research* involves intense data collection on many variables over an extended time period in a naturalistic setting. Data collection is done via interviews and both participant and nonparticipant observation techniques. Qualitative research could be applied to transition by observing many aspects of the environment to identify variables associated with effective and ineffective adult adjustment. A variety of strategies and instruments may be utilized.

Qualitative research usually results in the formulation of tentative hypotheses from the data to explain observed behavior. In this type of research, the investigator does not find support or nonsupport (as in other research) for a hypothesis. The qualitative approach is often used in anthropology. Much information is accumulated that is usually difficult to analyze or replicate. The reader is directed to Edgerton's (1967) book, *The Cloak of Competence,* for a more thorough understanding of the use of qualitative research with disabled populations.

Single-Subject versus Group Research

Single-subject and qualitative research designs have been presented as a valuable alternative to group study for several reasons applicable to the study of transition. The adult population with mild disabilities is a heterogeneous one. Individual responses to treatment are highlighted in the single-subject or case study approach. In group research differential responses to treatment would be averaged across a number of individuals. For example, a selected strategy might substantially increase the rate of interactions between a group of subjects and peers, which would produce a group difference of significant magnitude to validate a program's effectiveness. The investigator, however, would be hard-pressed to determine for whom the given educational program was or was not effective without a further individual analysis. Single-subject research allows the researcher to immediately determine the effectiveness for individuals.

Another advantage of single-subject research is that statistical significance obtained through inferential statistics used in group designs does not necessarily support the clinical or applied significance of the treatment. For example, a reduction in reliably measured negative interactions with fellow employees from 30 to 5 per day for a group of 15 individuals may be statistically significant. A number of these individuals, however, would still be considered as unacceptable by fellow employees. The effectiveness of applied or single-subject research, on the other hand, is judged by the difference between the strength of an individual's behavior before and after treatment.

A third problem with group designs is the failure to control for variability within groups, which has been a major obstacle in special education research (Cronbach & Snow, 1977). Many potentially effective educational practices have not demonstrated statistical success because of differences in the characteristics of subjects in the experimental groups. While some students excel as a result of specific educational practices, others show little progress. These within-group differences obscure the potential value of these procedures for some individuals.

The single-subject approach also minimizes the interference of between-subject differences. Single-subject designs evaluate the variability of behavior within the individual across program conditions, without relying on the presence or absence of variability between one subject and another. For example, a self-instruction program may be demonstrated to be effective in increasing on-task behavior in a job setting for a worker with a learning disorder. In the process, no comparison is made between the individual and that of other workers.

The major disadvantage in the use of single-subject and qualitative research methodology lies in the limited confidence one may place in generalizing the findings from one individual to another (Kiesler, 1971). This can be remedied by systematic replication of single-subject designs, which can be time-consuming but holds several advantages over group designs. One is that replication usually takes place in a somewhat different setting, thus expanding the validity of the treatment to a new environment. Hersen and Barlow (1976) suggest that four guidelines are necessary for sound replication. First, single-case research reports should include a clear and concise description of the setting, change agents, behavior, and subjects; initial and subsequent replications should vary one of these pertinent factors. Second, investigators should identify differences across variables when contrasting systematic replications. Third, if no exceptions are found as replications proceed, wide generality of findings can be established. Fourth, systematic replications are over when all relevant replications are finished and when all relevant exceptions are identified.

An approach to increasing the external validity of single-subject and/or qualitative research designs is advanced by Bergin and Strupp (1972). The authors advocate the use of single-case studies to develop specific treatment packages potentially applicable to well-defined treatment groups. A group design could then be used to evaluate the treatment approaches, which would thereby increase one's confidence in the generalizability of the findings.

Finally, it is likely that ideas for group research may evolve from single-subject replications or from qualitative case study designs. However, as the preceding discussion illustrates, it is unlikely that group designs will result in intervention procedures for specific individuals. It is also unlikely that a significant population of adults with mild disabilities who share homogeneous characteristics and can be studied as a group will be identified in the near future.

🌿 🌿 🌿

SUMMARY

A review of the literature indicates that over the past 20 years interest in transition for persons with mild disabilities has grown. In the past, investigative efforts with this population have primarily focused on the use of survey, descriptive, and group research methodologies for the purposes of identification and diagnosis. Such research has served to define the characteristics of this population and provides basic insights into the problems faced by adults who are learning disabled. The need for services has also been identified. However, the use of single-subject designs to develop effective strategies to remediate and accommodate the cognitive, social, personal, and vocational problems faced by adults in community employment and postsecondary settings has not been vigorously pursued.

Since laws now mandate the provision of services for adults with mild disabilities and today's population is very sophisticated in terms of advocacy, we can expect that the demand for effective services will increase. We need to establish basic guidelines for such programs through research dealing not only with the characteristics and needs of adults and adolescents with mild disabilities but also the unique characteristics and demands of the settings (community, employment, and postsecondary) with which they will be interacting. In addition, future research must direct itself to the pertinent indicators (or skills) dictated by the academic, vocational, and extravocational domains, within each setting. In short, the primary thrust of research now, and in the immediate future, should involve the development of data-based intervention techniques to be used in such programs and settings. Finally, we need to do research on the service delivery network to ensure that it is capable of maximizing the effective transmission of proven interventions that will facilitate the transition to adult life.

REFERENCES

Baller, W. R. (1936). A study of the present social status of a group of adults who when they were in elementary school were classified as mentally deficient. *Genetic Psychology Monographs, 18,* 165–244.

Balow, B., & Bloomquist, M. (1965). Young adults ten to fifteen years after severe reading disability. *Elementary School Journal, 66,* 44–48.

Bergin, A. E., & Strupp, H. E. (1972). *Changing frontiers in the science of psychotherapy.* New York: Aldin-Atherton.

Cobb, R. B., & Neubert, D. A. (1992). Vocational education models. In F. R. Rusch, L. DeStefano, J. Chadsey-Rusch, L. A. Phelps, & E. Szymanski (Eds.), *Transition from school to adult life.* Sycamore, IL: Sycamore.

Cronbach, L. J., & Snow, R. E. (1977). *Aptitudes and instructional methods.* New York: Irvington.

Edgerton, R. B. (1967). *The cloak of competence: Stigma in the lives of the mentally retarded.* Berkeley: University of California Press.

Eldredge, J. L. (1988). A 52 year old dyslexic learns to read. *Reading, Writing and Learning Disabilities, 4,* 101–106.

Fafard, M., & Haubrich, P. (1981). Vocational and social adjustment of learning disabled young adults: A follow-up study. *Learning Disability Quarterly, 4,* 122–130.

Geib, B. B., Guzzardi, L. R., & Genova, P. M. (1981). Intervention for adults with learning disabilities. *Academic Therapy, 16,* 317–325.

Hersen, M., & Barlow, D. H. (1976). *Single case experimental designs.* New York: Pergamon Press.

Kiesler, D. J. (1971). Experimental designs in psychotherapy research. In A. E. Bergin & S. L. Garfield (Eds.), *Handbook of psychotherapy and behavior changes: An empirical analysis* (pp. 36–74). New York: Wiley.

Silver, A. A. (1969). More than 20 years after—A review of developmental language disability: Adult accomplishments of dyslexic boys. *Journal of Special Education, 3,* 219–222.

Simpson, R. G., & Umback, B. T. (1989). Identifying and providing vocational services for adults with specific learning disabilities. *Journal of Rehabilitation, 55*(3), 49–55.

Temple, C. U. (1988). Developmental dyslexia and dysgraphia persistence in middle age. *Journal of Communication Disorders, 21,* 189–207.

White, W., Schumaker, J., Warner, M., Alley, G., & Deshler, D. (1980). *The current status of young adults identified as learning disabled during their school career* (Research Report No. 21). Lawrence: University of Kansas Institute for Research in Learning Disabilities.

Chapter 18

The Future of Transition: Theoretical and Practical Issues

*I*n our discussion to this point, we have identified a number of issues, goals, and trends in the areas of legislation; models of transition; barriers to transition; secondary and postsecondary programming; and prevocational, vocational, and rehabilitation services. Theoretical underpinnings for each area have been described. In this chapter we address the need for a sound theoretical base for transition curriculum and program development. We view this need as a critical one for the development of transition. Then we consider the future of transition within the systems framework described by Bronfenbrenner (1977). (For a discussion of this system, refer to the preview to Part I and chap. 5.) Finally, we conclude the chapter by discussing several important practical questions about the future of transitional services for persons with mild disabilities.

THEORETICAL CONSIDERATIONS

We believe that for transition and transitional services to grow and become more effective, a more extensive, sounder theoretical base must be developed. This theoretical base should provide an overarching view of how transition, both successful and unsuccessful, occurs. Such a theory would allow researchers and, more importantly, practitioners to identify the important variables and patterns that impact on an individual's transition. From this, modifications in curricula and practice could be planned, implemented, and evaluated. Currently, there is no cohesive theoretical framework on which to plan growth and elaboration. However, there are elements of theory that we can use to build a theory of transition. We will describe here some of the applicable theories and how they might be useful in constructing an effective transition system of the future.

Cummings and Maddux (1987), in a comprehensive text on career and vocational education for individuals with mild disabilities, emphasize that

career development approaches or programs designed for disabled populations appear to have evolved spontaneously. They postulate that the place of
theory in design and development of programs has been ignored or given
minor attention. We agree that a theoretical framework is essential not only
for career and vocational training but also for each of the elements and disciplines of the transition process. The following discussion of a number of theoretical approaches is adapted from Cummings and Maddux's chapter on
career development theory and disabled populations.

Personality Theory

Theorists working in this area indicate that factors such as early experiences,
attitudes, interests, and abilities relate to vocational and life choices. Although
early childhood experiences are an important component of this theory,
genetic and ability factors are also emphasized. Roe (1956) hypothesizes that
parent-child interactions exert an influence on the adult life of an individual.
In *overprotective environments,* parents baby children, encourage dependence,
and restrict any self-initiated activity. In *avoidance environments,* parents reject
or neglect the child. In *accepting environments,* children are treated as equals in
the family circle. According to personality theory, children from overprotective environments choose vocations that are service or people oriented,
children from avoidance environments pick professions that are not people
oriented, and children from accepting environments choose occupations that
may or may not be people oriented.

Osipow (1983) indicates that little empirical evidence exists to support the
tenets of personality theory and its application to transition. Osipow points out
that the theory lacks clear implications for transition counseling goals and recommendations, and it does not present remedial measures to correct inappropriate vocational goals. Therefore, personality theory is not terribly useful for
transition practitioners.

In contrast, Cummings and Maddux (1987) suggest that personality
theory has some implications for youth with disabilities, but these implications
are important at a time long before we usually begin to think about transition
(i.e., in early childhood). However, if parents, counselors, and pertinent others
are made aware of early environmental influence, vocational and life decisions
faced by young adults with disabling conditions may be facilitated.

Developmental Theory

Two different models, developmental and self-concept, are incorporated within
this theoretical framework. Self-concept theorists postulate that self-concept
becomes more clearly defined as individuals mature. Occupational and life
choices are influenced by the individual's perception of self in relation to life
and occupational opportunities. Developmental theorists believe that individuals pass through a number of life stages that determine behavior. For

example, Buehler (1933) describes four stages of development (with implications for transition): (a) the growth stage (0–14 years), (b) the exploratory stage (15–25), (c) the maintenance stage (25–65), and (c) the decline stage (65–on).

Cummings and Maddux (1987) identify Super's (1976) developmental self-concept theory of vocational behavior as an example of a theory that incorporates both the self-concept and developmental theoretical framework. Super's theory encompasses the work of self-concept theorists such as Rogers (1942; 1951), Carter (1940), and Bordin (1943), plus Buehler's (1933) work in developmental psychology.

Super (1957, 1976) identifies five levels of career development: (a) the growth stage (0–14 years), (b) the exploration stage (15–24), (c) the establishment stage (25–44), (d) the maintenance stage (45–65), and (e) the decline stage (65–death). During the growth stage, individuals develop first an awareness of self followed by an awareness of self in relation to others. Fantasies centered around "What will I be when I grow up?" are based on these concepts. During the exploration stage, the individual explores a number of different opportunities to an extent dependent on the results of the previous growth stage. Self- and other's perceptions of ability, talent, and so forth may exert an influence on what is attempted and what is viewed as possible. Toward the end of this stage, an individual may make tentative life, occupational, and career commitments. During the establishment stage, decisions made during the exploratory stage may become firmly established or changed. Changes are influenced by experiences. Also at the end of this stage, life and occupational decisions are solidified. During the maintenance stage, individuals continue to progress in directions chosen during the establishment stage. During the decline stage, career activity gradually or abruptly ceases. In short, this theory implies that an individual will make occupational and life decisions dependent on his or her self-concept (which is often determined by successes or failures in previous stages) and on the stage of life that the individual is experiencing.

In a discussion of the implications of Super's (1957) theory for those with mild disabilities, Cummings and Maddux (1987) state that "because handicapped individuals are less likely than nonhandicapped persons to have clearly defined self-concepts, and since they have a more limited view of various occupations, they may not be capable of making adequate career decisions" (p. 89). If self-concept is not well developed and accurate, an individual with a disability may have either an overly high or low expectation of his or her capabilities. Based on the premise that adult success with occupational and personal choices is influenced by experiences in previous developmental stages, the implications of this theory are apparent: students with mild disabilities should be encouraged to explore themselves, their attributes, and how they relate to work and other adult roles.

Ginzberg, Ginsburg, Axelrad, and Herman (1951) are the originators of a second developmental theory that Cummings and Maddux (1987) identify as having implications for individuals with mild disabilities. The Ginzberg et al.

theory incorporates three distinct and irreversible developmental periods. During the *fantasy period* (approximately 0–12 years), youngsters play out a number of make-believe adult roles. During the *tentative period* (approximately 12–24), the individual passes through four stages of development: *interest, capacity, value,* and *transition.* Behaviors during this period include exhibiting an interest for certain occupations and activities, relating one's capabilities to performing within these areas of interest, establishing a value base for future activities, and choosing a route for achieving selected occupations and/or lifestyles. During the *realistic period* (approximately 24 on), which incorporates the *exploration, crystallization,* and *specification* stages of development, the young adult focuses on making a choice among a number of selected interests or options. This stage is followed by the development of a clear selection of activities and finally a refinement of these choices.

The three periods of the Ginzberg et al. (1951) theory are characterized by a number of decisions based on an individual's aspirations and opportunities. In addition, environmental, educational, emotional, and values variables have an impact on personal and occupational decisions within each of the periods (Osipow, 1983). Cummings and Maddux (1987) believe that the Ginzberg et al. theory has relevance for individuals with mild disabilities. This relevance is partially because the theory incorporates deviant patterns of development. For example, Ginzberg et al. describe a possible stage of *pseudocrystallization* during the realistic period. During this stage, an individual acts as though he or she has made clear choices, yet succeeding events prove otherwise. The theory is limited by the lack of development of intervention techniques for individuals who exhibit deviant patterns of development and by the fact that the theory was developed based primarily on the behaviors exhibited by males in the upper socioeconomic class (Osipow, 1983).

Social Systems

Adherents of this approach postulate that socioeconomic status and cultural expectations exert the major influence on individual occupational and life decisions. A number of specific social variables that exert influences on individual occupational and life choices have been identified. Hollingshead (1949) identifies several variables (e.g., models, values, rewards, and punishments) that are influential and that are dependent on social class membership. Osipow (1983) indicates that socioeconomic status influences educational, and hence vocational, decisions. Additional important variables identified by researchers include family size (Blau & Duncan, 1967); father's income (Rosenberg, 1957); environmental influences such as the home, family, school, and church (Osipow, 1983); and industrial organization influences such as job requirements and salary.

Cummings and Maddux (1987) indicate that an acceptable theory for use with persons with disabilities and based on the social systems approach to adult development has not been developed. They believe that the approach has "less relevance for handicapped individuals than do other models" (p. 91)

because the research utilizing this theory has neglected varial
socioeconomic status. According to the theory, children from lc
ilies will not be as successful as children from high-income fan
children with disabilities from high-income families are apt t(
low-income individuals than like their nondisabled peers. The
ficient because the interactions among socioeconomic status, c
environments, and physiological variables (including disabi
addressed and have not been adequately investigated.

We believe that the fault lies not in the basic premise of
much as in the incompleteness of the variables included i
Certainly, it is possible to expand this theory to include other ;
such as the impact of disabilities and the interactions of disabili
characteristics, and social systems. If that were done, the social
might prove to be very useful and comprehensive. It might ;
practical tool to identify variables that can be manipulated t(
transition "odds" of persons with disabilities.

Trait Factor Approaches

Supporters of the trait factor theory assume that if an individual
interests are matched with an occupational choice, success in
follow (Osipow, 1983). A number of instruments for assessing
interests and aptitudes have been developed based on this the
the Strong-Campbell Interest Inventory (Campbell, 1974:
Hansen, 1981) and the Kuder Occupational Interest Survey (
Kuder & Diamond, 1979). According to Osipow, this theoretic;
used, often exclusively, by career counselors.

Cummings and Maddux (1987) discuss two specific trait fa
the *theory of work adjustment* (Dawis, 1973) and the *theory of v
sonalities and work environments* (Holland, 1985). The th
adjustment is based on a belief that occupational adjustment d
individual achieving a correspondence, balance, and/or harm
work environment. Tenure, job satisfaction, employer satisfactio
of an individual's employment are dependent on maintaining
dence between the demands of the occupational environment ;
and needs brought to the environment by the individual or th
work personality. In short, there is a balance between the employ
isfied with the skills brought to the job by the employee and t
being satisfied with the rewards offered by his or her employmer
Dawis, 1969).

The work personality strives to achieve the required balance l
and the environment. If correspondence does not exist, some wc
the environment to change it, whereas others react to the env
order to initiate change. Dawis (1973) describes these in(
responding in either an *active* or *reactive* fashion. In addition,

-ribed as *flexible* or *rigid,* depending on how much discorrespondence the ~~k~~er can tolerate, and as *fast* or *slow,* depending on how quickly the worker ~~l~~ates change when discorrespondence occurs.

Similarly, Holland's (1985) theory of vocational personalities and work ~~e~~nvironment postulates that an individual will be satisfied with his or her occu-~~pat~~ion if it is suited to his or her personality. Holland identifies six personality ~~and~~ corresponding work environment categories:

The *realistic* category includes individuals who seek manual and physical employment in an environment that demands little or no contact with other people. Occupations in this area may include heavy machine operation, forestry, and farming.

The *investigative* category contains individuals who seek activities that require organizing and analyzing in an environment that demands the ability to solve abstract and scientific problems. Occupations in this area include physicists, chemists, and mathematicians.

The *artistic* category includes persons who seek an egocentric existence but are willing to express deep emotion. Occupations in this area entail employment in theater, dance, and other arts.

The *social* category includes individuals who possess excellent interpersonal skills and choose occupations that are conducive to helping others (social work, counseling, etc.).

The *enterprising* category includes individuals who use their excellent interpersonal skills to manipulate others and to attain high occupational status. Careers in this area include employment in politics, sales, and corporate environments.

The *conventional* category includes individuals who adapt their personal needs to the work environment. Individuals in this category often work in clerical, secretarial, and bookkeeping positions.

Holland's (1985) theory incorporates three important dimensions to be ~~co~~nsidered within the six personality and environmental categories. The first ~~di~~mension, **congruence,** refers to the degree that a work environment is con-~~du~~cive to the individual's personality. The more congruent, the more satisfied ~~th~~e person will be. For example, artists will be happy in a setting where they ~~ca~~n express their creative personality. The second dimension, **consistency,** is ~~th~~e degree to which an individual selects an appropriate occupation or vacil-~~lat~~es between occupations. Persons who are consistent are likely to be more ~~su~~ccessful than those who are not. The third dimension, **differentiation,** is the ~~de~~gree to which a person exhibits an extremely high preference for an occu-~~pa~~tion. Persons who work in occupations for which differentiation is high will ~~be~~ successful in that area, whereas a person who exhibits many interests across ~~oc~~cupations will experience difficulty in identifying successful employment. ~~Th~~e undifferentiated person, however, once he or she finds employment, may ~~be~~ happier than the differentiated person because he or she will have the ~~ca~~pability to enjoy leisure and family ventures and accept job changes.

According to Cummings and Maddux (1987), "the trait factor approaches are as relevant as developmental approaches in explaining occupational behavior of handicapped persons" (p. 92). Developmental approaches center on the self-concept of the individual in relation to the environment across developmental stages. Trait factor approaches focus on the personal characteristics of the individual and how these characteristics interact with the adult occupational environment. An advantage of the trait factor approach is that counselors do not have to be concerned about previous or early development; they need consider only where the individual stands in the present. Occupational choices are determined by individual preferences and valid vocational instrumentation. This, however, does little for our need to know how to improve and expand realistic occupational choice for persons with disabilities. The Holland theory presents a viable foundation for directing some curriculum and programmatic decisions when the individual is at the career choice stage, but it does little to help us shape the decisions that must occur in the years before that stage is reached. The Holland theory does, however, identify the interaction between the individual's attributes (e.g., knowledge, attitudes, skills) and the environment (e.g., classroom, workplace, home, community) as the critical element in transition.

❦ ❦ ❦

THEORY AND PRACTICE

In chapter 4, we present a model for transition consisting of the individual, a facilitator, settings, and setting agents, all of which are linked by various methods and relationships designed to achieve transition goals. By relating this model, which we called "the process of transition," to the theoretical concept advanced by Holland (i.e., the unique interaction between individual traits and environments), we are able to create a theoretical foundation for future curriculum and program decisions.

We have postulated that transition is broader than just movement from secondary education into employment. It is movement from one set of personal and environmental expectations to another. For example, one transition may involve the movement of a student from secondary education, family, community, and leisure settings to adult employment, postsecondary education, family, community, and leisure settings. If we apply Holland's theory to this movement, success will be determined by not only the characteristics of the individual but those of the various environments in which the individual finds him- or herself and the interactions among those characteristics. For individuals with mild disabilities, the most effective integration and interaction of individual and environmental variables is difficult to identify. Every important model of transition (such as those identified in chap. 3) calls for a coordination of services for people with mild disabilities by an individual or a team of individuals. This phenomenon is a recognition that persons with mild disabilities need assistance in identifying and modifying environments so as to maximize their transition opportunities. In chapter 4 we identify the person or persons who would provide this assistance as the facilitator of transition. Depending on the environments (secondary or postsecondary as described in Part II, vocational as described in Part III, extravocational as described in Part IV), the facilitator would identify the best ways to enhance the interaction of individual and environmental characteristics. Curriculum, policy, and program decisions should follow.

Integration of theory and practice is often difficult to accomplish. If, however, we are committed to facilitating the transition process, we must continuously refer to and refine a theoretical foundation for our practices and procedures. In the remainder of this chapter we discuss some practical issues for the future. We advance this discussion with the aforementioned theoretical notions in mind, employing Bronfenbrenner's (1977) systems framework.

The Future within the Microsystem of Transition

Successful transition for an individual with mild disabilities will be determined, to a great degree, on what happens within the individual's microsystem. Adult success or failure is heavily influenced by interactions with close, important others (parents, employers, teachers, counselors, etc.), and within various immediate environments (secondary, employment, community, etc). As described in chapter 5, stereotypes, inappropriate training, and poor social skills often present obstacles to the transition process. We hypothesize that stereotypes are often supported by questionable formal and/or informal assessment procedures. The emphasis on labeling and identification has resulted in stereotyping. Identification procedures that highlight specific disabilities have set the foundation for negative attitudes across individuals and settings that are cast in a concrete expectation of failure in all areas. The absence of useful social, vocational, and learning skills assessment especially at the secondary level, has resulted in poor self-advocacy and inappropriate interactions in different environments.

Assessment and Training. Assessment of individuals with mild disabilities has received a great deal of attention in the literature. In elementary settings, assessment is conducted for the purpose of identification. In addition, assessment at the elementary levels of education includes an evaluation of ability and mastery of basic skills. Placement and the remediation of basic skill deficiencies are often prescribed based on this assessment. At the secondary level, the purpose of assessment becomes more complicated. Although identification remains a function, the continued assessment of basic skill deficiencies to the exclusion of other abilities is not only questionable, it is damaging.

Historically, assessment has been conducted for the purpose of identification. Shepard (1983) states that "roughly half the LD resources are spent on identification" (p. 6). Currently, as the individual progresses from elementary into secondary and postsecondary settings, the number and kinds of assessment multiply. Depending on the individual and the discipline with which he or she becomes involved, a number of evaluations often become available—medical, psychological, psychoeducational (conducted by school or private personnel), and vocational (conducted by school or vocational rehabilitation personnel). Coordination of different evaluations, however, is seldom undertaken. According to Trapani (1990), "The assessment process should not be a separate, fragmented entity, but should serve as a catalyst for initiating the design of individual, creative instructional plans for high school students" (p. 20). In addition, Sapir and Nitzburg (1973) note:

> Too often professionals look at the disabled child from a narrow limited perspective. Rather than seeing and treating the disabled child as a whole person with emotional, social, physiologic, and cognitive problems, they see only the specific problem . . . depending upon their specialization and training. (p. xiii)

Trapani (1990) provides a statement of the components of an educational evaluation at the secondary level including the following:

1. General intellectual functioning
2. Academic strengths and difficulties
3. Behavioral strengths and difficulties (including social, study, time, and self-management skills)
4. Problem-solving strategies employed by the adolescent
5. Efficacy of current placement and/or programs of instruction
6. A design for longitudinal programs and resources that will maximize academic, social, and vocational development

It is doubtful that many adolescents with mild disabilities in secondary school programs are benefiting from a functional assessment like the one just described. Comprehensive Individualized Transition Plans incorporating the various setting and setting agents with which the student must interact are nonexistent. If transition is to be truly successful for the majority of young adults with mild disabilities, future transition plans must include not only the coordination of the plethora of evaluations but also subsequent services.

In chapter 4, we present the concept of facilitator, either an individual or a team of individuals who would be responsible for coordinating transition activities. The facilitator must gather information from as many sources as possible—family, educators, vocational trainers, employers, medical personnel, rehabilitation workers—and then coordinate this information into a comprehensive transition plan. Furthermore, if we are to empower students or adults with mild disabilities, we must find ways to bring them into the evaluation and planning process so that they can begin to manage the process when the supports have been removed.

Social Skills. In chapter 5 we spoke of the barriers in various settings that individuals with poor social skills encounter. We believe that the training of social competence is of comparable importance to the training of academic or vocational skills. As indicated by Schumaker, Pederson, Hazel, and Meyen (1983), problems with social skills may be more detrimental to successful employment and adult functioning than deficits in academic or employment skills. Transition plans must, therefore, include social skills assessment and training, within the microsystem of transition.

In a chapter on social integration in employment and postsecondary settings, Chadsey-Rusch and O'Reilly (1992) state, "Social integration is an important outcome for all youths as they make their transition from school to adulthood" (p. 258). Although this outcome is generally acknowledged, specific skills and behaviors that contribute to social integration have not been researched. Chadsey-Rusch and O'Reilly suggest that there are three main outcomes associated with social integration: (a) the variety and extent of social events and activities, (b) acceptance and treatment by others, and (c) personal satisfaction with relationships. It is not known, however, if these outcomes are equally important in the successful social integration of adults with mild disabilities or whether these outcomes are more or less dependent on the environment or setting.

Finally, Chadsey-Rusch and O'Reilly (1992) suggest three categories of variables that can be manipulated to bring about successful social integration during the transition process. These include (a) *contextual* variables—changes in the physical setting, (b) *individual* variables—changes in the social behavior of individuals with disabilities, and (c) *interactant* variables—changes in the way others interact with an individual with mild disabilities. Although outcome measures and variables related to social integration have been suggested, the relative importance of the various outcomes and associated variables is not known. Research is sorely needed in the areas of social skills training and the desired outcomes of successful social integration. It is essential that educators address these issues if successful transition is to become a reality.

Trapani (1990), in an evaluation of future needs in the area of social skills training for students with mild disabilities, presents a number of research goals, reproduced here in their entirety:

1. Reliable measures of social skills to separate youths with disabilities who have social skills deficits from those who do not and to isolate the social skills that separate people with disabilities from people without disabilities should be designed (Hazel, 1987; La Greca & Mesibov, 1981; Schumaker & Hazel, 1988).
2. The developmental aspects of social skills training should be explored. Questions such as, "Which skills are essential to social competence in adolescence?" need to be asked. A hierarchy of social skills should be designed in order to develop a comprehensive curriculum (Furnham, 1986; Van Hasselt, Hersen, Whitehill, & Bellack, 1979).
3. The relationship of cognitive abilities and social competence must be considered (Furnham, 1986; Schumaker & Hazel, 1988).
4. Training for generalization must be included in the design of the social skills training program (Berler, Gross, & Drabman, 1982).
5. More information is needed about teacher feedback and the maintenance of social skills training (Berler et al., 1982). For example, the question "Does social skills training affect teachers and peers perceptions of students with disabilities?" should be answered.

6. Methods of incorporating social skills training into the curriculum must be implemented and evaluated (Cartledge & Milburn, 1978; Furnham, 1986).
7. Social validation of social skills training programs must be tested (Gresham, 1981; Michelson, Sugai, Wood, & Kazdin, 1983).
8. The effects of sex, demographics, and cultural diversity on the repertoire of essential skills must be addressed (Furnham, 1986; Schumaker & Hazel, 1988). (pp. 69, 73)

All of these points are critical issues that must be addressed in the near future if transition programs are to become more effective. We know that social skills have a profound influence on adult adjustment, and we know that social skills can be taught, but presently we are assuming that the instruction of social skills translates into better social integration of people with mild disabilities.

The Future within the Mesosystem of Transition

A number of future issues, goals, and trends within the mesosytem can be identified. Agency characteristics and requirements, and the large number of agencies available to serve the individual with mild disabilities, have historically diluted the quality of transitional services by creating confusion, competition for funds, and contradictory rules. This dilution of effective transitional planning has been described in Parts II, III, and IV.

As stated in chapter 5, community, employment, state, school, and federal agencies or settings and individuals (setting agents) who function within the various environments have specific goals and agendas. These agendas do not always correspond to individual requirements.

It is beyond the purpose of this text to describe our view of future directions for each agency involved with the transition process. General statements, however, can be made. A specific agency's requirements and characteristics are often at odds with the requirements of the individuals they serve. Each agency seeks to maintain its own identity and enhance its position in relation to other agencies. Serving this identity to the exclusion of knowledge and communication with other agencies or individuals presents a barrier to successful transition for persons with mild disabilities. In the following section, we use secondary and postsecondary education and their roles in the transition process as illustrations of this phenomenon. Furthermore, we describe some goals for these agencies that we think would enhance their effectiveness in transition.

Secondary and Postsecondary Education. The national call for "excellence in education" and the belief that students should master basic skills are admirable. In response to this call and as we described in chapter 6, secondary education programs and agencies in many states (e.g., Texas, Georgia, Florida, Oregon) have established graduation criteria including the completion of a certain number of credit hours and the passage of minimal competency testing (Knowlton & Clark, 1987). Knowlton and Clark question whether this movement will impede the provision of appropriate education in high school programs for students with mild disabilities. They state that disabled students may "transit into adult life only to experience the exclusion and inaccessibility their school-age counterparts faced 15 years earlier" (p. 563). Secondary education agencies have created requirements to meet the challenge of "excellence in education," but they have neglected to take into consideration the fact that many students with mild disabilities will not pass minimal competency testing requirements under standard conditions or may not pass the minimal number of credit hours needed within the specified time.

A goal for the immediate future should be that secondary schools develop accommodating and compensating arrangements such as oral testing and extended time lines so that the call to excellence does not become just another way of excluding persons with disabilities from the benefits of PL 94-142 and other legislation that was designed to enhance equity. If transition is to work, agencies must be flexible in determining the conditions under which requirements are accomplished.

Postsecondary programs are involved in transition in many ways. One way that has not been addressed in this text is training professionals to work in the area of transition. In our experience, postsecondary teacher training programs do not cooperate. Vocational education, regular education, special education, school psychology, reading education, and rehabilitation counseling are often impermeable to the ideas and influence of other disciplines. For example, special education teacher trainers may not see the value of courses in areas such as cultural foundations of education, vocational assessment, reading, and math methods in education. Regular education teacher trainers often do not see the value of courses in areas such as assessment and programming for special populations, the place of behavioral techniques in education, or characteristics of persons with disabilities. In addition, each discipline creates its own certification requirements. This adherence to agency specifications and loyalty to what we define as a territorial type of training hinders the transition process because it makes coordination and communication difficult. Furthermore, because new professionals are channeled through a narrow experience, they are apt to resist changes when they become employed. In addition, successful interaction among agencies and subsets within the agency (i.e., interaction within the exosystem) is made much more difficult.

Knowlton and Clark (1987) state that a principle implicit in many of the programs of personnel preparation for high school special education and special needs teachers is that these persons are preparing for specialization in the area of "transition specialist, job developer" and that this role requires differential role preparation on the part of training programs.

> The emphasis on interagency involvement in transition and the changing nature of the high school require training programs to act rather than react, reaction being the characteristic response to the aftermath of P.L. 91-142's passage when school personnel were asked to perform role functions for which they were not trained. (p. 563)

We believe that the future must experience a change in the role of some special needs teachers. This change should be an expansion to include the role of the transition facilitator (see chap. 4). This role must be clearly defined and financed, and not just mentioned in passing as it has been in most transition models (chaps. 3 and 4) or tacked on to the duties of the already over-burdened secondary special educator. The role and job description of the current secondary special education teacher does not encompass these skills, and these skills do not come from the traditional course of study of the special educator but rather from business, organizational psychology, public administration, and management. Therefore, training and certification programs must set a goal to reduce insular thinking and promote and incorporate knowledge from other disciplines and environments.

The Future within the Exosystem of Transition

In chapter 5 we outline the barriers to successful transition when individuals and agencies in one setting do not communicate with individuals and agencies in another setting. The exosystem must be developed to break down this lack of communication. Although federal and state mandates have been passed in the attempt to create or facilitate interagency cooperative and consultative agreements, most of these have not succeeded (Wehman, Kregel, & Seyfarth, 1985). The reason for this lack of success is similar to the "territoriality" described in the preceding discussion.

Again, it is beyond the scope of this text to outline the myriad of possible interagency agreements or areas in which improved cooperation and consultation would facilitate the transition process. General statements, however, can be made about agencies associated with the different setting categories (e.g., school, employment, community, and family). The following examples of goals for school, community, employment, and family agency cooperation are presented as illustrations.

School, Community, Employment, and Family Goals.   Communication across agencies within specific environments should be a starting point for future programs. Described here are some specific goals that should be attained.

Infrequent or absent communication and coordination among special, regular, and vocational education, social service, and health agencies inhibits successful transition efforts (Edgar, Horton, & Maddox, 1984; Halpern & Benz, 1984; Okolo & Sitlington, 1986). Research on the conditions conducive to successful communication and cooperation among professionals in educational settings for students involved in the transition process is imperative. This goal is absolutely applicable to rehabilitation programs, postsecondary settings, and so forth.

Another problem that must be addressed is lack of coordination and understanding among agencies in various *settings*, which leads to efforts that are at cross purposes or result in dead ends. For example, Trapani (1990) indicates that vocational education professionals involved in the transition process must get involved with linkages to the community (primarily employers) and private agencies. If these linkages are not established, students may be trained in vocations that are not marketable or that are disappearing (e.g., clerical skills without word processing). Thus, professionals working in transition must keep abreast of what is happening in the rapidly changing world into which they send their graduates.

Different expectations across individuals, agencies, and settings must be reconciled. For example, family expectations may differ from school expectations. In addition, family purposes for children may differ from what is available in a school setting. Trapani (1990) states, "Many parents fear . . . that the services provided at the junior high and high school level are inadequate and inappropriate. This appears to increase their anxiety over the future welfare of their children" (p. 88). In addition, she notes:

> Interdisciplinary team efforts that include family participation hold the greatest promise for comprehensive intervention (Vigilante, 1983). Working cooperatively, parents, teachers, and other professionals should use their power and expertise to conduct relevant assessments, design and implement effective academic and vocational programs and evaluate the realization of these goals (Biklen & Zollers, 1986; Vincent, Laten, Salisbury, Brown, & Baumgart, 1981). (p. 88)

These three examples provide some insight into the myriad individual and agency interactions that must be faced in the future. Within this context, a major goal is to answer these questions: (a) When should an agency become involved in the process? (b) What criteria should be used to determine success? (c) Which agency is responsible, and what roles does each agency play? In addition, the problems of conflicting classification and labeling procedures, confusing language systems among agencies, and differing philosophies across agencies must be tackled.

The Future within the Macrosystem of Transition

Legislative, economic, social, political, and philosophical trends influence the macrosystem for an adult with disabilities.

The Future of Legislation. Provisions of the 1990 amendments to the Education of the Handicapped Act (PL 101-476), currently known as the Individuals with Disabilities Education Act (IDEA, especially Section 626), and the Americans with Disabilities Act (PL 101-336) provide a strong foundation for the transition process. In combination, these two laws extend the transition focus to community and independent living, provide incentives for state education and state vocational rehabilitation agencies to develop, implement, and improve transition systems and services for young adults, and prohibit discrimination against adults with disabilities. Although additional mandates may be desirable, it is our opinion that the legal mandate for providing transitional services for adults with mild disabilities is now in place. However, the economic, social, political, and philosophical environment to support these mandates does not exist, and we should recognize that the mandates of PL 94-142 and the Rehabilitation Act of 1973 have never been fully funded, supported, or realized. A similar fate could befall the concept of transition.

Economic and Political Considerations. Following a decade of social, political, economic, and legislative growth, individuals and agencies involved with transition are increasingly asked to justify the cost of services. Crowner (1985) states, "Special education is now faced with political and economic consideration which may shape and limit the future of services for exceptional students" (p. 203).

Crowner (1985) proposes a taxonomy of special education finance broken into four categories: (a) base, (b) formula, (c) types, and (d) sources. *Base* refers to the element(s) on which revenues are figured, such as the number of pupils eligible for services. *Formula* refers to the method used to compute revenues, such as weighted excess cost. *Types* indicates any restrictions on how revenue is to be spent, such as continuing education and targeted education. *Sources* refers to agencies from which revenues flow, such as federal, state, and local agencies.

Crowner (1985) indicates that biases in funding can be shown by use of his taxonomy. For example, if students with severe disabilities (base) are weighted highly for generating financial support (formula) in the area of supported employment (type) and financed by federal incentives (source), then "local districts may be inclined to identify more students in those categories" (pp. 506–507).

We agree that bias in funding for students with mild disabilities can be identified by Crowner's (1985) taxonomy. As support for this belief, we offer the following argument: (a) the number of students identified as learning disabled or mildly disabled during the 1970–80 period (base) has been weighted highly for financial support during the 1970–80 period (formula); (b) the formula was dependent on providing special education services (type); and (c) the source for funding was federal, state, and local agencies. The base, formula, type, and source of funding were directed toward a specific group. The result was an overidentification of students with mild disabilities and in need of services.

These students were identified simply because they became a source of additional funds. Overidentification then became a drain on funds, which resulted in restrictions. Based on this overidentification and the subsequent restriction of economic resources that changed the source and the formula, the education community has responded with an alternative known as the ***Regular Education Initiative (REI).***

The Regular Education Initiative has become a new and, we believe, overused answer to services for students who have been identified as mildly disabled. It involves the wholesale provision of services for students who are in academic difficulty within regular education settings. This is a form of mainstreaming that, we believe, is often based on fiscal rather than educational need. In short, education's answer to the restrictions imposed after overidentification has been to return students with mild disabilities back to regular classrooms. This response is readily accepted by administrators, especially during periods of limited finances. We believe that fiscal restraints must be addressed, but we do not believe that responses should be applied across the board to fall heavily on the backs of one group.

In response to this new REI direction, Trapani (1990) states, "American society has chosen to provide equal education without defining what equality means. Does equality mean the right to sit in a mainstreamed class during one's youth but be separated from high-achieving peers in adulthood?" (p. 108).

Economic support exerts an influence on programs for persons with mild disabilities. According to Crowner (1985), the base, formula, type, and setting determine economic support for special education and serve as bases for funding priorities. Historically, funding priorities have changed quickly and alternated between students identified with mild disabilities or those with severe disabilities. Although we certainly do not advocate abandoning efforts to improve services to students who are severely disabled, our position is that in the face of economic constraints, we must maintain support for both and consider the relative prognosis for eventual independent adult functioning. It is destructive and frustrating for policymakers to continuously change priorities. The result is a system that never quite matures because it is constantly expanding and contracting.

Social Considerations. The social changes needed to bring about improvements in the lives of persons with mild disabilities have been addressed in legislation. Mandates have provided the legal means for accomplishing the intent of transition: reduction of barriers to training, employment, housing, and even political participation. Economic support, however, has not been given to the extent required, and one need only look at the notable failures to enforce Sections 501, 502, 503, and 504 of the Rehabilitation Act of 1973 to see that legislative intent without economic muscle is ineffective. We fear that in the absence of meaningful and long-term economic support, political and social support for transition mandates will gradually erode.

🌿 🌿 🌿

SUMMARY

In the past, the design and development of programs for populations with mild disabilities has not been solidly based on theoretical principles. Transition revolves around the movement from secondary to postsecondary environments and involves the making of vocational and life decisions that will affect the individual for a lifetime. Career development theory (personality, developmental, social, and trait factor approaches) offers some basic framework for the design of transition policies and programs for persons with mild disabilities. In combination, these theoretical approaches underscore the importance of both individual (self-concept, aspirations, emotions, values, abilities, interests, etc.) and environmental (early influences, education, socio-economic status, culture, occupational, etc.) variables. If they are to be successful, future transition policymakers and programmers for people with mild disabilities must recognize the interactions among individual and environmental characteristics within the micro-, meso-, exo-, and macrosystems of society.

REFERENCES

Berler, E., Gross, A., & Drabman, R. (1982). Social skills training with children: Proceed with caution. *Journal of Applied Behavior Analyses*, *5*, 41–53.

Biklen, D., & Zollers, N. (1986). The focus of advocacy in the LD field. *Journal of Learning Disabilities*, *10*, 579–586.

Blau, P. M., & Duncan, D. D. (1967). *The American occupational structure.* New York: Wiley.

Bordin, E. S. (1943). A theory of interests as dynamic phenomena. *Educational and Psychological Measurement*, *3*, 49–66.

Bronfenbrenner, U. (1977). Toward an experimental ecology of human development. *American Psychologist*, *32*, 513–531.

Buehler, C. (1933). *Der menschliche Lebenslauf als psychologisches Problem.* Leipzig: Hirzel.

Campbell, D. P. (1974). *Manual for the Strong-Campbell Interest Inventory.* Stanford, CA: Stanford University Press.

Campbell, D. P., & Hansen, J. C. (1981). *Manual for the SVIB SCII.* Stanford, CA: Stanford University Press.

Carter , H. D. (1940). The development of vocational attitudes. *Journal of Counseling Psychology*, *4*, 185–191.

Cartledge, G., & Milburn, J. (1978). The case for teaching social skills in the classroom: A review. *Review of Educational Research*, *1*, 133–156.

Chadsey-Rusch, J., & O'Reilly, M. (1992). Social integration in employment and post-secondary educational settings: Outcomes and process variables. In F. R. Rusch, L. DeStefano, J. Chadsey-Rusch, L. A. Phelps, & E. Symanski (Eds.), *Transition from school to adult life* (pp. 245–263). Sycamore, IL: Sycamore.

Crowner, T. T. (1985). A taxonomy of special education finance. *Exceptional Children*, *51*, 503–509.

Cummings, R. W., & Maddux, C. D. (1987). *Career and vocational education for the mildly handicapped.* Springfield, IL: Thomas.

Dawis, R. (1973). A theory of work adjustment. In J. G. Cull & R. E. Hardy (Eds.), *Adjustment to work* (pp. 51–63). Springfield, IL: Thomas.

Edgar, E., Horton, B., & Maddox, M. (1984). Postschool placements: Planning for public school students with developmental disabilities. *Journal of Vocational Special Needs Education*, *6*(2), 15–18, 26.

Furnham, A. (1986). Social skills training with adolescents and young adults. In C. H. Hollin & P. Trower (Eds.), *Handbook of social skills training* (Vol. 1, pp. 33–57). Oxford: Pergamon Press.

Ginzberg, E., Ginsburg, S. W., Axelrad, S., & Herman, J. L. (1951). *Occupational choice: An approach to a general theory.* New York: Columbia University.

Gresham, F. (1981). Social skills training with handicapped children: A review. *Review of Educational Research, 51,* 139–176.

Halpern, A., & Benz, M. (1984). *Toward excellence in secondary special education: A statewide study of Oregon's high school programs for students with mild disabilities.* Unpublished manuscript, University of Oregon, Eugene.

Hazel, S. J. (1987). *LD: A report to the U.S. Congress prepared by Interagency Committee on LD.* Washington, DC: Department of Health and Human Services.

Holland, J. (1985) *Making vocational choices: A theory of vocational personalities and work environments* (2nd ed.). Englewood Cliffs, NJ: Prentice-Hall.

Hollingshead, A. B. (1949) *Elmtown's youth.* New York: Wiley

Knowlton, H. E., & Clark, G. M. (1987). Transition issues for the 1990s. *Exceptional Children, 53,* 562–563.

Kuder, F. (1966). *Kuder Occupational Interest Survey.* Chicago: Science Research Associates.

Kuder, F., & Diamond, E. E. (1979). *General manual for the Kuder DD Occupational Interest Survey.* Chicago: Science Research Associates.

La Greca, A. M., & Mesibov, G. B. (1981). Facilitating interpersonal functioning with peers in learning disabled children. *Journal of Learning Disabilities, 13,* 20–29.

Lofquist, L. H., & Dawis, R. V. (1969). *Adjustment to work.* New York: Appleton-Century-Crofts.

Michelson, L., Sugai, D., Wood, R., & Kazdin A. (1983). *Social skills assessment and training with children.* New York: Plenum Press.

Okolo, C. M., & Sitlington, P. (1986). Instructional environments in secondary vocational education programs: Implications for LD adolescents. *Learning Disability Quarterly, 11,* 136–148.

Osipow, S. H. (1983). *Theories of career development* (3rd ed.). Englewood Cliffs, NJ: Prentice-Hall.

Roe, A. (1956). Early determinants of vocational choice. *Journal of Counseling Psychology, 4,* 212–217.

Rogers, C. R. (1942). *Counselling and psychotherapy.* Boston: Houghton Mifflin.

Rogers, C. R. (1951). *Client-centered therapy.* Boston: Houghton Mifflin.

Rosenberg, M. (1957) *Occupations and values.* Glencoe, IL: Free Press.

Sapir, S. G., & Nitzburg, A. D. (1973). *Children with learning problems.* New York: Brunner/Mazel.

Schumaker, J., & Hazel, J. S. (1988). Social skills training. In K. Kavale, S. Forness, & M. Bender (Eds), *Handbook of learning disabilities* (Vol. 2, pp. 111–156). Boston: Little, Brown.

Schumaker, J., Pederson, C. S., Hazel, J., & Meyen, E. L. (1983). Social skills curricula for mildly handicapped adolescents: A review. *Focus on Exceptional Children, 16*(4), 1–16.

Shepard, L. (1983, Fall). The role of measurement and educational policy: Lessons from the identification of learning disabilities. *Educational Measurement: Issues and Practice*, 4–8.

Super, D. E. (1957). *The psychology of careers.* New York: Harper & Row.

Super, D. E. (1976). *Career education and the meanings of work.* Washington, DC: U.S. Government Printing Office.

Trapani, C. (1990). *Transition goals for adolescents with learning disabilities.* Boston: Little, Brown.

Van Hasselt, V. B., Hersen, M., Whitehill, M., & Bellack, A. (1979). Social skill assessment and training for children: An evaluative review. *Behavior Research and Therapy, 17*, 413–437.

Vigilante, F. (1983). Working with families of learning disabled children. *Child Welfare, 62*, 429–436.

Vincent, L., Laten, S., Salisbury, C., Brown, P., & Baumgart, D. (1981). Family involvement in the educational processes of severely handicapped students: State of the art and directions for the future. In B. Wilcox & R. York (Eds.), *Quality educational services for the severely handicapped and the federal perspective.* U.S. Department of Education, Division of Innovation and Development.

Wehman, P., Kregel, J., & Seyfarth, J. (1985). Transition from school to work for individuals with severe handicaps: A follow-up study. *Journal of the Association for Persons with Severe Handicaps, 10*(3), 132–136.

Author Index

447

Subject Index

ISBN 0-675-21373-8